The Developing Child

The Developing Child

Third Edition

Helen Bee
University of Washington

Harper International Edition
Harper & Row, Publishers
New York

Cambridge
Hagerstown
Philadelphia
San Francisco

London
Mexico City
São Paulo
Sydney

1817

Sponsoring Editor: Bhagan Narine
Special Projects Editor: Peggy Waldman
Project Editor: Julie Segedy
Assistant Production Manager: Marian Hartsough
Cover and Text Design: Nancy Benedict
Illustrators: John Foster and Cyndie Clark-Huegel
Photo Researcher: Roberta Spiekerman
Compositor: Ruttle, Shaw & Wetherill, Inc.
Printer & Binder: R. R. Donnelley & Sons Company

Library of Congress Cataloging in Publication Data
Bee, Helen L   1939–
The developing child.

Includes bibliographies and index.
1. Child development. I. Title.
RJ131.B36   1981   155.4   80-19629
ISBN 0-06-040579-1

Harper International Edition
35-01343
Cover design by Lorna Laccone
Cover photography by Tom Keller

Photo Credits

Cover Photo Elizabeth Crews

Chapter 1 Fig. 1.1 Suzanne Arms/Jeroboam; Fig. 1.3 Suzanne Arms/Jeroboam; Fig. 1.4 Suzanne Szasz; Fig. 1.5 Elizabeth Hamlin/Stock, Boston; Fig. 1.6 Bennett Hall/ICON; Fig. 1.8 Cary Wolinski/Stock, Boston.

Part One Mark Memann/Silver Pony School

Chapter 2 Fig. 2.1 Peeter Vilms/Jeroboam; Fig. 2.3 Lois Inman Engle © 1980; Nancy Hays/Monkmeyer; Fig. 2.6 Dr. Landrum B. Shettles; Fig. 2.7 Sybil Shelton/Monkmeyer; Fig. 2.8 Mimi Forsyth/Monkmeyer; Fig. 2.11 Paul Conklin/Monkmeyer.

Chapter 3 Fig. 3.2 Suzanne Arms/Jeroboam; Fig. 3.3 Elizabeth Crews; Fig. 3.4 H.F.R. Prechtl & B. Beimtema "The neurological examination of the full term, new born infant," *Clinics in Developmental Medicine* #63/2nd ed. Spastics International Medical Publications; Fig. 3.5 SUVA/DPI; Fig. 3.6 Jim Harrison/Stock, Boston; Fig. 3.8 Suzanne Szasz.

Part Two Tony Zane/Silver Pony School

Chapter 4 Fig. 4.1 Elizabeth Crews/ICON; Fig. 4.5 Raimondo Borea; Bob East/Photo Trends; Fig. 4.7 E. Johnson/DeWys; Raimondo Borea, ASMP; Larry Trone/DPI; Fig. 4.8 J. M. Tanner/Institute of Child Health, London; Fig. 4.9 Bruce Kliewe/Jeroboam; Fig. 4.10 Roger Lubin/Jeroboam; Fig. 4.11 Jim Engle.

Chapter 5 Fig. 5.3 The Seattle Times; Fig. 5.4 William Vandivert, Scientific American; Fig. 5.5 Zimbel/Monkmeyer; Fig. 5.7 Jean-Claude Lejeune/Stock, Boston.

Part Three Amber Teagle/The Art Co-op of Berkeley

Chapter 6 Fig. 6.1 Susan Kuklin; Fig. 6.2 H. S. Terrace.

Chapter 7 Fig. 7.1 Bill Owens/Jeroboam; Fig. 7.3 Eileen Christelow/Jeroboam; Fig. 7.4 Jane Scherr/ICON.

Chapter 8 Fig. 8.1 Monkmeyer; Fig. 8.2 Elizabeth Crews; 8.3 R. DeVries and The Society for Research in Child Development, Inc.; Fig. 8.6 Eileen Christelow/Jeroboam; Fig. 8.7 Ellis Herwig/Stock, Boston; Fig. 8.9 William Rosenthal/Jeroboam.

Chapter 9 Fig. 9.3 Kent Reno/Jeroboam; Fig. 9.4 Jim Vincent/The Oregonian; Fig. 9.5 Jean-Claude Lejeune/Stock, Boston.

Part Four Ben Dolvyn

Chapter 10 Fig. 10.1 John Garrett/Woodfin Camp; Fig. 10.2 Lois Inman Engle © 1980; Fig. 10.4 Elizabeth Hamlin/Stock, Boston; Fig. 10.5 Jim Harrison/Stock, Boston; Fig. 10.6 Suzanne Szasz; Fig. 10.7 Donald Deitz/Stock, Boston; Ed Buryn/Jeroboam; Elizabeth Crews/ICON.

Chapter 11 Fig. 11.1 Suzanne Arms/Jeroboam; Fig. 11.2 R. Duane Cooke/DPI; Fig. 11.3 Chester Higgins/Photo Researchers; Fig. 11.4 Christopher Morrow/Stock, Boston; Fig. 11.5 The Seattle Times; Fig. 11.6 Ken Graves/Jeroboam; Fig. 11.7 Lois Inman Engle © 1980; Fig. 11.8 Conklin/Monkmeyer; Fig. 11.9 Marion Faller/Monkmeyer; Fig. 11.10 Bruce Roberts/Photo Researchers.

Chapter 12 Fig. 12.1 Elizabeth Crews/ICON; Fig. 12.2 Tana Hoban/DPI; Fig. 12.4 Cheryl Traendly/ICON; Fig. 12.5 Lois Inman Engle; Fig. 12.6 Elliott VarNerSmith; Fig. 12.7 Peter Menzel; Fig. 12.8 Frank Siteman/Stock, Boston; Fig. 12.9 Cheryl Traendly/ICON; Fig. 12.10 Olive Piercel/Stock, Boston.

Chapter 13 Fig. 13.1 UPI: Fig. 13.2 B. Kliewe/Jeroboam; Fig. 13.3 Mimi Forsyth/Monkmeyer; Fig. 13.4 Susan Ylvisaker/Jeroboam; Fig. 13.5 Elizabeth Crews/ICON; Fig. 13.6 Eileen Christelow/Jeroboam; Fig. 13.7 Roberto Borea; Fig. 13.8 Paul Conklin/Monkmeyer.

Part Five Tony Zane/Silver Pony School

Chapter 14 Fig. 14.1 L. Roger Turner/Wisconsin State Journal; Fig. 14.3 Jim Vincent/The Oregonian; Fig. 14.4 Stephen Potter/Stock, Boston; Fig. 14.5 Stock, Boston; David Powers/Stock, Boston; Fig. 14.6 Irene Bayer/Monkmeyer; Fig. 14.7 Raimondo Borea.

Chapter 15 Fig. 15.1 Paul Fortin/Stock, Boston; Fig. 15.2 Bill Anderson/Monkmeyer; Fig. 15.3 The Seattle Times; Fig. 15.4 Michael Rothstein/Jeroboam; Fig. 15.5 Hartmann/Jeroboam; Fig. 15.6 Mimi Forsyth/Monkmeyer; Bennett Hall/ICON; Fig. 15.7 Bruce Roberts/Photo Researchers.

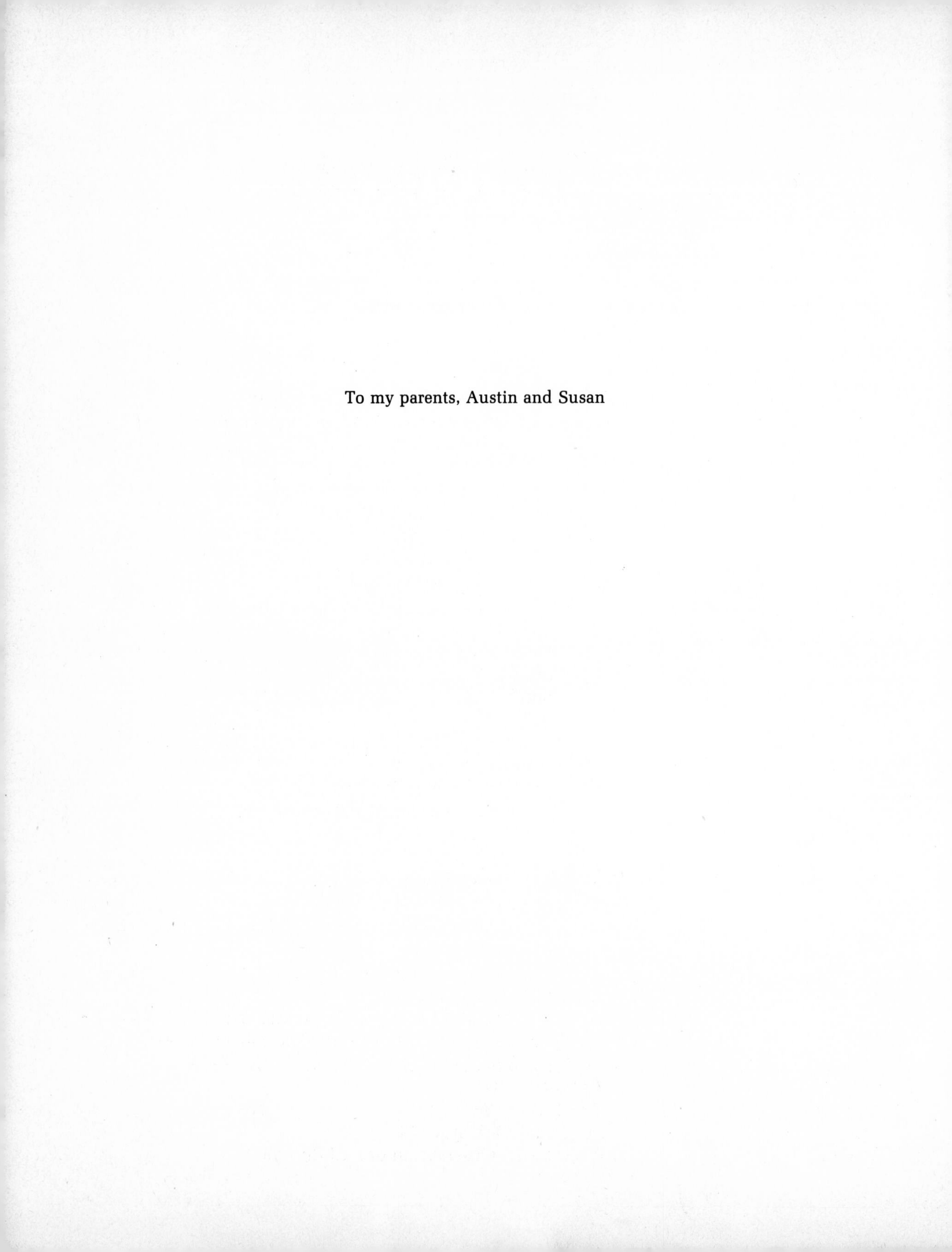

To my parents, Austin and Susan

Contents

Part One The Beginnings of Life 39

Chapter 2 Prenatal Development 40

Chapter 3 Birth and the Newborn Child 72

Part Two The Physical Child 103

Chapter 4 Physical Growth and Development 104

Chapter 7 Explaining Language Development 198

Chapter 8 The Development of Thinking in Children 222

Part Four The Social Child 293

Part Five The Whole Child 423

Preface

Goals of the Third Edition

The third edition of *The Developing Child,* like its predecessors, is intended for use in any first course in child development, whether that course is in psychology, education, home economics, family life, nursing, or elsewhere. From the beginning, I have aimed for a relatively brief, readable text that could form the backbone for a child development course without being encyclopedic. Each instructor has favorite topics or special emphases to be added; a good text should be brief enough to leave room for such expansions and excursions.

My second major goal, which has been especially significant in preparing the third edition, has been to provide a book that has as good a balance as possible between basic theory and research and practical applications. Instructors familiar with the earlier editions of the book will find this third edition has the same strong theoretical flavor as before, strengthened by expanded discussion of specific, current research. At the same time, the practical applications for educators, child care workers, and parents are also highly visible, both in examples throughout the text and in boxes in each chapter.

Organization

There are two time-honored ways of presenting human development. In the "ages and stages" approach, the book and the instructor begin at conception and move through the life cycle using age as the organizing principle. In the "topics" approach, the sequence of development from conception through childhood is discussed separately for each facet of development, such as physical growth, language, cognition, social interactions, and moral behavior. Neither one of these approaches is without pitfalls, but my own strong preference is for a topical organization. I have always felt that this gives the student a better feeling for the full sweep of development and for the links between early and later steps in each area. Thus, the basic organization of this book is topical.

The major topical chapters have been organized into three parts: The Physical Child (physical and perceptual development), The Thinking Child (language, intelligence, and cognition), and The Social Child (personality, social interactions, sex roles, self-concept, and moral development). As in early editions, a separate chapter on atypical development has also been included.

The greatest possible drawback of the topical approach is that the student may lose sight of all the things that are happening at the same time in the developmental process. So to "put the child back together," I have included a final part, The Whole Child, in which I integrate the several threads of development. Prenatal development and early infancy have also been handled as "ages and stages" chapters at the beginning of the book.

Key Strengths Retained

In revising the book, every effort has been made to keep and strengthen those special qualities or features that instructors and students have found useful.

The Personal Voice This edition, like all of my books, is written in the first person. I have also used examples from my own experience where they seemed natural and useful. My goal has been to write a book that reads as if I am talking directly to the student, which both maintains the student's interest and, at the same time, helps to "demystify" the scientific process.

Brevity The book continues to be one of the briefer child development texts, so it is readily usable in both semester and quarter courses, and leaves room for the instructor to add supplemental readings on special topics.

Projects Many of the projects from earlier editions have been retained and new ones added. Nine of the 15 chapters include at least one project, ranging from rather lengthy observations of children on playgrounds to TV monitoring. New projects in this edition include observation in a newborn nursery and the testing of the object concept in young infants. To complete some of the projects, students may need assistance in arranging permission to observe in day-care settings, newborn nurseries, or school playgrounds, but at least some of the projects should be feasible for all students.

Suggested Readings Each chapter includes an annotated list of suggested readings, intended as next sources for students particularly interested in that topic. The lists have been updated with recent material.

Chapter Summaries Each chapter also includes a numbered summary of key points, intended to assist students in the synthesis of ideas and recall.

Strong Coverage of Early Childhood While the full span of child development is discussed (and coverage of the elementary school years has been expanded), the discussion of the period from birth to about 5 is particularly strong, with emphasis on early attachments, early cognitive development, and language.

Balanced Discussion of Important Issues Despite the brevity of the book, I have tried not to side-step or water down the difficult theoretical and practical issues. Instead, I have tried to give the several sides of each problem and then my own conclusion.

New Features Added

Two goals of the third edition are reflected in major new features. First, the balance of theory and practical applications has been improved, and second, the organization and presentation of the material has been made more usable for both instructor and students.

Expanded Applications Each chapter now includes two to three boxes focused on practical or applied issues that specifically relate to teachers, nurses, parents, and others. For example, there are new boxes on breast versus bottle feeding, the application of Piagetian theory to early education, child abuse, the uses of IQ tests in the schools, bilingual children, obesity in childhood, and attachment to fathers. At the same time, coverage of basic theory and research has not been sacrificed.

Clearer Teaching Format Outlines have been added at the beginning of each chapter, more headings have been used throughout, and key ideas have been defined more fully.

New Glossary In each chapter, key terms have been highlighted in boldface in the text. At the end of the chapter, each of the key terms has then been defined in a glossary.

Lively New Design The book has been brightened by a new second color and a more attractive format. There are also almost double the number of photographs, showing children from all socioeconomic groups growing up in a wide range of urban and rural settings.

New Referencing System The standard APA referencing system has been adopted, with a full bibliography listed at the end of the book. Almost twice as many studies are cited as in the second edition, including many very recent papers and books.

Expanded and Updated Coverage

Every section of the book has been reconsidered, revised, and updated in light of new research and theory. Inevitably this has meant that some sections have changed more than others, since researchers have focused more on some topics than others and since some topics were covered too briefly in earlier editions.

Major Changes and Expansions The most substantial changes and expansions include discussions of the following:

> The process of birth, the father's role in the birth process, and the impact of birth conditions on the child and her parents

- The parents' attachment to the infant
- The impact of alcohol and other drugs on prenatal development
- The effects of prenatal malnutrition on later development
- The development of thinking during the preoperational and formal operational periods, both of which have received extensive research attention in recent years
- Friendships and relationships between peers
- The development of the gender concept and sex roles
- The gifted child
- Behavior problems and other nonpsychotic emotional disturbances
- Treatment of children with atypical development

Other Significant Updating

In addition to these major changes, new material on temperamental differences among infants and children, early language development, heritability of IQ, moral development and cognitive level, and many other topics has been included. The final "age overview" chapter has also been extensively revised to reflect my evolving thinking about the processes of development.

Overall, I think you will find that this revision gives *both* a sense of greater scientific rigor and greater applied relevance.

Supplements

Instructor's Manual

The IM, which I prepared, includes three main features: (1) 40 to 50 multiple choice questions per chapter; (2) suggestions for lecture topics, new material, or helpful sources for the instructor; and (3) a brief list of potential films for class use.

Study Guide

The Study Guide has been thoroughly revised and rewritten to correspond with the third edition. A dual format allows for either traditional or programmed Personalized System of Instruction (PSI) review. Each chapter includes chapter objectives, key terms and concepts, a multiple-choice self-quiz, open-ended study questions, and an end-of-chapter Programmed Review Unit.

Acknowledgments

In preparing the third edition, I have been fortunate to have had the help of a group of excellent reviewers. Mel Ciena, from San Jose City College, Santa Clara College, and Stanford University; Janice Bryan, from Middlesex Community College; Margaret Appel, from Ohio University at Athens; and Paul Kaplan, from Suffolk County Community College, reviewed the second edition and provided detailed and helpful comments about needed changes.

Sharon Antonelli, from San Jose City College; Charles Halverson, University of Georgia; Shirley Miller, Southwest Texas State University; and Roger Burton, SUNY Buffalo, read and commented on the early drafts of the third edition. Special thanks go to Jane Stormer, of Cuyahoga Community College; Robert Orr, of the University of Windsor; and Philip O'Neill, from Orgeon State University, who valiantly read both the second edition and versions of the third.

All of their comments were extremely useful. I am sure that this edition is far better because of the thoughtful suggestions of these colleagues. My thanks to them all.

Thanks are also due to the several Harper & Row editors who have been involved with this text, including Bhagan Narine, Peggy Waldman, and Julie Segedy. Peggy in particular did yeoman's work, evaluating comments, nudging reviewers, and helping to plan needed changes. I appreciate the strong support I have received from all the Harper & Row staff.

Finally, I want to say a special thank you to my colleague Sandra Mitchell, who has truly been a friend in need during the months I have worked on this edition. On those inevitable days when I just couldn't find the reference I needed, or couldn't figure out how to say something clearly, her humor has always helped to put the task into perspective.

Helen Bee
University of Washington

The Developing Child

Preview of Chapter 1

1 Basic Processes and Theories

The other day I came across a "test" in an article called "How Long Will You Live?" I don't know if other psychologists react in the same way to tests and questionnaires like this, but I find them irresistible. I dutifully answered the 58 questions about my health habits and life-style and discovered that I would probably live to be 84—a nice prospect since it means I'm not yet even halfway there. It occurred to me, reading the article, that you, too, may find such "tests" irresistible (or interesting at the very least), so let me start you off with a quiz: "How Much Do You Already Know About Child Development?"

See what you can do with the ten questions in Table 1.1. (The correct answers are upside down at the bottom of the table.) If you can answer all ten correctly, you may not need a course or a book on child development. But if you've missed some (and most of you will), you will obviously have new areas to explore in reading this book.

I use the word "explore" intentionally. For me, the study of human development is an adventure, an exploration of unmapped, or only partly mapped, territory. There is a great deal that we know, but so much more about which we understand only a little. What has always excited me is the process of trying to find out, of devising ways to study children and families that might give us another line on the map. I hope in this book to be able to convey some of that excitement to you.

Let me see if I can give you some flavor of the adventure and, at the same time, introduce you to several of the major theories underlying the study of human development by taking two brief journeys into the territory of research.

Table 1.1 How Much Do You Already Know About Child Development?

1. Which of the following aspects of a day-care center makes the most difference in a child's development?
   a. How many children there are per teacher
   b. How many children are in each class or group
   c. Whether the teachers have degrees in child development
   d. Whether children of different ages are in each class
2. Which sex is better at tasks that require the ability to visualize spatial relationships?
   a. Boys
   b. Girls
   c. Boys before adolescence
   d. Girls after adolescence
3. How early should a mother handle her newborn to maximize attachment of the mother to the child?
   a. Right away
   b. 6 hours
   c. 10 hours
   d. Any time in the first 24 hours
4. What is the youngest age at which most children have a complete understanding of their own gender?
   a. 1 year
   b. 3 years
   c. 5 years
   d. 7 years
5. What is the earliest age an infant can see and hear most things going on near her?
   a. Immediately after birth
   b. 1 month
   c. 2 months
   d. 3 months
6. Which group of boys ends up tallest as adults?
   a. Those who have early puberty
   b. Those who have late puberty
   c. Those who go through puberty at average time
   d. None of the above; timing of puberty doesn't affect adult height
7. Which of the following sentences spoken by a child is the most advanced developmentally?
   a. "See Dad."
   b. "Allgone cookie."
   c. "Sarah shoes."
   d. "Want more."
8. Which of the following types of thinking is found in the adolescent but not the younger child?
   a. Inductive logic
   b. Deductive logic
   c. Classification skill
   d. Reversibility
9. Which of the following types of discipline is most likely to lead to honesty or moral behavior in a child?
   a. Physical punishment
   b. Withdrawal of love
   c. Isolation
   d. Persuasion by reason
10. At what age do we first see a consistent IQ difference between poor and middle-class children?
    a. 6 months
    b. 18 months
    c. 36 months
    d. 60 months

1.(b) 2.(a) 3.(a) 4.(c) 5.(a) 6.(d) 7.(c) 8.(b) 9.(d) 10.(c)

Journey 1: Hospital Care and Attachment

Many of you know from firsthand experience that for at least the past generation it has been customary in American hospitals for a mother and infant to be separated after birth, except at feeding time, until they go home. Several years ago, two pediatricians, Marshall Klaus and John Kennell, along with several colleagues (Kennell, Jerauld, Wolfe, Chesler, Kreger, McAlpine, Steffa & Klaus, 1974; Klaus & Kennell, 1976; Kennell, Voos & Klaus, 1979) began to wonder whether or not this was really a good way to handle things. What was this separation doing to the important emotional bond between a mother and her infant? They knew of several studies of low-birth-weight infants —who were separated from their mothers for weeks or even months after birth—showing that their mother-infant relationship was different than for full-term babies. Aimee Leifer and her colleagues (Leifer, Leiderman, Barnett & Williams, 1972), for example, found that after taking their infants home from the hospital, the mothers of low-birth-weight children smiled at their babies less and held them close less often. Klaus and Kennell wondered whether the typical hospital practice for full-term babies was also interfering with the formation of a "bond" between the mother and the child. More specifically, was there some period immediately after the child's birth when the mother was physiologically and emotionally most "ready" to form such a bond with her infant?

The Original Klaus and Kennell Study

To check this possibility, Klaus and Kennell studied two matched groups, each including 14 mothers with their firstborn infants. The first group experienced the normal hospital procedure. They had a glimpse of their infant at birth, had another short visit at 6–12 hours after birth, and then saw the infant every four hours for feeding. A second group, called the "extended-contact" group, had in addition a total of five hours per day of extra cuddling with their infants. The contact began within the first three hours of birth and then continued regularly afterward. Figure 1.1 shows one mother with her baby immediately after delivery.

After their hospital experiences, the two groups of mothers went home and began caring for their infants on their own. A month later, Klaus and Kennell interviewed the mothers, examined the infant in the mother's presence, and filmed the mother feeding her baby. They interviewed and observed again when the babies were a year old. Remember that the two groups had been treated differently for only the first three days of the

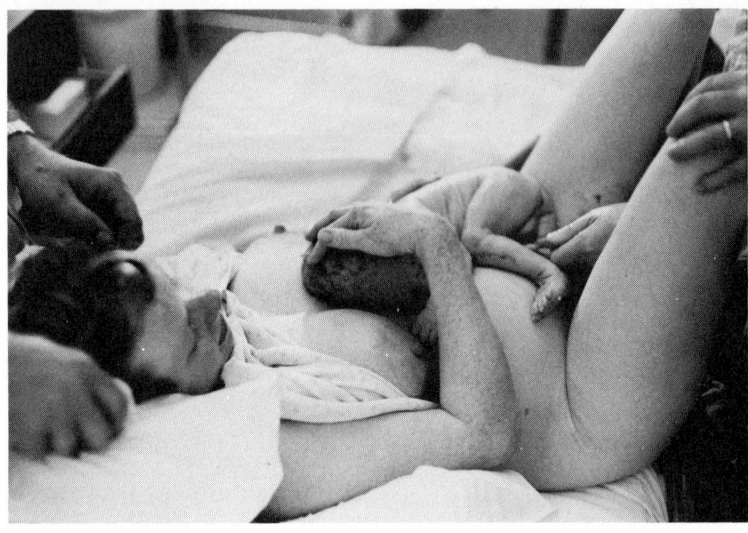

Figure 1.1 **This kind of skin-to-skin contact, in the hours immediately following birth, is what the mothers in Klaus and Kennell's "extended contact" study experienced.**

child's life. Would there still be a difference between them a month later? It turns out that there was. The extended-contact mothers held their month-old infants closely while feeding, while those with "normal" hospital experiences were more likely to use distant contact. Figure 1.2 illustrates these two types of caregiving.

When the babies were a year old, remarkably enough there were still several differences. Some of the mothers in each group had gone back to work or school. When the researchers asked about that, nearly all the extended-contact mothers talked about missing their baby or worrying about him while they were away, while the mothers who had been through the normal hospital practice rarely mentioned their child when talking about their work. The two groups also behaved differently while their child was being examined by the doctor. The extended-contact group mothers stayed closer and were quicker to come to the aid of their child if he cried or showed other signs of stress.

The Practical Applications What did all this mean? On the practical level, this research definitely called into question the normal hospital practices at delivery. Kennell and his colleagues put it this way:

> We now enter an era in which it will be necessary to closely review each of our traditional procedures and techniques for the birth of a baby. It will be necessary for those responsible for the care of

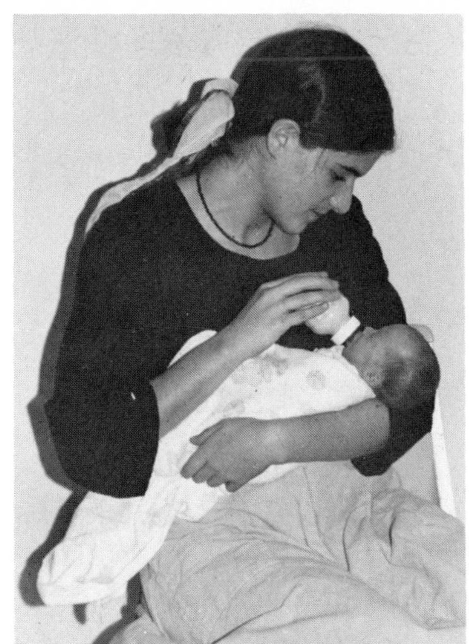

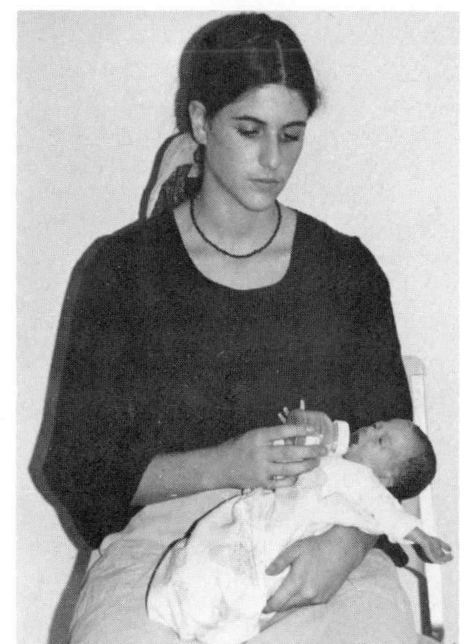

Figure 1.2 This mother is demonstrating two different positions in which a child might be held for feeding. On the left, the mother and baby are closer and have their faces fully turned to one another. On the right, the contact is more distant. In Klaus and Kennell's studies, mothers who had more close contact early on showed more of the type of holding and feeding shown on the left. (Source: Klaus and Kennell, 1970, p. 1024.)

> mothers and infants to evaluate hospital procedures that interfere with early and sustained mother-infant contact and consider introducing practices that promote a mother's immediate interaction with her infant. . . . In every hospital, keeping parents and infant together should be the rule, not the exception.
>
> (Kennell, Voos & Klaus, 1979, pp. 796–797)

In fact, many hospitals have already changed their procedures.

The Theoretical Applications But what do these results mean for psychologists? What do they tell us about the processes involved? The first and most logical possibility was that Klaus and Kennell were right in their basic hypothesis that human mothers—like females of other species—have some basic "readiness" to become attached to their infants immediately after birth but that the "glue" needed for this bond to hold completely is a lot of physical contact right away between the mother and the child. Other researchers have also begun to explore this possibility.

Later Studies of Early Bonding

A later study by another group of researchers, Elise Gaulin-Kremer, Jeffrey Shaw, and Evelyn Thoman (1977) supports the possibility of a special "readiness" of the mother for attachment to her infant immediately after the birth of the child. They observed a group of 28 mothers who experienced normal hospital routine. Because of differences in the time of day of delivery, some of the mothers had their first extended contact with their infant for feeding about ten hours after delivery, others at times ranging up to 25 hours after delivery. Gaulin-Kremer observed the mothers and infants during those first extended encounters to see whether this simple difference in the timing of the first contact would affect the mother's behavior with her baby.

What they found was that mothers who saw their baby early (ten hours or so after delivery) did more caressing and talking to their babies than did the mothers with a long interval before the first contact. The "early" mothers also held their babies longer before they began to feed them.

These results seem to tell us that it is the *timing*, and not the extended nature, of the first contact that is most critical. Other researchers, such as John Hopkins and Peter Vietze (1977), have found that the effect is even stronger if the mother handles and cuddles her baby within the first 1–3 hours after delivery.

Both of these studies provide support for the notion that a mother is especially ready to form a bond with her infant immediately after she gives birth. But why? One possible explanation is that there may be some set of hormones present at the time of delivery that augment the mother's interest in her infant. Kennell (Kennell, Voos & Klaus, 1979) believes there is. In fact, he argues that there is a "maternal sensitive period" for attachment that occurs in the hours right after birth.

But What About Fathers?

Until quite recently, the notion of some hormonal "readiness" in the mother made sense to me. But then I encountered a study of *fathers'* involvement in delivery that forced me to think again.

Gail Peterson and her co-workers (Peterson, Mehl & Leiderman, 1979), studied the effects of birth conditions on fathers' attachment to their infants. Peterson found that those fathers who were the most involved with the birth—and thus presumably had the greatest chance to see and handle the infant right after birth—were most attached (bonded) to their babies six months later.

It turned out that it was the actual experience during the birth that was crucial and not the father's earlier ideas about whether he wanted to be present or whether he thought he'd have much to do with his child. One man, for example, was not very pleased about having a child, didn't think he wanted to be present at the birth, but agreed to do so because his wife felt strongly about it and because it was a home delivery. The researchers describe what happened:

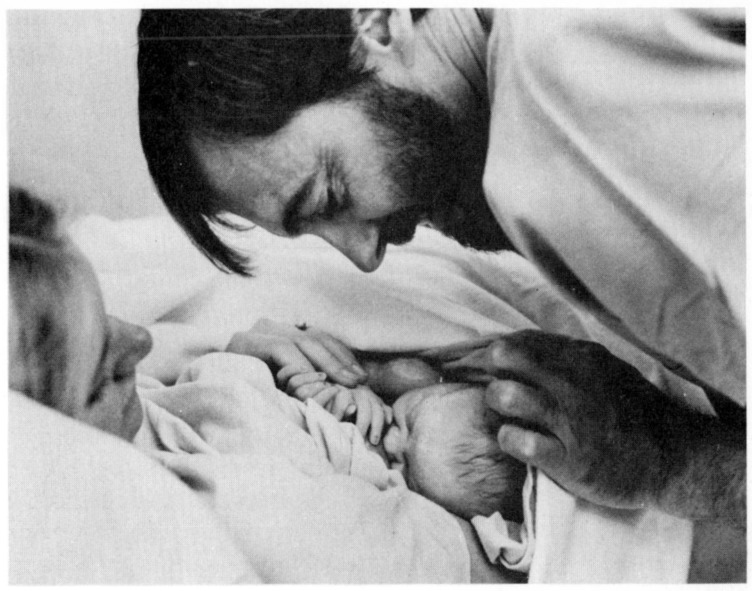

Figure 1.3 More and more fathers are participating in the delivery of their children. Recent research makes it appear that fathers who are present are more likely to be strongly attached to their infants.

> The husband's behavior was the opposite of what we had expected, based on his prenatal attitude. After an initial period of severe discomfort for his wife, he became very concerned about her and supported her both physically and emotionally by massaging her back and engaging in frequent touching and reassuring talking. At times he seemed overwhelmed and occasionally withdrew from the room, but he always returned. His disinterest and apathy were replaced by concern, amazement, and involvement. Following the birth of the baby he proceeded to cry and within 30 minutes held, rocked, and talked to his new son. After the birth, he reported feeling very close to his son and very involved in the caretaking. This was corroborated by direct observation and by his wife's report of his behavior.
>
> (Peterson, Mehl & Leiderman, 1979, pp. 335–336)

This study makes me think again because it calls the role of hormones into question. While it might make sense to think about the possible role of hormones in the *mother's* earliest attachment to her infant, it is hard for me to think of how hormones would account for the behavior of the fathers in the Peterson study. Possibly the general physical arousal that we all experience at a time of high excitement or fear could be involved—a possibility that needs to be checked with later research—but what we see in the fathers who participate in delivery seems to go beyond that. Something that happens during the process of observing the delivery and holding and caring for the infant immediately afterward seems to serve as a special "glue" for the fathers . . . and if that glue isn't hormonal, what is it?

One possibility is that there is something special about the *baby* immediately after birth that helps to "hook" both parents into a stronger attachment. In fact, there *is* something different; babies (if they have not been anesthetized) are very awake and alert for the first few hours after delivery, even managing to make eye contact with those around them. After that they get very dopey and sleepy and are not alert again for several days. So those first hours may be special simply because the infant can then respond to the parents.

Summing Up the First Journey

Where does this leave us in this particular journey? We know now that there is something important about the first hours after a child's birth, but we don't really know what it is. Is it something about the newborn baby that elicits unique reactions from the adults who are present? Is it some hormonal "readiness" in the mother, or some high level of physical arousal in the father, that forms the glue for the first bond?

Much of the research that has been done thus far on these questions has involved relatively few subjects, and the families haven't been followed much past the first year of the child's life. We don't yet know how important these early events are for the long-term relationship between the parent and the child. In addition, the studies of fathers' involvement during delivery suffer from a major problem: fathers who choose to be present at their child's birth are probably different to begin with. Is their later relationship with their infant different *because* they were present at his birth, or would those particular fathers have behaved that way with their children anyway?

Despite these problems, however, intriguing and important questions have been raised by Klaus and Kennell's research and by all the work that has followed. Time-honored hospital practices have been changed as a result. But the journey is not over. Each new bit of knowledge has raised new questions. We'll find the same thing true on our second journey.

Journey 2: "Am I a Boy or a Girl?"

The second journey takes us into territory that has become especially relevant since the beginning of the women's movement. Most women in our society occupy positions that are lower in status and salary than those occupied by men. They are secretaries instead of vice-presidents, classroom teachers instead of principals, or housewives instead of salaried workers. If we want to change this situation (as I do), we have to understand not only how people get channeled into different kinds of jobs, but also how and when our ideas and attitudes about men and women come into being. The most basic set of questions has to do with how a child comes to understand that she is a girl (or he is a boy) in the first place.

In this case, recent research has given some fairly clear answers to the factual question: We know quite a lot now about the concepts of gender that a young child has and how they change with age. The interesting puzzle here is *why*. How can we explain this developmental sequence?

The Basic Facts

Before we look at the explanations, let me fill you in on the basic facts. There are several good studies of this aspect of development, but let me use an especially interesting piece of research by Ronald Slaby and Karin Frey (1975) to lay the groundwork.

They found that a child goes through three distinct stages in developing an idea of his or her gender. First he figures out that he is a boy (which Slaby and Frey call *gender identity*), then he figures out that he will be a boy for the rest of his life (*gender stability*); and finally he figures out that this won't change even if he were to *look like* a girl (*gender consistency*). In the Slaby and Frey study, the 3-year-olds didn't understand any of these concepts; the 4-year-olds understood only gender identity; and most of the 4½–5-year-olds understood all three.

In more recent studies, researchers have not always found precisely these ages for the steps of gender development. Deanna Kuhn and her colleagues (Kuhn, Nash & Brucken, 1978) found full gender constancy in some 3- and 4-year-olds, while both Dale Marcus (Marcus & Overton, 1978), and Walter Emmerich (Emmerich, Goldman, Kirsh & Sharabany, 1977) found that full gender constancy didn't occur till much later, at age 6 or 7. Still, the same *sequence* has been found in every study.

How do children learn this concept? More broadly, how do they come to acquire and to *value* behaviors and attitudes that are like those of adults of their own sex? In other words, how do they acquire a sex role? When we arrive at this question, agreement ceases. There are three quite separate explanations of how sex roles come about, each representing a major theoretical approach within developmental psychology. Let's take a look at the three views.

The Three Theories

Mischel's Theory Of the three, perhaps the easiest to explain is a learning-based theory proposed by Walter Mischel (1966, 1970). Mischel used two basic principles of learning to explain the development of the gender concept and sex roles in general. The first is the principle of **reinforcement** which, stated broadly, is that actions which bring pleasant consequences are likely to be repeated. A child who is praised or given more attention when he does "boy things," uses the correct pronoun to refer to other men, or who selects appropriate "boy clothing" is likely to learn both that he is a boy and also to value boy behaviors.

The second principle involved is that of **observational learning.** It isn't necessary for the child (or the adult, for that matter) to be praised or otherwise reinforced in order to learn something. Each of us also learns just from observing other people doing things. We learn new ways of talking from watching TV; we learn something about how to ski from watching our instructor; and the child learns about how boys behave from watching his father, his brother, or other men in his life.

When Mischel put the two basic principles together, he concluded that children learn their gender and their sex roles because they are reinforced for **imitating** (for watching and copying) people of the same sex.

Freud's Theory Sigmund Freud, too, thought that imitation was a crucial part of the child's understanding of her own gender, except that he called the process **identification** (Freud, 1960). In Freud's theory, identification happens when a child "incorporates" or takes into herself all the qualities, behaviors, and values of some other person, usually her same-sex parent. This is not just imitation. A child who has identified with her mother will certainly attempt to "be like" her mother. But more than that, the child who is identified tries in some sense to *be* her mother.

Freud thought identification arose out of conflicts that occur at about age 3 or 4, which he called the *Oedipal crisis.* During this time, a child comes to love the parent of the opposite sex while growing afraid of the parent of the same sex. So the boy comes to love, and in some way desire, his mother, but fears his father, who is obviously bigger and stronger than he is. The boy assumes that the father could easily win out in any test of their rival affections for the mother. Specifically, the father has the power to castrate.

To handle his fear of his father, according to Freud, a boy tries to make himself as much like his father as he can, on the theory that if he's enough like him, the father won't harm his son. Freud called this process *identification with the aggressor.* Obviously, the boy has to understand some aspects of the dif-

Figure 1.4 This father's attention is probably reinforcing his son's imitation of his behavior and clothing style. Mischel argues that most of a child's learning of gender and sex roles occurs through processes like these. (Source: Szasz, 1978, p. 146.)

ferences between males and females before all this happens; but in Freud's view, the critical steps in both the gender concept and the broader sex-role concept come only after identification has occurred.

Kohlberg's Theory Finally, there is a quite different theory, this time in the **cognitive-developmental** tradition, proposed by Lawrence Kohlberg (Kohlberg, 1966; Kohlberg & Zigler, 1967). Kohlberg was most struck by the fact that the gender concept seems to develop in a particular *sequence,* and that this sequence parallels changes in the child's intellectual development during the same period. The concept of gender is, after all, a concept, just like the concept of bigness or smallness. Some things are big, some are small; some are male, some are female. From this point of view, we'd expect that as the child's general understanding of such classification improves, her understanding of gender should improve, too, which is precisely what Slaby and Frey found.

Kohlberg also argued that the child will try to imitate an adult of the same sex only *after* she has fully understood that she is a girl. In his view, then, it wouldn't matter if you rewarded a 2- or 3-year-old girl for imitating her mother until you were blue; only when the child figures out what is a girl and what is a boy, and that she is the former, will it have any effect. But *after* she has figured out her gender, Kohlberg thought she would quite naturally begin to pay more attention to and imitate others of the same sex.

All of these theories seem to account for at least some of the facts I've given so far. So how do we choose among them?

Choosing the "Right" Theory

Basically the way any psychologist chooses the "right" theory is to do more research, trying to design the research so that it tests the alternatives as well as possible. For example, if Freud is correct, children of 2 or 3 need to have noticed and made some sense of the anatomical differences between males and females; for Mischel to be right, we'd have to find that parents systematically reward their sons for imitating their father and their daughters for imitating their mother; for Kohlberg to be right, we'd have to find that children imitate same-sex adults only *after* they have figured out the gender concept.

As you will see when we get to Chapter 12, *none* of these expectations is fully supported. Nor do any of the three theories do the entire job, while each seems to describe a *part* of the process. The problem researchers now face is to work out some new theory—perhaps borrowing from all three views—that will do a better job of explaining this particular developmental sequence.

Figure 1.5 This picture doesn't quite fit our stereotypes about men and women. Children who see pictures like these, or of female doctors and male nurses, are likely to remember them with the roles switched back to the "normal" pattern. So the stereotypes affect what we think we see and what we remember.

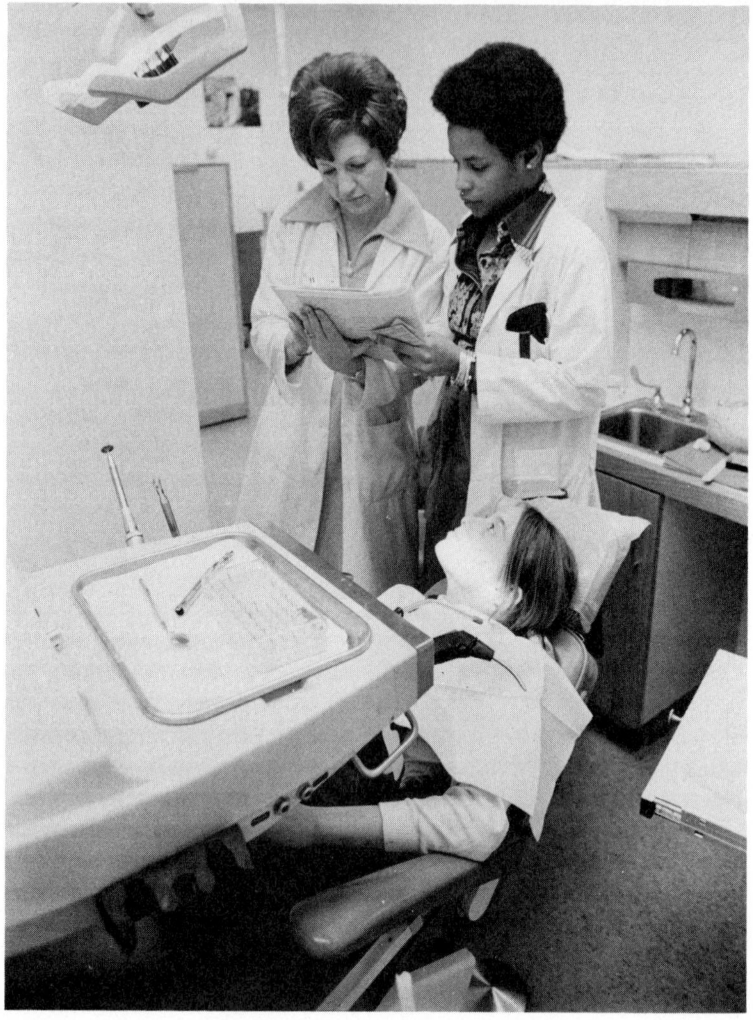

This journey, like the first, is a continuous process. It's a little like playing with the child's toy in which there is a tiny box inside a slightly bigger box, inside a bigger box, and so on. We start with the biggest box and figure out how to open it, only to find there is another one inside, and still more inside that. Similarly, each "answer" we come up with only raises more questions. Each new piece of research points to issues we hadn't considered before. I find this process exhilarating, both in my own research and when I read about other people's studies. Some of you may find the process frustrating, since there are so few absolutely firm answers, but I hope that most of you can share in the exhilaration.

Basic Questions About Development

These two journeys illustrate many of the basic issues, questions, and theories that are central to the study of human development. But I need to switch from the specifics involved in each of these two research areas and look at the issues and questions more broadly.

Reporters are taught to answer five basic questions about any story: who, what, when, where, and why. Psychologists must answer exactly the same questions about human behavior.

Who? The *who* in this case is primarily children. We are talking here about *child* development, so I will nearly always be describing studies of children or adolescents, and only rarely studies of adults.

More narrowly, we have to ask who participated in any given study. Did the researchers observe only fathers who *chose* to be present at their child's birth? Were only middle-class, or only poor, children observed? Can we explain the behavior of the two groups equally well? These questions become especially relevant when we try to generalize the results from one study to a whole group, or to children in general.

What? In many ways, this is the most basic question, the one most psychologists spend their time answering. Our most fundamental task is to *describe* behavior or development. What does a newborn baby do? What is an older child's reaction to a stranger? What does a 7-year-old do when confronted with a difficult intellectual task? What is the effect of a poor diet on the child's development? What are the effects of poverty? In what ways do boys respond differently than girls do? In nearly every chapter of this book, I will begin by trying to describe what we know about some aspect of development.

When? This question is perhaps more relevant for developmental psychologists than for others. The central question here is whether there are times when a particular type of experience will have a distinctly different effect than at any other time. Baby ducks, for example, will become *imprinted* on (become attached to and follow) any duck, or any other quacking, moving object that happens to be around them about 15 hours after they hatch. If nothing is moving or quacking at that critical point, they don't follow anything (Hess, 1972). So the period just around 15 hours after birth is a **critical period** for them to develop the proper following response.

Few psychologists suggest that there is anything quite so narrow or precise in human development, but broader **sensitive periods** have been suggested. John Kennell (Kennell, et. al, 1979) suggests exactly such a sensitive period for a mother immediately following the birth of her child. Kennell thinks the mother is then particularly attuned to cues from the child and particularly ready to become attached. Erik Erikson (1963) has argued that the whole first year of the child's life is an especially sensitive period for the development of trust in or attachment to the parents. If a firm, secure attachment is not formed during the first year or 18 months, Erikson thinks that it is very difficult to do so later.

The importance of such critical or sensitive periods is still being hotly debated among developmental psychologists. Most specifically, we are still arguing about whether the first two or three years of a child's life should be considered an especially sensitive period for many aspects of development. If a child is deprived of affection or enrichment during those years, can she ever recover? Can such deficiencies be made up later is she gets more enrichment or more affection? We will be meeting this issue in one form or another throughout the book.

Where? Until about five years ago, I would have left this word out of my list. A reporter certainly needs to describe where something happened. But as a rule, psychologists have paid relatively little attention to location. Recently, however, Urie Bronfenbrenner (1974, 1977) has taken us to task on this point.

Bronfenbrenner makes essentially two points, the first of which has to do with the way psychologists do business. A great deal of what we "know" about development is based on studies in artificial situations. We arrange some special set of circumstances, put children into that setting, and see what they do. If we want to know about fear of strangers among 10-month-old children, we may systematically expose children to a particular stranger, who acts in the same way toward each child. This *does* tell us something about the way babies react to strangers. But we also need to observe the same babies, or other babies of the same age, in their natural, complex environments to make sure that what we think we learned from the controlled situation still holds in the "real world."

Bronfenbrenner's second point is that every child grows up in a specific environmental network. The characteristics of that network have a major impact on the child. It matters whether the child is growing up in a slum, as opposed to a middle-class suburban neighborhood. And within a slum, it matters whether the child's own family is intact, whether his mother bothers to go to school to talk to the teacher, whether she takes him to the library, and so on. These are all part of the total *ecology* of childhood. If we are to understand development, we have to understand how different "ecological niches" change the ways a child grows or learns.

Bronfenbrenner is clearly correct on both points. *Where* matters as much as when or what.

Why? This final question takes us beyond the realm of description and into explanation. It leads us directly into theory.

A *theory* is basically an attempt at a general explanation that not only accounts for things that we have already observed but also tells us what *ought* to be true. A good theory thus makes order out of chaos and directs further research by focusing our attention on different aspects of the total problem and suggesting new solutions.

When several different theories are developed to explain the same basic descriptive facts—as in the case of the three theories of gender concept development I already talked about—good research is often stimulated. The issues are sharpened, and researchers can see what needs to be done next. The *why* and *what* questions thus interact constantly. You develop a theory to explain what you have observed, but then you make more observations to check on your theory.

Within the field of developmental psychology, there are four major theoretical approaches, three of which you have already met. I'll be describing each of them in more detail in later chapters, but let me give you some of the basic contrasts among the four at this stage. As you can see, I've summarized them in Table 1.2.

Obviously, the four approaches differ in significant ways. Among other things, they have focused on different aspects of development. Cognitive-developmental theorists like Jean Piaget, for example, have looked primarily at intellectual development. In contrast, psychoanalytic theorists like Freud have focused heavily on social and personality development and have had little to say about intellectual development. The maturational view represents still a third set of emphases: Arnold Gesell and other maturational theorists have looked almost exclusively at physical growth and development. Because of this specialization by theorists, you will find that only some of the theories apply to any given question we might have about development. The development of the gender concept and sex roles is one of the few areas in which three different theories have been offered—which is exactly why I chose to talk about it in this chapter.

Table 1.2 The Four Major Theoretical Approaches to Human Development

Approach	Major theorists	Aspect of development most studied	Typical questions asked
Learning	B. F. Skinner Walter Mischel Albert Bandura Robert Sears	Social behavior, such as dependency, aggression, or sex roles. Also concept development.	How does a child learn new concepts or new social skills? How do some children come to be more aggressive than others? What do children learn from watching TV?
Psychoanalytic	Sigmund Freud Erik Erikson	Personality development; sex roles; social behavior.	How do relationships between parent and child influence personality? How does deviant personality develop?
Cognitive-Developmental	Jean Piaget Heinz Werner Lev Vygotsky L. Kohlberg	Intellectual development, with some new emphasis on social interactions.	How does the child come to understand the world around her? How does her experience alter the way she approaches new tasks? What is the sequence of development of concepts like gender?
Maturational	Arnold Gesell Erik Lenneberg	Physical development; lately also language development.	How can we explain similarities among children in their physical and language development? What are the sequences in learning to walk or talk?

One of the risks in presenting the four theories to you in a brief table is that you may come away with the feeling that they don't overlap at all. You may also assume that one of them must be more right than the others.

I think there is some virtue in making the contrasts between the four approaches as distinct as possible. By focusing on a different set of questions, each theory has led to important new research that might not have been done had we tried to combine all four or select a single one.

But at the same time, I want to emphasize that the contrasts are not as sharp as they used to be. Many developmental psychologists are beginning to blend one or more of these approaches. For example, those of us who were attracted to the cognitive-developmental view (as I was) found after a period of years that we wanted to be able to say something about social and personality development as well. As a result, there is now a whole new area of research, often called "social cognition," that blends some elements from Piaget's work with elements from learning theory. Similarly, there has been a resurgence of interest in maturational approaches. More and more, we recognize that we have to begin with an understanding of the child's physical state or physical "readiness" before we can understand the effects of the environment or the way a child approaches some new task.

My basic point is that neither you nor I must choose a single one of these four approaches and apply it religiously or narrowly. Each theory has its strengths, and combinations of them are both possible and fruitful.

One Last Question: How Can We Use the Information?

Many psychologists would be completely satisfied with answering the five basic questions—who, what, when, where, and why. But there is a sixth question that is crucial for many of you as it is for me: How can we *use* the information we have about development? What is the practical relevance of a particular theory or a particular set of facts?

We've already seen one direct practical application in the case of Klaus and Kennell's studies of early attachments. In many places, hospital practices have been changed as a result of their research. Other findings we'll encounter throughout the book have had equivalent applications, which I'll try to point out as we go along.

The Basic Processes in Development

Over the past 80 years or so, developmental psychologists have been trying to answer these basic questions. In the course of their explorations, a number of basic processes have been emphasized, including heredity, maturation, and learning.

Internal versus External Influences

Historically, many of the discussions of such basic processes have been cast as a black and white argument between those who advocated a *nature* position, and those who argued for *nurture* as the basic processes.

The most extreme form of a "nurture" (environmental) position was proposed several hundred years ago by the philosopher John Locke (1690). He believed that an infant's mind was a **tabula rasa** (blank slate) at birth and that the slate was filled as a result of the baby's experiences.

By contrast, Jean Jacques Rousseau, a French philosopher, (1762) took an equally strong "nature" position. He believed that the child is born with an innate moral sense. The phrase "noble savage" was first used by Rousseau. He thought that if the child were allowed to develop naturally, exploring the world in his own way, he would grow into a fully moral and knowledgeable adult.

The modern versions of this argument can be seen in the

contrast between some learning theory approaches to development, which share Locke's emphasis on the environment, and the cognitive-developmental view, which shares Rousseau's emphasis on the child's active construction of concepts and understanding of the world. The same contrast can be seen in the **heredity versus environment** arguments over the sources of differences in IQ scores.

Sometimes casting issues in such black and white, either/or terms is useful. It may sharpen our thinking. But in the real world, *nothing* is entirely internally or entirely externally determined. There is always some interaction between the two.

In the next few pages, I will be talking about each of the basic processes as if each one worked independently. But you should keep in mind that the developmental outcome for a given child *always* results from a mixture of internal and external influences.

Heredity

Let me begin with the most obvious internal influence, namely, **heredity.** Each of you inherited from your parents a specific set of characteristics or tendencies (I'll describe the process by which this occurs in Chapter 2). For example, I inherited blue eyes, tallness, and a tendency to prematurely gray hair.

Beyond such physical characteristics, the direct effects of heredity are much harder to pin down. Probably we inherit some characteristics that affect our ability to handle intellectual tasks, as measured by an IQ test, although just how large an influence this may be has been and is still actively debated. In fact, this particular debate has been so extended that many of us wearied of the argument and set the issue aside. But in the past decade or so, the possible impact of heredity on a wide range of behaviors has reemerged as an important possibility.

For example, temperamental patterns such as a tendency to be slow or fast paced, or to be outgoing or shy, may be partly inherited (Buss & Plomin, 1975). We may also inherit some potential for certain patterns of emotional disturbance, such as schizophrenia, or manic-depressive psychosis (Gottesman & Shields, 1972). I confess that I begin with a bias against such hereditary explanations, but we both need to keep an open mind about potential hereditary influences on behavior.

Maturation A special subcategory of heredity is **maturation,** genetically programmed *sequential patterns of change* in such physical characteristics as body size and shape, hormone patterns, or coordination. These sequences, which begin at conception and continue until death, are shared by all members of our species. The "instructions" for these sequences are part of

Figure 1.6 These children obviously have different heredities. They are all about the same age, but differ greatly in height; one has poor eyesight while the others do not. But they also share basic maturational patterns. They all crawled before they walked; they will all go through adolescent changes in the same order. So hereditary "information" affects the ways we are the same as well as the ways we differ.

the specific hereditary information that is passed on at the moment of conception.

In its pure form, maturationally determined development occurs regardless of practice or training. You don't have to practice growing pubic hair; you don't have to be taught how to walk. But these changes do not occur in a vacuum. The child is maturing in a particular environment, and even the very powerful maturational patterns can be disturbed by deprivation or by accidents.

A child who does not get enough to eat may walk later than one who has a good diet. During prenatal development (the period from conception until birth), the sequence of changes that unfolds can be disturbed by such things as diseases in the mother. Even the physical changes at adolescence can be altered in extreme circumstances, particularly by malnutrition. Severely undernourished girls do not menstruate, for example.

One famous study that shows this kind of environmental interference with maturational timetables was carried out by Wayne Dennis (1960). Dennis observed the physical development of children raised in orphanages in Iran during the late 1950s. In one of the orphanages, the children were placed in cribs on their backs, in mattresses that had developed hollows so that it was very difficult for the baby to roll over. Since they were rarely on their stomachs, these babies had little chance to practice the movements that are the first stages in the sequence leading to crawling and walking. As a result, many of these babies never did crawl. Instead, they learned to get around by "scooting," a form of locomotion in which the child sits on her rump and pulls herself along by bending and unbending her knees. All the children did learn to walk eventually, but the "scooters" were very much delayed and their sequence of prewalking movements was altered. So although maturational sequences are powerful, they are affected by the kind of stimulation available to the child.

Maturation versus Growth I need to touch on one other possible point of confusion about the term "maturation." Maturation is often used as a synonym for "growth," but the terms do not mean exactly the same thing. Growth refers to some kind of step-by-step change in quantity, as in size. We speak of the growth of the child's vocabulary or the growth of his body. Such changes in quantity *may* be the result of maturation, but not necessarily. A child's body may change in size because her diet has changed, which is an external effect, or because her muscles and bones have grown, which is probably a maturational effect.

Physical State

Another internal influence, more short-term, is a person's immediate physical state. The mother's physical state changes as her hormones vary during pregnancy. The changes in alertness we all experience during a normal day are also variations in state, as is our overall health. A child who has a bad cold is not likely to achieve as high a score on an IQ test as a child in good health.

There has been an increasing emphasis on state in studies of development, particularly studies of infants, whose states change rapidly from one moment to another—from alert awake, to crying, to sleeping. The results of any study of infants will be affected by the physical state of the babies when they are observed. And what a child learns from a given situation, or is able to perform, will depend on her state at that moment.

Environmental Influences

There has been a great deal of research in developmental psychology on the effects of major external influences such as poverty or social class. This research, and equivalent studies of the effects of family patterns, diet, or ethnic differences, essentially involves comparisons of groups who have had widely differing experiences. The basic questions being asked are *what* questions rather than *why* questions. What is the effect of poverty on children's language development or on physical growth? What is the effect of having no father or no mother in the home on a child's gender concept?

A great deal of useful information has been generated from research focused on questions like these, but it only takes us so far. We may find, for example, that children raised in poverty-level families know fewer words than do children raised in more financially secure families. But why? Inevitably this *why* question leads us to much more detailed examinations of the environments of the two types of children. Who talks to the child? How often? What kind of words are used? When we get to questions like these, we have moved from the very broadest environmental effects down to specific individual experiences.

Learning

Learning is one of the fundamental processes by which individual experiences affect a child. Some of you may have encountered the basic principles of learning in earlier courses in psychology. But let me review the concepts here. There are three basic types of learning, all of which enter into our understanding of the developing child.

Classical Conditioning This type of learning involves the acquisition of new signals for existing responses. If you touch a baby on the cheek, he will turn toward the touch and begin to suck. In the technical terminology of classical conditioning, the touch on the cheek is the **unconditioned stimulus;** the turning and sucking are **unconditioned responses.** The baby already knows how to do all that; in fact, these are automatic reflexes. But suppose that the sound of the mother's footsteps and the feeling of being picked up always come just before the baby is touched on the cheek. Now what happens? The sound and the feelings eventually "trigger" the responses of turning and sucking. They have become **conditioned stimuli.** The steps in the process are described in Figure 1.7.

This might seem a relatively minor sort of learning, but it is particularly important in the child's developing emotional responses. Things or people that are present when you feel good come to be associated with "feeling good." Those that are associated with uncomfortable feelings may later trigger fear or anxiety or embarrassment. Since a child's mother is present so often when nice things happen—when the child feels warm, comfortable, and cuddled—"mother" usually comes to be a conditioned stimulus for pleasant feelings. A tormenting older sibling, however, may come to be a conditioned stimulus for angry feelings.

Sometimes it can take only one occasion to create an emotional conditioned response. I remember an occasion at least

Figure 1.7 The three steps in the development of a classically conditioned response. In the first step, the unconditioned stimulus automatically triggers the unconditioned response. In step 2, some additional stimulus occurs at the same time as the unconditioned stimulus. In the final step, the new stimulus—called the conditioned stimulus—is also able to trigger the original response.

Step 1		Step 2		Step 3	
Stimulus	Response	Stimulus	Response	Stimulus	Response
Touch on the cheek (Unconditioned Stimulus: UCS) →	Head turn (Unconditioned response: UCR)	Touch on the cheek (UCS) → Mother's voice (Conditioned stimulus: CS)	Head turn (UCR)	Touch (UCS) → Voice (CS) →	Head turn (UCR)

ten years ago when I was invited to give a talk to a group of psychologists in a town near Seattle. It turned out to be one of the worst talks I have ever given—not only controversial but poorly organized and unclear. I felt embarrassed. Ever since then, every time I even drive by that particular town on the freeway, I feel embarrassed. The sight of the place has become a conditioned stimulus for my discomfort. The feeling has weakened somewhat over the years, but it is still there.

The important point here is that from the earliest months of life, children learn new cues through classical conditioning, particularly cues for emotional responses.

Operant Conditioning This type of learning, also called *instrumental conditioning*, involves the use of rewards and punishments to change a person's behavior. It is this type of learning that Mischel thinks is involved in a child's learning of his gender, for example. The basic principles are these:

1. Any behavior that is reinforced will be more likely to occur again in the same or similar situation. There are two types of reinforcements. **Positive reinforcements** are pleasant consequences such as praise, a smile, food, a hug, or attention. Any time one of these occurs, the child is likely to try to repeat whatever it was that produced the goodies.

   Negative reinforcements, in contrast, are unpleasant events that when *removed* tend to strengthen whatever you did to remove them. This is a confusing concept, so let me give you an example. If you scold your child when she is drawing on the walls with a crayon, she will probably stop drawing and you will stop scolding. In this way her stopping has been strengthened by the removal of your scolding. A third concept is that of **punishment.** Many people assume that punishments are the same as negative reinforcements, but the terms are used differently by most psychologists. While a negative reinforcer *strengthens* behavior by its *removal,* a punishment is intended to *weaken* some behavior by its *application.* If you spank your son after he throws his glass of milk at you or take your daughter's allowance away after she stays out past her curfew, you are applying punishment in the hope that the children won't repeat their unacceptable behavior.

This use of the word punishment fits with the common understanding of the term and shouldn't be too confusing. What *is* confusing is the fact that punishments don't always do what they are intended to do. Your child may have thrown his milk glass to get your attention, so spanking him may be a positive reinforcement instead of a punishment, as you had thought. Because of this difficulty with the concept of punishment, some strict learning theorists (such as Sidney Bijou and Donald Baer, 1961) prefer not to use the term at all. I'm not that strict. In the rest of the book, I will use the term punishment in its common sense—something unpleasant done with the intent of eliminating some unacceptable behavior.

2. When you reinforce someone part of the time, but not all the time—a procedure called *partial reinforcement*—not only is his behavior strengthened, but it is also harder to get rid of. If you only smile at your daughter every fifth or sixth time she brings a picture to show you, she'll keep on bringing pictures for a very long stretch, even after you quit smiling altogether. In the technical words of learning theory, the partially reinforced response is highly resistant to **extinction.**

3. Reinforcements do not have to be from the outside. There are also internal reinforcements, called *intrinsic rewards* or *intrinsic reinforcements,* including such things as the pleasure a child feels when she finally figures out how to draw a star or the sense of satisfaction you may experience after strenuous exercise. Pride, discovery, that "ah ha" experience are all powerful intrinsic reinforcements.

All three of these basic principles of learning theory have direct relevance for day-to-day child-rearing practices. Some of the applications are discussed in Box 1.1.

Box 1.1 Some Applications of Learning Principles to Child Rearing

All parents, whether they are aware of it or not, reinforce some behaviors in their children by praising them, giving them attention, or treats. And all parents do their best to discourage unpleasant behavior through punishment. Often, however, parents think that they are rewarding behaviors they like and ignoring those they don't like, and yet the results don't seem to meet their expectations. When this happens, it may be because they are dealing with the operation of more than one learning principle at once.

For example, suppose you have a favorite armchair in your living room that is being systematically ruined by the dirt and pressure of little feet climbing up the back of the chair. You want the children to *stop* climbing up the chair. So you scold them. You may even carefully time your scolding so that it should operate as a negative reinforcer by stopping your scolding when they stop climbing. But nothing works. They keep on leaving those muddy footprints on your favorite chair. Why? It could be because the children *enjoy* climbing up the chair. So the climbing is intrinsically reinforcing to the child, and that effect is clearly stronger than your negative reinforcement or punishment. One way to deal with this might be to provide something *else* that they could climb.

A second example of the complications of applying learning principles to everyday dealings with children is what happens when you inadvertently create a partial reinforcement schedule. Suppose your 3-year-old son repeatedly demands attention while you are fixing dinner. Because you don't want to reinforce this behavior, you ignore him the first six or eight times he says "Mommy" or tugs at your clothes. But after the ninth or tenth repetition, with his voice getting louder and more whining each time, you can't stand it any longer and finally say something like "All right! What do you want!" Since you have ignored most of his demands, you might well be convinced that you have not been reinforcing the whining or the demanding. But what you have actually done is create a partial reinforcement schedule; you have rewarded only every tenth whine. And we know that this pattern of reinforcement helps to create behavior that is *very* hard to extinguish. So your son may continue to be demanding and whining for a very long time, even if you succeed in ignoring it completely.

Because many parents have difficulty with situations just like this and with seeing just what it is they are reinforcing, many family therapists have begun to ask families to keep detailed records of their child's behavior and their responses to it. Gerald Patterson (1975) has done this in his work with families of highly aggressive or destructive children. When the families see, through their own record keeping, just what it is they are doing to reinforce destructive behavior, it is much easier for the therapist to help the family by helping the mother and father alter their responses to their child.

Observational Learning Reinforcements clearly do affect behavior. But they are not necessary for learning to occur. Learning can also occur merely as a result of watching someone else perform some action. This is the second principle Mischel used in accounting for the child's learning of the gender concept and sex role. The child learns how to be a boy by watching his father's behavior.

Learning of this type, called observational learning or **modeling,** is involved in a wide range of behaviors. Children learn ways of hitting from watching other people (in real life and on TV); they learn generous behavior by watching others donate money or goods; they learn attitudes by copying the words and actions of their parents; they learn physical skills such as bike riding or skiing partly from watching other people demonstrate them.

Traditionally, all three types of learning—classical and operant conditioning and observational learning—have been thought of as essentially automatic processes. The child has been viewed as a passive recipient of these environmental influences—the environment is writing on the blank slate. But increasingly, researchers and theorists are coming to understand that the child is actively involved in the learning process. The concept of intrinsic reinforcement obviously puts the child back into the picture. Observational learning also requires the child's involvement. She can only learn from what she sees, and she is in control of what she looks at. Her understanding of what she has observed also affects what she learns, so her learning will change as her cognitive development proceeds.

Transactions and Interactions

As I pointed out earlier, most psychologists today assume that development results from a combination of influences or processes. It is not wholly environmental and not wholly internally determined; it is both. The basic task is therefore to describe the particular mixture of forces that affects each aspect of development.

One kind of mixture would be an additive one. For example, a child's diet might add to the effects of his heredity: good intellectual heredity plus good diet would produce the brightest children. Either good diet and bad heredity or good heredity and bad diet would result in people of medium brightness, and poor diet and poor heredity would result in the least-gifted individuals.

There may be some additive mixtures like this, but most often what we see instead is an *interaction* between several influences. Both heredity and diet may matter, for example, but some children may inherit qualities that make them less vulnerable to poor diet or to unstimulating environments. The outcome we observe is the result of both the child's internal characteristics and the environmental influences, but the relationship is more complex than just adding the two together.

Recently, developmental psychologists have also begun to focus on another complexity in the process, namely, the child's influence on the environment around him. A temperamentally difficult baby calls forth different behaviors from her parents than does a temperamentally easy child; a child who complies right away to requests or demands develops a very different relationship with his parents than a child who is more defiant. The parents bring their own tendencies to these encounters, but the child is a dynamic partner in the developing patterns. It is this *transaction* between the parent and the child, between the child's qualities and the environment, that is now seen as important.

Because the causes of behavior lie in such interactions and transactions, it is often hard to answer the *why* questions. But if we are to understand how an individual child turns out the way she does, it is precisely this complex set of relationships we will have to untangle.

Answering Questions

I've raised a great many questions in the course of this chapter. I've talked about "research" as if you all know what is involved in doing research to answer the sorts of questions we'll be exploring. But many of you may not have much familiarity with the techniques of psychological research. At a minimum, you will need to understand a few terms and concepts that you'll encounter in the rest of this book.

The Three Main Ways of Answering Questions

Psychologists interested in development (or in other aspects of behavior) have three main techniques available to them:

1. Watching people, which is usually called *observation*
2. Asking people, by the use of *interviews, questionnaires,* or other tests
3. *Experimental procedures*

Observations There are a great many techniques for observing children or adults, some of which are outlined in the Appendix. The most frequent procedure is to watch for some specific behaviors and simply count how often they occur. This can be done in natural settings, or in a controlled laboratory environment. Klaus and Kennell used observation in their study of mothers and infants: They counted smiling, close body contact, face-to-face encounters, and other specific events.

Questionnaires and Interviews Written lists of questions are not often used in developmental research with young children, but interviews are rather common. Slaby and Frey interviewed the children in their study by asking them questions about whether they'd be daddys or mommys when they grew up.

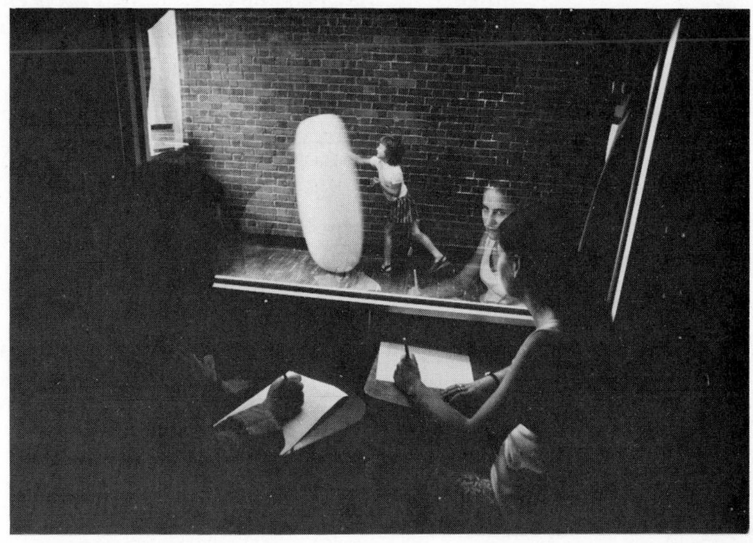

Figure 1.8 These observers, watching through a one-way mirror, can count the number of times the child performs particular behaviors of interests—such as, perhaps, aggression in this case. Arrangements like these are quite common in research laboratories, but observations are also done in natural settings, too.

Experiments Experimental procedures are also common in studies of children. In an experiment, as opposed to a *naturalistic* study (one in which the subjects are observed or studied in their own natural surroundings without intervention), the experimenter has control of and intentionally manipulates the critical conditions or behaviors under study. Ordinarily, there are at least two groups to which subjects are assigned randomly. The **experimental group** is given some special experience, such as the extended contact in the Klaus and Kennell studies; the **control group** has everything the experimental group has *except* that special experience, like Klaus and Kennell's "regular hospital routine" group. If, after the treatment, the behavior of the two groups differs, the experimenter can be fairly sure it is because of the particular experiences provided.

Figure 1.9 shows the design of the Klaus and Kennell study so you can see the contrast between the experimental and control group more clearly. Note that the *only* difference between the two groups was the amount of contact with the infant in the first days after birth. All the other observations and measures of the mother-infant pair were the same.

Another contrast that may highlight the features of an experiment is to compare the Klaus and Kennell study with the Gaulin-Kremer study of contact between mothers and infants, which I described earlier. Gaulin-Kremer's study is *not* an experiment; it is a naturalistic study. She did not alter any experience the mothers had. Instead, she observed the effect of a *natu-*

Figure 1.9 The basic design of the Klaus and Kennell study. This is an experimental design rather than a naturalistic study, since the experimenters deliberately varied the experiences of the subjects.

	Treatment	Measures of the effect of the treatment		
		at birth	at 1 month	at 1 year
Experimental group	"Extended contact" during the 2–3 days of hospitalization	Observed mothers and infants for smiling, and style of physical contact	Interviewed mothers; examined baby in mother's presence; filmed mother feeding baby	Interviewed mothers; examined infant in mother's presence; filmed feeding of infant, and tested infant
Control group	Normal hospital experience; no extra contact	Same as above	Same as above	Same as above

rally occurring variation in the length of time between delivery and the mother's first extended contact with the baby. Such a strategy will work fine for many purposes, as long as the naturally occurring variation is really random and not produced by some other factor you're not aware of. For example, if the mothers who are given more drugs during delivery regularly wait longer before they see their infants, then the drugs, and not the timing of the contact, might be the crucial factors. An experimental study like Klaus and Kennell's avoids this problem, since the mothers involved were assigned randomly to the two groups.

Combinations of Techniques The three techniques for answering questions are often used in the same study. Observation, interviews, or questionnaires may be used as part of an experimental design, as they were in Klaus and Kennell's study. Or they may be part of naturalistic studies, as they were in the Gaulin-Kremer research. Unstructured studies are often used in the early stages of research on a particular question, with experimental studies coming later, when the researchers want to answer the "why" questions.

Special Features of Developmental Research

The three techniques I've just described can be used to study any aspect of behavior. But when we study *development*, special techniques are needed. Very often, we want to ask questions about changes that occur with age. When the questions do concern age, there are basically two kinds of studies that can be done.

Longitudinal Studies In a **longitudinal study,** the *same* individuals are studied repeatedly over a period of time. The Klaus and Kennell study is a short-term longitudinal study, since they observed the mothers and infants in the hospital, at one month, and at one year. This kind of procedure is absolutely essential if we want to answer questions about consistency of individual characteristics over time or about the long-term effects of some experience.

Cross-sectional Studies Obviously, longitudinal studies take a great deal of time; and for many age comparisons, we can do just as well by studying *different* groups of children at different ages, which is called a **cross-sectional** design. The Slaby and Frey study of gender concepts is cross-sectional. They interviewed one group of 2-year-olds, another group of 3-year-olds, and so on. This can be a very useful strategy; but is has distinct limitations, particularly when we want to talk about the *sequence* of some developmental pattern.

How to Judge the Quality of Research

A final piece of information you will need at this stage is how to judge the quality of research you read. Not all research is equally good or equally well designed, particularly when it comes to studies of applied or practical problems with children. Table 1.3 gives you a checklist you might use as a starting point in making a judgment about research.

This checklist won't be crucial in evaluating research I will describe throughout this book. I've already applied my own standards to the studies I have chosen to discuss. But you need to keep these ideas in mind when you come across reports of research in magazines or newspapers. If a woman's magazine reports on a reader-response survey about parental discipline techniques, for example, I'd be wary about the results because of the choice of subjects. Only parents who read that magazine and chose to send in their answers are included in the results. You have no way of knowing how those people are different from a random group of parents. But even research like this can promote new ideas and lead to additional, better-controlled studies.

Table 1.3 A Checklist of Things to Look for in Evaluating Research

Clarity	Can you understand what was done and what was found?
Importance of Findings	Does the study have some obvious practical relevance? Does it help to untangle a theoretical puzzle? Does it advance our understanding of some problem?
Promotion of New Ideas	Good research should lead to new ideas, new theoretical insights, new questions, as well as answering old questions. Does this study do that?
Consistency	Are the findings from this study consistent with the results of other research? Are they consistent with your own experience? This may be hard for you to judge, since you don't know all the other research on a given question, but it is important to keep it in mind if you can. Don't throw out inconsistent results, but look carefully at any study that doesn't fit with other evidence.
Replicability	If the same research were done again, would the same result occur? Exact replications aren't often done in social science research, but they probably ought to be more often.
Choice of Subjects	Were all the children or families studied middle class? Or all from poverty environments? Did all the subjects volunteer? Can we generalize the results to other groups?
Appropriateness of Method	Was the method chosen for the study consistent with the questions being asked? For example, is the researcher using a cross-sectional design to study consistency of behavior? If so, it's the wrong design for that question.

Summary

1. The study of human development, like the study of any other aspect of human behavior, can be seen as a kind of adventure, even a detective story, in which clues are followed from one study to the next, leading toward greater understanding.
2. One example of such a process is the work of Klaus and Kennell on the early attachment process between a mother and her newborn infant. The existing clues suggest that the earlier the contact between mother and in-

fant, the stronger her initial bond to the child.
3. A second example is the work on the development of the gender concept. Three distinct theories have been offered to account for this development, each of which has led to new research.
4. When psychologists study children and their development, six basic questions are relevant: who, what, when, where, why, and how can the information be used?
5. Most of the effort of psychologists has gone into answering *what* questions—into describing basic patterns of development. Answering *why* questions nearly always involves devising and testing some theory about the developmental process.
6. Four major theories of development have been proposed over the past decades: learning theory, psychoanalytic theory, cognitive-developmental theory, and maturational theory. The four differ in the questions they ask, the aspect of development they study, and the assumptions they make about the relative importance of internal and external influences on behavior.
7. Historically, the contrast between internal and external explanations has dominated theoretical arguments. Theorists who emphasize internal influences point to heredity, maturation, physical states, and inborn abilities as crucial for development. Those who emphasize external influences point to the impact of specific learning and broad environmental experiences.
8. Maturational effects can be seen in the unfolding, sequential patterns of physical change that are shared by all members of our species.
9. Hereditary effects can be seen in those individual physical and possibly emotional and intellectual qualities each of us inherits from our parents.
10. Three major types of learning occur: classical conditioning, operant conditioning, and observational learning. Recent thinking about learning processes places more emphasis on the role of the child in any learning.
11. Development of any skill or knowledge in the child is a complex product of the effects of these several processes and influences. The combination of effects is rarely simply additive. More often, there is some interaction of forces. In particular, the complexities of the transaction between parent and child, and child and parent, needs to be taken into consideration.
12. In doing research to test theories or to answer *what* questions, there are three major ways to obtain information: by watching people, by asking questions, and by designing controlled experiments.
13. In an experiment, the researcher ordinarily assigns subjects randomly to an experimental group and to one or more control groups. The experimental group is then given some specific experience that the control group does not have. The effects of the experiment can be seen if the two groups later behave differently.
14. In studying developmental issues, two other types of research are important: a longitudinal study, in which the same subjects are observed or tested repeatedly over time, and a cross-sectional study, in which children or adults of different ages are each observed under the same conditions.
15. In deciding on the value of any piece of research, the major points to watch for are clarity, the importance of the finding, whether it promotes new questions or insights, the consistency and replicability, the suitability of the subjects chosen, and the appropriateness of the method used.

Key Terms

Classical conditioning One of three major types of learning. An automatic, unconditioned response such as an emotional feeling or a reflex comes to be triggered by a new cue, called the conditioned stimulus (CS), after the CS has been paired several times with the original unconditioned stimulus.

Cognitive-developmental theory Major theoretical approach associated primarily with the work of Piaget and his followers; focuses on the interaction of the child's internally developing understanding of the world with his environmental experiences; major emphasis on intellectual development; heavy emphasis on sequences of development.

Conditioned stimulus In classical conditioning this is the cue that, after being paired a number of times with the unconditioned stimulus, comes to trigger the unconditioned response.

Control group The group of subjects in an experiment who do *not* receive any special treatment.

Critical period A period of time during development when the organism is especially responsive to and learns from a specific type of stimulation. The same stimulation at other points in development has little or no effect.

Cross-sectional study A study in which different groups of individuals of different ages are all studied at the same time.

Experimental group The group (or groups) of subjects in an experiment who are given some special treatment.

Extinction A term used in learning theory to describe the weakening or disappearance of a response in a person's behavioral repertoire.

Heredity The unique set of "instructions" for physical and possibly emotional and intellectual skills that makes each individual different from every other.

Identification The process proposed by Freud by which a child attempts to "incorporate" the actions, values, and attitudes of another person, usually the parent of the same sex.

Imitation A general term describing the copying of a behavior of another person. Similar to the concept of modeling.

Instrumental conditioning Another term used to describe operant conditioning—conditioning in which the principles of reinforcement are operating.

Interviews A broad category of research strategy in which people are asked about themselves, their behavior, their feelings.

Longitudinal study A study in which the same subjects are observed or assessed repeatedly over a period of months or years.

Maturation The sequential unfolding of physical characteristics, governed by "instructions" contained in the genetic code and shared by all members of the species.

Modeling A term used by Bandura and others to describe observational learning. The child or adult models (copies or imitates) the behavior of some other person.

Negative reinforcement Any event whose removal strengthens the probability of the behavior associated with its removal.

Observational learning Learning of motor skills, attitudes, or other behaviors through observing someone else perform them.

Positive reinforcement Any event whose presence strengthens the probability of the behavior coming immediately before.

Punishment Unpleasant consequences, administered after some undesired behavior by a child (or an adult) with the intent of extinguishing the behavior.

Reinforcement An event that, following some response, increases the likelihood of that response the next time the same cue is present.

Sensitive period Similar to a critical period except broader and less specific. A time in development when a particular type of stimulation is particularly important or effective.

Tabula rasa Literally a "blank slate." The condition that John Locke and other "nurture" philosophers thought a child's mind was in at birth.

Unconditioned response In classical conditioning this is the basic unlearned response that is triggered by the unconditioned stimulus.

Unconditioned stimulus In classical conditioning this is the cue or signal that automatically (without learning) triggers the unconditioned response.

Suggested Readings

Achenbach. T. M. Research in developmental psychology: Concepts, strategies, methods. New York: The Free Press, 1978. This is a difficult book but an excellent source for more detailed information about developmental research. The author also includes information about topics such as ethics, which are important for researchers to be aware of.

Chukofsky, K. From two to five. Berkeley: University of California Press, 1963.

An absolutely delightful book by a Russian poet about his observations of children, the kinds of language they use, the concepts they have, and the poetry of their speech. Entirely nontechnical, it may turn you on to children if you aren't already.

Lavatelli, C. S., & Stendler, F. Readings in child behavior and development (3rd ed.). New York: Harcourt Brace Jovanovich, 1972.

This collection of readings has an excellent selection of papers on the major theoretical alternatives, including papers by Piaget, Erikson, Skinner, and Anna Freud. If you are interested in getting some sense of the flavor of these different approaches, this is a good single source.

Project 1.1 Observation of a Child

I have several purposes in suggesting this project. First, many of you will have had relatively little contact with young children and need to spend some time simply observing a child to make other sections of the book more meaningful. Second, I think it is important that you begin to get some sense of the difficulties involved in observing and studying children. So I am suggesting here, as a preliminary step, that you keep a straightforward observational record, noting down each thing that the child does or says. You will find, I think, that the task is less straightforward than it seems, but this type of observation is the simplest place I know to begin.

Step 1. Locate a child between 18 months and 6 years of age; age 2, 3, or 4 would be best.

Step 2. Obtain permission from the child's parents for observation. Tell them that it is for a course assignment, that you will not be testing the child in any way but merely want to observe a normal child in her normal situation.

Step 3. Arrange a time when you can observe the child in her "natural habitat" for about one hour. If the child is in nursery school, it's all right to observe her there, if you get permission from the teachers. If not, the observation should be done at home or in some situation familiar to the child. You must not baby-sit during the observation. You must be free to be in the background and cannot be responsible for the child during the observation.

Step 4. When the time for the observation arrives, place yourself in as unobtrusive a place as possible. Take a small stool with you if you can so that you can move around as the child moves. If you are in the child's home, she will probably ask what you are doing. Say that you are doing something for school and will be writing things down for a while. Do not invite any kind of contact with the child; don't meet her eyes; don't smile; and don't talk except when the child talks directly to you. If the child talks to you, say that you are busy and will play a little later.

Step 5. For one hour, write down everything the child does insofar as possible. Write down the child's speech word for word. If the child is talking to someone else, write down the other person's replies, too, if you can. Describe the child's movements. Throughout, keep your description as free of evaluation and words of intent as you can. Do not write "Sarah went into the kitchen to get a cookie." You don't know why she went originally. What you saw was that she stopped what she had been doing, got up, and walked into the kitchen. There you see her getting a cookie. Describe the behavior that way rather than making assumptions about what is happening in the child's head. Avoid words like "try," "angrily," "pleaded," "wanted," and so on. Describe only what you see and hear. (This may turn out to be harder than you expect.)

Step 6. When you have completed the observation, reread what you wrote and consider the following questions: Did you manage to keep all description of intent out of your record? Were you able to remain objective? Were you able to write down all that the child did? If not, what sort of things were left out? What kind of information about this child could be extracted from your record? Could anyone get a measure of the child's level of activity or count the number of times the child asked for attention? What changes in the method of observation would you have to introduce to obtain other sorts of information? What was the effect, do you think, of your presence on the child's behavior?

Part One

The Beginnings of Life

Preview of Chapter 2

Prenatal Development

I had lunch recently with my friend Jane, who had just discovered she was pregnant for the first time at age 36. She had been to see her doctor, of course, to confirm the pregnancy, but she had thought of a lot of questions since then. She wanted to know whether there were any extra risks involved in having a first baby at 36. She'd heard there was an increased risk of some kinds of abnormalities. Was that true? She also wanted to know more about exercise and diet. Would it be okay for her to keep on running while she was pregnant? Jane and I run together occasionally, three or four miles at a time. Should she stop that? And what about an occasional glass of wine or a cocktail now and then? I told her what I knew, and we made up a list of other questions that she would want to discuss with her doctor—questions about testing for hereditary diseases or disorders, about exercise, and about diet.

Most of you will not be 36 when you or your spouse becomes pregnant for the first time (although delayed first pregnancies are becoming more common); but all the other questions are good ones for both prospective fathers and mothers to think about seriously.

There are equally important theoretical questions. The broad problem for psychologists, physicians, and biologists is to understand the basic process of development from conception to birth. How does that development proceed? What can influence it? Drugs? Diseases? Diet? Characteristics of the mother such as her age or general health? What general principles can we come up with that describe prenatal development and the influences of the environment on it?

Figure 2.1 The period of pregnancy is normally one of excited anticipation for both the father and the mother.

Conception

The first step in the development of a single human being is that moment of conception when a single sperm cell from the male pierces the wall of the ovum of the female. That sounds so simple when it is put into one sentence; but since the sperm and the ovum both have to be in the right place at the same time, it is more complicated than it sounds.

Ordinarily, a woman produces one **ovum** (egg) per month from one of her two ovaries. This occurs roughly midway between two menstrual periods. If it is not fertilized, the ovum travels from the ovary down the **fallopian tube** toward the uterus, where it gradually disintegrates and is expelled as part of the next menstruation.

When a woman has intercourse, millions of sperm are deposited in her vagina. They travel through the cervix and the uterus, and several thousand of them survive to make their way up the fallopian tubes. If the timing is right and there is an ovum in the fallopian tube or about to be released by the ovary, then one of the sperm may manage to penetrate the ovum, and a child will be conceived.

Once conception has occurred, the ovum continues on its journey down the fallopian tube, where, instead of disintegrating, it implants itself in the wall of the uterus and begins the long developmental process. Figure 2.2 shows part of this sequence of events in schematic form.

Figure 2.2 Schematic diagram of the female reproductive system showing how conception occurs. The ovum has traveled from the ovary partway down the fallopian tube, where it is met by one or more sperm, which have traveled from the vagina, through the cervix and the uterus.

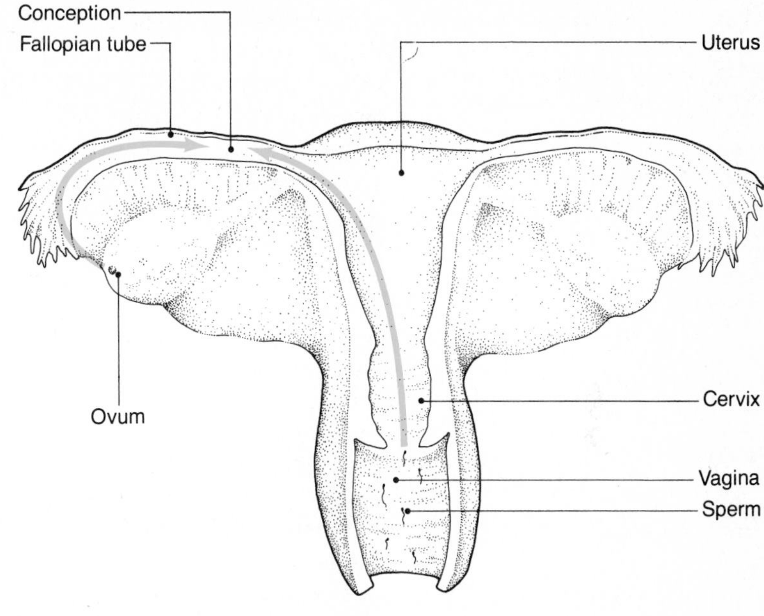

The Basic Genetics of Conception

As most of you no doubt know, the nucleus of each cell of our bodies contains a set of 46 **chromosomes,** arranged in 23 pairs. These chromosomes include all the genetic information for that individual. They control unique physical qualities, shared growth patterns, and possibly temperament, intelligence, and other characteristics.

Whenever a new cell is needed for growth or tissue replacement, an existing cell divides in a process called **mitosis.** Just before the division, the chromosomes double up so that when the division is complete, both the old cell and the new cell have the full set of 23 pairs of chromosomes.

Germ Cells

The process differs only in the case of **germ cells,** which is the technical term for the sperm and the ovum. In the early stages of development, germ cells divide by mitosis, just as other cells do. But the final step, called **meiosis,** is different. In meiosis, the chromosomes do *not* double themselves when cell division occurs. Instead, both the old cell and the new cell receive 1 chromosome from each of the 23 pairs. Germ cells, then, have only 23 chromosomes each instead of 46.

A second characteristic of meiosis is a process called **cross-**

ing over. At one point in the cell division sequence, the two chromosomes that make up each pair line up directly opposite one another, and some portions of each chromosome may be exchanged from one member of the pair to the other. One of the effects of crossing over is to increase immensely the number of possible combinations of "instructions" in each set of 23 chromosomes in sperm and ova.

When a child is conceived, the 23 chromosomes in the ova and the 23 in the sperm combine to form the 23 pairs that will be part of each cell in the newly developing body.

Males and Females

Just as there are two kinds of cells, there are also two kinds of chromosomes. In 22 of the pairs, called **autosomes,** the members of the pair look alike and contain information relating to the same set of characteristics. But one pair, called the *sex chromosomes,* both look different and perform a different function. They determine the sex of the child.

In the normal female, each of the chromosomes in this pair is large and under a microscope bears some resemblance to an X. In the male, there is only one X chromosome, and one smaller Y chromosome.

Given what I have just said about the special characteristics of germ cells, you can see how the sex of the child is determined by the X or Y chromosome from the sperm. Since the mother has *only* X chromosomes on this pair, every ovum carries an X. But the father has both X and Y chromosomes. When the father's germ cells divide, half the sperm will carry an X, half a Y. If the sperm that fertilizes the ovum carries an X, then the child inherits an XX pattern and will be a girl. If the fertilizing sperm carries a Y, then the combination is XY, and the infant will be a boy. (Thus, contrary to historical belief, it is the father, and not the mother, who determines the sex of the child.)

Twins and Siblings

At this stage, many people begin to wonder why all the children in a given family don't turn out to be exactly alike. If each of you receives 23 chromosomes from your mother and 23 from your father, why don't you look and act just like your brothers and sisters?

The answer should be clear from what I've already said about meiosis and crossing over. Not only does each germ cell have a different combination of 23 chromosomes, but because of crossing over, the chromosomes themselves may contain different sets of information. In view of the vast numbers of possible combinations, the wonder is that brothers and sisters are anything like one another at all.

The exception to this rule is in the case of identical twins,

Figure 2.3 Identical twins, like the ones on the left, come from the same fertilized ovum and have exactly the same heredity. They look alike and frequently act alike, too. Fraternal twins, like the ones on the right, are no more like one another than any other pair of brothers or sisters.

who come from the same fertilized ovum. In such cases the ovum divides into two distinct entities *after* it has been fertilized by the sperm. Each of the two developing organisms then has the same genetic material in the same combination, and the two children should turn out to be alike in all those areas affected by heredity.

Fraternal twins, in contrast, develop out of separately fertilized ova. This can happen if the woman ovulates more than once in a given month (something which is fairly common among women taking fertility drugs), so more than one ovum is available for fertilization. Because two separate combinations of chromosomes are involved, fraternal twins don't even need to be of the same sex (as you can see in Figure 2.3) while identical twins are always same-sex pairs.

Genes

Each chromosome, in turn, is made up of thousands of *genes*, which are even tinier particles. If we go down to a still finer level, we find that the genes are themselves composed of molecules of a chemical called **deoxyribonucleic acid,** DNA for short. According to a theory originally proposed by James Watson and Francis Crick (1958), DNA is in the shape of a double helix, a kind of twisted ladder. The remarkable feature of this ladder is that the rungs are made up in such a way that the whole thing can "unzip" and then each half can reproduce the missing part. It is this characteristic of DNA that makes it possible for the full set of genetic "instructions" contained in the fertilized ovum to be doubled and then reproduced in each new cell.

Dominant and Recessive Genes One of the intriguing questions about the genetic mechanisms is what happens when the instructions from the father's genes (in the sperm) and the instructions in the mother's genes (in the ovum) are not the same. If the father transmits a gene signaling blue eyes and the mother transmits a gene signaling brown eyes, what color eyes does the baby end up with?

The basic rules for combining genetic information were worked out many years ago by an Augustinian monk, Gregor Mendel (the rules are usually called "Mendelian laws"). For our purposes, the crucial bit of information is that some genes are **dominant,** and others **recessive.** A dominant gene is one that always "wins" in the case of an unmatched set of instructions. A gene for brown eyes, for example, is dominant; so if you receive a brown-eye gene from either parent, you will have brown eyes, no matter what the other gene may signal.

A recessive gene, on the other hand, "loses" in any contest with a dominant gene. The gene for blue eyes is recessive. The primary way a recessive gene can be expressed is if a child receives the *same* recessive gene from *both* parents. If you receive a blue-eye gene from both parents, you will have blue eyes.

This set of rules is important not only for such physical characteristics as eye or hair colors, but more vitally for inherited diseases. It turns out that there are a number of diseases that are transmitted on recessive genes, including sickle cell anemia and Tay-Sachs disease. An understanding of the mechanisms of hereditary transmission can help to predict the incidence of diseases like this and makes prevention possible in some cases as well.

Development from Conception to Birth

The Period of the Ovum Some time during the first 24 to 36 hours after conception, mitosis begins. The single cell splits in two. During the splitting, the DNA making up the genes "unzips" so that each of the new cells contains the full 23 pairs of chromosomes. Mitosis continues; and within two to three days, there are several dozen cells, with the whole mass about the size of a pinhead.

You can see the steps in this process in Figure 2.4. In the early stages of cell division, there is an undifferentiated mass of cells. But within about four or five days after fertilization, several different types of cells appear. Fluid appears in the ball of

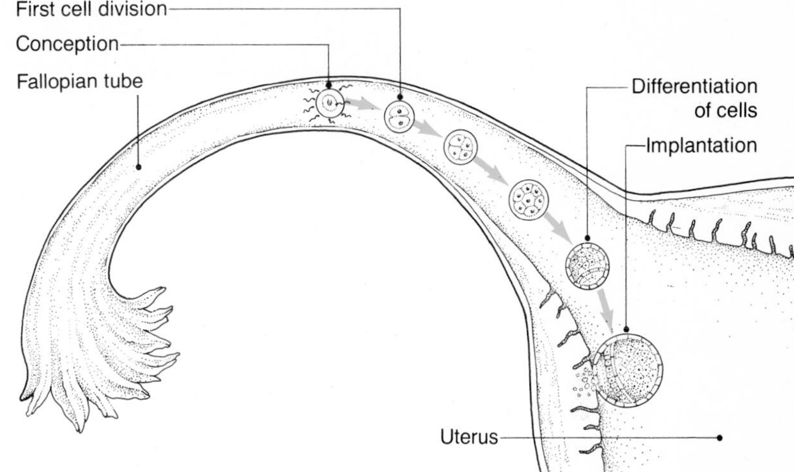

Figure 2.4 This drawing shows the sequence of steps from the moment of conception to the point of implantation in the wall of the uterus.

cells which separates the mass into two parts. The outer cells will form the **placenta,** and the inner mass forms the **embryo.** As it comes into contact with the wall of the uterus, the outer shell of cells breaks down at the point of contact and small tendrils develop which attach the cell mass (called a **blastocyst** at this stage) to the uterine wall.

Once implantation has occurred, about two weeks after conception, the period of the ovum is completed, and the period of the embryo begins.

The Period of the Embryo

This second major phase of prenatal development lasts from implantation until about eight weeks after conception. During this period, rapid cell division and differentiation takes place. A series of membranes develops around the embryo, with a liquid substance (the amniotic fluid) filling the cavity. The embryo floats in this liquid and is attached to the enveloping sac by the umbilical cord.

The umbilical cord, in turn, is attached to the placenta, a remarkable organ that lies next to and is attached to the uterus. The placenta serves as a sort of filter for the embryo and later for the fetus. The mother's bloodstream opens into the placenta. The blood passes through membranes in the placenta before it passes into the embryo's separate circulatory system. Useful substances such as proteins, sugars, and vitamins can pass through the placental membranes, while many (but not all) potentially harmful substances, such as viruses, are filtered out. As you'll see shortly, though, some disease organisms *do* pass through the placenta and affect the developing child. You can see all of these separate organs in Figure 2.5.

Growth during the embryonic period is extremely swift. By eight weeks of age, the embryo, now about 1½ inches in length, has all of the following:

Eyes

Ears

Mouth that opens and closes

Nose

Liver that secretes bile

Heart that beats, and a circulation system

Arms with elbows and legs with knees

Fingers and toes (although webbed, rather like a duck's foot)

Tail (that grows smaller after this stage; the tail bone at the end of your spine is the remnant of this tail)

Spinal cord

Cartilage that will become bone

The Fetal Period

Beginning in about the third month of pregnancy, the embryo becomes the **fetus** and is called the fetus for the remainder of the prenatal period. During the embryonic period virtually all major organs, parts of the body, muscles, and nerves are present in at least rudimentary form. The remaining seven months involve primarily a process of refining what has already been developed. It's a bit like the process of building a house. You first put up the floor and then the framework for the walls and roof. This skeleton of the house has the full shape of the final house; you can see where the windows and doors will go, what the shape of the rooms will be, how the roof will look. This stage is reached quickly, but after that, there is a very long process of filling in around the skeleton already established. So it is with the embryo and the fetus. At the end of the embryonic period, the main parts are all there at least in some basic form; the next seven months are for the finishing process.

The Nervous System The main exception to this developmental pattern is the nervous system, which is present in only very rudimentary form at the age of eight weeks. At that point only a small part of the brain and only the suggestion of a spinal cord have developed. The major development of the brain and the nervous system does not occur until the last three months

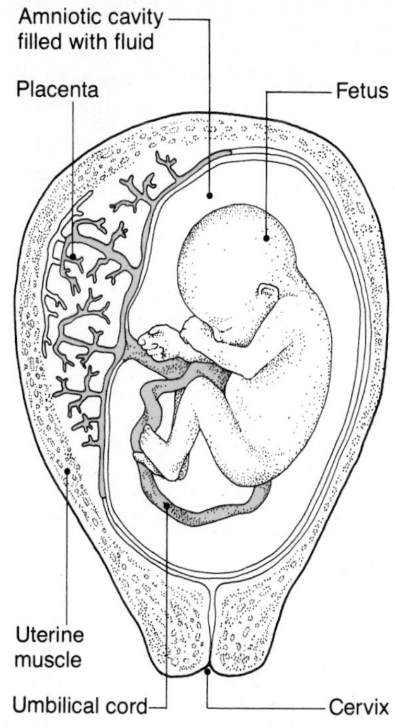

Figure 2.5 The organization of body structures during the fetal period. Note especially the placenta and the umbilical cord and the fact that the fetus "floats" in the amniotic fluid.

Table 2.1 Major Milestones of Fetal Development

Gestational age	Average size of fetus	Major new developments
12 weeks	3 inches	Sex of child can be determined; muscles developed more extensively; eyelids and lips present; feet have toes and hands have fingers.
16 weeks	4½–6 inches 3½–4 ounces	First fetal movement usually felt now; bones begin to develop; fairly complete ear is formed.
20 weeks	10 inches 10 ounces	Begins to grow hair; very human looking at this age; may show thumbsucking.
24 weeks	12–14 inches 1½ pounds	Eyes completely formed (but closed); fingernails, sweatglands, and taste buds all formed; some fat deposit beneath skin; capable of breathing if born prematurely, but low survival rate if born this early.
28 weeks	14 inches 2½ pounds	Nervous system, blood, and breathing systems all well enough developed to support life; prematures born at this stage have poor sleep/wake cycles and irregular breathing.
29–40 weeks	18–20 inches 5½–pounds	Nervous system develops further; general "finishing" of the body systems.

of gestation and the first six months to twelve months after the baby is born.

I've summarized the major steps in fetal development in Table 2.1. Notice how early the major organ systems and the facial and body features develop. But notice too that the largest gain in length and weight occurs in the final 12 weeks. You can see these changes more vividly in the photos in Figure 2.6.

Prenatal Sexual Differentiation

I've already said that the sex of the child is determined at the moment of conception by the XX or XY combination of chromosomes. You'd think that was the end of the story; but inter-

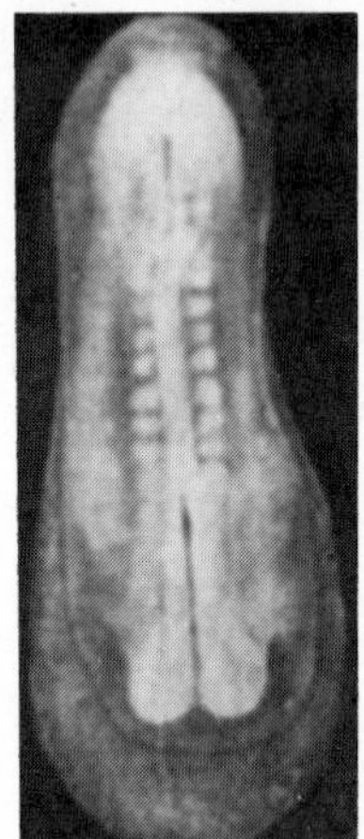
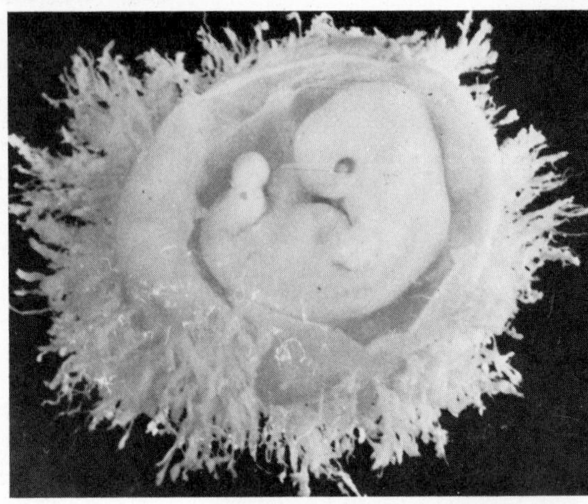
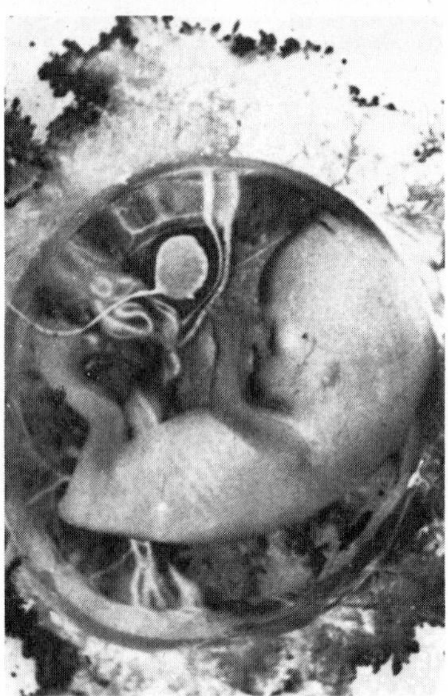
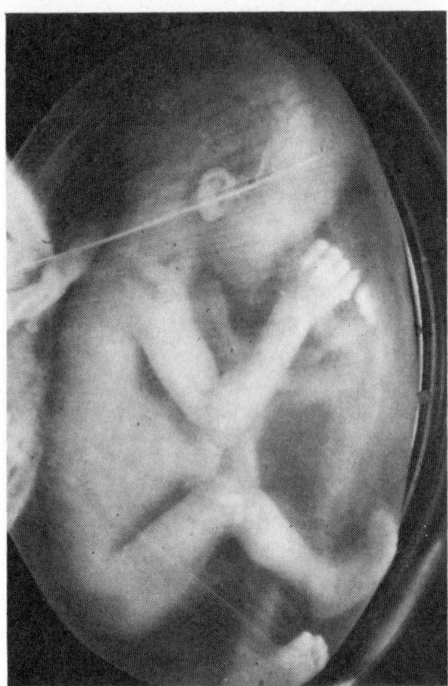

Figure 2.6 These four photos show the rapid changes in the embryo and fetus from 3 weeks of gestation in the first picture, to 4-6 weeks in the second, 12 weeks in the third, and 6 months in the fourth. In the 6-month fetus, you can see the development of facial features and the nearly complete development of the hands.

estingly enough, it is not. The basic genetic patterning does not *guarantee* the later sexual development of the infant. In the normal course of development, a second step is necessary for the male, but not for the female. Sometime between the fourth and eighth week after conception, the male hormone testosterone is secreted by the rudimentary testes in the embryo. If this hormone is *not* secreted, the embryo will develop as a physical female, even if genetically it is XY. If by some accident, male hormone is present at this stage of development of an XX embryo, the infant may have ambiguous genitalia—that is, some characteristics of a male and some of a female.

This two-step process of sexual differentiation is a good example of the difference between a **genotype** and a **phenotype.** Geneticists use the word genotype to refer to the specific set of characteristics described by the information in the genes. This is the basic map for later development we each inherit. But our *actual* characteristics are a product both of the basic map and of our experiences from conception onward. Geneticists refer to the actual characteristics as the phenotype. In this instance, an XY genotype results in a partly male/partly female phenotype because of the absence of the necessary hormone.

Explanations of the Normal Sequence of Development

One of the most important points about the child's prenatal development is how remarkably regular and predictable it is. The various changes occur in what is apparently a fixed order, in a fixed time period. To be sure, things can go wrong. But for the vast majority of children, the entire process runs off in a predictable, fixed pattern.

We don't have to look far for an explanation. Whenever there is that much regularity in a fixed sequence, maturation seems the obvious answer. The fetus doesn't learn how to grow fingernails. She doesn't have to be stimulated from outside to grow them. Rather, the fingernails, along with all the other parts of the complex system, apparently are controlled by the developmental code contained in the genes. This sequence of development is not immune to outside influence or modification, but it takes a fairly sizable intervention to make very much difference.

A second important point is that the effect of any outside influence depends heavily on the *timing* of that intervention or interference. This is an example of a "critical period" or a "sensitive period," as I described in Chapter 1. The general rule seems to be that each organ system—the nervous system, heart, ears, reproductive system, and so on—is most vulnerable to disruption at the time when it is developing most rapidly. At that point, it is "sensitive" to outside interference, from disease, inappropriate hormones, or whatever.

Before I begin talking about things that can go wrong, I want to emphasize that the maturational system is really extremely robust. Prenatal development must proceed in an adequate environment to be normal, but "adequate" seems to be a fairly broad range. *Most* children are quite normal. The list of things that *can* go wrong is long, but many of these possibilities are quite rare. More important, a very great number of them are completely preventable. As I go along, I'll try to point out the sort of preventive action that is possible in each instance.

Genetic Influences on the Normal Sequence

The first point at which something can go wrong is at (or even before) the moment of conception. There are two main types of problems that can occur at this stage: (1) improper chromosome division and (2) single gene defects, in which a disease or physical problem is passed on through either a dominant or recessive gene or on the X chromosome.

Chromosomal Problems

The particular chromosomal problem you've probably heard most about is **Down's syndrome** (also called mongolism and trisomy 21), in which the infant has a particular eye fold pattern, a flattened face, often heart defects or other internal disorders, and is usually mentally retarded to some degree. You can see some of the distinctive facial features in the photo in Figure 2.7.

This pattern, which occurs in about one out of every 600 births (Reed, 1975), occurs because the twenty-first chromosome does not separate properly during meiosis. One of the resulting germ cells ends up with two number 21 chromo-

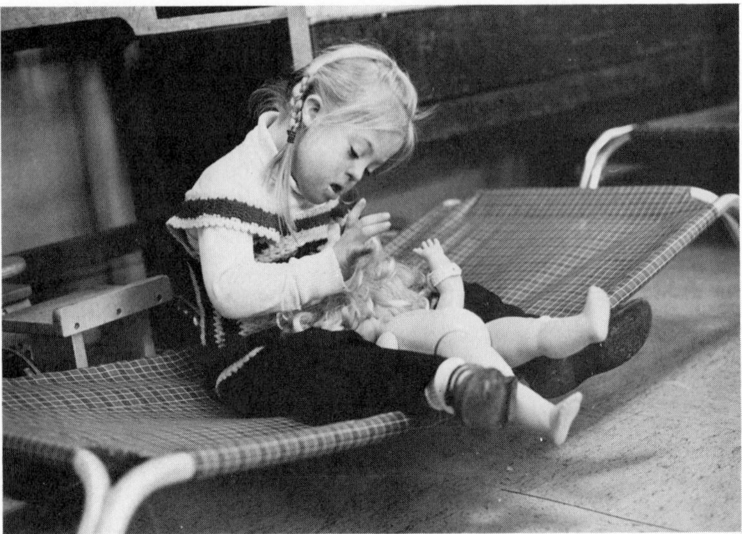

Figure 2.7 A Down's syndrome girl. Note the distinctive eye characteristics and the flattened face.

somes, while the other has none. The cell with too few chromosomes ordinarily does not survive, but the cell with an extra one may. Among women, the risk of this deviant pattern occurring is far greater for mothers over 30 or 35 than for those in their twenties.

Until quite recently, it had been thought that the faulty cell division occurred only in the ova and not in the sperm. But recent work by R. E. Magenis (1977) and his colleagues shows that perhaps 25 percent of Down's syndrome cases occur because of improper cell division in the sperm. So either the father or the mother can be the source of this particular abnormality.

Other types of genetic anomalies may occur if there is incomplete or incorrect division of the sex chromosome. Children with Klinefelter's syndrome, for example, have an XXY pattern of sex chromosomes; those with Turner's syndrome have only an X; and those with a "double Y" pattern have XYY. Many, *but not all,* individuals with these abnormal genetic patterns are mildly retarded.

Single Gene Defects

Dominant Gene Defects Some physical abnormalities, diseases, or other unfortunate outcomes are caused by a dominant gene. For a child to inherit such a problem, she must receive that particular gene from *either* her father or her mother. In every instance, the parent who passes along the problem *also* has the same disorder. An example of a problem of this type is a form of blindness called retinoblastoma, which is caused by a dominant gene.

Fortunately, dominant gene defects, although numerous in variety, are not all that common. There are two reasons. First, the number of defective genes in the population is simply not very large. More important, many people who inherit serious dominant gene defects do not have children and so do not pass on the problem to the next generation.

The situation is quite different, however, in the case of recessive gene defects, which may be passed on to children quite unknowingly.

Recessive Gene Defects A sizable number of crippling or fatal diseases is carried on recessive genes. I've listed some of the major diseases inherited in this way in Table 2.2.

It is important to understand two points about the recessive gene diseases. First (unless the disease is carried on the X chromosome), *both* parents must carry the recessive gene for it to be expressed in the child. And second, even if both parents carry the gene, on average only one in four of their offspring will inherit the disease. In Table 2.3, I have shown the probabil-

Table 2.2 Some of the Major Inherited Diseases

Phenylketonuria	A metabolic disorder; the child is unable to digest many types of food, including milk. If not placed on a special diet shortly after birth, the child usually ends up quite retarded. Can be diagnosed at birth, but not before.
Tay-Sachs Disease	An invariably fatal degenerative disease of the nervous system; virtually all victims die within the first 3–4 years. This gene is most common among Jews of Eastern European origin. Can be diagnosed prenatally.
Sickle Cell Anemia	A sometimes fatal blood disease, with joint pain, increased susceptibility to infection, and other symptoms. The gene for this disease is carried by about 2 million Americans, most often blacks. Can be diagnosed at birth, but not easily before.
Cystic Fibrosis	A fatal disease affecting the lungs and intestinal tract. Many children with CF now live to adolescence, a few to adulthood. The gene is carried by over 10 million Americans, most often whites. Cannot be diagnosed prenatally.

ities so you can see how it works more clearly. In this table, I have used Tay-Sachs disease as an example, labeling the recessive gene for this disease "T-S" and the normal gene "N." As you can see, *only* the child with the T-S/T-S pattern will inherit the disease, although half the children born to these parents would be carriers of the recessive gene (T-S/N and N/T-S).

Sex-Linked Defects The third category of single gene defects is those that are carried on the X chromosome and are also recessive. Since a boy has only one X chromosome, inherited from his mother, any genetic disorder she carries on that X chromosome will be passed on to the son, without being overruled by information on the Y chromosome. For the girl, the likelihood of inheriting such a disorder is very much smaller, since she would have to inherit the defective gene from both the father and the mother.

The most famous example of a sex-linked recessive defect is the blood disorder hemophilia, which affects the clotting of the

Table 2.3 The Inheritance of Tay-Sachs Disease from Parents Who Are Carriers of the Recessive Gene

If both parents are carriers, with gene patterns of normal/Tay-Sachs, then the following combinations of offspring are possible:

		Inherited from Mother	
		Normal	**Tay-Sachs**
Inherited from Father	**Normal**	N/N	N/T-S
	Tay-Sachs	T-S/N	T-S/T-S

blood. Queen Victoria was a carrier of this disease and passed it on to some of her sons and to her daughters as carriers. Her daughters, who married into many of the ruling houses of Europe, passed the disease on to their children in turn.

Diagnosing Chromosomal Anomalies and Single Gene Defects

I pointed out in Table 2.2 that phenylketonuria (PKU) can be diagnosed immediately after birth and then treated. Most of the other anomalies, and some of the single gene defects, can be diagnosed before birth by the use of a process called **amniocentesis.** A sample of the amniotic fluid is taken at about 15 weeks after conception and a chromosomal analysis of the cells in the fluid is then done. If there is some abnormality present, and if such an action is consistent with their moral judgment, the parents may elect to abort the fetus at this stage. Down's syndrome and all the sex-chromosome anomalies can be diagnosed in this way, as can Tay-Sachs disease.

Our increased knowledge about genetic abnormalities and inherited diseases, along with improved diagnostic technology, has made it possible to reduce the number of children born with crippling problems. But there are also very difficult ethical and practical questions for individual couples, some of which I have discussed in Box 2.1.

Environmental Influences on Prenatal Development: Disease, Drugs, and Diet

Once the child is conceived and the genetic pattern (the genotype) laid down, development ordinarily proceeds normally.

Box 2.1 Genetic Counseling: Better Information but Difficult Decisions

Not so many years ago, a couple married, conceived a child, and the child was born with whatever good or bad qualities happened to come along. For the vast majority of families, that is still the pattern. But for those couples who want to take advantage of it, or who are advised to do so by their physician, it is possible to take specific steps to reduce the risk of disease or abnormality in a child. There are three kinds of steps, each at a different point in the childbearing process.

First, before conceiving, both parents can have blood tests done that will tell them whether they are carriers of recessive genes for specific diseases. This can be done for Tay-Sachs and for sickle cell anemia, for example. Cystic fibrosis, however, *cannot* be diagnosed in this way. One couple I know had the tests done because they were both Jewish, of Eastern European extraction, and knew that their risks of Tay-Sachs were higher than normal. To their dismay, they found that they *were* both carrying the recessive gene for Tay-Sachs.

What are their options? They could decide not to have any children at all or to adopt children. Or they could figure that they had a three out of four probability of having a normal child and take the chance. Or they could conceive, have an amniocentesis done at the appropriate point, and abort the fetus if he had the disease.

Amniocentesis, then, is the second step available. It can be used to diagnose Down's syndrome. It is widely used to diagnose Tay-Sachs. (My friends who were carrying Tay-Sachs genes went through an amniocentesis and discovered their child was normal.)

But not all diseases or disorders can be diagnosed this way. Sickle cell anemia, for example, cannot be detected from amniotic fluid. So parents can find out if they each have a recessive gene for sickle cell but cannot know until the child is born whether the child has inherited the disease. For them, then, the decision is more difficult.

The case of cystic fibrosis is even more problematic and illustrates the third type of genetic counseling that is available. Carriers of CF cannot be identified ahead of time, and the disease cannot be diagnosed by amniocentesis. Only those couples who have already had one child with CF know that they both carry the recessive gene. For them, the decision is whether to have further children, knowing that the risk in each pregnancy is one in four that the child will have CF.

There are obviously extremely difficult ethical and religious decisions embedded in this process. Should you make an effort to find out if you carry any diseases? If you undergo amniocentesis and find that the fetus has a genetic abnormality or an inherited disease, are you prepared to abort? If you do have the initial blood tests done but do not wish to go through amniocentesis, are you prepared to risk having children knowing that there is some likelihood of their inheriting a serious problem? Genetic counseling is becoming more common, and our knowledge of inheritance patterns is improving, so these issues will become more compelling for individual couples over the next decades.

But there are specific types of outside events that can still have an impact.

Diseases of the Mother

Most diseases contracted by the mother cannot be passed through the placental membrane to the embryo or fetus, but there are a few exceptions in which the disease agent is small enough to pass into the child's bloodstream. Rubella and rubeola (both forms of measles), syphilis, diphtheria, influenza, typhoid, and chicken pox all may be passed to the child in this way. Of this list, the riskiest diseases for the child appear to be **rubella** and **syphilis.**

Rubella Rubella (also called German measles) is most risky for the child if the mother contracts it during the first three months of the pregnancy, especially if it occurs during the first month (Berg, 1974). This is a good example of the effect of the timing of the external influence. The particular organ systems most affected by rubella are the ears, eyes, and heart—all of which are developing rapidly during the first three months of gestation. The single most common effect is deafness in the child.

Estimates of the likelihood of the infant being affected if the mother contracts rubella during the early months of pregnancy range from 5 percent to nearly 85 percent (Sheridan, 1964; Berg, 1974), so we are obviously quite a long way from understanding the mechanism involved. It may be that the range of times during which rubella has negative effects is very narrow; or it may be that some fetuses, for one reason or another, are more vulnerable to stresses of this kind.

In any case, rubella is preventable. Vaccination is available and should be given to all children as part of a regular immunization program. Adult women who were not vaccinated as children can be vaccinated later, but it must be done at least three months before a pregnancy to provide complete immunity. (Those women among you who are not sure whether or not you have ever had German measles or who have not been vaccinated for rubella should be checked for immunity. If you are not immune, you should be vaccinated, but only if you are absolutely sure you are not pregnant at the time of vaccination. A vaccination for rubella during the first three months of a pregnancy has the same effect on the embryo–fetus as does the disease itself.)

Syphilis This disease, too, may cause significant problems, including mental retardation and physical deformities such as blindness or deafness. But again there is a preventive measure available. If a mother who has syphilis receives treatment and the disease is cleared up within the first 18 weeks of pregnancy, the fetus is unlikely to be infected.

Drugs Taken by the Mother

Ours is a drug-taking culture. We pop aspirin into our mouths at the first sign of pain, decongestants when we have a cold, tranquilizers when we are nervous, and sleeping pills when we cannot sleep. We also drink a lot of alcohol and many of us smoke.

Pregnant women are no exception. Several recent studies (Stewart, Cluff & Philp, 1977; Hill, Craig, Chaney, Tennyson & McCulley, 1977) show that the average pregnant woman takes about six to seven prescribed drugs and another three or four over-the-counter drugs such as aspirin during the course of her pregnancy. What are the consequences of such drug taking for the developing fetus?

Some drugs prescribed specifically for pregnant women have been later found to have significant negative effects. *Thalidomide*, for example, was a tranquilizer prescribed fairly often (particularly in West Germany and England) during the early 1960s. Some years later it was found that this drug, if taken during the first 52 days of pregnancy, greatly increased the risk of a particular kind of physical deformity in which the infant was born with foreshortened or missing limbs.

The thalidomide case aroused the concerns of the medical community; and since then, the effects of other drugs on embryonic or fetal development have received more careful scrutiny. Current findings suggest that any of the following drugs can have harmful effects in at least some cases: antibiotics such as tetracycline, anticoagulants, antihistamines, amphetamines, and tranquilizers. Even caffeine has come under suspicion lately, although I think the data are not yet good enough to be sure of the effect. Obviously, given this list, any pregnant woman would be well advised to consult with her physician before taking *any* medication, particularly "over the counter" drugs.

On a day-to-day basis, though, the drugs most of us have most contact with are not antihistamines or anticoagulants, but alcohol and nicotine. Should a pregnant woman drink or smoke?

Smoking In the last edition of this book, I suggested that we still could not be sure that smoking had a *direct* negative effect on the developing embryo and fetus. Now I think we *do* have enough information. The clearest single statement I can make is that women who smoke during their pregnancy are likely to have infants with lower birth weight. This finding has been reported again and again and seems to be reliable (Meredith, 1975).

Pregnant women who smoke are also more likely to have stillborn infants or infants with some kind of malformation (Naeye, 1978). Some recent research also points to long-term consequences for the infants: In three different longitudinal studies (Nichols, 1977; Butler & Goldstein, 1973; Dunn, McBurney, Ingram & Hunter, 1977), school-age children whose mothers smoked during their pregnancy were found to have

Figure 2.8 Sights like this used to be fairly common, but now that we know more about the potentially harmful effects of both drinking and smoking for the unborn child, most women are abstaining from both during pregnancy.

more difficulties in school and were more likely to be hyperactive.

The moral to be drawn from this research seems plain: do not smoke during pregnancy. If you cannot quit entirely, then at least cut back, since all these studies show a relationship between the "dose" (the amount of nicotine you are taking in) and the severity of the consequences to the child.

Alcohol An equally clear moral emerges from a look at the recent work on the effects of maternal alcohol ingestion on prenatal and postnatal development.

In the early 1970s, Kenneth Jones and his colleagues (Jones, Smith, Ulleland & Streissguth, 1973) identified a syndrome characteristic of children born to alcoholic mothers, which they labeled **fetal alcohol syndrome** (often abbreviated FAS). Infants with this syndrome are generally smaller than normal, with smaller brains; their faces are distinctively different, with small eye openings as one feature; they ordinarily show mild to moderate mental retardation, and they are uncoordinated.

Since the first identification of this syndrome, researchers such as Henry Rosett (Rosett & Sander, 1979), and Ann Streissguth and her colleagues (Hanson, Streissguth & Smith, 1978; Streissguth, 1978) have confirmed the fact that *heavy* drinking (two drinks per day minimum, with as much as five or six on occasion) is associated with FAS and with minor abnormalities.

But what about moderate drinking—a few glasses of wine with dinner or a cocktail now and again? This is much tougher to study, but the current evidence points to risk here, too. In recent research, Ann Streissguth (Streissguth, Martin & Barr, 1977) has studied a group of middle-class women, some of whom were "social drinkers" who continued to drink about 1 ounce of alcohol daily during their pregnancies. These women were more likely to have more sluggish, hard-to-arouse babies, often with low birth weights, compared to women from similar backgrounds who did not drink or drank very little. Once again the moral seems clear, even though the evidence is not all in. If you want to be on the safe side, do not drink while you are pregnant.

The Mother's Diet

Does it matter what you eat while you're pregnant? Does it matter how much or how little? The answer to both questions is "yes," although no one knows *exactly* what is the best diet or the precise effects of too much or too little.

The best information we have is about the effects of malnutrition during pregnancy. When malnutrition is severe, there is a greatly increased risk of stillbirths, low birth weight, and infant death during the first year of life.

Zena Stein and her colleagues (Stein, Susser, Saenger & Marolla, 1975) have done some of the most careful studies of these effects. They looked at the effects of a period of extreme famine in Holland toward the end of the Second World War (1944–1945), when whole sections of the country were allotted only about 1000 calories per day per person or less. By going back and looking at hospital, birth, and death records, they could trace the effects of the famine. Since the diet had been adequate both before and after this particular period, they could see whether malnutrition had a greater effect if it occurred early or late in the pregnancy.

What Stein found was that in general the effects of malnutrition were worse if it occurred during the last half of the pregnancy, particularly in the final three months. These babies were lighter at birth and had a greatly increased risk of dying during the first year. You can see one of the patterns in Figure 2.9. Famine during the first three months (point E) had essentially no effect; but if the mother was malnourished during the final three months (point B), there was a big effect.

When you think back to the general rule I gave earlier—that interference with prenatal development has the biggest effect during the time of maximum growth of any system—this pattern makes good sense. The final three months is when the major gain in weight occurs; so we'd expect these babies to be small, as they are, and perhaps therefore more vulnerable to disease.

The final three months of gestation is also a time of rapid growth of the nervous system, so we might also expect that malnutrition then would have some impact on the brain or nerves. And this is exactly what has been found, most clearly in research with animals. Malnutrition seems to result in fewer connective links between the nerve cells in the brain and in slower development of the sheathing around the nerves in the developing fetus.

Long-Term Consequences Virtually everyone agrees about these general conclusions about short-term effects. Where the agreement stops is on the question of the long-term consequences of prenatal malnutrition. You'd think that if there were effects on the nervous system, we ought to see long-term consequences in such things as the child's intellectual ability later on. But not everyone finds this. Stein and her collagues, for example, did *not* find any permanent effects for those children who survived the famine. But others, such as Stephen Richardson (1972), have found long-lasting effects, such as lower IQ and poorer school performance.

Figure 2.9 These results from Stein's study on the famine in Holland show that the number of deaths between 1 and 12 months of life was much greater for infants whose mothers had experienced malnutrition during the last part of the pregnancy. (Source: Adapted from Stein, et. al., 1975, p. 161.)

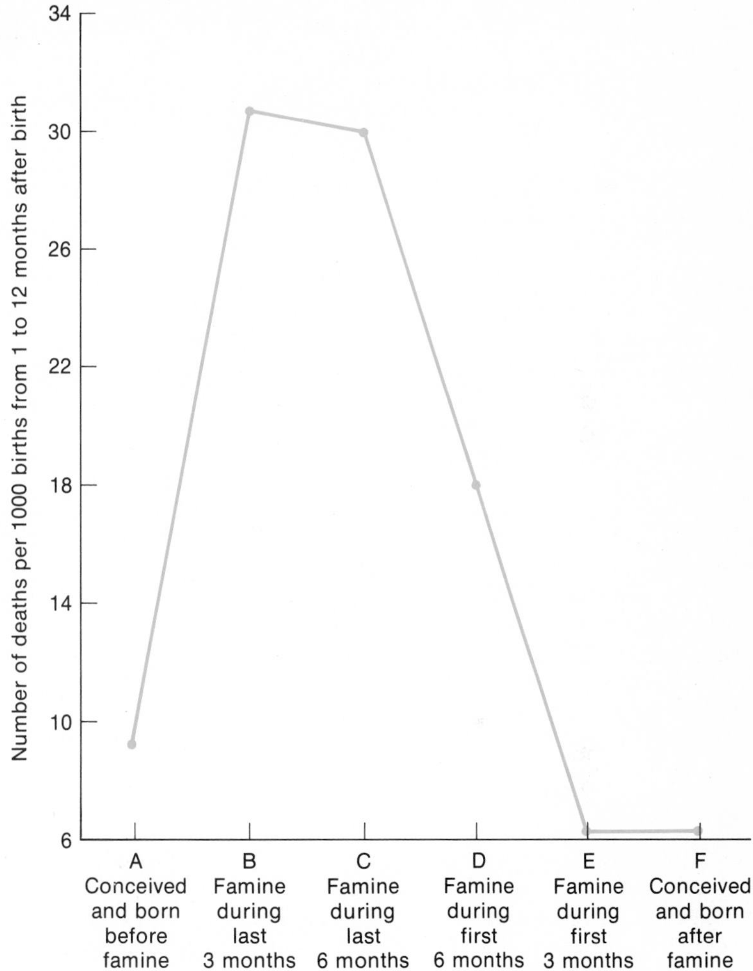

The solution to the disagreement seems to lie in whether the children were malnourished *both* before *and* after birth. If children are malnourished only before birth, then there seems to be no permanent effect (assuming they live through the first year). But if they are malnourished after birth as well, then the effects seem to last. Once again, then, the timing and duration of the deprivation is critical. Brain growth continues rapidly during the first year or more after birth, so it continues to be affected by malnutrition. If the deprivation goes on long enough, the impact is big enough for us to see on IQ tests or other measures of intellectual ability.

Of course, most mothers in developed countries are not malnourished, at least not as severely as those in Stein's or

Box 2.2 Diet and Exercise During Pregnancy

Weight Gain

Recent research by Pedro Rosso (1977a, 1977b) and by Roy Pitkin (1977) has helped to challenge some old established notions about weight gain during pregnancy.

For many years, physicians thought that the fetus acted as a sort of "parasite" on the mother's body, taking whatever nourishment it needed even at the expense of the mother. Rosso's research shows that this isn't so. If the mother is even a little underweight or malnourished, the fetus may not compete successfully for nourishment and may be born underweight, with the attendant risks. Only if the mother is at her ideal body weight, or heavier, and gains at a sufficient rate during pregnancy, does the fetus get all the nutrients he needs. The current rule of thumb, replacing the old 2-pounds-per-month rule, is that a gain of about 24–28 pounds is about right for most women.

Roy Pitkin takes this information a step further. He argues that the *timing* of the weight gain is as important as the total amount. Two to four pounds is a reasonable gain for the first three months of pregnancy; but after that, nearly a pound a week (14 ounces) is needed, particularly during the final three months, when the baby gains the most weight. One practical consequence of this is that a woman who has gained 20 pounds in the first four or five months should *not* cut back in order to hold her weight gain to some magic total number. Restricting calories during those final months is exactly the wrong thing to do.

A Good Diet

Pure poundage is not enough to ensure optimal development for the child. It also matters *what* the mother eats. Caloric requirements go up 10–20 percent; protein needs go up about 50 percent; and the need for calcium, phosphorus, and vitamin C go up by about 100 percent. Specifically, that means about 100 grams of protein per day (equivalent to about 12 ounces of lean meat, fish, or poultry or 2½ cups of cottage cheese). Milk or other dairy products are good sources of extra calcium, and the rest of the diet should include the usually recommended green and yellow vegetables and fruit and whole grain breads or cereals.

Exercise

In my opinion, we know far too little about the effects of exercise during pregnancy. The most widely given advice currently is that whatever regular exercise a woman is accustomed to – tennis, running, swimming, or the like – can be continued but that any new vigorous exercise is not recommended. But this advice is based on very little data. There is no evidence I know of – other than anecdotes – that would tell us whether women who have exercised vigorously before and during pregnancy have easier or harder labor or larger or smaller babies. I have several friends who continued to run while pregnant (and I was badly beaten in a 6-mile race by a very pregnant woman). But I know others who did not, and I have no way of choosing between the two options at this stage. Regretably, all I can say at this point is that we don't know.

Richardson's studies. For most of us, the question is whether it makes any difference – within a normal range – what we eat while pregnant. Oddly enough, there isn't a whole lot of information about this, but I've put together what we know in Box 2.2.

Characteristics of the Mother that Affect the Normal Sequence

Aside from diet, drugs, and diseases, there are three characteristics of mothers that seem to make a difference in prenatal development: her age, how many children she has already had, and her overall state during the pregnancy.

The Mother's Age

Older Mothers My friend Jane, pregnant for the first time at 36, was right to be concerned about increased risks. Any mother over 35 faces increased risks of having a Down's syndrome baby, and this risk goes up rapidly after 40. While for all mothers as a group the risk is about one in 600, for mothers between 20 and 30, the risk of a Down's baby is about one in 1000. For mothers between 40 and 45, the risk goes up to about one in 100. Since Down's syndrome can be diagnosed with amniocentesis, many pregnant women over 35 are undergoing this procedure.

For a *first* pregnancy over 35, there are some other risks, including a higher chance of a stillbirth and longer labor (Kessner, 1973). But all these increased risks, except for the chance of a Down's syndrome child, are more likely in mothers from poverty environments, which suggests that age is not the only factor. Rather, the mother's overall physical health is probably critical. Older mothers, particularly if they live in poverty, are more likely to be less healthy. So if you are going to have a late baby, the message seems to be "stay in shape."

Young Mothers At the other end of the age range there are also added risks, and these can't be reduced just by good physical condition. For any mother under 20, there is added risk of a premature birth, stillbirth, and difficulties during delivery (Kessner, 1973). These effects are strikingly clear for mothers 15 or younger. Since the rate of pregnancies among very young teenagers is on the increase, these facts are of considerable importance to us as a society. At the moment, something like 30,000 babies are born each year to mothers age 15 or younger. In these cases, the mother herself has not finished growing and has extra nutritional needs of her own. When the strain of carrying an infant is added to her other body stresses, there are distinct hazards to both the mother and the child. You can see the increased risk of stillbirth (fetal death) and death immediately after birth (neonatal deaths) for very young and for older mothers very clearly in Figure 2.10.

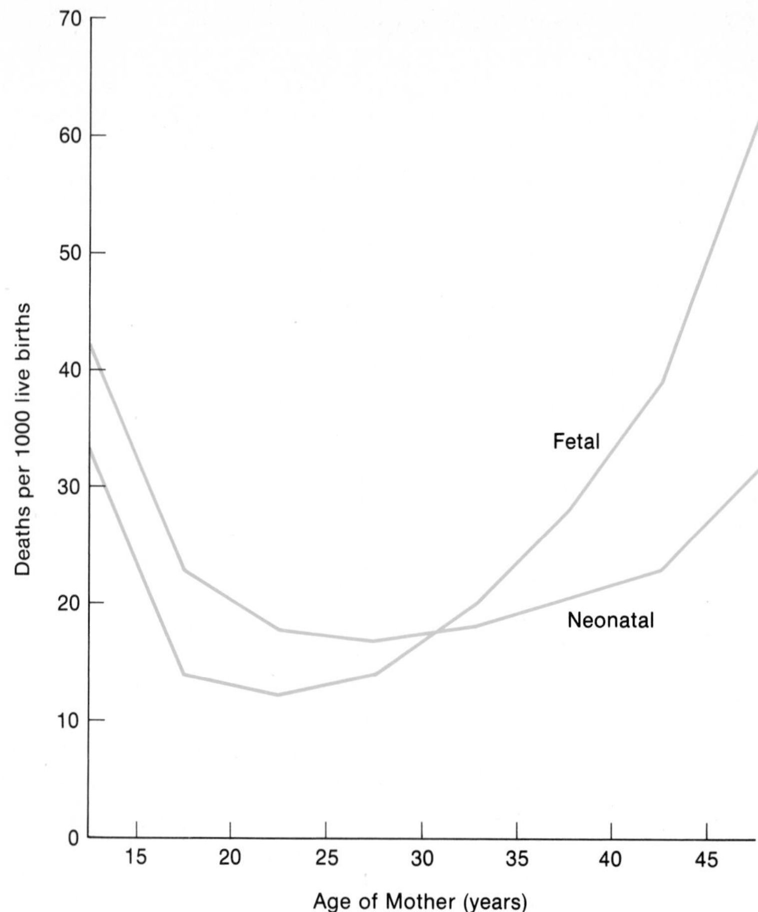

Figure 2.10 The relationship between the mother's age and the risk of death for the fetus or neonate is very clear in these findings. (Source: Reproduced from D. Kessner, *Infant death: An analysis by maternal risk and health care,* 1973, p. 100, with the permission of the National Academy of Sciences, Washington, D.C.)

Number of Pregnancies Women who have had more than four pregnancies are also at greater risk. The babies are more likely to be stillborn and to be smaller at birth (Kessner, 1973). Eleanor Maccoby and her colleagues (Maccoby, Doering, Jacklin & Kraemer, 1979) have also recently found that any child after the first, especially if the pregnancies are closely spaced, has lower levels of hormones in his blood at birth. In particular, firstborn boys had much higher levels of testosterone (the male hormone) at birth than did laterborn boys. We don't yet know what the implications of such a difference may be for development, but this study does point to the possibility of some kinds of physical "depletion" in the mother as a result of pregnancy that can affect later children.

The Mother's Emotional State

Does the mother's state of mind during the pregnancy make any difference? What if she is nervous? What if she didn't really want to be pregnant in the first place or is under some kind of continuing strain while pregnant? All these things do seem to matter. Arnold Sameroff and Michael Chandler (1975) have concluded that a woman who experiences prolonged or severe anxiety during the pregnancy—for whatever reason—has increased risk of any or all of the following:

Premature delivery

Longer or more difficult labor

Miscarriage

More difficult pregnancy, including more nausea and vomiting

It doesn't seem quite fair that the women who are the most anxious are more likely to have their worst fears confirmed, but that's the way it seems to work. Of course, not all women who are anxious or unhappy about their pregnancies have difficulties, and we don't know why this relationship holds for only some women and not for others. Some women may be anxious or upset for most of their pregnancy, others only for a short while. Some may eat poorly or drink or smoke more because of their nervousness, while others may not react to their anxiety in this way. We don't understand the links yet, but the basic relationship does seem well established.

One other effect of the mother's nervousness or anxiety has also been found. The infants born to tense or anxious mothers are also more irritable, cry more, and are more likely to spit up or have intestinal problems (a pattern called *colic*) (Lakin, 1957). There may be a kind of "self-fulfilling prophecy" here—mothers who expect to have more trouble with their infants may in fact have more troublesome babies because of the way they respond to their children. But the connection may be physiological rather than purely psychological. Prolonged anxiety during the pregnancy changes the chemical composition of the mother's blood, which may have some effect on the developing fetus that would account for his later irritability. Whatever the explanation, staying calm and unstressed during pregnancy seems like a useful thing to do if you can manage it.

Summary of Risks and Long-Term Consequences

The first point I need to emphasize again is that *most* babies are normal. Nonetheless, there are a lot of things that can make a difference in prenatal development; and the more we study the effects of drugs, diet, and emotional stresses, the more connections we are discovering. In view of all those potential problems, it's easy to get discouraged or to panic a bit, so I want to make two points to put the issue into perspective.

First, as I've already said, there are very specific preventive steps that any woman can take to reduce the risks for herself and her unborn child. She can be properly immunized; she can quit smoking and drinking; she can watch her diet and make sure her weight gain is sufficient; and she and the child's father can have genetic counseling. In addition, she can get early and regular prenatal care. It's *very* clear from a number of studies, including Kessner's major study of pregnancies in New York City (1973), that mothers who receive adequate prenatal care reduce the risks to themselves and their infants.

The second positive point to be made is that many of the risky consequences of poor diet, disease, and drugs are fairly short term. There aren't a whole lot of *permanent* effects of these early problems, although all the evidence isn't in yet on the long-term effects.

For example, premature birth or small size at birth is one of the frequent outcomes of many types of prenatal problems. Premature babies do have more difficulty right at the time of birth, and some don't survive. But of those who do, most catch up to their full-term peers by school age (Drillien, 1964; Werner, Simonian, Bierman & French, 1967; Sameroff & Chandler, 1975).

Some effects, though, do seem to last. The studies of babies with fetal alcohol syndrome point to long-lasting effects. There are hints of similar lasting effects in the studies of smoking. And, of course, children born with physical deformities, such as deafness resulting from maternal rubella, must live with those deformities for life.

In sum, while the consequences of prenatal problems are not as bleak as you might think, there is still every reason for caution and care.

Sex Differences in Prenatal Development

Since nearly all prenatal development is controlled by maturational codes that are the same for all members of our species—male and female alike—there aren't very many sex differences in prenatal development. But there are a few, and they set the stage for some of the physical differences we'll see at later ages.

1. As I've already pointed out, boys secrete testosterone during the early months of gestation, which leads to the "fixing" of the brain so that the proper male hormones are secreted at the right moments later in life. Girls do not secrete any equivalent hormone prenatally.
2. Girls are a bit faster in some aspects of prenatal development, particularly skeletal development. They are about 3–4 weeks ahead in bone development at birth.
3. Despite the more rapid development of girls, boys are heavier and longer at birth.
4. Boys are considerably more vulnerable to all kinds of prenatal problems. Many more boys than girls are conceived—on the order of about 120 to 150 male embryos to every 100 female—but more of the males are spontaneously aborted. At birth, there are about 105 boys for every 100 girls. Boys are also more likely to experience injuries at birth (perhaps because they are larger), and they have more congenital malformations.

The difference in vulnerability is particularly intriguing, especially since it seems to persist. Older boys are more prone to problems as well. One possible explanation for this may lie in the basic genetic difference. The XX combination affords the girl some protection against "bad" genes that may be carried on the X chromosome, since she would have to inherit the same one from both parents in order to develop some specific problem. The boy, on the other hand, could inherit a disorder by receiving the gene for it only from his mother, since he has only the one X chromosome. This seems to be the explanation of greater male susceptibility to infectious disease, since a gene that affects such susceptibility is carried on the X chromosome (Brooks-Gunn & Matthews, 1979). The greater number of spontaneously aborted male fetuses may be partly explainable the same way. Malformed fetuses are more likely to be spontaneously aborted, and there may be more inherited malformations in males because of the lack of the second X chromosome. Whatever the cause, the difference in vulnerability is intriguing.

Social Class Differences in Prenatal Development

The basic sequence of fetal development is clearly no different for children born to poor mothers than children born to middle-class mothers. But many of the problems that can afflict prenatal development are more common among the poor. For ex-

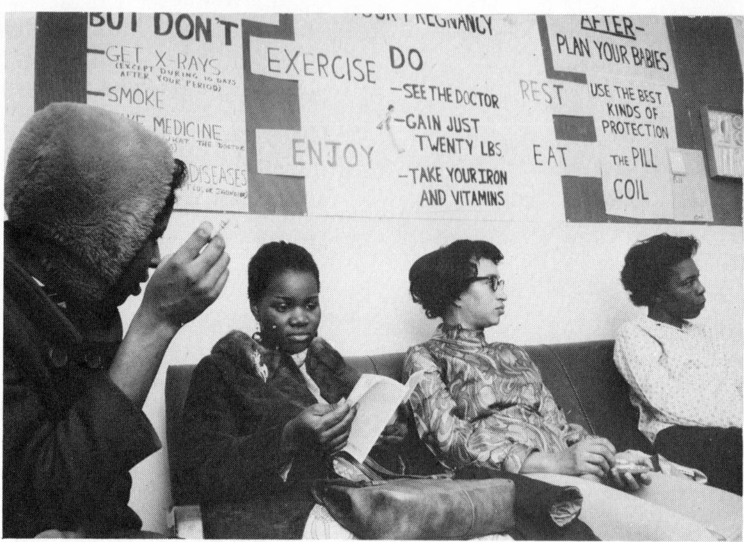

Figure 2.11 These women, by seeking out prenatal health care, are reducing the chances of risk for both themselves and their infants.

ample, mothers who have not graduated from high school are about twice as likely as mothers with a college education to have a low-weight infant or to have an infant stillborn (Kessner, 1973).

The explanation for the greater risks among poor women seems to lie mostly in their life-style, and perhaps most clearly in a lack of prenatal care. Among the poor, women are likely to have their first pregnancy earlier; they have more pregnancies on the average, are less likely to have been immunized against such diseases as rubella, and are *far* less likely to have adequate prenatal care.

Obviously, good prenatal care won't make a 15-year-old mother 25, but it can go a long way toward eliminating the differences in infant mortality between the poor and the middle class. Kessner (1973) found that those poor mothers who did get good care had fewer problems and healthier infants than those with bad or no prenatal care. What is particularly striking is what has happened in very poor areas when an intensive effort has been made to improve the prenatal care available to mothers. Kessner describes one area of New York City, for example, where the infant mortality rate dropped from 33.6 to 18.8 (per 1000 births) in three years after a massive prenatal care program was introduced.

Two points are worth remembering: First, the factors that affect prenatal development negatively don't operate any differently in the poor; but they are much more likely to occur among the poor and to occur in combinations. Second, many of these negative effects can be prevented if adequate prenatal care is provided. If we were willing to devote the resources needed for such an effort, we could significantly reduce not only the rate of infant death but also the rate of physical abnormalities and perhaps even mental retardation. Obviously, better prenatal care is not the only answer. But it would be a big step in the right direction. At this stage, however, it looks as if we have the way but not the will for the job.

Summary

1. Conception occurs when the male sperm penetrates the female ovum, ordinarily in the fallopian tube.
2. At conception, 23 chromosomes from the sperm join with 23 from the ovum to form the 46 that will be reproduced in each cell of the new child's body.
3. The child's sex is determined by one of the 23 pairs of chromosomes, XX for a girl and XY for a boy. The father's contribution of either an X or Y chromosome is the critical ingredient.
4. Chromosomes are made up of genes, which are in turn made up of deoxyribonucleic acid.
5. Individual genes may be either dominant or recessive. If dominant, they will "win" in any mixed pairing of genes from the father and mother.
6. During the first days after conception, the initial cell divides (mitosis), travels down the fallopian tube, and is implanted in the wall of the uterus.
7. Over the next weeks, cell differentiation takes place, with the placenta, umbilical cord, and amniotic cavity all formed.
8. From two to eight weeks, the developing organism is called the embryo; from eight to 40 weeks, it is called the fetus.
9. Most organ systems are developed in rudimentary form during the embryonic period; the fetal period involves enlargement and refinements.
10. During the embryonic period, the XY embryo secretes the hormone testosterone, which stimulates the growth of male genitalia. Without that hormone, the embryo develops as a girl.
11. The normal sequence of development prenatally seems heavily determined by maturation—by a "roadmap" contained in the genes.
12. Problems in prenatal development can begin at conception if a genetic abnormality, such as Down's syndrome, occurs or if the child receives recessive genes for inherited diseases from both parents.
13. Prior to conception tests in the form of chromosomal analysis for carriers of inherited-disease genes are available for many disorders. Following conception, amniocentesis may be used to diagnose diseases and genetic abnormalities prenatally.
14. Some diseases contracted by the mother may affect the child, most notably rubella and syphilis. Both may result in physical abnormalities.
15. Both alcohol and nicotine have harmful effects on the developing fetus; the greater the dose, the greater the potential effect.
16. The mother's diet also makes a difference, particularly if she is severely malnourished. In that case, she runs increased risk of stillbirth, low-birth-weight infant, and infant death during the first year of life.
17. Older mothers and very young mothers, along with those who have borne four or more children, also run increased risks.
18. The mother's emotional state may also affect the developing child. The more anxious the mother, the more difficulty she is likely to have with pregnancy and delivery and the more irritable her infant is likely to be.
19. There are a few sex differences in prenatal development worth emphasizing: hormone secretions, rate of skeletal development and size, and vulnerability to disorders and deformities. Boys are slower in skeletal development, bigger, and more vulnerable.
20. Social class differences also are present, with poor women more prone to virtually every problem of pregnancy and delivery and to higher rates of infant mortality. Many of these differences can be lessened with improved prenatal care for the poor.

Key Terms

Amniocentesis A medical test for genetic abnormalities in the embryo/fetus that may be done at about 15 weeks of gestation.

Autosomes The 22 pairs of chromosomes in which both members of the pair are the same shape and carry parallel information.

Blastocyst The name used for the small mass of cells, about two weeks after conception, that implants itself into the wall of the uterus.

Chromosomes The portion of each cell in the body that contains genetic information. Each chromosome is made up of many genes.

Crossing over The process that occurs during meiosis in which genetic material from pairs of chromosomes may be exchanged.

Deoxyribonucleic acid Called DNA for short, this is the chemical of which genes are composed.

Dominant gene A gene that "wins out" over a recessive gene in cases in which the individual inherits mixed signals from the father and the mother.

Down's syndrome A genetic anomaly in which there are three number 21 chromosomes rather than two. Children born with this genetic pattern are usually mentally retarded and have characteristic physical features. Also called mongolism and trisomy 21.

Embryo The name given to the organism during the period of prenatal development from about one week to eight weeks after conception, beginning with implantation of the cell mass into the uterine wall.

Fallopian tube The tube down which the ovum travels to the uterus and in which conception usually occurs.

Fetal alcohol syndrome (FAS) A pattern of physical abnormalities found often in children born to alcoholic mothers, including mental retardation and minor physical anomalies.

Fetus The name given to the developing organism from about eight weeks after conception until birth.

Germ cells Sperm and ova. These cells, unlike all other cells of the body, contain only 23 chromosomes rather than 23 pairs.

Meiosis The process of cell division that produces germ cells in which only one member of each chromosome pair is passed on to the new cell.

Mitosis The process of cell division that occurs throughout prenatal development.

Ovum The germ cell produced by women which, if fertilized by a sperm from the male, forms the basis for the developing organism.

Placenta The organ that lies between the fetus and the wall of the uterus, through which the mother's blood is filtered.

Recessive gene A gene that "loses out" in competition with a dominant gene. When two recessive genes are inherited, however, the characteristic will develop.

Rubella A form of measles that, if contracted by the pregnant woman during the first three months of the pregnancy, may have severe effects on the embryo or fetus.

Suggested Readings

Apgar, V., & Beck, J. Is my baby all right?: A guide to birth defects. New York: Trident, 1972.

An excellent source for more information about any of the genetic and environmental sources of defects described in this chapter.

The Boston Women's Health Book Collective. Our bodies, ourselves: A book by and for women (2nd ed.). New York: Simon & Schuster, 1977.

Although this book is really focused on the adult female's body, it has an excellent discussion of health during pregnancy. You may not be entirely in sympathy with all of the political views included, but there is no better compact source of information (including long bibliographies) on pregnancy.

Lewin, R. "Starved brains." Psychology Today, 1975, **9** (No. 4), 29–33. If you are interested in the problems of malnutrition and diet, this is an excellent place to start.

Nilsson, L. A child is born. New York: Delacorte Press, Seymour Lawrence, 1977. This book is full of marvelous photographs of the embryo and fetus. It also has a good basic text describing prenatal development and problems of pregnancy.

Preview of Chapter 3

Birth and the Newborn Child

Not long ago I overheard two mothers of newborns talking in a pediatrician's waiting room. One mother was describing the marvelous mobile she had just hung over her baby's crib. The other mother was doubtful: "I haven't bought anything like that yet for David. I don't think he can see very well yet, and he doesn't seem to reach for things. I thought I'd wait for a few months before I started worrying about mobiles and toys." The first mother was sure that her baby *could* see. "Jennifer seems to love looking at the one I got her, especially when the light shines on it or it moves."

Which mother is right? Certainly the doubting mother has a lot of company. In one study I was involved in (Barnard & Eyres, 1979), we asked 200 mothers of newborns how soon their babies could see, hear, and learn. Almost half thought that babies couldn't do any of those things until they were a month or two old. But while this view is clearly common, it is wrong. Newborns *can* see, hear, and learn. Over the past two decades, researchers have discovered that the newborn is really quite remarkably skillful—far more so than pediatricians or psychologists (or parents) had thought in earlier years.

Before we can look at some of the new knowledge about infant skills, though, I want to go back one step and talk about the process of birth itself.

Birth

The Normal Process

Once labor has begun, there are three broad stages in the birth of a child.

First-Stage Labor Stage 1 involves the **dilation** (opening up) of the cervix (take another look at Figure 2.2 for the location of the cervix). This part of labor has been likened to putting on a sweater with a neck that is too tight. You have to pull and tug and stretch the neck of the sweater with your head in order to get it on. Eventually the neck is stretched wide enough so that the widest part of your head can pass through. It is this widening and stretching that occur in the first stage of labor.

Second- and Third-Stage Labor The second stage is the actual delivery, when the baby's head moves past the stretched cervix, into the birth canal, and finally out of the mother's body. Once the baby is born, there is yet a third stage when the placenta is delivered. You can see all these steps schematically in Figure 3.1.

The First Acquaintance Process That brief description, and the figure, give the basic information, but the emotions that go with birth are somehow lost in the telling. Aiden Macfarlane (1977) has tape-recorded conversations between mothers and fathers immediately following delivery just after the baby had been given to the mother to hold. These conversations show some of the amazement and some of the joy, too. Here's one excerpt (pp. 64–65):

> *Mother:* Hello darling. Meet your dad. You're just like your dad (baby yells).
>
> *Father:* I'm going home!
>
> *Mother:* Oh, you've gone quiet (laughs). Oh darling, she's just like you—she's got your little tiny nose.
>
> *Father:* It'll grow like yours.
>
> *Mother:* She's big, isn't she? What do you reckon? (doctor makes a comment) Oh look, she's got hair. It's a girl—you're supposed to be all little. Gosh. Oh, she's lovely. Oh, she's opened her eyes (laughs). Oh lovely (kisses baby).

Notice both the pleasure the mother shows here and her concern about the child's physical features. Klaus and Kennell (1970) as well as Macfarlane have found that most parents are intensely interested in having the baby look at them right away. They are delighted if the baby opens her eyes, and will try to stimulate her to do so if she doesn't. Klaus and Kennell also noticed that mothers would first touch the infant rather gingerly with the tip of the finger and then proceed gradually to stroking with the full hand. All of this seems to be part of the acquaintance process that occurs immediately after birth, whenever the

Figure 3.1 The sequence of steps during delivery are shown clearly in these drawings. You can see the dilation stage, the delivery itself, and the delivery of the placenta.

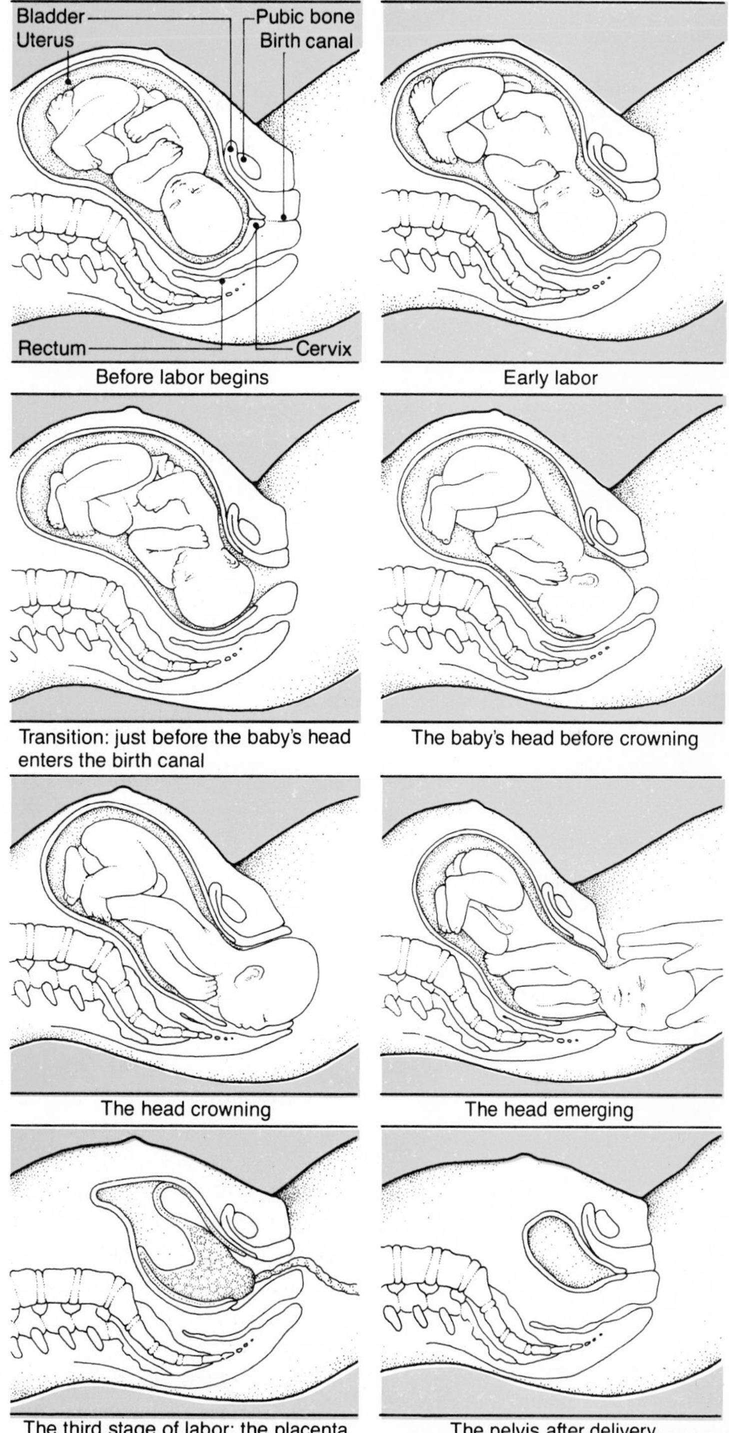

mother (or father) first has an opportunity to hold and examine the infant.

In 95 percent of all births (Macfarlane, 1977), there are no complications. The whole process is normal and satisfying to the mother. Most infants emerge from the process looking healthy. Still, there are some aspects of the birth process or setting that can affect the child's health or the mother's satisfaction with the delivery.

Effects of Drugs During Delivery

One of the major current issues about delivery concerns the use of drugs. In modern times, drugs were first given for a woman in labor in 1847, by James Simpson, a Scottish physician, who gave his patient ether. The use of painkillers for childbirth became widespread quite rapidly after that. Today, despite a move toward "natural" (largely drug-free) childbirth among some groups of women, the use of drugs is still the norm rather than the exception. Yvonne Brackbill (1979), for example, has found that approximately 95 percent of deliveries involve some drug administration.

The obvious purpose of the drugs has been to reduce the discomfort of labor for the mother. But what about the infant? Questions about the potentially harmful effects of obstetrical medications on the infant have been raised only in the past ten years or so, primarily by developmental psychologists such as Brackbill. There is still a great deal to be learned about such effects, but let me at least describe the current state of our knowledge.

Types of Drugs Three types of drugs are commonly given during labor and delivery: (1) *analgesics* (such as Demerol), which are given during the first stage of labor to reduce pain; (2) *sedatives or tranquilizers* (such as Nembutol, Valium, or Thorazine) given during stage 1 labor to reduce anxiety; and (3) *anesthesia*, given during the second stage of labor to block pain either totally (general anesthesia) or in portions of the body (local anesthesia). Many women receive all three types of drugs; others may receive only one or two of them.

It would be very helpful to physicians and to mothers if we knew the consequences of each of these types of drugs for the fetus. But because of the very large numbers of combinations of drugs given, it is extremely difficult to sort out the consequences. Still, a few conclusions are emerging from the current research.

Short-Term Effects on the Infant Nearly all drugs given to the mother during labor pass through the placenta and enter the fetal bloodstream. So the infant is obviously going to show some short-term effect. Infants whose mothers have received any type of drug are ordinarily found to be more sluggish, to suck less vigorously, to gain less weight in the days and weeks immediately after delivery, and to spend more time sleeping (Brackbill, 1979). The mother who was given medication may thus find herself dealing with a less-responsive baby and may experience more difficulty feeding her infant.

Long-Term Effects Most physicians and psychologists assumed that the effects of delivery medication on the infant would wear off during the first few days and weeks as the drugs were eliminated from the child's bloodstream. But there are now hints that this may not be the case. Brackbill (1979), who has reviewed all the existing evidence, reports that there are now several studies in which infants have been followed for the entire first year. In several cases, the effects of the delivery medication can still be detected at these later ages. For example, 8-month-old children whose mothers were given anesthetic scored more poorly on tests of motor development—they sat and stood a little later, among other things. This effect was not as evident for infants whose mothers had been given only analgesics or sedatives.

Practical Implications What does this mean for an individual mother? Unfortunately, it is very difficult to translate the existing evidence into clear recommendations. There is so much we don't know, particularly about long-term consequences to the infant. But the most cautious approach is to argue for as little use of drugs as possible during delivery.

Hospital versus Home Delivery

A second issue of concern to many parents has to do with *where* the baby is born. Home deliveries are on the increase, as are nontraditional delivery settings in hospitals. "Rooming in" arrangements in which the mother and newborn can be together continuously after delivery are now more common again (as they were several decades ago), and **birthing rooms** in hospitals are also being developed (see Figure 3.2). These are rooms designed to be as like a home as possible, in some cases with a nurse-midwife rather than a physician in attendance.

The arguments made for home or birthing room deliveries are primarily that they are more natural and that the birth is likely to be less traumatic if the mother is in a comfortable, familiar setting. The counterargument (particularly against home deliveries) is that they are less safe. If anything should go wrong, full hospital facilities are not readily available. Obviously the birthing room in a hospital is an attempt at a middle ground in this controversy.

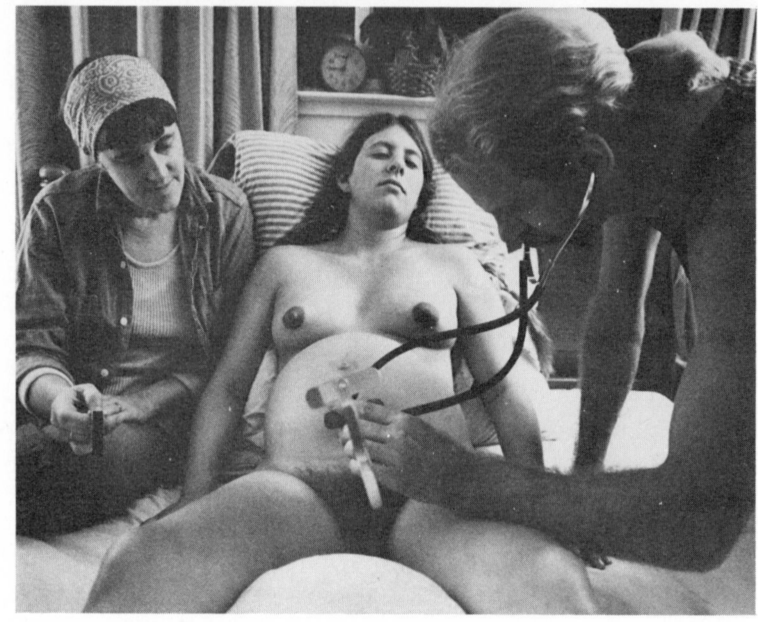

Figure 3.2 This is not a home delivery. Rather, it is a delivery in a "birthing room" in a hospital, designed to be as much like a home setting as possible but with the added safety of the hospital. The room is furnished like a home bedroom, and the mother may ordinarily have anyone she wishes present at the delivery.

These are vital questions for parents, who must make a decision about what sort of situation they prefer for the delivery. From my perspective as a developmental psychologist, the questions are a bit narrower: (1) Does the location of the delivery, or the conditions of delivery, make any direct difference in the development of the child? (2) Is there an indirect effect? Does the location of delivery affect the mother or father in some way so that their response to the child changes?

I wish I could give you clear answers to either of these questions, but I cannot. It is clear that no greater physical risk for the child *necessarily* accompanies home delivery. For example, in Holland, home deliveries are still extremely common; any woman who shows no signs of prenatal difficulty and has no history of such difficulty can have her baby at home. The rate of problems in these home deliveries is *very* low (Macfarlane, 1977), so it can obviously be done safely for the child. But whether babies born at home or in birthing rooms are *better* off than infants born in more traditional hospital settings is simply not clear from the information we have. One of the difficulties is that women who choose home delivery, or a birthing room, are different in other ways from women who opt for accustomed procedures. They may have used fewer drugs during pregnancy, or eaten differently, or have different attitudes about delivery and motherhood. If we found that home-delivered infants were better off, we couldn't be sure of the cause.

Box 3.1 Fathers' Involvement in Birth

Participation by fathers in the delivery process varies widely from one hospital to another, from one part of the country to another; but such participation is clearly on the increase. Most mothers report that having the father present was a great help, especially if the father had gone through prenatal classes with the mother. In one study by William Henneborn and Rosemary Cogan (1975), mothers who had their husbands present during delivery reported less pain and used less medication—both highly desirable effects.

But what about the effect on the father and on his involvement with or attachment to the baby? The data we have make it look as if it does have an effect. I've already talked about the study by Gail Peterson and her co-workers (1979) in Chapter 1. They found that the more involved the father was in the delivery—being present and helping the mother—the more attached he was to the infant. Martin Greenberg and Norman Morris (1974) found something very similar. They describe the quality of fathers who had been present at the birth, or who had had early contact with the baby, as *engrossment*. These fathers were preoccupied with the infant, wanted to touch and hold him, and were generally absorbed by the baby. They were more comfortable holding their babies and thought they were better at distinguishing their own infant from others in the newborn nurseries than were fathers who hadn't had early contact with their baby. Once again, then, there are signs of a possibly greater "attachment" by the father to the infant if he has had an opportunity to handle the baby shortly after the infant's birth. I should point out, however, that in the Greenberg and Morris study, the father didn't have to be present at the actual birth for this effect to occur; it was enough for him to have had early contact.

Similarly, Ross Parke (1979) has found in several studies that fathers hold and touch their newborns, smile and care for them in very much the same way as do mothers. And this was true whether they had been present at the child's birth or not. Parke's studies suggest that fathers may be "natural" caregivers, just as mothers are, but leave open the question of whether participation in the birth of the child significantly alters the father's short-term or long-term relationship with the baby. What does appear to be true is that *early* contact between father and infant—in the first few hours—enhances the father's reported feelings of involvement with his baby.

The indirect effect is even harder to pin down. Aiden Macfarlane (1977), in his discussion of this issue, reports that women who have home deliveries are less likely to be depressed in the days after giving birth than are women delivering in a hospital. But whether the depression accompanying hospital deliveries is long-lasting, or whether it has any long-term effect on the mother's relationship with her infant, we do not know. As home deliveries become more common, no doubt the research evidence will improve. In the meantime, assuming there are no signs of difficulty in the pregnancy, it seems to be very much a matter of personal choice.

A related issue for many parents is the potential role of the father during delivery. I've described some of the information we have about that question in Box 3.1.

Conditions During Birth: The Leboyer Method

Still another new direction in childbirth procedures has been suggested by a French obstetrician, Frederick Leboyer (1975). Leboyer is convinced that the process of birth is extremely traumatic and painful for the baby and that physicians need to try to reduce the stress as much as possible. Deliveries done using the **Leboyer method** are usually referred to as "gentle" births.

Leboyer suggests that as soon as the baby's head is delivered, the lights in the room should be lowered and everyone should speak as quietly as possible. Immediately after birth, the baby is placed on his mother's belly and allowed to begin breathing naturally before his umbilical cord is cut. A few minutes later, the baby is placed in a warm bath to recreate the warm liquid he has been accustomed to in utero.

There are two legitimate questions to be raised about Leboyer's proposed methods. First, is the baby really traumatized at birth? Are gentle methods needed at all? Opinions differ. Some psychoanalytically oriented theorists, such as Otto Rank (1929), have been convinced that birth is traumatic. Rank went so far as to suggest that "birth trauma" left an emotional scar that lasted throughout life. Other observers, including Macfarlane (1977), have been struck instead by how capable and adaptable the newborn is. The infant seems to adjust rapidly to the demands of the environment he finds himself thrust into. Obviously, this is a difficult question to study systematically, so opinions are about all we will have to go on.

The second question is whether the "gentle" method has any lasting effect on the child. Do "Leboyer children" turn out better in later months or years? Again I have to say that we really don't know. The only study I know of in which Leboyer children have been studied over a period of time was one by Danielle Rapoport (1978). She observed and tested a group of 129 such infants when they were 1–3 years old and reports that they walked a bit sooner than average and had few sleeping or feeding difficulties. The mothers reported that the babies had been calm and alert. This sounds very encouraging, but the catch is that Rapoport did not include a control group of "normal delivery" babies from similar families in her study. As a result, we don't know whether such slightly advanced development is typical of children from the backgrounds common to Leboyer infants.

Despite the lack of firm evidence, I suspect that Leboyer's methods, or at least portions of them, will become fairly widely accepted. Certainly they seem to do no harm, and they *may* be beneficial to the child.

Problems at Birth

While it is true that most deliveries are quite normal, as with prenatal development, there are some things that can go wrong.

Anoxia: Lack of Oxygen Sometimes during the process of delivery, the newborn has her oxygen supply cut off for a short while. Most often this occurs because the umbilical circulation system fails to continue the supply of blood oxygen until the baby cries or because the umbilical cord has been squeezed in some way during delivery. In severe cases, where the loss of oxygen has been prolonged, there can be brain damage. Many cases of cerebral palsy, a major motor disability that may involve loss of muscle control over the legs and arms or head, result from **anoxia** at birth or prenatally.

Shorter-term anoxia at birth, however, does not seem to have permanent effects in most cases. Arnold Sameroff and Michael Chandler (1975), in reviewing all the studies on the long-range effects of anoxia, report that in most instances, the infants catch up with their normal-birth peers. So while anoxia *may* have serious consequences, in most instances it does not.

Cesarean Section In some cases, because the mother's pelvis is shaped so that normal delivery is difficult, or when there are complications that call for instant delivery in order to save the child, or when the baby is positioned feet-downward ("breech") at the time of delivery, the baby may be delivered through an abdominal incision rather than vaginally. This is called a **cesarean section**—a name that derives from the legend that Julius Caesar was delivered in this way.

C-sections (as they are usually abbreviated) are becoming remarkably common in the United States, amounting to as many as 10 or 15 percent of all deliveries in some hospitals (Brackbill, 1979). There are good medical reasons for this increase. But as a note of caution, let me also point out that there are some hints of possible problems for C-section infants. Specifically, Helfer (1975) notes that child abuse is more common at later ages among C-section than among normal delivery infants. This *could* be because of a lack of opportunity for the initial attachment to be formed, or it could be for other reasons. But we obviously need to know more about the psychological consequences of this type of delivery.

Low Birth Weight Another fairly common complication is for the infant to be born weighing less than the normal or optimum amount, a condition labeled generally **low birth weight.** Infant weight is the single best predictor of infant mortality. For example, in one very large study of all the births in New York City during one year (Kessner, 1973), the mortality rate was 609 per 1000 for infants who weighed less than 1500 grams (about 3¼ pounds). For babies who weighed between 1500 and 2500 grams (3¼–4¼ pounds approximately), the mortality rate was 55 per 1000. By contrast, babies with optimum weight (between

Figure 3.3 This premature baby looks fairly typical. He has the body hair and slightly puffy appearance found in most full-term babies, but is smaller. Like many newborns, he is not overly attractive!

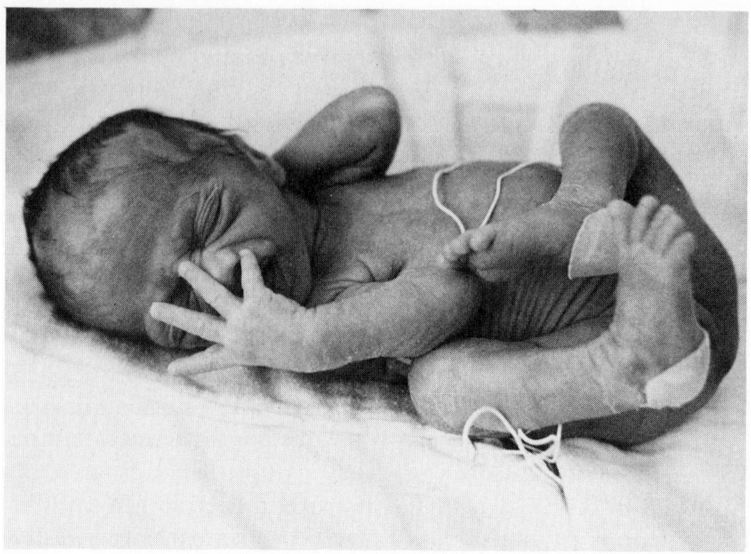

3500 and 4500 grams) had a risk of mortality of only about six per 1000.

Several types of infants make up the low-birth-weight group. First, there are those whose gestation has been too short. These babies are currently referred to as **short gestation infants;** in earlier years, they were called **premature,** a term with which you may be more familiar.

A second type of low-birth-weight infant is the **small for date** baby. These are infants who may have spent the normal number of weeks in utero (40) but who are just small for some reason. Pedro Rosso, whose work I described in the last chapter, finds that these small babies are more common among women who gained too little weight during their pregnancies, particularly if they gained too slowly during the final three months. The mother's nutrition thus seems to be a vital causative factor in this group of low-birth-weight babies.

As I already indicated, the risk of infant death is greatly increased among all small babies. But for those who survive—and more and more of them do—there are also added short-term risks. They are more likely to experience respiratory distress in the days and weeks immediately after birth; they are less alert and less responsive; and they are slower than their full-sized peers in motor development over the first few years.

Until quite recently, most physicians and psychologists had concluded that the disadvantage for the low-birth-weight baby continued throughout childhood. But recent evidence (Sameroff & Chandler, 1975) suggests that most short gestation and small for date babies catch up by about age 7, particularly if they are raised in a supportive and stimulating environment. The group that does show a long-term problem is low-birth-weight infants who are raised in a poverty environment (Werner, Simonian, Bierman & French, 1967; Drillien, 1964; Sameroff & Chandler, 1975). This is an excellent example, by the way, of an interaction between a physical influence and an external environmental influence.

The Newborn: What Can He Do?

The baby has been born. He cries, breathes, looks around a bit. But what else can he do in the early hours and days? On what skills does the infant build?

Reflexes

Infants are born with a large collection of **reflexes,** which are automatic physical responses triggered involuntarily by a specific stimulus. Many of these reflexes are still present in adults, so you should be familiar with them—the knee jerk the doctor tests for, your automatic eyeblink when a puff of air hits your eye, or the involuntary narrowing of the pupil of your eye when you're in a bright light.

In addition to these long-lasting reflexes, the newborn has a set of primitive reflexes, some of which are useful for his survival. I've listed some of the more helpful and interesting of these in Table 3.1 on the next page.

Clearly, the rooting/sucking/swallowing reflexes are essential if the baby is to get fed, and the Moro reflex is helpful in moving the baby away from unpleasant things. The Babinsky and grasp reflexes, though, are less useful. They are primitive reflexes, governed by the midbrain—the part of the brain that develops earliest. Both of these drop out at about six months or so, when the more complex parts of the brain begin to dominate.

Perceptual Skills: What the Infant Sees, Hears, and Feels

Again I've summarized what we know about the abilities of the newborn in a table (see Table 3.2 on page 85), but I want to expand on a couple of these points.

First of all, each item of information in the table represents more than one study—in some cases, there are dozens of studies involved. I've given references where the study is a "classic"—such as Wilton Chase's study of color vision in the infant or Kai Jensen's study of taste perception—or when the study is very recent.

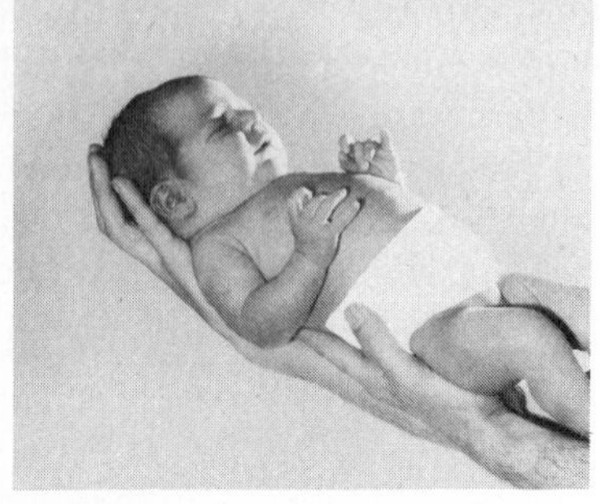

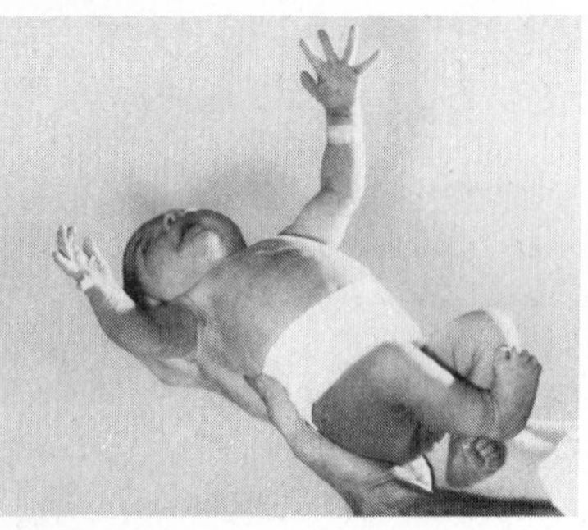

Figure 3.4 These two photos show the Moro reflex very well. In the top photo the baby is fairly relaxed, but when the adult drops the baby suddenly (and catches him again), the baby throws his arms out in the first part of the Moro reflex. The baby will later close his fingers, too. This reflex may be left over from our ape ancestors; young monkeys do this when their mother lets go briefly. The result is that the baby grabs hold of a bunch of fur and thus clings. In human babies it has little usefulness, but remains for the first six months or so.

Table 3.1 Major Reflexes in the Newborn Baby

Reflex	Description
Rooting	An infant touched on the cheek will turn toward the touch and search for something to suck on.
Sucking	When she gets her mouth around something suckable, she sucks.
Swallowing	This is present at birth, though it is not well coordinated with breathing yet.
Moro	This is also called the "startle reflex." You see it in an infant when she hears a loud noise or gets any kind of physical shock. She throws both arms outward, and arches her back.
Babinsky	If you stroke an infant on the bottom of his foot, he first splays out his toes and then curls them in.
Grasp	A baby will curl his fingers around your hand or any graspable object. The signal for this is a touch on the palm.
Stepping	If you hold a very young infant up so that his feet just touch the ground, he will show walkinglike movements, stepping his feet alternately.

Second, I've carefully put a "maybe" in some statements, where the evidence is just not complete or not consistent. Testing newborn babies is extremely difficult. They aren't awake very much and aren't terribly responsive during the first few days. So getting any kind of accurate information is a very hard job indeed, and sometimes we just can't get answers. Other times the results are simply inconsistent.

A good example of such inconsistency is the statement about babies being soothed by rhythmic sounds. Lee Salk first reported in 1960 that babies were soothed by the sound of a heartbeat, presumably because it was like the conditions of the womb. Other rhythmic sounds have been used by mothers over the centuries to soothe babies—lullabies, the creak of a rocking chair—so Salk's finding fits with folklore as well. But Douglas Detterman (1978), in a recent and very well designed and controlled study, has *not* found this kind of effect. In his study, the babies who listened to the heartbeat sound didn't cry less, as Salk had found in his babies. It's not obvious just what we do when we have two directly opposing results. But in this case, the Detterman study is technically a better piece of research, so

Table 3.2 Perceptual Skills of the Newborn

Sense	The baby can . . .
Seeing	Focus both eyes on the same point; the best focus point is about 8 inches away (Haynes, White & Held, 1965). Follow a moving object with the eyes; not a well-developed skill at birth, it improves rapidly (Kremenitzer, Vaughan, Kurtzberg & Dowling, 1979). Discriminate some colors; we know this can be done by two weeks (Chase, 1937), but we are not sure about birth (Werner & Wooten, 1979).
Hearing	Respond to various sounds, particularly those in the pitch and loudness range of the human voice. Make discriminations among very slightly different sounds like *pah* and *bah* (Trehub & Rabinovitch, 1972). *Maybe* locate the direction from which sounds come (Muir & Field, 1979). Clearly able to do this at six months, and *may* happen earlier. *Maybe* respond by being soothed by rhythmic sounds such as the heartbeat (Salk, 1960).
Smelling	React strongly to some smells, such as ammonia or anise (licorice).
Taste	Tell the difference between salty and sweet tastes and prefer sweet tastes (Crook, 1978); tell the difference between sour and bitter (Jensen, 1932).
Touch	Respond to touches over most of the body, especially on the hands and mouth.

it calls the old conclusion into question. Whether this means that all the traditional rocking chairs and lullabies don't really do what we all think they do I can't say at this point, but we have to take a further look at this whole question.

A third interesting thing about the information in Table 3.2, which you may have noticed, is that the baby seems to come into the world especially sensitive to stimulation that comes from people. She responds most to sounds that are about in the range of the human voice; and she can focus her eyes best about 8 inches away from her, which is just about the distance between the infant's face and the mother's during nursing.

Overall, if you look at the skills already present at birth, you can't help but be impressed. The newborn can see and hear remarkably well and seems to be able to make the major taste and smell discriminations. To be sure, all these skills improve with age. The baby develops better skill at following a moving object with her eyes and she gets better at focusing her eyes on

Figure 3.5 Newborn infants have very poor motor control. Their heads must be supported when they are held; they cannot even raise their heads off a mattress. This baby, who is about 1 month old, has just developed enough muscular strength to lift his head.

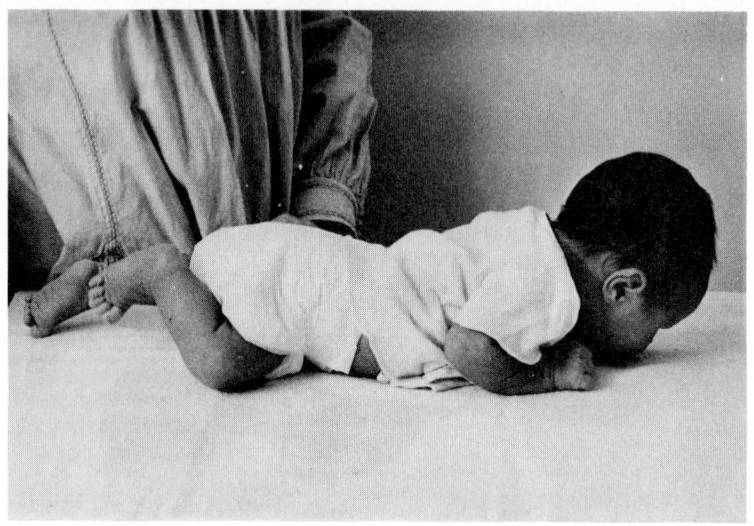

the same spot. But at birth, she has far more abilities than any of us thought ten or twenty years ago.

Motor Skills: Moving Around

The motor abilities of the newborn, in contrast, are not very impressive. He can't hold up his head; he can't coordinate his looking and his reaching yet; he can't roll over or sit up. The baby does *move* a lot, but we don't know whether the movements of arms and legs and head are attempts by the baby to explore the world around him or whether they are more like reflexes – automatic movements in response to sounds or sights or other stimulation.

During the early weeks, there are fairly rapid improvements in motor ability. By one month, for example, the baby can hold her chin up off the floor or mattress (Figure 3.5). By two months, she is beginning to swipe at objects near her with her hands. Still, by contrast with perceptual abilities, the baby's motor abilities are primitive and develop only slowly during the first years of life.

Learning and Habituation

Both the perceptual abilities and the child's motor skills seem to be pretty heavily influenced by maturation. At birth, seeing and hearing have matured, while moving hasn't very much. But what about learning? How early can the baby learn from her environment? For the theorist, these are important questions because they touch on the general issue of maturation versus learning. For the parent, they are equally important. If the baby begins to learn from the first day, then it makes sense to talk to and try to stimulate the baby—to give her things to learn from and learn about.

Classical Conditioning Researchers are still arguing about whether newborn infants can be conditioned classically. Arnold Sameroff, for example (Sameroff & Cavanaugh, 1979), has argued fairly consistently that while newborns do learn, they don't do so through standard classical conditioning. Most other researchers, however, are convinced that it is possible to condition a newborn. Lewis Lipsitt and Herbert Kaye (1964) have been successful in conditioning the baby's sucking reflex, for example. The babies in their experiment learned to suck in response to a loud sound, as well as to the feeling of a nipple in the mouth. More recently, Leighton Stamps (1977) has been able to condition the baby's heart rate.

These results show that the newborn *can* be classically conditioned, although it is equally clear that it is difficult to do so. By three to four weeks of age, however, classical conditioning is quite easy to demonstrate in an infant. So the conditioned emotional responses I talked about in Chapter 1 may begin to develop as early as the first weeks of life.

Operant Conditioning There is essentially no disagreement about whether newborns can learn through operant conditioning. They can and do. In particular, the sucking response and head turning have both been successfully increased by the use of reinforcements such as sweet-tasting liquids (Sameroff & Cavanaugh, 1979).

The fact that conditioning of this kind can take place means that whatever neurological "wiring" is needed for learning to occur is present at birth.

Habituation Still a third capacity of the newborn is for something called **habituation,** which I haven't discussed before. Habituation is the automatic reduction in the strength or vigor of a response to a repeated stimulus. An example would probably help: Suppose you live on a fairly noisy street—as I do. The sound of cars going by is repeated over and over during every day. But after a while, you not only don't react to the sound, you quite literally *do not hear it* or don't hear it as loudly. The ability to do this—to dampen down the intensity of some repeated stimulus—is obviously vital in our everyday lives. If we reacted constantly to every sight and sound and smell that came along, we'd spend all our time responding to these repeated events and not have energy or attention left over for things that are new and deserve attention.

It turns out that capacity to habituate is present in the new-

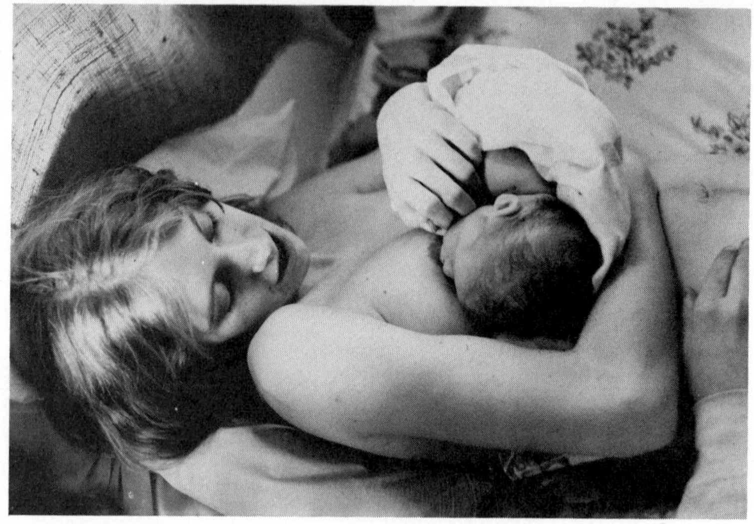

Figure 3.6 **This baby is in the sucking part of the suck-pause-jiggle-pause-suck "conversation" with his mother. Notice how the mother has turned her head and body so that her face and the infant's are parallel.**

born (Lipsitt, 1979). She will stop looking at something you keep putting in front of her face; she will stop showing a startle reaction (Moro reflex) to loud sounds after the first few presentations. This is not a voluntary process; it is entirely automatic. But the fact that the newborn is equipped with this capacity means that she can respond each hour, or each day, to the genuinely novel things that are occurring.

Social Skills

When you think about a newborn baby, you probably don't think of him as being particularly social. He doesn't talk; he doesn't smile often during the first weeks; he doesn't flirt. But even at this very early stage, the baby is remarkably good at enticing other people—particularly parents—into social encounters. I'll be talking more about this whole process in Chapter 11, but it's important to point out here that the baby comes equipped with very good social "elicitors."

She cries when she needs something, which ordinarily brings someone to her to provide care. And then she responds to that care by being soothed, which is very reinforcing for the caregivers. She adjusts her body to yours when you pick her up; after the first few weeks, she gets quite good at meeting your eyes; she begins to smile occasionally during those early weeks and by four to six weeks smiles regularly, especially to faces. All of these things bring people close and keep them close.

One other thing the baby does from the beginning, which seems to be critical for any social interaction, is to take turns.

As adults, we take turns in a range of situations, including conversations and eye contacts. In fact, it's very difficult to have any kind of social encounter with someone who does *not* take turns. Kenneth Kaye (1977) argues that the beginnings of this "turn taking" can be seen in very young babies in their eating patterns. As early as the first days of life, the baby sucks in a "burst-pause" pattern. She sucks for a while, pauses, sucks for a while, pauses, and so on. Mothers enter into this "conversation" too, often by jiggling the baby during the pauses. The eventual conversation looks like this: suck, pause, jiggle, pause, suck, pause, jiggle, pause. The rhythm of the interaction is really very much like a conversation and seems to underlie many of the social encounters among people of all ages. The fascinating thing is that this rhythm, this turn taking, can be seen in an infant 1 day old.

The Daily Life of Infants

Thus far I have described what an infant experiences and what she can do. But a more important issue for many parents, daycare workers, or others caring for an infant day to day is what he does with his time. How is the infant's day organized? What sort of natural rhythms occur in the daily cycles? Researchers such as Heinz Prechtl and his colleagues (Prechtl & Beintema, 1964), who have studied newborns have described five different **states of consciousness**—states of sleep and wakefulness in infants, which I've summarized in Table 3.3

You can see that the baby spends more time sleeping than doing anything else; and of the time awake, only about two to three hours is "quiet awake" or unfussy active awake.

The five main states tend to occur in cycles, just as your own states occur in a daily rhythm. In the newborn, the basic period in the cycle is about 1½ or 2 hours. Most infants move through the states from deep sleep to lighter sleep to fussing and hunger and then to alert wakefulness, after which they get drowsy and drop back into deep sleep. This sequence repeats itself about every two hours. Before very long, the infant can string two or three of these periods together without coming to full wakefulness, at which point we say that the baby can "sleep through the night." One of the implications of this rhythm, by the way, is that the best time for really good social encounters with a young infant is likely to be just after she is fed, when she is most likely to be in a quiet awake state.

Let me take a somewhat more detailed look at some of the major states.

Table 3.3 The Five Basic States of Sleep and Wakefulness in an Infant and Their Frequency at Birth and 1 Month

State	Characteristics	Average amount of time spent in that state: At birth	At 1 month
Deep sleep	Eyes closed, regular breathing, no movement except occasional startles	16–18 hrs.	14–16 hrs.
Active sleep	Eyes closed, irregular breathing, small twitches, no gross body movement		
Quiet awake	Eyes open, no major body movement, regular breathing	6–8 hrs.	8–10 hrs.
Active awake	Eyes open with movements of the head, limbs, and trunk; irregular breathing		
Crying and fussing	Eyes may be partly or entirely closed, vigorous diffuse movement, with crying or fussing noise		

Source: Based on the work of Prechtl & Beintema, 1964; Hutt, Lenard & Prechtl, 1969; Parmalee, Wenner & Schulz, 1964.

Sleep in Infants

Sleeping may seem like a fairly uninteresting part of the infant's day. Parents obviously find the child's sleep periods helpful, particularly as they develop into a pattern with a long nighttime sleep. But there are two other aspects of an infant's sleep that are intriguing to psychologists.

First, irregularity in the child's sleep patterns may be a symptom of some disorder or problem. You may remember that I mentioned in Chapter 2 that one of the characteristics of babies born to drug-addicted mothers is that they seem unable to establish a pattern of sleeping and waking. Brain-damaged infants have the same kind of difficulties in many cases, so any time an infant fails to develop clear sleep-waking regularity, it *may* be a sign of trouble.

The other interesting thing about sleep in newborns is that they show the same external signs of dreaming as do older children or adults. In adults, the outward sign of dreaming is a fluttering of the eyeballs under the closed lids called **rapid eye movement** sleep, or REM sleep. Newborn infants also show REMs during active sleep. Even premature babies as young as

Figure 3.7

32 weeks of gestational age show REM sleep. In fact, Howard Roffwarg and his associates (Roffwarg, Muzio & Dement, 1966) have found that newborns spend about half of their sleep time in REM sleep; while in young adults, by contrast, only about 20 percent of sleep time is REM sleep.

Of course, we don't know whether the infant "dreams" in our sense of the word. He may. But we do know that during the infant's REM sleep, there is a kind of intense stimulation of the central nervous system. So the sleep time of the newborn is full of internal activity of some kind.

Crying To many parents, the infant's crying may be mainly an irritation, especially if it continues for long periods and the infant is not easily consoled. But crying serves important functions for the child and for the parent-child pair.

For the child, crying helps to improve lung capacity (since the baby gulps in more air between cries) and helps to organize the workings of the heart and respiratory system. So it is quite literally physically good for a child to cry at least a little. Perhaps more important, the cry serves as a signal of distress, and this is significant information for the parents or other caregivers.

What should the parent do in response to the child's cry? Will picking up the child right away when he cries only serve to reinforce crying? Or will it reassure the infant in some way that his needs will be met?

Mary Ainsworth and her colleagues Sylvia Bell and Donelda Stayton (1972) tried to answer this question with a short-term longitudinal study of infants over the first year of life. They observed the infants' crying and the mothers' responses to it in a series of lengthy home visits every three weeks. Their findings seemed quite clear: Mothers who waited to respond to crying had babies who cried more often than did mothers who picked the babies up right away. They say about their results:

> These findings are, of course, inconsistent with the views of those who assume that to respond to crying is to reinforce it, so that mothers who respond promptly are likely to have "spoiled" babies who cry more, whereas mothers who refuse to reward this change-worthy behavior by responding to it should themselves be rewarded by having babies who cry little. According to our data, the reverse is true.
>
> *(Ainsworth, Bell & Stayton, 1972, p. 131)*

This conclusion stood largely unchallenged (and widely quoted) for about five years. Recently, however, Jacob Gewirtz and Elizabeth Boyd (1977) have argued that Ainsworth may have overstated the case. Gewirtz and Boyd agree that mothers who respond quickly may have infants who cry less, but they don't agree that this finding disproves the basic postulates of learning theory. A mother might be very attentive to the precrying and just-starting-to-cry signals and pick up her infant when she hears them. By doing this, she is reinforcing those precrying sounds, rather than crying, and the infant may in fact cry less. In contrast, if the mother ignores those early signals and doesn't respond until the child has reached a full-throated, long-winded wail, she may be reinforcing lengthy wailing. Either of these patterns of behavior on the part of mothers would help to generate the results that Ainsworth and her associates obtained, but both are entirely in keeping with the expectations of reinforcement theory.

No doubt this theoretical argument will continue for some years. For now, it does seem accurate to say that a parent who is sensitive to the infant's cues and responds appropriately and quickly is likely to have an infant who cries less.

Eating

Eating is not a "state," but it is certainly something that newborn babies do frequently. Given the approximately two-hour cycle, babies may eat as many as ten times a day. By 1 month, though, the average number is about five-and-a-half feedings (Barnard & Eyres, 1979), which drops to about five per day by 4

Box 3.2 Breast-Feeding versus Bottle-Feeding

Many people get pretty heated over this question. Advocates of breast-feeding argue that it is the only "natural" way to feed a baby. Those who prefer bottle-feeding are just as passionate in defense of their choice. My concern with the question, as usual, is with the potential effect on the baby or on the interaction of the infant and the mother.

Effects on the Baby

There are several potent arguments in favor of breast-feeding. First and most important, breast milk seems to provide important protection for the infant against many kinds of diseases. The baby receives antibodies from the mother—antibodies that he can't produce himself but that help to protect him against infections and allergies. Breast-fed infants have fewer respiratory and gastrointestinal infections than do bottle-fed babies (Marano, 1979).

Second, breast milk is easier for the baby to digest than is cow's milk or formula based on cow's milk. In particular, the fat in breast milk is almost entirely absorbed by the baby, while only about 80 percent of the fat in formula is absorbed. This is particularly troublesome for low-birth-weight infants, who have difficulty digesting fats. The high-cholesterol fats in breast milk may also have a long-lasting benefit. Isabelle Valadian (cited in Marano, 1979) has found that adults who were exclusively breast-fed for at least two months have lower cholesterol levels than those who were given formula.

Third, the risk of obesity or overweight appears to be higher in bottle-fed babies (Taitz, 1975; Marano, 1979). The most likely explanation of this is that the breast-fed infant has more control over the amount he eats. When he's no longer hungry, he stops sucking. The mother doesn't really know how much milk he's taken, but she watches for the cues he gives her that he's had enough. The mother of a bottle-fed baby, on the other hand, may feel that the baby should take all the milk in the bottle and keep urging him to continue even though he's giving signals that he's no longer hungry. So bottle-fed babies may be more often overfed. This is obviously not something that happens in every case, but the risk seems to be greater.

Mother–Infant Interaction

In contrast, mother–infant interactions do *not* seem to be affected by the manner of feeding. Bottle-fed babies are held and cuddled in the same ways, and their mothers are just as sensitive and responsive to their babies as are breast-fed infants' mothers. Tiffany Field (1977), for example, looked at the kind of "turn taking" that Kenneth Kaye describes and found that both breast-feeders and bottle-feeders entered into the "dialogue" equally well.

Advice?

The dietary evidence argues for breast-feeding if it is at all feasible and if the mother remains in good health and continues to eat a good diet. Many pediatricians are now urging this choice on their patients. But for some mothers this option is not possible. They may need to be away from their infant for long stretches each day, may be in poor health, or may want to share the feeding with the infant's father, to encourage his participation in the child's care. If any of these reasons prevail, the mother should know that her infant can receive his basic dietary requirements from formula and that her relationship with the child will not be adversely affected. When circumstances or philosophy permit, however, breast-feeding appears to be the best option for the child's short-term, and perhaps long-term, health.

months of age. From the point of view of the parents, one of the critical decisions about feeding is whether to breast-feed or bottle-feed. There are arguments on both sides, which I've summarized in Box 3.2.

Individual Differences Among Babies

So far I have been talking as if all babies were alike, and of course in most ways they are. Barring some kind of physical damage, all babies have similar sensory equipment at birth and can experience the same kinds of happenings around them. But they do differ quite markedly in **temperament.** In particular, babies range from placid to vigorous in their response to any kind of stimulation. They also differ in their rate of activity, irritability and restlessness, and in cuddliness. Some babies seem to enjoy being cuddled and adjust their bodies right away to the person holding them. Others seem to squirm from the beginning and do less body adjusting.

It turns out that these differences are usually found in clusters. The vigorous baby is often less cuddly, for example, and more irritable and restless. The placid baby is often cuddly and lower in activity generally. Alexander Thomas and Stella Chess (1977), who have done the best-known studies of temperamental differences among infants, describe three such types of children.

The Easy Child Easy children approach new events positively. They try new foods without much fuss, for example. They are also regular in biological functioning, with good sleeping and eating cycles, are usually happy, and adjust easily to change.

The Difficult Child By contrast, the difficult child is less regular in body functioning and is slow to develop regular sleeping and eating cycles. These children react negatively to new things, cry more and are more irritable, and respond vigorously (usually negatively) to new things. Thomas and Chess point out, however, that once the difficult baby has adapted to something new, he is often quite happy about it, even though the adaptation process itself is very difficult.

The Slow-to-Warm-Up Child Children in this group are not as negative in responding to new things or new people as is the difficult child. They show instead a kind of passive resistance. Instead of spitting out new food violently and crying, the slow-to-warm-up child may let the food drool out and may resist mildly any attempt to feed her more of the same. These infants show few intense reactions, either positive or negative, although once they have adapted to something new, their reaction is usually fairly positive.

Figure 3.8 These two pictures show consistency in temperament very graphically. Both are of the same pair of identical twins, in the same order. The child on the right in both pictures was consistently of a more "difficult" temperament, while her sister on the left was consistently "easy."

These differences in temperament can be seen in quite young infants and seem to persist throughout childhood—as you can see in Figure 3.8. Thomas and Chess have also found that the temperament makes a difference for the child's later adjustment to school. Children with difficult temperament are more likely to have school problems and are also more likely to show excessive aggressiveness, tantrums, speech problems, or stuttering in later childhood (Rutter, 1978).

Ethnic Differences in Temperament

Until the past few years, most psychologists assumed that differences in temperament among infants and children were essentially randomly distributed. There was no reason to suppose that children of particular ethnic or social class groups might have characteristic temperaments. But recent work by Daniel Freedman (1979) calls this assumption into question. Freedman finds systematic differences in the responses of newborns from different ethnic groups. He and his colleagues have observed and tested Caucasian, Chinese, Navaho, and Japanese infants. Of the four groups studied, the Caucasian babies were the most active and irritable and the hardest to console. Both the Chinese and the Navaho infants were relatively placid, while the Japanese infants responded vigorously but were easier to quiet than the Caucasian infants.

These differences are visible in newborns, so they cannot be the result of systematic shaping by the parents. Furthermore, there is at least some evidence that these differences persist into childhood. For example, classrooms of Chinese children are often observed to be much quieter than classrooms full of Caucasian children.

The persistence of such differences may result from basic temperament, as Thomas and Chess have suggested. But it is also possible that the parents of these different ethnic groups respond differently to their children as well. William Caudill (Caudill & Frost, 1972), for example, observed Japanese mothers and their infants and found that these mothers talked much less to their infants than did Caucasian mothers. Studies by Freedman and his colleagues show the same thing. Chinese mothers talked less and were much less likely to stimulate their infants. These differences in the mothers were present from their first encounter with their infants, so obviously the mother is bringing her own temperament to the interaction. When the mother and infant are of the same temperamental bent, they tend to reinforce each other's pattern so that the differences between the groups become more marked over time.

But what happens if the parents' and the child's temperaments are not well matched? How much impact does the infant's temperament have on the parents' interactions with her? As you will see on the following page, I've discussed some of these questions in Box 3.3.

Box 3.3 The Effects of Infant Temperament on Parents

One mother of a 2-year-old interviewed by Julius Segal and Herbert Yahraes said,

> *My two year old still won't fall asleep easily no matter what I do, and she's up every few hours. I can't figure out what I've done wrong. All my friends' babies have been sleeping through the night for months. Lately, I find myself getting desperate and angry. One night I just sat next to my baby's bed for 10 minutes and cried, and then I ran cursing from her room while she screamed herself blue in the face. I must be some kind of monster.*
>
> (Segal & Yahraes, 1978, p. 93)

It's possible that this mother had somehow, inadvertently, reinforced this particular behavior in her daughter. But it's equally possible—in fact, much more likely—that she's just dealing with a child of "difficult" temperament whose body clock does not run on the same predictable basis as do other children's. The end result is that the *mother's* behavior has been affected by the child.

For many years, psychologists had thought about the relationships of parents and children as if the parents always "shaped" the child. But the recent work on temperament points to the child's impact on the parents as well.

A child with a difficult temperament presents a very different stimulus to the parents than does an easy child. Michael Rutter (1978) finds that difficult children are more often criticized by their parents, for example, presumably because their behavior *is* more troublesome. The combination of the troublesome behavior and the higher level of criticism seems to increase the likelihood that such a child will end up with some problem in school later on. In other cases, parents may withdraw from their difficult child, spending less and less time with the infant or toddler. This, too, may help to create emotional problems for the child.

We often see the same kind of pattern in families with low-birth-weight children, who tend to be very passive and unresponsive babies. During the first few months after birth, the parents of these infants try especially hard to give the infants enough stimulation, enough cuddling, enough love (Beckwith & Cohen, 1978). But after about six months of that hard work, the infant is still not responding very much; the mothers and fathers begin to give up and are then *less* responsive to their babies, less involved with them emotionally (Field, 1977).

These findings illustrate just how much of a two-way street the interaction between infant and parents really is. Parents can and do adjust to the individual characteristics of their babies. But when an infant's behavior is unusually difficult or unusually unresponsive, the demand on the parent's adaptability is really severe; and not everyone can manage it. Some babies, in other words, are just darn hard to bring up. Others may be *very* easy, and the same set of parents may have both types of children.

Sex and Social Class Differences in Infancy

Remarkably enough, there aren't many sex or social class differences among infants. There are a few exceptions to that broad statement. As was true at birth, girls continue to be a bit ahead in some aspects of physical maturity, and boys continue to be more vulnerable. For example, more boys die during the first year of life. In addition, more of the boy's body is made up of muscle tissue than is true for girls, and there is *some* evidence that girls are a bit more responsive to touch than are boys (Maccoby & Jacklin, 1974).

Similarly, poor babies are more likely to be born with low birth weight and to have more problems at birth—a fact that's related to all the prenatal problems I mentioned in the last chapter. But if we look just at healthy babies, there are no differences between poor and middle-class babies in perceptual skills, motor development, or anything else I've discussed in this chapter (Bayley, 1965).

The most interesting thing about these facts is that boys and girls do *not* differ on the temperamental dimensions Thomas and Chess talk about. Boys are not more often "difficult" in temperament, and girls are not more often "easy," even though that is what our stereotypes might lead us to expect.

Having said that, I have to enter two cautions. First, there haven't been very many studies of temperament in infancy, so we can't be completely sure about the lack of sex differences. More important, most of the information we have about babies' temperaments comes from descriptions of infants by their parents. Since parents, like the rest of us, have stereotyped expectations about what boys and girls ought to be like, it is possible that they are simply more tolerant of "difficult" behavior in a boy than in a girl and don't think it's noteworthy enough to mention. Boys and girls might really be different on such dimensions as activity or acceptance of new things, but the differences might be masked by the way the parent *perceives* the behavior. It will take additional direct observations of young boys and girls to settle this question. For the moment, however, I think it is important to emphasize that at this stage we have no persuasive evidence for sex differences in temperament.

Summary

1. The normal birth process has three parts: dilation, delivery, and placental delivery.
2. Parents who handle their babies soon after delivery show intense interest in the baby's features, particularly the eyes, and go through an "acquaintance" process.
3. Most drugs given to the mother during delivery pass through to the infant's bloodstream. They have short-term effects on the infant's responsiveness and on feeding patterns. They may have long-term effects as well.
4. The location of the delivery—whether at home or in the hospital—*may* make some difference, but we know little yet about the effects of location on the baby or on the parent-infant bond.
5. Participation by the father during delivery appears to increase the father's attachment to his infant.
6. Several types of problems may disturb the normal delivery process. The child may have a reduced oxygen supply (anoxia), or conditions may require a Ce-

sarean section (abdominal delivery).

7. Another problem is low birth weight, either from premature delivery or because of insufficient growth during the normal gestational period.

8. Low-birth-weight infants have higher risk of death during the first year of life; but if they survive, many catch up to full-size peers by school age.

9. The newborn has far more skills than most physicians and psychologists had thought, including excellent reflexes, good perceptual skills, and effective social skills.

10. The important infant reflexes include feeding reflexes, such as rooting and sucking, and the Moro reflex.

11. Perceptual skills include focusing both eyes, tracking slowly moving objects, possibly color vision, discrimination of sounds, and possibly location of the direction of sounds. Babies also respond to differences in smell and taste and are sensitive to touch.

12. Motor skills, in contrast, are only rudimentary at birth.

13. Social skills, while rudimentary, are sufficiently developed to bring people close for care and to keep them close for social interactions. The baby can meet a gaze and smile within the first month of life.

14. Newborns can learn from the first days of life, by operant and probably also by classical conditioning.

15. Newborns also habituate to repeated stimulation.

16. Young infants spend the majority of their day sleeping and are in an awake and alert state only a fraction of the time. Rhythms and daily cycles of sleeping, waking, crying, and eating are established early.

17. Babies differ from one another on several dimensions, including vigor of response, general activity rate, restlessness, irritability, and cuddliness. These temperamental differences appear to persist into childhood and to affect the responses of those around them.

18. Male and female babies differ at birth on a few dimensions: Girls are more mature physically and more reactive to touch. Boys have more muscle tissue and are more vulnerable to stress. No sex differences are found, however, on temperamental dimensions such as cuddliness or sootheability.

19. No consistent differences between middle-class and poor infants are found on the usual measures of infant development.

Key Terms

Anoxia A shortage of oxygen. If it is prolonged, it can result in brain damage. This is one of the risks at birth.

Birthing room An arrangement, becoming more common in hospitals, with a homelike atmosphere for delivery.

Cesarean section Delivery of the child through an incision in the mother's abdomen.

Dilation The first stage of delivery when the cervix opens sufficiently to allow the infant's head to pass into the birth canal.

Habituation An automatic decrease in the intensity of a response to a repeated stimulus, which enables the child or adult to ignore the familiar and focus attention on the novel.

Leboyer method A "gentle" birth method proposed by Frederick Leboyer, including darkened lights and quiet, slow-paced birth.

Low birth weight The more precise term now used instead of "premature" to describe infants whose weight is below the optimum range at birth. Includes infants born too early (short gestation) and those who are "small for date."

Premature infant The term formerly used to describe short-gestation and other low-birth-weight infants.

Rapid eye movement (REM) sleep One of the characteristics of sleep during dreaming, which occurs during the sleep of newborns, too.

Reflexes Automatic body reactions to stimulation, such as the knee jerk or the Moro reflex. Many reflexes remain among adults, but the newborn also has some "primitive" reflexes that disappear as the cortex is fully developed.

Short-gestation infant An infant born before the normal 40-week gestation period has been completed.

Small for date infant A baby who weighs less than is normal for the number of weeks of gestation completed.

States of consciousness Five main sleep/awake states have been identified in infants, from deep sleep to active awake states.

Temperament Collections of typical responses to experiences that seem to be stable over time and that differentiate infants and young children from one another.

Suggested Readings

Brazelton, T. B. Infants and mothers: Differences in development. New York: Dell Publishing Co., 1969.
This is a lovely book, written by a remarkably observant and sensitive physician. It describes the first year of life in some detail and also chronicles the progress of three infants who differ in basic temperament.

Leboyer, F. Birth without violence. New York: Knopf, 1975.
Those of you interested in delivery options may find Leboyer's book about "gentle" birth of interest.

Macfarlane, A. The psychology of childbirth. Cambridge, Mass.: Harvard University Press, 1977.
Another lovely book, with both research information and opinions expressed in clear language.

McCall, R. Infants: The new knowledge. Cambridge, Mass.: Harvard University Press, 1979.
This is an excellent new book about the abilities and characteristics of infants, written in an easy style but describing the most current research.

Segal, J., & Yahraes, H. "Bringing up mother." Psychology Today, 1978, **12** (No. 6), 90–96.
A good recent, readable review of the research on the impact of a child's temperament on parental behavior.

Project 3.1 Observation in a Newborn Nursery

Despite the changes in birth practices, most hospitals still have newborn nurseries, and you can go and look through the window at the infants. Since there are ordinarily a fair number of friends and relatives peering at the babies, there's not likely to be a problem about your going to do some brief observation, but you should nonetheless obtain permission for such a visit. Probably it would be sufficient to go to a hospital and talk briefly with the nurse on duty, asking if you can stand at the window of the newborn nursery for about half an hour or less, and take some notes. If a more formal permission is needed, the nurse can let you know.

Once you have obtained permission and arranged a time for your visit, proceed with the following steps.

1. Set up a score sheet that should look something like this:

	Baby's State				
30-second intervals	Deep sleep	Active sleep	Quiet awake	Active awake	Crying, fussing
1					
2					
3					

   Continue the score sheet for sixty 30-second intervals.

2. Reread the material in Table 3.3 until you know the main features of the five states as well as possible. You will need to focus on the eyes (open versus closed, and rapid eye movement), the regularity of the baby's breathing, and the amount of body movement.
3. Select one infant in the nursery and observe that infant's state every 30 seconds for a half hour. For each 30-second interval, note on your score sheet the state that best describes the infant over the preceding 30 seconds. Do *not* select an infant to observe who is in deep sleep at the beginning. Pick an infant who seems to be in an in-between state (active sleep or quiet awake) so that you can see some variation over the half hour observation.
4. If you can arrange it, you might do this observation with a partner, each of you scoring the infant's state independently. When the half hour is over, compare

notes. How often did you agree on the infant's state? What might have been producing the disagreements?

5. When you discuss or write about the project, consider at least the following issues: Did the infant appear to have cycles of states? What were they? What effect, if any, do you think the nursery environment might have had on the baby's state? If you worked with a partner, how much agreement or disagreement did you have? Why?

Part Two

The Physical Child

hand - Stand on -
beam

Preview of Chapter 4

Physical Growth and Development

Several years ago, when my daughter Arwen was about 8½, I noticed that her normally shining and silky hair was looking lank and stringy. I'm supposed to be a knowledgeable developmental psychologist, and I should have known right away what was happening. But I didn't make the connection. She had fairly recently begun washing her hair herself, and I just thought she wasn't doing a very good job. So I reminded a few times and gave some further instructions. But her hair still didn't look the same. Finally (sometimes I'm a little slow!) it dawned on me that what I was seeing were changes in the oiliness of her hair that were part of puberty. I hadn't thought of 8½ as pubescent, but many of the changes of puberty begin that early for girls. When I figured it out, she and I talked about it, and it gave me a good chance to talk with her more generally about the changes that would be taking place in her body.

I think this anecdote illustrates very clearly that we have to keep the fundamental physical changes of development in mind as we look for explanations of behavior. There are several important ways in which physical development affects the behavior we see in a person. First of all, physical development *sets limits*. Obviously, it can limit actions directly. A child whose maturation hasn't reached the point where he has control over the anal sphincter muscle can't be toilet trained, no matter how hard you try. The mother who thinks she has toilet trained her 10-month-old is kidding herself; she has learned to interpret the baby's grunts or body movements and manages to get him onto the pot at the right moments. But the baby of this age does not have sphincter control.

Similarly, a young infant can't pick up objects easily because

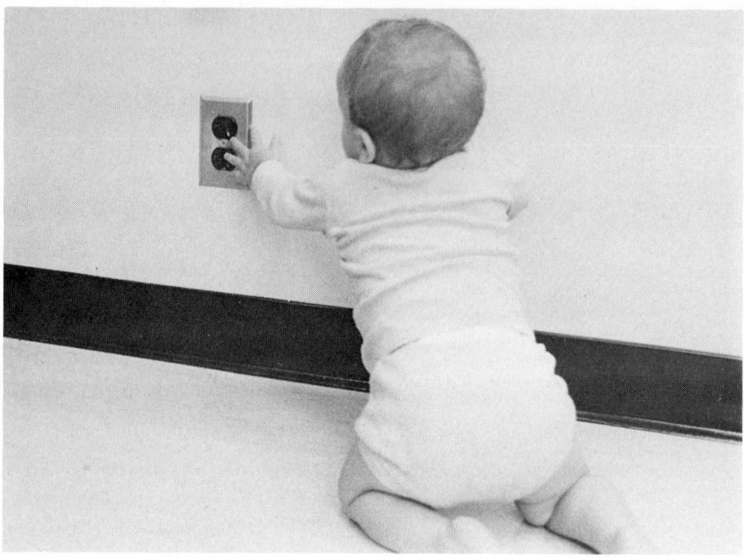

Figure 4.1 In many books about raising children, toilet training is described as the first major disciplinary battleground between parent and child. I don't agree. I think the first battle occurs when the baby begins to crawl, as this one is. The parent faces the task of teaching the preverbal child what he can and cannot touch.

the development of thumb–forefinger opposition hasn't occurred; an older child can't learn to ride a bike until the necessary coordination has developed; a girl can't get pregnant until she is fully mature sexually; and so on.

These limitations, in turn, affect the kind of experiences the child can have. In that way, they affect intellectual and social development as well. An infant who cannot crawl can only explore things that are brought to her or are within easy reach. When she begins to crawl, her horizons are opened. A physical change thus massively expands the range of experience the child can have. At the same time, it also changes the child's interactions with her parents. The parent who has grown accustomed to the relatively immobile baby must now adjust to a child who has to be chased all over the house.

Physical development also affects the child's self-image. Whether a child is small or large for her age, or an early or a late developer in adolescence, may affect the way she thinks about herself. Another personal example may help emphasize this point. As a child, I was unusually tall for my age. I was nearly 5 feet 6 inches at age 12; and when I finally stopped growing, I was just under 6 feet. There are some distinct advantages to being that tall: I can see over people at movies; I can reach into the top cupboards in kitchens; and I can get at books in the top shelves. But at age 12, the advantages weren't so obvious. During that two-year stretch when the girls all grew before the boys did, I was taller than everyone; and even after the boys grew, most did not catch up to me. I felt gawky and conspicuous.

Since social custom at that time dictated that a girl could not go out with a boy shorter than she, I felt my social life was greatly restricted, too. Now, of course, I wouldn't trade an inch; there are too many good things about being tall. But there was a period of about ten years when my image of myself, and a great deal of my behavior, was dominated by a sense of embarrassment about being so big.

Obviously, society's stereotypes about desirable physical characteristics for children and adults enter into this process. The child is comparing her own self-image with the ideal in her head. Her actual physical characteristics may be less important than her perceptions or feelings about them.

For all of these reasons, I think it is important to begin our exploration of development with a fairly detailed look at physical growth and change. What is the child physically able to do at various ages? And how is he affected by his own perceptions of his physical qualities and by the reactions of others to his pattern of physical development?

Answering the What Questions: Basic Sequences of Physical Development

Changes in Height and Weight

Babies gain in both height and weight very rapidly for the first two years. The usual rule of thumb is that an infant will double his birth weight by 5 months and triple it in the first year. The typical infant also grows about 10–12 inches in length, from about 20 inches at birth to over 30 inches at 1 year (Provence, 1979). By age 2, most toddlers are already *half* as tall as they will be as adults—something that is hard to visualize.

After this rapid growth during the first two years, the child settles down to a slower but steady addition of 2–3 inches and about 6 pounds per year (Eichorn, 1979). This continues until adolescence, when another period of rapid growth—usually called the "growth spurt"—occurs for several years. During the growth spurt, the child may add 3–6 inches per year. After this rapid increase, there is again a period of several years of much slower height gain until final height is reached in the late teens.

All of that is pretty straightforward. Since you probably remember your own adolescent growth spurt fairly well, there is not much in these facts that is especially intriguing. But there are some aspects of height and weight changes that may be less familiar.

First of all, the body proportions change systematically. In an adult, for example, the head is about one-eighth or one-tenth of the total height. But the toddler isn't built like this at all. In the 2-year-old, the head is about one-quarter of the total body

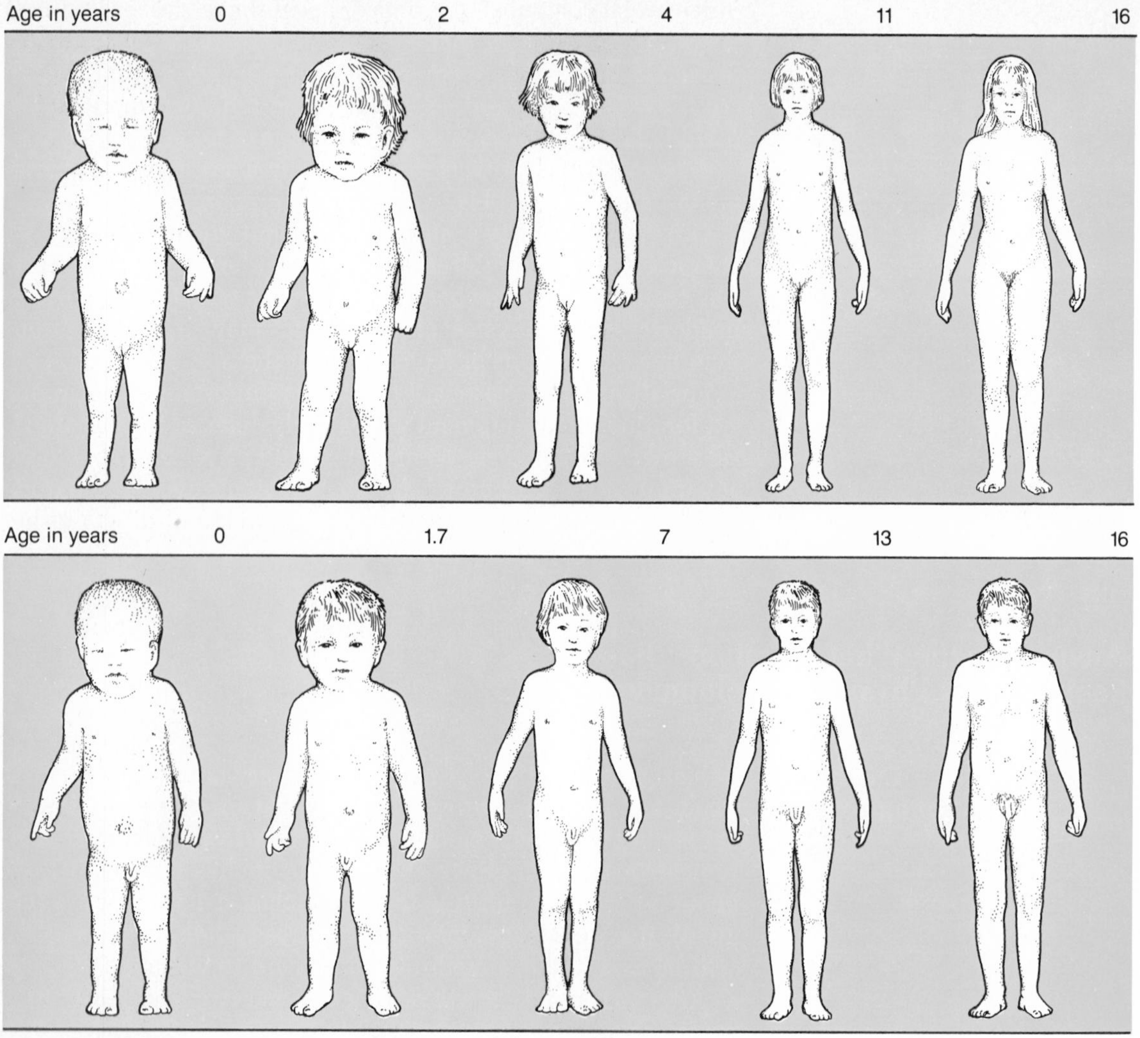

Age in years 0 2 4 11 16

Age in years 0 1.7 7 13 16

Figure 4.2 The change in body proportions from birth through adolescence. As you can see, the head represents a very large proportion of the body length in young children but a smaller proportion at final size. The legs also become relatively longer and the trunk slimmer with age. (Source: The Diagram Group, *Child's body: An owner's manual,* Paddington Press, 1977, section D-03.)

length. You can see the relative proportions of the different body parts in Figure 4.2.

A second point is that development of the different body parts is uneven, and this is particularly striking at adolescence. Hands and feet grow to their full adult size earliest, followed by the arms and the legs. The trunk is usually the slowest part to grow. We often think of an adolescent as "awkward" or uncoordinated. That turns out to be an inaccurate description. I think what people see in teenagers that may look like awkwardness is just the asymmetry of the different body parts. The child's body looks "leggy" and has proportionately large hands and feet. My 10-year-old daughter, for example, has feet as large as mine, even though she's almost a foot shorter.

For the developing child, this asymmetry requires rapid adjustments, too. Having gotten used to a particular body shape, the pubescent child must now adapt to change in proportions, and there may be periods when she is not always sure where her arms or legs are at any given moment.

Another interesting point about the adolescent growth spurt is that although there are big differences in the timing of it, with some kids growing very early, others not until much later, it turns out that the timing isn't related to final height. Many of you may have thought that children who grow early are more likely to end up taller. (Some of you may have missed this question on the "quiz" in Chapter 1.) But in fact, there is no connection between the two. Body *proportions* are related to early or late development. Early developers tend to be relatively shorter in the leg and longer in the trunk, while late developers tend to be more long-legged (Faust, 1977). But the two groups do not differ in average height as adults (Tanner, 1970; Faust, 1977).

Development of Bones

Bones change in three ways with development: They increase in number, become longer and larger, and grow harder.

Number of Bones The parts of the body that show the greatest increase in the number of bones are the hand, wrist, ankle, and foot. For example, in the wrist and hand of an adult, there are 28 separate bones. In the 1-year-old, there are only three. The remaining 25 bones develop over the period of childhood, with complete growth by adolescence.

Hardening of Bones In the infant, some bones are still mostly cartilage (like the bridge of your nose); and all bones are softer, with a higher water content than will be true later. The process of bone hardening, called **ossification,** occurs steadily from birth through puberty.

However, the rate of ossification varies for different parts of the body. The bones of the hand and wrist harden quite early, as do the bones of the head. By contrast, the long bones of the leg do not harden completely until the late teens.

The bone-hardening process may seem quite uninteresting, but it has important practical ramifications. Because of the greater pliability of his body, the infant can work himself into all sorts of postures (he can suck on his toes or put his foot behind his head, for example). But that very lack of stiffness is one of the reasons the baby has difficulty sitting up or holding up his head. As the bones stiffen, the baby is able to manipulate his body more surely—he becomes less floppy.

Increased Size of Bones While the composition of the bone changes and the number increases, the shape is also changing.

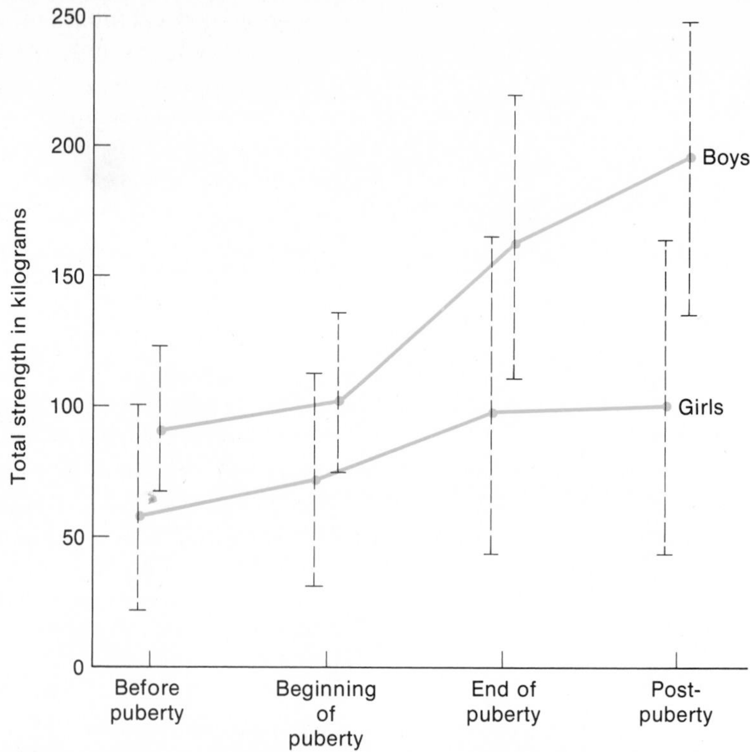

Figure 4.3 Changes in strength among boys and girls at adolescence. The heavy lines show the average strength scores for boys and girls at different stages of puberty. The dotted lines show the range of scores at each point. You can see that the least strong boy is stronger at every stage than the average girl, but there are some girls as strong as the average boy. (Source: Faust, 1977, p. 73.)

This is particularly noticeable in the long bones of the leg and arm, which get steadily longer throughout the years of childhood. Growth of these bones stops only when the ends of the bones (called *epiphyses*) finally harden completely, which does not occur until the middle or late teens.

The Fontanels One of the exceptions to the general rule of "more bones" with development are the bones in the head. In order for the fetal head to be flexible enough to move through the birth canal, the baby is born with several skull bones, with soft areas, called **fontanels,** in between. In most infants, the fontanels have been filled in by bone by about age 2, so there is now a single skull bone instead of several.

Development of Muscles

Unlike the bones, which are not all present at birth, the baby is born with all the muscle fibers she will ever have (Tanner, 1970). What changes is the length and thickness of the muscle fibers. Like bones and height, muscle tissue increases fairly steadily until adolescence, when it too accelerates. One of the clear results of this rapid increase in muscle tissue is that adolescents become quite a lot stronger in just a few years. This particular change is much more marked in boys than in girls, but both sexes do get significantly stronger. You can see the differences in Figure 4.3, from a study by Margaret Faust (1977). The usual way of measuring strength is to have someone pull against an instrument called a dynamometer, which measures the weight pulled. In the figure, Faust has reported the total number of kilograms pulled in several different tests. While boys get a great deal stronger, girls show only a slight increase.

As an aside, I should say that I will be very interested to see whether this difference will still be as large ten years from now. Adolescent girls are beginning to be much more athletic and physically active, and this may help to maintain or stimulate muscular growth. It seems pretty clear that on average males are still going to be stronger than females no matter how much exercise women engage in. About 40 percent of the final body mass of an adult male is muscle, while for women it is only about 24 percent. But it may be that the much greater increase in strength among boys comes about partly because they use their muscles more regularly and that girls too would show larger strength increases in adolescence if they were as physically active.

Development of the Nervous System

Growth in height and weight involve changes you can see. Even the changes in muscles and bones can be "seen" fairly easily in the child's longer legs or greater strength. But there are two enormously important types of changes in the body that are not so easy to perceive. The first of these is change in the nervous system. The most important point about the growth of the nervous system is that the brain and nerves are not "finished" at birth. As I pointed out in Chapter 2, most of the other organ systems are fully operative, even though they undergo some changes after birth. The baby's heart, lungs, and circulatory system, for example, are very much like an adult's. But that's not true of the brain or of the nervous system generally.

Cortical Development At birth, the parts of the brain that are most fully developed are those contained in what is usually called the **midbrain.** This section, in the lower part of the skull, regulates such basic things as attention and habituation, sleeping, waking, and elimination. These are all things the newborn does pretty well.

The least-developed part of the brain at birth is the **cortex,** which is the convoluted gray matter that wraps around the midbrain and is involved in perception, body movement, and all complex thinking and language. You can see the different parts of the brain in Figure 4.4. The cortex is present at birth,

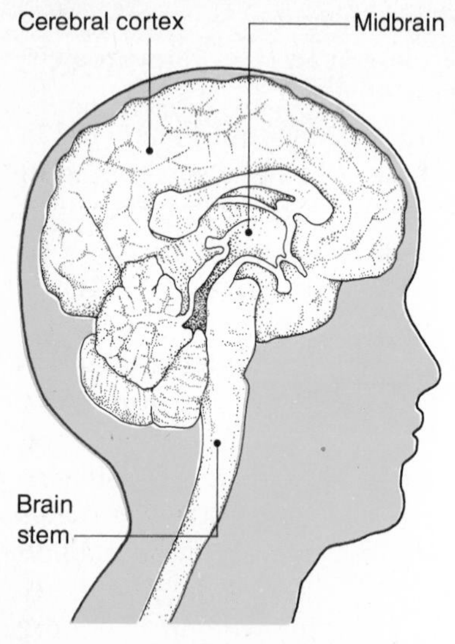

Figure 4.4 The three main sections of the brain. At birth the brain stem and the midbrain are more fully developed than the cortex; the cortex develops over the first few years of life.

but the cells are not well connected. During the first two years or so, some new cortical cells are added, the existing cells become bigger, and they build up many more connecting links. This process is about half complete at six months and about 75 percent complete by age 2. You should think back to the discussion of reflexes in the newborn in Chapter 3. Reflexes like the Babinsky drop out at about six months, when the cortical development is far enough along that the cortex is now dominating most of the baby's physical activities. Physicians use the Babinsky reflex to test for brain damage in older children or adults, since if it is present past about six months, it suggests that something may have gone wrong.

While it is true that about half of the changes in the cortex have taken place by six months after birth, the whole cortex doesn't develop evenly. At birth, the parts of the cortex involved in seeing and hearing are already well developed, and the areas controlling motor skills, such as head and trunk movements, develop fairly early. This sequence of cortical development is obviously going to be reflected in the kinds of movements the baby will be able to handle.

Myelinization A second important process is the development of sheaths around individual nerves, which insulate them from one another and make it easier for messages to pass down the nerves. This sheath is called **myelin;** the process of developing the sheath is called **myelinization.** At birth, for example, the spinal cord is not fully myelinized; and without this sheathing, the child has little ability to "communicate" with the bottom half of her body. The infant has sensation in her trunk and legs; but because messages can't be transmitted easily along the nerves, she has little muscle control. The process of myelinization of the nerves leading to and from the brain occurs rapidly during the early months and years and is almost complete by the time the child is 2 years old. In the brain, however, both myelinization and growth of connective tissues between cells continue into adolescence and perhaps adulthood.

You can understand the importance of the myelinization process very vividly when you realize what happens if it goes awry. **Multiple sclerosis** is a crippling disease of young adults in which the myelin begins to break down. The symptoms of the disease vary enormously, depending on the portion of the nervous system in which the deterioration takes place. But the general progress of the disease is such that the afflicted person gradually loses motor control.

Hormonal Changes

The second "invisible" set of changes is in hormones—secretions of the various **endocrine glands** that govern growth and

Table 4.1 Major Hormones Involved in Physical Growth and Development

Gland	Hormone(s) secreted	Aspect(s) of growth influenced
Thyroid	Thyroxine	Affects normal brain development and overall rate of growth
Adrenal	Adrenal androgen	Involved in some changes at puberty, particularly the development of secondary sex characteristics in boys
Testes (in boys)	Testosterone	Crucial in the formation of male genitals prenatally; also triggers the sequence of changes during puberty in the male
Ovaries (in girls)	Estrogen	Affects development of the menstrual cycle and secondary sex characteristics in girls
Pituitary	Growth hormone	Affects rate of physical maturation
	Activating hormones	Signal other glands to secrete

physical changes. I've summarized the major glands, the hormones they secrete, and their effects in Table 4.1.

Of all the endocrine glands, the most critical is the **pituitary,** since it provides the trigger for release of hormones from other glands. For example, the thyroid gland only secretes thyroxine when it has received a "signal" to do so in the form of a specific thyroid-stimulating hormone from the pituitary.

Let's take a quick look at how the various hormones affect development at different ages.

Hormones in the Prenatal Period There is still a great deal that we do not know about the role of hormones in prenatal development, largely because it is very difficult to determine just which glands begin secreting hormones during gestation. We do know that the thyroid hormone (thyroxine) is present by about the fourth prenatal month and is involved in stimulating normal brain development. Growth hormone is also produced by the pituitary, beginning as early as ten weeks after conception. Presumably it helps to stimulate the very rapid growth of cells and organs of the body. As I already pointed out in Chapter 2, testosterone is also produced in the testes of the developing male and influences the development of male genitals. In females, this secretion does not occur, and there is no equivalent prenatal secretion from the ovaries.

Hormones Between Birth and Adolescence As far as we know, the rate of growth from birth to adolescence is governed largely by the thyroid hormone and by the pituitary growth hormone. Thyroid hormone is secreted in greater quantities for the first two years of life and then falls to a lower level and remains steady until adolescence. This pattern of rapid early development followed by slower and steadier secretions matches the pattern of rapid early change and slower later change in height and weight during the same years.

Secretions from the testes and the ovaries, as well as adrenal androgen, remain at extremely low levels during this period. None of these sex-related hormones is of any particular importance during the first 9–12 years after birth. In fact, the particular cells in the testes which secrete testosterone (called **Leydig cells**) virtually disappear until puberty.

Hormones in Adolescence Obviously, this picture changes at adolescence. Before we can see any changes in the child's body, there are important hormonal changes. First, the pituitary begins to secrete hormones that signal the growth of cells in the testes and ovaries. The testes then begin to secrete testosterone, which is responsible for stimulating the development of male sexual characteristics. In girls, the ovaries begin to secrete estrogen; this secretion becomes cyclic, which in turn triggers the beginning signs of puberty and later the menstrual cycle.

That brief summary makes it sound as if we know quite a lot about the role of hormones in growth. In fact, we really know relatively little. We don't know why girls have a briefer growth spurt than boys do, for example, or what it is that signals that it is time to begin pubertal changes. But in this area, as in many others, our knowledge is increasing as new techniques for measuring hormones are developed.

Motor Development

So far I've dealt with all the basic changes in the body—height, muscles, bones, nervous system, and hormones. All these changes operate together to affect how the baby, toddler, child, or adolescent can use his body, a process called *motor development*. For the parent or the teacher, this is the most visible part of physical development. But it's important to keep in mind that when the child learns to skip or ride a bike, those new skills are built upon a great many less obvious or totally invisible changes in body composition or chemistry.

Basic Trends Two basic trends describe the child's motor development, especially during the first few years. The development moves from the head downward (called **cephalocaudal**) and from the trunk outward (**proximodistal**). In practical terms,

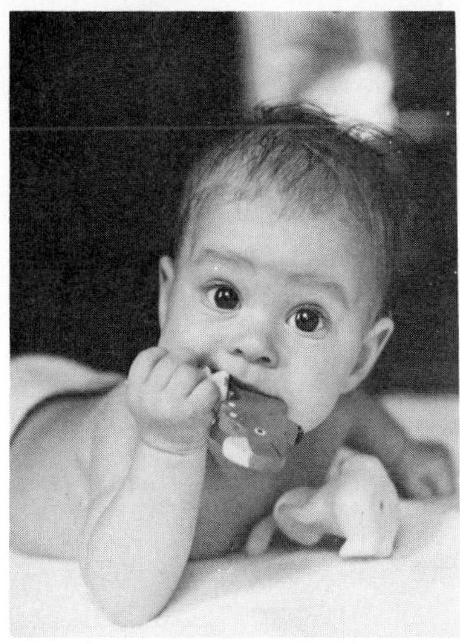

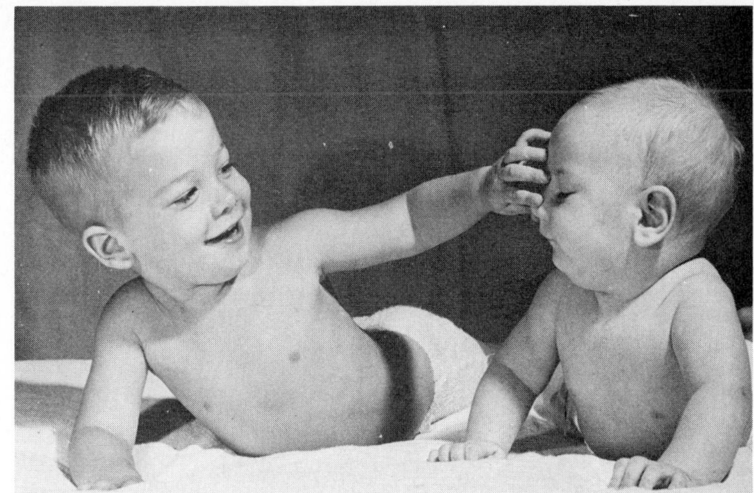

Figure 4.5 These two photos show the transition from whole-hand grasping to thumb-forefinger opposition. Once the child has reached the final step, he can pick up small objects, turn door knobs more easily, and perform many other tasks.

this means that the baby can hold up his head before he can sit up (a cephalocaudal development) and lift his chest off the mattress before he can aim his arm and hand efficiently toward an object (a proximodistal development). If you think back to what I said about the brain, you can see that the sequence of motor skills is built upon the sequence of brain development. The parts of the brain that govern the movement of the head and trunk develop before the parts that govern the movement of the legs and arms.

Some Basic Sequences The basic sequences of motor development are easier to show with pictures than to describe with words. Figure 4.5 shows a very important sequence in the child's growing ability to grasp objects. The baby starts by grasping things with the fingers pressed against the palm; the thumb isn't used much at all. You can see this in the top-left photo. The next step is the thumb used in opposition to the four fingers; and finally the child is able to use the thumb against just one other finger, as you can see in the child of about 18–24 months in the right-hand photo.

Figure 4.6 shows the sequence the baby goes through from standing to walking to stair climbing. Still later, at about 6 or 7, comes bicycle riding and other skills that require even more balance. Meantime, coordination of the arms and shoulders progresses as well. You can see the changes in these skills in the three photos in Figure 4.7. The young child catches the ball using his whole body. He can't yet catch the ball with just his hands and can manage at all only if the ball is large. A child of 5 or 6 can throw a smaller ball and can catch it some of the time, but the coordination is not yet smooth. By 8–10, however, both

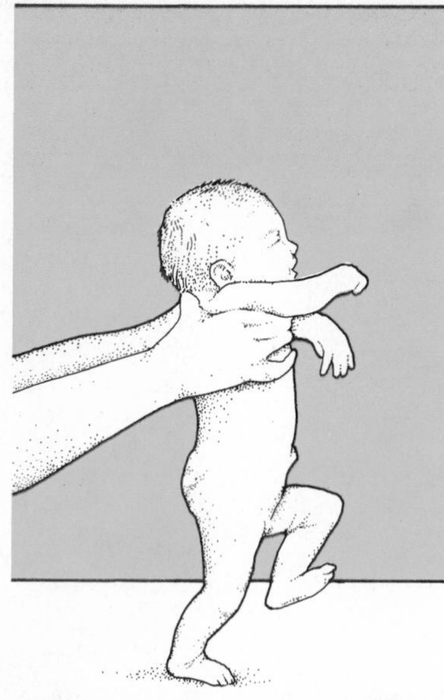
A newborn baby held with the sole of the foot on a table moves his legs in a reflex walking action.

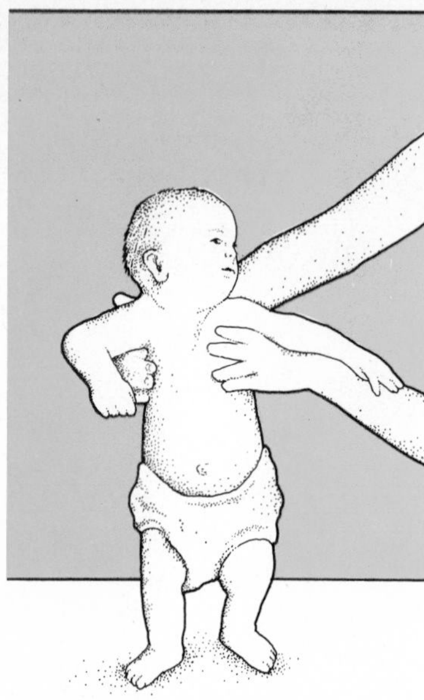
At eight weeks the baby briefly keeps his head up if he is held in a standing posture.

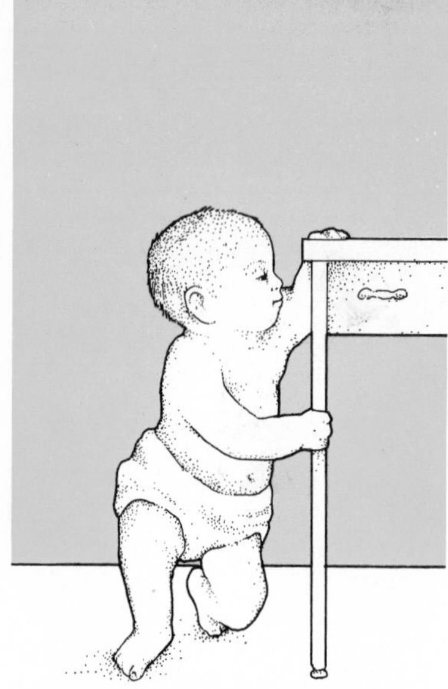
By 36 weeks he can pull himself up and remains standing by grasping hold of furniture.

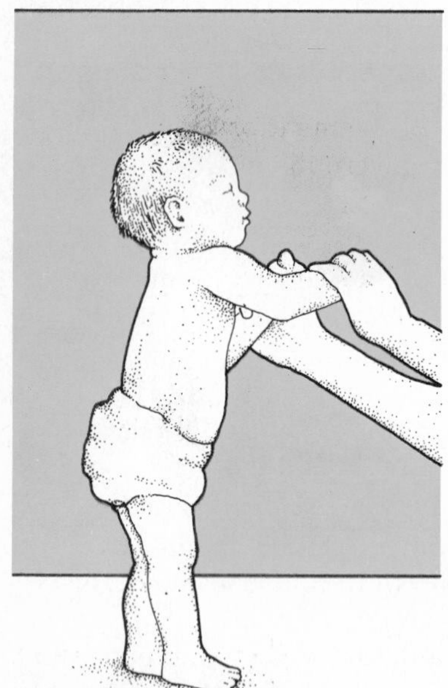
By 48 weeks he can walk forward if both hands are held (or sideways, gripping furniture).

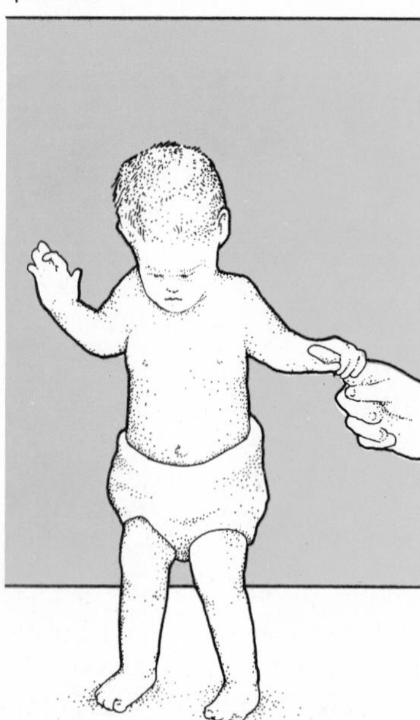
At one year the child walks forward if someone holds one of his hands.

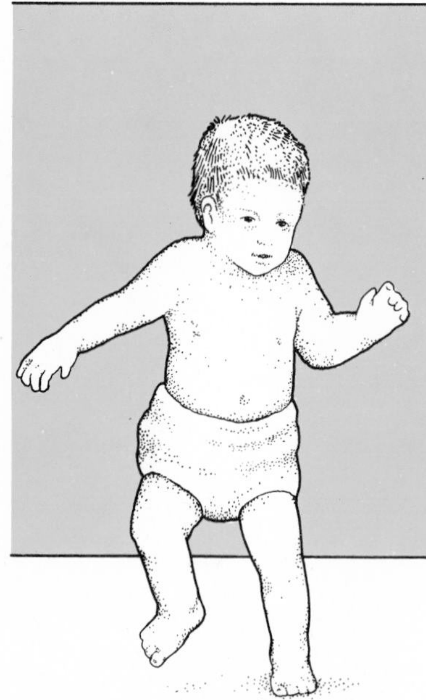
By 13 months the child has become capable of walking without help.

Figure 4.6 These drawings show very nicely the transition from standing to walking, and then to more complex skills. (Source: The Diagram Group, *Child's body: An owner's manual,* Paddington Press, 1977, section D-13.)

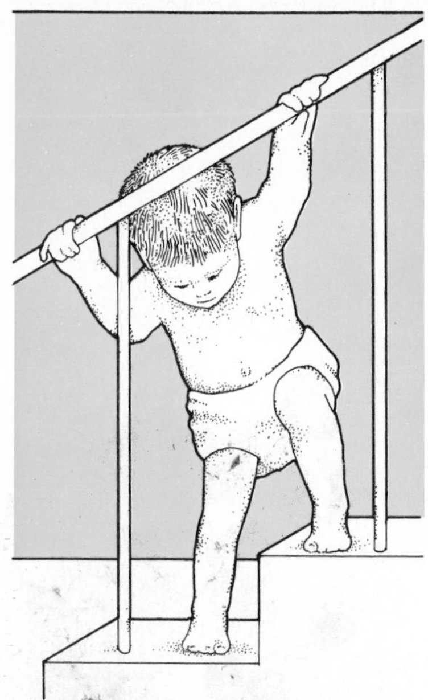

At 18 months he can go up and down stairs without assistance.

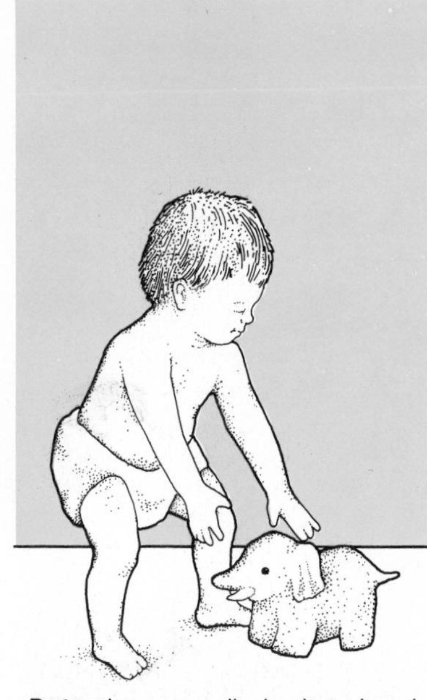

By two he runs, walks backward, and picks things up without overbalancing.

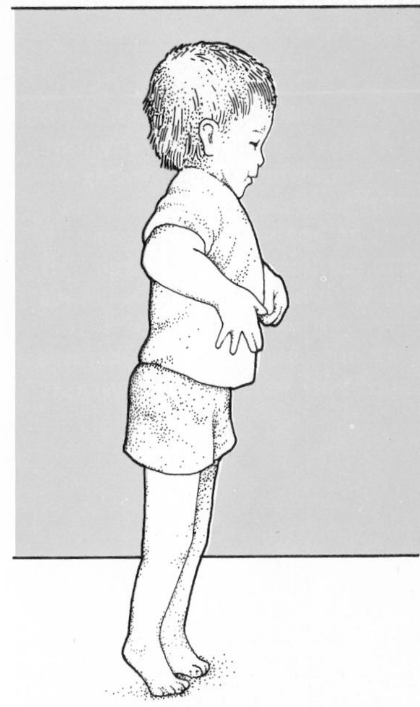

At 2½ he can balance on tiptoe, and jump with both feet.

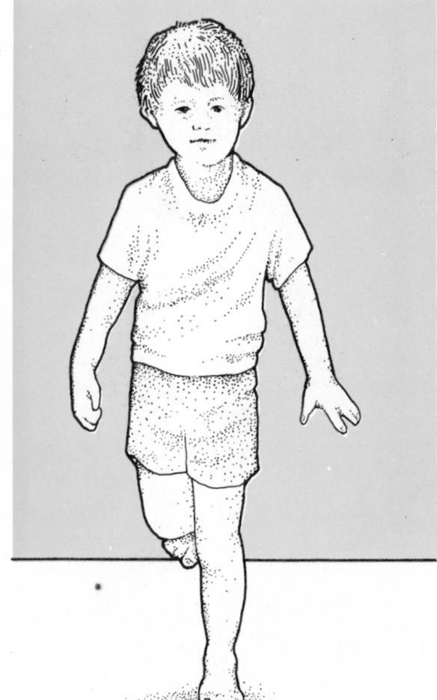

At three he can balance for some seconds while standing on one foot.

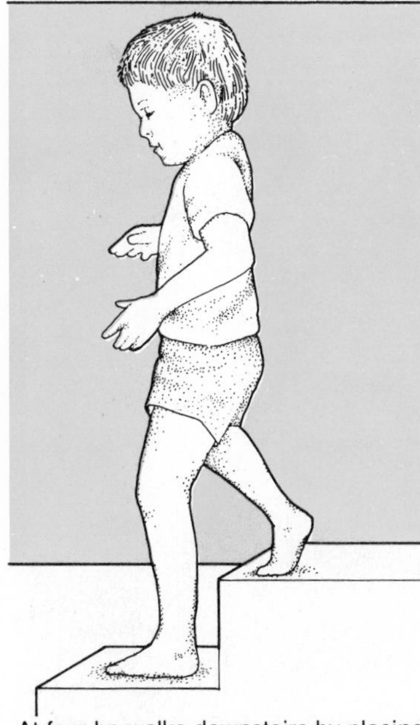

At four he walks downstairs by placing only one foot on each step.

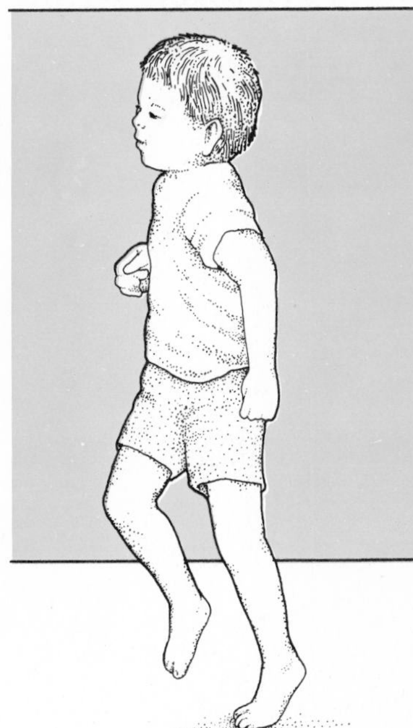

At five he skips on both feet.

Figure 4.7 The child's ability to throw and catch a ball shows systematic changes throughout early childhood. The young child uses her whole body as well as her hands and can only manage with a fairly large ball. But with age, the skill becomes more refined so that the 8–10 year old can catch and throw a small ball with some accuracy.

boys and girls can catch and throw quite small objects and aim them where they want them to go.

I've explored some of the practical implications of all these changes in Box 4.1. There are less obvious, but enormously sig-

Box 4.1

Implications of Motor Development for Toys and Games

Given what I've said about the child's physical development and motor coordination, what sort of toys and games would be appropriate for a child of each of several ages? Let me see if I can construct a beginning list for you.

Birth to 6 Months
Things that can be handled but not dropped are best, so mobiles or other toys attached to the crib are good, as is a cradle gym. They allow the baby to do what she does well, with hands and eyes, but don't require her to pick up a toy again when she drops it.

6 to 12 Months
The baby now sits up, stands, crawls, maybe walks. The main thing is to allow the child as much mobility as possible to exercise those new skills. Walkers or jumpers *may* be good, but free roaming is probably better. This means that playpens are probably not good as a steady diet. For the hands, stacking or nesting toys are good at this age. (A set of pots or pans is just as good as more expensive nesting toys, by the way.)

Second Year
The child begins to be able to manage things that require thumb–forefinger opposition and may like to play with small objects—though you have to watch out for things that can be swallowed. Toward the end of this year, the child can hold a big crayon or pencil and can do some drawing. Big balls (8–24 inches) are also enjoyed by children this age, as are push and pull toys. Push toys are generally better at this age than pull toys, since the child is better able to see where the toy goes. Simple, inexpensive toys that can be used in many ways, including the beginning of fantasy play, may also be enjoyed. Cardboard boxes are an example.

Third Year
Stable wheeled toys, such as a trike or equivalent, can be managed by the end of this year; and children of this age also enjoy smaller toys such as trucks or large stacking blocks. They handle crayons and pencils better, too, and enjoy drawing; so paints, paper, and colored pens (the kind that have washable ink!) are good choices.

Fourth to Seventh Year
Toward the end of this period, the child is well enough coordinated to manage a bicycle, or at least begin learning to ride one. The child can also manage toys that require fine coordination, such as threading beads (though he can't thread a needle till the end of this period). Because of growth of the bones of the hand and wrist, he can also cut paper with scissors and handle smaller-sized balls.

Elementary School
Coordination is well developed by 8 or 9; children this age can usually ride a bicycle easily and can skip rope and play most games that require hitting, kicking, or throwing a ball. I should emphasize that children as young as 3 can do most of these things, too, *if* a large enough ball, a wide enough hockey stick, or a light enough racket is used. From age 3 through at least age 10, the development of play and athletic skills is more one of degree than of kind. So if you are interested in having your child develop specific abilities needed for later organized sports, you can begin quite early, as long as the materials are sized properly for the child's ability.

nificant, implications for the child's mental and social development as well. As the child is able to sit up, crawl, walk, and ride a bike, she can explore her world more fully, which is very useful for intellectual growth. At the same time, she becomes steadily more independent, which affects her relationships with her parents and peers. The day when your child hops on her bike and announces casually, "I'm going to ride over to Julie's house to play," is a remarkable one. Things are never quite the same again.

Puberty

Like motor development, **puberty** represents a combination of all the underlying changes I've talked about—changes in size, in strength, and, most important, changes in hormones. Table

Table 4.2 Summary of Pubertal Development in Boys

Characteristic	Average age	Range of normal ages
Beginning accelerated growth of testes	11½	9½–13½
Beginning accelerated growth of penis	12½	10½–14½
Period of most rapid increase in height	13½	12½–17
Full development of penis	14½	12½–16½
Full development of testes	15	13½–17

Source: Based on data in Tanner, 1975, and Faust, 1977.

Table 4.3 Summary of Pubertal Development in Girls

Characteristic	Average age	Range of normal ages
Breast buds	10½	8–13½
Axillary hair (e.g., underarm)	10½	8½–13
Pubic hair, beginning	11	9–13½
Period of most rapid increase in height	11	9½–14½
First menstruation	12½	10½–15½
Full breast development	13½	10½–18
Full pubic hair development	13½	10½–17

Source: Based on data from Faust, 1977.

4.2 gives the normal sequence and timing of changes for boys, and Table 4.3 gives the same information for girls.

Several things are clear from these two tables. First, as you all know full well, girls reach and complete puberty about two years earlier than boys do. But second, there are huge differences in both sexes in the timing of all these changes. A boy who does not begin to show a spurt in height until he is 16 is a late developer, but he is entirely normal; a girl who begins to show breast development at 8 and menstruates at 10½ is an early developer, but she too is within the normal range. You can see these differences in rate very graphically in Figure 4.8.

In addition to all the specific sexual changes, there are other body systems that change rapidly during puberty:

The heart increases markedly in size, and heart rate drops. Both of these changes are greater for boys than for girls.

The lungs increase in size, again more for boys.

Muscle development accelerates, with boys again showing more rapid increases.

Fat tissue changes. There is an initial increase in the production of fat cells, but the proportion of total body weight devoted to fat cells declines during puberty. This change is again greater for boys: A fully mature girl has proportionately more fat than does a fully mature boy.

One of the curious phenomena about all these changes is that the age at which puberty occurs has been dropping steadily over this century. This is perhaps easiest to show for girls, since the age at first menstruation is fairly easy to measure. Alex Roche (1979), who has put together all the data on changes in the rate of physical development, reports that whereas in 1900 girls in the United States first menstruated at about age 14½, in 1960 this had dropped to an average of 12½. The average may be even lower than that now. The decrease has been steady, with the average going down about four months every ten years. Boys, too, have been going through the changes of puberty earlier and earlier.

One of the significant consequences of this shift in the timing of puberty is that we have seen a sharp rise in teenage and preteenage pregnancies. I talked about some of the risks associated with these very early pregnancies in Chapter 2; but even if a girl does not get pregnant in her early teens (and of course most do not), there is still a major discontinuity created by very early physical maturity. Teenagers are sexually mature, but they do not acquire the full rights and responsibilities of adulthood for another six to ten years.

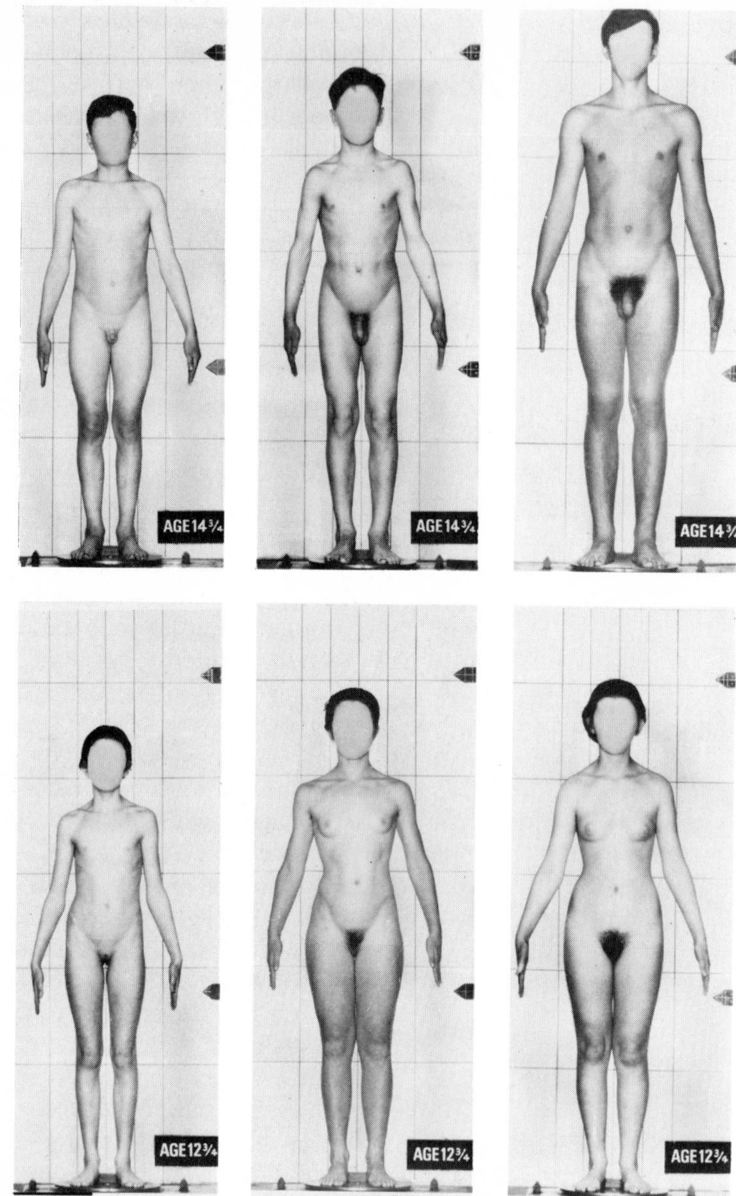

Figure 4.8 Teenagers vary enormously in the timing and speed of pubertal changes, as you can see clearly from these photographs. (Source: J. M. Tanner, "Growth and Endocrinology of the Adolescent." In L. J. Gardner (Ed.), *Endocrine and Genetic Diseases of Childhood and Adolescence,* 2nd ed. © 1975 by the W. B. Saunders Co., Philadelphia, Pa.)

Answering the Why Questions: Explanations of Physical Development

Maturation It seems very clear that some set of internal signals governs most of the growth patterns I have described. While the *rate* of development varies from one child to the next, the *sequence* is virtually the same for all children, even those with marked physical or mental handicaps (Kopp, 1979). For example, Down's syndrome infants are often slower in motor development than are normal children; they nonetheless move through the sequence from sitting to standing to walking in the same order (Carr, 1975; Dicks-Mireaux, 1972).

The precise mechanisms by which such regular sequences of development are controlled are not fully understood. We presume that the signals are contained in the genetic code in some way and thus shared by all members of the species.

Heredity

Our genetic heritage is individual as well as species-specific. In addition to being programmed for the basic sequences, each of us also receives unique growth tendencies. Height is one such individual pattern. Tall parents tend to have tall children; short parents tend to have short children. (There is also a process called *regression to the mean*. For example, *very* tall parents typically have children who are shorter than they are, since the set of genes required for extreme height is quite rare and not likely to be passed on to the children in precisely the same form. The same process occurs when two very short people reproduce: Their children are generally taller than they are.)

Rate of growth, as well as final height, seems to be an inherited trait, too. For example, J. M. Tanner (1970) describes several studies of twin girls, nontwin sisters, and random pairs of girls. The age of first menstruation is virtually the same for identical twins, somewhat similar in nontwin sisters, and not at all alike for random pairs of girls. This is exactly the sort of result we'd expect if there were one or more genes controlling the timing of physical changes. Since the same kinds of results have been found in studies of the rate of tooth eruption and bone ossification, it certainly looks as if both rate and final size and shape are influenced to at least some extent by specific inheritance.

Environmental Effects

But as usual, nothing is completely one sided. There are potent external influences on physical growth as well.

Practice If a child were completely immobilized and given no opportunity to practice crawling, walking, or grasping, would those skills develop anyway? Is the underlying growth of muscles and bones all that is needed; or does the baby have to have a chance to try out the coordination of muscles, bones, and senses?

There's still a good deal of disagreement about the answers to these questions. On the one hand, there is quite a lot of evidence that practice plays only a small role in the development of such skills as walking and climbing stairs. Several older studies of pairs of twins by Gesell and Thompson (1929) and McGraw (1935) were focused on this question directly. In each case, one twin of the pair was given a lot of early practice on the particular skill. Later, the second twin was given a brief period of practice, and then the two twins were tested. In general, if the "untrained twin" had been given even the briefest practice, the two children performed almost equally well on the task. For at least these early motor skills, then, a little bit of practice later is as good as a lot of practice earlier, presumably because physical changes have taken place in the intervening time.

Still, practice does matter. In the twin studies, the babies had at least some opportunity for normal physical exploration and body movement. The untrained twin was not kept completely immobile; she could practice parts of the acts of walking or crawling, even if special practice was not given. But when such opportunities for exercise and movement are *greatly* restricted, there *is* some retardation in motor development. The study of Iranian orphanages by Wayne Dennis that I described in Chapter 1 is the best example of this effect I know of (Dennis, 1960). You may remember that the babies in these institutions were routinely placed on their backs in cribs, and most never went through the normal sequence of learning to walk—presumably because they didn't have enough opportunity to practice all the on-the-stomach parts of the skill. They did learn to walk eventually, but they were about a year late.

Thus, what at first appeared to be only a simple maturational process is clearly more complex than that. Some minimum amount of practice is necessary just to keep the system working as it should. It is even possible that some chance to move and practice individual movements is necessary to stimulate the development of the brain, particularly the myelinization of the nerves. That is, the effects may work both ways—from the brain development to better motor skill and from practicing movements to faster brain development. Exactly this argument lies behind the common use of passive stimulation of body movements in physically handicapped children by parents and therapists.

Diet Another major influence on physical growth is the child's diet. Poorly nourished children grow more slowly, and they don't end up as large. More important, malnutrition in the early years seems to have a permanent effect on some parts of the brain and nervous system.

As I've already pointed out, the nervous system continues to develop rapidly during the first two years after birth, so we'd expect malnutrition to have an effect if it is severe enough during that time. The evidence we have (Lewin, 1975, for example) suggests that the effect is primarily to reduce the amount of connective tissue between individual brain cells. As a consequence, the cortex does not become as heavy. If the child is given a better diet during these early years, he seems to be able to catch up in brain development. But if the child's diet continues to be bad for the first two years or so, the effects appear to be permanent.

I have used the words "appear to be" and "seems to be" several times in the last paragraph. I wish I could state the case more positively than that, but at this point I can't. The research on the permanence of the effects of poor nutrition has been done almost entirely with laboratory animals, primarily rats and mice (Scrimshaw, 1969; Stein, Susser, Saenger & Marsella, 1975). In animals, the effects of poor nutrition do seem to be permanent. But we don't know for sure whether this is true for humans as well, although it's certainly a logical assumption.

Frequency of Malnutrition Just how common is malnutrition in children? Until fairly recently, we really didn't know the answer to this question for the United States—perhaps because few people wanted to believe that there could be significant malnutrition in this "land of opportunity." But there is.

Several major surveys, including an excellent one by George Owen and his colleagues (Owen, Kram, Garry, Lower & Lubin, 1974), show that almost a third of the children in the United States get too little iron. Among the poor, about a quarter have significant iron deficiency anemia (Eichorn, 1979). One of the effects of such a deficiency is a slowdown in the rate of growth. Owen finds that the poorer and less well educated the family, the shorter the child and the smaller his head is likely to be.

Interestingly enough, weight doesn't follow the same pattern. Middle-class children tend to be taller and leaner, while poorer children tend to be shorter and heavier, perhaps because their diets are made up of more starchy foods. The poor also consume fewer fruits and less milk. For most poor children, the dietary deficiency is not enormous: Only about 1–2 percent of children in the United States have serious shortage of protein or calories (Eichorn, 1979). But many children seem to suffer from potentially serious *sub*nutrition and to grow more slowly as a result.

At the other end of the nutritional scale are obese children, who also face a series of added risks. Box 4.2 gives some of the most recent thinking about obesity, its origin and treatment.

Illness A third type of experience that can affect a child's growth is a long-term illness. Usually a sick child grows more slowly—perhaps because she is less active, perhaps because

Box 4.2 Obesity in Children

In the United States, obesity has become a major national health problem. At least 15 percent of adults (and possibly many more) are more than 20 percent over the standard weight for their height. Life expectancy is reduced for people who are significantly overweight, and they are more prone to a number of disorders, including high blood pressure.

Perhaps because we've all become aware of fatness in adults, there has been a recent interest in obesity in children as well. Do fat children become fat adults? What contributes to overweight in children?

Do Obese Children Become Obese Adults?

The best answer to this seems to be "in most cases." But I have to point out that we don't have very good information—we don't have good *longitudinal* studies, and that's what we need. But the information we have points to a consistent pattern. In one study (Abraham, Collins & Nordsieck, 1971), of 19 obese children, 16 were moderately or markedly overweight as adults. Paul Zack (Zack, Harlan, Leaverton, & Cornoni-Huntley, 1979) has found the same kind of consistency between childhood and adolescent fatness.

At the same time, many obese adults were *not* obese as children. So there seems to be at least two kinds of obesity, childhood obesity, which persists, and adult obesity, which comes on later.

What Causes Obesity in Children?

There seem to be three causes. First, a tendency to fatness or thinness is partly inherited. Jean Mayer (1975) found in one study that only 7 percent of children of normal weight parents were obese, but 80 percent of those with two obese parents were themselves seriously overweight.

A second contributor seems to be the child's diet during the early years. Fat cells are added rapidly during the first two years and then again at adolescence. Once the number of fat cells is "set" at these two time points, you are more or less stuck with what you have (Garn, Clark & Guire, 1975). The more fat cells you have, the more likely it is that you will be overweight, and the harder it will be for you to lose weight. Children who are overfed as infants, then, may develop more fat cells and thus have a lifetime tendency toward overweight. I've already pointed out that bottle-fed infants seem to be a bit more prone to this pattern, but it can come from overfeeding of solids as well.

Still a third contributor is exercise. Jean Mayer, in some very interesting studies of overweight and average-sized children, has found that the obese children simply don't move as much, even doing the same things (Meyer, 1975). For example, normal weight girls were in motion about 90 percent of the time while playing tennis; obese girls moved only 50 percent of the time. This may reflect a basic temperamental difference. Meyer found that he could help the obese girls reduce simply by introducing a regular exercise program, without changing their diet.

In combination, these factors seem to work something like this: The child may inherit a tendency to add fat cells and may also be of an easy and placid temperament. The baby may eat whatever is given to him and thus add more fat cells. Inactivity then compounds the problem.

This combination of factors is very hard to combat. Once the fat cells have been added, they can't be removed. They will shrink and swell in size according to caloric intake for the rest of their lives. This means that the best line of defense against obesity in childhood is probably avoidance of overweight during the first two or three years. After the point of rapid fat-cell increase, however, the most effective strategy is probably to increase the child's activity. During the years of rapid physical growth, it is risky to restrict caloric intake too much, since there is a chance that the child may receive insufficient calories for proper bone and muscle development. Increase in exercise seems to be a safer route.

Figure 4.9 Mayer's research suggests that obese children often eat no more than their thinner peers; what makes them fatter is that they use far fewer calories. They simply move less, even when they are supposedly exercising.

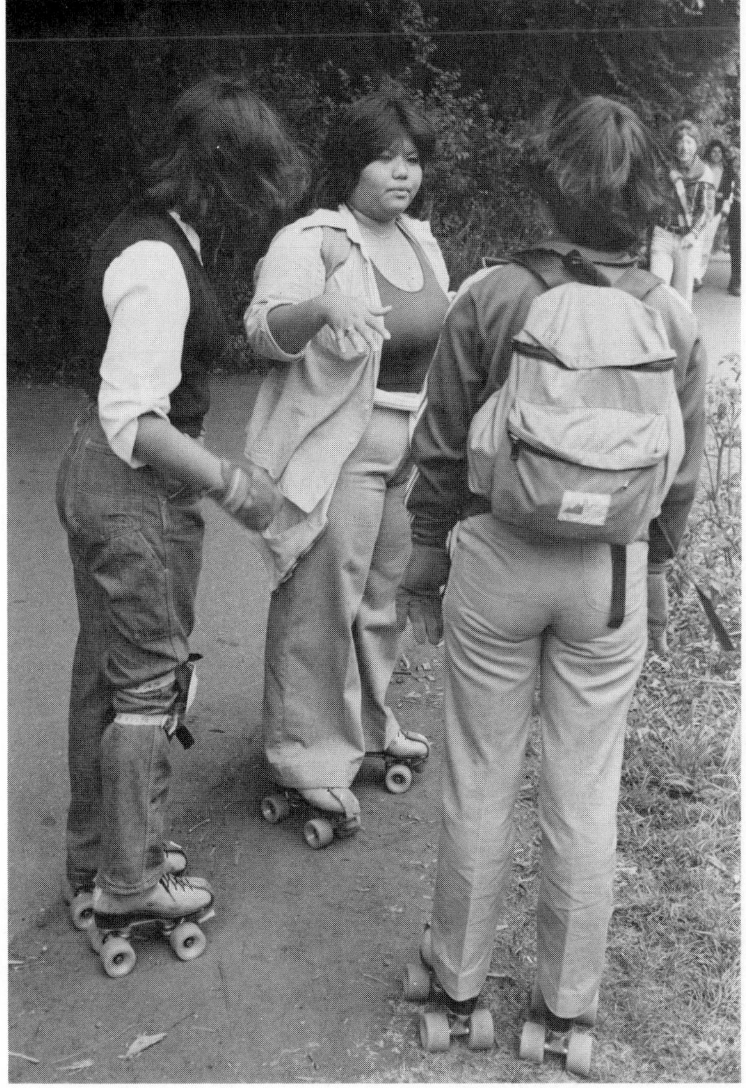

her diet has changed, perhaps because of the operation of the disease itself. But after she recovers, her growth spurts ahead, and she shows something Tanner calls "catch up" (Tanner, 1970). He describes the case of one child, as an example, who had had a tumor on the adrenal gland from ages 1 to 3 (Prader, Tanner & Von Harnack, 1963). By age 4, the child was extremely small – only about 30 inches tall, which is smaller than the average 2-year-old. When the tumor was removed, however, the child shot up. She grew about 8 inches in the next two years; and by adolescence, she was within the normal range. She was still smaller than average, so the catch up wasn't complete. But after several years of rapid growth, she returned to the *pace* of normal development shown before her illness.

Generally speaking, the earlier in the child's life an illness or malnutrition occurs, the more lasting the effect and the less successfully the child catches up to fully normal development. This is another example of a **sensitive period,** of the kind I discussed in Chapter 1.

Big or Fast versus Slow or Small: Some Individual Differences

What are the implications of differences in rate of development or differences in size? Do early developers turn out differently from late developers? Do big children have an advantage over smaller children? The short answer is yes to both questions, although it will take me several pages to give you the details.

Physical Growth and Mental Development

Children who are more rapid in physical growth are also slightly advanced in mental growth. They score a bit higher on standard IQ tests and do a little better in school than do their more slowly developing peers (Tanner, 1970). These differences are not terribly large, but they are found consistently.

Some of the relationship between rate of growth and mental development may be due to differences in diet. Some may be due to differences in confidence or self-esteem between larger, fast developing children and the slower developers. And some may be due to differences in responsibilities or opportunities offered by the people around the child. Whatever the reasons, the difference persists into adulthood, even after the differences in size between the two groups has faded.

Rate of Maturing and Personality

Faster developing children also have somewhat different personalities. In our society, physical appearance seems to be particularly important in adolescence, no doubt partly because the changes in the body that occur at puberty are signs of reaching near-adult status. At this stage, girls worry about whether or not their breasts are going to develop or whether they are too small or too big or the wrong shape. Boys worry about such outward signs of puberty as height, whether or not they need to shave, whether or not they have developed hair on their chest, and whether or not their penis and testes have developed fully. These changes are exciting and important events in teenagers' lives. It's a period in life when one is extraordinarily conscious of one's body and whether or not that body measures up to the standards of physical maturity held by our society.

Given that kind of preoccupation with the body, it's not surprising that the timing of puberty can have a significant psychological impact on the young person. I should point out that most of the research on the effects of early versus late maturing was done over two decades ago. We can't be sure that we would find exactly the same results now, since the social climate has changed. But these older studies do suggest a few conclusions.

First, either extremely early or extremely late development seems to have negative consequences. The child who matures exceptionally early faces the demands of adolescence before he is psychologically ready for it. Harvey Peskin (1967, 1973) found that early maturers were more anxious and more submissive to others. People may expect too much of the very early maturing child as well.

At the other end of the scale, Mary Cover Jones and Paul Mussen (Jones, 1957; Mussen & Jones, 1957) have found very late maturers to be more anxious and less popular. So either extreme poses real problems for the child.

Within the normal range of developmental rates, it seems to be psychologically easier to be early rather than late. Peskin found this in his studies, as did Jones and Mussen. Margaret Faust (1960) has matching findings for a group of late and early maturing girls. She found that in the seventh grade, girls who had begun to menstruate had higher status among the girls than did those who had not.

Finally, the effects of the timing of puberty appear to last into adulthood, especially among men. Jones and Mussen have found that, as adults, late maturers still had more difficulty with social relationships. The anxiety and feelings of inadequacy that accompanied delayed physical development carried over into adulthood in the man's image of himself. He still thinks of himself as inadequate and unlikable even after he has changed and grown physically.

These effects of the timing of puberty are partly or largely culture specific, but in our culture, they appear to be quite potent.

Body Build and Personality

Some of the differences between early and late maturers *may* be related to basic differences in body build as well as to cultural expectations. Nearly all the research on body build has been done on men and boys, so we can't say how true all this may be for girls; but at least for males, there appears to be a link between body type and personality and between body type and popularity with peers.

Figure 4.10 These two boys show clear differences in body type. The boy on the left shows the major features of mesomorphy, including square upper body, broad shoulders, and thick chest. The boy on the right is much more ectomorphic. Note the narrower chest and the more stooped shoulders, both of which are characteristic of ectomorphic body types.

Sheldon's Three Body Types One of the original exponents of the body type–personality link was W. H. Sheldon, who identified three components of human body types: the endomorphic, the mesomorphic, and the ectomorphic. Each man's physical build, according to Sheldon, can be described in terms of its degree of **endomorphy, mesomorphy,** and **ectomorphy.**

Very generally, endomorphy is the amount of fat, mesomorphy the amount of muscle, and ectomorphy the length of bone. An endomorphic man is generally soft and round. A mesomorphic man is close to the classic "all-American boy" image: well-muscled, thick-chested, broad-shouldered, and squarely-built. The ectomorphic man is tall, thin, and somewhat stoop-shouldered. Most boys and men have elements of all three; but in most cases, it is possible to identify a dominant theme.

Sheldon argued that these body types were matched by personality types, and there is some research that supports him. Richard Walker in one study (1962) found that endomorphic preschool boys were rated as aggressive and assertive; the ectomorphs were thoughtful and considerate; the mesomorphs were leaders and had high self-confidence. John Clausen (1975) has found similar patterns in adolescents. He found that the tall skinny ectomorphs were unpopular with their peers, particularly among working-class boys. In contrast, mesomorphs were more likely to be leaders, to make decisions, and to give orders to the group.

This research links up with the research on early and late maturing boys, since mesomorphs are usually earlier to mature. They seem to have the dual advantage of earliness and the mesomorphic body type.

Origin of Body Build–Personality Links Where do the links between body type and personality come from? One possibility is that in our society we have specific expectations about people with different sorts of body build. Muscular boys are viewed as athletes and we expect them to be "stars" in their group. We may think of the thin, ascetic-looking child as a future professor and encourage him to read. Perhaps we force children into personality molds, to some extent, because of their body build.

An alternative possibility is that body build is itself the result of particular patterns of hormones in the child's bloodstream and that the hormones also have an effect on personality. The data on this question are not at all good, but what evidence we have is at least consistent with the notion that hormonal differences among men and boys or women and girls may well influence both physique and personality.

Sex Differences in Physical Growth

I have mentioned a number of sex differences in physical growth as I've gone along in this chapter, but let me pull together all the bits and pieces for you here. Table 4.4 summarizes the major findings.

As you'll see from the table, most physical differences between males and females become more pronounced after puberty. Preadolescent girls and boys are about equal in strength and speed. After adolescence, boys become stronger and faster, as well as larger. One of the implications of this is that a 12-year-old girl is probably just as strong and just as good at throwing balls and stealing bases as a 14-year-old boy, since they are both at about the same point in pubertal development. At this age, girls should be able to compete effectively in little league or other sports. A few years later, though, it will be the unusual girl who is able to compete successfully with boys in sports that call for considerable strength or speed.

Despite the general difference, you should keep in mind that the distributions overlap. There are many girls with excellent strength and speed (see Figure 4.11) and many boys who are less physically developed.

Table 4.4 Summary of Sex Differences in Physical Growth

Characteristic	Nature of difference
Rate of maturation	Girls are on a faster timetable throughout development. For example, their teeth erupt sooner; their bones harden sooner; and puberty arrives sooner.
Predictability or regularity of maturation	Girls' physical growth is more regular and predictable, with fewer uneven spurts. It is easier to predict the final height of a girl, for example, than of a boy.
Strength and speed	There is little difference until adolescence; but after puberty, boys are stronger and faster.
Heart and circulation	At adolescence, boys develop a larger heart and lungs and a greater capacity for carrying oxygen in the blood than do girls.
Fat tissue	Girls from birth on have a thicker layer of fat tissue just below the skin and have a larger percentage of body weight devoted to fat after puberty.

Social Class and Racial Differences

As a group, poor children grow a bit slower and are a bit shorter than middle-class children, most probably because of dietary differences. Where diets are equivalent, the differences disappear.

One other difference is worth mentioning. Black children, even those in poor environments with poor diets, grow a little *faster* and are a little taller than their white counterparts. Nancy Bayley (1965) found this among infants, and George Owen found the same pattern in his nationwide study of nutrition and growth (Owen, Kram, Garry, Lower & Lubin, 1974). So girls are on a faster maturational timetable than boys, and blacks seem to be on a faster timetable than whites.

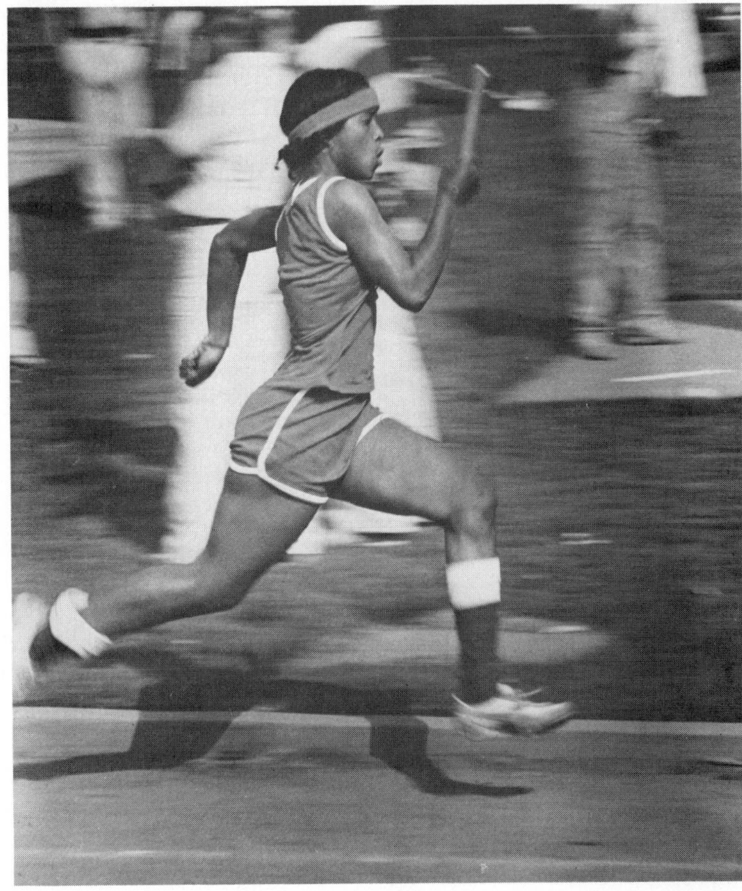

Figure 4.11 While it is true that the average teenage girl is not as strong or as fast as the average boy, there are many girls who are very swift and very strong.

Summary

1. It is important to know something about physical growth and development because the child's level of physical development sets limits on the kinds of interaction she may have with the environment and because her feelings about her own body may also affect her very broadly.
2. Changes in height are rapid during the first year, then level off at a steady pace until adolescence, when there is a sharp "growth spurt."
3. Muscles and bones develop in a similar pattern, with an increase in muscle density and length of fibers, particularly during adolescence.
4. The bones are not hard at birth. They harden in sequence, beginning with the bones of the hands and arms, then feet and legs.
5. The brain is not fully developed at birth; over the first two years, connective tissue and the myelin sheath covering the nerves develop.
6. Within the cortex, the portions governing vision and hearing and motor areas governing hands, head, and trunk are developed early.
7. Hormones are vital influences throughout growth, particularly during adolescence. The pituitary gland secretes triggering hormones at the beginning of

puberty, which stimulate the development of sex hormones.

8. Motor skills are extremely poor at birth and develop gradually over the first 15 years. In the infant, important sequences are the move to full thumb–forefinger opposition and the sequence from lying, to sitting, to standing, to walking, to running. More complex skills such as skipping, bike riding, and ball throwing and catching do not develop until about school age.

9. Maturation is the most important process underlying physical growth and development. Most sequences require only minimal environmental support.

10. Some individual differences in rate of development are apparently inherited, such as the timing of puberty.

11. The environment has an impact, however. Some practice is necessary for the child to develop motor skills, and adequate diet and good health are also critical.

12. There are substantial differences in rate of maturation among children. These are particularly noticeable during adolescence, when some children may go through puberty four or five years sooner than their late developing peers.

13. The child's stature, or early or late maturity, has an impact on her relationship with her peers. In general, larger and faster developing children are more likely to be popular and leaders in their groups.

14. Males and females have some differences in patterns of growth. Girls are accelerated in physical growth; but in adolescence, boys show more muscle and heart and circulatory system development than do girls.

15. Social class differences also exist, apparently the result of less-adequate diet for children from poverty environments.

Key Terms

Cephalocaudal A term describing the head-to-foot pattern of physical growth from conception through the first years of life.

Cortex The convoluted gray portion of the brain which governs most complex thought, language, and memory, among other functions.

Ectomorphy One aspect of male body build suggested by Sheldon; the degree of long-boned thinness in build.

Endocrine glands Those glands, including the adrenals, the thyroid, the pituitary, the testes, and the ovaries, that secrete hormones governing overall physical growth and sexual maturing.

Endomorphy One aspect of male body build suggested by Sheldon; generally the proportion of fat tissue and rounded build.

Fontanels The "soft spots" in the skull present at birth, where the skull bones have not yet fully joined.

Mesomorphy One aspect of male body build suggested by Sheldon; generally the degree of muscle.

Midbrain The section of the brain below the cortex that develops earlier than the cortex and regulates attention, sleeping, waking, and other "automatic" functions.

Myelin The sheath around all the nerves of the body. This sheath is not completely developed at birth.

Myelinization The process by which myelin is added.

Pituitary One of the endocrine glands that affects the rate of physical maturation and secretes hormones that control the secretions of other glands.

Proximodistal A term describing the trunk-outward pattern of physical development from conception through the early years of life.

Puberty The collection of hormonal and physical changes at adolescence that brings about sexual maturity.

Suggested Readings

The Diagram Group. Child's body. New York: Paddington Press, 1977.
This is a nifty book, designed as a parents' manual and full of helpful information about physical development, health, and nutrition.

Eichorn, D. H. "Physical development: Current foci of research." In J. D. Osofsky (Ed.), Handbook of infant development. New York: Wiley, 1979.
This is a more difficult source than any of the others listed here; but if you want to read about some of the issues that concern researchers studying physical development today, it is excellent. It has a particularly good section on nutrition.

Lewin, R. "Starved brains." Psychology Today, 1975, **9** (No. 4), 29–33.
This is a very readable paper reviewing some of what we know about the effect of malnutrition on children's developing brains.

White, B. L. The first three years of life. Englewood Cliffs, N.J.: Prentice-Hall, 1975.
For practical advice about toys, games, and other commercially available products for children, this is an excellent source. White also offers a range of specific suggestions about all aspects of infant development.

Winick, M. Childhood obesity. New York: Wiley, 1975.
This collection of individual papers covers most of the aspects of obesity I've described in Box 4.2. The papers by Weil and Mayer are particularly good.

Project 4.1 Observations of Body Types and Activities

This project needs to be done in pairs so that you can check for the degree of agreement on ratings of body types. With a partner, and after obtaining permission from the school principal, spend several recess periods observing children on a school playground. If this setting is not possible, a local park, playground, or day-care center may work as well. You and your partner should select a series of boys to observe for five minutes each. For each child you observe, do the following:

1. Decide whether the child is basically mesomorphic, endomorphic, or ectomorphic. Focus on breadth of chest and shoulders, length of limbs, and body fat. (I know that you are not skilled in this judgment, but do the best you can.)
2. Count the number of other children your subject is playing with.
3. Count the number of times other children speak *to* the child and how many times your child speaks to others. (You may have to follow the child discreetly to obtain this information.)

You should aim for as many as ten children observed in total. When you're done, you and your partner should compare results. Did you agree on the ratings of body types? Did you agree roughly on the number of talking episodes? What might account for your disagreement? What would you have to do to improve your agreement?

If you average the number of playmates and the talking episodes for the mesomorphs, ectomorphs, and endomorphs, are there any differences? Do mesomorphs have more playmates? Do they do more of the talking, or are they talked to more often? How do the results compare with information given in the chapter?

Project 4.2 Plotting Your Own Growth

This project will work only if your parents are among those who routinely stood you up against a convenient doorjamb and measured you—and if you still live in the house with the marked-up doorjamb. But those of you who can meet both criteria might find it interesting to go back and plot your rate of growth over the years of childhood. The maximum point of height spurt is considered to be that period during which you grew the most inches in a fixed period of time. When did that happen for you? During elementary school did you grow about the same number of inches per year? Does your growth curve look like the ones in Tanner's (1970) paper?

Preview of Chapter 5

Perceptual Development

Just last weekend I went sailing for the first time. In the beginning, everything was extremely strange and difficult. I kept calling things "ropes" only to be told that they were not ropes but "lines" or "sheets" or "halyards" or something else. I had to learn to notice the differences so I could tell what to reach for when I was given an instruction. I had to learn how to read all the various gauges and other markers, too, and to figure out what was important to watch for in the waves. I had a great time; but for all my effort, I only learned a fraction of what I would need to know to be a good sailor. Still, it's a very good example of **perceptual learning.** I didn't have to learn *how* to look; but I had to learn *what* to pay attention to, which discriminations were important and which irrelevant.

The infant can already perceive a great deal, as I described in Chapter 3. She has still more perceptual skill to develop over the first years, but she also has to learn how and on what to focus her eyes and ears, how to tell the difference between big and small things, how to discriminate one face from another. In older children, learning to read is another good example of a complex perceptual process, involving learning which of those funny squiggles on the paper are really important to look at and how they fit together. You go through a similar process just about every time you learn any new skill. If you're learning to ski, you have to learn not only how to move your body, but what to look for on the hillside and how to judge the different types of snow. If you take up playing the guitar, you have to learn to read music, and so on.

As I hope these examples illustrate, there are important practical reasons for studying the development of perception and perceptual learning. But there are equally significant theoretical issues at stake.

The Central Theoretical Issue

One of the major theoretical disputes that runs through all the discussion of perceptual development is the "nativism-empiricism" issue—one of the basic theoretical controversies in psychology. The essence of this issue—stated in extreme form—is whether we as humans are born with already developed or maturationally determined systems for dealing with experience (the nativist position) or whether our methods of analysis and our skills are developed solely as a result of experience (the empiricist position). If a child were raised in a black box without any visual or auditory experience but were fed and cared for, would she develop normal visual and auditory skills? Alternatively, can the child's experiences after birth account for all the perceptual abilities she develops? The question is a restatement of the basic question I've been asking all along about every aspect of behavior: How much is determined internally, how much by external events and experience? In fact, as is always true, there is a third alternative, namely, the combination or interaction of internal and external forces.

I've stated the nativism-empiricism issue in extreme form so that the issues are as clear as possible. In fact, few psychologists would take either position today. But it is still reasonable to ask just how much inborn or maturationally determined skills and later experiences contribute to the child's improving perceptual abilities.

You can see that as usual we have both "what" and "why" questions to answer. What is the developmental course of the basic perceptual skills? What perceptual learning occurs, and at what ages? And why or how do these changes occur? Are they purely the result of experience, or are basic maturational timetables important? Let me begin, as usual, with the what questions, and save the theoretical arguments until the end.

Answering the What Questions: Development of Basic Perceptual Abilities

Acuity

The word **acuity** refers to how well or how clearly you can perceive. When you go to apply for a driver's license and take the "eye test" that involves reading the letters on one line of a large chart, that's a test for visual acuity. Some of you may have had

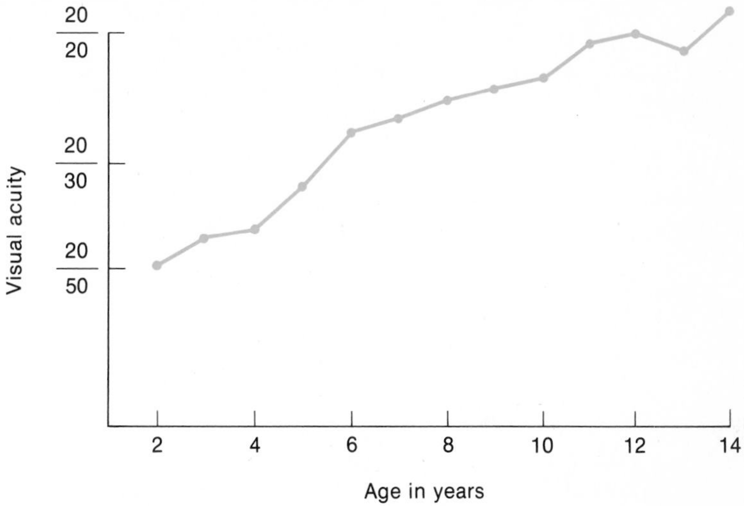

Figure 5.1 Children's visual acuity improves over the first 10 to 12 years, as you can see in the figure. Children younger than age 2 have still poorer acuity—20/100 or worse. (Source: Weymouth, 1963, pp. 132 & 133.)

tests for auditory acuity, too, when you were in school. Sounds of varying loudness and softness or high-pitched and low-pitched sounds were played, and you indicated in each case whether you heard a sound or not.

Vision "Twenty/twenty" vision is considered the standard of visual acuity. If you have 20/20 vision, it means you can see and identify properly something that is 20 feet away that the average person can also see clearly at 20 feet. If you have 20/15 vision (as I do), it means that you can see at 20 feet objects or letters that the average person has to be 15 feet from to see or read clearly.

As you can see in Figure 5.1, the child doesn't reach the level of 20/20 vision until he is about 11 or 12. By this standard, infants don't see very well. But then they don't really have to. Most of what they deal with is quite close to them, and their vision is perfectly adequate for that task.

Hearing Like vision, auditory acuity appears to improve steadily until adolescence. I've already pointed out that newborns can hear and respond to sounds in the general range of pitch and loudness of the human voice. As they get older, they become able to hear and respond to a wider range, particularly to softer and lower-pitched sounds.

Another hearing skill (not strictly an aspect of acuity, but very basic) that improves with age is the ability to determine the location of a sound. You can tell roughly where a sound is coming from because your two ears are separated from one another, so that the sound arrives at one slightly before the other. If the sound comes from the "midline," then the sound arrives at the same time. Newborns aren't very good at locating sounds; and since their heads are growing, infants and young children have to keep adjusting the judgments of location as their ears get farther apart. Still, by 6 months, most infants are quite good at making judgments of this kind (Bower, 1977).

Other Senses Psychologists haven't studied the development of taste, smell, and touch sensitivity very much; so we know very little about changes in these skills. Newborns don't have as many smell and taste receptors in the nose and mouth as adults do, so presumably they can't discriminate quite as well. But we don't know just how rapidly the additional receptors are added. Similarly, the sense of touch probably becomes more finely tuned over childhood, but we know almost nothing about those changes with age.

As you will see through the rest of this chapter, nearly all the research on perceptual development has focused on visual abilities, with only a little on auditory skills. As a consequence, I'll be talking mostly about vision. But that doesn't mean that other senses are unimportant—only that we know little about how they develop.

Perceptual Learning

Obviously, changes in acuity are only a small part of the picture. Much more important is figuring out what to look at, what to focus on, what to pay attention to, and what to ignore. It is this process that Eleanor Gibson (1969) calls perceptual learning. Whether it is all learned or whether there are some built-in "rules" for limiting or focusing attention is still a matter of debate. In any case, it is clear that the child does gradually focus her attention more effectively on those aspects of stimulation that are really critical.

Let me explore these developmental patterns in three ways. First, let's look at the changes in what an infant or child pays attention to. What do we know about the change in focus of the child's attention over time? Second, we'll narrow our own focus somewhat and look at a particular set of perceptual "rules"—the perceptual constancies, such as size and shape constancy. Finally, using the discussion of attention and of constancies as background, I want to look at the problem of learning to read. What are some of the perceptual tasks the child faces in learning to read?

Development of Attention

In the past ten years, there have been literally hundreds of studies of attention in infants, so we know quite a lot about changes during the first 6–12 months of life. Researchers have studied attention in babies partly because they are genuinely interested in perceptual processes. But partly the focus on this type of research has arisen because the baby can't talk, so she can't "tell us" much about what is happening internally, what she's thinking or feeling. But she can look at and listen to things; and by designing studies that give the baby a choice of things to look at or listen to, we may find out a great deal about her general makeup.

Studies of Infants The research technique most often used by investigators exploring the development of attention in infants is a preference technique developed by Robert Fantz (1956). If an infant is shown two pictures simultaneously or several pictures in series, the experimenter can measure the amount of time the infant spends looking at each picture and the number of shifts back and forth. If there are differences in the amount of time the infant gazes at each picture, this can be taken as evidence that the infant can tell the difference (discriminate) between the two pictures. It also may tell us something about the sort of visual features the child "chooses" to focus on.

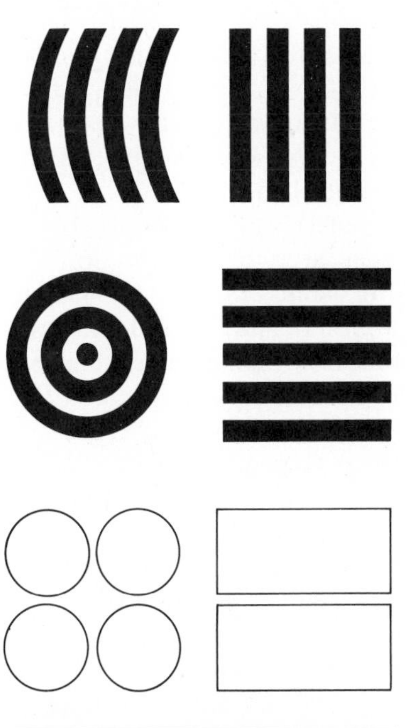

Figure 5.2 These figures are like the ones used by Fantz and his colleagues in their studies of visual preferences in infants. After about 2 months of age, babies will look longer at the curved figure of each pair. (Source: Fantz, Fagan & Miranda, 1975, p. 227.)

Since Fantz first began using the preference technique in the late 1950s, a large number of researchers have used this strategy to explore a whole series of perceptual dimensions with infants. Infants have been shown checkerboards with varying numbers of squares, bull's eyes versus striped patterns, designs with varying numbers of corners, pictures of faces with pieces of the face left out or rearranged, and nearly endless other combinations. To give you some feeling for the research and for the results that emerge from research of this sort, let me take just one example.

Fantz and his colleagues Joseph Fagan and Simon Miranda (1975) have done a series of experiments exploring infants' preferences for curved versus straight contours. Figure 5.2 shows some pairs of pictures that are like the ones Fantz used in these studies. Babies as young as a few days old were shown these pairs of pictures, and the investigators kept track of the amount of time the babies' eyes were focused on each one of the pair. What they found was that up to about six or eight weeks, infants showed no preference for curved or for straight lines. But after about eight to twelve weeks, most babies looked more at the curved figures than the straight-line figures. Extensive research using this general strategy points to a few conclusions.

Basic Changes at Two Months First of all, there seems to be a major change in infants' visual preferences at about two months of age. Several different theorists, including Gordon Bronson (1974), Philip Salapatek (1975), Marshall Haith (1979), and Bernard Karmel and Eileen Maisel (1975) have argued that for the first six to eight weeks, the baby is operating with what Bronson calls the **second visual system.** He is mostly concerned with *where* an object is. The baby focuses his eyes on objects near him, moves his eyes to track a moving object, and looks at the edges of things. These are all things that deal with the location of the object. At this age, the baby's attention is "captured" by movement and by sharp contrasts—things that tell him there is an object out there and help him locate it.

After about two months, though, the emphasis changes to what Bronson calls the **primary visual system,** which is mostly concerned with *what* something is. So the baby begins to pay attention to details of objects, such as curved versus straight lines, the individual parts of a picture, or the features of a face. The infant of two months also begins to move his eyes back and forth across a picture rather than getting hooked onto one part and staying there.

Probably this shift occurs because of a basic maturational change in the nervous system that happens at about two months. The cortex is developing during the first weeks; the part of the cortex that is required for close, detailed analysis of figures may not be fully developed at birth.

There are some important practical applications for these hypotheses about physical changes at two months. For example, during the first weeks of life, babies are not at all skillful at discriminating one face from another. They don't look carefully at the individual features of faces but focus their attention on the edges and the parts of the face that move, such as the eyes and mouth. Only after two months is the baby regularly capable of telling Mom from Dad or Grandma from the local babysitter by looking at their faces.

The Discrepancy Principle A second basic finding from the studies of infant preferences is that babies seem to like to look at things that are at least somewhat novel. Jerome Kagan (1971) calls this the **discrepancy principle:** A baby will look at, listen to, touch, or play with things that are moderately discrepant from what she has already experienced.

Piaget, too (Piaget & Inhelder, 1969), emphasizes that from the earlier months it is important for the child to encounter a moderate level of novelty. Piaget argues that the child is constantly "assimilating" (taking in) new experiences and comparing them with old experiences. As she builds up experience, more and more things are familiar; and she has less to learn from them. But in the same way, something completely novel—completely unlike anything she has encountered before—can't be absorbed at all, since she has nothing to relate it to from her previous experience. So things that are moderately novel should be the most helpful to and most preferred by the child.

Generally speaking, the discrepancy principle seems to hold, although there are some exceptions. If a baby has been looking at a red picture, she may prefer a moderate change in color, such as to yellow, rather than a very large change, such as to green. But if you give older babies a group of pictures, they may look the longest at the photo they have never seen before. So Kagan and Piaget are certainly right that babies prefer things that are not completely familiar. But "moderate novelty" may cover quite a large range of newness or strangeness.

Attention in Older Children Eleanor Gibson (1969) suggests that there are four basic dimensions of change in attention from infancy throughout childhood.

1. *From capture to activity.* This is a good description of the change that takes place at about two months, when the infant switches from "automatic pilot"—from having her attention captured by movement and edges—to active search and exploration. But Gibson thinks that this trend continues later on as well, with the child's explorations becoming more and more guided by her intentions.
2. *From unsystematic to systematic search.* The baby a few months old does look at more than just the edges of pictures or objects, but it isn't until much later—age 2 or even 5 or 6—that the child really begins to explore systematically, examining each feature carefully. Because of inefficient exploration, it is often harder for the young child to pick out something later on that he may have seen or played with before.
3. *From broad to selective pickup of information.* Older children get better and better at focusing their attention on a single aspect of a complex situation. In a classroom, the child has to be able to pick out and pay attention to the teacher's voice above the babble of other voices and noises or to select the red and green lights at an intersection out of all the myriad visual signals around. Children become increasingly good at this selective attention right up to adolescence.
4. *Ignoring irrelevant information.* It may seem as if I just talked about this. After all, isn't focusing on one thing the same as ignoring everything else? Not quite. The young child in the classroom may be able to focus well enough to hear the teacher's voice but may still hear the words of the other children. Very often it isn't necessary to shut

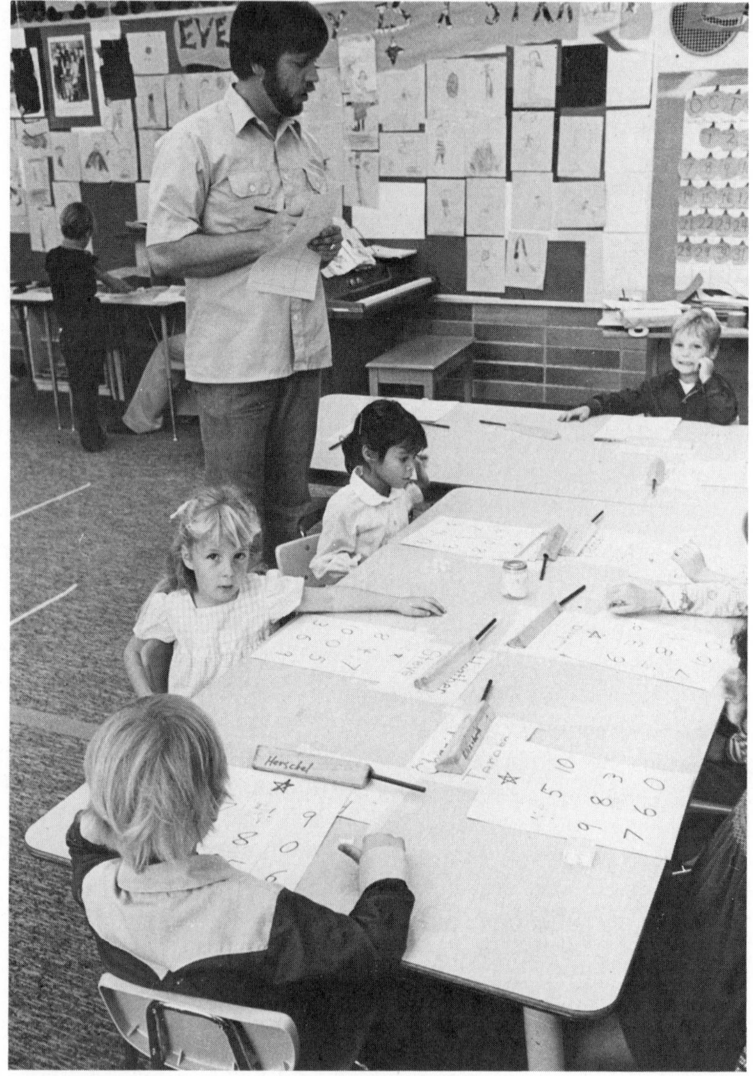

Figure 5.3 **A classroom like this is perceptually very complex, and children have to focus their attention on only some portions of it at any one time if they are to be able to work effectively. The ability to focus in this way, and to ignore the irrelevant, improves over the elementary school years.**

everything else out; but in complex situations, the child will do better at a task if she can concentrate so fully on one set of information that she really doesn't see or hear anything else. Remember last time you took an important test, such as perhaps the college board tests. You needed to be able to shut out everything else and focus all your attention on the questions and answers. Young children gradually acquire this ability to ignore the irrelevant, but the ability continues to develop up to and through adolescence.

Overall, then, the child's attentional processes seem to become more voluntary and more focused as she gets older.

Perceptual Constancies

Let me focus my own attention more narrowly. Let's look at one specific set of perceptual "rules" that the child must acquire in order to make sense out of the physical world around her, namely, the **perceptual constancies.**

When you see someone walking away from you, the image of the person on your retina actually becomes smaller. But you don't see the person as getting smaller. You see him as the same size but moving farther away. When you do this, you are demonstrating **size constancy;** you are able to see the size as constant even though the retinal image has become smaller or larger.

Other constancies include the ability to recognize that shapes of objects are the same even though you are looking at them from different angles, which we call **shape constancy,** and the ability to recognize that colors are constant even though the amount of light or shadow on them changes, which we call **color constancy.**

Taken together, the several specific constancies add up to the larger concept of **object constancy,** which is the recognition that objects remain the same even when they appear to change in certain ways. The evidence we have suggests that babies may be born with rudimentary forms of several constancies but that they become much more skillful over the first several years.

Size Constancy The aspect of size constancy that has been studied the most in infants has been **depth perception.** In order to maintain your size constancy when you see a man walking away from you, you have to be able to judge how far he has gone, which requires depth perception. Next time you're in an airplane, just before landing or just after taking off, when you can see the cars and people on the ground, take a good look out the window. The usual experience is that the cars look like toys and the people like midgets. Because you have no way of estimating the distance, you can't maintain your size constancy either. You know they are real people and cars, but they look smaller to you.

Obviously, for the infant, depth perception is not only an essential ingredient in size constancy, it is also essential for all sorts of everyday tasks, like aiming the hands properly to reach a toy, mobile, bottle, or breast. Can the baby judge depth?

One of the early studies to show depth perception in infants was the work of Eleanor Gibson and Richard Walk (1960), who observed babies 6 months old and older on an apparatus they called a "visual cliff." You can see a picture of the apparatus in

Figure 5.4 The "visual cliff" apparatus used by Gibson and Walk in their studies of depth perception in infants. In this photo, the mother is trying to coax the baby out on the "cliff" side.

Figure 5.4. It consists of a large table with a barrier around the outside edges. In the center is a slightly raised runway, and on either side are slightly lower sheets of glass. On one side, there is a checkerboard pattern immediately below the glass; on the other side—the "cliff" side—the checkerboard is some feet below the glass.

In the standard procedure, the baby is placed on the runway in the middle, and either the parent or the experimenter stands on the cliff side (as in the picture) or on the shallow side and tries to coax the baby to crawl out onto the glass. If the baby has no depth perception, she should be equally willing or unwilling to crawl out on either side. But if she has some depth perception, some ability to use the cues of depth that are contained in the checkerboards, then she should be unwilling to go "over the cliff." From the baby's perspective, the cliff side would indeed look like a cliff, and she should stay away.

The results of these studies show clearly that babies of about 6 months do *not* crawl out on the cliff side but are quite willing to crawl on the shallow side, which indicates that they have some depth perception.

This study was reported in 1960 and showed us all that babies had more perceptual skills than we had given them credit for. But this procedure wouldn't tell us just how early depth perception exists in infants. Babies younger than about 6 months can't crawl, so some other procedure had to be found for younger babies. Joseph Campos (Campos, Langer & Krowitz, 1970) solved the problem by attaching equipment to younger infants to allow him to record their heart rates while they were on the visual cliff apparatus. He put the babies out on the cliff side and on the noncliff side and watched to see if their hearts responded differently. As it turned out, they did. In babies as young as 2 months of age, the heart rate went down a little when they were over the cliff side and didn't change when they were placed on the noncliff side. So they were noticing some difference between the two. In this same study, though, 1-month-old infants did *not* show any different reactions to the two sides—perhaps because their acuity is simply not good enough to detect the depth cues.

To sum up, 6-month-old infants clearly have depth perception, and 2-month-old babies seem to have at least some form of it. Researchers are still debating about whether newborns respond to depth. If they do, of course, it would be a point for the "nativists," but we simply don't have the answer yet.

Shape Constancy Shape constancy is extremely important for the baby. She has to realize that the bottle is still the bottle even though it is turned slightly, and thus presents a different shape, or that her toys are the same when they are in different positions. You do this constantly without being aware of it. Look at the door or window nearest to where you are sitting right now. You "see" the window or door as rectangular, but in fact, unless you are looking absolutely straight on, the actual shape you see is probably a trapezoid of some kind.

Studies of shape constancy in infants such as those by Thomas Bower (1966) and Albert and Rose Caron (Caron, Caron & Carlson, 1979) lead to about the same conclusions as I drew about depth perception: Babies of 2–3 months have at least some shape constancy, but we don't know how much earlier it is present.

Object Concept The infant has to learn at least three different basic things about objects. She has to learn that objects remain the same even when they appear to be different. It is this set of skills we have just been discussing and have called **object constancy.** But she also has to develop an **object concept,** which has two facets. The infant must learn that objects continue to exist even when she can't see or feel them any longer—that when her mother goes out of sight through a doorway, the mother continues to exist or that when a toy disappears beneath the sofa, it still exists. This understanding is usually called **object permanence.** Finally, the infant has to learn that individual objects retain their unique identity from one encounter to another. When the mother goes away and then comes back again, it is the same mother both times; the crib is the same object each time she is placed in it, and so on. This understanding is usually called **object identity.**

These understandings about objects and people may seem so basic that you may not be able to imagine the child's not having them. But she does not, at least not at first. And the three aspects develop at different speeds. Object constancies such as size and color constancy, although probably present in some rudimentary forms in the very young infant, may not be completely developed until the child is 2 or 3 years old. Object identity by contrast seems *not* to be present at all at birth. It apparently develops first at about five months of age. For example, Thomas Bower (1975) has studied infants' reactions in a situation in which the infant, seated in an infant seat, looks at her mother through a window. The mother's image is then artificially multiplied so that the infant sees three mothers. Young infants show no signs of surprise at this multiple image. If anything, they seem to be more delighted with three mothers than with one. But at about 22–24 weeks of age, infants begin to be extremely upset at this multiple image, which suggests that they have in some sense understood that there should be only one, and the multiple image violates this expectation.

The Development of Object Permanence Object permanence also develops over the first year or two of life, apparently through a series of moderately distinct stages. Through the first month of life, there is little evidence that infants respond to anything that is not immediately present, visible, or touchable. By about two months of age, there are some signs that the infant is developing a rudimentary notion of object permanence. If you have an infant this age look at a toy, then put a screen between the child and the toy, remove the toy, and then remove the screen, the 2-month-old infant will show some surprise, which suggests that she has some expectation that the toy will continue to be there. But infants of this age will not try to search for the missing toy if you leave the screen there or if you cover a toy with a cloth.

By about six months, the infant is showing still more signs of object permanence. For example, if she drops a toy over the edge of her crib, she will look over the edge to see the toy. Occasionally, she will also look to see if she can find something that someone else dropped, although this is slower to develop (which may suggest that things the infant has handled herself

Figure 5.5 These photos show very graphically the change in object permanence from the baby of 6 months or younger, who stops looking for the elephant when someone puts a screen in front of it. An older baby would keep searching, pushing the screen aside, and reaching for the toy.

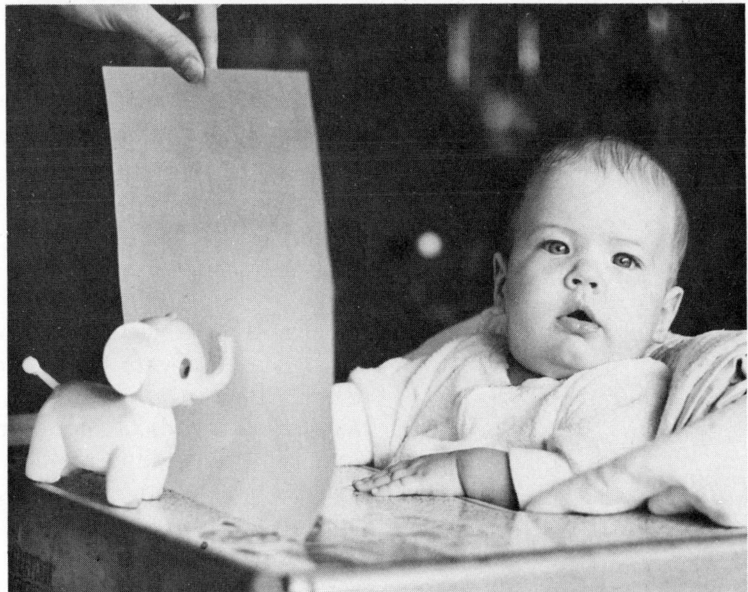

are in some sense more "real" to her than those other people have handled). At this same age, an infant will search for an object that has been *partially* hidden. If you put a favorite toy under a cloth but leave part of it sticking out, the infant will reach for the toy, which suggests that in some sense the infant "recognizes" that the whole object is there even though she can see only part of it. But if you cover the toy completely with the cloth, the infant will stop looking at it and will not reach for it, even if she has seen you put the cloth over it.

This changes somewhere between 8 and 12 months; infants this age will reach or search for a toy that has been covered

Figure 5.6 This is a schematic drawing of the apparatus used in the Mundy-Castle and Anglin experiment. The object is seen at A, then moves to B, and is later seen at C and then D. A 4-month-old child anticipates the movement of the object between B and C. What does this tell us about object permanence? (Source: Bower, 1977.)

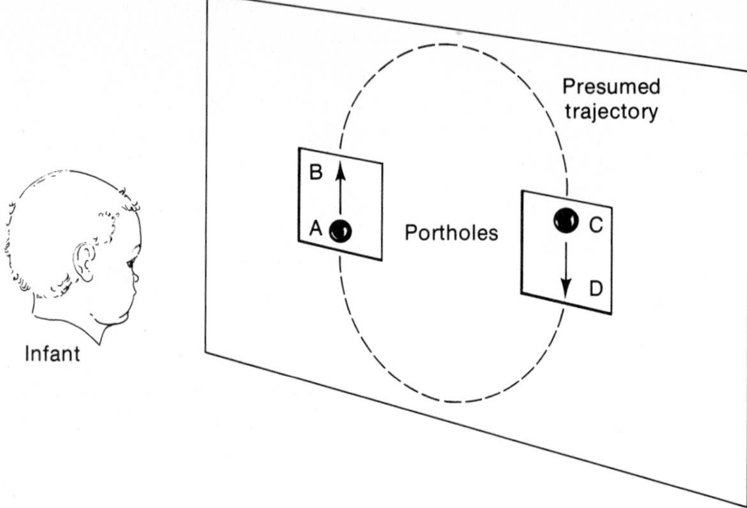

completely by a cloth or hidden by a screen. There are further refinements of object permanence, which develop during the second year of life; but by 12 months, most infants appear to grasp the fact that objects continue to exist even when they are no longer visible.

Puzzles About Object Permanence What I have just given you is the "standard version" of the development of object permanence. This is the sequence that Piaget (1954) describes and that has been widely confirmed. But there are some puzzles—some hints that younger babies understand more about objects than we give them credit for. Let me give you two of the puzzles, both suggested originally by Thomas Bower (1975).

First, Bower describes an earlier study by Mundy-Castle and Anglin (1969), which showed that a 4-month-old baby would follow the *presumed* path of a moving object with his eyes. The general situation used in the experiment is shown in Figure 5.6. The infant can see the object only when it passes by one of the two portholes. The object moves behind the screen in an oval pattern, so all the baby actually sees is that the object goes from the bottom to the top of the left porthole and then from the top to the bottom of the right porthole. What the babies in this experiment did was to move their eyes in an oval pattern, thus *anticipating* the reappearance of the object in the next porthole. This is a pretty sophisticated response and seems to show that the baby understands that the object is still there and moving even when he can't see it.

An even more intriguing bit of information comes from a study by Bower (1975). He found that 5-month-olds would not reach for an object which had just been covered in their sight but that the same babies *would* reach for the same object if you turned out the lights. They can't see it, just as they can't see it when you cover it with a cloth, but they'll keep reaching in the dark.

These puzzling findings do not fit nicely into the developmental sequence I sketched earlier. It certainly appears that young babies have more grasp of the object concept than we have given them credit for, but we are still a long way from understanding the steps in the process.

One final point about the object concept: Some of you will have already noticed that the development of the object concept may have important implications for the child's developing relationship to or attachment to the people around him. I've discussed some of those implications in Box 5.1.

Learning to Read: An Application of the Principles of Perceptual Learning

I have talked about how the child gets better at focusing her attention on the relevant things going on around her. The development of perceptual constancies is an example of this, since the child must learn *not* to pay too much attention to the apparent shape or color or size of objects but to pay attention instead to the whole context in which the object appears.

Some Perceptual Problems in Reading Learning to read represents another whole set of perceptual cues. One of the particularly interesting things about reading, in fact, is that the child has to *unlearn* some of the shape constancy she so carefully acquired during infancy. For ordinary objects, whether they are seen turned to the left or the right, right side up or upside down, doesn't matter. It's still the same object. But that's not true for letters. Letters like *b* and *d* are the same shape, except with the direction reversed. The letters *p* and *q* are the same kind of pair, and *p* and *b* are the same shape but one is "upside down." So in order to learn to read (at least the Latin alphabet), the child must now learn to pay attention to something she'd learned to ignore—namely, the rotation of the letter in space.

If this is a correct analysis of at least part of what goes on when a child learns to read, then we ought to find that children would have the most difficulty with the reversal pairs of letters or with words that make sense whether they are read from either end, like *saw* and *was*.

Another kind of shift of attention also has to take place in learning to read. The child of 5 or 6 has just spent three years learning to speak and understand *oral* language. He has learned which words are likely to go in particular places in sentences,

Box 5.1 Object Concept and Attachment in Babies

All the information I've given about the development of the object concept in infants may seem like pretty unimportant stuff until you realize that some kind of object constancy is probably required before the baby can become attached to an individual person, such as his mother. Babies younger than 6 months may be more soothable by someone familiar with their habits and may smile more to Mom and Dad than to strangers; but the full-fledged attachment of the baby to a single other person—usually the mother—doesn't seem to take place until about six or seven months, just about the time that the child begins to understand that Mom continues to exist even when he can't see her.

The fact that these two things happen at about the same time has led some cognitive-developmental theorists, such as Rudolph Schaffer and Peggy Emmerson (1964), to argue that the child's grasp of the object concept is a *necessary* condition for full attachment. At the very least, it is clear that the baby can't become attached to someone until he can consistently discriminate between that person and others, using the smell or touch or sight of the familiar person as cues. So perceptual development is involved in the process to at least that extent.

For some babies, there is also an intermediate step somewhere between about five and eight months, when they have figured out who mom or dad is and begun to develop one or more strong attachments; but they haven't yet completely grasped the principle of object permanence. When the parents leave such babies, the infants may show fairly extreme signs of distress, such as loud and persistent crying.

Some parents, faced with this "separation protest," simply don't leave the child at all, even for short periods. But an alternative is for the parent to separate from the child for a brief time—perhaps 15 or 20 minutes to start with—always returning and holding the child at the end of the separation. The time apart can then gradually be increased. Such a procedure may help the child to learn that the parent really will return after he or she disappears. During the same period, of course, the child is acquiring information about object permanence through her play, too. Once this concept is fully grasped, the extreme separation protest usually fades.

Another link between the development of the object concept and attachment is provided by some intriguing research by Sylvia Bell (1970). She found that babies who had a more secure attachment to their mother—who were easily soothed by the mother and used her as a safe base for exploring—were more rapid in their development of the concept of object permanence than were babies with an insecure attachment. In fact, the insecurely attached babies seemed to pay more attention to vanishing objects (such as toys) than they did to a vanishing mother. This study might make you think that the process works the other way—that the attachment comes first and the object concept later.

As is true of most things we'll talk about, probably it works both ways. The baby has to make some basic progress in perceptual development before he can be attached at all. But once he's reached that stage, a secure attachment may help to further the development of the object concept.

for example. But when he begins to read, he has to look at the *written* language. That's a major change in the focus of attention. We might expect that in the beginning, when a child learning to read came to a word he didn't know, he might put in

Figure 5.7 When children are first learning to read, they often "read" words that would make sense in the sentence but have no connection to the letters on the page.

a word that could fit into that sentence, regardless of what the little squiggles on the paper might show. Later on, when the child has figured out that reading involves decoding the squiggles, we might expect him to make more mistakes in which he *misreads* the word.

Coping with the Problems: The Basic Steps in Learning to Read Research by Eleanor Gibson and Harry Levin (1975), among others, suggests that children go through three basic steps in learning to read. The first strategy seems to be that any sentence that makes sense can be "read." Children using this strategy substitute words that are totally unlike the ones on the page but that make sensible sentences. In the next step, the child figures out that what he "reads" out loud has to have *some* connection to the letters on the page. At this stage, when he comes to a word he doesn't know, he is likely to stop short. He may stop reading or just leave out that word. Finally, instead of staying silent, the child will begin to try to decode the word – to figure out what it must be on the basis of the letters in it. So the kind of mistakes the child makes depends on what he's paying attention to – the sense of the sentence, the letters on the page, or both.

To take this one step further, Andrew Biemiller (1970) has found that children who reach the no-response phase (stopping short when they come to an unknown word) early are better readers by the end of first grade. As Gibson and Levin say:

Many children start school with the notion that reading is speaking with books open in front of them. The speech is not nonsensical. Still, the earlier the realization by the child that what he says must be determined by what is printed, the better the prognosis for early reading achievement.

(*Gibson & Levin, 1975, p. 282*)

Once the child *does* begin to pay attention to the individual letters, though, she still has to figure out that reversals like *b* and *d* are really different from one another. Eleanor Gibson's research on this shows that 4- and 5-year-old children still treat reversals as "the same," but 6- and 7-year-old children rapidly learn that *p* is not the same as *b*. In the process of learning this "exception" to the shape constancy rules, the child initially makes a lot of reversal mistakes in her reading, but these drop out naturally as she begins to pay attention to the direction of the letters.

"Whole Word" versus "Phonics" Methods for Teaching Reading You will notice that so far I have steered clear of that hotly debated issue of how reading should be taught. Should children learn whole words in one chunk? After all, it is whole words that we read, not individual letters in isolation. So perhaps it is better to emphasize whole words from the beginning. Alternatively, perhaps children would learn more readily if the teacher emphasized the sounds associated with individual letters or letter combinations, a procedure called *phonics training* or *decoding*.

Advocates of these two basic approaches among both researchers and teachers (such as Liberman & Shankweiler, 1977, on the phonics side and Perfetti & Lesgold, 1977, on the "whole word" side) often feel very strongly about their particular position. But the issue is obviously complex and has no single answer. I can't settle the issue here, but let me give you a few pieces of information to illustrate the complexity.

The type of instruction that works best seems to depend partly on the child's stage in the three steps I have just described. In the early stages, when the child is focused more on the meaning than on the actual letters, the whole word method works fine, especially if the words are short. It may be a good method for getting the child started on reading. But Jeanne Chall (1967), in her review of reading programs, concludes that some phonics training is essential for the child to move to the final step of decoding the individual words. By the second or third grade, children who have had no phonics training have fallen behind children trained in decoding. In particular, they are less good at reading new words. This debate has not ended; both educators and psychologists will no doubt still be arguing

Box 5.2

Problems in Learning to Read

As many as 15 percent of children in the United States have significant difficulty learning to read. A small segment of this group has obvious brain damage or is generally retarded in development. But the majority of children with reading problems show essentially normal development in other respects. They have no obvious brain damage, frequently do well in school in subjects other than reading, and show no substantial emotional disturbance. Two labels have been applied to children in this larger group. Most frequently today they are described as having a **specific learning disability.** A somewhat older term for this syndrome, still in use, is **dyslexia.**

What might account for this type of problem? After years of debate and a great deal of research, the one thing that is clear is that there is no *single* explanation of reading problems that will explain all children's difficulties. There seem to be many different sources of difficulty, among them the following:

1. *Visual perception problems.* Some children seem to have trouble decoding the visual information, probably because of some minimal (and nonobvious) brain damage. This does not, however, seem to be a major cause of difficulty for most children.
2. *Integrating visual and auditory information.* Reading involves, in part, matching the sound of a word with the sight of it. This is particularly true in the early years of reading, when children are asked to read aloud a lot. Herbert Birch (Birch & Lefford, 1963), among others, has argued that poor readers just don't integrate information from these two senses very effectively. In fact, this does seem to be the case for many poor readers.
3. *Hearing the parts of words.* Perhaps some children have difficulty because they genuinely don't hear words as separate combinations of sounds. So when they have to decode new words by breaking apart the word into separate sounds, they have great difficulty. Isabel Liberman and her colleagues (Liberman, Shankweiler, Liberman, Fowler & Fischer, 1976) have found that preschool children who have the greatest difficulty "hearing" the separate sounds in words do in fact have the hardest time learning to read.
4. *Problems with language.* Finally, we have to remember that when we read, we read *language*, so that any child who is having difficulty with language may have difficulty with reading as well. Frank Vellutino (1977), for example, argues that this is the *major* source of problems for most poor readers. "Our findings indicate that when dyslexics call *b* 'd' or *was* 'saw,' it is not because these figures are literally misperceived, but because dyslexic children cannot remember their names" (Vellutino, 1977, pp. 337–338). A reading problem, then, may be just one facet of a broader language problem.

The important point is that each of these explanations is probably true for *some* poor readers, but not all. This makes the teacher's problem extremely difficult, since she must try to diagnose, and then solve, a wide range of potential difficulties.

about whole words versus phonics at the turn of the next century. But practically speaking, the debate may not be so important, since virtually all current reading programs sensibly include both types of training. Despite the best efforts of educators, however, many children have great difficulty learning to read, a problem I've discussed in Box 5.2.

Individual Differences in Perception

Perceptual Styles in Children and Adults

So far I've talked as if all children are pretty much alike in what they look at and how. But it turns out that there are some interesting ways in which we differ systematically in the way we go about our perceptual explorations.

Reflection versus Impulsivity Go to a museum some time and watch the people looking at the paintings. Some get up fairly close and look at each picture for a long time, taking in the details and perhaps comparing one picture with another. Others stand back and get a general view and move from one picture to the next fairly quickly. The particular dimension of individual differences involved in this case is what Jerome Kagan calls **reflection versus impulsivity** (Kagan, Rosman, Day, Albert & Phillips, 1964; Kagan, 1971).

This dimension can be seen most clearly when a child (or adult) is faced with a problem that has many solutions. The impulsive child chooses quickly and typically makes more mistakes than does the reflective child, who may spend a very long time examining the alternatives. Kagan describes the entire dimension, from impulsivity to reflection, in terms of **conceptual tempo.**

Tempo differences appear as early as infancy. In babies, the one with the slower tempo will remain still and look at something new with fixed concentration, whereas the baby with the faster tempo will thrash around, become excited, gurgle, and look away after only a short period of examination.

In older children, Kagan has measured this dimension by showing the child one drawing and then asking her to find another one that is just like it. One of the items from Kagan's test is in Figure 5.8. The "reflective" children look at the alternatives slowly and carefully and are likely to select the right one on the first try. The "impulsive" children, by contrast, look quickly at the alternatives and simply choose one. They make their choice more rapidly but are more often wrong on their first choice.

This dimension of "style" is at least somewhat stable during childhood. For example, Kagan and his colleagues Deborah Lapidus and Michael Moore (1978) have recently reported that they could predict at least some of the differences in children's general tempo at age 10 from knowing what their tempo had been when they were 8 months old. Kagan also found that reflective children had a somewhat easier time learning to read, which makes sense when you think about the sort of careful ex-

Figure 5.8 A sample item from Kagan's test of "reflection versus impulsivity." The child taking the test must try to select the picture from among the bottom six that exactly matches the figure at the top. (Source: Kagan, J., B. L. Rosman, D. Day, J. Albert & W. Phillips, 1964, p. 23. Copyright 1964 by the American Psychological Association. Reprinted with permission.)

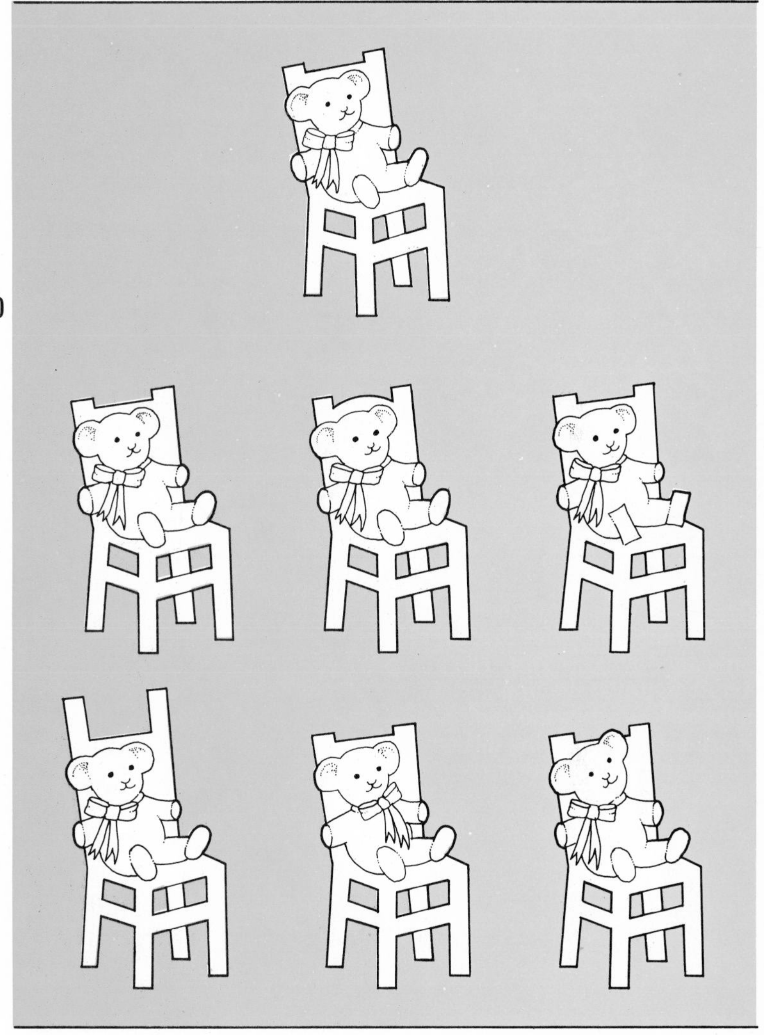

amination of letter forms that is needed in the early stages of reading (Kagan, 1965).

But reflectiveness is not always best either. If you're driving down a street looking for a sign that says "Connecticut Avenue," you don't need to stop at every corner and carefully examine the street sign. You can tell just by the length of the name whether it could be Connecticut or not, and you only have to take a quick look at other long words. Any time a simple glance is enough, the impulsive person will be more efficient. It is only when a detailed examination is needed to make a discrimination or a judgment that the reflective style is required.

Figure 5.9 A sample item taken from the Coates Preschool Embedded Figures Test. The simple figure at the upper right must be located in the complex figure below. How long does it take you to find it? (Source: Coates, 1972.)

Field Dependence and Independence A second dimension of perceptual style, studied originally in adults by H. A. Witkin and his associates (Witkin, Dyk, Faterson, Goodenough & Karp, 1962), is field dependence versus independence. What is at issue in this case is whether you are "captured" (or distracted) by the context something appears in or whether you can examine something independent of its background.

One of the tasks that is used to measure this dimension is called the *Embedded Figures Test.* In this task, the person is shown a simple figure, such as a square or a pie shape, and then asked to find a figure like that in a complex drawing. The problem is for the subject to ignore the other features of the drawing (the field) and pay attention only to the abstract shapes. (You might want to see how good you are at this yourself. One of the items on a children's version of the Embedded Figure Test is in Figure 5.9.) Those children or adults who are good at ignoring the irrelevant context are called **field independent,** while those who are "captured" by the total context area are called **field dependent.**

Generally speaking, children get more and more field independent as they get older, which is certainly what we'd expect in view of all the basic developmental changes in perceptual learning strategies I've already discussed. But at any given age, there are individual differences.

Conceptual Styles and Personality Conceptual styles appear to affect the way we look at things. But could they also reflect more basic aspects of personality or temperament? Witkin has argued all along that field dependent individuals are also more dependent in other ways. There has been little research on such a link, but a recent study by Stanley Messer and David Brodzinsky (1979) shows a partial link between conceptual tempo and aggressiveness. They found that among fifth graders, impulsive children were rated by their teachers and by other children as more physically aggressive than were reflective children.

Research like this raises some intriguing questions about the possible existence of very basic personal "styles" that cut across our traditional categories of analysis.

Sex Differences

We know relatively little about sex differences in perceptual skills, preferences, or sensitivities; so it's hard to give you nice clear statements. In general, the research we have shows few sex differences. There are hints that girls may be more sensitive to touch than are boys and other hints that they may be more sensitive to odors (Maccoby & Jacklin, 1974). But beyond that, there are no consistent differences.

In perceptual *style*, though, there is a consistent sex difference. Girls are usually found to be more field dependent than are boys, perhaps because most tests of this dimension involve some aspect of spatial visualization. Boys as a group are generally better at any task that requires visual–spatial skills. (More about that in Chapter 9.) On tests of reflections versus impulsivity, in contrast, no consistent sex differences have been found.

Social Class Differences

There are no social class differences that I know of in the basic maturation of perceptual skills. Middle-class children don't shift from looking at contours to looking at the middle of pictures any sooner than do poor children, for example. But in older children, there are differences in conceptual tempo, with poor children more often being impulsive and middle-class children being more reflective. I don't have any very good hunches about why this might be so, but this difference may help to explain why poor children have more difficulty learning to read. Of course, there are many other reasons for greater reading difficulties among the poor, including less experience with books and reading in the home; but an impulsive visual search style also makes it more difficult to examine the words carefully.

Answering the Why Questions: Explanations of Perceptual Development

Nativism versus Empiricism

As I emphasized at the beginning of this chapter, one of the issues that has run through all research on perceptual development, particularly in infancy, is the old question of internal versus external causes. In this case, the issue is stated in terms of **nativism** versus **empiricism.** Does the baby have to learn what to pay attention to, how to see depth, and so on; or are these skills present at birth? Even if skills are present at birth, does practice matter? Does it matter what kind of learning experiences the child has?

As with most psychological issues originally stated in black-and-white terms, we rapidly discover that the answer is a sort of gray. Neither the extreme nativist position nor the extreme empiricist position is entirely correct. As usual, both experience and initial abilities are involved, and both are affected by the continuing maturation of the body.

Arguments for Nativism We know that at birth the baby has considerable perceptual acuity, probably some depth perception, and perhaps some rudimentary constancies. More important, the studies of attention in infants show very clearly that babies do not have to be taught what to look at.

Kagan puts this point very nicely: "Nature has apparently equipped the newborn with an initial bias in the processing of experience. He does not, as the nineteenth-century empiricists believed, have to learn what he should examine" (Kagan, 1971, p. 60). The initial biases include the tendency to look at movement and contour. These basic tendencies change during the early months of life. In particular, there seems to be a shift of some kind at about two months of age, as well as gradual changes over the early months and years. Some of these changes seem quite obviously to be maturationally based, such as the change in looking "preferences" at two months.

Arguments for Empiricism Other changes in the child's perceptual skills are equally clearly affected by specific experience. First of all, we know from research with cats and monkeys that a basic minimum of visual stimulation is needed in order for any perceptual development to occur. D. H. Hubel and T. N. Weisel (1963), among others, have found that in animals deprived of all light during the early months of life, the eye actually deteriorates. Wayne Dennis's study of orphanage babies in Iran, a study I've touched on before, suggests that the animal research may be generalizable to human subjects as well. The infants who didn't have a chance to look at things, to explore objects with hands and eyes and tongue, and who were deprived of the opportunity to move around freely were retarded in the development of both perceptual and motor skills.

On the other end of the scale, there is evidence that extra enrichment may help to speed up the process of perceptual development. In another study of orphanage children, by Burton White (1967), some babies were given extra visual and tactile stimulation. These infants were more rapid than were the less-stimulated babies in their development of "visually directed reaching"—a skill requiring good depth perception.

Studies like these suggest that perceptual development in the infant is linked to the quantity of stimulation available. But the quality of the stimulation may be important, too. Bell's (1970) study, for example, points to the possibility that the course of perceptual development may be affected by the child's pattern of attachment or her relationship generally with the adults around her. Work by Leon Yarrow and others (Yarrow, Rubenstein, Pederson & Jankowski, 1972) points also to the importance of having complex and varied stimulation. Children who have a variety of different toys, or have toys which move or change when they are played with, show more rapid development of some perceptual skills.

Still, despite these few studies, we really know very little about the effects of early stimulation on perceptual development. We know enough to say that the environment makes some difference, but we're a long way from defining the critical aspects of the environment.

But although the "why" and "how" questions are still largely unanswered, we have come a very long way in the past 10 or 15 years in answering the "what" questions. We know an enormous amount about the earliest visual skills of babies and about what they pay attention to. All of this is important new knowledge to be built upon by future research.

Summary

1. The study of perceptual development is important because of the great role that perception plays in the early life of the child and because of the important theoretical issues involved.
2. Perceptual acuity is not perfect at birth; it improves over the first 10 years or longer.
3. For the first two months of life, infants primarily pay attention to movement and sharp contrast, including the edges of objects. After two months, they look more at *what* the object is, examining the middle as well as the edge.
4. The overall development of attention may be guided by four major principles suggested by Gibson (1969): a shift from (1) "capture" to activity, (2) unsystematic to systematic search, (3) broad to selective pickup of information, and (4) inability to ability to ignore irrelevant information.
5. Perceptual constancies are developed over the first several years of life. Babies as young as 1 or 2 months may have rudimentary depth perception and size constancy, but these develop further over the early months.
6. Object permanence and object identity also develop over the first several years.
7. The development of object permanence may be a necessary precursor for the development of a full-fledged attachment by the child.
8. Basic perceptual learning principles may be applied to the study of reading. Children have most difficulty discriminating letters that are reversals of one another. They must, generally, learn to pay attention to the specific configurations of letters.
9. Difficulties in learning to read may arise because of perceptual problems, integration of perceptual and auditory information, or problems with language.
10. Individual differences in perceptual style include the dimension of reflection versus impulsivity and field dependence versus independence.
11. There are few consistent sex differences in perceptual skills, although girls *may* be somewhat more sensitive to touch and taste. Girls are also somewhat more field dependent.
12. Social class differences are also scarce, although poor children tend to be more impulsive than middle-class children.
13. Both the empiricists and the nativists are correct to some extent about the origin of perceptual skills. Some basic perceptual skills, and strategies for examining the world with them, seem to be inborn. But they are modified by experience as well.

Key Terms

Acuity Sharpness of perceptual ability—how well or clearly you can see or hear or use other senses.

Color constancy The ability to see the color of an object as remaining the same despite changes in illumination or shadow. One of the basic perceptual constancies.

Conceptual tempo A dimension of individual differences

in perceptual/conceptual style suggested by Kagan, describing the general pace with which objects are explored.

Depth perception The ability to judge the depth of an object from your body, based on a number of cues.

Discrepancy principle A proposed preference on the part of infants and children for experiences that are moderately discrepant from previous experiences.

Dyslexia Significant difficulty in learning to read that is unaccounted for by mental retardation or substantial brain damage.

Empiricism Opposite of "nativism." The theoretical point of view that perceptual skill arises from experience.

Field dependence versus independence A dimension of individual difference in perceptual/conceptual style suggested by Witkin; people vary in the extent to which they are affected by the embedding context in which an event occurs.

Nativism See "Empiricism" above. The view that perceptual skills are inborn and do not require experience to develop.

Object concept A general term including the concepts of object permanence and object identity.

Object constancy The general phrase describing the ability to see objects as remaining the same despite changes in retinal image.

Object identity Part of the object concept. The recognition that objects remain the same from one encounter to the next.

Object permanence Part of the object concept. The recognition that an object continues to exist even when it is temporarily out of sight.

Perceptual constancies A collection of constancies, including shape, size, and color constancy.

Perceptual learning An increase in the ability to extract information (via the senses) from the environment, as a result of practice or experience.

Primary visual system Proposed system in the infant older than two months of age, governed largely by cortical activity and involving identification of *what* objects are.

Reflection versus impulsivity The same dimension as described under "Conceptual tempo."

Second visual system Proposed system in the infant that operates for the first two months of life, governed by the midbrain rather than the cortex, and involving primarily the location of objects —where the object is rather than what it is.

Shape constancy The ability to see an object's shape as remaining the same despite changes in the shape of the retinal image. A basic perceptual constancy.

Size constancy The ability to see an object's size as remaining the same despite changes in size of the retinal image. A basic perceptual constancy.

Specific learning disability The phrase commonly used to describe children with no obvious brain damage or mental retardation who show significant problems learning to read or doing other school tasks.

Suggested Readings

Bower, T. G. R. The perceptual world of the child. Cambridge, Mass.: Harvard University Press, 1977.

This brief book (about 85 pages) covers in readable fashion most of the major aspects of perceptual development during the early years.

Gibson, E. J., & Levin, H. The psychology of reading. Cambridge, Mass.: MIT Press, 1975.

I am a little hesitant to recommend this to you, since it is quite technical; but as professionally aimed books go, it's readable. And it is certainly encyclopedic.

Ross, A. O. Learning disability: The unrealized potential. New York: McGraw-Hill, 1977.

If you are interested in the question of reading problems, this would be a good first source. It is written for students and interested laypeople and has a great deal of useful information.

Project 5.1 Development of the Object Concept

For this project, you will need to locate an infant between 6 and 12 months of age. Obtain permission from the baby's parents, assure them that there is nothing harmful or difficult in the tasks you want to use, and inform them that you would like them to be there while you're presenting the materials to the baby.

Obtain from the parents one of the baby's favorite toys. Place the baby in a sitting position or on his stomach in such a way that he can reach for the toy easily. Then perform the following steps:

Step 1: While the baby is watching, place the toy in full view and easy reach. See if the infant reaches for the toy.

Step 2: In full view of the infant, cover part of the toy with a handkerchief, so that only part is visible. Does the baby reach for the toy?

Step 3: While the infant is reaching for the toy (you'll have to pick your moment), cover it completely with the handkerchief. Does the baby continue reaching?

Step 4: In full view of the child, while the child is still interested in the toy, cover the whole toy with the cloth. Does the baby try to pull the cloth away or search for the toy in some way?

You may need to use more than one toy to keep the baby's interest or spread the tests out over a period of time.

Steps 2, 3, and 4 should develop in the order listed. Jackson, Campos, and Fischer (1978) report that the first step is "passed" at about 26 weeks, step 2 at about 28 or 29 weeks, and step 3 at about 30 or 31 weeks. The closer to these ages your infant is, the more interesting your results are likely to be.

Did your subject's performance conform to those expectations? If not, why do you think it might be different? You might read the Jackson, Campos, and Fischer paper to see some of the reasons they give for differences in results from several studies. Do you think it mattered, for example, that a familiar toy was used? Or that the mother or father was present?

Part Three

The Thinking Child

Preview of Chapter 6

"Allgone Sticky." The Development of Language in Children

A friend of mine listened one morning at breakfast while her 6-year-old and her 3-year-old had the following conversation about the relative dangers of forgetting to feed the goldfish versus overfeeding the goldfish:

6-year-old: It's worse to forget to feed them.

3-year-old: No, it's badder to feed them too much.

6-year-old: You don't say badder, you say worser.

3-year-old: But it's baddest to give them too much food.

6-year-old: No it's not. It's worsest to forget to feed them.

The conversation is delightful all by itself, but what I want you to look at here is the language. One of the striking things about the language of these two children is how good it is. The 3-year-old, particularly, is creating remarkably good sentences. What makes the exchange funny, of course, is the one "mistake" they make, with the word "worse" or "worst." Both children are searching for some way to make the English language regular—which it isn't—and in the process they come up with some delightful errors.

Young children's language very often has exactly this delightfully inventive quality. Even elementary school-age children use language this way. Donald Brenneis and Laura Lein (1977, p. 55) recorded some arguments among children, including the following:

Bob: You're skinny.

Tom: You're slimmy.

Bob: You're scrawny.

Tom: You're . . . I don't know.

Bob: You're weakling.

Tom: You're the slimmiest kid in the whole world.

Bob: You're the weaklingest.

This creative aspect is one of the most remarkable features of language in children. But equally remarkable is the speed with which language develops. At 6 or 8 months, the child makes babbling sounds like "kikiki" or "diddlediddlediddle." Only a few months later you can hear the first words; and by 18 or 24 months, the child is beginning to put two words together into beginning sentences like "allgone shoe." By 3 or 4, the child is putting together both well-constructed sentences like the ones the 3-year-old used in the goldfish argument and such creative marvels as "Why it can't turn off?"

How does the child learn the complexities of language so quickly? Language in a child is one of those things that seems simple and obvious at first; but the longer you think about it and the more you learn, the less simple and obvious it becomes. Because of a burst of interest in and research on children's language in the past 15 years, we know a lot more now than we did even a few years ago. I will try to explain some of the current thinking to you.

What Is Language Anyway?

Let me begin at the beginning. What do we mean by language? Roger Brown has defined it as an arbitrary system of symbols,

> which taken together make it possible for a creature with limited powers of discrimination and a limited memory to transmit and understand an infinite variety of messages and to do this in spite of noise and distraction.
>
> *(Brown, 1965, p. 246)*

The critical element in this definition is the phrase "infinite variety of messages." Language is not just a collection of sounds. Very young babies make several different sounds, but we do not consider that they are using language. Chimpanzees, in the natural state, have "vocabularies" of sounds, each used in particular situations, such as danger. But they apparently do not naturally *combine* the individual sounds into different orders to

Figure 6.1 A chimpanzee—Nim, in this case—showing the sign for an individual word, *ears*. There is complete agreement among researchers that chimps can learn a large sign vocabulary of this type. (Source: Terrace, 1979.)

create new and different meanings. Human language speakers can say more than just "Help!" or "Danger!" We can say "Please help me" or "Help is on the way." The number of possible sentences is infinite, yet each of us learns to use and understand language in this creative way.

Language in Other Animals

While it appears that nonhuman species do not naturally use symbols in this creative way, there has been a continuing question about whether other animals could *learn* to use inventive language. Is a chimpanzee, for example, capable of some form of complex language?

The earliest answers were a clear "no." Several psychologists tried raising chimps in human families to see if they would learn a spoken language. They did not (Hayes, 1951). But then several independent groups of psychologists hit upon the idea of teaching chimps some form of *sign language* rather than spoken language. Allen and Beatrice Gardner (1964, 1974) worked with a chimp named Washoe, and Ann and David Premack (1972) had a star pupil named Sarah. These researchers found that the chimps not only learned the signs for individual words, such as in Figure 6.1, but also seemed to create new, complex sentences. Washoe created the phrase *water bird* to describe a swan and made longer sentences, such as *Washoe more eat*. Sarah eventually created such sentences as *Mary give Sarah apple*. Instances like these seemed to show that the chimps *could* invent new word combinations.

Figure 6.2 This sequence of photographs (among others) has led Terrace to doubt whether Nim was really creating complex sentences on his own. In the first photo, Nim signs "me," but the researcher, Susan Quinby, is signing "you" at the same time. In the third photo, Nim is signing "cat," and Susan is signing "who?" In previous training, Nim had been taught to respond to "who" with "cat," so if Susan's sign "who" came before Nim's sign "cat" in this sequence, then Susan has cued him. (Source: Terrace, 1979, p. 71.)

In the past year, however, some doubts have been raised. H. S. Terrace and his colleagues and students raised a chimp named Nim (Terrace, 1979). At first, Terrace was convinced that Nim was inventing new sentences. But after looking at photographs of the teaching sessions and at the types of sentences Nim used, Terrace concluded it was also possible that Nim's complex sentences were really cued by the trainers. Look at the photographs in Figure 6.2. Nim's sentence in this sequence was *me hug cat*—a fairly complex combination. But now look at what the adult is doing. Is she signaling the signs? We can't tell from the photographs whether the adult made the signs *before* Nim did, but sequences like these do raise some questions. The Gardners, in reply, insist that Washoe frequently invents sentences in situations in which no prompting is possible.

No doubt the debate will rage for some years, until more conclusive tests can be devised. In the meantime, several conclusions seem reasonable. First, species other than humans are capable of learning fairly large vocabularies of individual words. Second, at best, the quality of the chimps' sentences is at about the level of a 2- or 2½-year-old human child and does not seem to develop beyond this level. So the chimp—and perhaps other species such as the dolphin—is capable of complex language, but the capacity appears to be limited.

By contrast, language learning in children takes no endless hours of careful training by parents. It happens naturally and rapidly in the course of the first few years of life. But how?

Let me set aside that question for the moment and begin (as I have in other chapters) with the "what" question: What is the normal course of language development? I'll come back to the "why/how" questions in the next chapter when I take up theories of language acquisition.

Before the First Word

The sounds a child makes before 10 or 12 months of age, when she speaks her first words, are really not language at all. Usually, linguists call this period the **prelinguistic phase.** Within this phase, there is evidence that development occurs in rough stages or steps. Although children differ quite widely in the ages at which they pass from one step to another, the sequence does seem to be the same for most if not all children.

Crying

From birth to about 1 month of age, very nearly the only sound an infant makes is a cry. Infants may have several different cries with somewhat different sound patterns, and those different sounds may well signal different kinds of discomforts or problems. But in most cases, listeners have a hard time linking a specific pattern to the baby's particular problem, such as hunger or pain.

Interestingly, though, listeners *can* tell the difference between the cries of sick babies and those of healthy babies. Philip Zeskind and Barry Lester (1978) have found that sick babies' cries are higher pitched and more piercing and grating than are the cries of healthy babies. So the mother who tells her pediatrician that her baby just "doesn't sound right" to her may well be correct.

Cooing

Starting at about 1 month, the baby begins to add some noncrying sounds to his repertoire, of which a kind of **cooing** sound is the most common—the vowel *uuuu* is heard sometimes for long stretches. It seems to be associated with pleasurable times for the child—times when he is dry and awake and well fed. Quite understandably, most parents find this cooing sound to be pleasurable for them, too; and it may signal "social" encounters between the parent and the baby, where whole conversations take place, like the one I heard recently between my sister-in-law and her 2-month-old son, Stacey.

Figure 6.3 Echolalia strikes again! (Source: Johnston, 1978, p. 8.)

Stacey: Uuuu (gurgle).

Mother: Oh (on a rising inflection). You're going to be awake now. This is your Auntie Helen.

Stacey: (eyes open, looking at mother) Uuuuu.

Mother: That's nice. Are you going to smile for your momma?

Stacey: (smiling) Uuuu.

This seems to be another example of the kind of "turn taking" Ken Kaye talks about as part of the early interactions of mother and child.

Babbling By about 6 months, the infant begins to use a much wider range of sounds, including a lot of what we would call consonants, such as *k* and *g*. Frequently, the baby combines a consonant sound with a vowel sound and produces a kind of syllable, such as *ba* or *ga*. Toward the end of the **babbling** period, the baby frequently repeats such syllables over and over, so that you may hear "dadadadadadadada" or "gigigigigigigi" or

Box 6.1 The Links Between Babbling and Words

Many linguists have concluded that the child's preword sounds have little or nothing to do with the later development of words and sentences. We know, for example, that deaf children babble, although they do not spontaneously form words or sentences, which suggests that babbling may be a quite independent phenomenon. Perhaps the child is merely exercising her vocal cords or "playing" with her sounds.

In addition, analysis of the actual sounds children use in babbling and in the early words shows that while babbling may involve quite a wide range of sounds, the early words use only a few sounds. So there is a sharp *reduction* in the infant's sound repertoire (at least those he uses) between the babbling and the word stages. The sound repertoire heard in babbling is very similar among infants exposed to different languages, but the sounds the child uses in forming his first words tend to be those used in the actual language he is hearing.

Erik Lenneberg (1967) and others have suggested that the shift from babbling to words occurs as a result of fundamental changes in the child's neurological development. The baby can't learn to create words and sentences until a certain amount of brain growth has taken place, and that necessary growth has not occurred until about the end of the first year. Before this development, the baby's babbling and other sounds may be more in the nature of play, just as wiggling his fingers is a kind of play. With the beginning of real language—words and sentences—his activity seems to be more purposive, more guided by the intent to communicate.

But there are *some* connections between the early babbling and later development. For example, Kiki Roe (1975) has found that boys whose babbling peaked early (at 3–5 months) had higher scores on "infant IQ tests" at 9 months than did infants whose babbling peaked at 7 months. It may simply be that the early babblers are on a faster maturational timetable than the late babblers, which would be consistent with Lenneberg's position. But it may also be that the parents of the early babblers talked more to them. Gertrude Haugan and Roger McIntire (1972) have found that babies will babble more if you imitate their sounds, smile at them, or just pay attention when they are vocalizing. So the early babblers may just have more attentive parents.

If we put these two studies together, we might guess that infants whose parents talk to them a lot may babble earlier and may show more rapid intellectual development. We might also guess that their later language would be speeded up, too. There isn't a whole lot of information on this point, but there does seem to be a link. In one study, J. McV. Hunt taught the caregivers in an Iranian orphanage to provide lots of extra verbal stimulation to the babies in their care (Hunt, 1976; Pines, 1979). The infants who experienced this extra stimulation later had very rapid vocabulary growth. So early stimulation and later language may well be linked. But this still doesn't tell us whether babbling *by the infant* is a requirement for later words or sentences.

more complex combinations. This apparently endlessly repetitive game is one example of a process called **echolalia.** Children often repeat (echo) the sounds or words they have just heard. During the babbling phase, the baby echoes herself.

Several features distinguish the babbling period from what has gone before. First, the child simply spends more time making noises, particularly when she's alone. Second, the sounds the infant makes begin to have **intonational patterns** that are something like speech. The baby may use rising inflections or a speechlike rhythm, even though she is still babbling apparently meaningless sounds.

Understanding Language

Most babies do not use their first words until they are about 11 or 12 months old. But can they understand some of the things adults say to them even before they use words themselves? Stated another way, does *receptive language* (comprehension) develop before *expressive language* (spoken language)?

Among 2- and 3-year-old children, the answer is clearly yes. Such children understand most forms of sentences before they use them spontaneously in their own speech. For example, a 2-year-old may understand negative sentences but may not use words like "not" correctly (or at all) in her own creations (Fraser, Bellugi & Brown, 1963).

Among prelanguage infants, the evidence is not so clear-cut. Virtually every parent of a 6–12-month-old baby can give you examples of sounds the child appears to understand. The baby may look toward his father when the word *dada* or *daddy* is spoken or reach for a favorite toy when its name is given. This certainly looks like comprehension of the words, and it probably is. But just as in the case of the chimp language, we have to be sure that the child's looking or touching or choosing is not cued by some signal other than the sounds of the words. If your baby looks upward when you say *look up,* you might easily conclude that she understood the words. But perhaps you are inadvertently moving your eyes, your hand, or your chin upward, too.

The sort of careful experiments we will need to check on early comprehension haven't been done yet, so we can't be sure. But it is a reasonable bet that the 8- or 12-month-old understands at least some of what is said to her.

The First Words

The first word is an event that is eagerly awaited, but parents often miss the very earliest words because they are frequently sounds that are not at all like the words in the language the child hears. A baby does not one day say "dog" in a loud, clear voice. Even "dada" is often unrecognizable, or it may not mean "daddy" at all. To give you some idea of the sort of words a child may "invent," take a look at Table 6.1.

This is the full word vocabulary of 1-year-old Brenda. For a sound to be considered a word at this stage, it doesn't have to be the same as any sound spoken by the adults around her; it doesn't even have to be used to refer to a *single* event or object.

Table 6.1 Brenda's First Words at Age 1

Word	Used to refer to, or apparent meaning
nene	"milk," "juice," "bottle," "mother," "sleep"
awa	"I don't want"
da	"doll"

Source: Scollon, 1976, p. 44.

But it does require, as Scollon (1976, p. 42) puts it, "A systematic matching of meaning and form." Brenda used one word (*da*) only when referring to a doll. She used *awa* in a lot of different situations, but always when the apparent meaning was "I don't want." She used *nene* to refer to a whole collection of objects or people that have something to do with nurturing or comfort.

Brenda's first words illustrate the two ways in which young children seem to use their early individual words. First, they use words merely to label objects, such as cookie or doll. But second, they use single words as **holophrases**—the single word, when combined with the context in which it is used, conveys a whole sentence of meaning. If the baby slams his cup down on the highchair and says "*milk!*" a whole message is involved, such as *Bring me my milk right now!* If the baby sees the milk bottle being brought out of the refrigerator and says "*milk*" in a quieter tone, something like *There's my milk* is conveyed. Patricia Greenfield (Greenfield & Smith, 1976) has argued that these holophrases are the precursors of later, more complex sentences; the child is using gestures, tone of voice, and situations to add the full meaning to the individual words. Later the child learns how to add other words to make longer sentences that will do the same job.

Adding New Words

The rate of acquisition of the early words is fairly slow. Katherine Nelson (1973) found that most of the 18 children she studied took three to four months after the first words to achieve a ten-word vocabulary. But past the ten-word point, words seem to be added quite rapidly. In Nelson's study, the average age at which children had 50-word vocabularies was about 19–20 months. Children differed in the age at which they began the vocabulary growth process, but nearly all of the children in this study showed a pattern of slow initial growth followed by a spurt after the first ten words.

Brenda, the child whose first words are listed in Table 6.1, developed new words rapidly in the months that followed. By 14 months, she had an eight-word (sound) vocabulary; by 19 months, she used 39 different words.

Types of New Words But what *kind* of words does the child use in the early months of this stage? The old-style attempts to study this problem involved analyses of the child's speech into the same parts of speech categories as those used by adults, such as adverbs, adjectives, and verbs. But such a procedure artificially applies an adult category system to the child's language. A better strategy is to group the words into categories that appear to represent different functions in the child's speech. Nelson (1973) arrived at six such categories:

1. Specific nominals—words the child uses to name unique objects, such as people and animals.
2. General nominals—words the child uses for classes of objects, animals, and people, such as ball, car, milk, doggie, girl, he, that.
3. Action words—words the child uses to describe or accompany actions or to express or demand attention: go, bye bye, up, look, hi.
4. Modifiers—words that refer to properties or qualities of things: big, red, pretty, hot, all gone, there, or mine.
5. Personal-social words—words that say something about the child's feelings or social relationships: ouch, please, no, yes, or want.
6. Function words—words that have only a grammatical function, such as what, where, is, to, or for.

Table 6.2 shows the percentages of words in each category used by Nelson's 18 subjects in their first 50 words. As you can see, the vast majority of the child's earliest words are used to name or refer to classes of objects.

Another thing Nelson noticed was that most of the earliest words, even those that named objects or people, had something to do with action, with things that the child could do. For example, names of the child's toys are quite common (ball), as are names of foods (milk, cookie). The interesting point is that it appears that the amount of exposure to the object or word is not the only factor that determines whether or not the child will learn the word at this early stage. Each child's selection of

Table 6.2 Percentage of Words in Six Main Categories Used by a Group of Children in Their First 50 Words

Type of Word	Percentage
General nominals (ball, car)	51
Specific nominals (Spot, Daddy)	14
Action words (go, look, hi)	13
Modifiers (big, hot, all gone)	9
Personal-social words (please, yes)	8
Function words (what, is, or)	4

Source: Nelson, 1973, p. 18.

words is different, but each vocabulary seems to contain a great many labels for things the child can play with or manipulate, that make interesting noises, or that move in interesting ways. Perhaps, like that of the very young infant, the toddler's attention is still captured to some extent by things that move. But she also learns early the words for things she can act on herself in various ways.

Later Vocabulary Growth

Beyond the first 50 words, as any parent knows, vocabulary growth continues at a rapid pace. There isn't much recent research on this aspect of language, since most psychologists and linguists in the past decades have been more interested in *which* words a child learns than in how many. But the older data we have are probably still valid. Figure 6.4 shows the findings from a study by Smith over 50 years ago.

The First Sentences

Much more interesting than the mere addition of words to the child's vocabulary is her growing ability to string those words into sentences. The first two-word sentences usually appear at about 18 months. For some months after this, the child continues to use single words as well as two-word sentences. Eventually, the one-word utterances drop out almost completely, and the child begins to use three- and four-word sentences and to create more complex combinations of words.

Again, there seems to be order in the process of the develop-

Figure 6.4 The increase in vocabulary over the first six years of life. Notice that after a slow start, the rate of increase becomes very rapid and is maintained at that rapid level throughout early childhood. (Source: Adapted from Smith, 1926.)

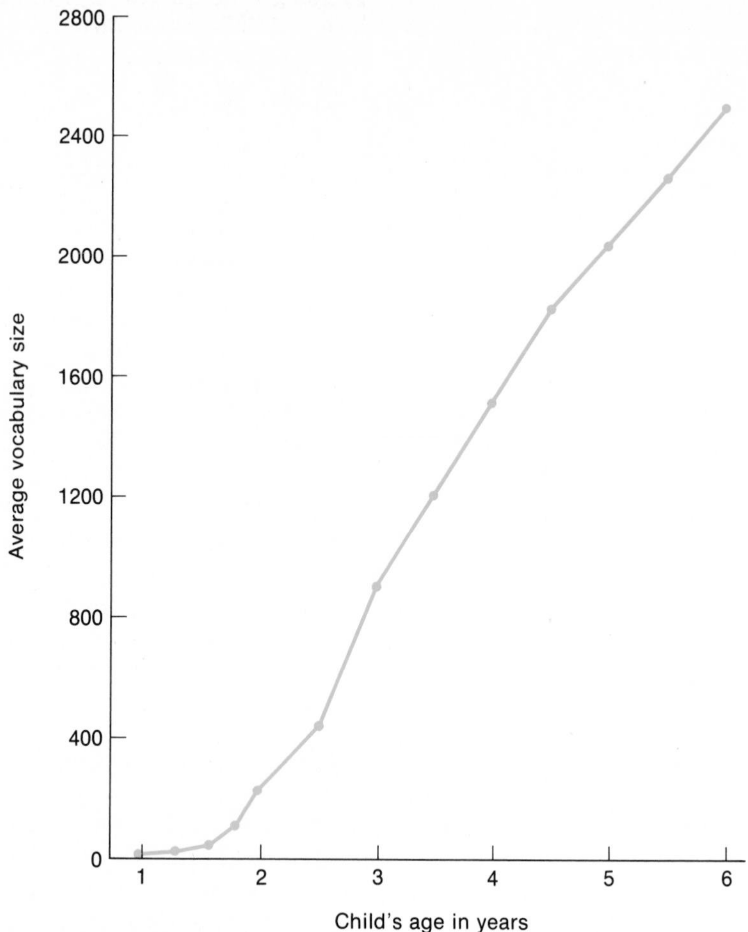

ment of grammar (or **syntax,** to use the more technical term). Linguists now commonly divide the process into two stages.

Stage-1 Grammar

There are several distinguishing features of the earliest sentences. First, they are shorter—usually two or three words. Second, the first two- and three-word sentences are *simpler.* Nouns, verbs, and adjectives are usually included; but virtually all the other grammatical markers (which linguists call **inflections**) are absent, including the *s* for plurals, the *ed* for verb endings, the possessive markers, and auxilary verbs. Because only the really critical words are present, the sentences of the very young child are sometimes referred to as **telegraphic speech.** The child's language is rather like what we use when we send a telegram. We keep in all the essential words—

usually nouns, verbs, and modifiers—and leave out all the prepositions, auxiliary verbs, and such.

Not only is the child's spontaneous speech simpler in this way, but her imitations are as well. If you ask a child of 20 to 24 months to say "I am playing with the dogs," the child is likely to say "Play dog" or "I play dog"—thus omitting the auxiliary verb (*am*), the verb ending (*-ing*), the preposition (*with*), the article (*the*), and the plural ending (*s*).

The other feature of this earliest sentence construction I want to underline is that from the beginning, the child's sentences are *creative*. Just as you can create totally new sentences following the rules of our grammar, so the very young child seems to construct totally new sentences as well. Children make sentences they could not have heard, for example, "A more water," "Out a car," or "Allgone sticky." Older children construct more complex, but still novel, utterances, such as "Cowboy did fighting me." What all of this sounds like is that the child has a grammar of his own and that he is constructing sentences that conform to that grammar, just as you follow the rules of adult grammar. As Katherine Nelson says, "If we take care to look at the child's system, however, we can see that the child does not make mistakes. The child's system may not match the adult system in various ways, but it is our job to determine what the nature of the system is, and how it develops, not to identify its 'errors,' which are errors only from a different systematic point of view" (Nelson, 1977, p. 118).

Following this logic, linguists have attempted to study the child's earliest sentences as if they were a foreign language and to write a grammar for it. What kind of rules does the child seem to be following? Do all children use the same kind of rules? And how do the rules change?

Early Attempts at Writing a Stage-1 Grammar Martin Braine was one of the first to attempt to write a grammar for the sentences of young children. He listened to three children—Gregory, Andrew, and Steven—all of whom were in the beginning stages of concocting two-word sentences. He began simply by collecting as many different sentences as he could from each child and then tried to see if there were any rules built in. You can see Braine's preliminary analysis of Gregory's first sentences in Table 6.3. Gregory had a small collection of words that he used in many different combinations: *see, pretty, my, it, nightnight, byebye, hi, big, more,* and *allgone.*

Braine called this small list of especially important words *pivot words;* the bigger group of words, which the child combined with the pivot words, he called *X words.* Other linguists have called the second group *open words.*

Table 6.3 Gregory's First Sentences

14 combinations with *see*, such as: see boy, see hot, see sock	nightnight office
31 combinations with *byebye*, such as: byebye plane, byebye man, byebye hot	nightnight boat
pretty boat	hi plane
pretty fan	hi mommy
my mommy	big boss
my daddy	big boat
my milk	big bus
do it	more taxi
push it	more melon
close it	allgone shoe
buzz it	allgone vitamins
move it	allgone egg
	allgone lettuce
	allgone watch
	Plus 20 unclassified sentences, such as: mommy sleep, milk cup, oh my see

Source: Braine, 1963, p. 5.

After studying Gregory's sentences, as well as those of Steven and Andrew, Braine came to the conclusion that at the simplest possible level, the child seems to use a rule something like this: Pick a pivot word, and then combine any X word with it. If this description of what the child is doing is valid, then any adult should be able to follow that rule and "speak childese" as well as the child does.

To me one of the most intriguing aspects of this approach to the study of child language is that it begins to make sense out of the really peculiar combinations that children come up with. Look again at Gregory's sentences. "Byebye hot" is a combination that we would never make, as is "Allgone shoe" or "Allgone vitamins." But given the child's grammar, those sentences make perfectly good sense—both to the child and to the adult listeners.

Later Grammatical Analyses While a *pivot grammar* (as Braine's description came to be called) seemed to be a good first approximation of what young children were doing, it became clear rather quickly that the child's early sentences were actually more complex than Braine had supposed.

Most important, the pivot grammar concept seems to gloss over some interesting **semantic** (meaning) distinctions that occur in the child's first sentences. For example, young children frequently use a sentence made up of two nouns, such as *Mommy sock* or *sweater chair* (to use some examples from Lois Bloom's 1973 analysis). In a simple pivot grammar, the word *Mommy* would probably be considered a pivot word. But such a classification misses what the child was saying in some instances. The child in Bloom's study who said *Mommy sock* said it on two different occasions during a day. The first time was when she picked up her mother's sock and the second was when her mother put the child's own sock on her foot. In the first case, *Mommy sock* seems to mean Mommy's sock—a possessive relationship. But in the second instance, the child seems to convey "Mommy putting on my sock," which is an *agent* (Mommy)—*object* (sock) relationship.

So hidden within the apparent simplicity of the pivot grammar are important complexities. From the very earliest two-word sentences, the child appears to be able to express a series of different relationships. She can express location, as in *sweater chair*, possessive, as in *Mommy coat*, recurrence, as in *more milk*, and so on. In adult language, each of these different relationships is expressed with different grammatical forms. Since the young child often uses the same kinds of word combinations to express these different relationships, it is easy to miss this complexity. But if you listen to the child's language in context, you can see that the child is indeed expressing a rich array of relationships from the very earliest sentences.

Stage 1 continues for about a year or less, depending on the overall rate of the child's linguistic development. During this time, the child's sentences get longer. In the terminology of linguistics, his **mean length of utterance** (abbreviated MLU) increases. But he still doesn't add the grammatical inflections (such as plurals, past tenses, or auxiliary verbs).

Stage-2 Grammar

The beginning of stage 2 is defined by the first use of any of the grammatical inflections and continues for several years. Children differ markedly in the ages at which they arrive at this stage and in the rate at which they move through it, but within this stage, there are some important regularities.

Adding Inflections Roger Brown (1973) has found that among English-speaking children there is a general order in which the various inflections are added. The preposition *in* appears very early, for example, as do plurals. Some irregular verb endings are also heard early, such as *went* or *saw*. Auxiliary verbs such as *am* or *do* and possessives such as *its* come along later in the series. In some recent research, Stan Kuczaj (1979) has added to this list. He finds that suffixes are learned before prefixes.

Overregularization A second intriguing phenomenon of stage-2 grammar is **overregularization** or overgeneralization. This is what the two children arguing about the goldfish were doing, and we see it in the use of past tenses as well.

In English, many of the most frequently used verbs have irregular past tenses (*go/went; see/saw; am/was; come/came; do/did*), while most of the less-used verbs have regular past tenses, adding *ed (play/played)*. Many young children learn a small number of irregular past tenses and use them correctly for a short time. But then, rather suddenly, the child seems to discover the rule of adding *ed* and overgeneralizes this rule to all verbs. Stan Kuczaj (1977, 1978) has found that 3–5-year-olds are particularly prone to show this kind of "error." In fact, 5-year-olds make the more complex "error" of adding *ed* to the *past* tense, as in *ated* and *wented*.

Development of Questions Still a third regular development during stage 2 is in question asking. Let me look at just one type of question, those that begin with a *wh* word (who, what, when, where, why), to illustrate the changes.

Take the following sentence (that describes me once a day): *The red-faced jogger is wearing fancy shoes.* How do you turn that into a question with a *wh* word at the beginning? There are three necessary changes:

1. We must add a *wh* word.
   The red-faced jogger is wearing what?
2. We must move the *wh* word to the beginning of the sentence.
   What the red-faced jogger is wearing?
3. We must move the auxiliary verb (in this case, *is*) to a position just after the *wh* word.
   What is the red-faced jogger wearing?

Obviously, when adults create questions of this kind, we are totally unaware of having gone through those three processes. But the child doesn't go from statements to questions in a single leap. In fact, each of the three steps I've listed represents a distinct stage in development of questions in the child's language.

In the very earliest stage of asking questions, the child doesn't add the *wh* word at all. She simply speaks ordinary two- or three-word sentences and raises her voice at the end, such as:

See hole?

Adults do this, too. It's perfectly legal in adult English to imply a question with the tone of voice, as in "You're coming?" rather than "Are you coming?" But *all* the child's early questions take this form.

Somewhat later the earliest *wh* questions emerge, but what the child apparently does is to stick the *wh* word onto the beginning of one of her ordinary sentences without changing the sentence around at all (McNeill, 1970), such as:

Where my mitten? or *What me think?*

Still later the child begins to cope with the auxiliary verbs, such as *is*, *do*, and *are*. These words show up in the child's questions but not in the right place:

What my trailer he should pull?

Why it's resting now?

Finally, as a last stage, the child manages to turn the verbs around the right way and produces *wh* questions that sound more or less like those of an adult.

This series of changes is delightful to listen to. But it is important for theorists, too, since in the process, the child creates sentences she could not have heard but which make excellent sense within the rules of her own grammar.

Later Language Development

By age 5 or 6, a child's language is remarkably like that of an adult. She can construct most kinds of complex sentences and can understand most. Despite this excellent skill, however, there are some specific kinds of "errors" that still occur and some systematic changes that take place over the elementary school period. For example, children of 5 and 6 have difficulty with passive sentences such as "The food is eaten by the cat." Children don't spontaneously produce many passive sentences at this age and have more difficulty understanding this construction than they do the active version ("The cat is eating the food"). They also make more mistakes with pronouns (as in "Him and me went to the movies") than do teenagers (although this error is still fairly common among adults). The 5- or 6-year-old also has to relearn the irregular verbs after the period of overregularization, and this process may take several years.

This continuing growth in language usage and understanding by the child can be seen well past age 5 or 6. The child's vocabulary also continues to grow rapidly, and her sentences become more varied in structure and more complex during elementary and high school years. So language development does not end at kindergarten or first grade. Still, the really giant strides in language development occur between 1 and 5 years of age, as the child goes from single words to complex questions, negatives, and commands. Changes after that are more in the nature of refinements of the basic skills rather than acquisition of completely new skills.

Overview of Grammatical Development

Several points deserve emphasis before we go on to other topics:

1. From the very earliest point in the child's sentence construction, there are clear regularities. The child constructs sentences by some kind of rule system, however simple.
2. The rule system is not the same as that for adult English (or adult Urdu, Greek, or any other language) but is unique to children.
3. As far as is known now, the same kinds of rules, in roughly the same order, are used by children learning all sorts of different languages. We find something like a stage-1 grammar in children learning Russian, French, or whatever.
4. The child's grammar changes gradually in a sequence that seems roughly the same for all the children who have been studied. There are vast differences among children in the *rate* of language development, but the sequence seems to stay about the same.
5. Children's language is creative from the very beginning. The child is not just copying sentences that she has heard; she is creating new ones according to the rules of her own grammar.

Box 6.2 Bilingual Children

There are two groups of **bilingual** children we need to think about. The first are those who are exposed to two languages at home from the earliest days of life. One child I know, for example, has a father who speaks English to her and a mother who speaks Hebrew to her. In the second group of bilingual children are those who are basically monolingual until they reach preschool or school age, at which point they have to learn a second language for school. This has been the case for many Spanish-speaking children in parts of the United States, as well as other minority groups. Until recently, it was also frequently the case for French-speaking children in Canada.

The first group—the fully bilingual child—is more interesting to those who study language, since such children may help us to understand more about the normal process of language development. The second group is of greater concern to educators, who must work out ways to teach English as a second language.

Despite these interests, there isn't a great deal of research about bilingual children. But let me summarize what we think we know at this stage.

There is both good news and bad news about children raised with two or more equal languages. On the negative side, their early language seems to be a bit slower. It takes them longer to get to, and through, stage-1 grammar, for example. On the positive side, they seem to understand quite early that there is a distinction between a word and its meaning. Since a child learning French and English, for example, learns two words for dog (*dog* and *chien*), he works out pretty early that a given meaning can be expressed several ways (Ianco-Worrall, 1972).

Dan Slobin (1978) observed this process in his daughter Heida, who lived in Europe with her family from about age 2½. By age 3, she was asking for the words in other languages: "What does bread mean in German?" Sometimes she would even ask, in English, for the English translation, as in "What is spoon called in English?" It is as if she had understood that she was hearing several languages but did not realize that she herself spoke one of them.

Despite a slower start, the bilingual child quickly makes up the ground. In later years, these children do as well as monolingual children on measures of language skill and on IQ tests (Peal & Lambert, 1962).

Children learning the second language at school age, or a bit earlier, pose a different problem, particularly if they must be taught in the second language. These children find the early grades in school very tough going indeed, and many of them never catch up later. Nicholas Anastosiow and Michael Hanes (1976) argue for two strategies in dealing with school children for whom English is a second language:

> *(1) Delay the teaching of reading until the child has mastered English, or preferably (2) teach the child to read in (his first language) and after the third or fourth grade switch to English.* (Anastasiow and Hanes, 1976, p. 144)

Many school systems, faced with the need for bilingual education, have opted for the second strategy. They provide instruction in the child's native language while simultaneously teaching English as a second language. The results are not all in on this procedure, but given what we know about reading and about language development, it seems like a sensible option.

Semantic Development: Word Meanings

Thus far I have been talking primarily about the development of grammar (syntax), the way in which words are strung together into sentences. But an equally important issue, which has only lately drawn the attention of psychologists and linguists interested in language development, is the development of **semantics,** or word meaning. How does the child come to understand the meanings of words? What meanings does she attach to the words she uses?

When my daughter was about 4, she would come to me and ask when "Sesame Street" was going to be on. "In a little while," I would say. Thirty seconds later she would be back asking again. She used the word *little* and the phrase *little while* herself, but she did not attach the same meanings to them that I did. Fifteen minutes is a little while to me, but it was a long time to her.

The fundamental task for the researcher studying semantic development is to discover how the child uses a particular word. What meaning does it have for him? Let me look at just one set of research studies—studies of early nouns—to illustrate this point.

The basic issue in this research has been whether the child attaches too-specific or too-general meanings to the words. Does the child use the word *dog* to refer only to the family collie (a too-specific usage), or does he use the word to refer to all four-legged creatures, including cats, cows, horses, and others (a too-general usage)? The answer seems to be that most children do some of both.

Of the two, *overextention* of a word is perhaps the more common. Eve Clark (1975) has collected a whole set of examples of this kind of usage by children from age 1 to 2 years and has found that most overextensions are based on the shape of objects or on their movement, sound, or texture—all perceptual aspects of objects. Some of Clark's examples are in Table 6.4.

From the child's point of view, part of the problem is that he doesn't know very many words. So if he wants to talk about something, point out something, or ask for something, he has to use whatever words he has that are fairly close. So overextensions may arise out of the child's desire to communicate and may *not* tell us that the child's underlying concepts are overextended. The example Clark (1977) uses is of a child who wants to call attention to a horse. She may recognize that the horse is different from a dog, but she doesn't know the word. So she says "doggie!"

Table 6.4 Some Examples of Overextensions in the Language of 1- and 2-Year-Old Children

Word	Object or event for which the word was originally used	Other objects or events to which the word was later applied
mooi	moon	cakes, round marks on windows, writing on windows and in books, round shapes in books, tooling on leather book covers, round postmarks, letter *O*
buti	ball	toy, radish, stone spheres at park entrance.
sch	sound of train	all moving machines
em	worm	flies, ants, all small insects, heads of timothy grass
fafer	sound of trains	steaming coffee pot, anything that hissed or made a noise
va	white plush dog	muffler, cat, father's fur coat

Source: Adapted from Eve V. Clark. "Knowledge, context, and strategy in the acquisition of meaning." In Gurt 1975: Developmental Psycholinguistics: Theory and Applications. Edited by Daniel P. Dato. Copyright 1975 by Georgetown University, Washington, D.C., 83, 84.

Regardless of the reason, overextensions of word usage are common in the language of young children. But very narrow word usage also occurs. Lois Bloom (1973), for example, observed that one of her daughter's earliest words, *car,* was used only to refer to cars moving in the street; she did not use the word when she was riding in a car or for cars that were standing still.

Nelson (1973) has also found both broad and very specific words in the 50-word vocabularies of the children she studied. Paul, at 18 months, included the words *bear, duck, frog, bird,* and *fish* among his 30-word vocabulary, whereas Jane at age 15 months had seven words for different kinds of food in her 50-word vocabulary: *cracker, cookie, cake, water, noodles, turkey,* and *pea.*

What these several bits of information tell us is that the earliest vocabularies of children refer to concepts that may be either quite specific or quite broad. But do we have any evidence that the earliest vocabularies, or the earliest concepts, are ever **superordinates**—that is, words that refer to several different classes? Does Paul have a word (or a concept) for *animals?* Does Jane have a word for *food?*

Until fairly recently, most psychologists and linguists agreed that the 1–2-year-old child did *not* have superordinate concepts or words that were used that way. But Katherine Nelson (1977), among others, has recently argued that we may be underestimating the child in drawing such a conclusion. As it happens, in Nelson's own study of early vocabulary, Jane did not use the word *food* and Paul did not have a word for *animal.* But other observers have noted examples of superordinates. Many children, for example, use the word *toys* quite early to refer to several different kinds of things to play with, for which they also have separate words. So the child might use the word *ball, doll,* or *blocks* and also use the word *toys,* apparently to refer to the whole batch. It may well be, then, that even children this young have some rudimentary idea that words can be grouped together into larger classes and that those larger classes have different words, although there is still considerable debate about this point.

Overall, the process of semantic (word meaning) development seems to be less regular and more individual than that of syntactic (grammar) development. Whether this seems to be so because we have not yet devised the techniques that will reveal the underlying orderliness or whether there really is less systematic order is just not clear at the moment. What we do know is that meanings children attach to their early words are different from meanings used by adults and that the development of full adultlike semantic understanding is a long and apparently gradual process.

Individual Differences in Language Development

I have emphasized throughout this chapter that the *rate* of development differs considerably from one child to the next. The range of "normality" is quite large. The first word usually is heard when the child is somewhere around 1 year old. Yet it's not at all uncommon for the first words to be delayed until he is 14 or 16 months, and a few children don't speak a single word until they are 18 months old. These children are normal, not retarded or brain damaged. On the other side, there are a very few children who begin using words as early as 7 or 8 months. The range of normality, then, is almost a full year, from 8 to about 18 months.

The spread is even wider in the construction of early sentences. The earliest two-word sentences recorded for any child studied thus far were uttered at about 10 months. The average

Figure 6.5 This shows the rapidly increasing sentence length for three children studied intensively by Roger Brown and his colleagues. The break between stage-1 and stage-2 grammars occurs at about 2½ words per sentence. As you can see, the pattern of change is very similar from one child to the next, but the ages at which the steps occurred differed markedly among the three children. (Source: Adapted from Brown, 1973, p. 55.)

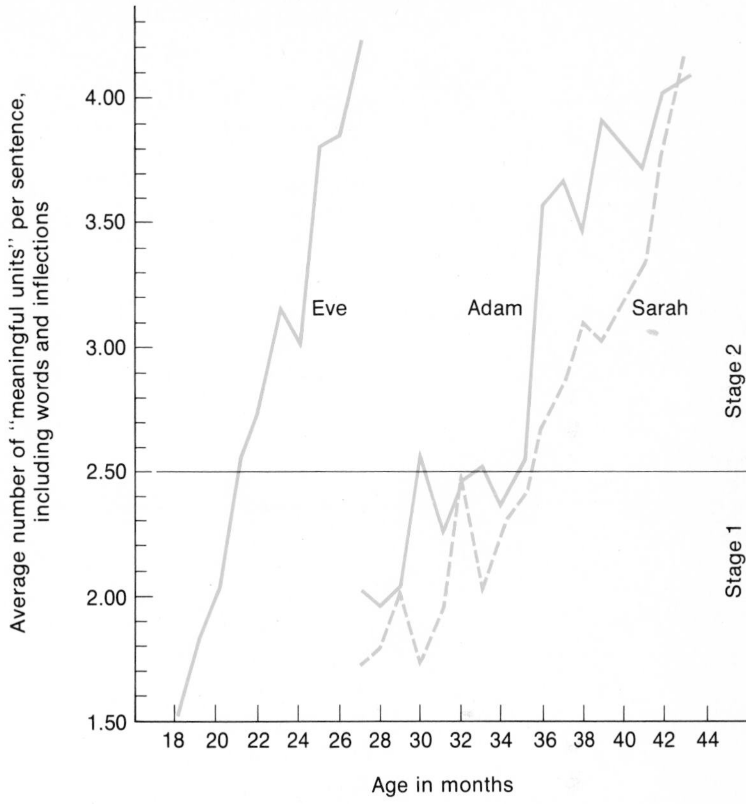

age is about 18 months, but again it is quite normal for the first sentences to be delayed until perhaps 24 months or even 26 or 28 months. You can see some of this normal range in Figure 6.5, which shows changes in sentence length for three children studied by Roger Brown.

What do we know about those differences in rate? Are boys or girls consistently faster? Are children from poor families consistently slower or faster in language development?

Sex Differences

One of our cultural stereotypes about women is that we are more talkative, more "verbal." As you can see in the summary of sex differences in language in Table 6.5, there is *some* basis for this stereotype, although much less in the early years than among teenagers.

Among infants and young children, there are relatively few sex differences, and there is disagreement about those. In the early research on language development (up to about 1950), the results seemed to show that girls were consistently superior in language development in the first few years of life. But more

Table 6.5 Summary of Sex Differences in Language Development and Skill

Skill	Direction of
Infancy and Early Childhood	
Vocabulary	Girls *may* be a bit ahead up to about age 3, but many studies show no difference.
Amount of talking	Girls again may talk a bit more in the early years, although this finding, too, is not consistently reported.
Grammatical skill	There is probably no difference.
Articulation (speaking clearly)	Girls are better and remain better through school; more boys need the help of speech therapists in elementary school.
Adolescence	
Spelling	Girls are better on the average.
Punctuation	Girls are better on the average.
Comprehension of complex written material	Girls are better on the average.
Verbal reasoning	Girls are better on the average.

Source: Based on an analysis by Maccoby and Jacklin, 1974.

recent research doesn't always show this. My conclusion is that there may be some slight advantage for girls at this age, but it is not large and doesn't last long. At the same ages, girls do *not* seem to have any advantage in grammatical development.

Among adolescents, nearly all measures of language ability show girls to be superior on the average. This doesn't mean that every female is better than every male. The two distributions overlap a great deal. But if you take a number of girls and a number of boys and give them tests of these skills, the average score for the girls will ordinarily be higher than the average score for the boys.

Social Class Differences

The usual assumption is that poor children have less good language. That turns out to be true for vocabulary but probably not for grammatical development. Poor children seem to know fewer words (Lesser, Fifer & Clark, 1965) but they appear to go through the same sequence of grammatical development at about the same rate.

Box 6.3 Black English

Many black children in the United States speak differently from whites. Until fairly recently, teachers and others who dealt with black children assumed that this "difference" was really a "deficit," that the children just hadn't learned properly. But a number of linguists, perhaps most notably William Labov (1972), have argued that what black children learn is a perfectly legitimate dialect of English. Anastasiow and Hanes give a lovely example:

A petite five-year-old black girl sits across from an experimenter. He asks her to repeat a sentence spoken in typical school English and played on a tape recorder. The tape recorder plays the sentence: "I asked him if he did it and he said he didn't do it." She smiles, presses down the folds of her thin dress and says, "I asks him if he did it and he says he didn't did it but I knows he did." (Anastasiow & Hanes, 1976, p. 3)

This child had simply translated the Standard English sentence into Black English.

When linguists have analyzed Black English, they have found that there are very specific differences, particularly in the use of verbs. In the Green Road Housing Project in Ann Arbor, Michigan (a largely black neighborhood), the children say "He be gone" when they mean "He is gone a good deal of the time." They say "He been gone" when they mean "He's been gone for a long while." Other translations are from such sentences as "He is going home" into "He going home" or "Every day when I come he isn't here" into "Every day when I come he don't be here."

The Black English versions are predictable enough so that it is quite possible for someone to learn the dialect. But is the Black English dialect less complex? Philip Dale (1976), among others, argues that it isn't. When the black child says "She come home" instead of "She came home," it doesn't mean that there is no past tense in Black English; rather it means that both the present and the past tense are formed with the word *come*.

Putting all this together, we find that the English spoken by most school-age black children is about as complex *within its own rules* as is the English spoken by whites. It is a different dialect, but it is as subtle and varied as Standard English.

Virtually everyone—educators and linguists—agree on this basic point. The argument now is over whether the black child should be allowed or encouraged to use the Black English dialect in school or whether he should be required to use Standard English. Parents in the Green Road Housing Project went to court to force the Detroit school system to provide better training for their teachers so that the children could use their dialect in school. They won the suit (*Time*, August 20, 1979.)

Some of you will have noticed the parallel between this issue and the problem of bilingual education for children who come to school speaking an entirely different language. Perhaps we ought to apply the same argument to the Black English dialect and begin the teaching of reading and other school subjects using the child's primary language. Standard English could then be taught later as a second language.

The other side of the argument is taken by many black leaders who emphasize the fact that, like it or not, Standard English is the basic language of the culture and black children need to become skillful in its use. They think that children should use the standard language from the beginning.

At the moment, we simply lack the evidence that would permit us to choose. The whole issue will no doubt be with us for a long time to come.

Probably the differences in vocabulary come about simply because the middle-class child gets talked to more from the earliest days of life (Kilbride, Johnson & Streissguth, 1977) and is exposed to many more words. But although the poor child may hear fewer words and sentences, the array of sentences she hears seems to be sufficiently rich for her to extract the grammatical rules.

The study of grammatical development among the poor is complicated by the fact that many poor children, particularly those from minority groups, are exposed to a dialect of English rather than Standard English. In Box 6.3 I've discussed some of the arguments about one such dialect, **Black English.**

Summary

1. Language is an arbitrary system of symbols that permits us to say, and to understand, an infinite variety of messages.
2. Prior to about age 1, linguists talk about the "prelinguistic" phase, which is broken up into steps: crying, cooing, and babbling.
3. Babbling does not seem to be a necessary precursor to later language, although that is still being debated.
4. At about 1 year of age, the earliest words appear. The child begins to use sounds with consistent references.
5. By age 2, most children have a vocabulary of 50 words; many children have much larger vocabularies by then.
6. The first two-word sentence is usually heard at about 18–24 months. Stage-1 grammar continues until the child begins to add grammatical "inflections" like plurals and past tenses.
7. The child's language is creative from the time of those earliest sentences; she constructs sentences she has never heard.
8. Stage-2 grammar involves the sequential addition of grammatical inflections and the construction of longer and more complex sentences. There is orderliness in this stage, too, with some prepositions and plurals added very early; auxiliary verbs come later.
9. Elementary school-age children continue to improve, particularly in the use of passive sentences and in the development of appropriate use of irregular verbs.
10. The development of word meanings (semantic development) follows a less-predictable course. Most children use both overgeneralized and undergeneralized words in their early vocabularies.
11. There are marked individual differences in the rate at which children develop language. Variations in rate of as much as a year are within the normal range.
12. There are hints that girls may be a little faster in early vocabulary and pronunciation, but not in grammar. This difference disappears until adolescence, when girls become clearly better at most verbal tasks.
13. Poor children are also somewhat slower in vocabulary development, but apparently not in grammatical skill.
14. Many black children, particularly those living in poverty, learn a distinct dialect called Black English. It has different grammatical rules but appears to be as complex as Standard English.

Key Terms

Babbling The repetitive sounds, usually involving at least one consonant and one vowel, shown by a baby from about 6–12 months.

Bilingualism The comprehension and use of two languages.

Black English The dialect of Standard English spoken by

many black children in the United States.

Cooing An early stage during the prelinguistic period in which vowel sounds are repeated, particularly the *uuu* sound.

Echolalia A characteristic of the babbling period. The child repeats (echoes) the same sounds over and over.

Holophrases The expression of a whole idea in a single word. They are characteristic of the child's language from about 12–18 months.

Inflections The grammatical "markers," such as plurals, possessives, past tenses, and equivalent.

Intonational patterns Variations in voicing, such as loudness and pitch variations, that help convey meaning.

Mean length of utterance Usually abbreviated MLU; the average number of meaningful units in a sentence. Each basic word is one meaningful unit, as is each inflection, such as the *s* for a plural or the *ed* for a past tense.

Overregularization The tendency on the part of children to make the language regular, such as using past tenses like "beated" or "goed."

Prelinguistic phase The period before the child speaks his first words.

Semantics The study of word meaning.

Superordinates Any word (or concept) that subsumes other words or concepts, such as *fruit*, which includes apples and oranges.

Syntax Grammar or sentence structure.

Telegraphic speech A characteristic of early child sentences in which everything but the crucial words is omitted, as if for a telegram.

Suggested Readings

Anastasiow, N. J., & Hanes, M. L. Language patterns of poverty children. Springfield, Ill.: Charles C. Thomas, 1976.
If you are interested in Black English and in comparisons between this and the language used by poor whites and other groups, this is an excellent book.

Bloom, L. "Language development." In F. D. Horowitz (Ed.), Review of child development research (Vol. 4). Chicago: University of Chicago Press, 1975.
If you need a shorter summary of language development than offered in Dale's book (see below), this is a good source.

Brown, R. "Development of the first language in the human species." American Psychologist, 1973, **28,** 97–106. Reprinted in N. S. Endler, L. R. Boulter & H. Osser (Eds.). Contemporary issues in developmental psychology (2nd ed.). New York: Holt, Rinehart and Winston, 1976.
A wonderful, brief description of some of the major findings in language development, written in Roger Brown's usual clear style. Bear in mind when you read this, however, that a great deal of research has been done since 1973 that changes some of his conclusions.

Dale, P. S. Language and development: Structure and function (2nd ed.). New York: Holt, Rinehart and Winston, 1976.
There are several other texts about language development, but I like this one the best. Not simple, but very informative and complete.

Pines, M. A head start in the nursery. Psychology Today, 1979, **13** (No. 4), 56–68.
Maya Pines interviews J. McV. Hunt in this article, and Hunt describes his study of orphanage children in Iran. The article also touches on some of the findings on the effects of Head Start, and on the question of a "critical period" for language development.

Premack, A. J., & Premack, D. Teaching language to an ape. Scientific American, 1972, (Oct.) **227,** 92–99.
An extremely interesting account of language training of Sarah the chimpanzee.

Terrace, H. S. How Nim Chimpsky changed my mind. Psychology Today, 1979, **13** (No. 6), 65–76.
This is the paper that has sparked the current controversy about whether chimps "really" create complex sentences or not. Very interesting paper.

Project 6.1 Beginning Two-Word Sentences

In Table 6.3, I've given you the sentences used by Gregory when he was at stage 1 of grammatical development. In this project, I want you to collect a similar sample of sentences from a child.

You will need to find a child as close to 20–24 months as you can. He or she should be speaking at least some two-word sentences. Arrange to spend enough time with the child so that you can collect a list of 50 different utterances, including one-word utterances and two-or-more-word sentences. Write them down in the order they occur and stop when you have 50. It may take several sessions with the child before you get this many, and you may find it helpful to have the child's mother or some other adult play with the subject while you listen and write things down. Whenever you can, make notes about the context in which each sentence occurred.

When you have your list of 50 utterances, consider the following questions:

1. Are there pivot words? Which words are they?
2. What are the X words in your child's grammar?
3. Is your child still at stage 1, or has he moved into stage 2? How can you tell?
4. How many different *meanings* can you detect, such as subject-object relationships or attribution (for example, *big boat*).
5. What is the mean length of utterance (MLU)? If you want to figure this out more precisely, follow the rules suggested by Brown (1973, p. 54) or Dale (1976, p. 19).

Preview of Chapter 7

Explaining Language Development

In the last chapter, I tried to give you some feeling for early language—what it sounds like and how it changes. Children's words and sentences have a lilt and cadence all their own and are a delight to listen to, even if we cannot always understand them. There is still a great deal to be done in describing the process of early language development, and perhaps I should leave it at that. But to me the *why* questions are equally fascinating and worth exploring.

I have several reasons for taking an entire chapter for such an exploration. From my point of view, the most important reason is that the whole topic is full of intriguing puzzles. Some of you probably share my fascination with puzzles. Put a puzzle in front of us and we want to solve it! But for you nonpuzzle lovers, explanations of language development are also important because they illustrate vividly the differences between the several types of theories of development. In particular, we see in this area a very clear contrast between learning approaches and maturational approaches—between external and internal explanations.

Finally, there are some issues I want to raise about the application of our knowledge of language development to special groups of children, specifically, deaf children and children whose language is delayed.

The Basic Alternatives

Stop and think about a child learning language within a family. What is your first notion about how that learning occurs? The first thought most people have is that children must learn through imitation. In fact, it seems so obvious that children learn to talk by imitating others around them that most nonpsychologists (or nonlinguists) don't bother to think any further.

Imitation Obviously, imitation has to play some part. After all, a child growing up in a family speaking English learns English, not Chinese or Greek. The child also ordinarily learns to speak with the same accent as the one spoken around him. As an example, in the United States, people in New England speak with a different accent than those in the South, and this is clearly the result of imitation.

A form of imitation is also involved in the sort of exchange in which the child asks "What's that?" or points to some new object. The adult supplies the word and the child repeats it. There is a period during the child's second year when this is a fairly common exchange, so this type of imitation may be involved in learning new vocabulary words.

But imitation does *not* work very well as an explanation when we take a closer look at the acquisition of grammar. When we do that, we immediately come up against some difficult facts.

First, from the very beginning, children create sentences that are quite unlike any that an adult would construct. These sentences cannot be imitations because no adult uses them. The overgeneralized *ed* endings, like *wented, goed,* or *beated,* are good examples. Some of the sentences children create while they are learning about questions, such as *"Why it can't turn off?"* illustrate the same thing.

Second, when children do imitate sentences spoken by adults, they reduce or convert them to conform to the forms of their own grammar. I have already made this point in talking about the "telegraphic" quality of children's language. It turns out that their imitations are as telegraphic as their spontaneous speech. This is illustrated nicely in the following exchange quoted by Dan Slobin (1968, p. 441):

Mother: It fits in the puzzle someplace.
Adam: Puzzle? Puzzle someplace?
Mother: Turn it around.
Adam: Turn around?
Mother: No, the other way.
Adam: Other way?
Mother: I guess you have to turn it around.
Adam: Guess turn it round. Turn round.

Adam imitated his mother, but he converted her sentences into ones like those he was producing spontaneously.

Still a third argument against imitation as the sole explanation of language development lies in the fact that most of us don't actually speak very well. We don't use complete sentences a lot of the time, and we do make a lot of grammatical mistakes. This becomes startlingly clear if you read a written transcript of an oral conversation. Some of you may have read the Watergate transcripts, for example. Aside from all the "deleted expletives," one of the most notable things about those White House conversations was what poor language they were! Obviously, the conversations were clearer to those who were actually there, since the tone of voice, gestures, and pauses all helped to convey the meaning. But objectively speaking, the sentences themselves were pretty unclear.

When we talk to children, most of us manage to be a bit clearer than that—a point I'll be coming back to later. But a great deal of what a child hears is in the form of incomplete or grammatically incorrect sentences. Yet despite that, the child seems to learn a basically correct grammar, just as you and I know how to speak "correctly," if we put our minds to it, and can write correctly most of the time as well. So we "know" the correct language, even if we do not always speak it. If the child learned all her grammar from listening to other people talking, how would she ever learn the basic, correct forms?

Imitation, then, plays some role in language development, but it can't be the central process, no matter how much common sense says otherwise. Where does that leave us? What other alternatives do we have? The next thought most people have is that the child must be *taught* language in some direct way, mostly by her parents. This leads us to the various reinforcement theories of language development.

Reinforcement

B. F. Skinner (1957) made a major attempt to apply his general reinforcement theory to language development in his 1957 book, *Verbal Behavior*. At one point he says, for example,

> A child acquires verbal behavior when relatively unpatterned vocalizations, selectively reinforced, gradually assume forms which produce appropriate consequences in a given verbal community.
> *(Skinner, 1957, p. 31)*

In this sentence, and throughout his book, Skinner is clearly arguing that the adults around the child *shape* the child's first sounds into words, and then the words into sentences, by selectively reinforcing those that are understandable or "correct." In addition, the assumption is that the child will use whatever "verbal behavior" (to use Skinner's term) that gets her what she wants. This second part of the theory has come to be called the **communication pressure hypothesis** by students of language development. Perhaps, according to this view, it is the pressure to communicate clearly—leading ultimately to the reinforcement of getting what she wants—that pushes the child toward better and clearer pronunciation and longer and more complex sentences. Let me explore both these types of reinforcement theory more fully.

Direct Shaping For direct shaping to be a major factor in language development, at least two things have to be true. First, we must observe that parents do *in fact* show systematic shaping of the child's language. For example, do parents pay more attention to a child when he speaks in grammatically correct sentences? Do they correct his grammar directly? Do they withhold treats like cookies until the child says "I want a cookie" instead of just "Want cookie"?

Second, assuming that parents *do* use some kind of system of reinforcement to shape language, do such patterns of reinforcement have any noticeable effect on the child's grammar?

The available evidence suggests that the answer to both questions is "no." For example, in one study, Roger Brown, Courtney Cazden, and Ursula Bellugi (1969) recorded the conversations between mothers and children and checked to see if the mother's responses to the child depended on the grammar of the child's language or on the presumed meaning. They found that in nearly all cases, the mothers seemed to be responding to the "truth value" of what the child said and not at all to the grammatical complexity of the child's sentences. In fact, mothers are remarkably accepting of children's language efforts. They try to interpret incomplete or primitive sentences and very rarely correct the child's grammar or withhold treats or other reinforcements until the child says it better. So as far as we can tell, systematic shaping of the child's language just doesn't occur.

But what would happen if one *did* try to shape the child's language? Would this technique improve the child's sentences? Martin Braine (1971) provides a lovely anecdote about an attempt of this kind that he made with his daughter:

> I have occasionally made an extensive effort to change the syntax of my two children through correction. One case was the use by my two-and-a-half-year-old daughter of *other one* as a noun modifier. . . I repeatedly but fruitlessly tried to persuade her to substitute *other* + N [Noun] for *other one* + N . . . The interchange went somewhat as follows: "Want other one spoon, Daddy"—"You mean, you want THE OTHER SPOON"—"Yes, I want other one spoon, please, Daddy"—"Can you say 'the other' spoon?"—"other . . . one . . .

spoon"—"Say . . . other"—"Other"—"Spoon"—"Spoon"—"Other . . . spoon"—"Other spoon. Now give me other one spoon." Further tuition is ruled out by her protest, vigorously supported by my wife.

(Braine, 1971, pp. 160–161)

Braine's example, of course, is just one anecdote, and we don't have very much systematic information on this point. But what data we have support Braine's conclusion. For example, in her study of early vocabulary growth, Katherine Nelson (1973) found that those mothers who systematically corrected poor pronunciation of words and rewarded good pronunciation had children who developed vocabulary *more slowly* than did children whose mothers were more accepting of the child's pronunciation.

All of this certainly doesn't provide much support for this type of reinforcement theory of language development. In contrast, however, therapy for language delayed children is heavily based on reinforcement principles. Children who speak very little, or who seem to have no language at all, have been systematically reinforced for making sounds, and then sentences, with some success. I've described some of this research in Box 7.1.

Communication Pressure The other half of the reinforcement theory of language is that the child learns to speak better in order to get her needs met better. You'll hear parents saying things like "Jennifer didn't learn to talk right away because there was always someone right there to give her what she wanted. She didn't have to talk." If this really happened, it would be evidence in support of a communication pressure hypothesis. But it probably isn't true.

First off, when you listen to children's language, you notice that once they start to talk, they improve in their grammar and pronunciation pretty rapidly, *even though their early, imperfect versions were understood and produced the desired results*. Philip Dale gives a good example of this:

My son Jonathan at age twenty-six months requested the repetition of some favored activity by saying *'gain*, with a characteristic rising intonation; at age thirty-one months he said *Do that again, Dad*. The latter sentence is far more complex linguistically but no more effective.

(Dale, 1976, p. 141)

More formal evidence for this point comes from a study by Roger Brown and Camille Hanlon (1970). They recorded and then analyzed the conversations between three mothers and their children, beginning when the children were about 1 year old. They categorized the children's sentences into two groups,

Box 7.1 The Use of Reinforcement Principles for Children with Delayed Language

There are several distinct groups of children with delayed language. The preschool teacher may see children who seem to understand what is said to them but who talk very little. In this instance, the problem is to get the child to talk, to put sentences together, and generally to *use* language. A second group, usually labeled **autistic,** includes children with more serious problems who talk little if at all and who also relate poorly to the people around them. They often show ritualized behaviors, such as rocking or head banging, and their speech often consists of a kind of echolalia, in which they repeat whatever is said to them.

Both types of language delay have been successfully treated using reinforcement principles. For example, Nancy Reynolds and Todd Risley (1968) worked with a 4-year-old girl in a Head Start program who talked very little. The teachers were told to pay attention to the child *only* when she said something. If she asked for a toy, the teachers withheld the toy until the girl answered some questions about the toy. Under these conditions, the girl talked more and more. When the teachers later switched the pattern so that they paid attention when the girl was *not* talking, she quickly stopped talking again. Clearly, then, the *amount* a child says can be increased or decreased, depending on the reinforcements.

Several programs of group language training for Head Start children are based on the same principles, such as the Bereiter-Engelmann (1966) programs.

Much more difficult is the problem of teaching language to the child who seems to have no language to begin with. Ivar Lovaas (1966, 1976) has undertaken this task with a number of autistic children who made some noises but otherwise neither used nor understood language. The program has several steps. In step 1, the child is reinforced for *any* noise. Usually food is used as the reinforcer. The therapist carries around raisins or a bowl of applesauce and pops a bit into the child's mouth right after any noise. In step 2, the child is reinforced only if his vocalizations come right after some speech by the therapist; and in step 3, the child is gradually shaped until he is imitating the sounds the therapist made, such as "m" or "a." These steps are not achieved rapidly. Sometimes *thousands* of repetitions are required.

What Lovaas is doing in this procedure is teaching the child to imitate sounds. But this is still not language. Once the child imitates individual sounds, he still has to learn words and then combine words into sentences. Lovaas has found that autistic children who are totally mute at the beginning of therapy rarely get to the point of combining words into new sentences. Autistic children who already imitate sounds when therapy begins, however, frequently can be helped to develop fairly complete language.

It is important to point out that although both of these reinforcement systems for fostering language can help to increase or improve language in the children, neither one proves that *normal* language development works that way. The child Reynolds and Risley worked with obviously already knew the language; she just didn't use it. And the autistic children Lovaas works with rarely acquire the full creative use of language that the normal child develops without intervention. Nonetheless, behavior modification techniques are extremely helpful in cases in which the normal developmental system breaks down.

---

primitive sentences and *well-formed sentences*. For example, *This here, huh?* would be classed as a primitive sentence, while *This goes here, doesn't it?* would be called a well-formed sentence. The mothers' replies were also grouped into two categories, *sequiturs*, and *nonsequiturs*. A sequitur was any reply by

Figure 7.1 In a family like this one, in which there are many children, the youngest child frequently is slower in developing language. Many parents assume that this is because the child doesn't have to talk—everyone in the family leaps to give the baby what he wants or needs. That is, they assume that there is no "communication pressure," so the child doesn't use language. However, research does not support this variation of reinforcement theory.

the mother that answered the child's questions, gave the child what he wanted, or involved some clear continuation of the child's thought. For example, if the child said, *Where Christmas cookies?* and the mother said, *We ate them all*, that would be a sequitur.

Nonsequiturs, in contrast, included replies by the mother that didn't answer the question, answered it in some nonconnected way, or merely repeated what the child said. For example, if the child said, *What time is it?* and the mother replied, *Uh huh, it tells what time it is*, that would be a nonsequitur. She had apparently misunderstood the child's question, and answered the question she thought he had asked.

If there really is communication pressure, Brown and Hanlon should have found that the mothers more often used sequiturs after well-formed sentences, and nonsequiturs after primitive sentences. If that happened, it would "push" the child toward better sentences in order to be understood. But that did *not* happen. In this study, the mothers were just as likely to respond with sequiturs to primitive as to well-formed sentences. The child was just as likely to get a cookie saying *Want cookie* as *I want a cookie*. So why does his language become more complex? If the communication pressure variation of reinforcement theory were correct, it shouldn't. But it does.

As a final argument against reinforcement theories of language acquisition, let me call your attention once again to the genuinely *creative* aspect of the child's language. He puts together things he hasn't heard before, just as you constantly create sentences that you have never heard. Furthermore, remember that the child's early language, like yours, is apparently governed by rules. How could a child whose language learning has been entirely governed by the parents' reinforcements be creative and rule governed? And how can we explain the fact that all children apparently go through very similar stages in their sentences?

Overall, then, neither imitation nor reinforcement theories are adequate to account for what actually happens between parents and children, and neither accounts well for the child's own linguistic achievements.

Parents as Facilitators of Language Development

At this stage, you've probably concluded that parents don't do anything at all that is important in the child's language development. But we have still one more alternative to look at. Even though children don't learn language solely from direct imitations of their parents, and even though parents don't reinforce language in a systematically selective way, maybe parents *facilitate* language development in important ways.

There are at least three things that parents do that may make a difference: (1) They talk to their child. (2) They use simpler language with the child than with others. (3) They sometimes "expand" the child's primitive sentences into longer, grammatically complete sentences. Do any of these things make a difference?

Talking to the Child It may seem a little silly to get to this simple a level, but it *does* seem to matter how much the adults around a child talk to her. Children who get talked to a lot seem to develop vocabulary a little faster in the early years than those who are talked to less (Engel, Nechlin & Arkin, 1975; Elardo, Bradley & Caldwell, 1977; Clarke-Stewart, Vander Stoep & Killian, 1979). In one study, Alison Clarke-Stewart (1973) observed and listened to a group of 36 infants and their mothers. She found that the mothers who talked to their children more had children who knew and used more words at 17 months. You can see the main contrast in her results in Figure 7.2. Clarke-Stewart didn't analyze the specific content of what the more-stimulating and less-stimulating mothers said; it could be that it is something about *what* they said rather than how *much* they said that is critical. But for the moment, the simplest hypothesis is that sheer quantity makes a difference in the early stages of language development. The child who hears more has more information to work with. When *no one* speaks to the child, as in the case of severely abused children like Genie—whom I've described in Box 7.2 on page 208—no language develops.

Figure 7.2 These results show that mothers who talk to their children a lot have children who develop a larger vocabulary during the first two years. (Source: Clarke-Stewart, K. A., 1973, p. 82. With permission of the Society for Research in Child Development, Inc.)

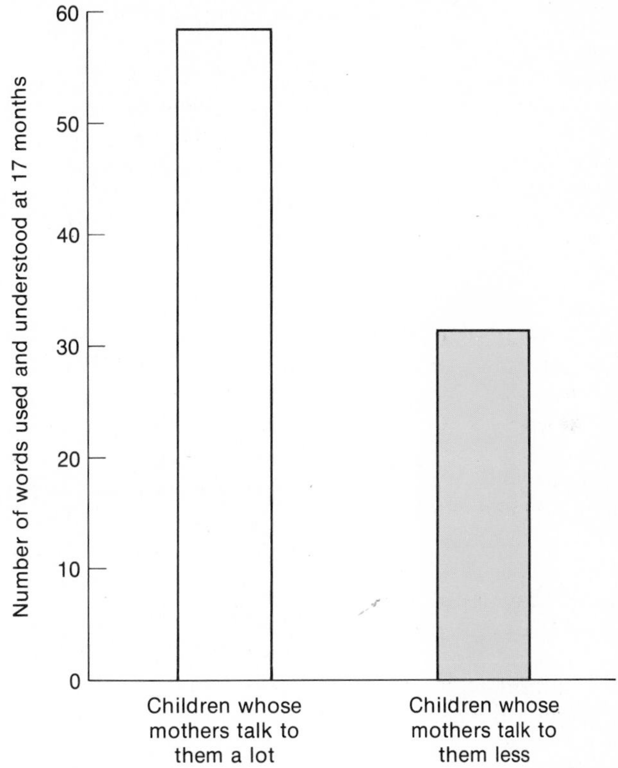

Simpler Language to the Child When adults talk to each other, we often use fairly long and complex sentences with clauses and subclauses. But when we talk to 2-year-olds, we use shorter, grammatically simpler forms. Linguists have come to call this talk to children **motherese** or sometimes "baby talk." Dan Slobin (1975) has given some marvelous examples of the difference between adult to adult speech and motherese from the recorded conversations of a black woman speaking to her 26-month-old son and to her sister. I've taken some excerpts from each for Table 7.1 to give you some feeling for the contrast.

The key features of motherese, as Rochel Gelman and Marilyn Shatz (1977) have found in their research are the following:

1. The sentences are grammatically well formed.
2. The sentences are fairly short.
3. The grammatical forms are fairly simple; there are many questions but few past tenses, for example.

Box 7.2 Genie: The Child No One Talked To

Genie's early months of life were relatively normal. She grew normally and seemed alert and interested to the pediatricians who saw her. From that point on, things went downhill. Her father didn't want her and refused to allow her mother to spend much time with her. She became very sick when she was 14 months old, and the pediatrician who saw her said he thought she was retarded, too. That was all the father needed. He used this "diagnosis" to justify the neglect and abuse that followed.

From the time she was about 2, Genie spent nearly all of her time in a single bedroom of their house, tied to an infant potty seat. Except for the harness that she wore, she was naked. She apparently spent years in this way. When she was taken off the potty seat at night, she was put into a kind of straightjacket and left to sleep in a crib with wire mesh sides and top. No one talked to her, and she couldn't hear other people talking to each other, since her room was in the back of the house.

If Genie tried to attract attention by making noise—to get food, for example—her father often beat her. Her father never spoke to her, even when he was beating her. He growled and barked at her like a dog.

They did feed her. But mostly she ate babyfood and soft foods. This incredible treatment continued until Genie was 13½, when her mother finally did something, and Genie's maternal grandmother found her and rescued her.

Despite the astonishing amount of abuse Genie had endured, she was alert and curious when she was found. She couldn't stand up, since she had spent most of her time sitting on the potty chair. She made almost no noises and didn't talk at all. She weighed 59 pounds and was only 54 inches tall.

After she was admitted to a hospital for treatment of her basic malnutrition, therapists began to record her language and to try to see if she understood anything that was said to her. She seemed to understand a few words, such as "red" and "blue" and "rattle." Over the next months and years, as Susan Curtiss (1977) has reported in her fascinating book, Genie gradually developed some language.

She began to pay attention to the speech of others. She watched people's mouths and tried to imitate sounds. She used a few sounds herself, beginning with *stopit* and *nomore*. And she began to understand a lot of what went on around her. Six months after she was hospitalized, for example, a "teacher asked [another child] who had two balloons how many he had. He said, '*Three.*' Genie looked startled and gave him another balloon" (Curtiss, 1977, p. 15).

At this point, her language development became fairly rapid and followed many of the same patterns as normal language development in the 1–2-year-old child. She seemed to have "pivot" words and had a kind of stage-1 grammar, in which she left out the inflections, just as the young child does.

One of the issues raised by this case study is whether there is some critical period for language development. Erik Lenneberg (1967), among others, has argued that children are most ready to learn language from about age 1 to 5; after that it is much more difficult—if not impossible—for a child to acquire language. Genie's case seems to say otherwise, although the fact that she was treated fairly normally for the first year or so makes it difficult to be sure. She did hear language in the early months, and perhaps that was enough. We also don't know yet if her final language skill will be really normal. But we do know that she is still improving in her language, social, and motor skills. She has come a long way.

Table 7.1 A Selection of Speech by a Mother

To her 26-month-old child:

Come play a game wit' me.
Come look at Mama's colorin' book.
Look at my coloring book?
Is that an Indian?
Can you say Indian?
Watcha been doin' today?
Look at that.
That's a funny picture, huh?

To her sister:

An' then well now his father an' I are separated so he sees me mainly. An' then I try to do things with him and for him an' all to, kinda make up y'know for this.
It gives me a certain amount of consolation which allows me to relax my mind and start thinking intelligently an' putting my effort all in one y'know force goin' in one direction rather than jus' y'know continually feeling sorry for yourself.
But they won't keep him at school because he's too sick.

Source: **Slobin, 1975, p. 287.**

4. The words are spoken in a higher-pitched voice, at a slower pace, and with a lot more variation in pitch and speed.
5. The vocabulary is fairly concrete, and only a small selection of words is used. Compare, for example, the vocabularies of the adult-adult and adult-child language in Table 7.1.

Beyond the basic simplification, the really fascinating thing about the whole business of motherese is that the adult appears to *adapt* her language very carefully to the complexity of the child's language and to the child's level of understanding. Juliet Phillips (1973), for example, has found that mothers gradually increase the length of sentences they use with their children as the children's own sentences get longer. The mother's sentences are always longer than the child's, but she moves ahead slowly, just a notch ahead of the child's language.

Jean Berko Gleason (1977) has also observed that the mothers respond to very specific signals from the child. When we talk to adults, we decide whether the other person has understood or heard us by watching for a whole set of signals. The other adult may nod in agreement, or look us in the eye, or say "um" or "uh huh." But 18–24-month-old children don't do those things when you talk to them, so it's hard to know whether the child has heard or understood. The result is that parents repeat themselves a lot when they talk to children this age: "Where's the ball? There's the ball. Give mommy the ball. That's right, give me the ball. Give it to me." In an attempt to make sure the child understood, the mother ends up repeating or making minor variations on basic, simple grammatical forms.

Obviously, mothers (and fathers and other adults) don't do all this in order to teach the child grammar. They do it in order to communicate with the child. But it's hard to imagine a more useful set of circumstances for the child trying to learn the language. She hears simpler forms and hears them repeated and varied. After many years of assuming that the child did most of the work in developing language, linguists are beginning to see that the conversations between adults and children are crucial elements, too (Brown, 1977; Snow, 1977).

Expansions Another thing that parents do when they talk to children that illustrates the process of adjusting in another way is to expand the child's sentences. If the child says *John shoe*, the mother might say *This is John's shoe*, if the child's meaning seemed to be possessive; or *John is putting on his shoe*, if the relationship seemed to be the action–object relationship. What the parent does, in cases like these, is to add inflections, auxiliary verbs, and all the other grammatical elements that make a complete adult sentence. Courtney Cazden (1965) called this process **expansion;** Keith Nelson (1977) calls it **recasting** sentences. Whatever the label, it is possible that this kind of activity on the part of parents aids the child by demonstrating the relationship between the child's more primitive forms and the "correct" adult forms.

There have been several attempts to check on the importance of expansions experimentally by exposing some children to a concentrated dose of expansions and comparing them to children who had had an equivalent amount of conversation without expansions. Keith Nelson (1977), for example, had adults talk for a total of five hours (in one-hour stretches) to individual children who had not yet developed either complex questions or the future or conditional tense use of verbs. The adults systematically expanded *either* the children's questions or their verbs during the five hours of conversation. What Nelson wanted to see was whether the children would start using the more complex forms in their conversations during the experiment. As it turned out, they did. The children who had listened to expansions of questions moved up a notch in their own questions, and those who had listened to expansions of verb forms began to use the more advanced verbs themselves. So the expansions seem to have helped.

Obviously, parents don't expand their children's sentences nearly as intensively as this. But Nelson's research certainly suggests that this "recasting" of the child's sentences helps her develop the next level of complexity in her own language.

The Child's Contribution

The theories and hypotheses about the child's language I have discussed so far focus primarily on what the child *hears* and how he is reinforced for what he says. The evidence we have certainly points to the importance of the quantity of language around the child, and the simplicity and repetitiveness of it are probably also crucial. But the emphasis thus far has been largely on externals—on what happens *to* the child. What I have left out of the equation is what the child is *doing* with what he hears. Given the evidence we have now, it is clear that no theory of language development can be complete without attention to the child's activity. But just what sort of activity does the child contribute?

Rehearsal

One of the things many children do is a kind of systematic practice or rehearsal of their language. They try out new combinations and new kinds of grammatical order. One linguist, Ruth Weir (1962), made a recording of her son Anthony practicing in this fashion by putting a tape recorder in his room. It was set to turn on automatically when he started to talk to himself. Anthony did a lot of talking before his nap, at night, and just after waking up. Some of the sequences of his soliloquies appear to be rehearsals of various grammatical patterns. Here he seems to be trying out different words in a single place in the phrase:

What color
What color blanket
What color mop
What color glass

In the following, he seems to be rehearsing negatives:

Not the yellow blanket
The white
It's not black

Figure 7.3 Children aged 2 through 4 or so often talk to themselves while they are playing or when they are lying awake in their cribs. Probably this child is carrying on quite a long "conversation" with her doll.

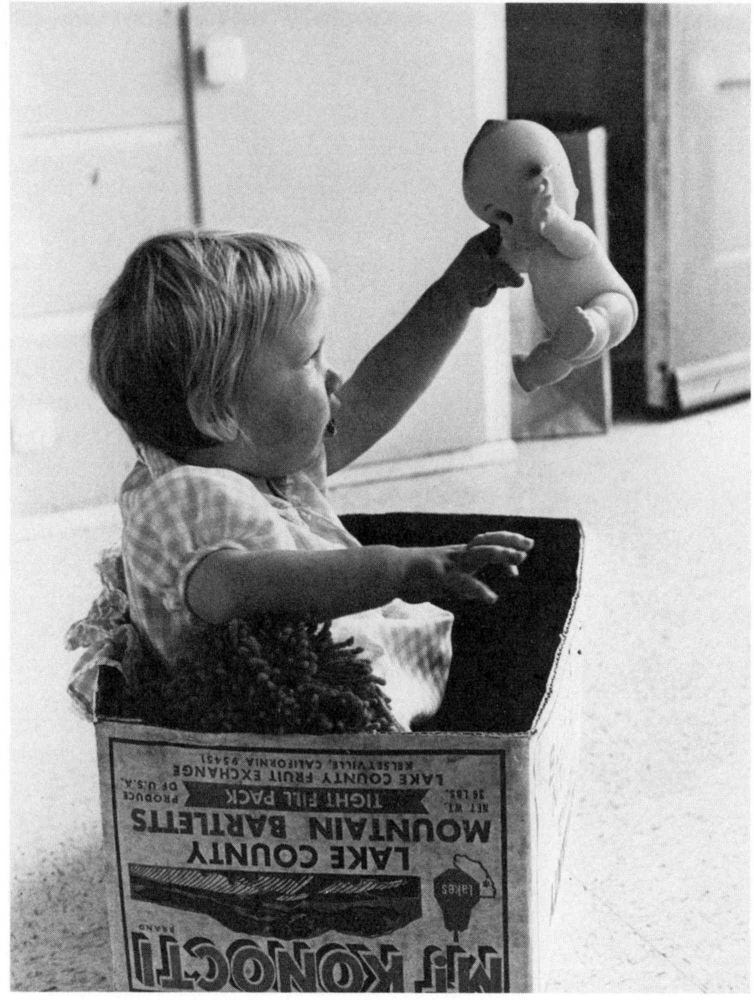

It's yellow

Not yellow

These and other examples from Weir's observations suggest that Anthony enjoyed playing with the sounds of the language. But they also seem to show that Anthony had noticed particular features of grammar or word relationships, and he was trying out the alternatives.

Most other children that linguists have listened to show this same kind of apparently joyful play with words. It reminds us that language is fun for children, not just a chore that has to be performed. But it doesn't tell us how the child learned the basic language forms to begin with. Rehearsal and experimentation of this kind may help the child get a better handle on the forms he does know, but it doesn't explain how Anthony learned such sentences as *What color* in the first place.

The Child's Linguistic Hypotheses

One notion about where the child's understanding of language forms comes from is that he progresses by noticing the regularities in the speech he hears and then applying those regularities to his own speech. In the early stages, he may notice only a few significant features, so his own language has only a few important variations. Gradually, he notices the more subtle aspects of adults' language, and his own language begins to mirror them.

This is basically a *hypothesis testing* model of language development. The process might go like this: The child concludes that "I say X this way," tries it out, sees if he is understood, and matches his try against what he hears back. If this is what happens, then expansions by the parents should be extremely helpful to the child since they provide feedback for his hypothesis testing. This is exactly what Keith Nelson thinks happens:

> To master syntax the child must in some way make comparisons between his or her own sentence structures and those of others. Recasting could aid these comparisons, as the child could compare the ways in which the contrasting sentence structures of the adult's reply and the child's preceding utterance serve to express very similar meanings.
>
> *(Nelson, 1977, p. 106)*

No doubt this is what happens to at least some extent. Nelson's own research shows that recasting helps to further the child's grammar. But I don't think that the hypothesis testing model can explain everything the child does, for several reasons.

First, even though the child hears a lot of motherese, he is still exposed to a lot of language that is ungrammatical or includes incomplete sentences. So the data he has to work with are not perfect, which would make hypothesis generation and testing very hard indeed. Martin Braine offers a delightful example of this problem:

> A case in point occurs on a tape of one of my subjects, Stevie, aged 26 months. Stevie complains to his mother about his elder brother, Tommy, and says "Tommy fall Stevie truck down." His mother, a little harassed, responds by turning to Tommy and saying somewhat threateningly, "Tommy, did you fall Stevie's truck down?" Obviously, his mother has concerns more pressing than the possibility that Stevie may be testing the hypothesis that *fall down*

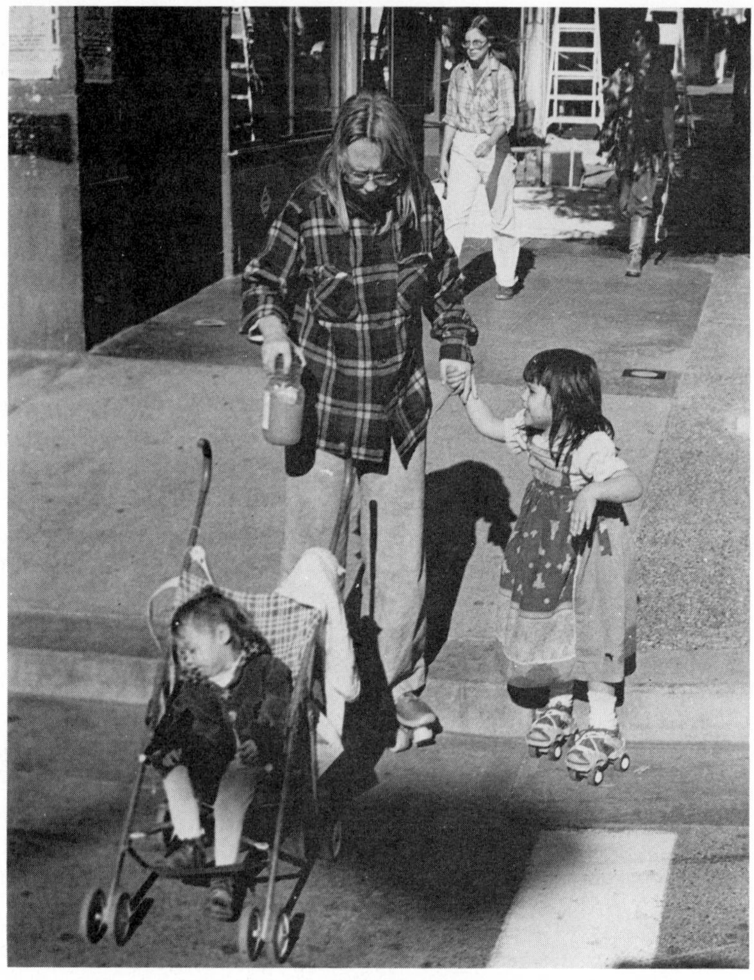

Figure 7.4 Mothers like this one, dealing with the complexities of everyday life, have little time or attention to correct their child's grammar. Yet these children do develop complex grammar anyway. Both research and observation suggest that neither specific training nor correction of improper forms is needed for a child to learn language.

is a transitive verb. When one considers the difficult circumstances under which huge numbers of children are raised, it becomes clear that correcting their infants' speech must be among the least of the concerns of very many human adults.

(Braine, 1971, pp. 159–160)

A second problem with the hypothesis testing idea becomes clear when you go back and think about the development of questions, as I described it in Chapter 6. In passing through the several stages from no questions to a complete form of *wh* questions, the child passes through stages not represented in any adult language she is hearing. If she is proceeding by some sort of analysis of adult speech, why would these intermediate stages be so unlike adults' speech?

A final problem is that the level of ability we have to assume the young child possesses in order to test linguistic hypotheses is very high. We are expecting the child to notice fairly subtle differences, figure out what those differences might mean, and then apply the new rules to his own new sentences. That is a complex process—far more complex than the cognitive skills 2- and 3-year-old children show on other tasks. In sum, it is simply not clear that the young child has yet developed the intellectual skills needed to learn language by hypothesis testing.

The Innateness Model

A number of linguists, perhaps most notably Noam Chomsky (1965) and David McNeill (1970), faced with this whole puzzle, concluded that the only answer was that children had a built-in **language acquisition device.** McNeill argued that basic language concepts are innate, or that they mature during the first year of life. So children's brains may be "programmed" to learn language, just as the newborn seems to be "programmed" to look at the edges of things.

Transformational Grammar But what exactly could it be about language that is built in? Chomsky argues that what is built in is what he calls **deep structure.** He proposes, in essence, that every sentence exists at two levels. The *meaning* of the sentence is contained in the deep structure. That meaning is then transformed into **surface structure,** which is the sentence we actually see or hear. The rules for turning basic meaning into sentences Chomsky calls transformational rules, and the whole system has come to be called **transformational grammar.**

If the basic deep structure meaning were something like

"I like cookies."

this could be transformed into a whole variety of actual sentences (surface structures), such as,

"Do I like cookies?" or

"What do I like?"

If the negative is needed, it becomes

"I do not like cookies."

If a negative question is needed, you apply two different rules and create

"Don't I like cookies?"

If you think back to what I said in Chapter 6 about the basic sequences of grammatical development, it begins to look like the child's earliest sentences are straight out of deep structure. The child uses a few words to convey whole meanings, and the adult listener fills in around the edges. As the child's language improves, what she seems to do is to learn the **transformations** —the rules for turning those basic meanings into various kinds of complex sentences.

The *wh* questions are a good example of all this. Each of the steps the child goes through in creating complete questions represents one part of the transformation from the deep structure to the final surface structure. She starts with the simplest transformation, using the deep structure with a rising intonation. Then she adds the "put a *wh* word at the beginning" rule and finally the rule about the order of the words in the sentence. The intriguing thing is that this explanation helps us to understand why the child goes through stages in her questions that are *not* like anything she is hearing. She's learning the transformational rules one at a time, while the adult applies them all at once.

There are some other bits of information that also fit well with this view of language development. Children learning to speak different types of languages all seem to go through the same kind of process. They all show some kind of stage-1 grammar, using basic two- and three-word sentences to express the same basic meanings (Slobin, 1970). Even deaf children whose parents use no sign language with them have been found to create a sort of stage-1 grammar with their gestures (Goldin-Meadow & Feldman, 1977). (I've discussed some other aspects of language in the deaf in Box 7.3).

Maturation and Language Development The other fact that lends considerable support to some form of biological explanation of language development is that the brain has to mature before the child can learn language at all.

Children are exposed to language from their earliest hours, but they don't begin to babble until they are about 6 months old or to use words until about a year. If you think back to Chapter 4, you'll remember that the cortex develops rapidly during the 6–12-month period and continues to develop during the second year of life as well. Studies of the brain show clearly that language is controlled by a particular section of the cortex, and it is simply not developed until about age 1 (Lenneberg, 1967). This match between the physiological development in the brain and the sequence of language development makes Chomsky's theory far more plausible.

Box 7.3 Language in the Deaf

Linguists have been interested in the language among deaf children for both practical and theoretical reasons. Can we use any of the information about basic language development to help the deaf child? And can the deaf child help us to understand the process of language development better? In particular, studies of the deaf have been used to address the now-familiar question of a critical period in language development. Many deaf children do not learn any language during their early years. Does this interfere with their ability to learn language later? Genie managed at least some language at 13; is the same thing possible for the deaf?

Let me deal with both sets of questions by giving you a summary of what we know at this point about language in the deaf child.

1. The vast majority of deaf children (about 90 percent) are born to *hearing* parents and thus grow up in a world dominated by spoken language.
2. Most deaf children have major deficits in both spoken and written language. They have difficulty speaking; most do not lip-read well; and most read only at the most basic level. Hilde Schlesinger and Kathryn Meadow (1972), for example, found that the teenage deaf children in their study read at about the fourth-grade level.
3. Among the deaf, those with deaf parents usually do *better* on measures of written and spoken language than do those with hearing parents.

It is this last fact that is the most surprising and which raises important practical and theoretical questions. Why would children raised by deaf parents have a better prognosis? Schlesinger and Meadow argue that the major reason is that these children are learning a language—in this case, sign language—at the normal time. Deaf parents use sign language with each other and with their children, so the children learn that language. And their early signs seem to go through the same stages as the spoken language of hearing children. There is a kind of stage-1 grammar of signs, for example; and the inflections are added later, just as with spoken language.

This basic finding provides some support for the existence of a critical period in language development. Children who learn to sign are able to learn spoken and written language later fairly well. But deaf children who are not allowed to use signs when they are small, and thus who do not learn a language at the "normal" time, have more difficulty later.

From the point of view of the parent of a deaf child, the message seems to be fairly clear: A combination of sign language and spoken language works well for the child and for the relationship between the child and the parent. Not only is the child exposed to a language at the normal time, but the child and parent can communicate with each other—something that is very difficult for the hearing parent who does not sign with a deaf child.

Not everyone who works with the deaf agrees with this conclusion. There are still those who argue for the "oral" method rather than the "total communication" method I am advocating here, particularly for elementary-age children. But I find the evidence persuasive.

Problems with "Innateness" Theory Plausible as it is, however, there are still weaknesses in this approach. Most basically, saying that something is "built in" really doesn't tell us very much. As Bruce Derwing puts it:

"Innateness" is a purely negative notion: it means that something has *not* been learned, hence that it can *not* be explained in terms of any known principles of learning. Explanation does not consist in substituting one unknown for another, but rather in accounting for what puzzles in terms of some general principle which *is* known and *is* understood.

(Derwing, 1977, p. 80)

What exactly is the language acquisition device? Does it exist in some physical sense in the brain? How is it programmed? And how does the biological base interact with the input the child receives? If the whole thing is automatic, why does it matter whether the mother expands on the child's sentences or speaks in simpler language?

Theorists like McNeill and Chomsky have rightly focused our attention on the essential biological underpinnings of language. But they have not yet offered us a complete theory of language development.

Putting It All Together

Where does this leave us in understanding language development? I can't offer you a complete theory either, but I can tell you what seems true at this point.

The child seems to learn word meanings first, before she learns grammar. Whether she is "programmed" to listen for the deep structure in what she hears, I don't know. It's equally possible that the child learns about the basic relationships between objects and actions through her own explorations of the world during the first year of life. At about 1, she begins to attach words to these basic meanings and later constructs sentences expressing them.

Second, when she begins to use more complex grammar, she does seem to learn a set of transformational rules. At least that concept comes the closest to describing what happens.

But third, it does matter what people around her are saying. Jean Berko Gleason puts it nicely:

We recognize now that language acquisition is an interactive process that requires not only a child with the appropriate neurological equipment in a state of readiness, but also an older person who engages in communicative interchanges with him, and some objects out there in the world as well.

(Gleason, 1977, p. 200)

So the labels the parents provide for objects, their simpler language to the child, the repetitions and variations on basic grammatical forms, and the expansions of the child's sentences all seem to be important in highlighting the transformational rules for the child.

What I am saying is that each of the theories is partly correct. Children do imitate to some extent; they will talk more if they are reinforced; they do need to have people speak to them in simple language. But they also bring their own concepts and their own analysis to the process. Finally, the child is probably neurologically "wired" to analyze the language he hears in specific ways. At the very least, some maturation of the brain is necessary before language can be fully developed.

Summary

1. Theories of language development are of interest because some of the central theoretical issues in developmental psychology can be contrasted and because there are important practical implications for children with language problems or language delay.

2. An imitation theory of language acquisition is weak because the child's language is creative from the beginning, because children do not imitate sentences wholly but "reduce" them, and because much of what the child hears is imperfect language.

3. A reinforcement theory is weak because reinforcement does not appear to be systematically applied to the child's grammar, and the child's language doesn't seem to be consistently modified by reinforcement. "Communication pressure" also does not seem to account for language change.

4. Reinforcement principles, however, have been successfully used to increase language usage in uncommunicative children and to introduce some sounds and basic language in mute autistic children.

5. The language spoken around the child plays an important role. The quantity of language a child hears and the extent to which the complexity of the adults' language is matched to the child's comprehension and grammatical skill both seem to matter. Expansions of the child's simple sentences also seems to aid the child in adding more complex grammatical elements.

6. The child's role in the process is vital, too. Some linguists argue that the child makes progress through "hypothesis testing"—extracting or noticing regularities in the language of others and then trying it out in her own language. This can be seen in children's rehearsals of sentence fragments, but it cannot account for all of language development.

7. A final theory is that the child's ability to acquire language is built in and matures further during the first year of life. In particular, some linguists argue that what is built in is some ability to scan for or notice transformational rules.

8. No one of these theories is yet a full theory of language development. None accounts for all of what is observed, and none deals extensively with the development of word meaning. There is agreement, however, that language development requires *both* a biological readiness and an appropriate level of linguistic input.

Key Terms

Autism A serious form of disturbance in children, usually appearing in the first year of life, characterized by delayed or bizarre language and problems relating to others.

Communication pressure hypothesis The hypothesis that children learn language in order to get their needs met better.

Deep structure The underlying meaning of a sentence—a concept first proposed by Noam Chomsky.

Expansions A reply to a child's incomplete sentence that repeats the child's sentence with added grammatical features.

Language acquisition device A hypothesized brain structure that may be "programmed" to make language learning possible.

Motherese The word linguists often use to describe the particular pattern of speech by adults to young children. The sentences are shorter, simpler, and higher pitched.

Recasting Another word for expansions. See above.

Surface structure The phrase used by Chomsky to describe the actual grammatical construction of a sentence.

Transformational grammar The phrase used broadly to describe Chomsky's theory of language and language development.

Transformations The rules by which deep structure is turned into surface structure.

Suggested Readings

Curtiss, S. Genie. A psycholinguistic study of a modern-day "wild child." New York: Academic Press, 1977.
This is the book describing the child I discussed in Box 7.2.

Schlesinger, H. S., & Meadow, K. P. Sound and sign. Berkeley, Calif.: University of California Press, 1972.
If you are interested in language in the deaf and in the overall development of deaf children, there is no better first source than this book.

Snow, C. E., & Ferguson, C. A. Talking to children: Language input and acquisition. Cambridge, England: Cambridge University Press, 1977.
This book has a collection of papers on the general topic of motherese and includes papers by most of the major researchers in the area. There is an excellent introduction by Roger Brown and good papers by Snow and others. Fairly technical, but informative.

Project 7.1 Conversation Between Mother and Child

Find a child between $2\frac{1}{2}$ and $3\frac{1}{2}$ years of age and arrange to spend time with the child while the mother is around. If you are working in a nursery school or day-care center or have access to such a setting, it is all right to study a child and the teacher; but you'll have to get the teacher alone with the single child for a period of time.

Record the conversation between the mother (or teacher) and child, making sure that you have the sentences of the two people in the right order. Continue to record the conversation until you have at least 25 sentences for each. You may use a tape recorder if you wish, but you'll find it helpful to write down the sentences as they occur as well.

When you have collected the sentences, reread the sections on imitation and on the parents' role in the child's language development. See if you can detect any of the following patterns in your adult-child conversation:

1. *Expansions:* instances in which the adult repeats what the child has just said, expanding it into a complete adult grammatical sentence
2. *Child's Imitations:* instances in which the child imitates what the adult has just said either exactly or with some kind of simplification so that her sentence is less complex than the adult's sentence
3. *Reinforcement from the Adult:* responses by the adult to the *form* for the child's sentence

Turn in your record of the conversation, along with a page or two of analysis and comment.

Preview of Chapter 8

The Development of Thinking in Children

In the chapters on language, I have had you listening to children. But now listen with a new ear. Listen for their logic and not only for the complexity of their sentences:

"Daddy, please cut down this pine tree—it makes the wind. After you cut it down the weather will be nice and mother will let me go for a walk."

(Chukovsky, 1963, p. 22)

On the subject of the sex of the new baby about to arrive in the family: "It's o.k. if it's a boy or a girl as long as it's a sister."

"As I came down our paved driveway, I said to myself, David, my eye hurts. I guess I'll just have to have some ice cream."

"Why did you make such a mess?" (addressed to his mother, who had spilled her milk. The mother replied, "I had an accident, Honey.") "But you're the Mommy; you're supposed to know your own thing."

All of these delightful conversations are with children between about 2 and 4 years old, when logic is still pretty primitive by adult standards. But there is *a* logic involved, just as the early language of children has *a* grammar. As is true of language, the child's logic gradually changes and becomes more and more like an adult's. It is this developmental process I will be talking about in this chapter.

Some of what I will be describing is fairly complex and theoretical. But I want to emphasize at the beginning that virtually everything I'll be talking about in this chapter has important practical applications, too. For example, the better we understand the thinking of a preschooler, the better we will be at designing day-care or Head Start programs. For parents, too, an understanding of the development of thinking is helpful, since it should tell them something about what they can reasonably expect their children to understand at different ages. As I go along, I'll try to make these applications as concrete as I can.

There are a number of different theoretical approaches to the study of thinking in children, but without any doubt the most influential theory over the past 25 years has been the work of Jean Piaget (Piaget, 1952; Piaget & Inhelder, 1969). Because his theory has structured so much of the current views of cognitive development, I'll be using his overall model in organizing the chapter.

Piaget's Basic Ideas

In order to explain just what it is that Piaget has contributed to the study of the development of cognition, let me start with his own history. Although he was trained as a biologist, in his student days Piaget worked briefly on the development of some of the first mental tests. His job was to give the same test to a whole series of children and to determine whether or not each child had given the "correct" answer on each item. But he soon discovered that the wrong answers were often more interesting than the correct ones (teachers take note). In particular, he noticed that children of the same age often gave the same wrong answers.

Piaget drew a number of important conclusions from these early observations. First, he argued that to understand the child's thinking, we have to shift our attention from *how much* the child could do and look instead at the *quality* of her problem solving. We should look not at what answer she gave, but at how she arrived at that answer.

Second, he suggested that when we begin to look at the quality of thinking, we will find that children of different ages have uniquely different ways of going about solving problems.

These conclusions were fundamentally different from the assumptions underlying the learning theories that had dominated American child psychology from the 1930s to the 1950s. Learning theorists assumed that the same rules, the same qualities or strategies, applied to all people, no matter what their ages. Classical conditioning was classical conditioning; it worked the same way in the newborn and in the adult. The intelligence testing movement, which had flourished in the first half of this century, was also based on an examination of changes in quantity rather than quality. So Piaget didn't fit. In fact, he began his major writing in the 1920s and 1930s but was thoroughly ignored by most North American psychologists until about 1960. The acceptance of Piaget's views in the past 20 years came about, I think, because we had discovered for ourselves that children of different ages approached basic learning problems in different ways. Younger children did learn things more slowly, but they also seemed to use different strategies. Results of this kind forced many learning-oriented researchers such as Tracy and Howard Kendler (Kendler & Kendler, 1962; Kendler, 1963), Sheldon White (1965) and Sonia Osler (Osler & Kofsky, 1966), among many others, to reexamine and expand on the basic concepts of learning theory. How could the changes with age be understood?

Since Piaget's theory had from the start been aimed at just such questions, many developmental psychologists turned to Piaget for new ideas. Since 1960, Piaget's ideas have been the major force in research on children's thinking. What has evolved from all of the work of the past 20 years is a set of basic assumptions about the development of thinking in the child. Let me try to put the assumptions in simplified form.

The Central Assumptions

Inborn Strategies Every child is born with certain strategies for interacting with the environment. The normal newborn can see, hear, touch, suck, and grasp. More important, from the beginning, the child's use of these skills appears to follow basic rules. Recall from Chapter 5 that newborn babies look most at edges and at movement. The baby "explores" the world around him in particular ways. Researchers have not yet studied infants' grasping or listening in as much detail, but there is every reason to suppose that there are built-in biases in the use of these skills as well.

Changes in Strategies These primitive strategies are the beginning points for the development of thinking. But the strategies change gradually as a result of the child's encounters with the world around her. The baby learns to grasp in several different ways, after she has had a chance to handle square, round, oval, and different shaped things; she learns to focus on different parts of objects when she is looking at them; her sucking becomes more skillful and more specific to the thing sucked on. As she gets older and her experience widens, the range of skills and the specificity of the skill increases steadily.

Voluntary Exploration In the beginning, the child's reactions to the world around her are more or less automatic. But over the early months and years, she begins to explore and examine

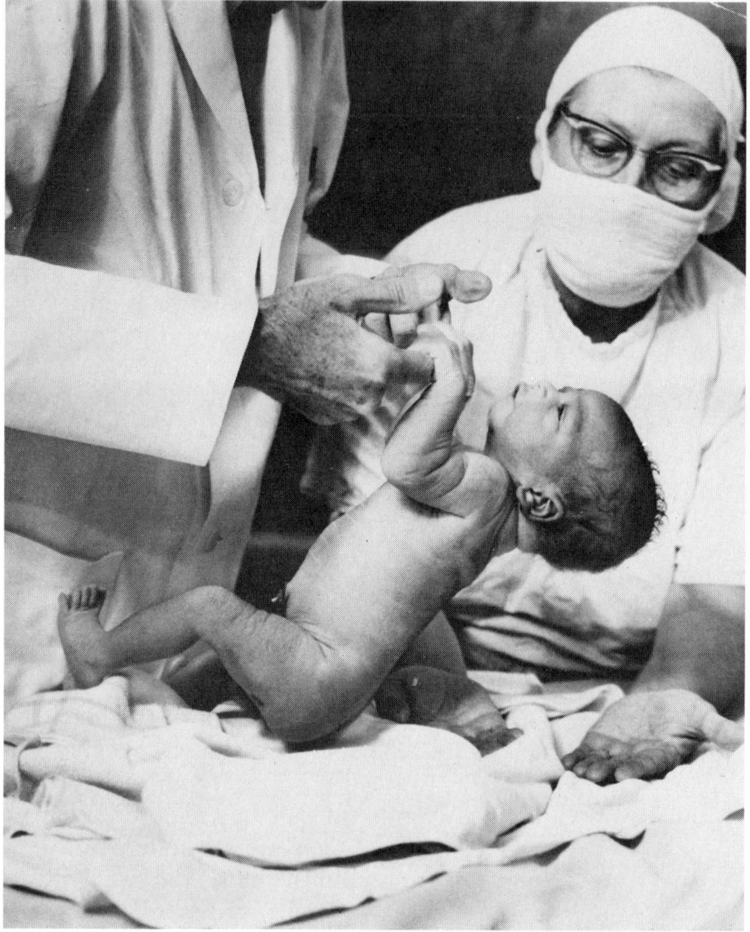

Figure 8.1 The newborn infant begins life with basic strategies, many of them reflexes like this grasping reflex, with which he deals with the world around him. Piaget and most other cognitive developmental theorists believe that these primitive strategies are the beginning points of intellectual development.

with purpose and direction, trying out new combinations, new experiments. In this way, each child "rediscovers the wheel." Each child discovers that objects are constant, that they can be grouped and classified, that things can be added to and subtracted from, and so on.

Sequences These rediscoveries appear to occur in particular sequences. For example, the child can't discover the principles of adding and subtracting until she has figured out that objects are constant. Progress through the sequence of discoveries occurs slowly; and at any one age, the child has a particular general view of the world, a particular logic for exploring and manipulating it. This basic logic changes as she encounters objects or events that don't fit into the system she has constructed, but the change is slow and gradual.

Table 8.1 Piaget's Major Concepts

Concept	Description	Examples
Assimilation	"Taking in" and adapting experience or objects to one's existing strategies or concepts; to "construe reality"	A baby assimilates when she reaches for a toy. In Piaget's language, she "assimilates the toy to her reaching scheme." You assimi late when you classify a new object as a vase or a new person as a Democrat.
Accommodation	Modifying and adjusting one's strategies or concepts as a result of assimilation of new experiences or information	When the baby changes the way she holds her hand as she reaches for round things as opposed to square things, she has accommodated. When you change your concept of what a Democrat is after talking with several self-proclaimed Democrats, you have accommodated.
Scheme	The "action" or strategy, either internal or external, to which the child or adult assimilates	In the infant, sucking, grasping, reaching, and other overt actions are all schemes. In older children and adults, classifying, adding, subtracting, and categorizing (all internal operations) are also schemes.

The Role of the Environment The environment in which the child is growing may affect the *rate* at which she goes through this sequence. A child needs "food for thought," just as much as her body needs food for growth. Some environmental diets are richer than others and seem to foster more rapid progress. Piaget calls the examination of environmental effects on the rate of development the "American question" and has been little interested in it himself. Yet it is an important question, particularly in any society in which there is inequality of opportunity.

I'll be exploring each of these basic assumptions in more detail as we go through the chapter. But before going on to describe the sequence of development Piaget proposes, you need one further tool, namely, an understanding of some of Piaget's specific terms. You will encounter these words in other reading and need to have some familiarity with them.

Piaget's Terminology

I've summarized the three most critical terms in Table 8.1. In order to understand Piaget's language, you have to remember that he started out as a biologist. He begins with the assumption that physical and mental functioning are basically the same, so the terms he uses to describe thinking are often biological terms.

Specifically, he suggests that in the functioning of a person's intellect, as in her physical functioning, there are two fundamental processes that occur at all times: **adaptation** and **organization.** It is the nature of human beings, Piaget says, to organize their experience and to adapt themselves to what they have experienced. Adaptation, at its most basic level, is simply the process of adjusting to the environment. The chameleon adapts by changing color so that its body matches the environment it is in. When you eat your morning granola, your body adapts by digesting it, by adding fat tissue (if you eat too much of it), by utilizing the vitamins and minerals, and so on.

Organization of experience includes such things as combining the information from several senses, such as when you both look at and feel the texture of material, as well as the tendency to classify, to group into sets or systems, which you do every time you see something new and say to yourself, "Oh, that's an ______."

These two processes are absolutely basic to everything we see in the human being. But Piaget doesn't stop there. As you can see in Table 8.1, he uses two new terms—**assimilation** and **accommodation**—to describe two aspects of the adaptation process. Assimilation is the process of taking in new experiences or information; accommodation is the process of changing your basic ideas or strategies as a result of the new experiences.

Finally, there is the concept of **scheme.** This is a hard word to explain, but the closest synonyms are probably *strategy* or *structure*. Schemes are organized patterns of behavior. They may be visible actions, such as grasping for a ball or looking at faces, or they may be internal patterns or strategies, such as classifying things into groups or comparing, adding, or subtracting. Piaget also uses the word **operation** to describe these more complex internal schemes.

It is important to understand that in Piaget's theory, the scheme is not just a passive structure of some kind. It involves activity; it is something the child *does*. This emphasis on activity is crucial. Piaget sees the child, from the beginning, as an active explorer, an *actor* rather than as someone passively *acted on* by the environment. Schemes are the ways of acting; and these ways, these schemes, gradually become more sophisticated, less and less overt, as the child progresses through the developmental process.

Another important aspect of the concept of scheme is that the processes of assimilation and accommodation are the mechanisms for changes in schemes. The child always approaches experiences or objects with her available repertoire of strategies (schemes). That is, she assimilates the experiences to her existing structures or collection of actions. But as a result of accommodation, the schemes change, become more specialized, more differentiated, more complex.

The process is a gradual one. But Piaget, and others who have studied cognitive development from a similar perspective, including Jerome Bruner (1966), Lev Vygotsky (1962), Jerome Kagan (1971), and Heinz Werner (1961), also suggest that there are broad "stages" through which children pass in their gradual progress from infancy to adult reasoning. The basic sequence of stages, as Piaget originally proposed it, has been supported by a great deal of research and is widely used as a framework for describing the development of thinking in children. So let us look at the stages as Piaget describes them.

The Sensorimotor Stage: From Birth to Age 2

During the **sensorimotor stage,** the baby operates almost entirely with overt, visible schemes—with actions such as looking, touching, grasping, and sucking. In the beginning, most of these schemes are basic reflexes; but by about 1 month, if not sooner, the baby has gone beyond the inborn reflexes and approaches objects and people in new ways.

The Substages

Piaget divides the sensorimotor period into six substages, which I've summarized in Table 8.2. The shift from substage 1 to substage 2 corresponds roughly to the shift I described in Chapter 5 from the *second visual system* to the *primary visual system*. There appear to be important changes in the brain that underlie this shift, but Piaget emphasizes that the child's experiences—her assimilations and accommodations—during the first 4–6 weeks of life are also crucial in bringing about this shift. Whatever the source of the change, it is clear that at about 1–2 months, there is a shift from reflexive action to more deliberate explorations.

A second important transition occurs between substage 2 and substage 3, at about 4 months of age. Up to about this time, the baby appears to make little distinction between his body and other objects. But at about 4 months, the infant seems to begin to distinguish between self and other, between body and objects. The most visible sign of this is that he begins to try to repeat actions that have resulted in interesting things happening with toys or other objects.

One excellent example of this given by Piaget is of his son Laurent, who had a mobile hanging over his crib (Piaget, 1952). When he was about 2½ months old, Laurent accidentally hit

Table 8.2 The Six Substages of the Sensorimotor Period Proposed by Piaget

Substage	Age	Characteristics of the stage
1	0–1 month	Almost entirely practice of built-in reflexes such as sucking and looking. These reflexes are modified (through accommodation) as a result of experience.
2	1–4 months	The infant tries to make interesting things with her body happen again, such as getting her thumb in her mouth. Visual and tactual explorations are more systematic. But infants in this stage still do not appear to distinguish between body and outside objects or events. They do not link their own actions to results outside themselves.
3	4–10 months	The infant tries to make external interesting things happen again, such as moving a mobile by hitting it. He also begins to coordinate information from two senses and develops the object concept. He understands, at some level that his own actions can have external results.
4	10–12 months	The infant begins to combine actions to get things she wants, such as knocking a pillow away in order to reach for a toy. She uses familiar strategies in combination and in new situations.
5	12–18 months	"Experimentation" begins; the infant tries out *new* ways of playing with or manipulating objects. Improved motor skills make wider exploration possible, too.
6	18–24 months	Internal representation is now readily apparent; the child uses images, perhaps words or actions, to stand for objects and can do primitive internal manipulations of those representations.

the mobile; it moved; and Laurent became excited, thrashed around, and gurgled happily. But he didn't seem to try to make it happen again. Several days later, Piaget attached a string to Laurent's hand and to the mobile so that when he waved his arms, the mobile moved. Laurent was delighted but still did not figure out that his arm movements controlled the movement of the mobile. But at about 3½ months, Piaget observed that

Figure 8.2 The opportunity to play—to manipulate objects, put them in the mouth, roll them around, or turn them upside down—is crucial for the development of the child in the sensorimotor period. You can see just that sort of exploration in the play of these babies.

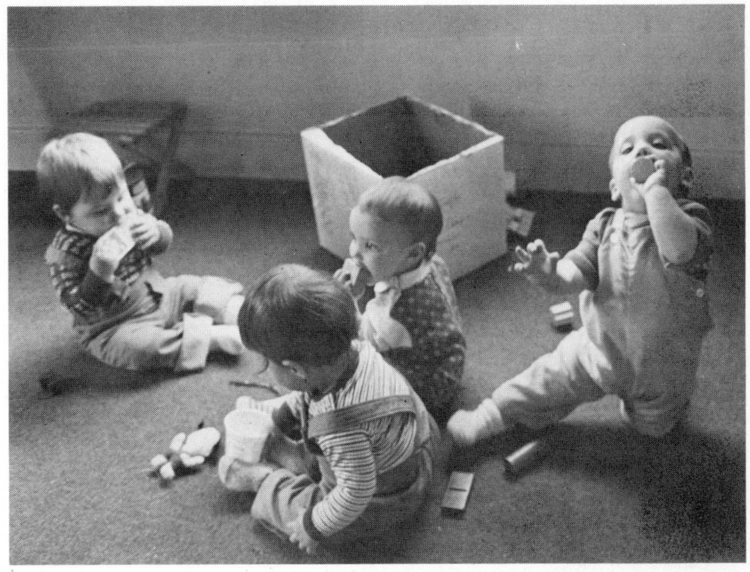

Laurent would move only the arm to which the string was attached. If Piaget moved the string to the other arm, Laurent shifted his movement to the other arm, too. Thus, over the period of about a month, Laurent shifted from substage 2 to substage 3. He began to relate to objects as things that can be affected.

The Beginning of Internal Representation

The transition from substage 5 to substage 6, when internal representation is first seen, is also particularly fascinating.

In your thinking, you have a word for an object and a mental picture of it. You can use that word and image in various ways. You can remember the object, compare it mentally with something else, or figure out how to fix it—all in your head. But this ability to form and manipulate mental images is not present in the baby until the sixth sensorimotor substage. Piaget has made one wonderful observation of his daughter Lucienne which illustrates this transition. At the time of this observation, Piaget was playing with Lucienne and had hidden his watch chain inside an empty box. He describes what happened then:

> I put the chain back into the box and reduce the opening to 3mm. It is understood that Lucienne is not aware of the functioning of the opening and closing of the match box and has not seen me prepare the experiment. She only possesses two preceding schemes [strategies]: turning the box over in order to empty it of its contents,

and sliding her fingers into the slit to make the chain come out. It is of course this last procedure that she tries first: she puts her finger inside and gropes to reach the chain, but fails completely. A pause follows during which Lucienne manifests a very curious reaction. . . . She looks at the slit with great attention; then, several times in succession, she opens and shuts her mouth, at first slightly, then wider and wider! [Then] . . . Lucienne unhesitatingly puts her finger in the slit, and instead of trying as before to reach the chain, she pulls so as to enlarge the opening. She succeeds and grasps the chain.

(Piaget, 1959, pp. 337–338)

Try to see the really enormous discovery this child has made. Faced with a new situation, instead of going immediately to trial and error, she paused and appeared to discover the solution through some kind of analysis. To be sure, she didn't do all the analysis in her head. She used her mouth to represent the box. But this behavior is nevertheless the very beginning of the child's ability to manipulate and combine, to experiment and explore, with images instead of real objects.

Overview of the Sensorimotor Period

Several aspects of the child's functioning during the sensorimotor period are worth some emphasis. First of all, you should understand that the baby is not really "thinking" in the sense of planning or intending, at least not at first. During the sensorimotor period, the child begins to show rudimentary aspects of intention and internal representation, but these are still very primitive in comparison to what will come later.

A second important point is that movement from one substage to the next is gradual. The baby doesn't suddenly wake up at age 1 month with a whole new set of skills. Internal representation doesn't happen overnight either. Each is built upon dozens and dozens of individual assimilations and accommodations. Nonetheless, although the changes are gradual, major new accomplishments do appear to develop in a particular sequence and at a fairly standard rate. It is for this reason that it makes sense to talk about "stages" rather than about continuous change.

Preoperational Thought: From Ages 2 to 6

In many ways, this stage is odd-man-out in Piaget's theory. A great deal of Piaget's description of children from 2 to 6 focuses on what they *cannot* do or on deficiencies in their thinking and reasoning. I'm not altogether sure why this is so, but perhaps it came about because Piaget was so struck by the major new accomplishments at the end of the sensorimotor period and by a second breakthrough at about age 6 that the years between seemed less interesting. Whatever the reason, the early descriptions of the **preoperational period** were largely negative. More recently, researchers have turned their attention to the many skills the preschooler does develop. The current view of young children's intellectual abilities is far more positive than the earlier one. Let me give you both views, beginning with Piaget's early descriptions.

Piaget's Description of the Preoperational Period

Several aspects of the preschool child's thinking stood out for Piaget: It was egocentric; it was focused on only one thing at a time; it was not reversible; and the reasoning was primitive.

Egocentrism The term "egocentric" or "egocentrism" refers to a tendency on the part of the child to be self-centered or, more literally, "centered in the self." The child sees things through his own perspective and does not realize that there are other possible ways of viewing things. Piaget saw this in children's language as well as in their thinking. In their conversations, children did not seem to take into account the needs of the listener. They talk as if the listener can see the things they see and know the things they know. In the child's thinking, you see egocentrism in his difficulty with understanding that you do not look at the physical space from the same perspective. If the child is standing in front of a chair and you are standing behind it, the child may not realize that you don't see the same parts of the chair that he sees.

Broadly stated, Piaget thought that one of the tasks of the preoperational period is for the child to become decentered—to shift from the self as the only frame of reference. As Herbert Ginsburg and Sylvia Opper put it:

> The [preoperational] child decenters his thought just as in the sensorimotor period the infant decentered his behavior. The newborn *acts* as if the world is centered about himself and must learn to behave in more adaptive ways. Similarly, the young child *thinks* from a limited perspective and must widen it.
>
> *(Ginsburg & Opper, 1969, p. 111)*

One Thing at a Time The second major feature of thought in the young child is really an offshoot of the decentering process. The child must learn to take more than one aspect of a situation into account at once. The 2- or 3- or 4-year-old tends to get stuck on one part. If he sees you pour water from a short, fat glass into a tall, thin one, he focuses on the height of the water in the two glasses and assumes there is more water in the tall glass. Only later, when he can keep track of more than one aspect at a time, does he realize that the water level is higher but that the glass is also narrower.

Lack of Reversibility The preoperational child, in Piaget's view, is unable to see that things can be undone as well as done—that water can be poured back into the short, fat glass and come to the same level it had reached before or that things that are added can be subtracted. The thinking of children in the next major stage, at about age 6, becomes reversible. The older child can run things forward and backward, both in action and mentally. But Piaget thought that the younger child could not do this.

Primitive Reasoning Piaget's daughter Lucienne announced one afternoon when she had not taken her nap, "I haven't had my nap so it isn't afternoon." This is a very good example of the kind of reasoning you'll hear in the preschool-age child. Lucienne knew that afternoon and nap usually go together, but she had the relationship between them wrong. She thought that the nap "caused" the afternoon. The child I quoted at the very beginning of the chapter who thought that the wind would go away if you chopped down the tree was showing the same kind of logic.

Piaget calls this **transductive** reasoning. Others, such as Carl Bereiter (Bereiter, Hidi & Dimitroff, 1979) call it *intuitive* reasoning, which is an easier term to remember. Whatever the label, the basic characteristic of this type of reasoning is that the child sees that two things happen at the same time and assumes one is the cause of the other.

Incidentally, you probably use reasoning like this yourself sometimes. I mentioned in Chapter 2 that women who smoke are more likely to have premature babies. Most people who hear that statement immediately jump to the conclusion that smoking *causes* prematurity. As it happens, there probably *is* a causal relationship in this instance, but it has taken years of research to demonstrate it. The mere fact that the two things happen together doesn't prove a causal relationship. The difference, though, between the adult who jumps to a too-easy conclusion and the child who does the same is that the adult is quite able to understand that there are other possible logical relationships. Piaget thought that the 4- or 5-year-old child couldn't do that.

Current Views of the Preoperational Period

Recent research suggests that Piaget may have been too pessimistic in his views of the potentials of the preschool-age child. Let me sample some of the findings.

New Work on Egocentrism The current evidence suggests that the preoperational child has far more ability to take other perspectives than Piaget believed. For example, Marilyn Shatz and Rochel Gelman (1973) have found that children as young as 4 would talk in simpler sentences when they talked to a 2-year-old than when they talked to an adult. As I pointed out in Chapter 7, adults do this when they talk to young children, presumably because they realize that the child will understand the simpler language better. The fact that 4-year-olds also make this adjustment shows they must have some ability to perceive the situation from the perspective of the younger child.

In another study, Helen Borke (1975) found that 3- and 4-year-old children could take the physical perspective of another person. They could tell, for example, that someone standing on the opposite side of a scene from themselves saw a different view than they did.

These studies point to the possibility that Piaget underestimated the preoperational child. But we have to be careful not to go too far in the other direction. The preoperational child may be less egocentric than Piaget believed, but she is still not able to take other people's perspectives all the time or in all ways. In particular, the preschooler has trouble when you ask her to understand that another person *knows* or *feels* different things than she does (Selman & Bryne, 1974).

Perhaps I can make this distinction clear with a personal example. In the house we lived in when my daughter Arwen was about 4, the dining room table was in a corner window. Our son Rex could see out of the window from his usual seat, but Arwen could not. One evening when she was about 4½, we got to talking about something outside, and she promptly described what her brother could see out the window. I was astonished. But at the same age, she was quite unable to understand that I didn't know what she was thinking about. She might say to me, "Where is it?" When I looked blank and said, "Where is what?" she was always surprised that I didn't know what object was in her mind. So she was good at taking someone else's *physical* perspective but not good at taking someone else's *mental* or *emotional* perspective.

New Work on Preoperational Reasoning Although it is certainly true that the preschool child's reasoning is less skillful than an adult's and less skillful than a 7-year-old's, Piaget's view may once again be too pessimistic. For example, Merry Bullock and Rochel Gelman (1979), in a very interesting study, have shown that children as young as 3 understand that a cause has to come *before* an effect rather than after it. So even these very young children seem to have at least rudimentary understanding of causes; all of their reasoning is not transductive.

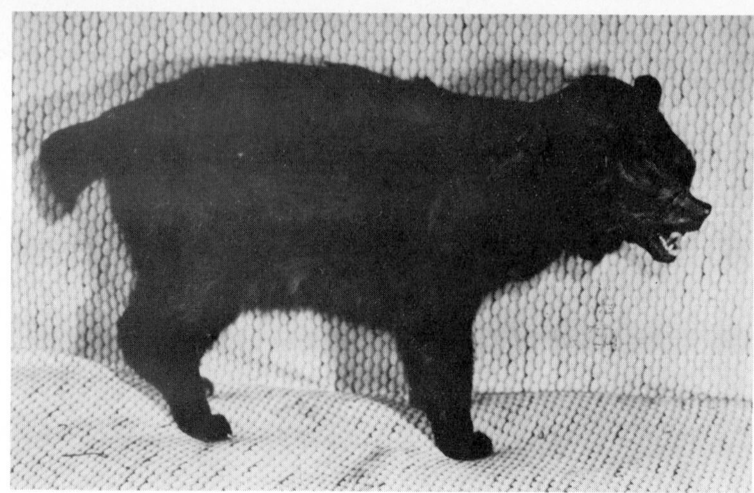

Figure 8.3 Maynard the amazing cat, with and without the dog mask. Young children thought that with the mask on, Maynard had essentially become a dog and could bark and do other dog things. But 4- and 5-year-olds understood that Maynard was still a cat. (Source: DeVries, R., 1969, pp. 8 & 9. By permission of the Society for Research in Child Development, Inc.)

Current Work on Understanding Identities Another focus of recent research has been on the child's continuing understanding of the constancy of objects. During the sensorimotor period, the infant discovers that objects remain the same even if you see them from a different angle or a different distance. This understanding is the first step on a long road for the child. During the preschool period, the child takes another step and begins to understand other things about constant objects. A delightful study by Rheta DeVries (1969) illustrates these changes nicely.

DeVries had children aged 3–6 play with a live cat—an apparently very friendly and docile beast named Maynard. After the child had petted the cat and was comfortable with him, DeVries took the cat to a table, hiding the front end of him behind a box. The child was told to watch the "tail end" and that the cat would look different later. Behind the screening box, DeVries put a very lifelike dog mask on Maynard's head and then brought out the transformed creature to face the child. (You can see Maynard in his several forms in Figure 8.3.) What DeVries wanted to know was whether the child understood that Maynard hadn't fundamentally changed. So she asked the child whether Maynard could now bark, whether he would eat dog food or cat food, whether the new animal would play like a cat or a dog, and so on.

The 3-year-olds in this study understood very little about the constancy of Maynard. They thought that with a dog mask on, Maynard had essentially become a dog. But by age 5, the children were doing very well. They knew that the mask was something external, which didn't change the *basic* characteristics of the cat, just as putting on different clothes doesn't make you a different person. This turns out to be an important basis for the child's understanding of gender, which I talked about in Chapter 1. The child of 5 or 6 understands that she won't change into a boy just by putting on boys' clothes or doing "boy things."

Classification Skills in the Preoperative Child A third area of emphasis in recent work has been the growing ability of the preschool child to classify objects – to put them into consistent groups.

The usual way of exploring the child's classification abilities is to give her a batch of blocks or paper cutouts of various sizes, shapes, and colors and ask her to "put the things together that go together." Nancy Denney (1972) used a procedure like this in a study with 2-, 3-, and 4-year-olds. You can see some of the different types of groupings that are possible in Figure 8.4. What Denney found was that even 2-year-olds created groupings that were at least partly based on similarity; and by age 4, nearly all the children's groupings were something like the "complete similarity on one dimension" shown in the figure.

So there is a lot of progress in this area over the preschool years. But as is true of egocentrism, logic, or any of the other areas I've talked about, there is still some distance to go. In the case of classification, the missing aspect is what Piaget calls **class inclusion.**

Suppose you give children a set of wooden beads (as Piaget did), most of which are brown, with a few white ones thrown in. You ask the child: "Are there more brown beads or more wooden beads?" A 5-year-old will usually tell you that there are more brown beads (Judd & Mervis, 1979). The child has failed to understand that the class of brown beads is *included in* the class of wooden beads and therefore has to be smaller. Only at age 7 or so does this important new classification concept develop in most children.

Overview of the Preoperational Child

If we add up the different bits of information I've just given you, we come up with a picture of a child who is a lot more logical than Piaget had thought – perhaps more logical than many preschool teachers had thought. But the 3- or 4-year-old child's thinking is still fairly primitive by adult standards. He tends to be quite rigid and static in his thinking; he often gets captured by what things look like and by his own view, feelings, and thoughts. He has a hard time understanding more complex logical relationships among things.

There are some important practical implications to be drawn from these qualities of the preschooler, which I've sketched briefly in Box 8.1.

Figure 8.4 Some of the kinds of groupings Denney found in her study of classification in preschool children. The youngest children tended to make the groupings shown at the top, while 3- and 4-year-old children made some of the groupings in the middle and at the bottom. (Source: Denney, N. W., 1972, p. 1165. By permission of the Society for Research in Child Development, Inc.)

Design

Design with similarity

Incomplete similarity on one dimension

Incomplete similarity on two dimensions

Complete similarity on one dimension

Complete similarity on two dimensions

Concrete Operational Thought: From Ages 6 to 12

Virtually all theorists and researchers agree that there is a major change in the child's thinking somewhere between ages 5 and 7. Piaget calls the new set of skills **concrete operations** and emphasizes several crucial new features. First of all, the child adds important new internal schemes, called operations, such as addition, subtraction, multiplication, division, and serial or-

Box 8.1 Some Practical Applications of Information about the Thinking of the Preschooler

Thomas Gordon, in his book *Parent Effectiveness Training* (1970), argues that it is possible to make "contracts" with children as young as 2 or 3. Suppose a parent comes home from work very tired and really needs some quiet time to read the paper before getting into the family fray, but the kids keep bugging her or him during that quiet time. Gordon suggests it is possible to explain to the child that "I'm really tired, and I need to sit quietly for a while" and that as a result of this explanation, the children will indeed be quiet for a while. I have my doubts. My doubts arise precisely out of what we know about children's "egocentrism" at age 2, 3, or 4.

In this case, the parent is asking the young child to step into his emotional shoes for a moment, and this is exactly the kind of perspective taking that is so very hard for a child this age. My basic point is that there are distinct limits to what the preschooler can understand—not only about logical relationships but about other people's feelings. Parents have to keep those limits in mind.

Another application of the research on egocentrism is that children are more likely to understand something if you explain it in very personal terms. Darlene Mood (1979) has found that preschoolers understand sentences in which their own name occurs more easily than equivalently complex sentences without their names. This might happen simply because using their name gets their attention. Or it could be that they understand better because they are able to look at it through their own perspective. In any case, it's worth remembering next time you want to explain something to a 2- or 3-year-old.

Still another practical effect of young children's limited logical abilities is that they don't understand a lot of what they see on TV, particularly cause and effect relationships. Many parents assume that it is okay for their preschoolers to watch crime programs (or most children's cartoons) because the "bad guy" gets caught and punished in the end. But the young child has a hard time grasping the links between the "bad behavior" and the consequence, between the cause and the effect, particularly when there is a long time gap between the two. So the child may take away a quite different message from a program than you do. If you want a child to learn a "moral" from some program, you may have to spend some time talking about it and making it as concrete and relevant to the child's own experience as possible.

Another basic quality of the young child that you should keep in mind when you work with preschoolers is that they are not *systematic*. If a 3-year-old child has lost his shoe, you can't expect him to search carefully, looking in all the places he's been (Wellman, Somerville & Haake, 1979). The boy may look in a few places and then give up. It's not that the child doesn't *want* to find his shoe, his toy, or whatever he's lost. Rather, he just doesn't understand yet about how to figure out where the missing object *might* be and how to search for it systematically.

The preschooler can do a great many things and understand so very much more than we had supposed; but there are limits, and it's important not to overestimate.

dering. The child becomes able to apply these very powerful new tools to her encounters with the world. Each of these operations is reversible. That is, the child understands that addition and subtraction are the opposite—that one is the reverse of the other. The understanding of the basic reversibility of actions is behind many of the gains made during this period.

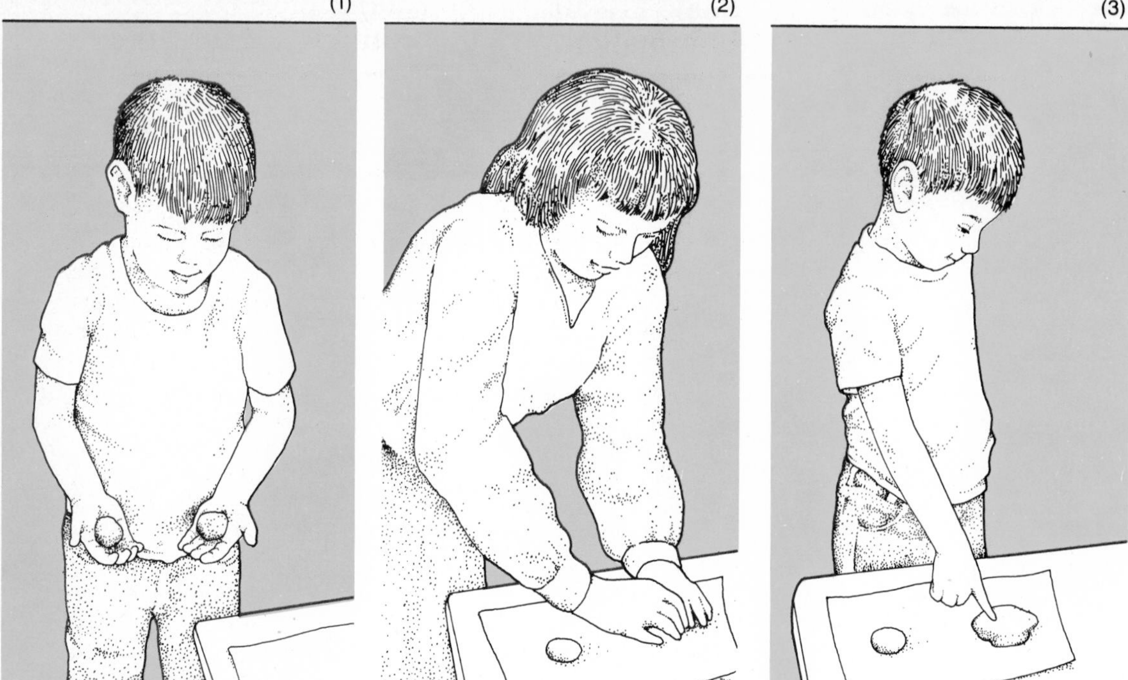

Figure 8.5 In the classic conservation experiment using balls of clay, the child first holds both and agrees they are the same. The experimenter then squishes one of them into another shape and asks the child whether they are the same or different.

The concrete operational child also is able to reason **inductively.** She can move from experience to general principles. She no longer treats each experience as an isolated instance but begins to add them up into new wholes.

In the case of concrete operations, Piaget's work and the work of more recent researchers converge quite closely. So I can describe the major findings in a more integrated way.

Understanding Identities: The Next Step

I've already described the preschooler's growing awareness that things may remain fundamentally the same even though their appearance changes. Maynard is still a cat even when he has a dog mask on. That's an important new level of understanding, but the child of 4 or 5 is still dealing with the surface qualities of objects—with clothing, masks, or changes in color, for example. During the concrete operational period, the child discovers another whole type of constancy, which Piaget calls **conservation.** I can explain this concept most easily by describing the way Piaget studied it.

The standard experimental situation begins with two equal balls of clay. The experimenter asks the child to hold them and to feel them in any way she wishes and asks her whether there is the "same amount" of clay in each. When the child agrees that they have the same amount, the experimenter takes one of the balls and squashes it into a pancake shape. The child is then asked, "Is there the same amount here (pointing to the pancake) as here (pointing to the ball)? Or is there more here, or more here?" The steps are shown in Figure 8.5.

A preschooler, when faced with this situation, will nearly always tell you that the ball and the pancake have different amounts. His attention gets captured by the change in shape and he can't keep in mind the fact that they were the same to start with.

Children of 6 or 7, however, will nearly always tell you that the pancake and the ball are still the same. They give various kinds of reasons for their conclusions, such as "If you put it back into a ball it would be the same," "It's bigger around, but it's thinner, so it's the same," or "You haven't added any or taken any away, so it must be the same."

Notice that the concrete operational child has been able to step back from the immediate, visible change and consider the logical relationships involved. He may rely on his new understanding of reversibility and see that if you made it back into a ball, it would be like it was before. Or he may rely on his new understanding of addition and subtraction. But he is able to avoid the trap of focusing too much on the immediate visual change. The fundamental principle the child has learned is that certain properties of objects, such as their quantity, weight, or number, stay the same even when the shape or spatial arrangement is changed. In some sense, this is a more advanced form of object constancy.

Classification: The Next Steps

The child of 7 or 8 goes beyond just grouping objects into clumps and begins to understand the relationships *between* classes, such as the class inclusion relationships. (Roses are also flowers; brown beads are also wooden, and so forth.)

But even this big advance doesn't take the child the whole way. The 7-year-old understands class inclusion when you put batches of beads or flowers in front of him, where he can see them and count them; but if you put the problem to him in the abstract, he still has difficulty.

Ellen Markman (1978) explored this. In one test she developed, she showed the children four toy couches and two toy chairs, collectively labeled as "furniture." Second graders could easily answer the standard class inclusion question: "Are there more couches or more furniture?" But then Markman hid all the toys behind a screen and said that she was going to take some of the furniture away. Then she asked, "Without seeing what I took away, can you tell for sure whether there is more furniture left or more couches left?"

To answer this question correctly, the child has to understand the basic *logical* relationship between the different classes. What Markman found was that children as old as fifth graders (10–11 years old) had difficulty with the abstract version of the problem.

This is a good example of the kind of progression in cognitive development that Piaget emphasizes. At each stage, the child makes significant new advances; but there are still further, more subtle, or more abstract versions of the same concept to be learned later.

Serial Ordering Besides class inclusion, the elementary school-age child learns other relationships among classes, such as **serial ordering.** She can put things into order from the tallest to the shortest or darkest to lightest. This is an important ability for learning about numbers, since numbers are a serial order.

One of the relationships within a serial order that the child learns at about this time is the concept of **transitivity.** For example, if Jane is taller than Sarah and Sarah is taller than Ann, then Jane is taller than Ann. Again, this concept is basic to an understanding of numbers.

All of these relatively abstract concepts about classification and the relationships among classes develop during the early years of the concrete operations period.

Memory

A shift in the way the child approaches a memory task also occurs between the preoperational and concrete operational stages. John Flavell and his several associates (Flavell, 1970; Flavell & Wellman, 1977; Salatas & Flavell, 1976), and John Hagen and his colleagues (Hagen, Jongeward & Kail, 1975; Kail and Hagen, 1977) have both focused a great deal of research attention on the development of memory strategies in children. How do children remember things? How do they recall lists, what to get at the store, or where they last saw their favorite toy?

In his early studies, Flavell most often approached this problem by giving children a set of pictures to remember in a particular order. There was then a period of delay during which the child had to remember what she had seen. Later the child was asked to reproduce the set of pictures in the right order. The experimenter observed and listened to see if there were any signs of the child's **mnemonic strategies** (techniques for remembering things). Did the child rehearse the order of pictures out loud? Did she mutter them to herself?

Flavell's research shows that children below approximately age 6 do not spontaneously use rehearsal or other mnemonic procedures. But 4- to 5-year-olds will use rehearsal if you suggest this strategy to them. They have the ability to rehearse,

Figure 8.6 Children of elementary school age can get very excited about scientific experiments, as this girl is. But their reasoning is still mostly inductive rather than deductive. Still, experiences like this one should help the child in her gradual development of more complex types of thinking.

but they do not do so spontaneously. Flavell calls this pattern a **production deficiency.** Six- to 7-year-olds often show spontaneous rehearsal, although they are not terribly efficient at it; and by 9 or 10, most children use rehearsal efficiently and silently.

But this is not the end of the memory story. Rehearsal and other fairly simple ways of remembering things only work when the amount you have to remember is not too great. When the load on your memory goes up, you have to switch to much more complex strategies to remember things. In particular, whether you remember something may depend on your ability to organize the material to be remembered into categories or analyze it in some way that reduces the load on your memory. Since older children have greater skill at organizing information, they have an easier time recalling complex sets of information.

Overview of the Concrete Operational Child

The elementary school child has made a great leap forward. He can understand a whole range of complex concepts and can apply his new understanding to such tasks as memory, mathematics, and searching for lost objects. But the child of this age is still tied down to the concrete, to some extent.

He can reason inductively—going from his own experience to a general principle. But he has trouble going the other way—from a general principle to some anticipated experience (called deductive reasoning). The 8- or 9-year-old has a hard time imagining things he has never experienced and has an equally hard time with abstract concepts when they are not linked to

Box 8.2 Piaget's Theory and Early Education

Piaget's theory is really not a theory of teaching. He says almost nothing about how a teacher confronted daily by a classroom full of children can apply his ideas. But a great many educators, both those dealing with preschoolers and those involved with elementary school children, have tried to apply at least some of Piaget's concepts in their teaching (Lavatelli, 1970; Weikart, 1972; Kamii & DeVries, 1974; Appel, 1977).

The most common application of Piaget's theory has been based on the understanding of the sequence of stages from preoperational to concrete operational thinking. Preschool educators map out the steps involved in such concepts as classification and then try to move the child along that sequence by presenting materials that "lead" the child from where he is "up" to the next step. You can see this in "Sesame Street" (which I urge you to watch occasionally, by the way) when they "teach" classification by having children figure out which things go together. You can see it in preschool programs like David Weikart's (1972), in which concepts are taught by first using sensorimotor experience, with more abstract experience added later. The word "boat," for example, might be introduced by having the children play in a life-sized rowboat (sensorimotor), then with a toy boat that stands for the larger boat, then with pictures of boats, and finally—with much older children—with the word "boat."

This same use of the basic sequences can be seen in some mathematics and science programs used in elementary and high school. Marilyn Appel (1977) describes one science program called PASE (Personalized Approach to Science Education). Science projects are arranged in a sequence from preoperational (involving basic classification, for example) through the transition to concrete operations (involving reversibility or conservation tasks, for example) and on upward in complexity. At each level, there are many different experiments, and the child chooses which one she wants to work on. A child may work on many at one level before moving on to the next group of experiments.

All of these efforts to "translate" Piaget into practical classroom procedures seem useful to me, but there are some pitfalls—some misunderstandings of Piaget that lead to misapplication of the theory. Let me mention just two.

First, from Piaget's point of view, the child's thinking is not created from the outside; it is *constructed* by the child. And this construction comes about through the child's own play and exploration. The teacher can help the process by providing things to play with and explore that are at a level of difficulty that will foster further growth in the child. Or the teacher can ask questions that will force the child to rethink old concepts. But in Piaget's view, the teacher cannot *force* the child along the sequence. It seems to me that the PASE science program follows this model well, but many other Piaget-based educational systems do not.

Second, American educators seem to be particularly vulnerable to the trap of paying attention to "right" answers. We want children to say that the two balls of clay are the same in the conservation experiment, for example. Piaget has always been more interested in *why* a child says something and not in whether the answer is right by some adult standard. Our preoccupation with rightness may lead teachers to listen too little to the child's logic and to focus instead on teaching the child the right words to say. In Piaget's views, the right words don't necessarily mean that the child has achieved the fundamental understanding.

Overall, American educators have seized on the stages Piaget describes and have tried to overlay them onto educational practice and onto curricula. But in the process, we have often missed the subtleties of Piaget's theory.

specific objects. He knows there is more furniture than couches only when the toys are right there to look at and count. So despite the huge advances, there are steps still to be taken.

Formal Operational Thought: From Age 12 On

Those next steps are taken during the final period of cognitive development, which Piaget calls **formal operations.** The major task of this period, according to Piaget, is to learn how to think about *ideas* as well as about objects. Ideas can be classified and organized, just as objects can. In fact, they can be manipulated much more flexibly.

From the Actual to the Possible

One of the first steps in this process is for the child to extend her reasoning abilities to objects and situations which she has not seen or experienced firsthand. Instead of thinking only about real things and actual occurrences, she must start to think about imaginary things and possible occurrences. This shift in the child's ability to reason is nicely illustrated in a study by Frederic Mosher and Joan Hornsby (1966) which involves the game of Twenty Questions.

The first task for the children in this study made use of a set of 42 pictures of animals, people, toys, machines, and the like. Each child was told that the experimenter was thinking of one of the pictures and he or she was to figure out which one by asking questions that could be answered "yes" or "no."

Many of you have played this kind of game before and already know that there are several ways to go about it. One way, especially with a set of pictures, is simply to start at one end of a row and ask "Is it this one?" about each in turn until you hit the right one. Another way is first to classify the pictures mentally into groups, hopefully hierarchically. You notice that there are red and blue toys. You can start by asking "Is it a toy?" If the answer is yes, you might ask whether it is a red toy, and so on. If the answer is "No, it's not a toy," then you go on and ask about other kinds of categories.

In this study, 6-year-olds did not ordinarily ask questions like "Is it a toy?" They used almost entirely the first kind of strategy, going from one picture to another, often in an apparently random order, hoping to guess the right one. Both 8- and 11-year-olds, on the other hand, did fairly well at narrowing down the possibilities through a series of more general questions. In this task, with the pictures in front of them, they made use of their ability to manipulate hierarchical classifications.

To make the problem more difficult, Mosher and Hornsby added a second task, which instead of using pictures used a story. The child was told, "A man is driving down the road in his car; the car goes off the road and hits a tree. Find out what happened." To approach this task systematically, the child has to be able to *imagine* all the possible reasons for such an accident and then to organize these imaginary possibilities into categories (such as weather, illness, or auto breakdowns). It is precisely this ability to imagine and organize unseen or unexperienced possibilities that the concrete child lacks, and so she reverts to guessing. Six-year-olds and even 8-year-olds asked questions like "Was the man stung on the eye by a bee?" Please notice that they *can* imagine things. What they cannot do is to organize the things they imagine logically. On the other hand, the 11-year-olds, who are just beginning to master formal operations, can begin *both* to think up the possibilities *and* to organize them into some kind of system. They asked questions like "Did the weather cause the accident?" or "Did the driver make a mistake to cause the accident?"

Systematic Problem Solving

Thinking up and organizing possible solutions to a problem still does not solve the problem, though. In order to do that, the child must learn to test each of the possible solutions mentally until he finds one that works. So another important feature of the stage of formal operations is that the child is able to search systematically and methodically for the answer to a problem. This aspect of formal operations has been extensively studied by Piaget and his colleague, Barbel Inhelder (Inhelder & Piaget, 1958).

Inhelder and Piaget present adolescents with a series of tasks, most of which come from the physical sciences (chemistry or physics). One of the most famous of these tasks involves a pendulum. Youngsters are given a long piece of string and a set of objects of various weights which can be tied to the string to make a swinging pendulum. They are shown how to start the pendulum by pushing the weight with differing amounts of force and by holding the weight at different heights. The subject must figure out which one or combination of these four factors (length of string, weight of object, force of push, and height of push) determines how fast the pendulum swings. As you might expect, Inhelder and Piaget are not very interested in whether the child gets the right answer. What they *are* interested in is *how* she goes about trying to find the answer.

If you give the pendulum problem to a child who is still in the stage of concrete operations, she will try out many different combinations of length and weight and force and height. But she will go about trying them in an illogical and inefficient way. Many children of this age, for instance, will first try a heavy weight on a long string and then a light weight on a short string. By changing *both* the weight and the length of the string, the child cannot make any conclusion about *either* of these factors. Some concrete operational children do solve the pendulum problem, but they do it by a lucky guess or a random try with several lucky combinations rather than by systematically searching for it.

Many adolescents proceed very differently. They apparently recognize that the only way to solve the problem is to vary just one of these factors at a time. So a 12- to 15-year-old may try a heavy object with a short string, then with a medium string, then with a long one. After that, she'll try a light object with the three lengths of string. Of course, not all adolescents (or adults, for that matter) are quite this methodical in their approach. But there is a very dramatic difference in the overall strategy used by formal operational and concrete operational youngsters.

Deductive Logic

Another facet of the change from concrete to formal operations is the shift from inductive to deductive logic. The concrete operational child is able to do inductive reasoning, which involves arriving at a conclusion based on a lot of individual experiences. The more difficult kind of reasoning, deductive reasoning, involves if → then relationships: "If all people are equal, then you and I must be equal."

A great deal of the logic of science is of this deductive type. We begin with a theory and propose, "If this theory is correct, then I should observe such and such." In doing this, we are going well beyond our observations. We are conceiving things that we have never seen that *ought* to be true or observable. We can think of this process as being part of a general decentering process that began much earlier in cognitive development. The preoperational child gradually moves away from his egocentrism and comes to be able to take the physical perspective of others. He becomes free of his own narrow perspective. During formal operations, the child becomes free of his reliance upon specific experience.

Some Questions about Formal Operations

The type of shift in thinking that Piaget has in mind between concrete and formal operations is quite clear. He thought that this began to occur at about age 12 or 13 and continued for several years, to perhaps age 16 or 17.

As it turns out, most recent research shows that children are much slower to develop formal thought than Piaget believed, and many do not develop formal operations at all. Unlike

Figure 8.7 By high school, students may be able to approach science problems using the deductive method—going from a theory to an experiment that tests some part of the theory.

concrete operations, which seem to be developed by virtually all children, only about half of the adolescents and young adults in most studies have developed formal operations. In one study by Suzanne Martorano (1977), only two out of 80 subjects used formal operations on *all* the different problems she gave them.

No one is terribly sure why some children develop formal operations and others do not. It may have something to do with the kind of schooling the child is getting (whether he takes a lot of mathematics and science, perhaps). It may have something to do with the child's basic style of approaching problems. Edith Neimark, for example (1975), has found that "reflective" children (those who examine options carefully) are more likely to develop formal operations than are "impulsive" children (look back to the discussion of these styles in Chapter 5). Pausing to consider alternatives may lead the child to question, to explore more fully, and thus to reach formal operations eventually.

My own hypothesis is that we all seem to use the simplest level of logic that works for the environment we live in. Any child who lives in an environment in which concrete operations are sufficient is not likely to develop formal operations. Only those young people who are in some sense "forced" by circumstances or experiences to work out more complex ways of relating ideas with one another seem to develop or show formal operations.

Overview of the Stages of Cognitive Development

The child comes a long way in only about 10 or 15 years. He moves from very rudimentary abilities to represent things to himself, with images and with words, to classifications, to conservation, to abstract, deductive logic. As Piaget sees it, the progress along this chain is continuous but marked off into stages, with each stage characterized by particular kinds of logic. In broad outline, that seems to be true; but there are some distinct problems with Piaget's theory, and I can't leave this chapter without pointing out some of them to you.

Problems with Piaget's Theory

American psychologists have several complaints about Piaget's theory. Two of these seem to me to be relatively unimportant, but there is one very serious difficulty.

Rates of Development

One of the unimportant problems (in my opinion) is that Piaget hasn't said very much about why children don't all seem to develop at the same rate. This is the "American question" again, and Piaget just isn't very interested in it. But that doesn't prevent others from doing research on this question—as you'll see later in the chapter.

Stages and Ages

The second, less-important problem is the issue of just when the various stages occur. Sometimes Piaget seems to underestimate the child, as we saw in the research on egocentrism; other times his ages seem to be too young, as in the case of formal operations. To me, the specific ages are not nearly so important as the sequences themselves. It may be interesting to know that a 4-year-old shows some signs of being able to use other people's perspectives, but that's not a disproof of the basic features of Piaget's theory.

Consistency of Development

The one body of research that does raise fundamental questions about Piaget's ideas is the study of consistency across tasks. Piaget suggests essentially that at each stage the child possesses a certain underlying structure of logic. If Piaget is correct about the existence of such structures, we should find that children at any given stage should apply the same type of logic to a range of different problems. A teenager who can solve one formal operations task ought to be able to solve another one; a concrete operational child who can solve conservation problems, or the Twenty Questions problem, ought to be able to do seriation tasks, too.

But many researchers do *not* find this kind of consistency across tasks (Uzgiris, 1973; Martorano, 1977; Roberge & Flexer, 1979; Keating & Clark, 1980). Often there isn't even consistency across different measures of the *same* task. Thomas Achenbach and John Weisz (1975) found that 4- and 5-year-olds might succeed at a serial ordering task involving colors from light to dark but fail one with sticks of different lengths. If serial ordering is a basic concept, why is it that the child can't apply it to many different tasks?

This lack of consistency across tasks is not a trivial matter. It has led many developmental psychologists to question whether Piaget's stages are really very meaningful (Brainerd, 1978). John Flavell (1977), a major American interpreter of Piaget as well as a theorist in his own right, argues that the lack of consistency shows that cognitive development occurs in a continuous, gradual process rather than in a few major mental reorganizations, as Piaget's theory suggests.

Despite the heavy weight of the evidence against consistency, Piaget and likeminded theorists have some reasonable replies.

First, Piaget is not unaware of the lack of consistency. In fact, he was one of the first to point it out. (He uses the term **horizontal décalage** to describe it.) Piaget does believe that there is an overall structure at each stage, but he does not believe that all the skills making up that structure emerge at precisely the same time.

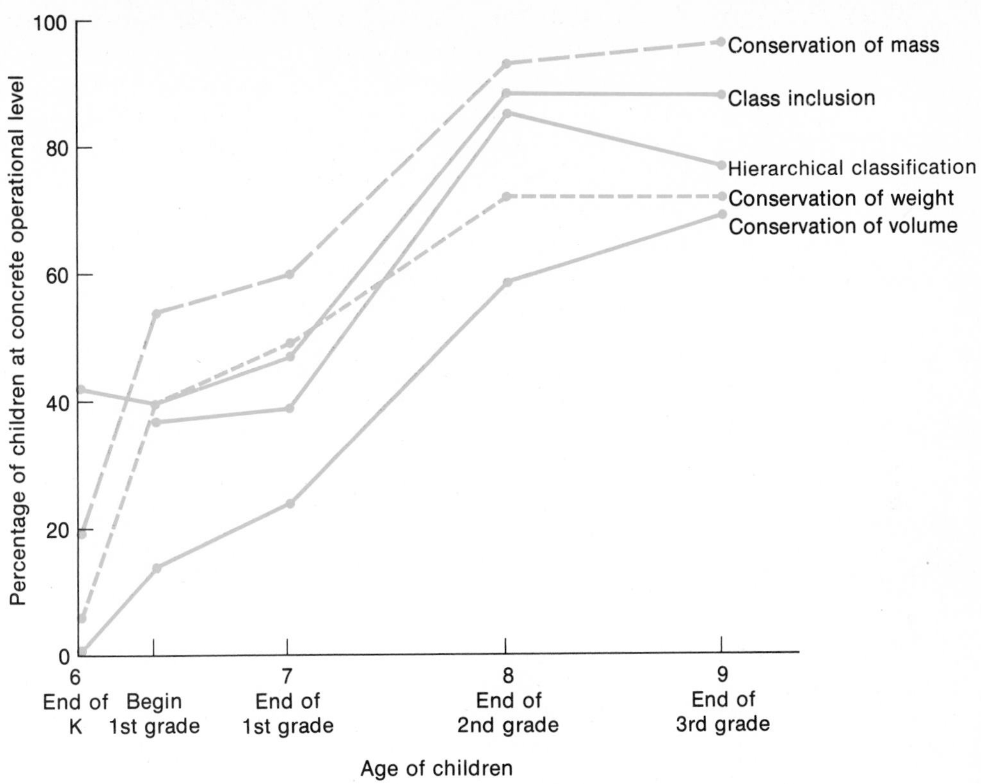

Figure 8.8 These results are from a longitudinal study in which the same children were given a set of concrete operations tasks five different times, beginning in kindergarten and ending in the third grade. As you can see, the percentage of children "solving" each type of problem increased, particularly at about age 7. But the tasks differed in difficulty, too. (Source: Tomlinson-Keasey, Eisert, Kahle, Hardy-Brown & Keasey, 1979, adapted from Table 2, p. 1158.)

Recent research shows that within each stage, there appears to be a specific order in which the several basic concepts are acquired. For example, Carol Tomlinson-Keasey and her colleagues (Tomlinson-Keasey, Eisert, Kahle, Hardy-Brown & Keasey, 1979), in an excellent recent longitudinal study, have looked at the development of some of the concrete operations. Figure 8.8 shows the percentage of children in this study at each succeeding testing who solved class inclusion, hierarchical classification, and several types of conservation problems. You can see that there was a spurt of development early in the sixth year and another during the seventh year, with less-rapid change in between. More important, the different tasks were not equally easy. Conservation of mass was easier than conservation of weight, with conservation of volume the hardest of the three. Class inclusion was also generally harder than conservation of mass. Even more interesting, Tomlinson-Keasey found that a child's relative position on these tasks stayed approximately the same throughout the three years of testing. A 6-year-old who developed conservation of mass early continued to be ahead of the other children later on; a late-developing child went through the same sequence about two years later.

This study and others like it (Almy, Chittenden & Miller, 1966; Little, 1972) show that while all concrete operations tasks are not mastered simultaneously, there is a *sequence* involved. Each new skill or understanding seems to rest on earlier ones. By the end of any given stage of cognitive development, the child ought to be able to perform most or all of the tasks associated with that stage. But at the beginning of a new stage, we will find inconsistency across tasks.

If this chain of logic is valid, it leaves Piaget's theory wounded, but not dead. Clearly there is much less generalizing of logical strategies across problems than Piaget thought. But there is more orderliness, more sequence, and more structure to the process than some critics have maintained.

The Effects of Environment on Cognitive Development

The sequences of cognitive development appear to be shared by virtually all children. But the *rate* of development is not. As I just pointed out, there is as much as a two-year difference among elementary school-age children in the timing of concrete operations and still wider differences at the formal operations stage. Could this result from differences in the children's environments?

Social Class Differences

One way to answer this question is to compare children from poor families with children from middle-class families. When researchers have done this, they have found that among infants, social class doesn't matter (Wachs, Uzgiris & Hunt, 1971; Golden & Birns, 1968). Poor children develop the object concept, for example, at the same speed as do middle-class children.

However, among children older than about 3, social class makes a difference. Middle-class children are usually found to be just a shade ahead of poor or working-class children on measures of conservation, classification, or formal operations (Gaudia, 1972; Overton, Wagner & Dolinsky, 1971).

These studies certainly point to the possibility that the environment makes a difference, but they tell us essentially nothing about what might be the critical variables. What do poor parents do or say, or fail to do or say, that makes a difference? Is it the opportunity for play with a variety of toys, the amount the child is talked to, or what?

Figure 8.9 Children raised in poverty like this usually show significant delay in their cognitive development. This "retardation" of development is usually observable beginning at about age 2 or 3 and continues throughout childhood.

Family Differences

The only way to answer questions like this is to look at actual families interacting with one another. Most of the studies like this have measured the child's IQ rather than his broad level of cognitive development (and I'll talk about the IQ studies in the next chapter). But there are a few bits of research relating to Piaget's stages.

For example, Theodore Wachs (1979) visited the homes of a group of 39 babies every two weeks for a year, beginning when the infants were about a year old. On each visit, he noted the types of stimulation available to the baby; and periodically he also tested the babies to see how rapidly they were developing such Piagetian concepts as object permanence, causality, and means-ends relationships. Wachs found that those babies who had the most physically responsive, uncrowded environment, with room to explore, showed the most rapid cognitive development. These babies had many toys or objects to play with and books to look at.

Leon Yarrow and his colleagues (Yarrow, Rubenstein & Pederson, 1975) have also found that the availability of interesting toys is important. In addition, the amount the baby is talked to, held, and generally stimulated by the adults around him matters.

In a third study, Richard Endsley and his colleagues (Endsley, Hutcherson, Garner & Martin, 1979) found that mothers of preschoolers who encouraged their children to explore had children who did more exploring. Presumably, the more the child explores new things, the more rapid her cognitive development will be.

Studies like these provide important first clues. It seems clear that both the quantity of exploratory experience and the richness and variety of that experience make a difference. But we can't go much further than that at this stage.

Sex Differences in Cognitive Development

Most comparisons of the intellectual abilities of males and females are based on IQ tests or equivalent. Studies comparing boys and girls on Piagetian-type tasks are more scarce. But the conclusions seem to be fairly clear.

Up through concrete operations, there do not seem to be *any* consistent sex differences. In contrast, at the formal operations period, there is growing evidence that boys begin to outstrip girls (for instance, Keating & Schaefer, 1975; Roberge & Flexer, 1979). The most reasonable explanation of this difference I can think of lies in the fact that many of the measures of formal operations used in Piagetian research involve some spatial visualization ability. We know from a great deal of other research that girls on average are less good at spatial tasks than boys are (Maccoby & Jacklin, 1974). So it may not be that girls are less "formal" in their thinking but that they have trouble with any formal tasks that *also* require them to use spatial skills. I must emphasize that this is only a hunch at this point. There isn't enough research on sex differences in formal operations to settle this question.

Summary

1. Most current researchers in the area of cognitive development would agree on basic assumptions that emphasize the child's active role in development and the sequential changes in her strategies for interacting with her environment.

2. At present, Jean Piaget's theories about cognitive development are still the dominant theoretical force.

3. The sequence of development, as proposed by Piaget and as validated broadly in many studies, is broken down into four main periods:

a. Sensorimotor period, from birth to age 2. Gradual movement from reflexive to intentional behavior. The beginning of internal representation marks the end of this period.

b. Preoperational period, age 2–6. The child develops beginning forms of reasoning and classification and shows some primitive ability to see things from others' perspectives.

c. Concrete operations, age 6–12. The child is able to perform various complex mental operations, such as addition and subtraction, in his head. Concepts like seriation and transitivity and conservation, all of which are probably required for mathematics, develop during this time.

d. Formal operations, age 12 and up. The young person becomes able to manipulate *ideas* as well as objects and can approach problems systematically. Deductive logic appears. Unlike earlier stages, which virtually all children go through, formal operations are achieved by only about half of adolescents.

4. Although this sequence is a fairly good general description, Piaget's theory suffers from significant problems, most notably the fact that children are not consistent in their performance on tasks that appear to demand the same levels of cognitive skill.

5. Children also differ in their rate of development, although we know less about the reasons for this than we'd like to. Past about age 3, poor children are generally a little slower. Families that encourage exploration and curiosity and provide the child with a rich array of toys and other materials have children who develop a bit faster.

6. No sex differences have been found in rate of development up to formal operations; but among adolescents, there are hints that boys are somewhat more likely to develop formal operations.

7. Piaget's theory has had some effect on educational practices; but the application is more difficult than it appears to be, and the verdict is still not in on the question of the impact of Piagetian educational programs on the development of cognitive skills.

Key Terms

Accommodation The process hypothesized by Piaget by which a person adapts existing structures—actions, ideas, or strategies, to fit new experiences.

Adaptation The basic process of biological existence according to Piaget, which characterizes intellectual as well as physical functioning. Both assimilation and accommodation are adaptive processes.

Assimilation The process of taking a new experience or new information and adjusting it to fit existing structures. A cornerstone concept in Piaget's theory.

Class inclusion The relationship between classes in which a subordinate class is included in a superordinate class, as bananas are part of the class "fruit."

Concrete operations The stage of development proposed by Piaget for the ages 6–12, in which mental operations such as subtraction, reversibility, and multiple classification are acquired.

Conservation The concept achieved by children from 6 to 10 years wherein objects remain the same in fundamental ways, such as weight or number, even when there are external changes in shape or arrangement.

Deductive logic Reasoning from the general to the particular, from a rule to an expected instance, or from a theory to a hypothesis. Characteristic of formal operational thought.

Formal operations Piaget's name for the fourth and final major stage of cognitive development, occurring during adolescence, when the child becomes able to manipulate and organize ideas as well as objects.

Horizontal decalage Piaget's term for the inconsistency of a child's performance across several similar tasks.

Inductive logic Reasoning from the particular to the general, from experience to broad rules. Characteristic of concrete operational thinking.

Mnemonic strategy A system for remembering things, such as repeating a list over to yourself.

Operation Term used by Piaget for complex, internal, abstract, reversible schemes, first seen at about age 6.

Organization One of the two basic processes of human functioning, along with adaptation, proposed by Piaget.

Preoperational stage Piaget's term for the second major stage of cognitive development, from age 2–6, during which the child develops basic classification and logical abilities.

Production deficiency A phrase used primarily to describe a stage in the child's development of memory skills when she possesses helpful strategies but does not produce them spontaneously when they would aid her.

Schemes Piaget's word for the basic actions, ideas, and strategies to which a new experience is assimilated and which are then modified (accommodated) as a result of the new experience.

Sensorimotor stage Piaget's term for the first major stage of cognitive development, from birth to about 18 months, when the child moves from reflexive to voluntary action.

Serial ordering Putting objects or events into a series that varies systematically along one dimension, such as small to large, or light to dark.

Transductive reasoning Reasoning from the specific to the specific; assuming that the two things happening together cause one another.

Transitivity The principle that if A is larger (or brighter or wider or whatever) than B, and B is larger than C, then A must be larger than C.

Suggested Readings

Flavell, J. H. Cognitive development. Englewood Cliffs, N.J.: Prentice-Hall, 1977.
This is a first-rate basic text in the field, written by one of the major current figures in cognitive developmental theory. Flavell has a fairly easy, anecdotal style, although the book gets technical in places. A very good next source.

Furth, H. Piaget for teachers. Englewood Cliffs, N.J.: Prentice-Hall, 1970.
Not a new book but an excellent discussion of the application of Piaget's theory to education, written as a series of letters to teachers.

Piaget, J. The stages of the intellectual development of the child. Bulletin of the Menninger Clinic, 1962, **26,** 120–128. Reprinted in N. S. Endler, L. R. Boulter & H. Osser (Eds.), Contemporary issues in developmental psychology (2nd ed.). New York: Holt, Rinehart & Winston, 1976.
An excellent, brief presentation by Piaget of the major stages of cognitive development.

Piaget, J. "Development and learning." In R. Ripple & V. Rockcastle (Eds.), Piaget rediscovered. Ithaca, N.Y.: Cornell University Press, 1964. Reprinted in C. S. Lavatelli & F. Stendler (Eds.), Readings in child behavior and development (3rd ed.), New York: Harcourt Brace Jovanovich, 1972.
This relatively brief paper is one of the clearest and most "chatty" of Piaget's writings. It presumes that you know something about his terminology, so it is not really easy; but it is an excellent place to read about his view about the role of maturation and experience in cognitive development.

Project 8.1 The Game of Twenty Questions

General Instructions

The first step is to locate a child between the ages of 5 and 10. Tell the parents that you want to play some simple games with the child as part of a school project, reassuring them that you are not "testing" the child. Obtain their permission, describing the games and tasks if you are asked to do so.

Arrange a time to be alone with the child if at all possible. Having the mother or siblings there can be extremely distracting, both for the child and for you.

Come prepared with all the equipment you will need. Tell the child that you have some games you would like to play. Play with the child for a while to establish some kind of rapport before you begin your experimenting. At the appropriate moment, introduce your "game."

The Task

"I am thinking of something in this room, and your job is to figure out what I am thinking of. To do this, you can ask any question at all that I can answer by saying yes or no, but I can't give you any other answer but yes or no. You can ask as many questions as you need to, but try to find out in as few questions as you can."

Choose the door to the room as the answer to your first game. (If there is more than one door, select one particular door as correct; if there is no door, use a particular window.) If the child asks questions that cannot be answered yes or no, remind her (or him) that you can't answer that kind of question, and restate the kind of questions that can be asked. Allow the child as many questions as needed (more than 20 if necessary). Write down each question verbatim. When the child has reached the correct answer, praise her and then say, "Let's try another one. I'll try to make it harder this time. I'm thinking of something in the room again. Remember, you ask me questions that I can answer yes or no. You can ask as many questions as you need, but try to find out in as few questions as possible."

Use your pencil or pen as the correct answer this time. After the child has solved the problem, praise her or him. If the child has not been successful, find something to praise. ("You asked some good questions, but it's a really hard problem, isn't it?") When you are satisfied that the child's motivation is still reasonably high, continue. "Now we're going to play another question-asking game. In this game, I will tell you something that happened, and your job will be to find out how it happened by asking me questions I can answer yes or no. Here's what happened: A man is driving down the road in his car; the car goes off the road and hits a tree. You have to find out how it happened by the way I answer questions you ask me about it. But I can only answer yes or no. The object of the game is to find out the answer in as few questions as possible. Remember, here's what happened: A man is driving down the road in his car; the car goes off the road and hits a tree. Find out what happened."

If the child asks questions that cannot be answered yes or no, remind him or her that you cannot answer that kind of question and that you can answer only yes or no. If the child can't figure out the answer, urge her or him to try until you are persuaded that you are creating frustration, at which point you should quit, with lots of positive statements. The answer to the problem is that it had been raining, the car skidded on a curve, went off the road, and hit the tree.

Scoring Score each question asked by the child on each of the three problems as belonging to one of two categories:

1. *Hypothesis.* A hypothesis is essentially a guess that applies to only one alternative. A yes answer to a hypothesis solves the problem; with a no answer, all that has been accomplished is to eliminate one possibility. In the first two problems, a hypothesis would be any question that applied to only one alternative, only one object in the room: "Is it your hair?" or "Is it the picture?" In the third problem, a hypothesis would be any question that covers only one alternative: "Did the man get stung in the eye by a bee?" "Did he have a heart attack?" "Was there a big snowbank in the middle of the road that the car ran into and then skidded?"
2. *Constraint.* A constraint question covers at least two possibilities, often many more. A yes answer to a constraint question must be followed up. ("Is it a toy?" "Yes." "Is it the truck?" "Yes.") A no answer to a constraint question allows the questioner to eliminate a whole class of possibilities. On the first two problems, any of the following would be constraints: "Is it in that half of

the room?" "Is it something big?" "Is it a toy?" "Is it something red?" (assuming there is more than one red thing in the room.) For the third problem, any of the following (or equivalent) would be constraints: "Was there something wrong with the car?" "Was the weather bad?" "Did something happen to the man?"

Data and Analysis

For your own analysis or for an assignment to be turned in to a course instructor, you should examine at least the following aspects:

1. How many questions did the child ask for each problem?
2. On each problem, how many were hypotheses and how many were constraints?
3. Did the child do better (ask more constraint questions) on the concrete problem than on the abstract (story) problem? Or was the performance the same on both?
4. Is the child's overall performance on this task generally consistent with the findings from Mosher and Hornsby's (1966) study? Does your subject behave in a way that would be expected on the basis of his or her age? If not, what explanation can you offer?

Preview of Chapter 9

Intelligence and Its Measurement

A friend of mine was recently called by the psychologist at her son's school and told—in rather solemn and ominous tones—that her boy had been given an intelligence test and that the psychologist was a "little concerned" about the way the child had performed. He wanted my friend to come and see him about the whole situation because he thought it might be appropriate for the child to be placed in a special class in the school.

Some of you have been through a similar experience. Your first reaction, like my friend's, was probably an awful sinking feeling in the stomach, followed by panic, followed in some cases by anger. "What do they mean telling me my kid didn't do well! He's perfectly all right at home." Or "IQ tests are a bunch of hooey anyway." Or "I don't want my kid labeled retarded."

All of these reactions are perfectly understandable. Intelligence tests, and test scores, seem mystifying—almost magical—to a lot of people. They are also widely misunderstood and misused. So if your child's school ever calls you with news like my friend got, you *should* be skeptical; you should go into the consultation with the psychologist well informed about what the tests do and do not mean; and you shouldn't let yourself be bulldozed!

What I want to do in this chapter is to demystify the whole subject. To do this, I need to tell you what we know about "intelligence" as measured by "intelligence tests," where the concept came from, and how it is used. Most important, I want to tell you about the *limits* of the tests and what kinds of things can affect the score an individual child, or a group of children, may receive on a test.

First, though, I need to link up this discussion with what I said about the development of thinking in the last chapter. Aren't intelligence tests supposed to measure the child's thinking ability? How are they different from what Piaget has been talking about?

Intelligence Tests and Cognitive Development

When Piaget uses the word "intelligence," he is talking about a *quality*. The child of a given age has a particular kind of intelligence, a particular sort of logic. These qualities of thinking change over the course of development as a result of the child's interactions with the environment. When I talk about "cognitive development," as I did in Chapter 8, it is that sequential process I am referring to.

But the word "intelligence" used by the people who developed "intelligence tests" means something quite different. It refers to a *quantity* of something rather than to a quality. Piaget asks how thinking changes over time. The test developers wanted to know how children (or adults) differed from one another in their *ability* to think and in how much they already know. Some children are quicker, more knowledgeable, or better able to learn new things; and those early psychologists wanted to find ways to measure such differences. For Piaget, the question "How intelligent is Jimmy?" has little meaning. But for the test developers, and those who have followed in that tradition, the question says, "In comparison to other children his age, how well does Jimmy do at problems and tasks that require intellectual skills?"

It is critical for you to understand the difference between these two views. Both have value, but they lead to very different kinds of questions and very different kinds of emphases in both research and education. The major differences are (1) an emphasis on the *quality* of logic or thinking skill on the part of Piaget versus an emphasis on the *quantity* of logical ability or knowledge on the part of the test developers and (2) an emphasis on the sequential *changes* in thinking skill and logic on the part of Piaget versus an essentially *nondevelopmental* view on the part of the test designers. Obviously, those who designed tests for children knew that older children could do more things, could remember more words, and could solve harder problems than younger children could. But the tests weren't designed to reveal how or why these changes took place. Instead, they were intended to permit comparison of children with one another.

The Nature of IQ Tests

Students are often bored by reading about the history of ideas and theories, but I think it is important for you to know something about the background of intelligence tests. Much of the confusion and misunderstanding about tests and test scores can be eliminated by knowing why tests were first developed and by understanding the beliefs and values of the men and women who devised them.

The First IQ Tests

Although there had been some earlier attempts to develop a global test of intellectual functioning, the first modern intelligence test was published in 1905 by two Frenchmen, Alfred Binet and Theodore Simon. The work of Binet and Simon was based on the generally held belief that individuals differed in mental ability and that it would be desirable to have a way of measuring these individual differences. Binet was asked by the French government to devise such a test in order to identify retarded children—those who would not, or could not, profit from a regular school program. From the very beginning, the purpose of the intelligence test was to predict school success.

The selection of tasks to be included on the tests was heavily influenced by Binet's and Simon's thinking about the nature of intelligence. They believed that intelligence is basically judgment:

> It seems to us that in the intelligence there is a fundamental faculty. . . . This faculty is judgment, otherwise called good sense, practical sense, initiative, the faculty of adapting oneself to circumstances. To judge well, to comprehend well, to reason well, these are the essential activities of the intelligence.
>
> *(Binet & Simon, 1916, p. 24)*

The tests they devised, not surprisingly, were composed of measures of comprehension, reasoning, vocabulary, and the like.

The system Binet and Simon worked out for measuring intelligence was later followed by Louis Terman and his associates at Stanford University (Terman & Merrill, 1937) when they translated and revised the test for use in the U.S. It consisted of a series of individual tests for children of each age. There were six tests for 4-year-olds, six tests for 5-year-olds, and so on. A child taking the test was given these age tests until a level was reached at which he failed them all.

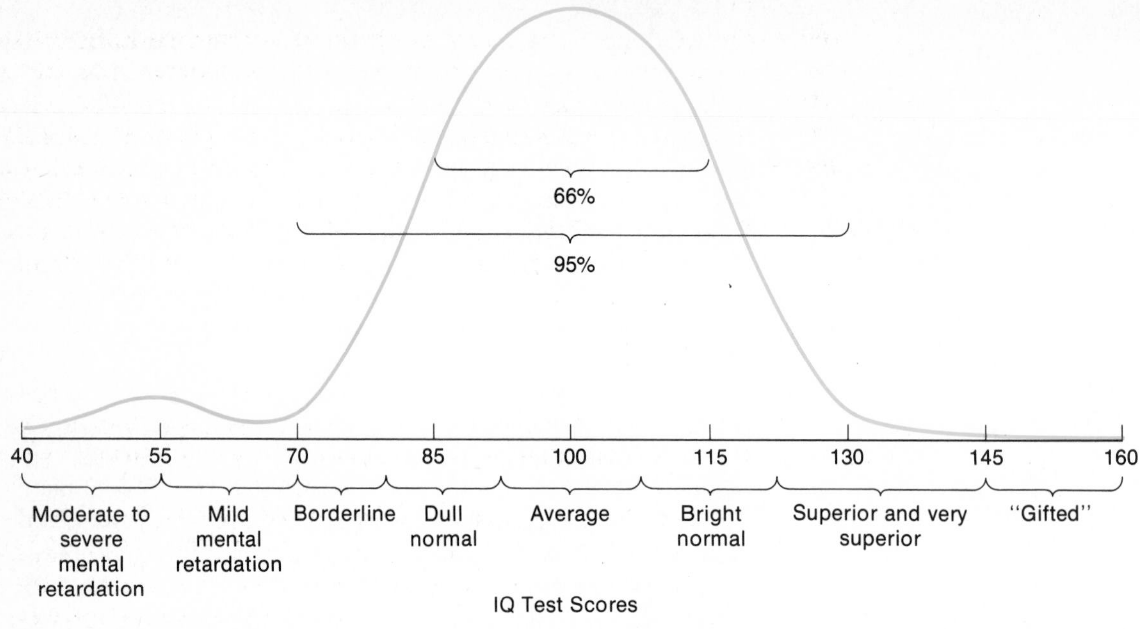

Figure 9.1 The approximate distribution of IQ scores on most modern tests. The tests are *designed* so that the average score is 100, and two-thirds of the scores fall between about 85 and 115. Because of brain damage or genetic anomalies, there are slightly more low-IQ children than there are very high-IQ children.

This procedure led to something called the **Intelligence Quotient,** which is where **IQ** comes from. It was originally a comparison of the child's actual age (chronological age) with his **mental age.** For example, a child who could solve the problems for a 6-year-old but not those for a 7-year-old would have a mental age of 6. The formula used to calculate the IQ was

$$\frac{\text{Mental Age}}{\text{Chronological Age}} \times 100 = \text{IQ}$$

This results in an IQ above 100 for children whose mental age is higher than their chronological age and an IQ below 100 for children whose mental age is below their chronological age.

This old system for calculating the IQ is not used any longer, even in the modern revisions of the Stanford-Binet (as Terman's revision of Binet's test is called). Nowadays IQs from any type of test are calculated by comparing a child's performance with those of a large group of other children his own age. The "average" child of any age is automatically given a score of 100; any child who does better than that average has an IQ above 100, and so on.

Modern IQ Tests

The tests used most frequently by psychologists today are the **Stanford-Binet** and the Wechsler Intelligence Scales for Children, usually called the **WISC,** which was developed originally by David Wechsler (1949). Because the Binet has items designed for testing preschool-age children, which the WISC does not, the Binet is more often used with 3–6-year-olds, while the WISC is more commonly used with older children. To give you some idea of the sort of items included in tests like this, I've described the WISC in some detail in Box 9.1.

Infant Tests Neither the Binet nor the WISC can be used with infants much younger than about 3. Infants don't talk well, if at all, and of course the usual childhood tests rely heavily on language. So how do we measure "intelligence" in an infant? This becomes an important question if we want to be able to identify, during infancy, those children who are likely to have intellectual or school difficulties later on. If we had a good "infant intelligence test," perhaps it could help locate such children.

Several attempts have been made. Arnold Gesell, whose maturational view of development I mentioned in Chapter 1, devised one of the first infant tests (Gesell, 1925). His major purpose was descriptive rather than predictive. He wanted to map out the typical maturational milestones, their sequence, and their rate of development. His test included measures of motor, language, and social development. For example, one item at the 4-month level involves ringing a bell near the baby. The baby "passes" this test if she turns her head toward the sound.

Two later tests were developed by Raymond Cattell (1940) and Nancy Bayley (1969). Bayley's test is probably the most widely used today and includes separate measures of motor development and mental development in the infant. Several attempts to develop tests of infant development linked more specifically to Piaget's theory have also been undertaken, particularly by Ina Uzgiris and J. McV. Hunt (1975).

The key thing for you to know about all these tests is that they do *not* do what we had all hoped. They do not predict later IQ scores or school performance very well (Rubin & Balow, 1979). The younger the infant is when you test him using any of these tests, the less help the infant test score will be in predicting his performance on the Stanford-Binet or the WISC later on. So babies who are quicker in motor development or who develop the object concept rapidly aren't necessarily the ones with bigger vocabularies or better block design performance when they are 6 or 10 years old.

This lack of continuity in the scores on intelligence tests between infancy and later childhood poses some problems. It obviously makes the identification of infants "at risk" for later low IQ very much harder. It raises some theoretical puzzles, too. Possibly we are just not measuring the right things in the infancy tests. Maybe there are aspects of infant functioning that

Box 9.1 The Wechsler Intelligence Scale for Children (WISC)

Unlike the Binet, which has separate tests for children of each age, on the WISC, all children are given the same ten types of problems, with each type running from very easy to very difficult items. The ten "subtests" are divided into two groups, those that rely heavily on verbal abilities and a group called "performance" tests, which involve less language ability and test the child's perceptual skills and nonverbal logic. The ten tests, with examples of items similar to those on the actual tests, are as follows:

Verbal Tests

General Information: "How many eyes have you?"

General Comprehension: "What is the thing to do when you scrape your knee?"

Arithmetic: "James had ten marbles and he bought four more. How many marbles did he have altogether?"

Similarities: "In what way are a pear and an orange alike?"

Vocabulary: "What is a radio?" "What is an emerald?"

Performance Tests

Picture Completion: The child is shown pictures of familiar objects in which a part has been left out. He has to identify the missing part, such as a comb with a tooth missing.

Picture Arrangement: Pictures like the frames of a comic strip are laid out in the wrong order. The child has to figure out the right order to make a story.

Block Design: Sets of blocks that are red, white, blue, and yellow on different sides and half red/half white or half blue/half yellow on other sides are given to the child. Using these blocks, he has to copy designs.

Object Assembly: Large pictures of familiar objects like a horse or a face have been cut up into pieces. The child has to put them together as rapidly as possible.

Coding: A series of abstract symbols like balls and stars are each shown with a paired symbol, such as a single line. The child then has several rows of the first set of symbols and must fill in the paired symbol next to each one.

Uses of the WISC Scores

One of the reasons many educators prefer the WISC to the Stanford-Binet is that it allows you to look at the variation in a child's performance. Gifted children typically do well on all the tests. Very retarded children typically do poorly on all the tests, although they may do a little better on the performance tests than on the verbal tests. But children with some kind of learning disability or brain damage may show a lot of variability. For example, children who have difficulty learning to read nearly always do better on the performance tests. But they often do quite well on the vocabulary subtests and very poorly on the coding test (Sattler, 1974). So it isn't just words that are the problem.

The key point is that significant *unevenness* in a child's performance on the WISC (or any other IQ test) may alert the teacher to a specific learning problem. Two children with the same total IQ scores may have very different patterns of test performance and may need very different kinds of special help.

do relate to later IQ. But it is equally possible that sensorimotor intelligence (to use Piaget's term) is just not very strongly related to the later types of intellectual functioning we measure with the WISC or the Binet.

Culture-Free Tests Because of the heavy verbal content of the Binet and the WISC, some psychologists, such as Florence Goodenough (1926), have tried to develop basically nonverbal tests. Verbal tests may underestimate the ability of children

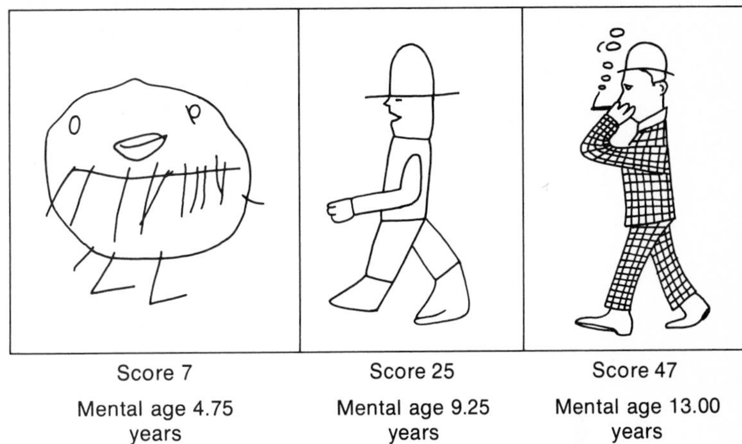

Figure 9.2 Examples of children's drawings of the human figure and the score they were given on Goodenough's draw-a-person test. The drawing on the right, which includes the plaid of the suit, a cigarette, and a moustache, gets a higher score than the drawing in the middle. (Source: From *Measurement of Intelligence by Drawings* by Florence L. Goodenough. Copyright 1926 by Harcourt Brace Jovanovich. Inc.; renewed 1954 by Florence L. Goodenough. Reproduced by permission of the publisher.)

who come from cultural backgrounds in which language is not stressed or who speak a different dialect—like Black English, as one example.

The most famous of the **culture-free** or **culture-fair** tests is probably Goodenough's **Draw-A-Person** test, which simply requires the child to draw a picture of a man or a woman. You can see some examples of children's drawings in Figure 9.2. The child's drawing is evaluated in terms of the normal amount of detail and elaboration found in the drawings of children that age. Since all children have observed people, it is assumed that they all have had the basic experience necessary to perform this task. There are other such culture-fair tests, although none is very widely used today for the simple reason that they have proven to be less predictive of other kinds of preformance than have the more standard IQ tests.

Achievement Tests Finally, let me say a word about a very familiar type of test, the **achievement test.** Nearly all of you have taken these tests in elementary and high school. They are designed to test *specific* information learned in school, using items like the ones in Table 9.1. The child taking an achievement test doesn't end up with an IQ score. But his performance is still compared to that of other children in the same grade across the country. Often the scores are reported in *percentiles.* A child who does just as well as the average child in his grade would be at the fiftieth percentile; one who did better than 90 percent of the other children would be at the ninetieth percentile, and so forth.

How are these tests different from an IQ test? The original intent was that an IQ test was supposed to measure the child's

Table 9.1 Some Sample Items from a Fourth-Grade Achievement Test

Vocabulary
jolly old man
1. angry
2. fat
3. merry
4. sorry

Spelling
Jason took the *cleanest* glass.
right _____ wrong _____

Language Expression
Who wants _____ books?
1. that
2. these
3. them
4. this

Mathematics
What does the "3" in 13 stand for?
1. 3 ones
2. 13 ones
3. 3 tens
4. 13 tens

Reference Skills
Which of these words would be first in ABC order?
1. pair
2. point
3. paint
4. polish

Mathematics Computation

$$\begin{array}{r} 79 \\ +14 \\ \hline \end{array} \qquad \begin{array}{r} 62 \\ \times\ 3 \\ \hline \end{array}$$

$$\begin{array}{r} 149 \\ -87 \\ \hline \end{array}$$

Source: From Comprehensive Tests of Basic Skills, Form S. Reprinted by permission of the publisher, CTB/McGraw-Hill, Del Monte Research Park, Monterey CA 93940.

basic capacity, her underlying **competence,** while the achievement test was supposed to measure what the child had actually learned.

This distinction between **competence** and **performance,** between "ability" and "achievement," is an important one. Each of us presumably has some upper limit of ability—what we could do under absolutely ideal conditions, when we are maximally motivated, rested, and so forth. But, of course, everyday conditions are never ideal, so we perform below our hypothetical ability. A teacher may help a child to perform better—come closer to his ability—by introducing new teaching techniques or motivating the child in a new way.

But important as this distinction is, it is a great mistake to assume that the IQ test somehow measures the child's basic ability or competence. It is *not* a benchmark against which you compare the child's day-to-day performance in the classroom. If you use it that way, you are led into some interesting logical fallacies.

Suppose, for example, that a child's IQ test score is higher than her achievement test scores and higher than her grades. If you assume that the IQ test measures her "real" ability, this child may be called an "underachiever"; and there may be parent conferences, much finger wagging and head scratching. Why is this basically "bright" child not doing well in school? How can she be motivated to do better?

That seems fairly logical, doesn't it? But now turn it around. What happens if the child's school performance is *better* than her IQ test score would suggest? These children are sometimes called "overachievers," and again the parents may get called in for a conference. Are they pushing the child too hard at home? But think about the logic. If the IQ test measures real capacity, then these "overachievers" are doing better than they can do. How is this possible?

The basic point, as John Horn states it flatly, is that "intelligence tests are achievement tests" (Horn, 1979, p. 237). The difference between tests called IQ tests and those called achievement tests is really a matter of degree. The intelligence tests include items that are designed to tap fairly fundamental intellectual processes; the achievement tests call for specific information the child has learned in school. But *both* measure performance and not competence.

If that's so, why bother with IQ tests at all in the schools? Some educators, in fact, don't think they are useful. But there are specific ways in which IQ tests are used in schools, as I've described in Box 9.2.

Stability of IQ Scores

Does a child's performance on an IQ test tend to stay fairly stable if she is tested several times? If she "has" an IQ of 115 when she is 10, is she likely to achieve the same score when she is 12 or 15?

If the two tests are given within a fairly short space of time—say weeks or even months apart—the scores do tend to be quite similar. But over the years of childhood, *most* children show wide fluctuations in their scores. Robert McCall and his colleagues (McCall, Appelbaum & Hogarty, 1973), for example, looked at the test scores of a group of children who had been given IQ tests at regular intervals from the time they were 2½ until they were 17. The majority of these youngsters had shown

Box 9.2 The Uses of IQ Tests in the Schools

The Sorting Function

The dominant use of IQ tests in public school systems today is for what Lauren Resnick (1979) calls the "sorting function." This is very much the purpose that Binet had in mind when he designed the first tests, and they are still used in this way.

Children who seem to be learning slowly in class may be given an IQ test to see if they might be "retarded." The test score would then be one of several pieces of information used to decide if the child should be in a special class. Or a child who is having difficulty learning to read but is otherwise doing okay may be given a test like the WISC or other special tests designed to diagnose specific learning disabilities or brain damage.

IQ tests are also sometimes used before school starts as a type of "readiness" test. When my daughter was not quite 5, she was given an IQ test because we wanted her to enter school a few months early. The school psychologist used the IQ test to help him determine if she would be able to handle the work of kindergarten.

All of these uses of the tests are for diagnosis and sorting. They help the teacher or the school to know which children need special help (either because of poor performance or very high performance), and they help to pin down the sort of help that may be most useful.

I should point out that not all educators or parents approve of this use of IQ tests. In a recent court case in California, a federal judge ruled that IQ tests could *not* be used as a basis for placing black children in classes for the retarded. He argued that the tests were biased against blacks and thus unfairly underestimated their abilities. In fact, a single IQ test score is almost never used alone as a basis for such placement. The child is normally given several tests, and his classroom functioning is also observed. Only when all the signs point in the same direction would a child be placed in a special class. Still, the court ruling shows the type of concern that has arisen recently about the use of IQ tests for sorting.

The Accountability and Justification Function

More recently, IQ tests are beginning to be used in another way as well—to justify educational practices to the public. "Accountability" is becoming a watchword in public life, and public schools are affected by the need to justify their actions, just as are other government groups. In many states, achievement tests are being used for this purpose. All the children in one or more grades may be given the same test, and then the results are made public. If the children in a given state are doing well by national standards, then all the educators pat themselves on the back. But if the children do poorly, what happens?

Poor performance by a group of children in a given class or a given school might come about because the school or the teacher just isn't doing a very good job. That's what parents are likely to conclude if they see low test scores, and they may pressure the schools to improve. In the face of pressure like this, some educators have fallen back on the IQ test as a measure of competence. If the children in a school have been given IQ tests and have performed poorly, then how can the school be expected to teach them as readily?

It should be obvious from what I've already said that I think this is fallacious reasoning. But I know it happens, because I have seen it in the school district on whose school board I served for several years. In one year, our fourth graders did poorly on the statewide achievement tests. The school psychologist suggested that we give them all IQ tests to see if they were "really" not very bright. The school board did not take his advice (I won that round!); but I suspect this use of IQ tests, as justification or legitimization of school policy, will become more prominent as schools come under increasing public pressure.

shifts of 20 to 30 points in their IQ scores during childhood, and nearly 15 percent of the children had shifted as much as 40 points one way or the other.

This type of shifting up and down in test scores is another good argument against using a single IQ test score as some kind of "upper limit" measure of a child's ability.

What IQ Tests Predict

The fact that IQ tests do not measure basic ability or competence doesn't mean they are useless. For many psychologists, the critical question is what they predict. If the IQ test scores can help us to make predictions about future problems or success, then it may still be a useful tool.

School Performance

In the case of IQ tests, psychologists have most often looked at predictions of school performance. After all, Binet designed the first tests specifically to predict school success, and that is still the major use of the tests. The research findings on this point are quite consistent: The correlation between a child's test score and her grades in school or performance on other school tests is about .60 (Sattler, 1974). So although some children with high IQ scores don't do all that well in school and some low-IQ children do quite well, on the whole, the children with the top scores will also be among the high achievers in school; and those who score low will be among the low achievers.

IQ scores not only relate moderately well to *current* school grades, they can also predict future grades. Preschool children with high IQ scores will tend to do better when they enter school than those with lower scores; children in fourth or fifth grade who test well are likely to be performing well in high school.

There's also a consistent finding that the higher a child's IQ, the more years of school she's likely to complete. Children with lower scores are more likely to drop out of high school or to complete high school and not go on to college. Partly this is because children with low IQ scores are more likely to come from poor families, and children from poor families are less likely to go to college anyway. But that's not the whole explanation. Of those kids who *do* decide to try college, those with lower IQ scores have more trouble finishing. So the test scores do predict school performance reasonably well.

I am *not* saying here that IQ *causes* good or poor performance in school—although that is one possibility and one that has been widely believed. All we know is that the two events—

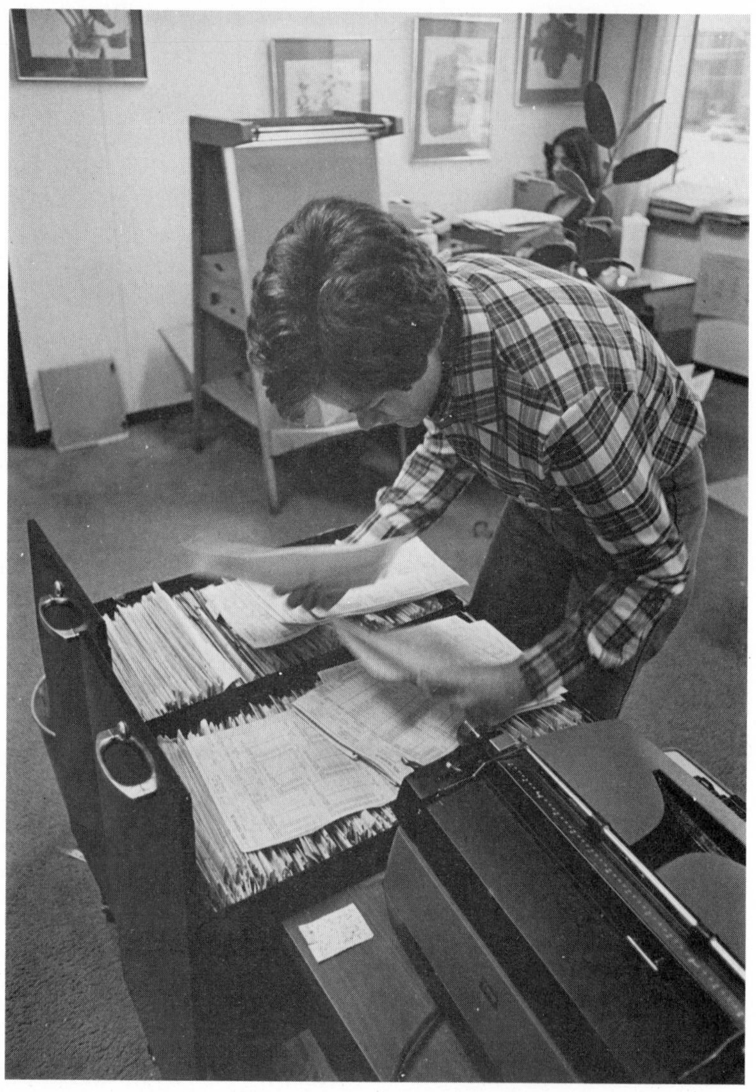

Figure 9.3 The job of secretary is one for which the IQ score predicts success. This job has no "entrance requirements," that is, you don't have to have a high IQ to get into this occupation. Once in it, however, adults with higher IQs are more successful than those with lower IQs.

high or low IQ scores and high or low school performance—tend to go together. The fact that makes the IQ test score potentially useful is that it can be used to predict school performance later on.

Later Job Success

Once a person gets out of school, does his IQ still predict anything important? Do people with higher IQs get better jobs, or do they do better in the jobs they hold? The answer is a cautious yes.

There is a relationship between IQ and the types of jobs people hold as adults. Most doctors and lawyers, for example, have fairly high IQs, while cooks and salesclerks, as a group, have lower IQs (Brody & Brody, 1976). This difference comes about partly because occupations like medicine or law have "entrance requirements." You have to be able to pass IQ-like entrance tests just to get into medical or law school, and you have to have finished college, too. That's not true for jobs like mechanic, cook, or salesclerk; so those jobs are open to people with less training or lower achievement.

The best general statement I can make is that people with high IQs and good education have many more options for their adult occupations. They can be mechanics or carpenters if they want, but they can also choose to be accountants or lawyers or dentists. People with lower IQs are more limited in their choices.

At the same time, once a person is in a job, his IQ doesn't tell us very much about how well he will succeed. Doctors with IQs of 150 don't make more money or have more satisfied patients than doctors with IQs of 130. And high-IQ carpenters don't hammer straighter nails than low-IQ carpenters. Only in those occupations where there are no entrance requirements and where there are intellectual demands, such as secretarial work or bookkeeping, does IQ predict performance.

Factors Influencing IQ Test Scores

There are really two questions here. First, why do some children fairly consistently do better on IQ tests than others do? And second, why does any one child's score fluctuate from one testing to the next?

The first question is at the heart of the now-familiar nature/nurture question. How much of the difference between children in their test scores is the result of built-in differences in such things as heredity (nature), and how much results from different experiences or different opportunities to learn (nurture)?

When Binet designed the early IQ tests, he did not make the assumption that he was measuring some fixed, inborn quality. He assumed instead that a child's intelligence could be modified. All he wanted to do was to measure it at a particular time. But in the United States, the psychologists who devised and revised intelligence tests by and large *did* assume that intelligence was inherited and thus fixed at birth. This assumption somehow got attached to the tests in many people's minds, so that most nonpsychologists (and many psychologists, I should add) are still convinced that intelligence is something you inherit and are then stuck with. How valid is that assumption? How much of a role do nature and nurture play in test scores?

The Influence of Heredity on IQ

The arguments about the heritability of IQ have been going on now for at least 50 years, and there is still no good agreement among the psychologists who do research in this area. Among current researchers and theorists, Arthur Jensen (1969, 1979) has taken one of the strongest genetic positions. He argues that as much as 80 percent of all the variation among IQ scores is due to genetic differences. In fact, his 1969 paper in the *Harvard Educational Review* sparked a whole new series of studies on the question. On the other end of the spectrum, Leon Kamin (1974) has taken an extreme environmentalist position. He contends that very little, if any, of the differences among people in IQ tests scores are due to genetic influence.

In between these two extremes are psychologists such as Robert Plomin (1978; Plomin & DeFries, 1980) and Sandra Scarr (Scarr & Weinberg, 1977, 1979), who argue that there is *some* genetic component in measured IQ but that environment plays an equal or even more dominant role.

I can't possibly settle this theoretical argument here. What I can do is to summarize some of the evidence and give you my own current synthesis.

There are two basic ways of searching for a genetic influence on IQ (or on any other trait, for that matter). You can study identical and fraternal twins or you can study adopted children. Identical twins share exactly the same genetic patterning, while fraternal twins do not. So if identical twins turn out to be more like one another in IQ than do fraternal twins, that would be evidence for the influence of heredity on IQ.

In the case of adopted children, you have a different situation. Here the child is being raised by someone other than her natural (genetic) parent. If the child's IQ should turn out to be more closely related to her *natural* parents' IQ, even though she didn't grow up with them, that would again be a point for the influence of heredity.

Both of those types of studies sound quite straightforward; but in fact, they are *extremely* difficult to do well, and the results are confusing.

Twin Studies Identical twins *do* have IQs that are more alike than fraternal twins (Loehlin & Nichols, 1976; Newman, Freeman & Holzinger, 1937; Wilson, 1977, 1978). Score one point for heredity. But isn't it possible that identical twins are *treated* more alike than are fraternal twins, too? Maybe they are dressed

Figure 9.4 These identical twin girls both have very high IQs and are both in a special program for gifted children. Are their IQs so similar because they share the same heredity? Or are they similar because they have been treated alike by their parents?

alike, spend more time together, are disciplined alike, have more similar toys, and so on. This seems to be true. Hugh Lytton (1977) found, in fact, that parents treat identical twins more alike, *even when they mistakenly think they are fraternal twins.* So part of the similarity in the IQs of identical twins may be their similar experiences and not just their identical heredity.

One way around this problem is to look at identical twins who have been reared apart from one another. If they are *still* alike in IQ, even though they are not together, that would surely show a hereditary effect.

Obviously, there aren't many pairs of identical twins who have been reared in different families. But there are a few, and there are several studies of them (Shields, 1962; Newman, Freeman & Holzinger, 1937; Juel-Nielsen, 1965). The general finding is that the identical twins are still pretty much alike. But as Leon Kamin (1974) points out, the more dissimilar the families in which a pair of twins is reared, the more dissimilar their IQs tend to be. So if the environments are very different, the intelligence tests scores are different, too. Both the "nature" and the "nurture" theorists can find some support from these results.

Adoption Studies Results from these studies are equally two-sided. The general finding is that adopted children's IQs can be predicted better from knowing the IQs or the level of education of their *natural* parents than from knowing the IQs of their adoptive parents. Again that sounds like a clear point for a genetic influence. But again there are some confusions.

First of all, when two adopted children are raised in the same family, their IQs turn out to be more similar than you'd expect by chance, even though they have *no* shared inheritance at all (Scarr & Weinberg, 1977). The environment, in this case, seems to be moving both children in the same direction.

Second, adopted children, as a group, tend to have much *higher* IQs than their natural parents. The effect of the adoptive environment seems to be to raise the child's IQ 10 or 15 points over what it probably would have been if he had been raised by his natural mother (Scarr & Weinberg, 1977; Skodak & Skeels, 1945). So obviously the adoptive environment has a major impact.

Summing Up the Role of Heredity in IQ Confusing, isn't it? After reading all of this research and all the heated comments by theorists on both sides of the issue, my own conclusion is that, as usual, neither extreme position is correct. The good recent research, such as that of Sandra Scarr on adopted children, does seem to me to show some genetic influence on measured IQ. But that influence seems to me to be a *lot* smaller than the 80 percent Jensen argues for or even the 50 percent Plomin suggests. In sum, we each appear to inherit particular characteristics that affect such things as the speed with which we learn, but the environment we grow up in plays a major role as well.

Racial Differences in IQ

If you thought that the evidence about hereditary influences on IQ was complicated, wait until you consider the evidence about racial differences! The basic troublesome fact is that, on the average, blacks achieve IQ test scores about 15 points lower than do whites. Obviously, this finding has aroused enormous controversy, and rightly so. The way you explain or interpret such a fact will have a big effect on social attitudes, educational practices, and governmental policy. To clarify this highly explosive question, if I can, let me first give you a further set of facts and then describe some of the alternative explanations that have been offered.

1. The average IQ difference between blacks and whites is found in numerous studies, those conducted in the North as well as in the South (Loehlin, Lindzey & Spuhler, 1975).

2. The difference is *not* found among infants. There are essentially no differences among racial and social class groups during infancy, except that black children exhibit somewhat faster motor development than do white children (Bayley, 1965). The difference between blacks and whites on IQ tests is first seen when the children are between 2 and 4 (Golden, Birns, Bridger & Moss, 1971).
3. Within both the black and white groups, there are social class differences: Middle-class blacks, on the average, achieve higher scores than do poor blacks, just as among whites (Loehlin, Lindzey & Spuhler, 1975).
4. School performance is about equally well predicted by the IQ test scores in each group: Black children who have high IQ scores are more likely to do well in school than are black children with low scores, again just as among whites (Kennedy, Van de Reit & White, 1963).

Genetic Differences? The most controversial explanation of these findings is that there is a genetic difference between the two racial groups. As I have just pointed out, many people are convinced that there is an important genetic contribution to the measured IQ score. On that basis, some people have argued that because heredity is an important determinant of measured IQ, differences between blacks and whites in measured IQ must be due to heredity, too. It sounds somewhat logical on the face of it, but it is not. It is entirely possible that individual IQ scores may be heavily influenced by heredity and that group differences may be entirely or largely the result of environmental differences. Let me give you an example that may make this point clearer.

Suppose that you go to a very poor village in Mexico (or any other less-developed country) and study the relationship between parents' and children's heights. You will find, to no one's surprise, that height is highly heritable: Genetic factors account for 80 or 90 percent of the variations among the heights of people in the village. Tall parents have taller children than short parents. Now go to Mexico City and do the same thing. Again you will find a strong genetic effect. But now measure the average height of the children in the village and of the children in the city. You will find that the village children are, on the average, quite a lot shorter than the children in the city, and this difference between the average heights of the two groups we know to be mostly a function of diet. The people in the village are not as well nourished, so they do not grow as tall as the people in the city. Here we have a situation in which there is a major genetic effect on height *within* each group but a difference *between* groups that is largely a result of an environmental variable.

The same logic can be applied to the observed difference between the IQ test scores of blacks and whites. Within each group, there might be some genetic influence, but the difference between the groups could be entirely the result of environmental differences.

Test Bias? A second explanation of racial differences in IQ is that there is something in the test itself—some built-in **bias**—that produces the observed difference. The argument is that the tests were originally devised for middle-class whites and have never been standardized for poor or black children. Furthermore, the tests tend to be heavily verbal; and as I mentioned in Chapter 6, many black children speak a dialect rather than Standard English.

There is probably some truth to the "test bias" argument, but in my opinion, test bias can't explain all the differences that are found. In particular, when systematic efforts are made to overcome such bias, a difference is still found. In the best-known study of this kind, conducted by Gerald Lesser and his coworkers (Lesser, Fifer & Clark, 1965), the children were tested by adults of their own race and cultural background. The tests were rewritten to include only words equally available to all groups. The testing was done in many sessions, with lots of time for each child to get to know her examiner, and so on. Under these testing conditions—the very best and fairest that could be devised—there were still differences. Results like these seem to me to show that bias isn't all of the answer.

Environmental Differences? If heredity doesn't explain it and bias can't explain it all, we are left with the very general notion that the environments of the two groups—blacks and whites—must differ in some ways that have important influences on test scores.

Diet may well be one such environmental influence. The evidence on malnutrition that I've already discussed points to the importance of nutrition for proper physical development. This may, in turn, affect the child's cognitive functioning, either directly, by affecting the growth of the brain, or indirectly, by influencing alertness and motivation. Since there are proportionately many more poor among the black population in this country and we know that the poor tend to have inadequate diets, it seems reasonable to look to nutrition to help explain some of the difference.

Alternatively, there may be aspects of the physical or interpersonal environment that are different in important ways. The typical statement is that the early environment of the black child is "impoverished," although precisely what impoverishment means in this context is not at all obvious. It is clear that the black child is likely to experience a different family structure (more often lacking a male figure), is more likely to be poor, and is likely to experience more prejudice and rejection from others, which may lead to a very different kind of self-image. There may also be different styles of interaction in black families, and different values may be assigned to learning and education.

Overall, although I cannot totally reject the possibility of a genetic difference on logical grounds, it seems to me that there is ample reason to suppose that the difference is largely, if not entirely, the result of environmental differences. With that in mind, let me turn to the question of environmental influences on IQ generally.

The Influence of the Environment on IQ

Let me start at the most global level, with social class differences, and work my way "down" to more specific kinds of experiences.

Social Class Differences

The most consistent finding in studies of IQ is that children from poor or working-class families have lower average IQs than do children from middle-class families. This difference is on the order of 10 to 20 points.

These differences are *not* found among infants. The rate of a child's sensorimotor development, as assessed by Bayley's test, for example, seems to be largely unrelated to the education or income of the family. But by age 3, consistent differences are found. The results from a study by Mark Golden and his colleagues (Golden, Birns, Bridger & Moss, 1971), shown in Table 9.2, show this difference very clearly. Generally speaking, the more affluent or the better educated a child's parents are, the higher the IQ he is likely to have.

There are about as many ways to interpret such findings as there are psychologists, as you might imagine. But from my perspective, the crucial point is that comparisons of social class groups will never tell us *why* there are differences. Studies like Golden's tell us that there *is* a difference, but to understand it, we have to do more detailed observations of what is going on in families between parents and children.

Table 9.2 IQ Scores of Children from Different Social Class Groups Tested at 1½ Years and 3 Years

Social class of children's parents	Average IQ scores	
	At 18 months on Cattell's test	At 36 months on Stanford-Binet
Middle class	106	115
Working class	113	110
Lower class, nonwelfare	114	102
Lower class, welfare	110	94

Source: Adapted from Golden, Birns, Bridger & Moss, 1971, Table 2, p. 41. With permission of the Society for Research in Child Development, Inc.

Specific Family Characteristics

I mentioned in Chapter 8 that the type of intellectual development studied by Piaget is affected by the child's early environment. Parents who provide a lot of both social and inanimate stimulation seem to have faster-developing children. The same kinds of environmental features emerge from studies of environment and IQ.

In my opinion, some of the most interesting research on this question has been done by Bettye Caldwell and her colleagues Robert Bradley and Richard Elardo (Elardo, Bradley & Caldwell, 1975; Bradley & Caldwell, 1976, 1977, 1978).

Caldwell has devised a measure of the environment she calls the HOME Inventory (Home Observation for Measurement of the Environment). An interviewer/observer visits a home, talks with the parent about various things, and observes the kinds of materials available to the child and the kind of interactions the parent has with the child. The observer then scores yes or no for each of a series of specific items about that family. Some examples of items from this scale are in Table 9.3.

Elardo, Bradley, and Caldwell's (1975) research using this technique shows that mothers who are emotionally responsive to their 6- or 12-month-old infant, provide appropriate play materials, spend time with their infant, and provide variety in the child's experience have children who later have higher IQs.

My colleagues and I at the University of Washington have replicated these findings in an ongoing longitudinal study of a group of about 200 infants. Craig Ramey and his colleagues at the University of North Carolina (Ramey, Farran & Campbell, 1979) have also partially replicated the Caldwell results. In

Table 9.3 Some Sample Items from the HOME Inventory

The mother spontaneously vocalizes to the child at least twice during the visit (excluding scolding).	Yes____	No____
When speaking of or to child, mother's voice conveys positive feeling.	Yes____	No____
Mother does not shout at child during visit.	Yes____	No____
Child gets out of house at least four times a week.	Yes____	No____
Child has push or pull toy.	Yes____	No____
Family provides learning equipment appropriate to age—mobile, table and chairs, high chair, play pen.	Yes____	No____
Mother structures child's play periods.	Yes____	No____
Mother reads stories at least three times weekly.	Yes____	No____

Source: Caldwell & Bradley, 1978.

Ramey's research, and in our own, the mother's level of punishment and restriction also emerges as a critical variable. Mothers who are more physically restrictive and more punitive toward their children, especially during the second year of life, have children with *lower* IQs later on.

Other investigators, using different measures of the environment, have reported parallel findings. Steven Tulkin and Fran Covitz (1975), for example, have found that the number of play materials provided for children at 10 months was related to the child's IQ at age 6. And Ralph Hanson (1975) found that the parents' involvement with their children, their emphasis on school achievement, and their encouragement of the child's verbal expression were all quite strongly correlated with the child's IQ scores from age 3 through age 10.

Two very recent studies also point to the importance of the quality of the mother's language to the child. Alison Clarke-Stewart (Clarke-Stewart, VanderStoep & Killian, 1979) has found that mothers who use more "descriptive" language—talking about objects and people with the child—have children with higher IQs. Even more interesting, Patrick Dickson and his colleagues (Dickson, Hess, Miyake & Azuma, 1979) have found that the mother's "referential communication accuracy" when

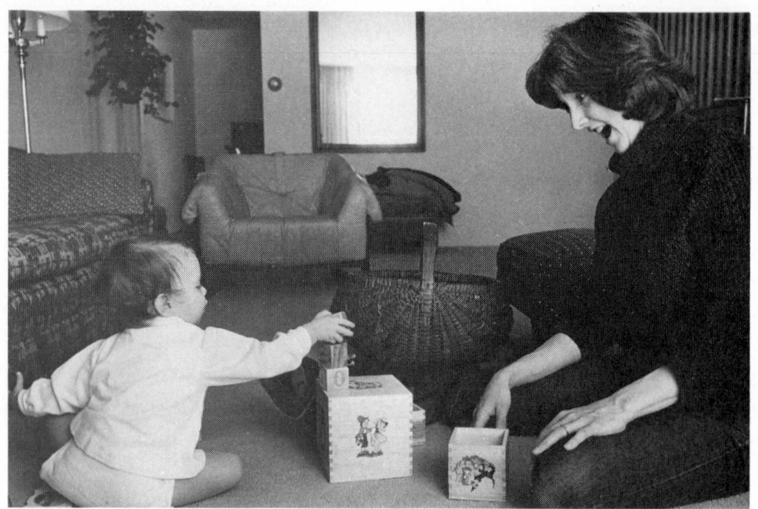

Figure 9.5 Parents who spend time with their child, encourage exploration, provide appropriate toys, and use complex language have children who later perform better on IQ tests.

the child was 4 predicted the child's IQ at 6 in both a United States sample and a Japanese sample. The task Dickson used to measure referential communication accuracy required the mother to describe a photograph to her child. The child then had to select the described picture out of a set of four. Whether the child could make a correct selection depended largely on how accurately and fully the mother had described the picture. Thus, the clarity of the mother's language appears to be an important determiner of the child's later IQ.

Summary of Family Effects Each of these groups of researchers has approached the task of assessing the environment in a different way, so adding up the results is complex. But there do seem to be consistent threads running through all the findings. Children who show the most rapid cognitive progress or highest IQ seem to be those whose parents do several things:

1. They provide *appropriate* play materials for the child. It is not the sheer quantity of play materials that is significant; rather, it is the appropriateness of the play materials for the child's age and developmental level that seems to be critical. A set of nesting pots or pans to play with is just as good as an expensive toy, so long as the child has access to it.
2. They are *involved* with their child. They spend time with the child, encourage the child's play and problem solving, and respond to the child's questions, actions, or activities.

Figure 9.6 **The relationship between birth order, family size, and IQ. Each line represents a family of a particular size, and each dot represents the average IQ of the first, second, third, or *n*th child in a family of that size. Clearly, the larger the family, the lower the scores for all the offspring. And later children in any sized family have lower scores than those born earlier. (Source: Zajonc, 1975, p. 43. Reprinted from *Psychology Today Magazine.* Copyright © 1975, Ziff-Davis Publishing Co.)**

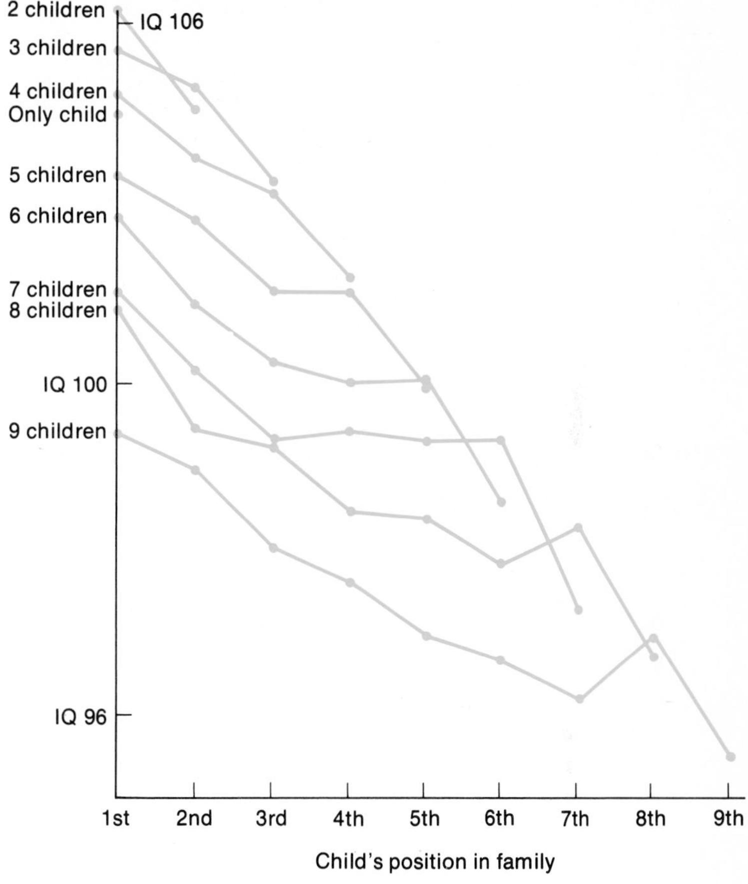

3. They *expect* their child to do well and to develop rapidly. They emphasize and press for school achievement.
4. They talk to their child, using language that is descriptively rich and accurate.

These patterns of parental behavior seem to begin when the child is still in infancy, but the full impact of the parent's behavior on the child's IQ is not felt until the child is 3 or older.

Birth Order Another aspect of family experience that seems to have some connection to measured IQ is the child's position in the family. On the average, firstborn children have the highest IQs, with the average IQ declining steadily as you go down the family (Zajonc, 1975; Zajonc & Marcus, 1975). One set of data that shows this effect very clearly comes from a study of nearly 400,000 young men in Holland (see Figure 9.6). You can see in the figure that later-born children on the average have lower IQs and that children in larger families have lower scores as well.

One possible explanation for these results is what I think of as the "tired mother" theory—an option I discussed in Chapter 2. The mother's general health seems to decline with repeated pregnancies, so that both the prenatal and the postnatal environment of each succeeding child is less good. If this is true, you'd expect that the second child in two very closely spaced pregnancies—when the mother's body would be most stressed—should have an even greater disadvantage on an IQ test, and this is what has been found. But it's difficult to see how physical fatigue or depletion could account for average differences in IQ within two- or three-child families in which the children are reasonably well spaced.

Robert Zajonc has suggested a second explanation (Zajonc, 1975). He thinks that the child's intellectual development is the product of the average intellectual level of the people around her as she is growing up. A firstborn child has only grown-ups around her in the early years, so she's exposed to fairly advanced kinds of intellectual functioning. But a second child has not only the adults but also a somewhat older sibling, who may be still at the sensorimotor or preoperational level (to use Piaget's terms). The average level of functioning the second child experiences is lower, and so her intellectual stimulation will be lower, too.

Zajonc's hypothesis makes a certain amount of intuitive sense, since we know that second-, third-, or later-born children do spend more time with other children than is the case with firstborns. But I'm still not totally convinced. There are some important unanswered questions. For example, Elardo's study shows that toys, materials, and variety in stimulation help to increase IQ. Why would a second or third child have fewer toys or less variety? Still, Zajonc's hypothesis is intriguing and will undoubtedly foster a whole collection of new studies on the effects of siblings on children's intellectual development.

School Experience

Obviously, family experiences affect the child's intellectual development. But what about school? Does it matter if the child has been to preschool or **Head Start?** Does it matter what sort of teacher the child has in elementary school?

Preschools: Head Start and Equivalent Experiences The answer to the first of these questions, about preschool experience, seems now to be yes. Early studies of Head Start, or of Head-Start-like preschools, showed that the children gained about ten points on IQ tests during their preschool year, but the effect

Figure 9.7 **The effect of a preschool enrichment program on children's school performance in grade school. Note that the children who had had preschool are very slightly ahead on achievement test scores all along, but the difference increases markedly from sixth grade on. This is the "sleeper effect" of preschool. (Source: *Bulletin of the High/Scope Foundation*, 1977, p. 5.)**

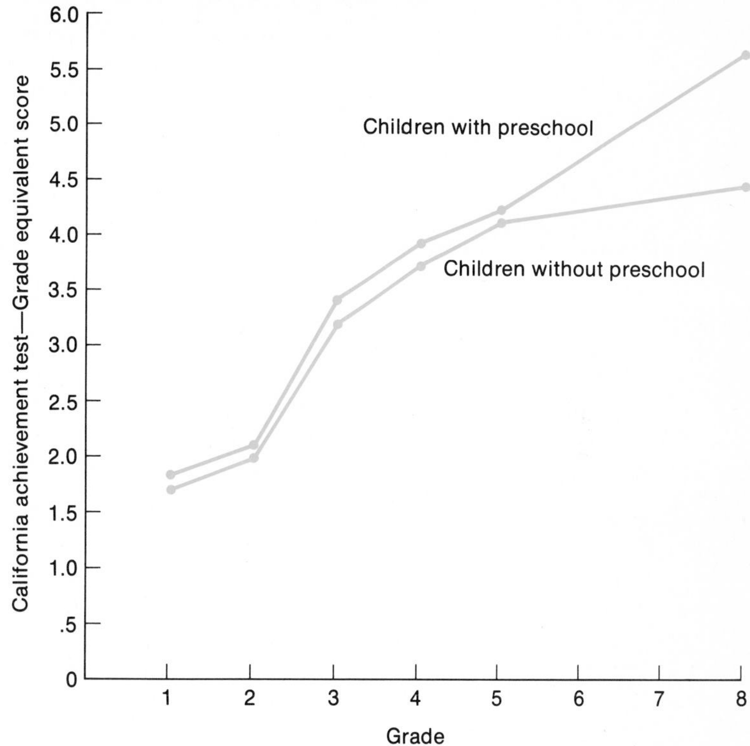

seemed to fade once they were in regular schools (Gray & Klaus, 1965; Klaus & Gray, 1968; Bissell, 1973; Weikart, 1972). This was discouraging news for those educators and psychologists who had argued that preschool education would be an effective way of providing needed additional stimulation for children from economically disadvantaged families.

More recent news has been much more encouraging. There seems to be a "sleeper effect" in the impact of Head Start and equivalent programs. If you keep track of the children long enough, by sixth, seventh, or eighth grade, a consistent and growing difference between those who attended preschool and those who did not shows up on achievement test scores. Some typical findings from David Weikart's study are in Figure 9.7. In this case, the difference becomes clear at about sixth grade and then gets larger over time. The preschool children in this study were also less likely to require remedial programs later on or to be assigned to special classes.

Phyllis Levenstein and her colleagues (Madden, Levenstein & Levenstein, 1976; Levenstein, 1970) have produced similar results by, in effect, bringing the preschool into the home. They visited mothers and children at home once a week, bringing special toys and teaching the mother how to play with the child

Box 9·3 The Remarkable Case of "Miss A"

In the process of looking at the long-term outcomes of a group of children who had all attended a single school in a poor neighborhood, Eigel Pederson and his co-workers (Pederson, Faucher & Eaton, 1978) came by accident on evidence of the effects of a remarkable teacher, whom they call "Miss A."

Miss A taught first grade in the same school for over 30 years. Pederson was able to track her former pupils through the school system and was later able to interview 14 of them as adults, along with 44 others who had had different first-grade teachers. It seems very clear from this study that Miss A had a lasting impact on her pupils.

The children in her classroom were more likely to show increases in IQ during elementary school. They were rated as more cooperative by their later teachers, throughout elementary school. They got better grades throughout elementary school. They finished more years of schooling and were *much* more successful as adults. Not a single one of Miss A's pupils whom Pederson interviewed as an adult was in the lowest level of adult success defined in this study, despite the fact that most of the children in Miss A's classes came from poor families, many from minority families.

All of Miss A's pupils remembered her, even 20 or 30 years later, while adults who had had other first-grade teachers often did not recall their teacher's name or anything about her.

This is only one study, and the number of people studied is not large. But those of you who are planning a career in elementary education should take heart. It does seem to matter what you do with and for children in the early years of school. As Pederson puts it:

> *If children are fortunate enough to begin their schooling with an optimistic teacher who expects them to do well and who teaches them the basic skills needed for further academic success, they are likely to perform better than those exposed to a teacher who conveys a discouraging, self-defeating outlook.*
>
> (Pederson, Faucher & Eaton, 1978, p. 11)

in a stimulating way. Children who went through this program had higher IQs and continued to do better in school later. Interestingly, their younger brothers and sisters also showed positive effects from the program.

The question about the impact of the quality of instruction once the child gets to elementary school is more difficult to answer. Christopher Jencks and his colleagues (Jencks, Smith, Acland, Bane, Cohen, Gintis, Heyns & Michelson, 1972) argue that most features of schooling matter relatively little in the long run. Adult success, they say, is not greatly affected by specific schooling experiences. In contrast, Robert Rosenthal argues in his well-known book *Pygmalion in the Classroom* (Rosenthal & Jacobson, 1968) that at least one aspect of schooling, namely, the teacher's expectations, has a powerful effect on the performance of an individual child. If she thinks the child is bright and will do well, the child in fact does better.

I'm not convinced we have the evidence to decide one way or the other at this stage, but there is one fascinating study which I've described in Box 9.3 that provides some support for Rosenthal's side of the argument.

The Testing Situation The final set of circumstances that can affect a child's test score is the specific conditions under which the test is given. Two things seem to matter.

First, the relationship the child has with the person administering the test can make a significant difference in his score. Elinor Sacks (1952) looked at this aspect in an excellent older study. She found that the children with whom she established a warm and friendly relationship increased about 15 points in their IQ scores between a first and second testing. So if a child is tested by someone he knows rather than by a stranger, he will probably achieve a higher score.

The procedure during the testing itself also can make a difference. The traditional procedure is to begin with the easy questions and work up to the hard ones until the child fails a whole series in a row. That can get discouraging for the child. But if you modify this procedure so that there are successes mixed in with the failures and so that the child is given lots of encouragement and time to respond, the child's scores again will go up. Edward Zigler and his colleagues have shown increases of as much as 10 or 15 points in IQ scores when these more positive conditions are used (Zigler & Butterfield, 1968, for example).

Both of these findings underline the fact that you have to be very cautious about interpreting a score from a single test given to a child on a particular day. Did the child know the examiner? Was the child feeling well that day? Was the examiner warm and encouraging? In other words, is the child's test score representative of what he can do under fairly optimal conditions, or is it a kind of lower limit of his performance under standard or even discouraging conditions? If the test was given in the first place because a decision is being made about placing the child in a special class, then caution in interpreting a single score is even more critical.

Sex Differences

On measures of overall IQ, there are *no* consistent sex differences. Boys and girls have about the same average IQ scores. But when the score is broken down into several separate skills or abilities, some patterns of sex differences do emerge. I've summarized the major findings in Table 9.4.

Table 9.4 A Summary of Sex Differences in Intellectual Abilities

Type of ability	Nature of difference
Spatial visualization (ability to manipulate abstract shapes, to visualize three-dimensional spaces from two-dimensional drawings, and so forth)	Boys quite consistently better at this from adolescence on. *No* consistent difference is found among younger children.
Mathematics	No difference is found, or girls are slightly better on such things as computational skill.
Numerical reasoning	Boys are better starting at about adolescence.
Verbal abilities	Girls are a bit more talkative and use a bit longer sentences.
Verbal reasoning	Girls are a bit better starting at about adolescence.

A crucial point needs to be made about the results described in the table. These are *average* differences. On *every* measure, there is a great deal of overlap between the scores of boys and girls, males and females. There are many girls good at spatial visualization and many boys good at verbal reasoning. It is also worth emphasizing that the pattern of differences doesn't fit perfectly with our cultural stereotypes about men and women. The stereotype for females is that they talk a lot but aren't very "logical." The male stereotype is that they are clear and logical, good at math, and maybe less verbal. The actual pattern is that each sex is good at some kinds of logical problem solving and neither is consistently more "logical" than the other. Girls are somewhat more verbal—so that much is accurate—but except for boys being better at mathematical reasoning, there are no differences in ability with mathematics.

Probably there are both environmental and biological forces at work in producing these differences. In particular, the difference in spatial skills seems to have some biological underpinning, perhaps having to do with hormone patterning. Deborah Waber (1977), for example, finds that girls who go through puberty later are better at spatial tasks than are girls who are early developers, which suggests that hormones may play some role.

But there are no equivalent biological explanations of the differences in mathematical or verbal reasoning. Are these differences the result of differing school experiences, such as more mathematics courses for boys? Are girls encouraged to talk more? We don't know the answers to these questions yet. In fact, it will be very interesting, over the next decade or so, to see whether these differences continue to be found at all as the various obvious and subtle effects of the women's movement begin to be felt.

Overview of IQ Testing

One of the questions that students often ask at about this point is whether, given all the factors that can affect a test score, it is worth bothering with IQ tests at all. I think that these tests do assess some important aspects of children's intellectual performance and that they can be helpful in identifying children who may have difficulties in school. But it is important to keep in mind that they do *not* measure a lot of other things we may be interested in, such as the child's level of cognitive development (as in Piaget's theory) or her motivation to achieve. An IQ test is a specialized tool, and like many such tools, it has a fairly narrow range of appropriate use. I don't want to throw out this tool, but you have to keep its limitations very firmly in mind when you use it.

Summary

1. Standard IQ tests do not measure all the aspects of a child's cognitive development that might interest us. They don't, as a rule, tell us where the child is in some sequence of logical development, as would a test based on Piaget's theory. But they do tell us something about the child's performance relative to that of her peers, and they do predict such nontest performance as school success with some consistency.

2. IQ tests do not measure a child's capacity or competence. They measure performance.

3. Psychologists are still arguing about whether IQ test scores are influenced by heredity. Most psychologists would agree that something between 20 and 50 percent of the variation in scores among people is due to heredity.

4. Hereditary explanations of the differences between blacks and whites in average test scores can probably be rejected, however. Large environmental differences between the two racial groups are a far more likely explanation.

5. The influence of the family environment on IQ test scores is substantial:

- **a.** There is a consistent relationship between social class and IQ, with middle-class children achieving higher scores.
- **b.** Firstborn and early-born children on the average have higher IQs than later-born children in the same families.
- **c.** Those families that provide appropriate play materials and encourage the child's intellectual development have children who test higher on IQ tests.

6. Special "enriched" preschools for disadvantaged children help to increase IQ; more important, they help to produce long-term improvements in school performance.

7. Within elementary school, individual teachers may have a lasting impact, although this case is still being argued.

8. The specific testing situation affects a child's test score. Children given more time and encouragement during testing will usually score higher, as will children who are familiar and comfortable with the examiner.
9. On total IQ scores, males and females do not differ; but males are better at spatial visualization and mathematical reasoning, while females are better at verbal reasoning and some other verbal tasks.

Key Terms

Achievement test A test usually given in schools, designed to assess a child's learning of specific material taught in school, such as spelling or arithmetic computation.

Bias Aspects of a psychological test, such as dependence on language or cultural experience, which may influence the scores of some subjects.

Competence The behavior of a person as it would be under ideal or perfect circumstances. It is not possible to measure competence directly.

Culture-fair test A test whose items are chosen so as to minimize test bias, that is, one that children from different cultural backgrounds would be expected to score equally well on.

Draw-A-Person test Nonverbal test of intelligence that requires the child to draw a picture of a human figure.

Head Start Federally funded program which offers compensatory education to preschoolers from poor families who would otherwise be expected to have poor school performance later.

Intelligence Quotient See IQ.

IQ Intelligence quotient. Originally defined in terms of a child's mental age and chronological age, IQs are now computed by comparing a child's performance with that of other children of the same chronological age.

Mental age A way to describe the level of mental tasks a child can perform. A child who can perform tasks normally done by 8-year-olds, for example, has a mental age of 8.

Performance The behavior shown by a person under actual circumstances. Even when we are interested in competence, all we can ever measure is performance.

Stanford-Binet The best-known American intelligence test. It was written by Louis Terman and his associates based upon the first tests by Binet and Simon.

WISC The Wechsler Intelligence Scale for Children. Another well-known American IQ test which includes both verbal and performance (nonverbal) subtests.

Suggested Readings

Bane, M. J., & Jencks, C. "Five myths about your IQ." Harper's, 1973, **246** (February), 28–40.
This is an excellent discussion of some of the same issues I have raised in this chapter. Not new, but representing a particular, mostly environmental, point of view.

Birns, B., & Bridger, W. "Cognitive development and social class." In J. Wortis (Ed.), Mental retardation and developmental disabilities. An Annual review. Vol. 9. New York: Brunner/Mazel, 1977.
A first-class review of the information on social class (and racial) differences in IQ and the possible explanations of those differences.

Brody, E. B., & Brody, N. Intelligence: Nature, determinants, and consequences. New York: Academic Press, 1976.
A very good, moderately difficult book covering the whole topic. An excellent next source of further references or more detail on some of the topics I've covered in the chapter.

Goleman, D. "Special abilities of the sexes: Do they begin in the brain?" Psychology Today, 1978, **12** (6), 48–59, 120.
A good recent discussion of some of the major findings on

sex differences in intellectual abilities and the provocative suggestions of some researchers that those differences originate in differing brain patterns.

Pederson, E., Faucher, T. A., & Eaton, W. W. "A new perspective on the effects of first-grade teachers on children's subsequent adult status." Harvard Educational Review, 1978, **48,** 1–31.
Very easy to read and fascinating. This is the study I've described in Box 9.3.

Rice, B. "Brave new world of intelligence testing." Psychology Today, 1979, **13** (No. 4), 26–41.
A very interesting current discussion of some of the newer tests and related facets of intellectual functioning.

Zajonc, R. B. "Birth order and intelligence: Dumber by the dozen." Psychology Today, 1975, **8** (No. 8), 37–43.
A highly readable account of Zajonc's argument regarding birth order and IQ.

Part Four

The Social Child

Preview of Chapter 10

Theories of Personality Development

I watched the two children on the playground for almost an hour, during their school lunch period. Michael was on the move almost constantly. He'd play with one group for a while, and then—almost restlessly—move on to another group of children. But when he was with a group, he seemed to take a dominant role. If he wanted to play kickball, his wishes seemed to carry the day. He had a loud, clear, voice and didn't hesitate to use it! Mostly he played with other boys, although occasionally a girl would be part of the group, too.

There were several teachers on the playground, but Michael never approached or called out to them. His attention was on the other children. But he was not aggressive. While I observed him, he never hit, threatened, or bullied another child.

Steven was also on the playground for the whole lunch period, but he presented a very different picture. He spent most of his time either alone or with one other boy, who seemed to be a special friend. They were playing in one corner of the area for nearly half an hour, building a sort of fort out of dirt. Neither child seemed to be the leader in this pair, and they didn't talk a great deal to one another. But they played companionably together. Several of the teachers spoke to Steven and his friend; and at one point, Steven pointed out his construction with apparent pride to the nearest teacher.

What I have emphasized about these two boys are aspects of their **personalities**—those individual, relatively enduring patterns of reacting and interacting with others and with the environment that distinguish each of us. Michael appeared to be active, talkative, dominant, but not aggressive. By contrast, Steven was quiet, less dominant, and perhaps slightly more attentive to adults. I couldn't tell from my brief observation whether he was normally shy with other children, but he was certainly less gregarious than Michael.

How did these two children develop such different patterns of relating to others? How consistent are those patterns across situations? Have these two boys been different from their earliest months of life? Were they "taught" these different styles of interacting? Will they still be different in the same ways 10 or 20 years from now?

There are really two sets of issues here. First of all, what do we know about the origins of those unique and consistent patterns of individual behavior that we call personality? What have various theorists said about how those differences come about?

Second, are there development stages or steps that we all go through in our interactions with other people? You can probably think of some adult you know who is highly dependent on others. We'd call that an aspect of his or her personality. But *all* of us were clinging and dependent when we were infants and toddlers. We became more independent as we grew older. So there seem to be both enduring characteristics and developmental patterns shared by all children.

It is not always possible to disentangle these two questions when we talk about personality and social development. But let me approach the problem by discussing several major theories of personality development in this chapter and then turning to what we know about the basic sequences in the development of social relationships in the next chapter. Inevitably, I'm going to slip back and forth somewhat, since several of the theories of personality development have explicit stages built into them and since an examination of patterns of social development leads naturally to theory building. But the focus in this chapter will be on the personality theory side of these issues.

What and Why Questions By talking about theory first, I am reversing my usual order: I'm putting the *why* before the *what*. Ordinarily, I would argue that that's putting the cart before the horse; but in this case, I think it's necessary. Unlike the area of cognitive development, in which there is one dominant theoretical perspective, in the study of personality and social development, there are many competing theories. More important, a good deal of the research that has been done has been explicitly guided by one or another of these theories. For example, most of the newer research on attachment in babies has been guided by Bowlby's (1969) ethological theory. It is almost impossible to describe the basic findings without describing the theory first. Because of such linkages between the what and the why questions in this area, it seems sensible to me to begin by telling you about the theoretical alternatives. I'll turn to the more factual side of the issues in Chapters 11 and 12.

Major Types of Personality Development Theories

Three of the broad approaches to development I described in Chapter 1 are represented here: the psychoanalytic approach, the learning approach, and several variations of a biological approach. The one theoretical view missing in this instance is the cognitive-developmental. Most theorists with a cognitive-developmental slant have focused on intellectual growth rather than on social interactions, so there is as yet no comprehensive cognitive-developmental theory about personality. But cognitive elements are creeping into other theoretical approaches—most notably into Bandura's (1977) social learning theory. I expect that within the next decade, we will be seeing a much fuller blending of cognitive and personality theories. For now, though, we have only three general categories of theory to explore.

Social Learning Approaches to Personality

The fundamental concept in social learning theories of personality is that we behave the way we do because we have been reinforced for that pattern of behavior. In fact, most learning theorists don't use the word "personality" at all. They don't see a child as having an "aggressive personality"—only aggressive behavior. The emphasis is on the impact of the environment on the child. Albert Bandura, who has developed perhaps the most systematic social learning theory, puts this basic proposition flatly:

> Except for elementary reflexes, people are not equipped with inborn repertoires of behavior. They must learn them. New response patterns can be acquired either by direct experience or by observation.
>
> *(Bandura, 1977, p. 16)*

Bandura is not rejecting biology. He goes on to say that biological factors such as hormones or inherited propensities can affect behavior. But he clearly comes down hard on the side of the environment as the major "cause" of the behavior we observe.

These are not new ideas. The question here is how to apply this theory specifically to such "personality" characteristics as dependency, nurturance, aggressiveness, and shyness. So let me restate the basic propositions of the theory and then see how they can be applied to social behavior or to more enduring "personality" characteristics.

Proposition 1 *Behavior is "strengthened" by reinforcement.* If this rule applies to all behavior, then it should apply to attachment, shyness, sharing, or competitiveness, too. We'd expect that children who are reinforced for clinging to their parents would show more of this behavior than do children who are not reinforced for it. A nursery school teacher who pays attention only to children when they get rowdy or aggressive should find that the children get steadily more rowdy and aggressive over the course of weeks or months.

In fact, this does seem to happen. For example, when experimenters have systematically rewarded some children for hitting an inflated rubber clown (a Bobo doll) on the nose and then watched the children in a play situation, the children who were rewarded show more hitting, scratching, and kicking than do children who haven't been rewarded for punching the Bobo doll (Walters & Brown, 1963).

Proposition 2 *Behavior that is reinforced on a "partial schedule" should be even stronger and more resistant to extinction than behavior that is consistently reinforced.* I talked about this phenomenon in Chapter 1 and already gave you some examples of the application of the principles of partial reinforcement (see Box 1.1). Parents are nearly always "inconsistent" in their rewards to their children, so most children are on partial schedules of some kind. Bandura and others have argued that we can understand why some children turn out to be more aggressive or more shy, and others less so, by looking at the kind of reward patterns at home.

These first two principles have been used successfully in therapy with families of children with troublesome behaviors such as tantrums, defiance, or extreme aggressiveness, as I've described in Box 10.1.

Proposition 3 *Children learn new behaviors largely through modeling.* Bandura has argued that the full range of social behaviors, from competitiveness to nurturance, is learned by watching others perform those actions. The child who sees her parents making a donation to the local Cancer Society volunteer or taking a casserole next door to the woman who has just been widowed will learn generosity and thoughtful behavior. The child who sees her parents arguing or hitting each other when they are angry will most likely learn violent ways of solving problems.

Box 10.1

Using Social Learning Principles to Modify "Problem Behavior" in Children

Many forms of therapy have been used successfully to modify unwanted behavior in children. One widely used strategy is the systematic application of reinforcement principles, often described as **behavior therapy.** Gerald Patterson's descriptions (1975) of behavior therapy with children showing severe problem behavior is particularly fascinating. One case study will give you some of the flavor of this approach.

Eric was ten years old and a practiced monster. He not only hit his younger sister, but had completely alienated himself from children in the neighborhood as well. He was so bossy that other children avoided playing with him. He was likely to settle disagreements with an all-out attack. At home he made derogatory remarks about his mother and his sister. He was large enough and aggressive enough so that his mother felt she could not handle him. . . .

Eric was so skilled at noncompliance that neither the father nor the mother asked him to do anything. As is the case for most aggressive boys, both parents had been trained to believe that Eric could not mind or do chores.

(Patterson, 1975, p. 130)

Having arrived at this awful state of affairs, what could Eric's parents do? Patterson's prescription follows distinct steps.

1. Select only *one* specific problem behavior to work on at a time, preferably beginning with one of the less awful. In this case, Eric's parents started with his noncompliance.
2. Observe and keep records. Eric's parents defined what they meant by "noncompliance" and then counted each time it occurred. At the beginning of the "treatment," Eric "noncomplied" about once every ten minutes.
3. Describe your records to the child and tell him precisely what you expect and what he'll get in the way of a reward if he changes his behavior. Eric was told that he would get a "point," which he could exchange for things he wanted, each time he did what he was told. During this step, the parents do *nothing* if the child does not comply.
4. After point earning has been well established, the parents introduce a type of punishment called "time out" whenever the child doesn't do what he's been asked. Time out involves having the child go to a separate room by himself for a specified period of time. In Eric's case, he had to spend five minutes alone in the bathroom each time.
5. Change the point programs as needed by adding other possible incentives or other goal behaviors. Eric could earn a fishing trip with his dad for 50 points, for example.

Children exposed to programs like these often get worse before they get better, and it can be a terrific strain on the parents to maintain the new system. Frequently, the parents need the assistance of an outside therapist (such as Patterson) to help them maintain consistent responses to their child. But many types of problem behaviors that had been the despair of parents have been modified in this way.

Children learn from TV, too, and from their playmates, their teachers, and their brothers and sisters. A boy growing up in a slum who observes playmates and older boys who hang around street corners, shoplift, or steal hubcaps is going to learn all those behaviors. His continuous exposure to all those unsavory models makes it that much harder for his parents to reinforce more constructive behavior. Teenagers are often irate when their parents get concerned about the "crowd" they run with.

Figure 10.1 **These children clearly show aggressive behavior and postures learned through observation, probably on television. The fact that the "victim" is not actually killed does not mean that the children have not learned the full set of responses.**

But from Bandura's point of view, such parental concern is justified, since the child is learning from observing.

Another interesting—and very practical—sidelight to the process of modeling is that when there is a conflict between what a model does and what he says, it is the *behavior* that is likely to be imitated. In one study, Joan Grusec and her coworkers (Grusec, Saas-Kortsaak & Simutis, 1978) found that telling children to be generous did little good, but showing them generosity led them to be generous, too. So the old adage, "Do what I say, and not what I do" doesn't seem to work.

These three basic propositions describe the fundamental "rules" for learning any behavior, including behaviors that we typically think of as "personality." According to this theory, children are gregarious, shy, aggressive, nurturant, generous, or stingy because they have been reinforced for behaving that way.

Recently, Bandura (1977) has also added a "developmental" aspect to his theory. He has recognized that what a child learns and performs from observing a model will change with age. What the child pays attention to, understands, or remembers about what the model did will be affected by the child's overall level of cognitive development.

I find this combination of learning and cognitive approaches extremely interesting and encouraging. It moves the

Figure 10.2 This child, the soul of helpfulness at nursery school, may be the despair of his mother's life at home. Bandura expects exactly this type of inconsistency in any case in which the reinforcement patterns are very different in the two locations.

learning approaches toward a recognition that how a child uses the information he has is as important as what the environment does to the child. It makes the whole reinforcement and modeling process far less automatic.

Strengths, Weaknesses, and Implications of Social Learning Approaches

Several implications of this theoretical approach are worth emphasis. First of all, you've probably gathered that most social learning theorists don't really want to talk about personality traits. A child's behavior is consistent from one situation to another not because she has a "trait" of shyness or gregariousness but because the reinforcement patterns are the same in the several settings. If the reinforcement patterns were different, the child would be different, too. This can explain the child who is a whiner at home but who is the soul of helpfulness and consideration at school or the child who never minds his mother but does whatever his father asks right away. Inconsistency in behavior can be explained just as readily as consistency with this approach.

A related implication is that this view of behavior is a very hopeful one. Change is quite readily possible, so "problem behavior" can be modified, as I described in Box 10.1. The same approach is used in currently popular behaviorally oriented weight loss or "assertiveness training" programs. The basic idea for these programs comes directly from social learning theories of behavior.

The great strength of this view of social behavior, in my opinion, is that it gives an accurate picture of the way in which many behaviors are learned. It is perfectly clear that children do learn through modeling; and it is equally clear that children (and adults) will continue to perform behaviors that "pay off" for them. The addition of the cognitive elements in Bandura's theory seems to me to offer the possibility of creating, eventually, a genuinely *developmental* social learning theory. The disadvantage of this view, for me, is that it still places too much emphasis on what happens *to* the child and not enough on what the child is doing with the information he has. Despite this drawback, there is no doubt that this has been one of the dominant views of "personality" among developmental psychologists in the United States for the past 30 years or more.

Biological Theories of Personality and Social Interaction

In contrast, biological views of personality have had little or no influence on the thinking of most developmental psychologists until quite recently, when there has been a resurgence of interest in the role of temperament and of biologically based patterns of social behavior.

Temperament Theories

I talked about temperamental differences among infants in Chapter 3, so I don't need to go into a great deal more detail here. But I do want to lay out the basic propositions more fully.

Proposition 1 *Each individual is born with characteristic patterns of responding to the environment and to other people.*

Table 10.1 Four Dimensions of Temperament Proposed by Buss and Plomin

Temperamental dimension	Description
Active versus Lethargic	The active person is usually busy and in a hurry, with vigorous actions.
Emotional versus Impassive	Intensity of reaction is involved; the emotional person is easily aroused and responds more intensely.
Gregarious versus Detached	The gregarious person is more "affiliative," has more desire to be with others, and is more responsive to others. People are strong reinforcers to the gregarious.
Impulsive versus Deliberate	Impulsive people respond quickly rather than inhibiting the response. (Note the similarity of this dimension to impulsive versus reflective perceptual styles discussed in Chapter 5.) The impulsive person is more likely to give in to urges and responds quickly, rather than planning.

Source: **Adapted from Buss and Plomin, 1975, p. 8.**

Alexander Thomas and Stella Chess (1977) have emphasized such qualities as activity rate, rhythmicity, adaptability to new experiences, intensity of response, general mood, and persistence as being basic properties of temperament in infants and young children. Combinations of these properties create the several distinctive temperaments of "easy," "difficult," and "slow to warm up" children Thomas and Chess have described.

An alternative formulation of basic temperament has been offered by Arnold Buss and Robert Plomin (1975), who suggest that there are four main temperamental dimensions, which I've listed in Table 10.1. Buss and Plomin argue that these temperamental qualities are inherited, a proposition with which Thomas and Chess would agree. In principle, temperamental differences could also arise from variations in prenatal environments, but all the temperament theorists I know of assume a genetic basis.

Proposition 2 *These temperamental characteristics affect the way any individual responds to people and things around him.* For example, a gregarious child (or adult) would tend to seek out contact with others; a detached person would not.

Proposition 3 *The individual's temperament also affects the way others respond to her.* Temperament affects the environment, as well as the other way around. The gregarious child, who may smile more than the detached child, "shapes" the parents' behavior toward her. The parents may smile, pick her up, and talk to her more simply because she has reinforced their behavior by her positively approaching temperament.

Obviously, theorists who emphasize temperament are not discarding reinforcement principles. What they are adding is the inborn (and probably inherited) patterning with which the child enters the world. These temperamental characteristics operate, then, as a sort of "filter" through which the environment must pass.

Strengths, Weaknesses, and Implications One of the major implications of a temperament view of personality is that consistency across situations *is* expected. A child should be active at home and at school or gregarious at home and at school rather than showing different patterns in different places. Furthermore, since these patterns are thought to be inherited, they should be very difficult to modify. Those who hold a temperamental view of personality are thus less optimistic about the possibilities of engineering major changes in behavior through behavior therapy or other interventions.

The major strength of this view, I think, is that it focuses our attention on the qualities the child brings to each interaction. Whether the temperamental qualities are inherited or not is an empirical question that has not yet been satisfactorily answered. But it is clear that babies and children differ in their typical responses. It seems important to me to acknowledge those differences rather than assuming that all children start out the same.

The weakness of the temperament theories at this stage lies largely in a lack of information. Both Thomas and Chess and Buss and Plomin offer evidence for the consistency of temperamental qualities throughout childhood. But we need more research. Just how dominating are these basic temperamental qualities? Do children with different basic temperaments respond to reinforcements differently? Do they pay attention to different aspects of a model's behavior? (If so, that would have major implications for social learning theory, too.) Do the temperamental qualities persist through childhood and into adulthood? Can they be changed? Until some of these questions can be answered, temperament theories will not be complete.

Ethological Theory

A quite different approach to the influence of inborn patterning is the **ethological** view. This approach to the study of behavior has its origins in studies of birds, bees, fish, and other animals by naturalists such as Konrad Lorenz (1966), Ekhart Hess (1972), and von Frisch (1974). These remarkable observers noted that in all animal species there seem to be very specific **instinctive** sequences of behaviors, such as mating rituals or the "dance" done by bees to inform their hivemates of the location of good flowers. All members of a particular species show these same behaviors, apparently without any learning. All it takes to trigger the instinctive pattern is the right cue. A male bird will attack a bird of another species who enters his territory. The attack is apparently triggered by the sight of the invader's particular shape or markings or by the sound of its distinctive cry. The attacker will show this aggressive pattern even if he has never seen another bird of his species attacking. These instinctive patterns seem to be vital to the survival of the species, too. They help to protect the individuals from attack, to produce mating, nest building, and the nurturing of the young.

But what does all this work on other animal species have to do with children's development? Are there instinctive patterns in humans as well? Several psychologists, most notably John Bowlby (1969), argue that there are. In particular, Bowlby thinks that the development of the child's attachment to his mother (or other regular caregiver) is dominated by instinctive patterns.

Strictly speaking, this is not a theory of "personality." Thus far within developmental psychology, the ethological approach has been applied to only a narrow range of human behaviors. Moreover, ethological theory is a theory about *similarities* among people rather than about differences. It tells us more about a normal developmental sequence that is the *same* for all children than it does about the ways in which children are consistently different from one another. But since Bowlby's work on attachment has come to be a dominant theoretical view for those studying the early attachment of parent and child, I want to sketch the main propositions for you here.

Proposition 1 *The baby comes into the world equipped with a set of prepatterned signals and responses to others.* These responses make up what Bowlby calls **attachment behavior.** The baby signals the need for help or contact by crying, fussing, or smiling. He maintains contact with the caregiver by clinging,

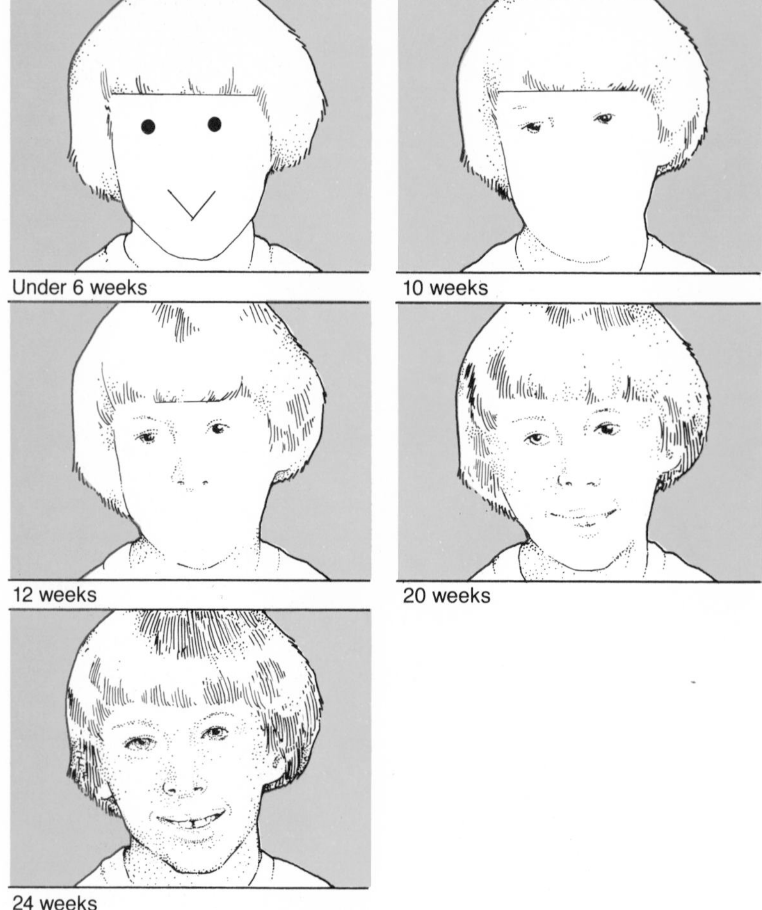

Figure 10.3 These drawings show the kinds of facial features that seem to be sufficient to elicit a smile from a baby of each age. Notice that initially, any facelike arrangement with a smiling mouth and eyes will do the trick. Later the eyes alone are enough, and still later the rest of the features are needed.

holding, or (in an older infant) by following his parents around. Bowlby thinks that in early infancy, the baby's actions are triggered automatically by various fixed signals like pain, separation, or threat. As he develops during the first year, however, he comes to use his repertoire of attachment behaviors less automatically and more intentionally.

For example, during the early months of life, babies smile a lot. From Bowlby's point of view, the most interesting thing about the smiling of the young baby is that it seems to be triggered (*elicited*, to use the ethologists' term) by quite specific stimuli. In very young babies (3–6 weeks old or so), the sound of a high-pitched human voice will often elicit a smile (Wolff, 1963). Then beginning at about 6 weeks, aspects of the human face seem to trigger smiling, too. Initially, as Rolf Ahren's (1954) research shows, it is the eyes that are the trigger. Later more of the face must be present before the infant will smile, as you can see in Figure 10.3. Still later, as the baby discriminates more reliably between one face and another, he begins to smile more to some faces than to others. So the initial smiling seems to be a built-in response to specific cues; later the smiling becomes less automatic, more directed. This is exactly the sort of pattern Bowlby emphasizes for all the attachment behaviors.

Proposition 2 *Whether or not the instinctive pattern is maintained depends on the responses of the people around the baby.* It takes two to do this particular tango, and if no one responds or if the responses are not properly tied in with the baby's signals, then the instinctive pattern may not persist. A 6-month-old will smile more at a face that smiles back, to take just one example.

Strengths, Weaknesses, and Implications The major attraction of the ethological approach to early attachment is that it has given us, at long last, a framework for understanding those earliest encounters between baby and adult. The richness and subtlety of those encounters are being uncovered by researchers following Bowlby's general theory.

But there are some obvious drawbacks as well. First and foremost, this is not really a *developmental* theory. How do the instinctive patterns change past the first years of infancy? Are there other instinctive patterns in babies? Do they persist through childhood? Should we expect children to show consistent behavior across many situations? In other animal species studied by ethologists, consistency is the watchword; if the proper signal is present, the animal responds in a predictable way. But is that true for humans past the earliest weeks of infancy? Can temperamental differences alter the "instinctive" patterns?

Until questions like these are addressed and answered, we can't really consider the ethological approach to be a full-fledged theory. But both the temperament and ethological theorists have helped to focus our attention on the significant unlearned aspects of behavior. That is no small achievement.

Psychoanalytic Theories

There is a whole family of theories called "psychoanalytic," beginning with Freud's and continuing with theories by Karl Jung (1916, 1939), Alfred Adler (1948), and Erik Erikson (1963, 1964, 1974), to name only a few. The word *psyche,* in Greek, refers to the soul, spirit, or mind. So psychoanalysis is the analysis of the mind or spirit. All the theorists who share this general tradition have been interested in explaining human behavior by understanding the underlying processes of the mind and the personality. And nearly all psychoanalytic theorists have begun by studying and analyzing adults or children who are disturbed in some way. They believed they could come to understand the normal processes by analyzing how it had gone wrong.

Of all the theorists in this large group, only Freud and Erikson have dealt very thoroughly with the *developmental* questions about the origin of personality in infancy and childhood. Since the two theories differ in important ways and have had differing impacts on research, I want to describe them to you separately.

Freud's Theory

Let me lay out the basic concepts in Freud's theory as a set of propositions, as I have done before.

Proposition 1 *All behavior is energized by fundamental instinctual drives.* Freud thought that there were three such instinctual drives or motivating forces: *sexual drives*, which he called **libido;** *life-preserving drives*, or instincts such as hunger and pain; and *aggressive drives.* Of the three, he thought the most interesting—and perhaps most important—were the sexual drives.

Proposition 2 *Throughout life, the child (and later the adult) is focused on gratification of these basic instincts.* The specific *form* of gratification sought and the strategies used to obtain it change with age, as we'll see later; but the inner push to obtain gratification remains.

Proposition 3 *Over the course of childhood, each of us develops three basic structures of personality that aid in gratifying the instincts.* These three structures Freud called the **id,** the **ego,** and the **superego;** and they are developed in the order listed. The id is the basic storehouse of raw, uninhibited, instinctual energy. Freud thought that this was all that was present in the infant. The baby tries to gratify his needs very directly. He has no ability to delay. He wants what he wants when he wants it.

This basic instinctual push for gratification remains a part of the personality; but because gratification can frequently be achieved more successfully by planning, talking, delaying, and

Figure 10.4 **A child of this age tries to get what he wants by being very direct—just as this child is grabbing away a toy. But two or three years later, the same child may try to get the toy indirectly, such as by asking to share, asking the teacher to make the other child share, or joining the play and gradually taking control. This illustrates the development of the *ego,* which operates on what Freud calls the "reality principle," as opposed to the *id,* which uses the "pleasure principle."**

other techniques than by instant demands, the child gradually transfers energy from the id to the ego. In Freud's terms, the ego is the planning, organizing, thinking part of the personality. The child is still trying to get what he wants, but now he is trying to gratify his desires by using more reality-based strategies.

Finally, there is the superego, which is roughly the same as what we call the **conscience.** This is the part of the personality that "monitors" the rest, that decides what is right and wrong. It is the internalized morality of the child's parents and of the society in which the child lives.

These three parts of the personality are, in some sense, at war with one another. The id says, "I want it now!" The ego says, "You can have it later" or "Take it easy; we'll get there eventually if we do it this way." The superego says, "You can't have it at all. It's wrong."

Proposition 4 *When conflicts arise between the different parts of the personality, the result is anxiety.* You all know the feeling of anxiety, so I don't need to try to define it for you. Many times the ego can handle the anxiety directly. If I send in a paper to a professional journal and have it rejected, I feel anxious. But I know what I'm anxious about and can handle it realistically by looking objectively at my paper to see how it could be improved, doing another study to prove the point I was trying to make, or doing something equivalent.

But sometimes the anxiety is too much to be handled this way, so we resort to **defense mechanisms**—automatic, unconscious strategies for reducing anxiety. I can *repress* the feelings when my paper is rejected and insist that I really don't mind at all. I can *rationalize:* "I didn't really want the paper published in that journal anyway; it would be much better published somewhere else." I can *project:* "The people who reviewed my paper for the journal are really stupid! They don't know what they're doing." In this way, I ascribe to the other people the qualities I fear may be true for me (stupidity, in this case). I can *displace* my anxiety. Instead of dealing with my fears about having the paper rejected, I may get angry at my co-workers over little things or have a fight with my husband.

There are many ways of defending against anxiety. The key things to realize about defense mechanisms, as Freud conceived them, is that they are *unconscious;* they involve *self-deception;* and they are quite *normal.* They can be taken to extremes, in which case they become neurotic. But Freud believed that defending yourself against anxiety is a natural process.

Proposition 5 *In the course of development, the child goes through a series of distinct psychosexual stages.* Two things develop in stages. First of all, the ego and the superego are not present in the infant and must be developed. And second, the goals of gratification change. At each stage, the sexual energy is focused on ("invested in," as Freud says) a single part of the body, which he called an **erogenous zone,** such as the mouth, the anus, and the genitals. The infant first focuses on stimulation in the mouth because that is the part of the body that is most sensitive. Later, when her neurological development progresses, other parts of her anatomy become sensitive, and her focus of sexual energy changes.

There is a strong maturational element in this part of Freud's theory. He thought that the transitions from one psychosexual stage to the next were determined largely by the changes in body sensitivity.

The Psychosexual Stages

Freud proposed five developmental stages, which I've summarized briefly in Table 10.2. But let me give you some more detail about each stage.

The Oral Stage: Birth–1 Year The baby's first contacts with the world are through his mouth, and he has great sensitivity there. Freud emphasized that the oral region—the mouth, tongue, and lips—becomes the center for pleasure for the baby. His earliest attachment is to the one who provides pleasure in the mouth, usually his mother.

Table 10.2 Freud's Stages of Psychosexual Development

Age	Stage	Erogenous zone	Major developmental task
0–1	Oral	Mouth	Weaning
2–3	Anal	Anus	Toilet training
4–5	Phallic	Genitals	Identification with parent of the same sex
6–12	Latency	No specific area; sexual energy quiescent	Development of ego defense mechanisms
13–18 and adulthood	Genital	Genitals	Mature sexual intimacy

The Anal Stage: 1–3 Years As maturation progresses and the lower trunk becomes more developed and more under voluntary control, the baby becomes more and more sensitive in the anal region and begins to receive pleasure from bowel movements. At about the same time, her parents begin to place great emphasis on toilet training and show pleasure when she manages to perform in the right place at the right time. These two forces together help to shift the major center of sexual energy from the oral to the anal erogenous zone.

Whether the child will get through the anal period unscathed, according to Freud, depends on whether the parents allow the child sufficient anal exploration and pleasure. If toilet training becomes a major battleground (as it often does) or occurs too early, then Freud thought that the child may bear the scars of that encounter throughout her lifetime.

The Phallic Stage: 3–5 Years At about 3 or 4 years of age, there is another shift, away from the anal region and toward the genital erogenous zone. Again there is a maturational basis for the shift; only at about this time does the child begin to receive pleasurable sensations from stimulation of the genital area. One sign of this increased genital pleasure is that children of both sexes quite naturally begin to masturbate at about this age.

According to Freud, the most important event that occurs during the phallic stage is the so-called **Oedipal conflict.** He

Box 10.2 Being Raised Without a Father

Four out of every 10 children born during the 1970s will spend at least part of their childhood in a one-parent family, and most often with the mother (Keniston, 1977). In 1977, there were nearly 10 million children living without a father in the home.

What is the effect on a child of living without a father? Freud thought that the impact could be substantial, even devastating. In particular, he thought that the damage would be greatest if the father was missing during the Oedipal period (age 3–5 approximately) and that it would be greatest for a boy. A girl still has her mother to identify with, so at least her sex-role identification is appropriate. But the boy, lacking a father, may never go through the identification process properly and may end up with a very confused sex-role orientation and perhaps a weaker superego.

From the social learning point of view, too, divorce or father absence should have an effect. If the behavior of the remaining parent (usually the mother, though that is changing) is altered, the children's behavior should change as well. Mavis Hetherington and her colleagues (Hetherington, Cox & Cox, 1975, 1977, 1979) have found that mothers become less affectionate and more inconsistent in their discipline in the first few years after a divorce. We might expect the children to become less tractable as a result. Social learning theorists also point to the lack of a male role model for the boy; this should affect the development of sex-role behaviors, particularly if the loss of the father occurs early.

The results of studies of children raised without fathers support some, but not all, of these depressing expectations.

First, there do seem to be greater effects on boys than on girls (Hetherington, Cox & Cox, 1979; Hetherington & Deur, 1972), particularly in the short term (Wallerstein & Kelly, 1980). Boys are more disorganized after a divorce, and there is some indication that their behavior is "feminized," which is what both Freud and the social learning theorists would expect. Second, the effects do seem to be worse if the separation from the father occurs before the age of 5, again what Freud would expect (Hetherington & Deur, 1972).

described the sequence of events more fully (and more believably!) for boys, so let me trace that pattern for you.

The theory suggests that first the boy somehow becomes "intuitively aware of his mother as a sex object" (Rappoport, 1972, p. 74). Precisely how this occurs is not completely spelled out, but the important point is that the boy at about age 4 begins to have a sort of sexual attachment to his mother and to regard his father as a sexual rival. His father sleeps with his mother, holds her and kisses her, and generally has access to her body in a way that the boy does not. The boy also sees his father as a powerful and threatening figure who has the ultimate power to castrate. The boy is caught between desire for his mother and fear of his father's power.

The result of this conflict is anxiety. How can the little boy handle this anxiety? In Freud's view, the boy responds with a process he calls **identification.** By trying to make himself as like his father as possible, the boy may feel as if he is taking on some of his father's power, too. Freud talks about the process

Third, the greatest short-term effect seems to be an increase in negative behaviors in the children (Hetherington, Cox & Cox, 1979). They become more defiant and aggressive, which is what we'd expect, given the changes in the mother's discipline and affection. The greatest long-term effects appear to be in the area of sex roles, or heterosexual adjustment. Hetherington (1972) found in one study of girls of divorced and widowed mothers that the daughters of divorce showed a heightened, almost promiscuous sexuality; daughters of widows were extremely inhibited with boys and men.

So much for the bad news. The good news is that many of the worst effects seem to diminish after a year or two. Hetherington finds that the mother's disorganization and the child's negativity both diminish. In addition, other researchers (Nye, 1957; Landis, 1962) have not found any indication that children from divorced families are more likely to be juvenile delinquents or have serious school problems or fewer friends.

A recent and extremely interesting study of 60 divorced families by Judith Wallerstein and Joan Kelly (1980) gives us some clues about what affects successful versus unsuccessful adaptations to divorce. In their group, about a third of the children were coping very well five years after the divorce. Another third were doing reasonably well, and a final third were still depressed or otherwise not handling problems effectively. One of the key differences between these groups was whether they continued to have good, loving contacts with *both* parents. The most depressed children tended to be those who no longer saw their fathers or saw them only infrequently. But when the father continued to be involved, saw the children regularly, and cared for the children, the youngsters had a good chance for a successful resolution of the crisis. Wallerstein and Kelly also found that for young boys in particular, the presence of an affectionate stepfather was helpful. Apparently, the presence of a loving male model is an important ingredient for healthy growth, particularly (but not exclusively) for boys.

of identification as being one of "incorporation" (taking in) of the father's qualities. It is this "inner father," with his values and moral judgments, that forms part of the child's superego or conscience.

A parallel process is supposed to occur for girls, although neither Freud nor his followers has been too clear about just how it should work. Supposedly, the girl sees her mother as a rival for her father's sexual attentions, but her fear of her mother is less (perhaps because she assumes that she has already been castrated). As a result, since the girl's anxiety is thought to be weaker, her identification is supposed to be weaker, too.

Successful resolution of the Oedipal crisis, with identification with the appropriate parent, is critical for healthy development. Any condition in a family that would tend to alter the identification process should create real problems. For example, if the mother is more powerful within the family than the father, this should create problems for the boy, who would

Figure 10.5 About 10 percent of children whose parents are divorced live with their fathers. Most of them are older children, rather than infants or toddlers, but the number at all ages is increasing. What will be the effect of such an arrangement? Would it have a greater impact on girls? We don't know the answers to such questions yet because there has been almost no research on children reared by their fathers.

then not fear his father sufficiently to lead to a strong identification. And if there is no father figure at all—as in many divorced families—this could affect both the boy and the girl. I've explored some of the consequences of father absence and divorce in Box 10.2.

The Latency Stage: 5–12 Years Freud though that after the phallic stage there is a sort of resting period before the next major change in the child's sexual development. The child has presumably arrived at some preliminary resolution of the Oedipal crisis, so that there is a kind of calm after the storm. Then, too, the child starts school during this period, and this new activity absorbs the energies rather fully.

During these years, the child's peer interactions are almost exclusively with members of the same sex. The identification with the same-sex parent at the end of the phallic stage is followed by a long period during which the identification and interaction extends to others of the same sex.

The one significant event of this period, in Freud's view, is the further development of defense mechanisms. Among those thought to be developed in the latency period are *denial*, in which the child simply denies that he feels or thinks a certain thing (for example, "I am *not* tired" when he is clearly at the edge of exhaustion) and *repression*, in which unacceptable thoughts or feelings are simply forced out of conscious awareness. The child literally forgets unpleasant things.

The Genital Stage: 12–18 and Older The further changes in hormones and the genital organs that take place during puberty reawaken the sexual energy of the child; and during this period, a more mature form of sexual attachment occurs. From the beginning of this period, the child's sexual objects are people of the opposite sex. Freud placed some emphasis on the fact that not everyone works through this period to a point of mature heterosexual love. Some have not successfully completed the Oedipal period, so they may have confused identifications which affect their ability to cope with rearoused sexual energies in adolescence. Some have not had a satisfactory oral period and thus do not have a foundation of basic love relationships; this too will interfere with full resolution of the conflicts of puberty.

Strengths, Weaknesses, and Implications of Freudian Theory

Freudian theory has several attractions. First, it is a *sequential* theory, and there is now increasing evidence (as we've seen in earlier chapters) that there are sequences built into many of the child's developing skills. Second, it focuses our attention on the importance of the relationship of the child to the caregivers, although Freud was not very specific about the sort of nurturing behavior on the part of the parents or other caregivers that would be optimal. Still, the emphasis is on the *interaction* between the child's qualities and preoccupations and the responses of the caregivers, and that seems to me to be an appropriate emphasis.

Third, Freudian theory offers several useful additional concepts that are missing from the nonpsychoanalytic views, such as the defense mechanisms and the concept of identification. Identification, in particular, has been an influential concept and has been widely adopted in one form or another. For example, Bandura's concept of "modeling" may be thought of as a variation of the identification concept.

Despite these attractions, however, there are drawbacks to Freud's theory. A major weakness is that Freud didn't provide very much detail concerning precisely what it is about experiences at particular stages that would lead to health versus later emotional disorder. Various researchers have tried to extract specific hypotheses from Freud's writings, but a lot of such theorizing is fairly chancy.

A second weakness is that much of what Freud said about the early stages, particularly the phallic stage, with its Oedipal conflict, just doesn't seem to be true. For example, there is no research evidence to support Freud's expectation that girls will be more weakly identified with their mothers than boys are with their fathers. Because of these drawbacks, Freud's theory is less influential today than it was several decades ago.

Erikson's Theory

Erik Erikson belongs firmly in the psychoanalytic tradition; but he has focused his attention on the ego—on the conscious self—rather than on unconscious drives or instincts. He has always been much more interested in the cultural and social demands made on the child than in the sexual drives. So Erikson's stages are referred to as **psychosocial stages,** whereas Freud's are called **psychosexual stages.** Most broadly, Erikson has been interested in how the child (and later the adult) develops her *sense of identity*. In Erikson's view, this process takes a full lifetime. As usual, let me break down the theoretical concepts into a series of basic propositions.

Proposition 1 *Over the life span, each individual goes through a series of distinct developmental periods (stages) with a specific developmental task at each stage.* The central task of each period is the development of a particular "ego quality," such as trust, autonomy, or intimacy.

Proposition 2 *The developmental periods are partially defined by the society in which the person grows.* A stage may begin at age 6 in our culture because that is when the child goes off to school. In a culture in which schooling was delayed, the timing of the developmental task might change as well. In this view, Erikson obviously differs from Freud, who emphasized the dominant maturational basis for the sequence and timing of stages.

Proposition 3 *Any developmental task that is not successfully completed leaves a residue that interferes with later tasks.* Actually, Erikson thinks that no task is ever fully completed. There are always bits and pieces left over. But the number and size of those bits and pieces may be critical for later health. A teenager who does not complete the task of developing her sexual or occupational identity, for example, will have a harder time later on entering into a fully intimate relationship at age 20 or 25. In this proposition, Erikson is very like Freud, who also thought that truly "mature" adult functioning required the successful sequential resolution of all the different stages or tasks.

With this brief background in mind, let me describe for you the stages Erikson proposes, which I've summarized in Table 10.3.

Table 10.3 The Eight Stages of Development Proposed by Erik Erikson

Approximate age	Ego quality to be developed	Some tasks and activities of the stage
0–1	Basic trust versus basic mistrust	Trust in mother or central caregiver and in one's own ability to make things happen.
2–3	Autonomy versus shame, doubt	Walking, grasping, and other physical skills lead to free choice; toilet training occurs; child learns control but may develop shame if not handled properly.
4–5	Initiative versus guilt	Organize activities around some goal; become more assertive and aggressive. Oedipal-like conflict with parent of same sex may lead to guilt.
6–12	Industry versus inferiority	Absorb all the basic cultural skills and norms, including school skills and tool use.
13–18	Identity versus role confusion	Adapt sense of self to physical changes of puberty, make occupational choice, achieve adultlike sexual identity, and search for new values.
19–25	Intimacy versus isolation	Form one or more intimate relationships that go beyond adolescent love, marry, and form family group.
26–40	Generativity versus stagnation	Bear and rear children, focus on occupational achievement or creativity, and train the next generation.
41+	Ego integrity versus despair	Integrate earlier stages and come to terms with basic identity.

Source: Erikson, 1963.

The Psychosocial Stages

As you can see in the table, there are three adult stages and five stages describing the tasks of childhood. Erikson's theory is therefore one of the few genuinely life-span views of development.

Basic Trust versus Basic Mistrust: Birth–1 Year The first task (or "crisis," as Erikson sometimes says) occurs during the first year of life (Freud's oral period). What is at issue is whether the child will develop a sense of basic trust in the predictability of the world and in his ability to affect the happenings around him. Erikson believes that the behavior of the major caregiver (usually the mother) is critical to the child's successful or unsuccessful resolution of this crisis. Children who emerge from the first year with a firm sense of trust are those with parents who are loving and who respond predictably and reliably to the child. A child who has developed a sense of trust will go on to other relationships carrying this sense with him; but those infants whose early care has been erratic or harsh may develop *mis*trust; and they, too, carry this sense with them into the later relationships.

Autonomy versus Shame and Doubt: 2–3 Years Erikson sees the child's greater mobility as the major change at this time. She can now move around in the world, and this forms the basis for the sense of independence or autonomy. But if the child's efforts at independence are not carefully guided by the parents and she experiences repeated failures or ridicule, then the results of all the new opportunities for mobility and exploration may be shame and doubt instead of a basic sense of self-control and self-worth. The fact that toilet training occurs during this period as well may create additional difficulties for the parents, since this is an area in which there are many taboos and more occasions when ridicule or failure may occur for the child.

Initiative versus Guilt: 4–5 Years This phase corresponds to Freud's phallic stage and occurs some time around age 4 or 5. Once again Erikson is less concerned with the sort of "sexual" development that preoccupied Freud (although he acknowledges it) and more interested in the impact of the child's new skills and abilities. At this age, the child is able to plan a bit, to take initiative in reaching particular goals. Having achieved these new cognitive skills, the child tries them out and tries to conquer the world around him. He may try to go out into the street on his own; he may take a toy apart, then find he can't put it back together and throw it—parts and all—at his mother.

This is a time of vigor of action and of behaviors that parents may see as aggressive. The risk here is that the child may go too far in his forcefulness. He may break a favorite toy or strike out at his mother or father. When this happens, the child may be overwhelmed by guilt.

What the parents need to do is help focus the child on what *is* permissible—to direct all that energy and initiative toward acceptable activities so that the guilt may be kept to a minimum.

Industry versus Inferiority: 6–12 Years The beginning of schooling is a major force in this stage. The child is now faced with the need to win approval through productivity—through

Figure 10.6 This 6-year-old boy shows guilt very clearly—a quality that Erikson thought was central to the task for this age. The boy had been left alone with his infant brother and had played a bit roughly with him. When his mother came back, he pulled his hand back and turned toward his mother with this expression.

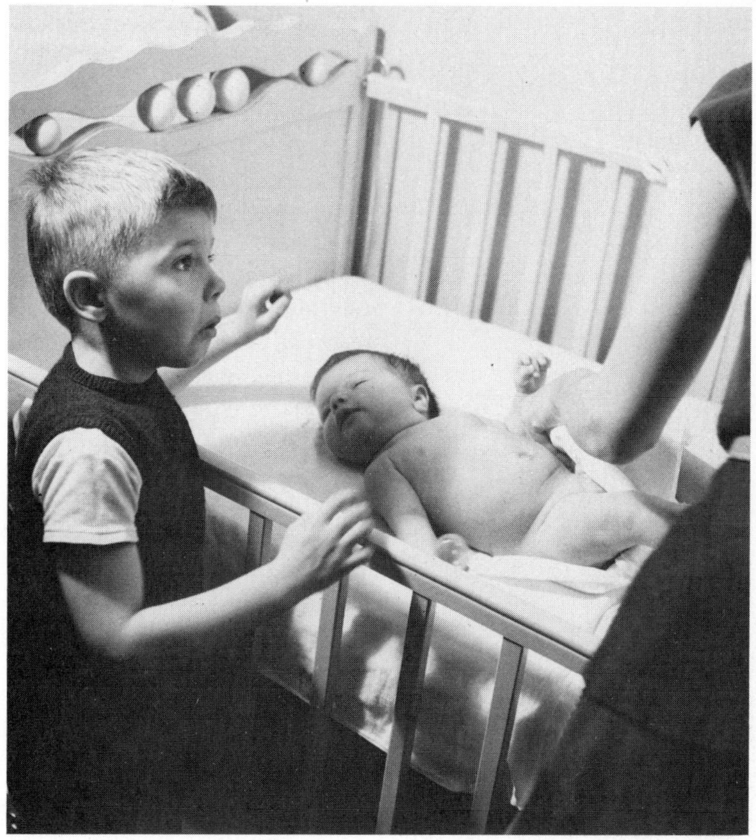

learning to read, write, do sums, and other specific skills. The task of this period is thus simply to develop the repertoire of abilities society demands of the child. The obvious danger is that for one reason or another the child may be unable to develop the expected skills and will develop instead a basic sense of inferiority.

Identity versus Role Confusion: 13–18 Years The task occurring during puberty—the genital stage in Freudian language—is a major one in which the adolescent reexamines his identity and the roles he must occupy. Erikson suggests that two "identities" are involved—a "sexual identity" and an "occupational identity." What should emerge for the adolescent from this period is a reintegrated sense of self, of what one wants to do and be, and of one's appropriate sexual role. The risk is that of confusion, arising from the profusion of roles opening to the child at this age.

Intimacy versus Isolation: 19–25 Years This is the first of the three adult stages. The central focus of this period is the need for intimacy—for merging one's identity with that of another. This is only possible if you have already developed a firm identity. If your basic identity is not strong enough to support real intimacy, then a sense of isolation may be the result.

Generativity versus Stagnation: 26–40 Years Erikson thought that at midlife, sexual maturity and intimacy with a partner were not enough. Each adult also feels a need to "generate" in some sense—to bear and rear children, to create something useful in a job, to train others, to produce works of art, or whatever. Any adult who is not successful at some aspect of generativity may feel a sense of stagnation. It is exactly that sense of stagnation—"what have I done with my life?"—that lies at the heart of many "midlife crises" in the forti

Ego Integrity versus Despair: 41 and Beyond The final step is to put it all together, to accept what you are, where you have been, and what you may be. Erikson thought that to reach real ego integrity you had to have successfully weathered the seven stages that came before. If you have not—if you have too many bits and pieces still left over—you are likely to experience despair, regret, and a sense of hopelessness in your later years.

Strengths, Weaknesses, and Implications of Erikson's Theory

Erikson made his basic proposals about the stages of development more than 20 years ago, but I think there has been a kind of delayed impact. His stages provided a good framework, but most of what he had to say was fairly sketchy and quite fuzzy. It wasn't clear just exactly what kind of experiences ought to matter. What would lead to trust rather than mistrust, for example?

But in recent years, there has been a kind of rediscovery of Erikson. I see this most clearly in two areas. First, the work on attachment in infancy has begun to link up to the concepts of "trust" and "mistrust." Children who are "securely" attached in infancy seem to fare better at later stages of development (Waters, Wippman & Sroufe, 1979), which is exactly what Erikson proposed.

Second, there is now an extremely interesting body of research on the development of identity during adolescence, spurred in large part by the development of a measure of "identity status" developed by James Marcia (1966, 1976). Not only is the struggle for identity clearly the focus for most teenagers, but that struggle seems to occur in a particular sequence. This work was designed specifically to test some of Erikson's general ideas and has proved fruitful. I think that in the next de-

Figure 10.7 One of the major attractions of Erikson's theory is that it is a life-span theory. These adults show three facets of generativity, which Erikson thought was the major task of middle adulthood. The major focus of generativity is on bearing and rearing the next generation, but dedication to work and creativity are also avenues through which generativity can be expressed.

cade we will see a great deal more work of this kind based at least loosely on Erikson's theory.

The reason for this new interest in Erikson's theory, in my opinion, is that he offers one of the few theories that blends cognitive and personality development. Erikson specifically suggests that changes in the child's thinking skills will change her social interactions and personality as well. Since the whole field of developmental psychology seems to be searching right now for just such a blending, Erikson begins to look better to a lot of us.

A further major strength is that Erikson is talking about the whole life span, so his theory may be used as a basis for exploring adult as well as childhood life stages. In addition, unlike Freud, Erikson saw the life crises and the disturbances of behavior and personality that often accompany them as occasions for personal growth—an optimistic view I find appealing.

The major drawback with the theory is still its impreciseness. The descriptions of the stages are not detailed, and the reasons for the transitions from one to the next are not explained fully. What current theorists are doing is using Erikson's view as a beginning point and providing their own detail.

Overview of the Theories

I'm sure you've gathered from this long description of theories that I'm not totally delighted with any of them. I don't think any one of these approaches really tells us everything we want to know about personality or about social development. Fortunately, we don't have to choose one. We can combine them. I don't see any reason why the temperament theories *and* the ethological theories *and* the learning theories can't all be true. Furthermore, either Erikson or Freud (or Piaget, for that matter) can provide us with a developmental framework that could be combined with Bandura's theory.

As we explore the process of social development in children in the next chapters, you should keep all that in mind. I think you will find that each theory helps to explain a portion of social development very nicely.

Summary

1. The word *personality* refers to those individual, relatively enduring patterns of acting with and reacting to the animate and inanimate world around you.

2. There are three major theoretical approaches to personality development: the learning theories, the biological theories,

and the psychoanalytic theories.
3. Social learning theorists assume that patterns of social behavior are learned through reinforcement or through modeling. Because they are learned, they may be specific to particular situations; we should not necessarily expect consistency across situations or over time.
4. Current versions of social learning theory, particularly Bandura's, have introduced some cognitive elements; Bandura argues that a child can imitate only what he has paid attention to and remembered.
5. Temperament theories of personality and social interaction emphasize inborn characteristics such as activity, gregariousness, and impulsivity, which persist throughout the life span.
6. Ethological theory emphasizes the infant's inborn, instinctive patterns of interaction. The baby provokes caregiving by crying or movement then prolongs it by cuddling, smiling, or making other responses. The adult, too, responds with instinctive caregiving, including smiling and cuddling.
7. Freud's psychoanalytic approach emphasizes a maturationally based developmental sequence of psychosexual stages. In each stage, a particular erogenous zone is dominant. Of particular importance is the phallic stage, beginning at about age 4, when the Oedipal crisis is met and mastered through the process of identification.
8. Erikson's emphasis is on psychosocial stages, each one shaped in part by the social demands and by the child's physical and intellectual skills. Each of the major stages has a central task or "crisis."
9. No one of these theories is totally satisfactory, but many combinations of the theories are possible. In particular, biological and learning approaches can be fruitfully combined.

Key Terms

Attachment behavior The collection of possibly instinctive behaviors used by infants, children, and adults to create and maintain proximity to significant others. Includes smiling, crying, mutual gaze, among others.

Behavior therapy A therapeutic intervention based on principles of reinforcement.

Conscience Roughly equivalent to the term *superego*. The part of the personality that monitors one's behavior, judging it to be acceptable or unacceptable.

Defense mechanisms Strategies of the ego, in Freudian theory, for coping with anxiety, including denial, repression, identification, and projection.

Ego That portion of the personality in Freudian theory that organizes, plans, and keeps the person in touch with reality. Language and thought are both ego functions.

Erogenous zones Portions of the body that in Freudian theory are thought to be sequentially the seat of heightened sexual awareness, such as the mouth, the anus, and the genitals.

Ethology A theoretical approach that focuses attention on inborn instinctive response patterns in subhuman species and in humans. Most often applied to the study of attachment in humans.

Id The first, primitive portion of the personality in Freud's theory; the storehouse of basic energy, continually pushing for gratification.

Identification The process of taking into oneself the qualities and ideas of another person, which Freud thought was the result of the Oedipal crisis at age 3–5. The child attempts to make himself like his parent of the same sex.

Instinct Instinctive behaviors are innate, predetermined patterns of behavior released or evoked in the presence of specific stimuli. They figure prominently in ethological theory.

Libido The term used by Freud to describe the pool of sexual energy in each individual.

Modeling Bandura's term for the process of learning through observation.

Oedipal crisis The pattern of events Freud believed occurred between age 3 and 5 when the child, because of fear of possible reprisal from the parent of the same sex and "sexual" desire for the parent of the opposite sex, identifies with the parent of the same sex.

Personality The collection of individual, relatively enduring, patterns of reacting and interacting with others that distinguishes each child or adult.

Psychosexual stages The stages of personality development suggested by Freud, including the oral, anal, phallic, latency, and genital stages. The sequence is heavily influenced by maturation.

Psychosocial stages The stages of personality development suggested by Erikson, including trust, autonomy, initiative, industry, identity, intimacy, generativity, and ego integrity. Influenced by social expectations as well as maturation.

Superego The "conscience" part of personality proposed by Freud, which is developed as a result of the identification process. The superego contains the parental values and attitudes incorporated by the child.

Suggested Readings

Bandura, A. Social learning theory. Englewood-Cliffs, N.J.: Prentice Hall, 1977.

Not easy reading, but the most up-to-date statement of Bandura's theory.

Erikson, E. H. Childhood and society. New York: Norton, 1963.

One of Erikson's major theoretical statements. His comments on the stages of personality development are mostly contained in Chapter 7.

Patterson, G. R. Families. Champaign, Ill.: Research Press, 1975.

As a general rule, I don't lean much toward behavior modification approaches, but this is a wonderful book—clear, easy to understand, and very helpful, particularly if you are struggling with a child whose behavior stymies you.

Preview of Chapter 11

Preview of Chapter 11

The Development of Social Relationships

Let me describe a fairly typical recent day of mine. At the office, I worked by myself for several hours on some research data, stood in the hall by the office for a while chatting with a longtime friend and colleague about a puzzling research finding, ran with two co-workers who are acquaintances but not good friends, and sat through a difficult and very irritating meeting with another group. My temper got a bit short during this meeting, and I spoke rather sharply to a graduate student who was describing her research. When I got home, I talked on the phone to my college-age son and to my father and wrote to my closest woman friend, who lives several thousand miles away. In the evening, I went out to dinner and to the movies with a man I have known for 30 years, who has been an off-and-on friend over that whole stretch.

Several things struck me when I thought about that day. First of all, I was surprised at the number of different people I had contact with who are personally close to me. There were encounters with acquaintances, too; but throughout the day, I "touched base" with friends and relatives with whom I have significant and enduring relationships.

There is also a hint of another important element of personal relationships in my description, namely, aggressiveness. I didn't yell at my younger colleague; I didn't tell her she was a dummy, as a child will often do to a playmate. But I did speak sharply and critically to her.

Both of these facets of personal relationships—close positive contacts and aggressiveness—are seen in children's encounters with one another and with adults. Thus far in this book, I have talked mostly about the child's physical and intellectual development and haven't said very much about her social relationships. In this chapter, I want to try to balance the scales a bit.

Since I dealt with the major theories of social and personality development in the last chapter, the focus here will be on answering the "what" questions. In particular, what do we know about developmental changes in social relationships, and what do we know about individual differences?

Attachment: A Definition

I want to begin this exploration by looking at that most central of human relationships, **attachment.** Mary Ainsworth defines an attachment as an "affectional tie or bond that one individual . . . forms between himself and another specific individual" (Ainsworth, 1972, p. 100). When you are attached to someone, you try to be near him or to maintain contact in some way.

Attachments exist between adults, between children, and between children and adults. Of the people I dealt with during the day I described to you, I am attached to at least some degree to my father, my son, my long-time colleague, and my close woman friend.

Most of the research on attachment, as you'll see shortly, focuses on the infant's attachment to her parents; but I think the attachment of parent to child and of child to child are equally interesting and important. To give all three types of attachment reasonably equal billing, I am going to begin by looking at parents' attachment to their children, then turn to the more extensive work on children's attachments to their parents, and deal finally with contacts between children.

As a final step in this chapter, we need to look at the less-positive side of children's interactions, namely, aggressiveness. How does aggression change with age? Why are some children more aggressive than others? And what impact do external influences such as television have on aggressiveness in children?

Parents' Attachment to Infants and Children

Before we can go any further in talking about the development of attachment, I want to emphasize an important distinction between **attachment** and **attachment behavior.** The attachment is the underlying link, the desire to make and maintain contact with a specific other person. Attachment behaviors are the various things each of us does to bring about the contact, such as smiling, moving close to the person, touching, crying, and making eye contact. This distinction is particularly vital when we talk about the child's attachments and attachment behaviors toward the parent, but it is relevant when we look at the parent's involvement with the child as well.

Research evidence we have so far points to a two-step process in the development of attachment between parent and child. There is an early bond formed at birth or shortly after birth. This bond is then strengthened by the opportunity to engage in mutual attachment behaviors with the baby.

Step 1: The First Bond at Birth

Unlike the infant, who does not seem to form a strong attachment to the parents until perhaps 4–6 months of age (as I'll describe shortly), many parents form a strong initial bond with their infant at birth or in the hours and days immediately following.

As I pointed out in Chapter 1, the work of John Kennell and Marshal Klaus (Kennell, Jerauld, Wolfe, Chesler, Kreger, McAlpine, Steffa & Klaus, 1974; Kennell, Voos & Klaus, 1979; Klaus & Kennell, 1976) suggests that mothers may be especially sensitive to their babies immediately following delivery. In the best-known study in this series (Klaus & Kennell, 1970, 1976), those mothers who were given an opportunity for extended physical contact with the infant in the hours immediately after birth, in contrast to those with less early contact, fondled their babies more, held them more closely, and soothed them more when the babies were a month old. One year later, the extended-contact group of mothers still differed in their behavior with their infants. They soothed them more when they cried and were more attentive and involved when a physician examined the baby.

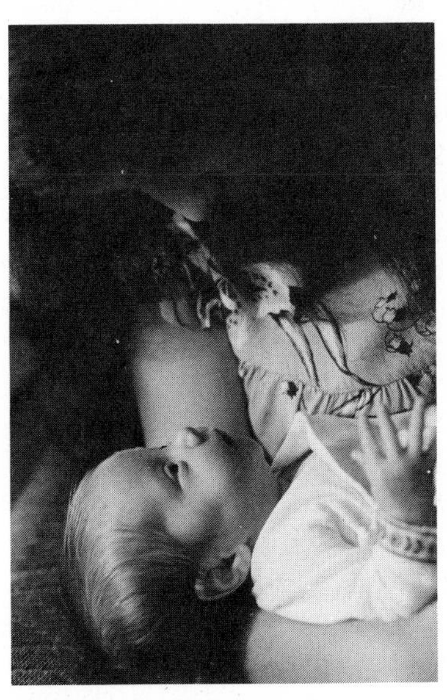

Figure 11.1 Kennell and Klaus's research show that this close, attentive position is more common among mothers who had extended contact with their infants shortly after birth. The phrase *en face* (roughly, face to face) is sometimes used to describe this position.

Later still, when the babies were 2 years old, five of the mother–child pairs from the extended-contact group and five from the regular hospital routine group were observed. The special focus in this case was on the language the mothers used with their children, and the researchers (Ringler, Trause & Klaus, 1976) found that the extended-contact mothers used more questions, more adjectives, longer sentences, and fewer commands.

The durability of the effect of early contact in this study is moderately astonishing. The mothers in the extended-contact group had had only 16 extra hours of handling and touching in the first three days after delivery. But those extra hours appear to have strengthened the mother's attachment to her infant enough so that the later course of her relationship with that child was altered. The specific effect seems to be to increase the mother's involvement with her child. That is, her stronger attachment is expressed in more consistent and persistent attachment *behaviors.* She spends more time near the baby, holds the baby more, and later talks to the child in a more elaborated way as well. This pattern of maternal behavior seems to be a beneficial one for the child, especially when you bear in mind all the information I described in Chapters 8 and 9 about the antecedents of intellectual skill in the child.

We do not yet know enough about the nature of the "glue" that is involved in forming this strong early bond between mother and child. Why is the glue stickier if there is extended early contact? Does the mother have some hormonal readiness, as Kennell and Klaus imply? Does the infant have special qualities in the early hours that enhance the mother's responses? We'll need more research to answer these questions. For now, however, it does seem reasonably clear that early extended contact has a persisting effect on the attachment of mother to child.

The father, too, can enter into this first phase. As I mentioned in Chapter 1 and in Chapter 3, if the father has contact with the child, his bond appears to be strengthened. At least fathers who have had an opportunity to be present at their child's birth or to hold and cuddle the infant in the early hours report that they are more strongly attached and that they spend more time caring for and playing with their baby (Greenberg & Morris, 1974; Peterson, Mehl & Leiderman, 1979). We have less information about the long-term effects of early father contact. So far as I know, no one has yet compared early-contact fathers with no-early-contact fathers a year or more after the birth of the child. But the existing evidence suggests that for fathers, too, early contact helps to create a somewhat stronger initial bond between parent and child.

Step 2: The Meshing of Attachment Behaviors

Not all parents are able to form the initial attachment at birth. The infant may require special medical treatment; there may be little contact between parents and child during the first days of life because of hospital routine or parental preference; the infant may be adopted. For any of these reasons, the child and parents may begin their home life together without a strong bond. Fortunately, there is a backup system.

Over the early weeks and months, there develops a mutual, interlocking pattern of attachment behaviors. The baby signals her needs by crying or smiling; she responds to being held by soothing or snuggling; she looks at the parents when they look at her. The parents, in their turn, enter into this two-person "dance" by coming near the baby when she cries or gurgles, by picking her up, by waiting for and responding to her signals of hunger or other need, by smiling at the baby when she smiles, and by gazing into her eyes.

Dan Stern (1977) has a wonderful description of a mother feeding a 3-month-old that illustrates this whole package of interlocking behaviors. In the early portion of the feeding, the mother was pretty neutral in her expression, and the baby was sucking away vigorously.

> Then a change began. While talking and looking at me the mother turned her head and gazed at the infant's face. He was gazing at the ceiling, but out of the corner of his eye he saw her head turn toward him and turned to gaze back at her. This had happened before, but now he broke rhythm and stopped sucking. He let go of the nipple and the suction around it broke as he eased into the faintest suggestion of a smile. The mother abruptly stopped talking and, as she watched his face begin to transform, her eyes opened a little wider and her eyebrows raised a bit. His eyes locked on to hers, and together they held motionless for an instant. The infant did not return to sucking and his mother held frozen her slight expression of anticipation. This silent and almost motionless instant continued to hang until the mother suddenly shattered it by saying "Hey!" and simultaneously opening her eyes wider, raising her eyebrows further, and throwing her head up and toward the infant. Almost simultaneously, the baby's eyes widened. His head tilted up and, as his smile broadened, the nipple fell out of his mouth. Now she said, "Well hello! . . . heello . . . heeellooooo!" so that her pitch rose and the "hellos" became longer and more stressed on each successive repetition.
>
> *(Stern, 1977, p. 3)*

There are many fascinating things about this whole process, but one of the most intriguing to me is that we all know how to do this particular dance. Adults will automatically shift into their "baby play act" (including the raised eyebrows, the higher-pitched voice, the smile, and the pauses for the child's response) any time they are holding or talking to an infant. And the baby runs through her half of the dance pretty automatically, too. But while we can perform all these attachment *behaviors*, we don't become *attached to* every baby we coo at or cuddle; and the baby doesn't become attached to every adult who smiles and raises her eyebrows.

For the adult, the critical ingredient for the formation of a genuine attachment seems to be the opportunity to develop real mutuality—to practice the "dance" until the partners follow one another's lead smoothly and pleasurably. This takes time and many rehearsals. The parents of a newborn, especially if it is a first child, may feel clumsy or awkward with their infant. They don't read the baby's cues easily, and the interaction may be out of synchrony. But as they care for the infant, play with him, and talk to him, the synchrony improves. The mother or father can reliably elicit a smile from the baby; they know when

Figure 11.2 Virtually every adult, when interacting with a young baby, shows this "mock surprise" expression, including the raised eyebrows, wrinkled forehead, and wide smile. This combination of features is in fact quite likely to elicit a smile from a young baby.

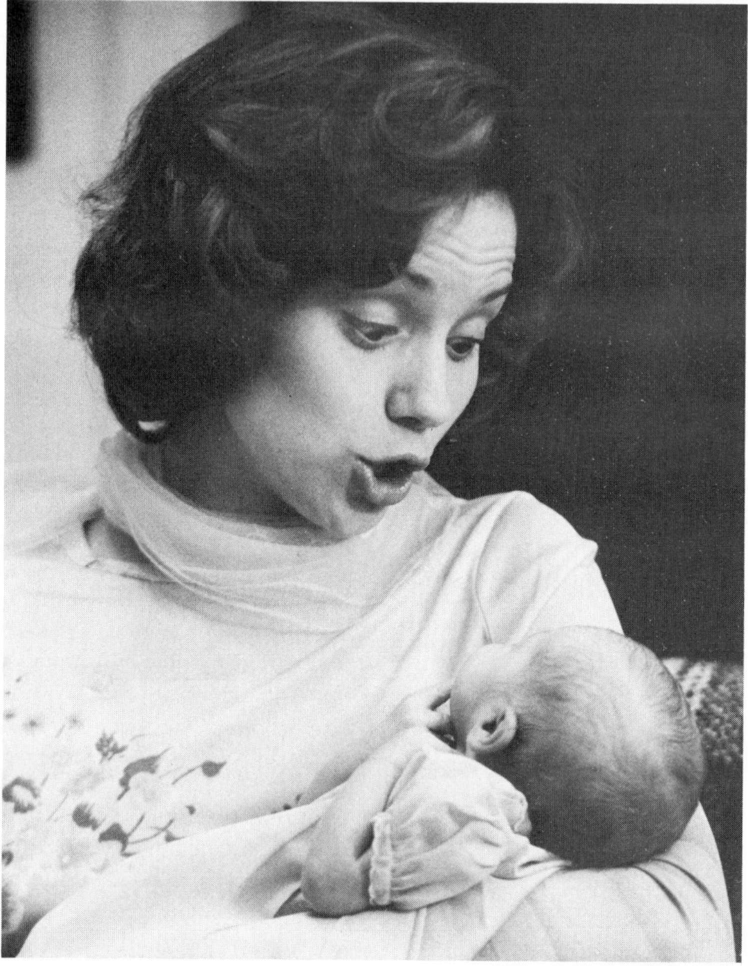

and how to get the baby to look at them; they have learned how to soothe and feed the baby. The smoother and more predictable the process becomes, the more satisfying it seems to be to the parents, and the stronger their attachment to the infant becomes.

When the Mutuality System Fails Even this very robust backup system for encouraging the formation of an attachment by the parents to the child can fail if the child has some disability that makes it difficult for him to enter fully into the mutual process. Selma Fraiberg (1974, 1975) has studied a group of blind babies, who smile less and don't show mutual gaze. Most parents of blind infants, after several months of this, begin to think that their infant is rejecting them; or they conclude that the baby is depressed. These parents feel less attached to their blind infants than to their sighted infants.

Similar problems can arise with parents of premature infants, who are usually separated from their parents for the first weeks or months. And when the baby does come home from the hospital, he may be more unresponsive than a full-term infant (Field, 1977).

Several things can happen if the parent's attachment to the child does not develop fully. In the case of the families Fraiberg studied, the mothers simply withdrew more and more from the infant. Another possible response is child abuse, which may be thought of, in part, as a failure of attachment. I've explored that possibility in Box 11.1. But whatever the parent's response, the consequences for the child are probably major.

Fortunately, it's possible to intervene to help the unattached parent become more attached. Fraiberg (1974) found she could help the parents of the blind babies to "read" the baby's hand and body movements instead of waiting for smiles or eye contact. Rose Bromwich (1976) has used a similar procedure with families of children with other physical handicaps. She begins by finding some activity that the child and parent can do together that brings pleasure to both. When that level is achieved, she tries to help the parent become more attentive to the child's signals. Through this process, the parents' attachment to the child can be enhanced.

Overview of the Parents' Attachment to Their Infant

In sum, the parents normally form a strong initial bond that is strengthened by the repetition of attachment behaviors and by the increasing mutuality and responsiveness of their interactions with their infant. The process is affected by the opportunity for very early contact and by the skillfulness or predictability of the child's half of the mutual system.

Development of the Infant's Attachment to His Parents

In contrast, the infant shows a wide range of attachment behaviors before he forms the attachment itself. That may seem like a contradiction, since the attachment behaviors are thought to be a reflection of the underlying bond. But Bowlby (1969) has argued that the baby's initial attachment behaviors—crying, clinging, soothing, smiling, eye contact, and the rest—are all part of a built-in system designed to elicit caregiving behavior

Box 11.1 Child Abuse: An Example of a Failure of Attachment

Every year in the United States, about 1 out of every 100 children is physically abused and another 1 out of 100 is severely neglected or sexually abused (Light, 1973). And even these numbers may be too low, since many types of abuse—particularly sexual abuse—go unreported. In about 4 percent of the cases of physical abuse, the child dies. In another 25 percent, the child suffers some lasting physical damage, such as brain damage or loss of sight or hearing (Helfer, 1975). These are horrifying numbers. And the act of abuse itself is horrifying. How does it happen?

There are many causes of abuse, but researchers are beginning to realize that many of the homes in which abuse occurs are the same homes in which attachment has failed. For example, about a quarter of abused children were premature babies, even though prematures represent only about 8 percent of the total population (Klein & Stern, 1971). Be careful about this statistic. I'm not saying that a quarter of all prematures are abused. But I am saying that prematures—a group in which the parents' attachments may be weakened—are vastly overrepresented in the group of abused children.

The parents' attachment to the baby is obviously not the only element. Most parents of prematures do not abuse their children; many parents of perfectly normal, "attachable" babies do abuse them. Two other factors seem to matter.

First, abuse occurs more often in any family under extreme stress. Families with many children are more likely to abuse their children than are those with fewer children (Light, 1973); and families that are undergoing high levels of "life change," with new jobs, new homes, perhaps a death in the family, a loss of job, or overcrowding at home, are also more likely to abuse their children (Justice & Justice, 1976).

Second, parents who abuse their children share certain histories and characteristics. They are likely to have been abused themselves, which may mean that their own basic bonds are not strong. They have also grown up seeing violence used as a way of dealing with problems. Abusing parents also tend to have very high expectations for their children and to expect the child to give them love right away (Steele & Pollock, 1974). One abusing mother said,

> *I have never felt really loved all my life. When the baby was born, I thought he would love me; but when he cried all the time, it meant he didn't love me so I hit him. (This infant was hospitalized at 3 weeks of age with brain damage.)*
>
> (Steel & Pollock, 1974, p. 96)

When we put these three factors together, we find that abuse is most likely when the parents' attachment to the infant is weak, when the parent has some personal potential for violent action, and when the parent is under stress.

Child abuse is certainly the most extreme form that a failure to form attachments can take, but it underlines the potentially critical importance of that first attachment of parent to child, as well as child to parent.

---

from the adults. The emergence of genuine attachments out of this initial, possibly instinctive, interaction system seems to occur in several steps.

Phase 1: Initial Preattachment During the first three or four months, the baby directs her attachment behaviors pretty much indiscriminantly to any face that looms into view or anybody that picks her up. Most of the attachment behaviors the infant shows at this age are *proximity-promoting behaviors*. They have the effect of bringing people close enough to respond to the baby's needs, and it doesn't seem to matter much just who it is who comes close.

Phase 2: Attachment in the Making

Sometime around 3–5 months of age, the baby begins to dispense her attachment behaviors more discriminantly. Remember from Chapter 5 that the baby can, by this age, tell the difference between one face and another. Now she begins to smile more at familiar faces and may be more easily soothed by someone familiar to her. Still, this is not yet a full-blown attachment to a *single* figure. There are still a number of people who are favored with the child's proximity promoting behaviors.

Phase 3: Clear-Cut Attachment

At about 6 or 7 months, there is a fairly sharp demarcation. In the vast majority of cases, the child now has only *one* person to whom he is primarily attached. In addition, the dominant mode of his attachment behavior changes from "come here" signals (proximity promoting) to what Ainsworth calls *proximity seeking*. The child now clings or moves nearer to the caregiver. He also begins to use this "most important person" as a safe base from which to explore the world around him. If you'll think back to Chapter 4, you'll remember that most infants learn to crawl at about this age. The child can now get *to* the parent as well as have the parent come to him.

Separation Anxiety and Fear of Strangers In some children, another sign of this strong single attachment is separation anxiety or separation protest. If the mother leaves the child with a sitter—even a familiar babysitter—or is otherwise separated from the child for a while, the baby of this age may cry, cling, or show other signs of distress at the impending departure. Mary Ainsworth points out that many babies do *not* show this pattern (Ainsworth, Blehar, Waters & Wall, 1978), so the lack of separation protest should not be taken as a signal that the baby is not attached. But it is a fairly common occurrence at about 6–8 months.

Several months later many children show still another facet of their strong attachment: They respond fearfully to strangers. Again, not all children show this pattern; but for those who do, it typically lasts for two to three months between the ages of 8 and 12 months (Sroufe, 1977; Batter & Davidson, 1979). Some children show only a brief wariness toward strangers; others show more striking withdrawal such as crying, clinging to the parent, or other signs of fear. Alan Sroufe (1977) has found that whether the baby shows fear or not depends a lot on what the stranger does. Most infants show no fear if a stranger just walks into the room. But if the stranger approaches or tries to pick up the baby or touch him in some way, then the strongest fear reactions occur.

Phase 4: Multiple Attachments

The most intense single attachment normally occurs during the period from 6–12 months. After that time, most babies show a spread of attachments, to older siblings, fathers, regular babysitters, grandparents, or other regularly seen adults. These attachments appear to have the same qualities as the attachments to the principal caregiver; the child uses all of her preferred adults as a safe base for exploration, smiles more at them, and turns to any of them for comfort in distress.

Attachments in Older Children

Two- and 3-year-olds seem to maintain their strong attachments to mothers, fathers, and other significant people in their lives. But the attachment *behaviors* change. Over the preschool period (from 2 to 5), most children become steadily less clinging; they check in with the parent less often and generally are increasingly independent in their activities (Maccoby & Feldman, 1972). I suspect that this change occurs partly because of the child's growing skill with language and with thinking. She can call to her mother from across the room, so she doesn't have to be close by to check in with her. And as she understands and explores more, fewer things are scary or new, so the child doesn't have to return to the "safe base" of the special person quite so often.

At the same time, a child of this age will still show all the strong, "immature" attachment behaviors such as clinging and being near if he is stressed or frightened. When you take 3-year-olds to the doctor's office, off to preschool for the first time, to the zoo, or any place new and potentially scary, they "regress" (return to an earlier pattern) and show strong proximal attachments. As soon as they feel comfortable in the new situation, their independence reasserts itself. All of this shows that the basic attachment is still there but that it doesn't show itself as often.

I think the same thing must be true of elementary school-age children and adolescents, too. Their fundamental attachments are probably still there, underlying everything else. But no one has studied attachments in older children in this way. Among

Box 11.2 Attachment to Fathers

One of the arguments still going on about the clear-cut and multiple attachment periods is about the quality of the attachment the child develops to the father. Is it as strong as the attachment to the mother?

Michael Lamb (1977) argues that it is, that infants normally form equally strong attachments to mother and father during the 7–8-month-old period when strong attachments are first seen. The available evidence shows that babies prefer both the father and the mother to a stranger starting as early as 6–7 months of age (Yogman, 1977; Lamb, 1977). And when both mother and father are available to the child, infants seem to smile at or approach both, *except* when they are frightened or otherwise under stress. When that happens, most children turn to the mother (Clarke-Stewart, 1978; Lamb, 1976).

But is all this true about *every* father? Some fathers spend a lot of time with their infants, helping take care of them, holding them, and playing with them. Others spend almost no time with the baby. This variation, understandably, seems to make a big difference in the infant's attachment to the father. Gail Ross (Ross, Kagan, Zelazo & Kotelchuck, 1975) found that she could predict a baby's attachment to the father by knowing how many diapers the dad changed in a typical week: the more diapers, the stronger the attachment. More generally, the more time the father has spent with the baby, the more the baby seems to choose his company. This shouldn't be surprising in view of what I've already said about the "dance" of attachment. It takes partners a while to learn to dance well together, and that smooth reciprocal process seems to be an important ingredient in the child's attachment to an adult. If the father doesn't practice, the baby is less attached. The moral of this, of course, is that the father who wants his infant to be strongly attached to him during the first year or so will need to invest some time with the baby, both in routine care (diapers!) and in play.

Figure 11.3 By about age 2, most children show this type of clinging, unhappy style of attachment only when they are under stress, such as visiting the doctor, as this little girl is doing. This same child is probably quite independent at home.

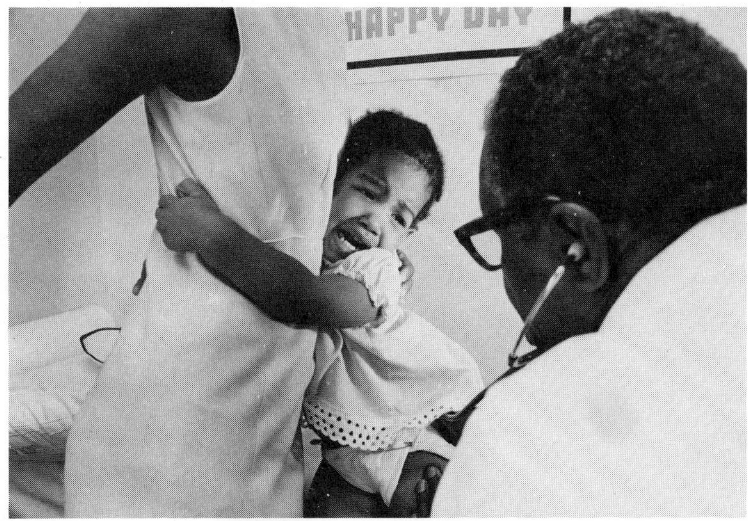

6–12-year-olds, the focus instead has been on individual differences in such relatively immature forms of attachment behavior as clinging, being near, and seeking contact or reassurance. Traditionally, the word *dependency* has been used to describe this dimension of individual difference. As a group, children become less dependent and more independent from infancy through childhood. But some children seem to retain the immature forms of dependent behavior while others move more rapidly toward independence. The study of such differences is a perfectly legitimate concern. But the heavy emphasis on dependency (that is, attachment behaviors) has meant that psychologists have not explored the development or maintenance of basic attachments during the school-age years.

Individual Differences in Attachment and Dependency

Virtually all babies seem to go through the sequence I've described. But the *quality* of the attachment they form to their parents differs. Mary Ainsworth, in particular, has suggested that there are important differences between infants who are **securely attached** and those who are **insecurely attached** (Ainsworth & Wittig, 1969; Ainsworth, Bell & Stayton, 1972; Ainsworth, Blehar, Waters & Wall, 1978).

Measuring Secure and Insecure Attachment

Most investigators, following Ainsworth's lead, have measured the security or insecurity of attachment using a procedure called the **strange situation.** It consists of a series of episodes, in a laboratory setting, in which the child is with the mother, with the mother and a stranger, alone with the stranger, completely alone for a few minutes, and then reunited with the stranger and then with the mother. The behavior of three groups of babies in this setting, one group thought of as securely attached and two groups seen as insecurely attached, is described in Table 11.1.

Effects of Secure and Insecure Attachment on Later Behavior

As I mentioned in the last chapter, I think the contrast between secure and insecure attachment comes close to what Erikson means by basic trust versus mistrust. If Erikson is correct, we should find that this early pattern affects later adjustment. And that's just what recent researchers have been finding.

Some of the most interesting work has been done by Everett Waters and Alan Sroufe and their colleagues. They observed a group of 50 infants in the strange situation at 1 year of age and then followed this group through the next four years, observing

Table 11.1 Behavior of Securely and Insecurely Attached 1-Year-Old Infants in the Strange Situation

Group	Behavior
Securely attached	Baby seeks and maintains contact or proximity to mother, especially when reunited with her after absence; clearly prefers mother to stranger; greets mother with smile or cry after separation.
Insecurely attached Detached/Avoidant	Child avoids or ignores mother at reunion; little tendency to seek contact with mother at any time; does not hold on if picked up; treats stranger about the same as mother.
Insecurely attached Resistant/Ambivalent	Both actively resists contact with mother (particularly at reunion) and seeks contact and nearness; baby seems ambivalent, as if he wants contact but resists it when offered; baby very distressed when separated from the mother.

Source: **Based on descriptions of Ainsworth, Blehar, Waters & Wall, 1978, pp. 59–63.**

them playing with other children, solving problems, and coping with kindergarten. Several points have emerged from this longitudinal study.

First, secure or insecure attachment seems to be fairly stable, at least over short periods of time. Waters (1978) observed the 50 babies in the strange situation again at 18 months and found that all but two were still in the same basic group of secure or insecure attachment that they had been in at 12 months.

Even more interesting, these researchers have found that at 2, those babies who had been securely attached at 12 months were more likely to take the lead in playing with other children and were more curious (Sroufe, 1978; Waters, Wippman & Sroufe, 1979). Still later, when the children were in kindergarten, those who had been securely attached as infants were rated as more "ego mature" by their teachers and were again found to be more curious about new tasks (Arend, Gove & Sroufe, 1979). Several other groups of investigators have found parallel results (Lieberman, 1977; Easterbrooks & Lamb, 1979), so the link between early attachment and later success with peers, and possibly with school tasks, is emerging more and more strongly.

The next question, naturally enough, is how the children get to be securely or insecurely attached in the first place. Maybe they just come that way. Some of you may have noticed that the characteristics of the insecurely attached baby sound a bit like those of the temperamentally "difficult" child Thomas and Chess (1977) have described. Some of them seem to be hard to console; they approach new situations with fear and lots of distress; and they adapt slowly. So perhaps "insecurely attached" really just means "difficult." Maybe. But it seems likely that what the parents do with the child makes a difference, too.

There is now a whole collection of studies that show differences in the maternal behavior of securely and insecurely attached infants (Ainsworth, Bell & Stayton, 1971, 1972; Blehar, Lieberman & Ainsworth, 1977; Sroufe, 1978; Main, Tomasini & Tolan, 1979). Mothers of securely attached infants are more supportive of their infant's independent play, more sensitive to their child's needs, and more expressive. They also show more of what Mary Blehar calls "contingent pacing," which is very like the "turn taking" Ken Kaye describes and that I mentioned in Chapter 3. The mothers of the securely attached infants are "dancing" well with their babies.

Attachment and Later Dependency

Studies of children older than about 2 or 3 have most often focused on dependency (that is, on the persistence of such immature forms of attachment behavior as clinging) rather than on basic attachments. The focus of this research (Sears, Maccoby & Levin, 1977; Kagan & Moss, 1962) has been on the question of consistency of a "trait" of dependency over childhood. For example, does the proximity-seeking 3- or 4-year-old still show signs of heightened dependency at 6 or 10 or 20?

Since the forms of attachment behaviors changed with age, this is a difficult question to answer. But generally speaking, there appears to be *some* consistency. For example, Jerome Kagan and Howard Moss (1962), in a major longitudinal study, found that preschool children who were high in what they called "affectional dependency," which included seeking acceptance, approval, and affection from adults, were still high in these behaviors at 8 or 12. But from adolescence on, the consistency got weaker. Among girls, those who were more passive and dependent on adults as teenagers were still dependent on their parents as adults. They chose secure, nonrisky jobs and stayed pretty close to home. But this pattern didn't hold for boys, perhaps because boys have learned to disguise their dependency more than girls have.

Since most of these studies on dependency were done before the newer conceptualizations of attachment appeared, we don't have good connective links between the two bodies of research. We don't know the connection, if any, between secure versus insecure attachment and later forms of consistent dependent behavior. Waters's and Sroufe's research suggests that there are some links, but we need more information. For the moment, what we know is that there is *some* (but not a great deal) of consistency in children's tendencies to be more or less proximity seeking or attention seeking throughout childhood.

Attachment and Separation

So far I have talked about mothers and children as if all mothers spent full time with their infants and toddlers. But at least 40 percent of mothers with children younger than 3 work part or full time (Hoffman, 1979) and other mother–infant pairs are separated for other reasons. What happens then? Is the attachment weakened? Does the child end up with an insecure attachment?

The practical issue is very clear for many of you: Will your infant be somehow "damaged" if you are working? But the theoretical issue is also important. Many years ago, John Bowlby (1951) used the term *maternal deprivation* to describe what happened to an infant who was separated from the mother during the early months of life. He was convinced that such "deprivation" did irreparable damage not only to the child's emotional stability but to his intellectual development as well.

Bowlby seems to be right that the early relationship is important, but he has turned out to be mostly wrong about the effects of separation (Rutter, 1972, 1979). Let me talk here about just one kind of "deprivation," namely, the sort of repeated separation that occurs when a mother works and the child is cared for by someone else. Specifically, what happens to the child's attachment?

Children in Day Care There is now a rich array of research on children in day care, so we are a great deal closer to answers to these questions than we were only a few years ago. Let me summarize.

The substantial majority of studies of attachment in which day care and home-reared children have been compared show *no* differences (Caldwell, Wright, Honig & Tannenbaum, 1970; Cornelius & Denney, 1975; Belsky & Steinberg, 1978; Kagan, Kearsley & Zelazo, 1978; Blanchard & Main, 1979). That is, children in day care show as strong an attachment to their mothers and fathers as do home-reared children. In fact, they almost always prefer the mother over a regular caregiver if given the choice (Farran & Ramey, 1977; Cummings, 1980).

For children from economically disadvantaged homes, day care appears to have a beneficial effect on intellectual develop-

Figure 11.4 At least 2 million children are cared for at least part of the day outside of their own homes. Most are cared for in someone else's home, but day-care centers, like the one in this picture, are becoming more and more common. What effect does this type of care have on children?

ment, as measured by standardized IQ and achievement tests (Robinson & Robinson, 1971; Ramey & Smith, 1976; Golden, Rosenbluth, Grossi, Policare, Freeman & Brownlee, 1978). The study by Mark Golden and his colleagues is the most interesting of these, since they observed and tested children enrolled in ordinary neighborhood day-care centers and family day care rather than in special, enriched, experimental day-care centers. ("Family day care" refers to the situation in which a mother cares for several young children in her own home.) Children in either center care or family care in this study were slightly ahead of their home-reared counterparts on IQ tests at age 3.

Some characteristics of day-care centers seem to be important in affecting the results for the children. The best evidence we have on this issue comes from the National Day Care Study (Ruopp, Travers, Glantz & Coelen, 1979), which was undertaken by the federal government in order to improve their written standards for day care. For this study, several thousand 3–5-year-old children in over 50 centers in three cities were observed and tested. Only two features emerged as critical. First, children in centers in which the youngsters were cared for in small groups (15 or less per group) did better on standardized tests and were more socially active than children cared for in larger groups. The ratio of adults to children was *not* vital.

Second, it mattered whether the caregivers had had specific training in the area of child development, particularly the development of young children. Formal degrees didn't make a difference, and years of day-care experience didn't matter, ei-

Figure 11.5 Owen is only 10 weeks old, but he is cared for in a day-care center near his mother's job. Day care for infants this young is still relatively rare, and we need to know more about the possible effects. So far, though, the research suggests that babies can adapt to stable alternate care without any ill effects.

ther. But knowledge about children's needs and development helped: Children whose caregivers had such knowledge did slightly better on standardized tests.

Taking all this evidence together, it seems reasonable to conclude that day care is an acceptable form of care for a young child. But I don't want to give the impression that all the needed research has been done or that we can answer all the questions. It hasn't and we can't. So I need to state some cautions.

We know less than I would like about the impact of the child's age at the time of entering day care on his eventual adjustment. In particular, there is little information about children under 1 year of age. Jerome Kagan (Kagan, Kearsley & Zelazo, 1978) studied a group of children who began in day care between 3 and 5 months and found no negative effects, which is encouraging. But what about children who enter day care just at the time when they are forming their strongest attachment to their parents? Does this have any negative effect?

We also know too little about the effect of day care on the *family*. For example, is the parent's attachment to the child affected?

Finally, we don't know enough about the long-term effects of day-care experience. Do children who have been in day care do better in school? Do they have an easier or more difficult time relating to peers later on? Do they show more or fewer behavior problems as teenagers or adults? We don't know the answers to any of these questions.

Figure 11.6 Recent research shows that babies under 1 year of age are more interested in one another than we had thought, as these two seem to show. Perhaps, though, babies this young consider each other to be just other objects to play with.

Despite the unanswered questions, I want to emphasize again that we do know a fair amount about the impact of day care on attachment, which is the central issue in this chapter. And what we now know suggests that the child's attachment to the parents is not adversely affected by the regular separation of day care.

Children and Their Peers: Another Type of Attachment

For the first few years, our strongest bonds are with our parents or other caregivers. But then a transition begins. Other children become more and more important. By the time we are teenagers or adults, friends, lovers, and spouse become the central attachments. How does this shift take place?

Developmental Patterns in Peer Relationships

Infancy and Early Childhood Until recently, most psychologists thought that peers weren't very important in the lives of children until perhaps 3 or 4. But that turns out to be wrong. Children as young as 10–12 months of age will play with each other, imitate each other's actions, and smile at each other (Eckerman & Whatley, 1977). Given a choice between a toy and another child to play with, children of this age will usually play with the toy; but if there aren't any toys, other little bodies will do, as you can see in Figure 11.6. This certainly doesn't show an attachment to other infants, but at least we know now that babies are not indifferent to one another.

Over the period from 1 to 2 years, children get more and more social. Edward Mueller and Jeffrey Brenner (1977) have found that over the period from age 1 to age 2, toddlers in play groups spend more and more time looking at each other, exchanging toys, and saying "hi" or the equivalent. But practice matters, too. The more time a 1- or 2-year old spends with other children, the more "social" he becomes, perhaps because there is some learning involved. He has to learn how to play, how to share, how those other little people will respond.

Despite the fact that there is more and more social interaction during these early years, the play of very young children is not yet really shared actively. Piaget describes the earliest play between children as **parallel play.** The children may be using the same materials or the same toys, but each one is working independently. Some time in the middle of the preoperational period – at about 3 or so – we begin to see **cooperative play,** in which two or more children join in the *same* activity. (You can see the contrast in Figure 11.7.) The amount of cooperative play increases after this age.

One of the side effects of cooperative play is that it increases the sheer amount of time children spend in close contact with one another, so the opportunity for conflict increases, too. The fact that aggressiveness increases among children at about the same age is probably linked to this shift in play patterns.

Another shift in the play of children with one another is in the amount they imitate each other. Three- and 4-year-olds imitate one another very frequently. If one child is making a block tower, another child may copy that. But by school age, this form of imitation decreases sharply (Abramovitch & Grusec, 1978).

In sum, children's relationships with their peers in the early years move from a kind of mild interest, to more intense interest, to cooperative play. Starting as young as 3 or 4, children also have "best friends" (Hartup, 1975), so there are individual bonds forming as well. What we do not know is the strength of these earliest attachments to peers. Could a 3- or 4-year-old use a best friend as a safe base from which to explore new territory? Could he be consoled by a friend? We don't know. But it is clear that the amount of time a child spends with other children, in comparison to time spent with adults, changes markedly during the preschool years.

School-Age Children Individual friendships continue to form during elementary school and increase in number over the school years. In one study, John Riesman and Susan Shorr

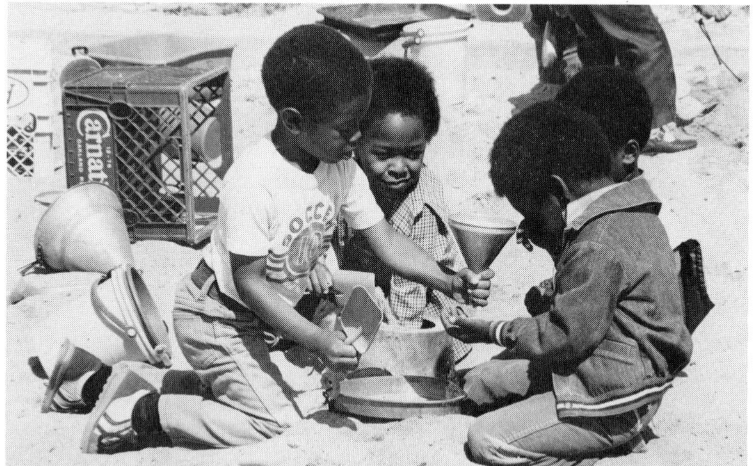

Figure 11.7 These two photos illustrate parallel play (on the top) and cooperative play (on the bottom). During the preschool years, there is a shift from a dominance of parallel play to a predominance of cooperative play.

(1978) found that second graders named about four friends each, while junior high school students named seven or eight friends each. But again we know less than I'd like about how strong or enduring these early friendships (attachments) may be and how significant they are in the lives of children. The *lack* of friends, however, does seem to be significant. Children in elementary school with few or no friends have an increased risk of emotional disturbance (Cowen, Pederson, Babijian, Izzo & Trost, 1973).

Aside from the growth of individual friendships, the most striking thing about peer relationships during elementary school is that the groups children form then are almost exclusively same sex. In classrooms, of course, children are with others of both sexes. But when the kids choose their own playmates, they nearly always choose others of the same sex. Remember that this is during Freud's latency period, when he thought that sexual feelings were quiescent. And remember, too, that this is the period when children seem to be learning their full sex role, which may require more attention to people of your own gender. Whatever the reason, the focus of friendships and peer relationships at this stage is very much same sex.

The groups children form during elementary school tend to be fairly fluid. A group of children will come together around some shared goal, such as a sports team or a hobby. Or a gang of children who live near each other will hang together informally for a few months. Most of these groups have a relatively short existence. But while they do exist, the children create special rituals or special "norms" for members of the group. There may be some particular thing everyone in the group is supposed to wear—a special kind of hat, blue jeans, quilted vests, or whatever. Or there may be an initiation rite or password of some kind.

Over the elementary school period, children's groups become more cohesive and durable. But there is nearly always some coming and going, new members arriving, or new groups forming.

Adolescence Peer interactions among adolescents have many of these same qualities. There are still "gangs" or other loose groups, but these become closer knit and more significant during the teenage years. Most of the groups at this age are formed on the basis of shared background or interests, such as the "jocks" or the "bookworms." Teen groups also tend to be segregated along social class and racial lines more than is true for groups of younger children.

The biggest change at adolescence is that peer relationships shift from being same sex to being heterosexual. This is not an instant change. In fact, most adolescents belong simultaneously to at least three levels of peer groups. There is a **crowd,** which is a loosely organized group made up of kids who share the same activities or interests. The crowd usually includes both boys and girls. Within the crowd, there are then smaller groups, sometimes called **cliques,** made up of young people with stronger ties to one another. At the beginning of adolescence, these cliques tend to be same-sex groups, but by later adolescence, the cliques may be made up of three or four couples who

Figure 11.8 This group of teenagers illustrates one of the features of adolescent groups: It is a mixed-sex group.

share many activities. Finally, the cliques may be made up of individual pairs of close friends or "steady" couples.

Conformity to the norms of these various groups is strongest early in adolescence at about ninth grade (Hartup, 1970; Bernat, 1979). By the end of high school, when the young people have moved toward Erikson's intimacy stage, the focus turns away from the group and more toward individual significant relationships.

Once more I want to emphasize that the friendships of teenagers have not been thought of in terms of attachments. But it seems very obvious to me that the relationship between best friends or between going-steady couples can certainly be thought of as strong attachments. One member of the pair turns to the other for support in stress; they smile more at one another, have more eye contact, and use all the other signals of special status. If Erikson is correct, then the ability to form satisfying attachments of this kind in adolescence and in adulthood is probably related to the security of the very first attachments formed in infancy.

Individual Differences in Peer Relationships

The point I just made raises the issue of "skill" in peer relationships. Are some children just plain better at relating to their friends and playmates? The answer is clearly yes.

Among 2- to 4-year-olds, skill with peers seems to be related to early attachment experience. As I mentioned, several recent studies show that securely attached infants are later more skillful than insecurely attached infants in playing with and relating to peers in the preschool years (Lieberman, 1977; Sroufe,

Table 11.2 Characteristics of "Popular" Children in Elementary School and High School

Friendliness	**The more friendly, the more popular a person is.**
Outgoingness	**Gregarious children are more popular than withdrawn children.**
Success in school	**Children who get better grades or have greater academic skill are more popular.**
Family position	**Youngest children in a family are usually more popular than firstborns.**
Physical attractiveness	**The more attractive the child, the more he is liked by peers.**
Physical size	**Tall or physically mature children are more popular.**
Specific task ability	**Children who are very good at sports, or at some other task valued by the group, are more popular.**

1978; Walters, Wippman, & Sroufe, 1979). Securely attached 1-year-olds are later more confident with other children, are more likely to be leaders, respond more fully to a partner's distress, and are less hesitant.

Whether these same children are still more skillful five or ten years later I don't know, but it seems reasonable to expect that they would be. Among other things, they build up a lot of successful experience with peers, so they are learning good skills as they go along.

Popularity A second way to look at individual differences is to ask who is "popular." In Table 11.2, I've given a list of the characteristics of children who are chosen as playmates or who are leaders of groups (Asher, Oden & Gottman, 1977). The list should offer few surprises, except perhaps the fact that first-born children are less popular than last born children. As a group, firstborn children tend to be more anxious and show more immature forms of dependence on others. Those qualities do not seem to promote popularity with peers.

The families of popular children also seem to differ in several ways: (1) They discourage aggression and antisocial behavior in their children. (2) They try not to frustrate the child and punish little. (3) They like their children and tell them so. For a boy to be popular with his peers, a strong, warm, and positive father figure seems to be particularly important (Hartup,

1970). The research on attachment I've already discussed suggests another item for this list. Parents of popular children have probably helped to foster a secure attachment in the first year of life.

In general, it looks as if children who feel good about themselves are liked by others, which is a not very surprising link.

Aggression in Childhood

Basic attachments to parents and to friends are important parts of a young child's development. But all is not sweetness and light on the playground or in the home. Children also show **aggression.** They hit each other and their parents, call each other names, snatch toys from each other, and generally try to do damage to each other's bodies and feelings. It's important to look at this aspect of personal relationships, too.

Definitions of Aggression

Before I go any further, I need to pause long enough to define what is meant by aggression. There has been a basic argument between social learning theorists such as Bandura (1973) and theorists influenced by Freud's drive concepts of aggression (such as Feshbach, 1970) about how to define aggressiveness. Bandura (1973, p. 5) defines aggression as "behavior that results in personal injury and in destruction of property." He emphasizes the *consequences* of the action, not the intent of the actor. Feshbach and others of similar persuasion emphasize the person's intent to injure. From this perspective, aggression is usually defined as any action intended to injure someone or something.

My own leanings are toward a definition that includes intent, even though this creates the difficulty that we must infer the intent from the behavior of the actor.

Most researchers also distinguish between two forms of aggression. **Instrumental aggression** is directed at achieving some reward other than the suffering of someone else. A child who grabs a toy away from another child has shown instrumental aggressiveness if his intent was to get the toy rather than to injure the playmate. **Hostile aggression,** in contrast, is aimed at hurting the other person.

Assertiveness is distinguished from aggression as well. An assertive action is the forceful expression of one's legitimate interest. A child who says, "That's my toy!" is showing assertiveness. If he then bashes his playmate over the head to reclaim it, he has shown aggression.

Frustration and Aggression

The basic "signal" for aggression, in most instances, seems to be frustration. In a famous book some years ago, Dollard and his colleagues (Dollard, Doob, Miller, Mowrer & Sears, 1939) argued that aggression is *always* preceded by frustration and that frustration is always followed by aggression. This extreme position seems clearly wrong. But it does seem to be the case that the human child is born with a fairly strong natural connection between frustration and aggression, just as she "naturally" exhibits attachment behaviors when she is hungry, frightened, or in need.

Since every child is frustrated at least occasionally, every child is going to show some aggression. The two issues we have to deal with are whether there are systematic changes with age in the frequency or form of that aggression and whether some children are consistently more aggressive than others.

Developmental Changes in Aggression

There are only a few studies of changes in aggression over the early years of life and none that I know of involving children older than about 8.

One of the good old studies is by Florence Goodenough (1931). She had mothers of 2–5-year-olds keep diaries in which they recorded the circumstances surrounding every aggressive outburst by their children. In a more recent study, Willard Hartup (1974) relied on direct observation of 4–7-year-old children in a school setting. These and other studies lead to some general conclusions.

First of all, the amount of aggression increases during preschool, with a peak at about age 4. As I mentioned, this corresponds to the time when children's play becomes more cooperative, so they spend more time in contact with each other.

At the same time, the form of aggression changes. In a 2- or 3-year-old, a physical attack is the most common form of aggression. Most often, though, this is instrumental aggression rather than hostile. Older children show less and less physical aggression and use words more to do the damage. But their aggression is more often hostile—aimed at hurting another person.

Many of these changes make good sense if we think about what else is changing in the child and in her life during the same years. She is getting much more skillful with language, so she can create elaborate insults instead of just hitting out. She is also becoming more aware of other people's intentions during the years from 2 to 7, so the older child is much more likely to decide that another child "meant" to hurt her, which leads to more hostile aggression.

Beyond early elementary school, we know essentially nothing about developmental changes. Physical aggression—actual

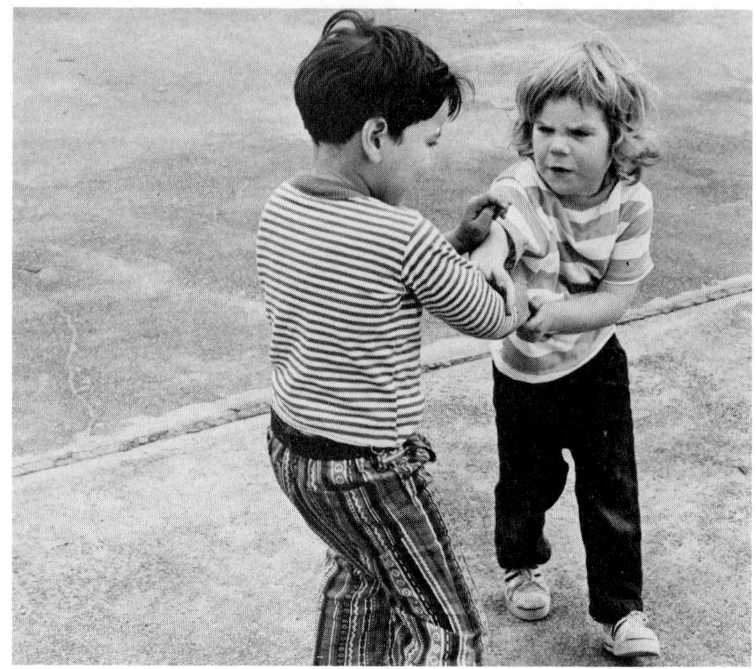

Figure 11.9 This is a good example of hostile aggression among preschoolers. Hostile aggression remains high during early elementary school, but it more often takes the form of verbal aggression in older children.

hitting, kicking, or equivalent—probably continues to decline during elementary school. But does it increase again during adolescence? Many delinquent acts are aggressive actions, but that doesn't necessarily mean that teenagers as a group are more aggressive than younger children. We just don't have the research to answer the question.

Individual Differences in Aggressiveness

Go to a school playground or a day-care center some time and just sit for a while and watch. It isn't hard to pick out some children who are consistently more aggressive than others. They get into more fights, yell more at other children, and generally have a hard time of it. Some children seem to be able to play for long stretches with others without getting into disputes. Where do differences like that come from?

The social learning theorists, such as Bandura (1973), argue that any child who is rewarded for aggression at home or in school and who has aggressive models around to learn from should show more aggressive behavior with others. In general, this all seems to be true.

For example, in most nursery schools, aggression is a pretty successful tactic. Children often find they get what they want this way. When that happens, we ought to see aggression increasing; and that's just what observers have found. In one study, Gerald Patterson (Patterson, Littman & Bricker, 1967) found that children who were already pretty aggressive when they came to nursery school got more aggressive as time went on. Even the children who had come to nursery school with low levels of aggression became more aggressive. After being victimized a few times, they found that fighting back paid off and began to fight back more often. Obviously, if the teachers set up the school situation so that aggression does not pay off, you wouldn't find this pattern. But Patterson's study does show that aggression will increase when it is rewarded.

The same rules seem to apply to family situations. The most consistent finding in studies of families is that children who are rejected or unwanted are likely to be highly aggressive. Among delinquent teenagers, for example, a common combination is rejection by parents along with large (and inconsistent) doses of physical punishment (Glueck & Glueck, 1950). Probably the pattern works in cycles. The child is rejected and frustrated, so he strikes out against the parents. The parents retaliate with physical punishment, which provides the child with a model of violence, involving more rejection and frustration.

Among less-rejecting families, the most aggressive children appear to come from families high in both permissiveness and punishment for aggression, a relationship reported by Robert Sears, Eleanor Maccoby, and Harry Levin in their study of several hundred 5-year-olds (1957, 1977). The sequence apparently runs something like this: The mother (or father) allows the child to beat up her brother or snatch a toy from her little sister. But when the noise level becomes too high or the screams of agony too piercing, the parent steps in with some fairly severe punishment, such as spanking, sending the offending child to her room for a protracted period, or taking away a cherished privilege. The parents in such cases may think that they are being consistently severe toward aggression and may be mystified that their children are so aggressive. What the parents have done, though (in addition to modeling aggression for the child), is to allow aggression some of the time and to punish it at other times. They have created a partial reinforcement schedule, which I described in Chapter 1.

The families with the least aggressive children seem to be those who practice a combination of nonpermissiveness, nonpunishment, and nonrejection. They try to avoid letting potentially explosive situations develop, and they head off quarrels and arguments by separating the children before the aggression begins. But when aggression does occur, they don't punish it severely.

Figure 11.10 This mother may think that by spanking her child she is "getting rid of the bad behavior." But she's also providing the child with a model of aggression, and this may have the effect of increasing his aggressive behavior.

Television and Aggression

If parents and teachers were the only people who had an effect on the child's aggressiveness, it might be easier to control. But children are influenced by many other things, including television. And since television is filled with violence and aggression, many psychologists, educators, and parents have been concerned about the possible effects on children. There have been endless Senate committee hearings on the subject of violence on TV. One result of the concern has been a great deal of government-sponsored research on TV violence. So we have better answers than we used to.

How Much Do Children Watch TV? Two facts are clear to begin with. First, most children watch a *lot* of television. The average preschooler watches about three to four hours a day, and the average 9–10-year-old watches four to six hours a day (Liebert & Schwartzberg, 1977).

Second, TV fare is very violent. The definition of violence used in most studies is "the overt expression of physical force against others or self, or the compelling of action against one's will on pain of being hurt or killed" (Gerbner, 1972, p. 31). By this definition, the average TV drama has 8 acts of violence each hour. Children's cartoons, in contrast, have about 20 to 30 episodes of violence per hour (Gerbner & Gross, 1974).

Even more disturbing is the fact that violence is concentrated in programs during the times of day when children are watching. Ronald Slaby and his colleagues (Slaby, Quarfoth & McConnachie, 1976) found that TV violence was high in the early morning, when young children watch cartoons, dropped during "nap time" in the afternoon, and then rose again during the after-school and after-dinner hours.

Characteristics of TV Violence I want to emphasize several points about the violence children see on TV: (1) All the violent episodes I have just listed involve *physical* aggression. If verbal aggression were counted, too, the rate of aggression on TV would be many times higher. (2) The "good guys" are just as likely to be violent as the "bad guys." (3) Violence on most TV programs is rewarded; people who are violent get what they want. In fact, violence is usually portrayed as the most successful way of solving problems. (4) The consequences of violence —pain, blood, damage—are seldom shown (although this is changing). The networks' own codes forbid the showing of such gore, so the child is protected from seeing the painful and negative consequences of aggression.

What effect does this barrage of violence have on the child viewer? Is she likely to be more aggressive because of all that exposure to aggression on TV? Can she tell the difference between the fantasy of television and the real-life encounters at home or school?

Summary of Research Findings Let me summarize what we know as briefly as I can. First, children *do* learn specific aggressive actions from watching them—on TV or in real life. So children are learning about guns, knives, karate, and other aggressive actions from watching TV.

Second, children who watch violent TV *are* more aggressive with their playmates than are children who watch less violent TV (Liebert & Schwartzberg, 1977). This is more clearly true of young children than of older children. Among elementary school and high school youngsters, watching aggressive TV seems to raise the level of aggression *except* when there is some situational inhibition. So if the child knows that Mom or Dad disapproves of aggression or they are in a situation in which aggression is discouraged, the effect of the TV violence is lessened to some extent.

Third, the effects of seeing violence on TV seems to be cumulative. The more violent programs the child sees, the more aggressive he seems to become (Steuer, Applefield & Smith, 1971).

Fourth, children who watch a lot of violent TV have different attitudes about aggression. Joseph Dominick and Bradley Greenberg (1972) found that elementary school-age children who watched a lot of violent programs were more likely to think that aggression was a good way to solve problems than were less-heavy viewers. This effect was weakened if the children came from families that disapproved of aggression, but the effect didn't go away entirely. What this means for us as a society is that whole generations of TV-watching children are growing up thinking of aggression and violence as useful and effective ways of solving their difficulties.

All of these effects can be lessened by parents who demonstrate nonaggressive ways of solving problems and who disapprove of aggressive actions in their children. More important, parents can control the sort of programs their children watch. The really crucial point is that whether we like it or not, television is an educational medium. Children learn sharing, counting, imaginative play, and other helpful things from "Sesame Street" or "Mr. Rogers's Neighborhood," both programs that are designed to instruct. But they also learn from Saturday morning cartoons, from "Charlie's Angels," and from all the other violent programs they watch.

Sex Differences in Social Interactions

So far I have steered clear of any discussion of sex differences in social interaction. But since this is an area in which the sex-role stereotypes are *very* strong, I need to address the question as squarely as I can. Take a look at Table 11.3. In the table, I've listed both the stereotype (the basic cultural expectation) and the actually observed differences, so you can see how well they match.

In many areas, the match is not good. Girls don't seem to be more dependent or consistently more nurturant (the offering of care and concern to others) or more socially oriented. They are somewhat more compliant, but they don't cry more. The one area in which there is a good match between the stereotype and the observed difference is aggression, assertiveness, and dominance. As expected, boys are more aggressive.

Where might such a difference in aggressiveness come from? Eleanor Maccoby and Carol Jacklin (1974), who have summarized all the studies done up to 1974, conclude that there is an important biological basis for the aggression differences:

> Let us outline the reasons why biological sex differences appear to be involved in aggression: (1) Males are more aggressive than females in all human societies for which evidence is available. (2) The sex differences are found early in life, at a time when there is no evidence that differential socialization pressures have been brought to bear by adults to "shape" aggression differently in the

Table 11.3 A Comparison of Sex-Role Stereotypes and Observed Sex Differences in Social Behavior

Behavior	Stereotyped expectation	Actually observed difference
Aggression/dominance/ competitiveness	Boys are expected to be more of all three.	Boys are fairly consistently found to be more physically aggressive (Maccoby & Jacklin, 1974; Barrett, 1979). Differences in verbal aggression are less consistent. Boys are also more dominant and more competitive in most situations.
Dependency	Girls are thought to be more.	No consistent sex difference has been found in such behaviors as clinging, being near, or attention seeking in children (Maccoby & Jacklin, 1974).
Nurturance	Girls are thought to be more.	No clear difference among children has been found (Maccoby & Jacklin, 1974). Both boys and girls will respond to the need of another child with a nurturing response.
Interest in others; sociability	Girls are though to be more.	The results are mixed. Boys seem to be more peer oriented in preschool (Maccoby & Jacklin, 1974; Roper & Hinde, 1978). In elementary school, boys have more friends and play in larger groups; girls seem to have fewer but stronger friendships (Laosa & Brophy, 1972; Omark, Omark & Edelman, 1973).
Compliance	Girls are thought to be more.	Preschool girls comply more with adult requests (Minton, Kagan & Levine, 1971; Maccoby & Jacklin, 1974). Among older children there is no consistent tendency for girls to be more compliant (Maccoby & Jacklin, 1974).
Crying	Girls are thought to do more.	There is no consistent difference among children. Among preschoolers, when there is a difference, it looks as if boys cry more (Maccoby & Jacklin, 1974).

two sexes. (3) Similar sex differences are found in man and subhuman primates. (4) Aggression is related to levels of sex hormones, and can be changed by experimental administration of these hormones.

(Maccoby & Jacklin, 1974, pp. 242–243)

As you might imagine, not all psychologists agree with this biological position. Jeanne Brooks-Gunn and Wendy Schempp Matthews (1979), for example, think that a combination of biology and training by parents is involved in the sex difference we see in aggressiveness. I'm sure this issue will be debated for some time to come. For me, though, the most striking thing to come out of the studies of sex differences in social interactions is that boys and girls are much more like each other than different in the way they relate to other people. They go through similar steps in developing attachments; they develop peer interactions in similar ways; the form of aggression they show changes with age in the same ways. So while it is worthwhile for researchers to go on exploring the differences, you should keep the fundamental similarities firmly in mind, too.

Summary

1. Relationships with adults and peers are of central significance in the development of all children. Of particular importance is the formation of basic attachments to others in infancy and later childhood.
2. An important distinction is between *attachment behavior* and underlying *attachment*. The latter is the basic bond between two people; the former is the form in which that bond is expressed in actual behavior. Attachment behaviors change with age.
3. The parents' attachment to the infant develops in two phases: (1) An initial strong bond may be formed in the first hours of the child's life. (2) A growing attachment results from the repetition of mutually reinforcing and interlocking attachment behaviors.
4. An infant shows a wide range of attachment behaviors, including smiling, cuddling, crying, and mutual gazing. The parent responds with matching behaviors, including holding, smiling, and mutual gazing.
5. The infant's attachment goes through several phases, from initial preattachment to formative attachment, to clear-cut attachment at 6–7 months of age.
6. In older children, the basic attachment remains; but the form of attachment behavior changes, becoming less clinging, *except* when the child is under stress, when the earlier forms reappear.
7. Children differ in the security of their first attachments. The secure infant uses the parent as a safe base for exploration and can be readily consoled by the parent.
8. Secure attachment appears to be fostered by attentive, loving, "contingently paced" interactions between parent and child.
9. Having an infant in day care does not appear to disrupt the child's basic attachment to the parents, and, in some cases, may foster cognitive development.
10. Attachments to peers also form during the first 3–4 years of life, with individual "best friends" chosen by many children as young as 3. Over the early years, peer contacts become more and more social.
11. Play with peers is at first parallel and only later, at about age 3 or 4, cooperative.
12. Children differ in their skill at peer play. Those differences are partly the result of sheer experience with peers and partly the result of security of early attachments.
13. Older children continue to form strong individual friendships but also play in looser groups or gangs. In elementary school, the groups are nearly all same sex; in adolescence, the groups are mixed sex.
14. Popularity among peers is affected by the child's intelligence, friendliness, physical attractiveness, and physical size.
15. Aggression among children seems initially to be a response to frustration. But the form and amount of aggression changes with age. The peak of physical aggression is at about age 4, with verbal aggression increasing after that.
16. Children who are reinforced for aggressiveness show more aggression with their peers. In the home, rejected children and those permitted to be aggressive and then punished for it show heightened aggression.
17. Children who watch a lot of violent TV also show heightened aggression and are more likely to approve of aggression as a

problem-solving technique.

18. The most consistent sex difference in the area of personal relationships is that boys are more aggressive than girls. In other areas, the similarities are more striking than the differences.

Key Terms

Aggression Usually defined as intentional physical or verbal behaviors directed toward a person or an object with the potential for damage or injury to that person or object.

Attachment The positive affective bond between one person and another, such as the child for the parent or the parent for the child.

Attachment behavior The collection of (probably) automatic behaviors of one person toward another that bring about or maintain proximity and caregiving, such as the smile in the young infant.

Cliques Groups observed in adolescence made up of dating couples or clusters of same-sex friends who share basic interests.

Cooperative play Play between two children in which both are joined in a common enterprise, such as building a block tower together.

Crowds The term used to describe larger groups of children or adolescents, usually made up of several cliques but held together by common background or common interests.

Dependency Term used to describe such relatively immature forms of attachment behavior as attention seeking, proximity seeking, and clinging behavior in children or adults.

Hostile aggression A subset of aggression aimed at other people rather than at objects.

Insecure attachment Includes both ambivalent and avoidant patterns of attachment in children; the child does not use the parent as a safe base and is not readily consoled by the parent if upset.

Instrumental aggression Aggression aimed at achieving some goal or object other than the pain or discomfort of another person.

Parallel play A pattern of play in which two or more children play next to each other but each at his own game or task, with no mutual activities.

Peers Other persons of roughly the same age as oneself.

Secure attachment Demonstrated by the child's ability to use the parent as a safe base and to be consoled after separation, when fearful, or when otherwise stressed.

Strange situation A series of episodes used by Mary Ainsworth in her studies of attachment. The child is with the mother, with a stranger, left alone, and reunited with stranger and mother in a specific sequence.

Suggested Readings

Brooks-Gunn, J., & Matthews, W. S. He & she. How children develop their sex-role identity. Englewood Cliffs, N.J.: Prentice-Hall, 1979.
If you are interested in sex differences, particularly in aggression, attachment, and other areas I've discussed in this chapter, this is an excellent, readable summary. These authors take a more environmental position than do Maccoby and Jacklin.

Kempe, R. S., & Kempe, C. H. Child abuse. Cambridge, Mass.: Harvard University Press, 1978.
An excellent, up-to-date summary of not only what we know about the origins of abuse but also treatment programs.

Maccoby, E. E., & Jacklin, C. N. The psychology of sex differences. Stanford, Calif.: Stanford University Press, 1974.
The classic discussion of sex differences; must reading if you are interested in this topic.

Schaffer, R. Mothering. Cambridge, Mass.: Harvard University Press, 1977.

This small book and Stern's (see below) are excellent places to begin if you are interested in the whole area of early attachments.

Stern, D. The first relationship: Infant and mother. Cambridge, Mass.: Harvard University Press, 1977.
A lovely book, full of good examples and clear descriptions of research.

Project 11.1 Television Aggression

Using the definition of violence offered by George Gerbner (given on p. 354), select a minimum of four half-hour television programs normally watched by children and count the number of aggressive or violent episodes in each. Count both verbal aggression and physical aggression. You may select any four (or more) programs, but I would strongly recommend that you distribute them in the following way:

1. At least one "educational" television program, such as "Sesame Street," "Mr. Rogers," or "The Electric Company."
2. At least one Saturday morning cartoon. "The Road Runner" is a particularly grisly example, but there are others. If you have time, it would be worthwhile to watch a whole Saturday morning of cartoons so that you can get some feeling for the fare being offered to young children.
3. At least one early evening adult program that is watched by young children: a family comedy, a western, a crime film, or one of each.

For each program that you watch, record the number of violent episodes, separating the verbal and physical violence.

In thinking or writing about the details of your observations, consider the following questions:

What kind of variation in the number of violent episodes is there among the programs that you watched?

Are some programs more verbally aggressive, some more physically aggressive?

Do the numbers of violent episodes per program correspond to the numbers found by Gerbner?

What about the consequences of aggression in the television films? Are those who act violently rewarded or punished? How often do reward and punishment occur?

In light of the discussion in the chapter, what do you think might be the consequences to a child of viewing the same programs?

What behaviors other than aggression might a child have learned from watching the programs you viewed? This question is particularly relevant for "Sesame Street," "Mr. Rogers," or other "educational" programs but applies to "entertainment" programs as well.

Preview of Chapter 12

12 Self-Concept and Sex Roles in Children

A friend of mine, who had just received her Ph.D. and was very proud of her new status, was discussing grown-up jobs with her 4-year-old daughter, Amanda. She explained to the little girl that she was a "psychology doctor." "No you aren't, Mommy," replied Amanda. "You're a psychology nurse!" As far as this child was concerned, men were doctors and women were nurses, and that was that.

My friend isn't the only one who has found this rigidity in young children. Glen Cordua (Cordua, McGraw & Drabman, 1979) showed preschool children films that included male nurses and female doctors. When they were later asked about the characters in the films, most of the children remembered all the doctors as being men and all the nurses as being women.

Even older children have fairly fixed expectations about future roles. Ask a group of 9- or 10-year-olds what they want to be when they "grow up." The boys are likely to tell you that they want to be doctors, firemen, or cowboys; the girls are likely to tell you that they want to be be teachers, nurses, or mommies. A few children will cross over these lines, but not many. A few girls may say they want to be doctors or cowboys (cowpersons?), but it is the very rare little boy who will tell you he wants to be a nurse.

Where do these ideas and attitudes come from? How and when do children develop their sense of what it means to be a girl or a boy?

This issue is part of a larger question: How does a child form his **self-concept,** his basic idea of his qualities, abilities, and his place in the world? The self-concept can be divided up into several parts, so let me begin with some definitions.

Definitions

At the most basic level, there is what Michael Lewis and Jeanne Brooks-Gunn (1979) call the **existential self,** the fundamental sense of being separate from others. Until this develops, we can't really speak of the child having a self-concept at all.

Second, there is the **categorical self** (again to use Lewis's and Brooks-Gunn's term). The child comes to define herself in terms of a set of categories, such as age, size, gender, color, and specific skills or knowledge. The specific set of category values a child applies to herself (for example, young, tall, female, black, smart, and slow) is her self-concept (sometimes called the self-image). As children progress along the lines of cognitive development I described in Chapter 8, developing more and more complex concepts and categories, we'd expect that their self-concepts would become more complex as well.

Finally, there is the *affective* aspect of the self-concept, the value the child gives to the qualities she sees herself as having. This aspect is usually described in terms of **self-esteem.** A child with "high self-esteem" places a positive value on her self-perceived characteristics; a child with "low self-esteem" places a neutral or negative value on her characteristics.

How do these several aspects of the self-concept develop over the years of childhood? I want to deal with this broad question first and then focus on just one facet of the self-concept, namely, the gender concept, and the concept of sex roles. Gender is just one of the many categories by which the self is defined. But it is a particularly interesting one, especially in light of the changing sex roles and sex-role concepts in our culture.

Development of the Self-Concept

Developmental Patterns

The First Stages The first step is for the infant to recognize that she is separate from others, that her mother's or caregiver's body is not part of her own. This is what Lewis and Brooks-Gunn call the existential self-concept. Freud talked about the child's early **symbiotic** relationship with her mother, in which the infant appears to consider the two of them a single unit. Piaget, too, emphasizes that the very young infant has not yet understood the separation of self from nonself. The awareness of this separation seems to develop during the first six to eight months, along with the development of the object concept, as I discussed in Chapter 5.

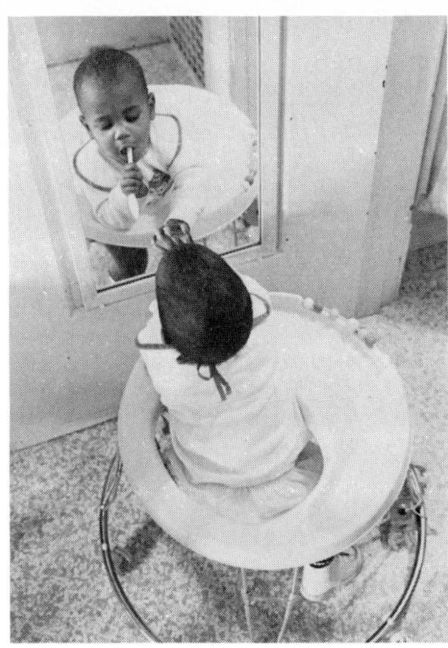

Figure 12.1 Research by Lewis and by Gallup shows that a child of about 20 months or older is able to recognize himself in a mirror, which is a sign that the "existential self" is well developed.

Once she realizes she is separate, the child has another big step ahead of her: She must see herself as a continuing "event." Just as she must realize that the mother who comes through the door today is the same mother who came through the door yesterday (and will come through the door tomorrow), so she has to begin to see herself as existing continuously in time and space.

One sign that the child has achieved this understanding is that she begins to be able to recognize herself or to use her own name. There has been a lot of research quite recently on self-recognition in infants (Gallup, 1979; Lewis & Brooks-Gunn, 1979; Dickie & Strader, 1974; Amsterdam, 1972) which shows that children of about 18–24 months recognize themselves in mirrors, look more at their own pictures than at the pictures of other babies, and name themselves in pictures. Gordon Gallup (1979) has found that adolescent chimpanzees also show self-recognition in mirrors, but that this is *not* true of chimps reared in social isolation. Apparently, some kind of social contact with members of the species is required for the animal to develop this basic aspect of the sense of separate self. Gallup argues that among humans as well, "one must have knowledge of others in order to have knowledge of self" (Gallup, 1979, p. 118). In the infant, then, the self-concept presumably grows out of the social encounters with the parents and others during the first months of life.

The Preschool Years Once the young child has achieved a basic understanding of his own separateness and distinctness, he begins the long process of developing the categorical self—of identifying dimensions on which people differ and locating himself on those same dimensions.

For example, Carolyn Edwards and Michael Lewis (1979) have found that 3- to 5-year-old children notice *age* as an important dimension. They can sort photographs into groups such as "little children," "big children," "parents," and "grandparents." The same children can also identify themselves as being "little children" or "big children." As we'll see later in the chapter, children of the same age (3–5 years) begin to categorize others and themselves by gender as well.

Another sign of the child's developing self-concept during this period is her growing independence and insistence on autonomy. Perhaps this reflects only desire for mastery; but as Erikson (1963) points out, this powerful push for independence may also be part of the child's exploration of herself. What can I do? Where can I go? What happens if I. . . ? The child is trying out the boundaries of her skills.

At the same time, 3- and 4-year-old children begin to show possessiveness about objects and people. The child has "my

Figure 12.2 During the preschool years, children become more and more independent and more able to do things by themselves, as this boy is doing. In the process of testing the limits of what they can do, they steadily change their self-concept.

dollie," "my daddy," "my blocks." Gordon Allport (1961) suggested that this represents a further extension of the concept of self to "things that belong to me."

School Age By age 4 or 5, the child's categorical self is well developed. He can describe himself on a whole series of dimensions and compare himself to others on those same dimensions. But as I suggested earlier, as the child moves through the school years, developing more and more complex concepts, his self-concept becomes more complex as well. This shift is shown very vividly in a study by Raymond Montemayor and Marvin Eisen (1977).

Montemayor and Eisen measured the child's self-concept in a very straightforward way. They asked fourth, sixth, eighth, tenth, and twelfth grade students each to write 20 different answers to the question "Who am I?" (You might want to try this yourself before you read any further.) Montemayor and Eisen found that the younger children's answers focused on such externally visible categories as their age, their size, their address, or their favorite activities. But older children listed their beliefs, their relationships with other people, and their personality characteristics. You can sense this change by reading the answers given by two different subjects in this study, the first a 9-year-old in the fourth grade, the second a 17-year-old in the twelfth grade:

> My name is Bruce C. I have brown eyes. I have brown hair. I have brown eyebrows. I'm nine years old. I LOVE! Sports. I have seven people in my family. I have great! eye site. I have lots! of friends. I live on 1923 Pinecrest Dr. I'm going on 10 in September. I'm a boy. I have a uncle that is almost 7 feet tall. My school is Pinecrest. My teacher is Mrs. V. I play Hockey! I'm almost the smartest boy in the class. I LOVE! food. I love fresh air. I LOVE school.
>
> I am a human being. I am a girl. I am an individual. I don't know who I am. I am a Pisces. I am a moody person. I am an indecisive person. I am an ambitious person. I am a very curious person. I am not an individual. I am a loner. I am an American (God help me). I am a Democrat. I am a liberal person. I am a radical. I am a conservative. I am a pseudo-liberal. I am an atheist. I am not a classifiable person (i.e., I don't want to be).
>
> *(Montemayor & Eisen, 1977, pp. 317–318)*

Clearly, the self-concept in the twelfth grader is much more abstract, which undoubtedly reflects the underlying shift from concrete operational to formal operational thinking. The concrete operational child (like Bruce C.) is still paying attention primarily to the external properties of objects or people, including himself. But the adolescent pays more attention to the inner

Table 12.1 Sample Items From Coopersmith's Measure of Self-Esteem

I often wish I were someone else.
I am often sorry for the things I do.
I'm pretty sure of myself.
I can make up my mind and stick to it.
I wish I were younger.
I don't like to be with other people.
I'm pretty happy.
There are many times when I'd like to leave home.
My parents usually consider my feelings.
I'm a lot of fun to be with.
I'm doing the best work that I can.
I often get discouraged in school.

Source: Coopersmith, 1967, pp. 265–266.

qualities of objects and examines herself using those same, more subtle categories.

Another difference you may have noticed between the statements given by the two young people is the positive or negative tone. Bruce writes mostly positive statements about himself, while the high school girl lists many negatives. This is one reflection of a difference in self-esteem between the two.

We don't know very much about the development of self-esteem in very young children, since it has been little studied. But by school age (5 or 6), children can tell you quite clearly whether they like themselves or not.

In older children, self-esteem is usually measured with a questionnaire, like the one developed by Stanley Coopersmith (1967). Table 12.1 shows some of the items from this instrument. In each case, the child is asked to say whether the statement is "like me" or "unlike me." In any group of children, some will select many positive statements as being "like me," while others will select mostly negative statements.

But like the categories children use, the focus of their self-esteem changes with age. Barbara Kokenes (1974), using Coopersmith's inventory with groups of children from fourth to eighth grade, found that the central theme in the self-esteem of fourth and fifth graders was their success in school and in friendships. Children who saw themselves as successful and as having good friendships generally selected more of the other positive items on the inventory. But among eighth graders in this study, the crucial ingredient in a positive self-image was a satisfying and supportive relationship with the parents. That is, young people who selected items like "my parents usually consider my feelings" as being "like me" were more likely to have a generally positive self-image on the other items.

One of the implications of this study is that a child's self-esteem is not fixed. It is heavily dependent on the child's success with currently important relationships or tasks. In the elementary school years, when school success is a central task, a child's skill in school weighs heavily in the self-esteem. But when the psychological tasks change, as they do in adolescence, a child who had high self-esteem at age 10 may shift toward a more negative view or vice versa. Self-esteem may also shift at adolescence because the teenager begins to go through a conscious reevaluation of his identity.

The Adolescent Search for Identity: A Transformation of the Self-Concept You'll remember from Chapter 10 that the stage Erikson describes for adolescence is "identity versus role confusion." He thought that there was a special crisis in a young person's sense of self that occurred at this time. The teenager has to reevaluate herself and her goals. More specifically, the teenager needs to come to terms not only with the question "Who am I?" but the question "Who *will* I be?" For many teenagers, this requires a complete transformation of the self-concept. At the very least, it requires a *reevaluation* and then a *commitment* to a new identity or a reaffirmation of the old identity.

A good deal of the research on identity formation in adolescence has been spurred by the work of James Marcia (1966, 1976). Following Erikson's lead, Marcia suggested that at any given moment, an adolescent or young adult could be described as being in one or another of four different "identity statuses":

> Identity achievement: The young person has been through the period of reevaluation and struggle and has made a commitment.
>
> Moratorium: The young person is in the midst of reevaluation and is struggling among alternatives.
>
> Foreclosure: The young person has continued a commitment to earlier self-concepts and goals without going through a period of reevaluation.
>
> Identity diffusion: The young person is not in a state of reevaluation and has not yet made a commitment.

Erikson thought that the struggle for identity took place during early adolescence. Marcia's work, and that of others who have used his measures, suggest that for many young people,

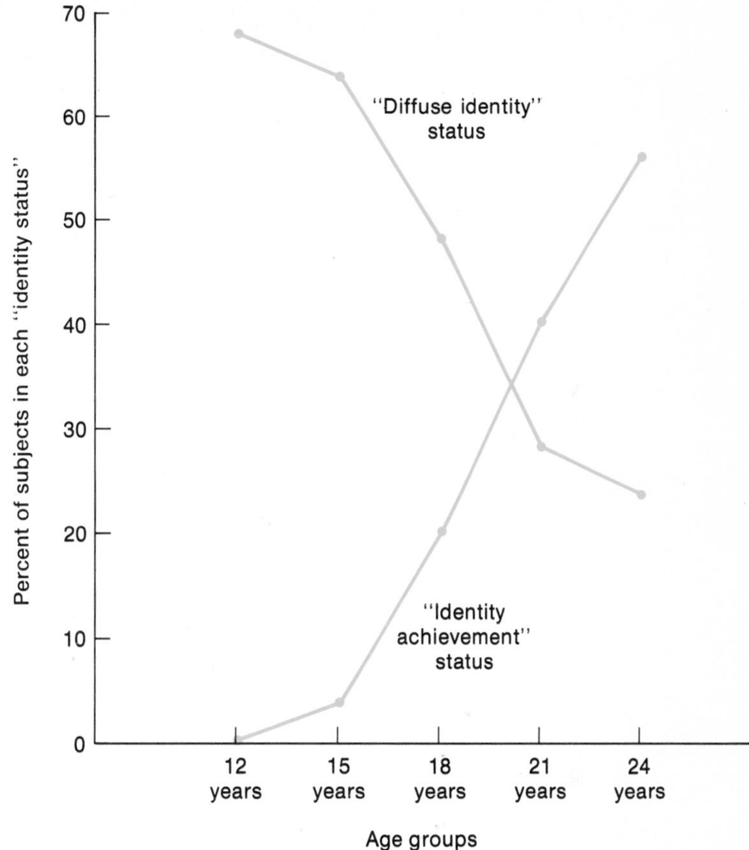

Figure 12.3 Although Erikson believed that the "identity crisis" occurred fairly early in adolescence, these results from Philip Meilman's study show that "identity achievement" (the resolution of the crisis) doesn't occur for most young people until they are in their late teens or early twenties. (Source: Meilman, 1979, p. 231. Copyright 1979 by the American Psychological Association. Reprinted by permission.)

the struggle comes much later—in the late teens and early twenties. Some results from a study by Philip Meilman (1979) (see Figure 12.3) show this very clearly. He classified separate groups of 12-, 15-, 18-, 21-, and 24-year-olds using Marcia's categories. As you can see, it isn't until age 18 that any significant number of young people in this study had reached the "achievement" status.

Other studies using Marcia's categories (Waterman, Geary & Waterman, 1974; Marcia, 1976) show that there is a developmental transition involved, with most college students moving from diffusion through moratorium (crisis) to a final identity.

Nearly all of the work on identity formation in adolescence and young adulthood has been done with male college students. We know much less about the situation for girls and for noncollege bound youth. Nonetheless, it does appear that Erikson was right to at least some extent. Teenagers do seem to go through an "identity crisis," and many of them emerge from the other side of the crisis with a new, firmer, more future-oriented self-concept.

Table 12.2 Characteristics of Children with High Self-Esteem Compared to Children with Low Self-Esteem

They get better grades in school and on achievement tests.
They see themselves as responsible for their own success or failure.
They have more friends.
They see their relationship with their parents more positively.
They may be more competitive (DeVoe, 1977).
As adolescents, they are more likely to have achieved "identity status" (LaVoie, 1976).

Summary of Developmental Changes in Self-Concept Let me sum all this up for you. The young child develops first a sense of her physical self, her continuity, her boundaries, her skills. By school age, she also has a sense of her self-worth and some sense of her physical "place" in the world. Over the period of concrete and formal operations (from age 6 through adolescence), the content of the child's self-concept becomes more abstract, less and less tied to outward physical qualities. But for most adolescents, there is also a significant reevaluation of identity. Who am I? What will I be? What should I be? These are all questions that become extremely important during the adolescent years.

Individual Differences in Self-Esteem and Identity Achievement

As usual, I have begun by talking about developmental patterns as if the process were exactly the same for all children. But here, as in every other area, there are important differences among children. In particular, there are differences in the positive or negative value children place on themselves. And at adolescence, there are important differences in the success the teenager has in passing through the "identity crisis."

Differences in Self-Esteem Children and teenagers who like themselves have certain other characteristics as well. I've listed some of them in Table 12.2.

Of all the qualities listed in the table, the one that is most significant for teachers is the fact that children with high self-esteem do better in school and, conversely, that those with low self-esteem do less well in school. Of course, there is a chicken/egg problem here. Does the child have high self-esteem because he succeeds, or does he succeed because he has high self-esteem? No doubt the process works both ways. A child who enters school with a strong positive self-image will approach the tasks of school with a different attitude, different motivation. This more positive view probably leads to greater effort and more success, which just reinforces the child's high self-esteem. Similarly, an "I can't do it anyway" attitude is not likely to lead to greater effort, which only reinforces the child's negative self-image.

But the attitudes and behavior of the teacher can make a significant impact on this spiraling process. Remember the case of Miss A (Box 9.3), the first-grade teacher who expected all her pupils to do well. Her expectation was confirmed, presumably because of the way she encouraged her students. Several other studies (Beez, 1968; Rosenthal & Jacobson, 1968) have also shown that when teachers are told that some children are very bright or are likely to learn easily, those children do in fact learn more, even though they were originally assigned to the "fast learning" group purely at random.

The last link in this chain of evidence is provided by an older study by Staines (1958), who measured the self-concept of a group of students and then had teachers give extra praise and encouragement to those students who had low self-esteem. After three months of this treatment, not only had the children's self-esteem risen, but their schoolwork had improved as well.

All of this research leads to the important point that a student's *perception* of or *belief* about his abilities, as well as his teacher's perceptions and beliefs, may be as important for his school success as his objective skill. The moral for teachers is to be very wary about the assumptions you make about your pupils. A more hopeful conclusion, though, is that it is possible to change a child's self-image by consistent use of positive treatment. In the process, you may improve the child's school performance as well.

Differences in Identity Achievement There are parallel differences between young people who successfully achieve a clear and firm identity and those who remain more diffuse. But during this period, some sex differences emerge, too. Ruthellen Josselson and her colleagues (Josselson, Greenberger & McConochie, 1977a, 1977b) have given us some of the most vivid pictures through a series of case studies of psychosocially "mature" and "immature" eleventh-grade boys and girls. She has not used Marcia's categories, but it is clear that the "mature" young people in her studies are those who are either struggling toward or have reached a completed identity.

Among boys, those with low maturity are heavily focused on the here and now. They make few plans for the future, and their behavior is guided by what other people think of them or do for

Figure 12.4 We can't tell just from looking at these teenagers which one has a "mature" identity and which has an "immature" identity. But Josselson's research suggests that the athletically and socially successful high school boy may be *less* mature, while this is not the case for girls.

them. Someone else decides whether they should go to college or get a job after high school; their self-esteem is dependent on being liked by their friends. Many of these boys are popular, and many are actively involved in sports. Sports is fun, and people who are good at sports get a lot of attention. Nearly all the boys in the "immature" group also had a steady girlfriend. One example:

> Leonard has given no thought to where he might like to go to college or what he might like to study. . . . Leonard seems to feel pessimistic about his own future . . . [saying] "Life is fun now, but I guess sooner or later, you're going to have to work." His friends are those who share his enthusiasm for sports, people who "like to do what I like to do." [He] says later on that having friends and fitting in with the gang are the most important problems a teenager faces.
> *(Josselson, Greenberger & McConochie, 1977a, pp. 33–34)*

By contrast, high-maturity boys in this study were very future oriented. They thought about what they would do with their lives. For them, self-esteem arises from what they do more than from what other people think. They are often quite introspective and try to understand why other people do the things they do.

One of the very interesting findings in this study was that among the boys, those who were *low* in maturity were the most popular, the most likely to be seen as leaders in their group. The low-maturity boys are very friend oriented, and care a great deal about being accepted by and being part of the gang. The higher-maturity boys are often active in school, but they are also more self-sufficient. Josselson's results suggested that "success" for a boy in the high school culture may not be a sign of overall health or growth.

Among girls, in contrast, it is the *high*-maturity girls who are seen as popular and as leaders. These are girls "who take themselves seriously," as Josselson puts it. They are introspective and have thought about who they are and where they are going. But their thinking is much less focused on an occupation than on their own inner nature. They want to find out *who* they are, not what they will do. So they differ from the high-maturity boys in their attitude about the future. Still, most of them have specific career plans and expect to work in addition to marriage.

Outwardly, the low-maturity girls are very similar to the high-maturity girls. Both groups are involved in school activities, in sports or cheerleading, or other school events. Both groups have friends, and both date. But inwardly, there are differences in values. "The world of the low-maturity girls is dominated by two concerns: having fun and having things" (p. 152). As one girl put it, "I like doing something every minute—I hate being bored" (p. 152). As a group, these girls are outgoing, often cheerful, sometimes successful with their peers. But they are "diffuse," in Marcia's terms.

What does the future hold for these different groups of young people? Since I don't have a crystal ball, I can't tell you whether Leonard will break out of his pessimism and work out some positive future for himself. But I can tell you what group differences have been found between teenagers who have achieved identity and those who have not.

Identity achievers, as a group, adjust more easily to and do better in college (Bourne, 1978). They are also more successful in establishing satisfying intimate relationships as young adults (Marcia, 1976; Orlofsky, Marcia & Lesser, 1973). Diffuse adolescents are more likely to experience a sense of personal isolation as adults. These are results we'd expect if Erikson is right about the need to move through the different stages in order. A student who has not completed the identity stage will have a much harder time achieving intimacy in his twenties.

These findings also emphasize, again, how central the self-concept and sense of identity can be to the overall functioning of a child or adolescent. So it becomes very important to understand how children get to be self-confident and high in self-esteem.

Origins of High Self-Esteem and Identity

Direct Experience and Attributions by Others A child's image of herself arises partly out of her own experience. What does she do easily? Can she run faster than the other children in her neighborhood? Can she yell louder? Is she good at reading, climbing trees, playing ball? By comparing herself to others, she gets some sense of her relative skill.

But what other people say about her—what qualities they attribute to her—is another significant source of information for the self-concept. I recall very vividly in my own early years that when something was broken in our house, no one asked, "Who broke the dish?" The question seemed (to me) to be instead, "Helen, when did you break the dish?" I have no way of knowing whether in fact I broke more things than other children did, but I *believed* that I did. My self-image then, and still, includes a sense of physical clumsiness.

The child whose parents, peers, teachers, and other significant people consistently emphasize her positive qualities is thus more likely to have high self-esteem; the child whose weaknesses are emphasized (accurately or not) will incorporate those negative impressions into her view of herself.

Family Influences But more than these specific types of "attributions" by other people, a child's self-esteem seems to

Figure 12.5 Studies of the origins of high self-esteem show that parents who are warm and affectionate, as this mother is, and who *also* set clear and firm limits, have children with the most self-confidence and highest self-esteem.

depend very much on the overall climate in her family. Several different researchers, including Stanley Coopersmith (1967) and Diana Baumrind (1972), have found that the most favorable pattern seems to be a combination of clear, strict limits with firm discipline along with warmth and affection. Baumrind calls this combination **authoritative parental style.** These parents like their children, tell them so, and explain the limits they have set. But they are firm about the rules. In contrast, both parents with a **permissive style,** who are loving but not firm, and those with **authoritarian style,** who are firm but less warm, have children who are less confident and less effective in their relationships with others.

All of these studies have been done with quite young children—preschoolers and elementary school age. But they

Box 12.1

Girls and Their Fathers: A Special Source of Self-Esteem

In Freud's theory, good "mental health" requires, among other things, that the child identify with the parent of the same sex during the Oedipal period. The "healthiest" girls, then, ought to be those who have most fully identified with their mothers. But there is now growing evidence that, at least in our society, girls with the highest confidence and self-esteem have either strongly identified with their fathers or have particularly significant and supportive relationships with their fathers (Baruch & Barnett, 1975).

Most of the studies that show this effect have involved college-age or older women, who have already shown independence, success, and self-confidence. When these women's early histories are explored, the researchers find that the father looms large.

One such study I find particularly fascinating, by Margaret Hennig and Anne Jardim (1976), was of a group of 25 highly successful, middle-aged, top-level women executives. These very successful women were *all* the firstborn in their familes, and *none* had any brothers. Virtually all described close and supportive relationships with their fathers, such as the following:

> *I think my dad never stopped hoping for a son but in the meantime I think he singled me out for the role. It was only after I was older that I realized that all girls didn't do the same things with their fathers that I did.*
>
> (Hennig & Jardim, 1976, p. 79)

Margaret Hennig found a very similar pattern in a much younger group of women who were enrolled in the masters in business administration program at the Harvard Business School, so this is not an isolated instance.

Caryl Rivers, Rosalind Barnett, and Grace Baruch (1979, p. 58) summarized this evidence by saying that

> *For a woman to be a healthy, self-confident individual, she must identify with virtues that have been associated with the male role in our society. While there is plenty of evidence that this will be healthy for her, there is no evidence that it will be harmful.*

Happily, more and more fathers seem to be involved with their daughters in just the way Hennig and Jardim's subjects' fathers were 40 years ago. Even 20 years ago, it was the rare father who spent time with his daughter, taught her sports or other activities, and encouraged her ambitions. Now it is much more common. What is more, girls growing up today have many more successful and achieving women models, including their mothers; so the intensive participation by the father in the daughter's rearing may be much less critical for female confidence and self-esteem than it once was. But it is nonetheless interesting that Freud was at least partly wrong about the basis of "health" among girls and women.

point to the fact that the roots of high self-esteem lie at least in part in the earliest interactions of the child with his family. Interestingly, the roots may be somewhat different for boys and girls—a possibility I've explored in Box 12.1.

The Self-Concept: A Summing Up

There are obviously many questions still to be answered. But I want to emphasize once again that a child's self-concept appears to be a highly significant mediating concept. Her beliefs about herself and her abilities color nearly all of her actions and interactions. The child who believes that she can't play base-

Figure 12.6 Fathers seem to be particularly important for the development of self-confidence and success among girls. Fathers who are involved in the rearing of their daughters, who spend time with them, and who teach them skills, as this father is doing, have daughters who are much more likely to be independent and competent adults.

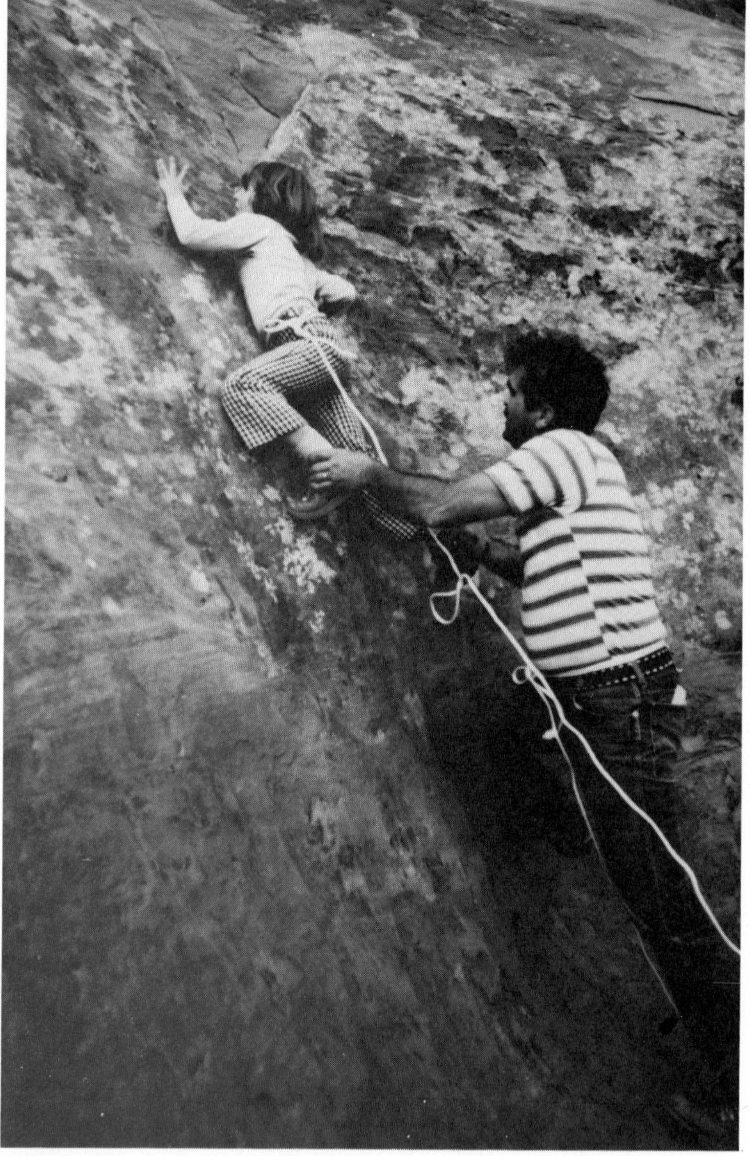

ball behaves differently from the child who believes that she can. She is likely to avoid baseballs, bats, playing fields, and other children who play baseball. If forced to play, she may make self-deprecating remarks like "You know I can't play" or she may play self-defeating games, such as refusing to watch the ball when she swings at it or not running after the ball in right field because she knows she couldn't catch it even if she did get there in time. (Those of you who were bad at baseball, as

I was, know that the poorest players are *always* put in right field!)

A child who believes that she can't do long division will behave quite differently in the classroom from the child who has more confidence in her academic skills. She may try to draw attention by cutting up and being noisy, or she may become silent and withdrawn. She may not try to work the long division problems on the theory that if you don't try, you can't fail. Or she may try much harder, paying the price in anxiety about failure.

The point is that these beliefs are pervasive, and they affect virtually all of the child's behavior. Further, they develop early and do not seem to be easily changed. We need to know much more about the origins of a child's feelings of worth, or worthlessness, if we are going to be able to counteract the latter.

The Development of Gender and Sex-Role Concepts

The element of the child's self-concept I have left out of the discussion so far is the gender concept and the accompanying concept of sex roles. This has been an area of hot debate for the past five or ten years, partly because of the women's movement and partly because of several significant books, such as Eleanor Maccoby and Carol Jacklin's *The Psychology of Sex Difference*, which have prompted a great deal of new research. So we know a lot more about the process than we did even a few years ago. Still, as you will see, there are some gaps in our knowledge.

Developmental Patterns

There are three separate developmental lines we have to follow: (1) the development of the child's understanding that she is a girl (or that he is a boy), called the **gender concept;** (2) the development of sex-role **stereotypes**—ideas about what males and females are *supposed* to be like; and (3) the development of distinctively different patterns of sex-role *behavior*, such as playing with "boy" toys or "girl" toys or choosing playmates of the same sex. The three are linked, but let me first look at them individually.

The Development of Gender Constancy This was the developmental sequence I talked about in Chapter 1, so I need only sketch it briefly for you here. How does a child figure out that he is a boy or she is a girl? There seem to be three steps involved. First, there is **gender identity,** which is simply a child's ability to label his own sex correctly and to identify other people as men or women, boys or girls. Spencer Thompson (1975) has found that 2½-year-olds are already pretty good at this. Hair length and clothing are important cues for gender for these children, but they can still accurately identify girls with short hair or trousers.

Second, there is **gender stability,** the understanding that you stay the same gender throughout life. Researchers have measured this by asking children such questions as "When you were a little baby, were you a little girl or a little boy?" Ronald Slaby and Karin Frey (1975) found that most children understood the stability aspect of gender by about age 4.

Finally, there is the development of true **gender constancy,** which is a kind of conservation—a recognition that someone stays the same gender even though he may appear to change by wearing different clothes or having different hair length. Remember from Chapter 8 that most children understand conservation of amount and number at about age 5 or 6. Gender constancy is grasped at about the same time (Slaby & Frey, 1975; Marcus & Overton, 1978). In sum, children as young as 2 or 2½ know their own sex and that of people around them, but they do not have a fully developed concept of gender until they are 5 or 6.

The Development of Sex-Role Stereotypes Once the child has figured out he's a boy or she's a girl, what do they think that means? What do they think men and women are like? What generalized expectations (usually called stereotypes) does the child have for males and females?

In our society, adults have very strong stereotypes about males and females. In some earlier research of my own (Rosenkrantz, Vogel, Bee, Broverman & Broverman, 1968), my colleagues and I found that the male stereotype was of someone who is competent, skillful, assertive, aggressive, and able to get things done. The female stereotype included the qualities of warmth and expressiveness, tact, quietness, gentleness, awareness of others' feelings, lesser competence and independence, and lack of logic.

Do children share these expectations about males and females? If so, how early do they develop? The youngest children who have been asked about their ideas about boys and girls or men and women are the 2½- and 3½-year-olds studied by Deanna Kuhn and her colleagues (Kuhn, Nash & Brucken, 1978). They focused on both the things that boys and girls *do* and on their feelings and preferences. Nearly all the 2½-year-olds they studied did have different expectations for the two sexes, and there was some agreement between the boys and girls about how the sexes differed.

Both boys and girls thought that girls like to play with dolls, like to help mother, like to cook dinner, like to clean house, talk a lot, never hit, and say "I need some help." Both boys and girls thought that boys like to play with cars, like to help father, like to build things, and say "I can hit you."

But that's where the agreement ended. In addition to these qualities, each sex saw its own gender as having special positive qualities. Girls saw other girls as looking nice, giving kisses, and never fighting; boys saw other boys as working hard. At the same time, each sex had some negative perceptions about the other. Girls saw boys as liking to fight and as mean and weak. Boys saw girls as crying and being slow.

Obviously, a lot of these ideas match the adult stereotypes. But at this early age, each sex tends to see itself as quite positive and the opposite sex as quite negative; while among older children and adults, the male stereotype contains more positively valued qualities (Rosenkrantz, Vogel, Bee, Broverman & Broverman, 1968; Broverman, Vogel, Broverman, Clarkson & Rosenkrantz, 1972).

In elementary school children, the sex stereotypes come closer and closer to those of adults. Deborah Best, John Williams, and their colleagues (Best, Williams, Cloud, Davis, Robertson, Edwards, Giles & Fowles, 1977; Williams, Bennett & Best, 1975) have found that fourth and fifth graders in the United States, Ireland, and England all see women as weak, emotional, softhearted, sentimental, sophisticated, and affectionate. They all see men as strong, robust, aggressive/assertive, cruel, coarse, ambitious, and dominant. Kindergartners in these studies showed some of these same themes, but not as strongly.

Another interesting finding from Best's and Williams's studies is that the male stereotype seems to develop a bit earlier and be stronger than the female stereotype. More children agree on what men are like than on what women are like. This could happen because children have seen women in more different roles (mother and teacher, for example) than they have seen men. Or it could mean that the female role in our society is more flexible than the male role. At any rate, it is clear that the qualities attributed to the male are more highly *valued* than are the female traits (Broverman, Broverman, Clarkson, Rosenkrantz & Vogel, 1970). It is "good" to be independent, assertive, logical, and strong. (Think back to Box 12.1; it is exactly those highly valued male qualities that the father encouraged in the confident and successful daughters.)

The Development of Sex-Role Behavior This is the third element in the whole developmental progression. Children's concept of gender develops steadily beginning at about age 2, and

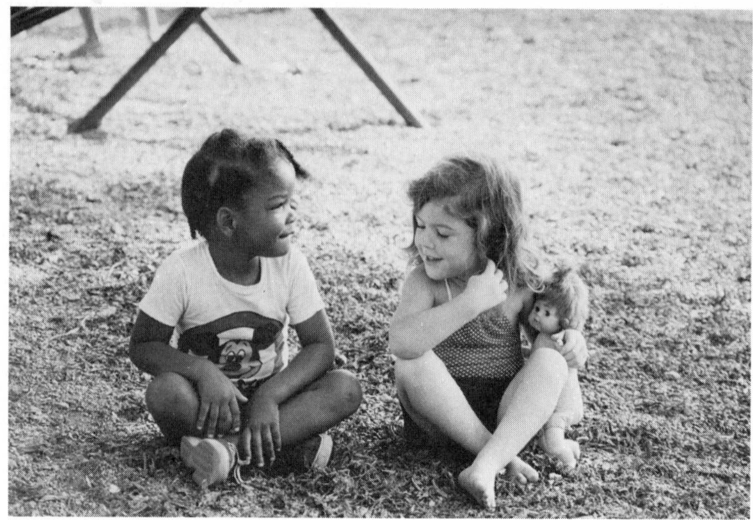

Figure 12.7 As early as 3, 4, or 5, children's play groups divide into all-girl and all-boy pairs or clusters, like this pair. This is one sign that preschoolers are aware of gender differences.

sex stereotypes begin at about the same time. But what about children's behavior?

The most common way to study this has been to look at children's toy choices. If children are observed while they play in a room stocked with a wide range of attractive toys, which toys do they choose? By about age 2 or 3, girls play at various housekeeping games, including sewing, stringing beads, or cooking. Boys play with guns, toy trucks, fire engines, and with carpentry tools (Fagot, 1974).

Another way of looking at sex-role behavior in young children is to check for the child's choice of playmates. Beginning at about age 3 or 4 (and sometimes earlier), preschoolers ordinarily choose to play with same-sex peers; and this tendency gets still stronger at school age, as I pointed out in the last chapter.

As early as 2 or 3 years of age, then, children's play is affected by their own sex and the sex of those around them.

Links Among the Developmental Patterns Obviously, these three developmental chains are related to one another. Until a child can reliably tell whether a playmate is a boy or a girl, we wouldn't expect to find same-sex peer choices. In fact, the two seem to develop at about the same time. Similarly, we might expect sex-role stereotyping to get clearer as the child's gender concept becomes more advanced, which is precisely what is found. In the study by Deanna Kuhn (Kuhn, Nash & Brucken, 1978), the researchers found that those children who had the most mature gender concept were the ones with the strongest

Figure 12.8 It's easy to tell just from looking whether this bedroom belongs to a boy or a girl. Rheingold and Cook's study suggests that this kind of stereotyping in toys and decoration is quite common among children around age 6, but we don't know how early parents begin to select different toys or activities for their sons and daughters.

sex stereotypes. What I don't know is which comes first. Probably they develop together; as the child notices physical differences between males and females, she also notices (or is told) of differences in attitude or occupation or feelings.

Still, there are some puzzles. For example, sex differences in toy preferences develop very early—earlier than there is clear gender identity. Why should boys choose trucks to play with even before they know they are boys? One possibility is that parents give boys more trucks to play with and girls more dolls. Unfortunately, we have very little good information about whether this actually occurs, and the information we have is contradictory.

For example, Harriet Rheingold and Kaye Cook (1975) went into the bedrooms of a group of 6-year-old boys and girls and made a list of the toys and the decorations. If we assume that most of the toys and decorations were selected by their parents, this study may tell us how much stereotyping is occurring. Rheingold and Cook found that boys' rooms contained more vehicles, educational-art materials, sports equipment, toy animals, machines, and military toys. Girls' rooms had more dolls, doll houses, and domestic toys. Boys' rooms were more often decorated with an animal theme; girls' rooms had more flowers and ruffles for decoration. These differences certainly fit the stereotypes. But remember that these children were 6. What about toy choices for younger children?

Carol Jacklin and her colleagues (Jacklin, Maccoby & Dick, 1973) watched mothers with their 14-month-old children in a playroom stocked with toys. They found no differences in the toys mothers chose to hand to sons and daughters, which suggests that with young children, there may be less toy choice stereotyping than we'd expect. Nonetheless, I suspect that there are differences in the toys parents buy for their sons and daughters, and this may be one of the origins of the very early sex differences in toy preferences among children.

Despite the puzzles, the broad outline of the developmental sequence is fairly clear. But how can we explain it?

Theories About the Origins of Sex Roles and Sex-Role Stereotypes

I described the three main theories in Chapter 1, but let me cover the alternatives briefly here as well.

Mischel's Theory Walter Mischel, strongly influenced by social learning theory (Mischel, 1966, 1970), argues that children learn their sex roles both by being reinforced for doing sex-appropriate things and for imitating same-sex models, particularly the same-sex parent. We know that children of 2 and 3 do imitate the behavior of other children and adults. So what Mischel is saying is that parents pay more attention to a child, praise him, or reinforce him in some other way whenever he imitates the "right" sexed person. In this way, the child learns not only about boyness and girlness but about what behaviors are supposed to go with his gender.

Kohlberg's Theory Lawrence Kohlberg (1966; Kohlberg & Ullian, 1974) approached the problem from a cognitive-developmental framework. He argues that the child's development of the basic concept of gender constancy is related to her overall intellectual development. And until that concept is fully understood, Kohlberg thought the child doesn't really imitate others of the same sex. After she grasps the gender concept, Kohlberg thought that the child would quite naturally try to figure out what people of her own gender were like and how they behaved. The child's imitation of the adults around her is important in Kohlberg's theory, as it is in Mischel's, but Kohlberg thought that it happened *after* the child's development of the gender concept, and not before.

Freud's Theory Imitation appears again as a critical element in Freud's theory, except that he called it identification. As you'll recall from Chapter 10, Freud thought that the child resolved the Oedipal crisis by identifying with the parent of the same sex and thereafter attempted to pattern herself after that parent as closely as possible, in attitudes and beliefs as well as in behavior. Obviously, this would include imitation of all the elements of sex role that the same-sex parent shows.

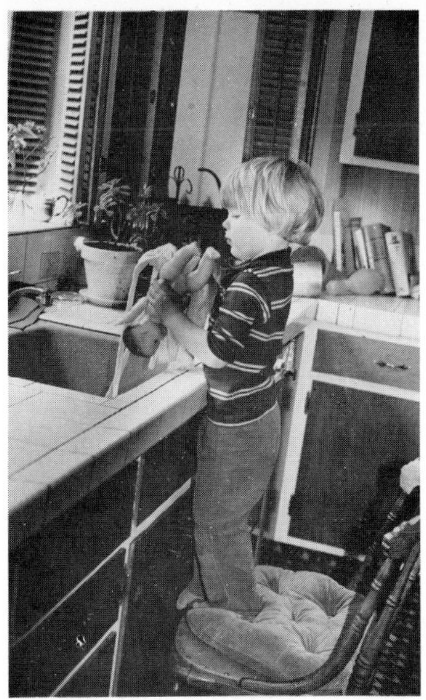

Figure 12.9 This boy is quite unusual. Most boys do not show this much of this kind of cross-sex play choice, and when they do, they are likely to get teased by their friends, or punished by their fathers. In contrast, "tomboy" behavior in girls is much more accepted by both peers and parents.

Implications and Accuracy of the Theories The differences among these theories have some practical relevance. If Mischel is right, then a child's idea about her sex role is formed very early—before school begins. So any efforts to promote a more equal view of male and female roles (something I would personally like to see) would have to be focused on the preschool-age child. But if Kohlberg is right, then the crucial years are during early elementary school. It might be possible to affect children's views, perhaps their stereotypes, by changing the way teachers treat boys and girls, altering the reading books and other school materials, and through other interventions.

As it happens, I think neither Mischel nor Kohlberg is entirely correct. If we follow Kohlberg's logic, we should find that there aren't many sex differences in behavior until after the child has achieved full gender constancy. And clearly that's not the case. Both toy preferences and same-sex playmate choices occur much earlier.

Mischel's view, on the other hand, requires that parents (or other significant people in the child's world) consistently reinforce boys for boy behavior and girls for girl behavior, as well as for imitating same-sex adults. On the whole, that does *not* seem to happen (Maccoby & Jacklin, 1974).

Tomboys and "Girlish" Boys While generally speaking, parents do not seem to reward boys more for boy behavior and girls for girl behavior, it *is* true that boys are quite consistently punished for doing girl things. Preschool teachers and other children will tease a boy who plays dressup (Fagot, 1977), and fathers are distressed when they see any "girlish" behavior in their boys (Lansky, 1967; Fling & Manosevitz, 1972). In contrast, it seems to be quite okay for a girl to show "tomboy" behavior. (This may be one reason that the male stereotype develops earlier and is stronger than is the female stereotype.) But keep in mind that preschool-age girls, as a group, still choose to play with dolls and play dressup just as much as boys choose trucks or carpentry toys. Where do the differences come from if it isn't from some kind of reinforcement or modeling?

It may well be that the reward patterns are more subtle than we've been able to pick up so far in observations of children with their parents or in nursery schools. Barbara Bianchi and Roger Bakeman (1978) found that some of the early signs of sex typing among preschoolers disappeared when they were enrolled in an "open" school in which there were both male and female teachers and the teachers encouraged equality of roles. In more traditional settings, there may be all sorts of clues that steer the children toward the "expected" roles. But so far, we haven't found much direct support for Mischel's view. Neither parents nor teachers reward boys more for aggressiveness, and young girls don't seem to be discouraged from playing with boys. Yet the differences appear.

Imitation of Same-Sex Adults One more possibility, suggested by both Mischel and Kohlberg, is that children will learn their sex roles by learning to watch (and imitate) adults and other children who share their gender. But even that doesn't seem to hold up when researchers study the process. As I pointed out in Chapter 1, so far it looks as if neither girls nor boys consistently watch same-sex adults until they are about 5 or 6; and after that age, only boys do (Slaby & Frey, 1975).

It looks as if what happens instead is that children imitate those behaviors in an adult that they see as being appropriate behaviors for their own sex. John Masters (Masters, Ford, Arend, Grotevant & Clark, 1979) found that 4- and 5-year-old girls would play with a toy labeled a "girl's toy" even after they had seen a man play with it; boys would play with a "boy's toy" even after they had seen a woman play with it. The child's play choice was dominated by the label attached to the toy, not the sex of the adult who served as a model. It certainly seems that children as young as 4 or 5 are on the lookout for clues about what behavior "fits" with their own gender. The sex of an adult who is performing some behavior is one clue, but apparently not the most important one.

A Tentative Synthesis Where does this leave us in our effort to understand the child's sex-role identify? The theorists and researchers are still arguing, but the best suggestion I have come across has been offered by Eleanor Maccoby and Carol Jacklin (1974). They argue that children learn *both* the male and the female roles through observation but perform whichever one is reinforced or is called for in a particular situation.

Remember that I said in the last chapter that we all seemed to know how to do the "baby act" with an infant. We all smile and coo and talk with a higher voice when we hold a baby. What Maccoby and Jacklin are saying is that in the same way children (and adults, too) know *how* to be both boyish and girlish. Once a child has understood the basic concept of gender constancy, she knows her gender isn't going to change. She can't *be* a boy, but she still knows how to *behave* like a boy as well as like a girl. How she actually does behave, whom she watches and learns from, will depend on what her parents and peers reinforce, what her teacher pays attention to, and what she sees on TV, in books, and with her friends (see Box 12.2).

Since stereotyped male qualities such as independence and logic are all more highly valued in our culture, girls may imitate men more than boys imitate women. And since tom-

Box 12.2 Sex Stereotyping on TV and in Books

I find myself very puzzled about the sex-role stereotypes that most of us—including children—carry around in our heads. I've pointed out in earlier chapters that there isn't a very good match between the stereotypes and what males and females are actually like. The people children watch don't *behave* very much like the stereotypes. If children are learning a lot of their behavior from the adults they observe, why don't the stereotypes get weaker and weaker with each generation? Of course, perhaps they will over the next decades as the influence of the women's movement is felt more fully. But there is not much sign of a weakening of the stereotypes yet. Why not?

One possibility is that the books children read and the TV they watch may show highly exaggerated views of males and females, thus reinforcing the stereotypes. In fact, that's what researchers have found.

Terry Saario, Carol Jacklin, and Carol Tittle (1973) analyzed the roles of males and females in children's reading books and found that there were very few major female characters at all, and those that were tended to be weaker, less able to solve problems on their own, and more dependent on male characters. The boys and men in the children's books are shown as strong, dominant, and problem solving. Let me give you just one example. In one reading book (O'Donnell, 1966), a little girl is shown having fallen off her roller skates. The caption said, " 'She cannot skate,' said Mark. 'I can help her. I want to help her. Look at her, Mother. Just look at her. She is just a girl. She gives up.' "

Fortunately, blatant examples like this have disappeared from children's reading books, partly as a result of the efforts of various parent groups. But on TV, women (and men) are still portrayed highly stereotypically. Jane Trahey (1979) recently went through an issue of *TV Guide* and picked out the descriptions of the female characters: "Heartbroken housekeeper, misguided housewife, restless housewife, student-victim, old flame, invalid wife, do-good nun, natural mother, rich society deb, nurse, and stage-struck singer." In the same issue, the male roles were described as "venerable physician, country-music veteran, private eye, lawyer, teacher, and handsome dentist."

When researchers have systematically counted the roles and behaviors of men and women on TV, they have supported Trahey's brief sample. Both George Gerbner (1972) and Sarah Sternglanz and Lisa Serbin (1974) found that women were more conforming, less effective, more dependent, and less physically active. They are most often in "handmaiden" roles—they hand the male character his coat, type his reports, and listen to his troubles.

A continuous exposure to these stereotyped males and females does seem to affect a child's vision of men and women. Terry Frueh and Paul McGhee (1975) found that elementary school children who watched more than 25 hours of TV a week had much more "traditional" views of sex roles than did children who watched less than 10 hours a week. And Emily Davidson (Davidson, Yasuna & Tower, 1979) found that when they showed either highly stereotyped or more equal sex role cartoons to young children, the kids who saw the stereotyped cartoons gave more stereotyped answers to questions about the qualities of men and women.

Clearly, TV is having an impact on children's ideas about men and women, just as it is influencing their ideas about aggression. Specifically, TV is strengthening inaccurate stereotypes about males and females. Since the children are learning from whatever they watch on TV, television could just as easily be used to portray equality of men and women. Perhaps one day. . . .

boyishness in a girl is acceptable, while "sissy" behavior in a boy is not, girls' sex roles are more flexible than boys' are, at least in the early years.

Individual Differences in Sex Roles and Sex-Role Stereotypes

Even though we can trace the development of stereotypes among children beginning at about age 5 or 6, not all children develop equally strong stereotypes. As a group, boys usually have stronger stereotypes (Angrist, Mickelsen & Penna, 1977; Best, Williams, Cloud, Davis, Robertson, Edwards, Giles & Fowles, 1977) and more "traditional" views of the roles of men and women in society than do girls.

In contrast, children whose mothers work tend to have *less* stereotyped views about men and women. They see women as more competent and positive than do children whose mothers do not work (Marantz & Mansfield, 1977; Broverman, Vogel, Broverman, Clarkson & Rosenkrantz, 1972; Derdiarian & Snipper, 1979).

Another group with weaker stereotypes (or, to put it positively, with more egalitarian views) is children who show cross-sex preferences—girls who would rather be boys and boys who would rather be girls. Deanna Kuhn (Kuhn, Nash & Brucken, 1978) found this in the 2- and 3-year-old children she studied, and it seems to be true for older children as well (Nash, 1975).

"Cross-Sex" Children Such "cross-sex" children are a particularly interesting group. How does a child come to prefer to be the other sex or to choose cross-sex playmates or toys?

One possibility is that they are trained that way. If it's true that children learn *both* boy and girl roles, then perhaps cross-sex children are merely those who have been reinforced for aspects of the opposite sex's role. Some girls are given trucks and blocks and taught carpentry and football by their fathers (or mothers). They may also come to wish that they were boys. In fact, there are far more girls who say they would rather be boys than there are boys who say they would like to be girls (Nash, 1975), which makes sense from a social learning point of view. Tomboy behavior is more accepted and reinforced than is "girlish" behavior in a boy. Also, as I've pointed out before, male behavior is more highly valued than female; so it's logical that more girls would want to be something that has high status.

But could there be a biological element, such as a different hormone pattern, in the cross-sex choice of some children? Again, maybe. There are some bits of information that support a biological view. Most strikingly, there are several studies of girls who have experienced heightened levels of androgen prenatally. (Recall from Chapter 4 that androgen is largely a

Figure 12.10 Among elementary school-age girls (and even among teenagers), it is fairly common for girls to say they would prefer to be boys. This "tomboyish" girl might have such a preference. At the moment, though, we don't know whether such cross-sex preferences are influenced by hormones or by training or both.

"male" hormone.) These "androgenized" girls, in comparison to their normal sisters, were later more interested in rough and tumble play, more often preferred to play with boys, and thought of themselves as tomboys (Ehrhardt & Baker, 1974).

But John Money, who with Anke Ehrhardt has done much of the research on the effects of prenatal hormones on sex roles, argues that biology is not destiny. He thinks that the child's experiences override the hormone patterning, so that it is the sex of *rearing* that determines behavior, and not the genetically determined gender or the hormone-determined gender behavior. His evidence for this somewhat sweeping assertion comes primarily from a series of case studies of children who, because of ambiguous genitals or other accidents, were assigned the "wrong" gender. The parents reared these children according to the assigned sex, and the children's behavior, toy preferences, playmate choices, and the rest matched the assigned sex, not the biological sex.

Money is making an important point. Clearly, the child's specific experience, and what he *thinks* he is, have a powerful effect on the sex role he adopts and the behavior he shows. But at the risk of being unpopular, I want to say that I don't think all the evidence is in yet on hormone effects. I'm not yet convinced that hormones are totally overridden by experience; I think we just don't know very much yet about their possible effects. Whatever the source of the difference, we need to know more about children who would prefer to be the other sex, since that might well tell us a great deal about how most children come to prefer to be their own gender.

Sex and Social Class Differences

The usual generalization—found in textbooks and other psychological articles—is that poor children and girls are generally lower in self-esteem than middle-class children and boys. Earlier research seemed to support this conclusion, and many writers argued that the negative self-concepts of poor children might account (in part) for their poorer school performance. Self-esteem among girls is also widely thought to be lower because so many of the qualities of "femininity" in our culture are less highly valued than are the qualities of masculinity.

More recent work, however, calls both parts of this generalization into question. There are now a number of studies of self-esteem that show no differences between poor and middle-class children. For example, in one study of nearly 4000 children aged 8–14, Norma Trowbridge (1972) found that children from lower social class families had consistently *more favorable* self-concepts than did children from middle-class families. Other researchers (such as Ristow, 1965) have found no difference. I'm not sure why there has been this change; perhaps our culture has changed enough over the past decades so that lower-class status in many communities no longer carries with it the seeds of low self-concept. This is not to say that all poor children have high self-esteem. They do not. But at the moment, there does not appear to be any *general* tendency for poverty and low self-esteem to go inevitably together.

Sex differences in self-esteem are equally inconsistent. There is just no evidence that girls generally value themselves or their qualities less highly than do males (Maccoby & Jacklin, 1974). However, teenage girls appear to be *less confident* than boys about their ability to succeed at new tasks. Other evidence suggests that while the two sexes are about equal in overall self-esteem, the particular positive qualities they see in themselves differ somewhat. Older boys and men are likely to see themselves as having such qualities as ambition, energy, optimism, or practicality; while older girls and adult women are more likely to see themselves as having the positive qualities of attractiveness, cooperation, frankness, sympathy, and ability to be leaders. In other words, the qualities men see in themselves are primarily *personal* qualities, while those women see in themselves appear to be more *social* qualities—skills and abilities that involve others.

I find these results puzzling, since among young children there appears to be no general tendency for girls to be more "affiliative" or more involved with or concerned about social encounters. In fact, young boys (preschool age) seem to spend more time with groups of peers than girls do. Why then, among teenagers and adults, should we find women defining themselves in terms of social skills rather than personal competencies? I don't have a good answer to this question, but it seems most likely to me that as the sex stereotypes grow stronger with increasing age, both boys and girls come to value those qualities that match their own sex-role stereotype.

One area in which there are fairly consistent sex and social class differences is in the strength of that sex role stereotype. I've already pointed out that boys are usually found to be more traditional in their views of sex roles than are girls. There is a parallel social class difference: Children from middle-class families tend to be more egalitarian in their views than are working-class children (Angrist, Mickelsen & Penna, 1977).

In sum, while neither boys nor girls have consistently more positive self-concepts, the sorts of things they value about themselves differ, particularly among adolescents. Such differences in the content of self-concepts may be influenced by the sex-role stereotypes prevalent in our society. Those sex-role stereotypes, in turn, appear to be particularly strong in boys and among working-class children.

Summary

1. The child's self-concept includes the "existential self" (I am separate and distinct from others), the "categorical self" (I have these specific characteristics), and the self-esteem (I like or dislike these aspects of myself).

2. The earliest stage in the development of the self-concept is the development of the "existential self," which occurs in the first months of life. The child must then discover that she (her body) is a continuous "event."

3. Most children show self-awareness or self-recognition by about 2 years of age, recognizing themselves in mirrors and in pictures.

4. By about age 3, children have learned their names; by age 3, autonomy is notable, as they assert their own identities. At about age 4, they show an increased possessiveness for "things that are mine." By age 5 or 6, they have developed (and verbalize) a fairly complete concept of self and have made positive and negative judgments about themselves.

5. Among younger school-age children, the self-concept is quite concrete, focusing on physical features and concrete activities. By adolescence, children's self-concepts begin to be more abstract, including beliefs and attitudes as well as physical qualities.

6. During adolescence, most young people go through a reassessment of their self-concept and then make a new commitment to a more mature sense of self. This is the "identity crisis" of adolescence.

7. Children high in self-esteem ordinarily do better in school, see themselves as in control of their own destiny, have more friends, and get along better with their families.

8. During the adolescent identity reevaluation, more-mature girls are also more popular and more likely to be seen as leaders. Among boys, however, the less psychological mature may be more popular.

9. Children with high self-esteem most often come from families in which their independent achievements are valued and praised, in which there is a warm, affectionate relationship between parents and children, and in which clear limits are set on the children's behavior.

10. Sex-role concepts, stereotypes, and behavior develop in parallel fashion, beginning at about age 2. Two-year-olds usually know their own gender and begin to show sex-typed toy preferences; 3–4-year-olds know they will stay the same sex and show fairly clear sex stereotypes; 5–6-year-olds have developed gender constancy.

11. The development of the gender concept is related to the child's overall cognitive development; gender constancy is a "concrete operations" accomplishment.

12. Three major theorists have described sex-role development. Mischel emphasizes the role of reinforcement and modeling and argues that children are reinforced for imitating same-sex models. Kohlberg suggests that such same-sex model imitation occurs only after the child has achieved gender constancy and that reinforcement plays little role in the process. Freud emphasized the process of identification as the resolution of the Oedipal crisis at about age 4.

13. No one of these theories does a very good job of explaining the current data on sex-role development.

14. Some groups of children seem to be consistently less stereotyped in their views of male and female roles: (a) girls, (b) children with working mothers, and (c) children with cross-sex preferences.

15. Cross-sex preferences may occur because of unusual environment forces, because of some hormonal patterning, or because of some combination of the two.

16. Stereotypes are portrayed in an exaggerated fashion both in children's books and on TV. Thus, the sex-role stereotypes are reinforced by many elements in our culture.

17. There are no consistently found sex or social class differences in self-esteem, although teenage girls are normally found to be less confident about new tasks. However, boys and working-class children tend to have more strictly stereotyped concepts of sex roles.

Key Terms

Authoritarian parental style Pattern of parental behavior described by Baumrind, among others, including high levels of directiveness and low levels of affection and warmth.

Authoritative parental style Pattern described by Baumrind, including high control and high warmth.

Categorical self The major content of the self-concept, descriptions of the self in terms of categories such as size, color, age, and beliefs.

Existential self The most basic part of the self-concept; the sense of being separate and distinct from others.

Gender concept The broad concept, developed by each child during the first 5–6 years, of his own gender and that of others.

Gender constancy The final step in developing a gender concept, in which the child understands that gender doesn't change even though there are external changes like clothing or hair length.

Gender identity The first step in gender concept development, in which the child labels herself correctly and can categorize others as male or female.

Gender stability The second step in gender concept development, in which the child understands that a person's gender continues to be stable throughout the lifetime.

Permissive parental style A third style described by Baumrind, among others, which includes high warmth and low levels of control.

Self-concept The broad concept of self, including the "existential self," the "categorical self," and the self-esteem.

Self-esteem The positive or negative quality of the self-concept.

Stereotypes A fixed set of ideas or expectations about a group of people, such as males, females, blacks, or other groups, that are applied to each new member of the group without sufficient adjustment for individuality.

Symbiotic Word used by Freud to describe the mutually interdependent relationship between the mother and infant during the earliest months of life. Freud believed that the infant was not aware of being separate from the mother at this stage.

Suggested Readings

Baumrind, D. "Socialization and instrumental competence in young children." In W. W. Hartup (Ed.), The young child: Reviews of research, vol. 2. Washington, D.C.: National Association for the Education of Young Children, 1972.
An excellent and not very difficult paper describing Baumrind's research on the development of "competence" in young children.

Hennig, M., & Jardim, A. The managerial woman. Garden City, N.Y.: Anchor Press/Doubleday, 1976.
This book is not primarily about children; it is about women in executive roles. But it describes the early childhood and adolescence of a group of highly successful women. I found it fascinating reading.

Maccoby, E. E., & Jacklin, C. N. The psychology of sex differences.. Stanford, Calif.: Stanford University Press, 1974.
This book is already the standard reference in this area. Because there has been so much new research in this area, Maccoby and Jacklin's literature reviews are no longer up to date, but the discussions are excellent. In particular, you will want to look at chapters 8 and 9.

Rivers, C., Barnett, R., & Baruch, G. Beyond sugar & spice. How women grow, learn, and thrive. New York: Putnam, 1979.
An excellent, very readable new book on sex-role development in girls. Since the book was designed for a lay audience rather than other psychologists, you will find it less technical than some other books I have suggested.

Project 12.1 Sex Roles on TV

In the last chapter, I had you watching TV for aggressive episodes; this time I want you to watch for sex-role stereotypes. By this time, you should be able to design your own specific project exploring this subject. You may choose among the following alternative projects or design one of your own, combining these elements or introducing elements of your own.

1. Watch at least eight hours of TV, spread over several time periods, and record the number of male and female characters and whether they are the central character or a minor character.
2. Watch four to six hours of TV, selecting among several different types of programs, and note the activities of each male and female character in the following categories: aggression, nurturance, problem solving, conformity, constructive/productive behavior, and physically exertive behavior.
3. Watch four to six hours of TV, selecting among several different types of program, and focus on the consequences of various actions by male and female categories: positive outcome resulting from own action; positive outcome resulting from the situation or someone else's action; neutral outcome; negative outcome resulting from own action; negative outcome resulting from the situation or the action of others.
4. Watch and analyze the commercials on at least ten programs, making sure that the programs cover the full range of types, from sports to soap operas. You might count the number of male and female participants in the commercials and the nature of their activity in each case, using some of the same categories listed in number 2.

Whichever one of these projects you choose, you must define your terms carefully and record your data in a manner that makes it understandable. In writing up your report, include the following: an *introductory* section, in which some of the background literature is described and your hypotheses are given; a *procedure* section, which must include details of the programs you observed, how you selected them, what specific behaviors you recorded, how you defined your behavioral categories, and any other details that a reader would need to understand what you actually did; a *results* section, in which the findings are reported, using graphs or tables as needed; and a *discussion* section, in which your results are compared to those of other researchers (as cited in the book or elsewhere) and any puzzling or unexpected findings are discussed and explained if possible. Additional research projects may also be suggested.

Preview of Chapter 13

Moral Development

Stop for a moment and think about some of the moral dilemmas you face in your everyday life. When the cashier at the grocery store gives you back too much change but you don't discover it till you're out in the parking lot, do you go back and return the extra money? If you have a friend who begins dating someone with whom you had a bad experience, should you tell your friend about it? If you see someone breaking the law, should you report it?

In my own recent experience, I can think of several very real issues of this kind. I have been asked to consult for various organizations, including charitable organizations like United Cerebral Palsy and noncharitable organizations like the Rand Corporation. Should I charge the same fee to both? A second issue came up at a recent meeting of the Society for Research in Child Development. Should the organization agree to have meetings in states that have not ratified the Equal Rights Amendment or should we join the boycott? If you live in a state in which there have been recent votes on capital punishment or abortion reform, you have faced difficult moral decisions before casting your vote.

Children face moral issues, too. They have to work out fair ways of sharing scarce things, like turns on the swing or time with the teacher. They have to decide whether to "tattle" on another child who has broken some rule; they have to resist temptations regularly, such as the temptation to steal the piece of candy in another child's desk when no one is looking.

Moral and ethical issues like these arise every day in the lives of children as well as adults. How do we learn to cope with these issues? How do we know what is "right" and what is "wrong"? How do we resist temptations, even when we don't think we'll get caught and how do we feel if we do *not* resist the temptation? How do we judge other people's moral actions?

Dividing Up the Issue

The central process involved in all of these questions is the development in the child of a set of culturally defined **internalized rules** to govern behavior. (The word **conscience** is often used to describe such a set of rules.) But we can break the subject down more conveniently into three subissues, each having to do with one facet of moral development.

Moral Behavior First, there is the development of moral behavior. Can the child match his behavior to the internal rules? It's all very fine to know that it's "wrong to steal," but can the child resist the impulse to shoplift when the transistor radio he wants is right there within reach and he sees that there is no one watching? Can he say no to friends who are urging him to do something he knows he shouldn't do?

Moral Feelings The second element is the *affective* part. How does the child (or adult) feel when he transgresses—when he takes the transistor radio, for example? *Guilt* is the most common feeling in this situation and is taken by many theorists to be a signal that the child has developed internalized rules.

Moral Judgment Finally, there is the cognitive element. The child must figure out how to determine if some particular action is right or wrong or whether someone else is guilty or not. How does this ability develop during childhood? Do the standards the child applies to actions change with age?

Probably all three elements are related to one another, but the theories and research on moral development have largely dealt with the three questions separately. Most of the traditional work on moral development, based on Freud's theory, has focused on the feeling part of the process—on guilt or the lack of it; most of the work based on the social learning approach has focused on moral behavior; cognitive-developmental theorists such as Piaget and Lawrence Kohlberg have emphasized the development of moral judgment. This is another case, then, in which the *what* and *why* questions can't be tidily separated. Each theory has generated a different type of research, aimed at answering a different set of questions. So let

Figure 13.1 When a group of adults serves on a jury like this one, they are asked to make a moral judgment—to determine guilt or innocence and to judge the circumstances. What logic do they apply? How do they go about their task? And how do children develop the ability to make judgments like this?

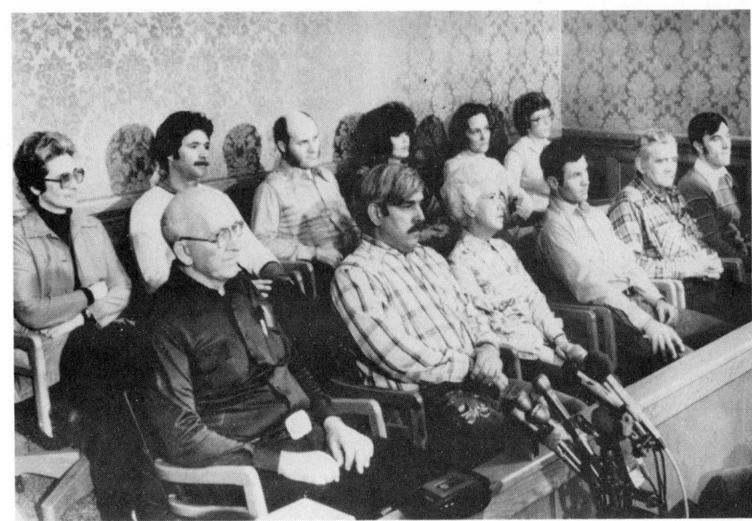

me approach the problem by looking at each of the aspects—behavior, feelings, and judgment—along with the theory that has given rise to the research on that aspect.

The Development of Moral Behavior

Social Learning Theories of Morality

Several learning theorists have proposed alternative explanations of both internalized rules and moral behavior. O. Hobart Mowrer (1950, 1960) tackled the problem of internalized rules, using a form of classical conditioning as his basic explanation. Remember from Chapter 1 that classical conditioning seems to be particularly potent in linking feelings with places or actions. The child feels good while being fed and cuddled and associates that feeling with mother or father. So just the nearness of the mother may come to trigger "feeling good."

Mowrer argues that the same principle can help to explain how a child develops a sort of internalized moral rule. If a child is repeatedly punished after doing some "bad" action, such as snatching a toy away from another child, then the bad feelings that accompany punishment will eventually come to be associated with snatching. The next time the child is about to snatch, the discomfort or fear associated with the punishment will be triggered, too, and that will inhibit the snatching. In this view, internalized rules are just a collection of **learned avoidance reactions.** You avoid doing things that have come to be painful.

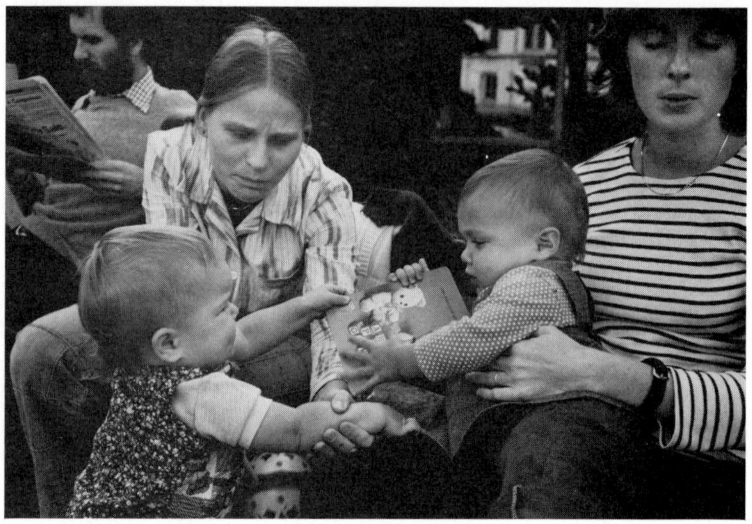

Figure 13.2 Experimental studies of resistance to temptation show that punishing before the child is able to complete the forbidden action, as this mother is doing, works better than waiting until the child has already gotten into trouble. In this way, the discomfort associated with punishment gets hooked to the cues of the beginning of the action, so the child is better able to resist the next time.

Rules about what you ought to do ("good behavior") can presumably be learned in the same way.

As you might expect, Albert Bandura and his colleagues (Bandura & Walters, 1963; Bandura, 1977) have approached the problem a little differently. He emphasizes the role of modeling for both the learning of the basic rules of right and wrong and the control of behavior.

According to this view, children learn right and wrong both by being told specifically by their parents what is good and bad behavior and by observing what their parents (and friends, teachers, TV characters, and all the other models) actually do. Since parents are often inconsistent about what they do and say —saying one thing and doing another—or are inconsistent from one time to another, Bandura thinks it is quite normal for children to develop inconsistent "moral" behavior, too. What the child does when faced with some temptation to transgress will depend heavily on the circumstances, on who else is around, on how similar the situation is to one he's seen his parents or others face, and on how likely he is to get caught.

In sum, Mowrer's theory leads us to expect that consistent punishment for wrongdoing ought to lead to stronger inhibitions and thus to more "moral" behavior. Bandura's theory leads us to expect that the behavior of models around the child is critical. The parent who states rules clearly and behaves in a manner consistent with those rules should have the child who shows the most resistance to temptation.

Table 13.1 Some Factors Influencing the Child's Ability to Resist Temptation

Timing of punishment	If the child is punished at the beginning of a "bad" behavior, he is more likely to avoid performing that behavior the next time; punishment given after the child has completed the undesired behavior is less effective.
Itensity of punishment	High-intensity punishment (a very loud noise accompanied by "no," for example) is more effective in inhibiting later behavior than is less-intense punishment.
Relationship to punisher	Punishment is more effective if it is delivered by someone the child knows and with whom he has a warm relationship.
Explanations	If the child is given a verbal rationale for the punishment, it has a greater effect than punishment given without explanation.
Observing a model	Seeing someone else deviate from a rule increases the likelihood that the child observer will later deviate, too.
Consequences to the model	If the model is punished for deviation, the observer is less likely to deviate later; if the model is rewarded for deviaion, the observer is more likely to transgress himself.
Verbalization of prohibitory rule	If the child repeats a rule stating that some behavior is prohibited, this helps him resist temptation. Observing a model rehearse a rule also helps.
Strength of desire for prohibited object or action	If a child very much wants the thing or action that is prohibited, he is more likely to give in to temptation, regardless of the other factors.
Risk of detection	If the child believes he is not likely to get caught, he is more likely to transgress.

Research on Moral Behavior

Both of these expectations are generally supported by experimental studies. The general strategy for this research has been to give a child an opportunity to perform some action, such as picking up an attractive toy. The child is then punished for this action or observes a model being punished for that action. Later the child is given another chance to play with the toy, apparently without observation, and the experimenter notes whether the child successfully resists the temptation or not.

In Table 13.1 I've given a list, drawn primarily from the work of Ross Parke (1969, 1972), of the factors that researchers have found to be associated with increased resistance to temptation in studies like these. You can see from the list that both punishment and modeling play significant roles.

You can also see from the table that the specific circumstances in which a child is tempted are important, too. If a child wants something badly and thinks he will not be caught if he transgresses, he is much more likely to give in to temptation than if he wants it less badly or thinks he might be caught. This finding is consistent with the expectations of social learning theorists. In general, they put much greater emphasis on specific situational factors and much less on the power of broad "internalized rules" or "conscience."

The practical conclusions to be drawn from the list in Table 13.1 are fairly clear. A parent who wants a child to be able to resist temptation or avoid wrongdoing of some form needs to intervene *right away* when he sees the child beginning to show the "wrong" behavior. If he also explains *why* the behavior is wrong or supplies a rule, the child's ability to resist will be strengthened. In addition, of course, parents need to be careful that their actions match their words—something that is not always easy to accomplish!

The Development of Moral Feelings

Psychoanalytic Theories of Morality

In Freud's theory, the key event in the development of morality is the process of identification. As I mentioned in Chapter 10, Freud thought that as an outgrowth of the Oedipal crisis, the child "incorporated" the parent's ideas and behaviors in one lump. Since the parents' rules about what is right and wrong are contained in that one lump, the child internalizes those rules, too. This "parent within you" functions as a kind of internal monitor, which tells you whether your behavior is good or bad, right or wrong, and punishes you with guilt when you transgress.

Whether the child *behaves* morally, however, is determined not only by identification, but also by the strength of the ego. As I mentioned in Chapter 10, the ego is the organizing, logical, planning, part of the personality in psychoanalytic theory. Only if the ego is strong will the child be able to follow the dictates of her conscience and avoid the feelings of guilt.

Differences among children in the amount of guilt they experience, according to Freud, ought to be related to the strength of their identification with the appropriate parent. The strength of the identification, in turn, should be connected to at least two things. First, Freud emphasized that the child's identification was based on fear, specifically, fear of the loss of the parents' love. We might find, then, that parents who use threats of loss of love as a way of disciplining children would have children with stronger consciences, and thus more guilt, and perhaps more moral behavior.

Second, the strongly identified child—particularly the boy—is thought to be physically afraid of his parents. So parents who use power-oriented discipline such as physical punishment or withdrawal of privileges, might have children who feel the effects of transgressions more strongly and be able to resist temptation more completely.

Studies of the Antecedents of Strong Conscience

In this case, Freud's theory doesn't fare as well when we look at the evidence. The usual way of studying this problem has been to put children one at a time into very tempting (but forbidden) situations and watch (1) whether they transgress and (2) whether they show signs of guilt later, such as saying they are sorry or trying to make amends. Then the child-rearing practices and parent-child interaction patterns in the families of the children are studied to see if there is a link.

Figure 13.3 This child is showing all the signs of guilt after transgression—one of the characteristics of a child who has identified with the appropriate parent and developed a strong conscience. This boy may confess to his mother or offer to do something to make up for it.

A Sample Study In one well-known study of this kind, Robert Sears, Lucy Rau, and Richard Alpert (1965) put the child in a small room full of extravagantly marvelous toys. Also in the room was a box with a live hamster in it. The experimenter explained that, unless the hamster was watched, he might get out of the box and run away; the child was given a rolled-up newspaper and asked to use it to keep the hamster in the box. The experimenter explained that the hamster was his pet and that he'd be very sad if anything happened to it. So would the child, as a special favor, watch the hamster for him? Of course, all the children agreed to do so, while looking longingly at all the fantastic toys.

The experimenter then left the child in the room with the hamster and the toys. At this point, the child thought he was unobserved and was tempted to stop watching the wretched hamster and play with the toys instead. Some children rather quickly turned to the toys; others watched the hamster faithfully for long minutes (up to half an hour in several cases!). But all the children did eventually turn to the enticing toys; and when they did, the experimenter, who was watching through a one-way mirror, pulled open a trapdoor on the bottom of the hamster's box and the animal disappeared down a chute. When the child went back to check the hamster, it was gone. Shortly afterward, the experimenter came back and exclaimed about his missing hamster.

What does the child do then? Does he confess that he stopped watching for a moment? Or does he insist that he never stopped at all and can't understand what happened? Does he offer to get another hamster? Does he show signs of guilt about the disappearance of the hamster? And just how long did he

Figure 13.4 **Careful, clear explanation of why something is right or wrong, and what the consequences are for the other person—as this parent seems to be trying to do—seems to help the child develop firmer internal rules.**

watch the hamster in the first place? All of these may be signs that the child has developed both a sense of right and wrong and the feelings that go with it.

General Conclusions from Research on Conscience Researchers who have used measures of conscience like this one, and who have also looked at the sort of discipline the parents use, have come to some broad conclusions.

First, physical punishment for "bad" behavior does *not* produce children who resist temptation. In fact, the exact opposite is true. The more physical punishment parents use, the *less* resistance to temptation or guilt a child shows and the less likely he is to confess after transgression.

Second, use of withdrawal of love as a discipline technique—such as saying, "I don't love you when you do that," or turning away from the child in disappointment have little effect one way or the other (Hoffman, 1970).

The one type of parental discipline that does seem to have some link to conscience-directed behavior is what Martin Hoffman (1970) calls **induction.** The parent attempts to persuade the child by reason that she should change her behavior. More important, the parent emphasizes the *consequences* of the child's actions: "When you hit me, it hurts me"; "It hurts your brother's feelings when you call him names"; "If you make a big mess on the kitchen floor, your mother will just have to go to a lot of extra work to clean it up"; "Don't yell at him. He was only trying to help."

The effectiveness of techniques like this is very clear in an extremely interesting recent study by Carolyn Zahn-Waxler and her colleagues (Zahn-Waxler, Radke-Yarrow & King, 1979). They had mothers keep a sort of diary record each time their 2-year-olds were faced with a situation in which another child or an adult was in distress. The mother wrote down what had happened, what she'd said or done to her child, and what the outcome was. Here's one mother's description of an incident:

> Today there was a little 4-year-old girl here, Susan. Todd and Susan were in the bedroom playing and all of a sudden Susan started to cry and ran to her mother. Todd slowly followed after and watched. I said, "What happened?" and she said, "He hit me." I said, "Well, tell him not to hit you," and I said "Todd!" He didn't seem particularly upset; he was watching her cry. I said, "Did you hit Susan? Why would you hit Susan? You don't want to hurt people." Then they went back in the bedroom and there was a second run-in and she came out. That's when I said sternly, "No, Todd. You musn't hit people."
>
> *(Zahn-Waxler, Radke-Yarrow & King, 1979, p. 322)*

Later this same little boy took some flower petals to Susan in an apparent attempt to make up or comfort her.

What Zahn-Waxler found was that the mothers who *both* explained the consequences of the child's actions (for example, that hitting results in hurt to the other person) *and* who stated the rules very clearly and explicitly ("You mustn't hit people"), as this mother did, had children who were much more likely to react to distress in another person by trying to make them feel better.

I think what is important about this study is that it shows us that induction, which sounds like fairly detached, unemotional reasoning when Hoffman talks about it, is really a very emotional process, too. The mothers in Zahn-Waxler's study made it very clear how they *felt* about their child's behavior as well as explaining why it wasn't good. And they also responded empathetically and compassionately to another child's distress by trying to soothe or offer some treat. So they modeled "good" behavior, too.

Connections Between Social Learning and Psychoanalytic Research on Moral Behavior

If you think about the two sets of information I've given you so far, you will probably be struck by some obvious parallels and some equally obvious disagreements.

Both the psychoanalytically oriented researchers and the social learning researchers have found that modeling and explaining (induction, in Hoffman's language) are important for the development of moral behavior and moral feelings. But the results concerning punishment seem to be totally inconsistent. Ross Parke and his colleagues (Parke & Walters, 1967; Walters, Parke & Cane, 1965; Parke, 1972) have found in controlled ex-

Box 13.1 How to Raise a Prosocial Child

Most of what I've said about "moral behavior" in children so far has been about the child resisting the temptation to do some "bad" thing. But what about the child doing "good" things, such as sharing, helping, or being compassionate to someone who is hurt? How can a parent or a teacher increase these positive behaviors in children?

Ervin Staub (1975, 1979) has done a good deal of the research on "prosocial" behavior; and he suggests that if you want to encourage such behavior, several things will help.

1. Reasoning and explaining does help some. Just as "inductive" control techniques work for reducing unwanted behavior, so explaining to a child why it is "good" to be helpful or kind does seem to encourage generosity and compassion.
2. Children also learn to be helpful by being helpful. That may sound simpleminded, but we often forget the simple things! You can get children to do helpful things in several ways. You might, for example, have children role play helpfulness or generosity. In a play-acting situation, children can take turns being in the role of the person needing help and the helping person. If you also talk about what's happening and get the children to talk about the way the actors behave and feel in the play, this strengthens the effect (Friedrich-Cofer, Huston-Stein, Kipnis, Susman & Clewett, 1979).

   A second way to encourage responsible behavior is to give children genuinely responsible tasks. This is the argument many parents use when they assign regular chores to their children, and the argument seems to be quite correct. Staub (1970) found that a child who is put in charge of the care of younger children is much more likely to respond to the sound of a child crying in a nearby room than is a child who has no responsibility.
3. Children can learn helpfulness or kindness by teaching these things to younger children, too. The role of "tutor" seems to be beneficial both for the learner and the tutor. So if you ask an older child to show a younger one "how to share," *both* children may show more sharing later (Staub, 1975).
4. Obviously, it's also important for the parents, teacher, or other adults to demonstrate in their own day-to-day actions the type of sharing, caring behavior they want their children to show.

Not all of these tactics are as easy as they may sound. The task isn't over when you assign your child a regular chore; you also have to make sure that he does it and that you explain often the reason for needing his help. But if all these different procedures are combined, it is possible to increase the amount of helpful and compassionate behavior children show toward one another and toward adults.

periments that punishment, applied consistently and at the appropriate moment, results in greater resistance to temptation. But in studies of real-life family settings, such as those discussed by Hoffman, parents who use a lot of punishment have children who are *less* able to resist.

I think the key to the discrepancy lies in the phrase "applied consistently and at the appropriate moment." Most parents are *not* very consistent, and most apply punishment only after the child has already completed some forbidden behavior. Inhibition is thus not built up, and the child is positively reinforced at least part of the time. Thus, while Mowrer's theory about the effect of punishment on inhibition seems to be generally correct, in real life the conditions required for the creation of a generalized inhibitory response are rarely met.

The Development of Moral Judgment

The third aspect of the child's developing sense of morality is the judgment of moral actions. How does a child—or an adult, for that matter—decide whether something is right or wrong? Partly, of course, it depends on what set of rules about good and bad behavior a child has learned or internalized from her parents and from the society around her. But there are other elements in the child's judgment, too, such as the overall type of reasoning she brings to the process.

Piaget's Stages of Moral Development

In some of his earliest work, Piaget was the first to suggest that there might be stages in the child's moral reasoning (Piaget, 1932). Specifically, he proposed two stages, with age 7 being the approximate dividing line between the two.

Figure 13.5 One way for children to learn such "prosocial" behaviors as helping and nurturance is to practice them, as this youngster is doing.

Stage 1: Heteronomous Morality The stage of **heteronomous morality,** also sometimes called **moral realism,** has several important features. First, there is **moral absolutism.** The young child of 5 or 6 thinks that rules are laid down in absolute, unchangeable form by higher authority. Rules of games, for example, are seen as completely fixed. A second feature of the first stage is a belief in **immanent justice.** The preschool child believes that if you break a rule, punishment will inevitably be meted out—by parents, by teachers, perhaps by God. Finally, the stage-1 child judges the goodness or badness of other people's actions largely on the basis of the consequences rather than the person's intent. By this reasoning, a child who breaks five glasses accidentally is seen as worse than a child who intentionally throws one down and breaks it.

Stage 2: Autonomous Morality Somewhere around age 7, a shift takes place, and the child develops **autonomous morality,** also called the **morality of reciprocity.** Social rules are accepted but seen as more arbitrary, more changeable. Rules of a game, for example, can be changed if the children playing the game agree on the change. The belief in immanent justice fades, too; rule violations are no longer thought to result in inevitable punishment. And the intent of the person performing some action is taken into account in judging the morality of the action. Overall, the child in this second stage sees fairness and reciprocity as the proper basis for relationships with others.

Piaget's Moral Stages and Cognitive Development Obviously, this shift at age 7 is intimately connected to the basic cognitive changes Piaget sees at the same ages. In particular, think back to what I said about the egocentrism of the preoperational child in Chapter 8. In order to be able to judge someone else's action on the basis of intentions, the child has to be able to put herself in the other person's place to at least some extent. And while preschoolers can do this in a limited way, they aren't very good at it yet. By age 6 or 7, though, they are much more skillful at taking another person's perspective; so it is quite reasonable to assume that they would also take intent into account in making moral judgments.

Recent studies of this aspect of young children's moral judgments provide some support for Piaget's proposals. As was true of studies of egocentrism, the newer studies show that preschoolers are more aware of others' intent than Piaget had believed; but there is also a steady increase with age in the use of intent as a basis for judgment. So while 4- and 5-year-olds pay some attention to intent, 7- and 8-year-olds do so much more fully (Bearison & Isaacs, 1975; Suls, Gutkin & Kalle, 1979).

Kohlberg's Stages of Moral Development

Lawrence Kohlberg has gone several steps further (Kohlberg, 1964, 1969, 1971, 1976, 1978). He thought that Piaget was quite right in seeing a link between cognitive development and type of moral reasoning. But he thought the process was much lengthier than Piaget proposed. Instead of a single early step from heteronomous to autonomous morality. Kohlberg thought there were many steps, beginning at about age 6 or 7 and extending into young adulthood. Specifically, he has proposed six steps, divided into three basic levels. Since virtually all the recent research on moral judgment has been based on Kohlberg's stages, I need to describe them, and the procedure he uses to measure them, in some detail.

In order to explore a child or young person's reasoning about difficult moral issues, such as the value of human life or the reasons for doing "right" things, Kohlberg devised a series of dilemmas. One of the most famous ones is the dilemma of Heinz:

In Europe, a woman was near death from a special kind of cancer. There was one drug that the doctors thought might save her. It was a form of radium that a druggist in the same town had recently discovered. The drug was expensive to make, but the druggist was charging ten times what the drug cost him to make. He paid $200 for the radium and charged $2000 for a small dose of the drug. The sick woman's husband, Heinz, went to everyone he knew to borrow the money, but he could only get together about $1000 which is half of what it cost. He told the druggist that his wife was dying, and asked him to sell it cheaper or let him pay later. But the druggist said, "No, I discovered the drug and I'm going to make money from it." So Heinz got desperate and broke into the man's store to steal the drug for his wife.

(Kohlberg & Elfenbein, 1975, p. 621)

After hearing this story, the child is asked a series of questions, such as whether Heinz should have stolen the drug. What if Heinz didn't love his wife? Would that change anything? What if the person dying was a stranger? Should Heinz steal the drug anyway?

Obviously, dilemmas like this are artificial, as a number of critics have pointed out (Baumrind, 1978). But in my opinion, the issues they raise are the same ones we all face in our day-to-day moral decisions. How can we weigh the value of laws and society against the rights of individuals? How do we weigh our own desires against the needs or values of the group? What Kohlberg is interested in is not the actual choice the child makes in answering the dilemma, but the kind of reasoning he uses in grappling with the problem.

On the basis of children's answers to dilemmas like this one, Kohlberg concluded that there were three main levels of moral reasoning, with two substages within each level. I've summarized the stages in Table 13.2 on the next page.

The transition from level 1 **(preconventional morality)** to level 2 **(conventional morality)** represents a shift from judgments based on consequences and personal gain to judgments based on the rules and norms of the group the child belongs to. Kohlberg asked one 10-year-old, for example, why someone should be a good son. The boy answered, "Be good to your father and he'll be good to you." This is a stage-2 answer, at the preconventional level. You are "good" because it will bring a reward. But some time in late elementary school, between 10 and 12 or so for most children, there is a shift. Andy, an older boy Kohlberg interviewed, said,

I try to do things for my parents, they've always done things for you. I try to do everything my mother says, I try to please her. Like she wants me to be a doctor and I want to, too, and she's helping me get up there.

(Kohlberg, 1964, p. 401)

Table 13.2 Kohlberg's Stages of Moral Development

	Level 1: Preconventional Morality
Stage 1: Punishment and obedience orientation	The child decides what is wrong on the basis of what is punished. Obedience is valued for its own sake, but she obeys because adults have superior power.
Stage 2: Individualism, instrumental purpose, and exchange	The child follows rules when it is in her immediate interest. What is good is what brings pleasant results. Right is also what is fair, what's an equal exchange, a deal, an agreement.
	Level 2: Conventional Morality
Stage 3: Mutual interpersonal expectations, relationships, and interpersonal conformity	The family or small group to which the child belongs becomes important. Moral actions are those that live up to what is expected of you. "Being good" becomes important for its own sake, and the child generally values trust, loyalty, respect, and gratitude, and keeping mutual relationships.
Stage 4: Social system and conscience, law-and-order orientation	A shift in focus from the young person's family and close groups to the larger society. Good is fulfilling duties you've agreed to. Laws are be upheld in extreme cases. Contributing to society is also seen as good.
	Level 3: Postconventional or Principled Morality
Stage 5: Social contract or utility and individual rights	Acting so as to achieve the "greatest good for the greatest number." Child is aware that there are different views and values, that values are relative. Laws and rules should be upheld in order to preserve the social order, but they can be changed. Still, there are some basic nonrelative values, such as the right to life and liberty, that should be upheld no matter what.
Stage 6: Universal ethical principles	The young person develops and follows self-chosen ethical principles in determining what is right. Since laws are usually in conformity to those principles, laws should be obeyed; but when there is a difference between law and conscience, conscience dominates.

Source: Adapted from Kohlberg, 1976 and Lickona, 1978.

Andy is in stage 3 at the conventional level. He is deciding what is good on the basis of the important relationships around him. What his family wants or thinks is right is what he wants and thinks is right.

The transition to level 3 **(postconventional level)** which takes place for some adolescents in the midteens or even later, is a shift to a still larger arena. It comes about, in Kohlberg's view, because the teenager recognizes that there are some issues that just can't be resolved by relying on fixed laws. Hitler, after all, was obeying the laws of Germany when he ordered the confiscation of Jewish property and created the extermination camps. And the laws of many southern states in the

United States in the early 1960s allowed poll taxes or required blacks to ride at the back of the bus. Faced with such a conflict between a law and individual rights and freedom, many teenagers reassess moral issues and come to the conclusion that while we need laws so that there won't be social chaos, the laws are changeable. Individual values are important, and the laws should reflect those values. But if they didn't, then the laws should be changed.

Young people who were active in the civil rights movement in the 1960s were operating with this level of moral reasoning, as were many of the Vietnam War protesters in the late 1960s and early 1970s. In fact, the entire legal system of the United States (as well as most other countries) is based on a level-3 type of moral reasoning. Laws are to be obeyed, but the individual circumstances are taken into account in rendering judgment. Furthermore, there are accepted ways of changing laws so that society can adapt to group and individual needs.

What I've just written about level-3 moral reasoning is really a description of stage 5. Kohlberg originally thought that there was a further, still more advanced stage. But his recent research suggests that very few people really operate at anything resembling stage 6. He says now:

> My sixth stage was mainly a theoretical construction suggested by the writings of "elite" figures like Martin Luther King, and not an empirically confirmed developmental construct.
>
> *(Kohlberg, 1978, p. 86)*

For most of us, then, stage 5 is the "final" stage of our moral reasoning, and many teenagers and young adults do not move fully into stage 5. Stage-4 reasoning is still a very common basis for moral judgments among adults.

Despite the examples I've given as I've gone along, I suspect that much of what I've said about these levels of moral reasoning is still pretty abstract. In order to make it more concrete for you, I've put together some sample answers given by young people to some of Kohlberg's dilemmas in Table 13.3. Several of these answers were to the "Heinz dilemma"; others were to a dilemma in which a fatally ill woman begged to be put out of her misery and the doctor had to decide whether to accede to her request. See if you can see why each of these answers is assigned to its particular stage.

Some Issues About the Stages of Moral Development

Kohlberg has made a number of claims about the stages of moral development. First and foremost, he argues that they are true stages, following one another in invariant order, with each stage built upon the one that preceded it. Erikson's psychosocial stages, in contrast, come in the same order, but you go on to

Table 13.3 Examples of Moral Judgments Relating to the Issue of the Value of Human Life

Stage	Age of Child	Judgment made by child
1	10	(Should the druggist give the drug to the dying woman?) "If someone important is in a plane and is allergic to heights and the stewardess won't give him medicine because she's only got enough for one and she's got a sick one, a friend, in back, they'd probably put the stewardess in a lady's jail because she didn't help the important one."
2	13	(Should the doctor "mercy-kill" the sick woman?) "Maybe it would be good to put her out of her pain, she'd be better off that way. But the husband wouldn't want it. It's not like an animal. If a pet dies you can get along without it—it isn't something you really need. Well, you can get a new wife, but it's not really the same thing."
3	16	(Should the doctor "mercy-kill" the sick woman?) "It might be best for her, but her husband—it's a human life—not like an animal, it doesn't have the same relationship that a human being does to a family. You can become attached to a dog, but nothing like a human you know."
4	16	(Should the doctor "mercy-kill" the sick woman?) "I don't know. In one way, it's murder, it's not a right or privilege of man to decide who shall live and who should die. God put life into everybody on earth, and you're taking away something from that person that came directly from God, and you're destroying something that is very sacred, it's in a way part of God, and it's almost destroying a part of God when you kill a person. There's something of God in everyone."
5	20	(Should the doctor "mercy-kill" the sick woman?) "Given the ethics of the doctor who has taken on the responsibility to save human life—from that point of view he probably shouldn't, but there is another side, there are more and more people in the medical profession who are thinking it is a hardship on everyone, the person, the family, when you know they are going to die. When the person is kept alive by an artificial lung or kidney it's more like being a vegetable than being a human who is alive. If it's her own choice, I think there are certain rights and privileges that go along with being a human being. I am a human being and have certain desires for life and I think everybody else does too. You have a world of which you are the center, and everybody else does, too, and in that sense we're all equal."
6	16	(Should Heinz steal the drug?) "Yes. A human life takes precedence over any other moral or legal value, whoever it is. A human life has inherent value whether or not it is valued by a particular individual." (Why is that?) "The inherent worth of the individual human being is the central value in a set of values where the principles of justice and love are normative for all human relationships."

Source: Kohlberg & Elfenbein, 1975, pp. 624–625.

the next one even if you haven't finished the current one. Kohlberg thinks that each new moral reasoning stage emerges only when the child has completely mastered the one before.

Kohlberg also argues that the moral reasoning stages are linked in important ways to cognitive development. His basic position is that new levels of cognitive functioning are necessary but not sufficient conditions for new levels of moral reasoning. What is needed, in addition, is for the child or young person to be able to take other people's perspectives in more and more sophisticated ways.

A third claim Kohlberg makes is that the stages of moral judgment are universal—that the same sequence will be found in all different cultures and not just in Western societies.

Finally—and most interesting perhaps to those of you who are educators—Kohlberg claims that it is possible to introduce concepts of moral reasoning into the schools and to raise the level of children's moral understanding through specific training.

Let me take a brief look at the evidence for each of these claims.

Are the Stages a Fixed Sequence? The answer seems to be a qualified "yes." In Kohlberg's own longitudinal study of 30 men who were interviewed every three years from their teens till about age 30 (Kohlberg & Elfenbein, 1975), the men either stayed at the same stage or moved up one stage at each interview. No one went backwards. And in many studies in which children have been exposed to moral arguments both one stage above their own and one stage below their own, the strong tendency is for the children to move upward in their own reasoning and not to go "downward" (Turiel, 1966; Rest, Turiel & Kohlberg, 1969; Rest, 1973).

There are occasional exceptions, but on the whole, Kohlberg does seem to have identified an invariant sequence.

Are the Stages Universal? Again the answer is a qualified "yes." Obviously, psychologists have not given Kohlberg's moral dilemmas to children in every culture. But there have been studies in Taiwan, Turkey, and Mexico by Kohlberg (1969), and in Kenya (Edwards, 1975), India (Parikh, 1975), and the Bahamas (White, 1975) by other investigators. In every case, the older children studied had higher levels of moral judgment than the younger children and used forms of judgment that were parallel to those found in United States children.

There are differences, though, in the *level* of moral reasoning found in children in different cultures. In the rural villages of Turkey and Mexico that Kohlberg has studied, stage 4 was the highest level reached by any of the 16-year-olds questioned. In contrast, in Kohlberg's United States sample, about 10 percent of the 16-year-olds were using stage-5 reasoning. Similarly, Charles White (1975) found that in his study of Bahamian children, the highest stage reached by any of the 13- and 14-year-olds was stage 3.

What these studies seem to show, then, is that while the sequence remains the same, both the rate at which a child moves through this sequence and the level or stage at which he finally stops are affected by the specific cultural experiences and values to which he is exposed.

Are the Stages Linked to Cognitive Development? Again, generally yes. Cognitive development appears to be a necessary precursor to change in moral reasoning. But there is *not* a one-to-one correspondence between the two.

If you think about Piaget's description of the stages of cognitive development and then look again at the stages of moral reasoning proposed by Kohlberg, there are some obvious parallels. In particular, the shift from level-1 to level-2 reasoning looks like it ought to come about some time during concrete operations; and the shift to level 3 looks like it ought to happen some time at adolescence, when the child is moving into formal operations. Stages 5 and 6 in Kohlberg's system require the ability to analyze a problem into its separate issues rather than just on the basis of past experience. And that sounds a lot like a formal operations reasoning.

Most of the research on the relationship between moral reasoning and cognition has focused on the period of formal operations, and once again Kohlberg's position has been supported. Carol Tomlinson-Keasy and Charles Keasy (1974), in one of the best studies, gave both moral dilemmas and tests of formal operations to a group of 12-year-old girls and to a group of college women. None of the 12-year-olds was using level-3 morality, but all those who used level-2 morality (stages 3 and 4) were *also* using some types of formal operations reasoning. Among the college students, those who were using level-3 morality (stages 5 and 6) were also using formal operations. So in both cases, the subjects with the higher levels of moral judgment also showed advanced cognitive reasoning.

In another study on the same question, Lawrence Walker and Boyd Richards (1979) have found that it is easier to train adolescents in the use of stage-4 reasoning if they are already reasoning at formal operations levels than if they still use concrete operations reasoning.

Both of these studies suggest that formal operations reasoning may be a prerequisite for the development of higher stages of moral judgment. But while formal operations may be *necessary*, it is *not sufficient*. In the Tomlinson-Keasey and Keasey

Figure 13.6 Moral education programs often involve having high school students discuss either hypothetical or real-life moral dilemmas, as this class is doing. The effect of this type of instruction is to raise most students' level of moral reasoning slightly.

study, for example, there were many adult women who used formal operations reasoning but who were still using conventional moral judgments. In other words, the ability to use complex forms of logic doesn't automatically lead to the sort of moral reexamination that seems to be part of the shift from stage 4 to stage 5.

Can Moral Reasoning be Taught? I suppose the more basic question, really, is whether one ought to try to teach moral reasoning. Kohlberg obviously thinks that we should: "Mature moral judgment is a necessary but not sufficient condition for mature moral action" (Kohlberg, 1975, p. 672). By this argument, raising children's level of logic about moral decisions is worthwhile because it lays the foundation for more just and moral behavior. I'll be coming back to the link between moral judgment and moral behavior in a moment, but for now let's take Kohlberg's argument as valid and see whether it is in fact possible to "teach" moral reasoning.

First of all, in experimental studies, it has proved possible (although difficult) to move a child from one stage of moral reasoning to the next highest level by exposing him to arguments at that next highest level (Turiel, 1974). So far so good. But can this be done in real-life situations, such as schools?

A lot of people have tried. The earliest efforts (Blatt & Kohlberg, 1975) were mostly just a direct translation of the dilemma procedure. Students in high school classes were given specific dilemmas and urged to discuss them fully. The teacher tried to lead the discussion in such a way that more advanced types of reasoning came out. For example, students might argue about whether a boy should give up a college scholarship in order to go to work to provide support for his family or whether a student should tell a teacher about cheating on a recent test. This type of discussion did seem to lead to slightly higher levels of reasoning on Kohlberg's dilemmas, but it didn't seem to change the students' behavior much.

More recent efforts have focused on changing action as well as talk. For example, Susan Crockenberg and Jennie Nicolayev (1979) studied a school system in which there were two junior high school programs. The "Traditional program" emphasized academic subject matter and was organized in the usual manner. The "Alternative program," in contrast, was organized so as to encourage student participation in decision making and to stimulate teacher-student discussion of relevant moral issues. Students were involved in discipline decisions and in creating school rules. After one year, Crockenberg and Nicolayev found that the students in the Alternative program showed slightly greater increases in stage of moral reasoning on Kohlberg's dilemmas than did students in the Traditional program. (An even broader effort to create a "moral atmosphere" in a school is described in Box 13.2.)

This study and other experiments with moral education point to the importance of applying the abstract discussion of moral dilemmas to real, everyday problems. When this is done, the change in moral reasoning seems to "stick" better.

Many of these techniques can be added to existing school courses without major changes in curriculum. For example, courses in "family living" or equivalent are already taught in many high schools and could be modified to use a moral education approach effectively. Whether an individual teacher or a school district thinks that is worthwhile depends very much on whether they agree with Kohlberg's basic point about the link between moral reasoning and moral action.

Moral Judgment and Moral Behavior

It seems to me that the point at which the several traditions of study of moral development come together is on the question of the link between moral judgment and moral behavior. For Freud, the question is stated in terms of the relationship between the internalized rules and the child's ability to follow those rules. For Kohlberg, the link is between the *level* of moral reasoning and moral behavior. Since Freud thought that the whole process of logic was part of the ego, the two positions are really not unconnected. As the child's logic gets more sophis-

Box 13.2 Creating a Moral Atmosphere: The Cluster School

In the early years of Kohlberg's writings about moral education, he argued that the crucial thing was to change each individual's level of moral reasoning and that that would lead to more mature moral behavior. But recently, he has begun to argue that the whole social group has such a powerful effect that it can override the individual's judgments. So if you really want to change moral behavior, you have to raise the level of moral reasoning of the entire group (Lickona, 1978). The Cluster school program has been an effort to do just that—to create a moral "atmosphere" in which steadily increasing levels of moral judgment are applied to real problems.

The Cluster School is a school within a school—an experimental high school contained within a larger public high school. It has about 70 students and six staff members (Power & Reimer, 1978). The school is governed largely through a weekly group meeting, including all students and staff. The staff tries to focus the students on the moral issues—such as what to do about stealing in the school—but the group decisions determine the rules of the school to a large extent.

In the first year of the school, the issue of stealing took up a lot of time at the weekly meetings. Staff members tried to state the issue in terms of the trust of community members in one another. But the students didn't buy the argument. They passed a rule against stealing and left it at that. But a year later, when the question of stealing came up again, it was the *students* who raised the issue of trust and community spirit. One girl said, "It's everyone's fault that she don't have no money. It was stolen because people just don't care about the community" (Power & Reimer, 1978, p. 108). The group decided this time that the just solution was for the group to collect the money and pay it to the student who had been ripped off. That was two years ago, and there have been no thefts in the school since that time.

What has happened here is not only that some of the students have switched from stage-2 to stage-3 reasoning, but that the entire *community* has begun to operate at a higher level. This supports and extends the change in the individual students.

Power and Reimer (1978, p. 115) conclude that if moral education is to be successful,

> *Attention must be given to the "hidden curriculum" of the school, composed of those values underlying school discipline and teacher/student relationships. It is only by becoming conscious of the moral atmosphere of the school that educators can begin to change it so that it is more just and more effective in harnessing the energies of the peer group for constructive action.*

ticated, he will be better and better able to resist temptation, better and better able to maintain "good" behavior.

Bandura, in contrast, thinks that "good behavior" is governed by a whole host of situational variables. A child can learn to be "good" in some circumstances and learn that it is okay to be "bad" in other settings. So he expects less consistency and has little to say about the child's level of judgment as it might affect his behavior.

What we know about the link between moral judgment and moral behavior provides some support for all these views. First of all, Kohlberg does seem to be at least partially right. Young people reasoning at higher levels do behave differently in real-

Figure 13.7 Research by Keniston and others suggests that these 1970s student war protesters are likely to be reasoning at the principled level.

life moral situations. For example, Kenneth Keniston (1970) found that nonviolent Vietnam War protesters in the late 1960s were more likely to be using stage-5 or stage-6 moral reasoning than were nonprotesting college students. On the whole, these students worked within the law, which is characteristic of stage-5 reasoning. They protested and marched, but they were prepared to go to jail for breaking the law in order to make their point.

As another example, Kohlberg (1975) found that only 15 percent of students reasoning at the principled level (stages 5 or 6) cheated when they were given an opportunity, while 55 percent of conventional level and 70 percent of preconventional students cheated.

A study of much younger children by Nancy Eisenberg-Berg and Michael Hand (1979) shows a similar link. The preschool children in this study who answered simple moral dilemmas with hedonistic reasoning (what feels good is right; what feels bad is wrong) were much less likely to share toys with other children in their nursery school than were youngsters who considered the needs of others in their moral reasoning.

But there is clearly no direct and automatic relationship between moral reasoning and moral behavior. As Kohlberg points out about his own study, 15 percent of the stage-5 and stage-6 students *did* cheat. As he says, "One can reason in terms of principles and not live up to these principles" (Kohlberg, 1975, p. 672).

What are the other things that matter? We don't have all the answers to this question yet, but some influences are clear. First, simple habits are involved—what Randy Gerson and

Figure 13.8 Teenage delinquents, many of whom belong to gangs like this, are likely to be reasoning at stage 1 or 2, while adolescents from the same kind of backgrounds who do not become delinquent reason at much higher levels.

William Damon (1978) call *habitual* moral reactions. Each of us faces every day small moral situations that we have learned to handle in a completely automatic way. Sometimes these automatic choices may be at a lower level of reasoning than we would use if we sat down and thought about it. These habitual moral actions are exactly what Bandura would emphasize: We have learned a particular response from watching other people or from direct instruction. And these habits go right on, despite changes in our level of moral reasoning.

Second, and perhaps more important, the group we are in makes a huge difference. This is what Power and Reimer are describing in the Cluster School (Box 13.2). The level of moral behavior changed when the *group* values changed. Gerson and Damon found the same thing in their studies. One of the tasks they used was to have a group of four children divide up ten candy bars. The candy was a reward for work the children had done on a project, and some of the group members had worked harder than others. Many children who would otherwise argue that the hardest-working child should have the greatest reward nonetheless agreed to divide the candy into four equal shares. As Gerson and Damon (1978, p. 51) put it, "A primary objective for most children, after some exposure to the group, was to get along with their peers." And when the peer group is collectively operating at a lower level of moral judgment than the individual child, most children go along with the group anyway. Again, this is what Bandura would expect. The child is getting important reinforcements from the group.

But every child does not seem to be equally vulnerable to this type of group pressure. There is some evidence, for example, that young people who are at stage 5 or 6 are less likely to be swayed by group pressure or pressure from authority than are youngsters reasoning at less-mature levels (Kohlberg, 1969).

I don't think we know nearly enough yet about a child's ability to resist group pressure. But at the very least, we know that the effect of the group is not automatic or uniform. The child's level of logic does seem to make a difference, and the type of discipline and explanations of moral behavior the child has been exposed to seem to make a difference, too. Perhaps the link between the two sets of research is that "inductive" discipline, which Hoffman and others find to be associated with greater resistance to temptation, is precisely the sort of discipline that is likely to further the development of the child's moral reasoning, which in turn helps to create greater resistance to temptation and to group pressure.

Where Do We Go from Here?

All of the questions I've been discussing in the last few pages demonstrate the range and richness of questions raised by Kohlberg's analysis of moral development. But there are important unanswered questions. We need to know more about how some children are able to resist group pressure. Most of the work on this problem has been done with quite young children, but it is during adolescence that the peer group seems particularly powerful. We need to know what helps one teenager maintain his own moral judgment in the face of group pressure while another does not.

We also need to know more about the long-term consequences of efforts at moral education. What will happen to the students from the Cluster School when they leave high school? Will they take their sense of community with them and apply it to other situations? Or is their new moral reasoning specific to the school setting?

Both of these questions have important practical ramifications. Perhaps over the next decade or so we will be able to come up with some answers.

Summary

1. The study of moral development can be divided into three issues: the development of moral behavior, moral feelings, and moral judgment.

2. The study of moral behavior is dominated by social learning approaches. Both direct reinforcement and modeling are thought to play a role.

3. Experimental studies of resistance to temptation show that the timing and intensity of punishment, the relationship of the child to the punisher, the amount of explanation given, and the consequences to the model all affect the child's "moral behavior." Situational factors, such as the level of desire for the forbidden object or action and the risk of detection, also make a difference.

4. Studies of moral feelings (such as guilt) have been based primarily on psychoanalytic theory, which emphasizes the process of identification as the basis for internalized rules and self-punishment for transgression.

5. Studies of child-rearing practices provide little support for psychoanalytic expectations; neither withdrawal of love nor "power" control techniques have a marked effect on the child's moral behavior or guilt. The use of reasoning ("induction"), however, is effective.

6. Studies of moral judgment have been dominated by cognitive-developmental theory. Piaget proposed two basic stages, heteronomous and autonomous, with the shift at about age 7. Heteronomous reasoning includes the concepts of moral absolutism and immanent justice. Autonomous morality is based on principles of reciprocity and fairness.

7. Kohlberg proposed six stages, divided into three levels. The child moves from preconventional morality, dominated by punishment and "what feels good," to conventional morality, which is dominated by group norms or laws, to postconventional (principled) morality, dominated by social contracts and basic ethical principles.

8. The six stages appear to occur in a fixed sequence, although not everyone moves all the way through the sequence. Stage-4 reasoning is still very common among adults.

9. The same sequence has been found in studies of children and young people in many countries.

10. The underlying progression of cognitive development, described by Piaget, seems to be a necessary but not sufficient condition for the transition from one stage of moral reasoning to another.

11. Levels of moral reasoning can be increased through exposure to someone else reasoning at a higher level. But some actual involvement in real-life moral choices and decisions seems to be important, too.

12. Application of these principles to "moral education" in the school system has been fairly widespread and moderately successful.

13. The link between moral reasoning and moral behavior is complex. Generally, the higher the level of moral reasoning a child or young person shows, the more likely he is to resist temptation, to follow social rules, and to be "good" or generous. But the effect of group pressure and habit make a difference as well.

14. We know less than we would like about the factors that make it possible for one person to resist group pressure while another person is swayed by it.

Key Terms

Autonomous morality Piaget's second proposed stage of moral reasoning, developing some time after age 7, characterized by judgment of intent and emphasis on reciprocity.

Conscience The term ordinarily used to describe the set of internalized rules Freud thought came about through the process of identification.

Conventional morality The second level of moral judgment proposed by Kohlberg, in which the person's judgments are dominated by considerations of group values and laws.

Heteronomous morality Piaget's first proposed stage of moral reasoning, characterized by moral absolutism and belief in immanent justice. Judgments are based on consequences rather than intent.

Immanent justice Principle that wrongdoers will be automatically and invariably punished for their transgressions.

Induction The form of discipline that includes clear rules, the use of reason, and emphasis on consequences of action.

Internalized rules A set of standards about what is right and wrong that each of us carries about "in our heads."

Learned avoidance reactions The process Mowrer thought accounted for learning what is "wrong" behavior. The child who is punished repeatedly for some action associates the bad feelings of punishment with the action and learns to avoid the prohibited action in the future.

Moral absolutism Belief characteristic of the first stage of moral judgment: Rules are completely fixed and unchangeable.

Moral realism Another description of heteronomous morality.

Morality of reciprocity Another description of autonomous morality.

Preconventional morality The first level of morality proposed by Kohlberg, in which moral judgments are dominated by consideration of what will be punished and what feels good.

Principled morality The third level of morality proposed by Kohlberg, in which considerations of justice, individual rights, and contracts dominate moral judgment.

Suggested Readings

Kohlberg, L., & Elfenbein, D. "The development of moral judgments concerning capital punishment." American Journal of Orthopsychiatry, 1975, 45, 614–640.
If you are interested in reading some of Kohlberg's own writings and seeing how his work can be applied to such practical questions as attitudes about capital punishment, this is a good source.

Lickona, T. "Moral development and moral education. Piaget, Kohlberg, and beyond." In J. M. Gallagher & J. A. Easley, Jr. (Eds.), Knowledge and development, vol. 2: Piaget and education. New York: Plenum Press, 1978.
An excellent review of current attempts to apply Kohlberg's work to moral education in the schools.

Staub, E. Positive social behavior and morality, vol. 2; Socialization and development. New York: Academic Press, 1979.
I think this is a very good book. Staub reviews the several theories I have talked about in this chapter and goes on to focus on the fostering of positive behavior in children.

Project 13.1 Moral Judgments Among Teenagers

Locate at least two teenage subjects, preferably at least three or four years apart in age. If you can manage to test more than two teenagers or young adults, that would be preferable. Try to space your subjects out on the age continuum so that you can maximize your chances of getting differences in level of moral judgment.

Read the Heinz dilemma to each subject, and then ask the following questions (allowing your subject to answer each one before you go on to the next):

1. Should Heinz have stolen the drug? Why?
2. What's to be said for obeying the law in this situation or in general?
3. If the husband doesn't love his wife, is he obligated to steal the drug for her? Why?
4. Why is it so important to save the woman's life? Would it be as right to steal it for a stranger as for his wife? Why?
5. Heinz is arrested for stealing the drug. Should the judge sentence him or let him go free? Why?

Analyze the answer of each of your subjects in terms of Kohlberg's six stages of moral development. I know this will be hard, since you haven't had enough exposure to the several stages to do a perfect classification job. But do the best you can. Do you find elements of several stages in your subjects' answers? Does the older subject appear to give a higher-level answer than your younger subject?

Part Five

The Whole Child

Preview of Chapter 14

Definitions
Frequency of Problems
Mentally Atypical Development
- The Mentally Retarded
- Learning Problems
- The Gifted Child

Box 14.1 Raising a Gifted Child: Pitfalls and Decisions
Emotionally Atypical Development
- Severe Emotional Disturbance
- Less-Severe Emotional Disorders: The Behavior Problems
- Some Causes of Behavior Problems

Physically Atypical Development
- The Deaf and Hearing Impaired

Box 14.2 Vulnerable and Invulnerable Children
- The Blind Child
- Other Physical Problems

Box 14.3 Basic Attachments between Blind Babies and Their Mothers
Sex Differences in Atypical Development
Interventions
- Treatment for the Child, Training for the Parents
- Intervention in the Public Schools: Mainstreaming versus Special Classes
- Residential Treatment

A Final Point
Summary
Key Terms
Suggested Readings

Atypical Development

Danny, who is 4 years old, has trouble in nursery school. His teacher says, "He can't hold on to what I tell him. He echoes what is said to him but he isn't able to act on it. It seems as if I can't teach him by talking." Danny's mother says he seems to "lose his train of thought" while talking (Osman, 1979).

Tommy is also 4 years old, and his nursery school teacher is also worried. He seems to be bright, but is fearful and inhibited. He is both imperious and anxiously complying with the other children (Solnit & Provence, 1979).

Vicki is 11. "She absolutely loves to roller-skate, and like any other 11-year-old, she squeals with delight when she's careening down the sidewalk in front of her house. But Vicki doesn't speak . . . sucks her thumb . . . and has a great deal of trouble making eye contact with others" (*San Francisco Chronicle*, Aug. 21, 1979).

When Jeffrey was 4, he couldn't walk or talk and spent most of his time in a crib. He was fed pureed baby food through a bottle. After six years with a loving foster family, Jeffrey is now in a special class in a regular elementary school and is learning to print and read.

All of these children are "atypical" in some way. In every case, the normal developmental processes I have been describing in the past 13 chapters didn't quite work in the normal way. Danny has some kind of **specific learning disability,** perhaps because of **brain damage.** Tommy has a **behavior problem,** while Vicki has a much more serious type of disorder, usually called **autism.** Jeffrey is a Down's syndrome child and is **mentally retarded.**

I have touched on some of the problems of atypically developing children in earlier chapters—problems in learning to read, problems of deaf children, and treatment of excessive aggressiveness in children. But in this chapter, I want to try to give you some sense of the range of problems that can occur and the sort of treatments that are used. The topic is enormous, so I will of necessity be giving you breadth rather than depth. Still, I can alert you to some of the difficult issues and questions still facing us in understanding the reasons for atypical development and in designing successful treatments.

Definitions

I need to make two important points about the group of children called "atypical" before I go further. First, the definition of atypical is very much a matter of degree. How much visual loss does a child have to have before she is considered "visually impaired"? How long does a period of depression or anxiety have to persist before a child is diagnosed as "emotionally disturbed"? How poorly does a child have to do in school before she is called "learning disabled" or "retarded"? At the extremes, there is little disagreement about diagnosing atypical development, but in every domain there is a fuzzy area in which the distinction between what is "normal" and what is "atypical" is a matter of judgment.

Second, children whose development is atypical in some respect are much more *like* normally developing children than they are unlike them. Blind and deaf and retarded children all form attachments in much the same ways that physically and mentally normal children do; children with behavior problems go through the same sequences of cognitive development that more adjusted children show. So the fact that a child is different in one way should not blind us to the fact that she is probably quite "typical" in many other ways. You should keep that basic point in mind as I talk about the various ways in which development can go off the tracks.

Frequency of Problems

Let me begin by taking a quick look at the frequency of various types of atypical development. Table 14.1 gives some recent guesses on the incidence of the major groups of children with problems. I've taken these estimates from several different sources, and there is considerable overlap in the categories. For example, the children with serious learning disabilities (700,000 of them) are also a part of the group with significant

Table 14.1 Estimated Incidence of Various Types of Atypical Development

Type of problem	Approximate number of children in United States	Approximate percentage of all children 0–18
Problems with language or cognition		
Significant reading problems	8,000,000	14.0
Speech and language problems, including delayed language, articulation problems, or stuttering	2,400,000	3.5
IQs below 70: mentally retarded	1,700,000	2.5
Serious learning disabilities	700,000	1.0
Problems in relating to others or to society		
Short-term behavior problems or relatively mild emotional disturbance	5,000,000	7.0
Relatively severe emotional disturbance	1,400,000	2.0
Juvenile delinquency (counting only those arrested)	1,100,000	1.6
Physical problems		
Significant hearing impairment or deafness	350,000	0.5
All other problems, including blindness, cerebral palsy, and epilepsy	120,000	0.2

Sources: Profiles of Children, 1970; Hobbs, 1975; Graham, 1979.

reading problems. Similarly, there is probably some overlap between the group with severe emotional disturbance and those with milder emotional problems, since the two numbers come from two different places and the definition of "mild" and "severe" is bound to vary from one investigator to another.

Still, even if we allow for some overlap, the numbers are astonishing. Something like 15–20 percent of all the children in the United States (and presumably in other countries as well) show at least one form of atypical development. At least one in six, and probably as many as one in five, will require some form of special help in school, in a child guidance clinic, or equivalent. When you think of these figures in terms of the demands this places on the school system and on other social agencies, the prospect is somewhat staggering.

Of course, not all the children listed in the table have long-term or terribly serious problems. Many children experience brief periods of emotional disturbance (just as adults do), which can be treated successfully or which fade without any intervention. Many children with speech problems or language delay can be helped, too, and the problem need not persist, just as many children with reading problems can be assisted with special programs. But many of the children represented in the table have long-term handicaps that require continuous assistance, such as major physical disabilities, serious emotional disorders, or significant mental retardation.

For society as a whole and for the several helping professions in particular, there are at least three tasks involved in coping with these large numbers of children in need. First, we have to understand the nature and origin of the problems we are facing. How do behavior problems, such as excessive shyness or extreme aggressiveness, come about? What are the causes of mental retardation?

A second task is to develop effective intervention programs. How can children with reading problems be helped? What works best with Down's children? How can deaf children be taught language?

A final task is to develop programs of prevention. Many of the disorders represented in the table could be avoided if we knew the right kind of early interventions.

Most of my time in this chapter will be focused on the first of these three tasks, but I'll talk about the significant treatment questions as well.

Mentally Atypical Development

The Mentally Retarded

Of all the atypical children listed in Table 14.1, probably those studied most thoroughly are those labeled retarded. Not too many decades ago, when mental ability was thought of as a fixed trait, mental subnormality was considered a kind of incurable disease. Labels like "idiot" or "feeble-minded" or "moron" were used to describe children or adults with very low IQ scores. But this older view has changed a great deal. Not only have the old negative labels been changed, but the basic assumptions about the nature of retardation have changed, too.

Mental retardation is now (correctly, I think) viewed as a *symptom* rather than as a disease. And like any symptom, it can change. A child's life circumstances or his health may change, and his IQ score may go up or down at the same time. Remember from Chapter 9 that *many* children's IQ test scores vary as much as 30 or 40 points over the childhood years. To be sure, many children with low IQ scores, particularly those with some form of brain damage, will continue to function at a low level throughout life. But it is important for educators and parents to understand that a single low IQ score need not invariably mean that the child will function at that level forever. For many children, improvement is possible.

The Assessment of Retardation Two criteria are usually used in deciding whether a given child is functioning at a mentally

Table 14.2 IQ Scores and Labels for Various Groups of Children Classed as Retarded

Approximate IQ score range	Label used by psychologists	Label used in schools
52–70	Mild retardation	Educable mentally retarded
36–52	Moderate retardation	Trainable mentally retarded
20–35	Severe retardation	--------
19 and below	Profound retardation	--------

retarded level. First and foremost, an individual IQ test score is used. Second, some measure of the child's **adaptive behavior** is often used as well. Can the child dress himself and go to the bathroom alone? Can he get along with other children and adapt to the demands of a regular classroom by being quiet for periods and paying attention to the teacher? Whether or not a child is labeled "retarded" by parents, teachers, or school psychologists will depend not only on his test score but on his success at such adaptive tasks. Still, in most cases, the individual test score is the most critical single element in classifying a child as retarded.

Labels Table 14.2 shows the customary labels attached to test scores of differing ranges. As you can see, there are two category systems, one normally used by school systems and one by psychologists. (There are no school system labels for children with IQs below about 35 since schools very rarely deal with children functioning at this level.)

The farther down the IQ scale you go, the fewer children there are. About three-quarters of all children with IQs below 70 are in the "mild" range; only about 2 percent (perhaps 3500 children in the U.S.) are profoundly retarded.

What are the causes of very low IQ scores like these? As you might imagine—especially in view of the still-continuing arguments about the hereditary versus environmental sources of intelligence—there is still hot debate about the causes of retarded levels of functioning. But conventionally, the causes are divided into two broad categories: *physical causes* and *cultural-familial* (also called *sociocultural*) *causes.*

Physical Causes of Retardation Included in this category are some of the **genetic anomalies,** such as Down's syndrome, I

Figure 14.1 Programs like the Special Olympics, in which Mark was participating when these pictures were taken, have helped to enrich the lives of Down's syndrome and other retarded children.

described in Chapter 2. In such children, the combination of chromosomes in either the ova or the sperm is not normal, and the child develops with this abnormality in every cell. Many, *but not all*, children with chromosomal abnormalities have retarded intellectual development. Among Down's syndrome children specifically, the most typical IQ is in the moderately retarded range (36–52), but intensive efforts by parents and special educators can raise that level somewhat (Robinson & Robinson, 1976).

A second group of physical causes of retardation is inherited diseases—again something I discussed in some detail in Chapter 2. One example is **phenylketonuria** (PKU), which is an inherited metabolic deficiency. If children who have this disorder are not placed on a special diet immediately after birth, the end result is severe retardation. But with the special diet, normal mental functioning can usually be achieved.

Still a third physical cause of retardation is **brain damage,** which can come from a very large number of sources. Diseases in the mother during pregnancy, such as rubella or syphilis, can produce damage in the brain; severe malnutrition in the mother during pregnancy can have a similar effect. Maternal alcoholism also frequently produces brain damage. As I pointed out in Chapter 2, children with fetal alcohol syndrome are usually mentally retarded to at least some degree. Finally, there can be damage to the child during birth or after birth through some accident.

Nearly all severely and profoundly retarded children have some type of brain injury or genetic anomaly. Most such children also have physical defects along with their mental retardation, such as deafness, cerebral palsy, or heart defects.

Before you get discouraged at this long list of rather awful things that can cause mental retardation, you should remember that a great many of the things I've mentioned here are preventable in one form or another. Some genetic disorders can be diagnosed in utero using amniocentesis (see Box 2.1); other disorders, like PKU, can be treated effectively if diagnosed early; diseases of the mother can be treated or prospective mothers can be immunized. Good *preventive* health care, then, should help us to reduce the number of children with physically caused mental retardation.

Cultural-Familial Causes of Retardation Included in the cultural-familial group are all those children whose IQ scores are below 70 but for whom no physical cause is obvious. That is, there seems to be nothing obviously wrong with the child except that he tests and functions at a fairly low level. Frequently, such children come from families in which the parents have low IQs, where there is serious family disorganization, mental illness in the parents, or emotional or cognitive deprivation in the home. Often several of these factors operate simultaneously. Most psychologists assume that the retarded level of functioning in such children is the result of a combination of two things: a very poor environment and a nonoptimal genetic inheritance.

As I pointed out in Chapter 9, psychologists are still arguing about the role of heredity in a child's measured IQ. But most agree that there is at least *some* effect. So it is reasonable to assume that many children who score below 70 on an IQ test start out in life with several strikes against them.

But genetic endowment is clearly not the only ingredient in this soup. When children with IQs below 70, from families like the ones I have just described, are given special enrichment programs, their IQs can be quite startlingly increased. Rick Heber and his colleagues (Heber, Garber, Harrington & Hoffman, 1972) selected a group of children from severely impoverished homes in which the mother had a retarded-level IQ and in which there were older children also functioning at a retarded level. From early infancy, the children spent most of their time in a special, enriched preschool. In Figure 14.2 you can see the comparison of the IQs of these specially educated children with a group of children from equivalent families who did not receive the special training. Obviously, the very high IQs shown by the enriched group in the preschool years (while the program was still in effect) has fallen off somewhat as the children have gotten older, but the contrast between the two groups is still striking.

Studies like this one point to the fact that at least some potential cultural-familial retardation can be prevented or the ef-

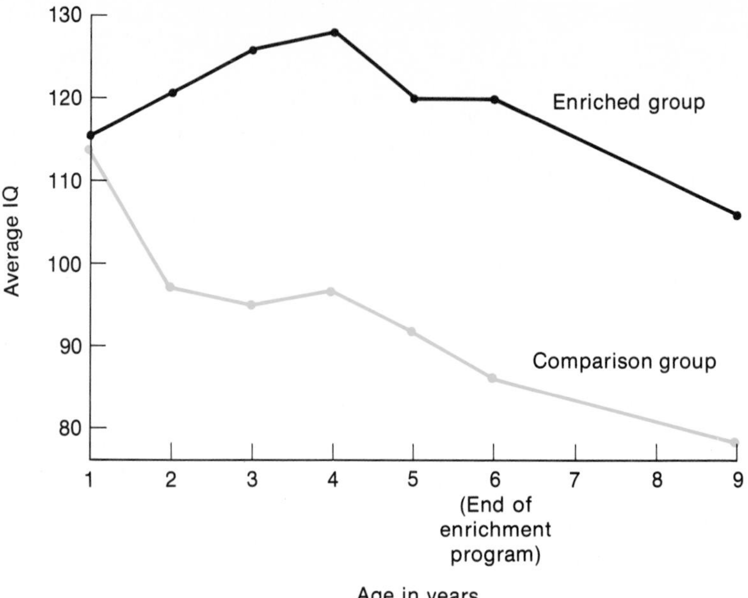

Figure 14.2 The results from Heber's long-range program for potentially retarded children show that large doses of individual attention and enrichment can help such children to develop normal intellectual abilities. Note that although the enriched group did show some decline in IQ after the program ended, they are still functioning above average. (Source: Adapted from data from Heber, Garber, Harrington & Hoffman, 1972; Heber, 1978; Garber, 1977.)

fects softened if the children are given maximum stimulation. But before you leap to the conclusion that we should immediately begin intervention programs like Heber's for all children who are likely to function at a retarded level, I have to caution you.

First, we know amazingly little about the specific kinds of early experiences that a child has to have to develop cognitive skills at the normal rate. I can give you a *general* prescription, including enough toys and materials to stimulate thinking, warm and responsive adults, and (within limits) a nonrestrictive and nonpunitive environment. But it is not always easy to turn this general statement into specific programs for children. Even more, we know next to nothing about the *long-range* effect of special programs.

Second, enrichment programs like Heber's may work well for the child whose retardation is primarily environmental in origin. But it works far less well for children with some physical abnormality. This is not to say that we should ignore environmental enrichment for children with physically caused retardation. Greater breadth of experience would enrich their lives and might well improve their functioning. Certainly, efforts to provide special schooling for Down's syndrome children have done both (Hayden & Haring, 1976). But even massive early interventions are not likely to make most brain damaged or genetically anomalous children intellectually normal, although they may foster a level of functioning closer to the child's intellectual limits and permit the child to function much more independently.

Third, interventions of the type Heber used are *expensive*. Other programs, like the one Phyllis Levenstein has used with mothers in their homes (described in Chapter 9), are less expensive, but the initial cost per child is still great. Obviously, if we knew more precisely just what kind of experiences a child needs for normal growth, we could "aim" our programs more narrowly, and they would probably cost far less. In the meantime, we use a sort of "shotgun" approach, doing everything we think might help; and that costs money. In the long run, I think that such an investment would pay off handsomely, since the cost to society over the lifetime of an individual child would be far less if he grows up to be a well-functioning, capable adult than if he emerges as a borderline retardate requiring public assistance. But even if we were sure that early interventions could have large and persisting effects, it is not at all clear to me that as a society we are prepared to pay the very high initial cost of intervening. It is even less clear to me that we have agreed that we have some shared responsibility to do so.

Learning Problems

A second group of children with "atypical" mental development are those who have IQ scores in the normal range but who seem to have trouble learning particular things in school. Such children are often described as having a **specific learning disability** (SLD).

Some so-called learning disabled children have difficulty with numbers, but by far the largest group are children who have trouble learning to read. In Table 14.1, I indicated that about 1 percent of children have *serious* learning difficulties. As many as 15 percent have at least some significant reading problem. I have already talked about some of the possible explanations of deficits like this in Chapter 5 (Box 5.2), but let me emphasize a couple of points here.

The most commonly offered explanation of specific learning disability—particularly by educators and parents—is that the child suffers from some kind of minimal brain damage. Such children rarely show any outward signs of major brain damage, but perhaps there is some smaller damage, undetected until the child is faced with a complex task like learning to read.

In fact, this may be a correct explanation, at least in some cases. But you should understand clearly that this is a *hypothesis*. We don't really know why these children have difficulty with learning to read or calculate. In fact, as I pointed out in Box 5.2, the symptoms are actually quite varied. Brain dysfunction is one possible explanation, but not the only one. Regrettably, however, the phrase "learning disabled" has come to be synonymous with "brain damaged" in the minds of many parents and educators. Nicholas Hobbs (1975) has offered a thoughtful comment about this usage of the term:

> The term *learning disability* has appeal because it implies a specific neurological condition for which no one can be held particularly responsible, and yet it escapes the stigma of mental retardation. There is no implication of neglect, emotional disturbance, or improper training or education, nor does it imply a lack of motivation on the part of the child. For these cosmetic reasons, it is a rather nice term to have around. However, no one has ever been able to find evidence of the implied neurological impairment. Furthermore, children with known neurological impairments often do not manifest the kinds of behavior associated with the learning-disability concept. . . . Many critics of the term regard the learning-disability classification as a middle-class nicety. Low socioeconomic-level children exhibiting the same behavior are likely to be labeled mentally retarded.
>
> *(Hobbs, 1975, p. 81)*

So where does this leave us? My own feeling is that probably some children who have difficulty with specific learning tasks do have some kind of brain dysfunction. But many do not. So it is premature for educators, parents, and psychologists to lock themselves into the assumption of minimal brain damage as the sole explanation. What about the role of language, as Vellutino's research (see Box 5.2) emphasizes? And what role does the child's family environment play? Do these children read less at home? Are they read to less? Is there less encouragement of reading, of speaking, or of writing at home? And what about the child's emotional state? Is the child inattentive in class because of depression or other emotional disturbance? Has there been some recent family upheaval, such as a divorce? Any or all of these factors may enter into a specific learning problem.

For the teacher or the school psychologist, who must first recognize and then try to deal with such a learning problem, all of these elements need to be explored. Exactly what does the child have trouble doing in school? Is it recognizing letters? Is it saying words? Is it paying attention? And is there a family situation that may be contributing to the child's problem? When all this detective work is done—and it is time-consuming and very difficult work—it *may* be possible to design a special type of training program that will help the child work around (or through) his difficulty. At the moment, I think it is fair to say that we know more about the diagnosis part of the task than we do about the "cure" part. Designing and implementing special training programs is still a very chancy business at best.

The Gifted Child

I can't leave the topic of "mentally atypical development" without saying at least a word or two about the group of children on the other end of the distribution, the **gifted.** Statistically, these children are just as atypical as the mentally retarded. And like the retarded, they place special demands on both parents and school systems.

One representative definition of giftedness was offered in 1972 by a U.S. Senate committee.

> Gifted and talented children are those identified by professionally qualified persons who by virtue of outstanding abilities are capable of high performance.
>
> (*Education of the Gifted and Talented*, 1972, p. 10)

Usually, the "professionally qualified person" uses an IQ test, or occasionally a test of creative ability, to identify children with special talent. Ordinarily, an IQ score of 140–150 or higher is used as a basic cutoff point in a definition of giftedness, although children with outstanding musical or artistic talent but lower IQ scores are now being included in groups of gifted and talented students.

A great deal of what we know about gifted children comes from a remarkable longitudinal study by Lewis Terman, who selected about 1500 children with high IQ from the California school system in the 1920s. These children—now adults of middle age—have been followed regularly throughout their lives (Terman 1925; Terman & Oden, 1947, 1959; Sears & Barbee, 1977; Sears, 1977; Goleman, 1980).

Terman found that the gifted children he studied were also better off in a great many other ways. They were somewhat healthier; they were interested in many things, such as hobbies and games; and they were successful in later life. Both the girls and the boys in this study went on to complete many more years of education than was typical for children of their era.

Most of the girls in this group did not go on to professional careers as adults (remember that these girls grew up in the 1920s and 1930s, before the women's movement), but some of the accomplishments of the 800 boys in the study are worth noting. By the time they were about 40, these men had published 67 books, more than 1400 scientific or technical articles, and over 200 novels or short stories. They had many patents for new inventions.

Later studies have painted a similarly rosy picture for the very bright child. They are friendly and are popular with their peers—although this is less true in high school than in elementary school. They have high self-esteem and are independent (Gallagher, 1975).

Box 14.1 Raising a Gifted Child: Pitfalls and Decisions

Compared to the problems faced by families with physically handicapped or retarded children, those encountered by parents of gifted children may seem minor. But they are very real.

Two problems in particular may be prominent. First, most gifted children are quite normal in their rate of development of social skills. As they get older, this means that there is an increasingly large gap between their mental level and their emotional level. As one example, Leah Levinger (1979) describes 3-year-old Debbie, who had already learned to read. On the playground at her nursery school one day, she had printed a sign saying GO on one side and STOP on the other side. She was trying to be the traffic cop for a group of trike riders but ended up weeping with frustration because the other children (who could not read) ignored her sign. In this case, Debbie's ability to read did not mean that she had eliminated her egocentrism or that she was able to handle her frustration any better than other 3-year-olds can. If this discrepancy between emotional and intellectual levels is not kept clearly in mind, parents and teachers can easily expect too much of the child.

A second problem for which parents and teachers must be alert is the gifted child who becomes so bored with school that he simply "turns off" and quits trying. He may show aggressive or other class disruptive behavior, become withdrawn, or simply do worse and worse on school tasks. Such children need more stimulation, more challenges. Helping classmates is one useful strategy, but tutoring others is not enough. The gifted child also needs an opportunity either to explore subjects in greater depth or to move more rapidly through a sequence of intellectual tasks.

For the parent, one of the most difficult decisions concerns the choice of school or school program. Should your child be "double promoted" (skip a grade)? This used to be quite a common practice but then virtually disappeared as educators began to worry about the potential emotional problems of children in classes with others much older than themselves. Recently, the practice has reappeared in the form of special programs for highly talented children, some of whom enter college in their early or mid-teens (Stanley, George & Solano, 1977). An alternative, if you are fortunate enough to live in a school district that has one, is to place your child in a special "enrichment" program for gifted children like the one in Figure 14.3. These, too, are becoming more common as districts realize the potential handicap for the understimulated gifted child.

Despite changes in the past decade, however, I think it is fair to say that programs for the gifted in public schools are both scarce and underfunded. Like all parents of "atypical children," the parents of gifted children find that they must play the role of advocate for their child within the school system, talking to teachers, visiting classrooms, and lobbying for change with school boards. In the case of physically handicapped and mentally retarded children, such parental lobbying has led to important new legislation and new school programs. I suspect that the same will be true for programs for gifted students.

Still, there are some thorns. Not every gifted or talented child is a paragon of self-confidence, independence, and popularity. Although they are less likely to show behavior problems, some nonetheless do have difficulties. Gifted girls, in particular, seem to be less likely to fulfill their early promise with significant accomplishment as adults, no doubt because of cultural pressures against achievement for girls. Those pressures

Figure 14.3 These girls are both in a special class for gifted children. They are working on a special science project that is typical of the programs now being developed for gifted children in schools. These new programs emphasize teaching problem-solving skills rather than just facts.

are changing, and we may well find that in the next decades, the sex differences in outcomes for gifted children will disappear.

Emotionally Atypical Development

In the last section, I talked about children who had difficulties in the whole area of cognitive development and language—topics I discussed originally in Chapters 6 to 9. Here I will be describing children who have problems in their relationships with others and in their self-concepts—topics I originally discussed in Chapters 10 to 12.

Problems in relating to others and in the child's emotional state can range from relatively minor (and basically normal) brief depressions or fears, to broader or more lasting patterns of behavior, such as extreme shyness or excessive aggressiveness, to still more severe problems, usually called **psychoses,** that affect all the child's encounters and make normal relationships virtually impossible. In the most extreme cases, the child requires continuous help just to get through the daily tasks of dressing, eating, and eliminating. In less-extreme cases, often called **behavior problems,** the child may need help in dealing with her fear, her depression, or her aggressiveness; but she does manage to deal reasonably well with the everyday tasks of living.

Figure 14.4 This autistic child, who makes little eye contact and shows few signs of friendliness or involvement with others, is being treated in an operant conditioning program. Every time he shows one of the desired behaviors, he is quickly reinforced with some food he likes.

Let me approach the description of emotional disorders in children by talking first, and rather briefly, about the extreme types of disorders and then moving to the much more frequent, but less-serious, behavior problems.

Severe Emotional Disturbance

The group of children with really severe emotional problems—those who just don't cope with the everyday world at all—is typically further subdivided into two groups, **autistic** children and **schizophrenic** children. One of the major distinctions between these two types is the time at which the disturbance is first shown. Autistic children show abnormal behavior from early infancy; schizophrenic children often are normal, or very nearly so, during early childhood and develop serious symptoms only at school age or during adolescence.

Autism Michael Rutter (1975a) describes three symptoms that are consistently found among autistic children:

> A profound and general failure to develop social relationships; language retardation with impaired comprehension . . . ; and ritualistic or compulsive phenomena.
>
> *(Rutter, 1975, p. 329)*

These children talk little, if at all, and are not affectionate or apparently even very interested in relating to adults or other children. As infants, they don't make regular eye contact with their caregivers.

Because of their very striking lack of attachment or affectionate relationships with other people, autistic children have traditionally been classed with the group of "emotionally disturbed." But recent work by Rutter, as well as others, points to the possibility that it may be the *language* problem that is really central. In fact, Rutter argues that there is some basic brain damage that makes it difficult for the child to make sense out of strings of sounds. Try to imagine what that would be like. So much of what happens around you, so much of what you understand about the world you live in, depends on sounds. What if the sounds just didn't make sense? If that were true, you might withdraw from people (who make confusing sounds), and you might find yourself arranging your time in very rigid ways so that you could create order out of chaos.

That's essentially what Rutter thinks happens with autistic children. But I should emphasize that not everyone agrees with the "language deficit" theory of autism. Researchers who argue from a social learning perspective, for example, see the reliance on physiological explanations as a kind of cop-out. It is too easy to say that such problems are the result of "the brain," just as explaining learning problems as "minimal brain damage" is a kind of empty reliance on a physiological explanation.

Researchers and therapists who adopt a psychoanalytic perspective are also unhappy with physiological explanations of autism, since the important child-environment, child–parent interactions are left out of the equation. Whatever the status of the child's neurological system at birth, the child does relate in some fashion to the world around her. If the child doesn't make eye contact early, for whatever reason, this affects the way the parents relate to her. So the child's later problem with relationships may come partly from some initial brain damage, but the problems may get worse because of the particular pattern of parent–child interaction that evolves in the early months.

Nonetheless, while both of these arguments are valid, I still find myself persuaded that the *original* problem for an autistic child is probably neurological.

Childhood Schizophrenia This second severe pattern of emotional disturbance seems to develop later, after a fairly normal early development. But for reasons that are not clear, some children, at about 4 or 5, show a kind of regression to earlier patterns. They may lose speech, become incontinent or overactive, or show bizarre behaviors of one kind or another. The symptoms, in fact, may be very much like what we see in autistic children.

In this case, however, the origin of the problem does seem to lie in the child's earliest relationships. The typical finding is that the families of autistic children seem to be basically normal, nurturing, and stimulating. The families of schizophrenic children, in contrast, are often disturbed, with neurotic patterns of relationships between the parents or with one parent showing serious emotional disorders (Werry, 1979). In the terms I have used in this book, very probably the schizophrenic child does not establish a sufficiently secure initial attachment to the mother or father. In Erikson's terms, it appears that the task of developing basic trust is not successfully accomplished. And when the child is later faced with the demands of the preschool years or of school, the lack of the basic foundation shows in disturbed behavior.

Still, not all children who have difficulty with their first attachments end up with schizophrenic symptoms. As yet we know very little about the special vulnerability of some children or about the particularly difficult family conditions that may increase the likelihood that a child will show severe emotional problems later on.

Less-Severe Emotional Disorders: The Behavior Problems

As far as I know, *all* children show some disturbed behavior at some time in their young lives. They may become briefly incontinent at the time a younger sibling is born or temporarily depressed or withdrawn after a favorite grandparent dies; they may throw occasional tantrums, have nightmares, or bite their fingernails. All of these symptoms *may* indicate lasting problems. More often, they are what clinicians call **transitory situational disturbances** (Quay, 1979a). Parents cope with these disturbances as best they can, with attention and affection, and the behavior fades.

But for some children, the disturbed behavior does not fade quite so quickly. In this case, the child may be accurately described as having a behavior problem or a behavior disorder.

Herbert Quay (1979a) argues that there are three basic groups of behavior disorders, which I've summarized in Table 14.3. Each of the three patterns involves "interpersonal alienation with peers: attack in the case of conduct disorder, withdrawal in the case of anxiety-withdrawal, and lack of engagement in the case of immaturity" (Quay, 1979a, p. 20).

Many other clinicians, including Keith Connors (1969), argue that there is still a fourth group of children, usually called *hyperactive*. These children are restless, distractable, impulsive, and inattentive (sometimes diagnosed as learning disabled, too). But since many also show aggressive or disruptive behavior, Quay has included these hyperactive children in the group of conduct disorders.

Many children who show these disturbed patterns of behavior recover spontaneously or with short-term therapy. In particular, anxiety-withdrawal patterns in preadolescents are nearly

Table 14.3 Three Main Types of Behavior Disorder

Name	Symptoms
Conduct disorder	Aggressiveness, disruptive and disobedient behavior, poor social relationships with both adults and peers. Many adolescents labeled "delinquent" are in this group, as are overly aggressive or disruptive preschool and school-age children. In younger children, temper tantrums are part of the syndrome.
Anxiety-withdrawal	The child withdraws from contact with peers or adults, is fearful, anxious, tense, shy, and often depressed. Frequently, feelings of worthlessness (low self-esteem) are part of the pattern.
Immaturity	The child has trouble dealing with everyday demands. The pattern is often seen in children with learning problems and includes inattentiveness, poor physical coordination, boredom, and lack of interest in events.

Source: Adapted from Quay, 1979a.

always short-term (Robins, 1979). Withdrawal or depression in adolescence tends to last longer, and conduct disorders at every age are less likely to disappear spontaneously than are the anxiety patterns. But as a group, behavior disorders are more temporary and less severe than the psychoses.

Another characteristic of behavior disorders is that they are more likely to develop at certain times in children's lives. In particular, there is an increase during the early years of elementary school, with the peak at about age 9, and then another increase during adolescence, with the peak rate of problems at about age 14 (Anthony, 1970). Suicide rates go up during adolescence as well. This pattern makes sense when you think of the extra demands placed on children at these time points—to adapt to school (Erikson's stage of industry versus inferiority) and to adapt to the demands of puberty and adolescence (Erikson's stage of identity versus role confusion).

Some Causes of Behavior Problems

Most psychologists and psychotherapists assume that the roots of behavior problems lie in the child's relationship with the significant people in his life, particularly his parents.

Figure 14.5 The teenager in the left picture shows signs of depression, which may be a short-term behavior problem of the anxious-withdrawn type. In the right photo, the child doing the hitting—if that is habitual behavior—may be showing a "conduct disorder." Heightened and habitual disruptiveness and aggression are characteristics of that type of behavior problem.

Conduct Disorders Children who show conduct disorders (aggressiveness, delinquency, or the equivalent) are most often from homes in which the parents are themselves maladjusted and arbitrary or inconsistent in their discipline. The parents use a lot of physical punishment with their children, argue more with each other, and lack warmth and affection in dealing with their children (Hetherington & Martin, 1979). In fact, the parents of highly aggressive children are often hostile and rejecting of their children. When you think of this cluster of parental behaviors in terms of what I said in Chapters 10 and 11 about social development, the whole thing makes a great deal of sense. In many instances, these children (like a schizophrenic child) lack a secure basic attachment. But more important, through observation and direct reinforcement, the child has learned a highly aggressive and violent pattern of relating to others. Children who are physically abused by their parents often abuse their own children, so the pattern is passed from one generation to the next.

Withdrawn Children Just as aggressive children usually have aggressive parents, shy, withdrawn, and anxious children tend to have parents who are also withdrawn and anxious. Usually at least one of the parents shows a consistently disturbed pattern, and usually there is conflict in the parents' marriage (Hetherington & Martin, 1979). The parents are not openly hostile and don't use a great deal of physical punishment, but they are restrictive, controlling, and not very loving. Diana Baumrind's study (1967), which I described in Chapter 12, fits here quite nicely. She found that the authoritarian parents—those who were restrictive and unloving—had generally less self-confident and competent children than parents who combined clear rules with affection.

One interesting exception to this pattern, however, comes from studies of children with school phobias—children who are fearful of school or who refuse to go to school. These children would ordinarily be classed with the withdrawn and anxious types, but their family background is likely to include *over*protection rather than restrictiveness (Waldron, Shrier, Stone & Tobin, 1975).

Immature Children Much less research has been done on the immature child, no doubt because this pattern has not been seen as a distinct class of behavior problems until fairly recently. One plausible hypothesis, however, is that these are children whose overall development, for one reason or another, is simply slower. When they are placed in a situation for which they are not ready, they respond simply by being inattentive. The fact that physical clumsiness often goes along with this pattern suggests the possibility of some physical problem as well. But we don't know at this stage whether immaturity is further encouraged by particular kinds of upbringing.

The Role of Short-Term Stress I don't think there's any doubt about the fact that the sort of relationship the child has with her parents makes a difference. The earliest attachments play a role, as do the particular forms of discipline the parents use with the child. But children who don't show serious behavior problems frequently experience nonoptimal family patterns, and some children show symptoms even though their childhood experiences seem to be supportive.

James Anthony (1970) suggests that, in any child, a behavior problem emerges only when there is some accumulation of risks or stresses above the threshold that the child can handle. If the parents divorce and the child starts school at the same time, that may be more than that particular child can handle, and you may see some disturbing symptom in the child. A very good example of the cumulative effects of stress comes from a study by Michael Rutter (Rutter, Yule, Quinton, Rowlands, Yule & Berger, 1975). He found that families who had only *one* stress at a time, such as divorce, marital discord, or the death of a family member, had children who were no more likely to have behavior problems than were children from families with no stresses. But *any two* stresses occurring together enormously increased the possibility that the child would show serious symptoms.

You can see the same thing in the study of school phobia by Waldron, Shrier, Stone & Tobin (1975). Mothers of school phobic children were more protective of their children, but about half of the phobic children had *also* experienced some significant stress in the family in the year just before the school phobia began.

The particular symptom the child shows in the face of too much stress—phobia, aggression, or whatever—may be determined by the pattern of early attachment and later discipline. But the presence of any symptom may reflect simply an excess of stresses, as Anthony suggests. When the level of stress goes down, the child's symptoms often disappear.

I find the concept of stress to be a very helpful way to look at behavior problems in children. It helps to explain why such problems are more common at particular times and also why they often go away without any intervention. The concept of stress also raises the very interesting issue of differences in children's vulnerability. Why do some children show symptoms in the face of only a few stresses, while others can handle a much greater load? I've discussed this issue in Box 14.2.

Physically Atypical Development

If you look back to Table 14.1, you'll see that children with major physical problems, such as blindness, deafness, or significant motor dysfunction, are relatively rare, especially in comparison to the frequency of other types of problems. Although the numbers may be small, the degree of difficulty encountered by the physically atypical child may be very great indeed. Most of the children I'll be talking about here require special schooling or special facilities in school; many require continued assistance throughout life. For the children and for their parents, the emotional (and financial) cost can be very great indeed. Still, with improved instruction, intervention, and mechanical assistance, many children with significant physical handicaps are leading full and satisfying lives.

The Deaf and Hearing Impaired

Most children with hearing loss can function adequately with the assistance of a hearing aid. In fact, many physicians are now fitting **hearing impaired** children (the phrase that is now used in place of "hard of hearing") with hearing aids during in-

Box 14.2 **Vulnerable and Invulnerable Children**

Throughout the book, when I've talked about the impact of the environment on a child, I've generally talked as though the effect were equal for all children. But that is clearly not the case. Some children, raised in the most punitive, rejecting, unstimulating homes turn out to be successful and distinguished adults; some children who face far fewer difficulties develop chronic emotional problems, delinquency, or other life problems. Why?

Psychologists have only recently begun to ask about "invulnerable" children, so we have few answers. But there are bits and pieces I can pass on to you.

First, males seem to be more vulnerable to stresses than females are—a point I'll be coming back to later in the chapter.

Second, the child's temperament seems to make a difference. The "difficult" child is much more likely to show emotional problems during the preschool period than is the "easy" child. This could reflect an inborn vulnerability of the difficult child or an inborn invulnerability of the easy child. Or it could reflect differences in the patterns of interaction that develop between the child and the parent. The difficult child is more likely to be criticized by his parents, as one example (Rutter, 1979). So the developing transactions between a parent and child may simply aggravate an already existing tendency in the difficult child to react strongly to stress or to change.

Most important, the *in*vulnerable child—the child who seems later to be able to cope with life's stresses without lapsing into serious behavior problems—seems to have one important thing going for him. He nearly always has at least one good, strong, secure relationship with a parent or with another adult (Rutter, 1971, 1978). The existence of this early secure attachment seems to "buffer" the child against the later slings and arrows of normal life.

I mentioned in earlier chapters that children with secure attachments have more successful peer relationships and better approaches to solving problems during the preschool years. Now we have another piece to the puzzle; children with secure early attachments seem better able to cope with such life stresses as their parents' divorce or a death in the family.

Let me be careful here not to make the mistake of placing too much emphasis on the first attachment. Important as it seems to be, a child *can* recover from a highly stressed early relationship if the family situation improves. Note, however, that "improvement" in the family situation almost by definition means that the child now has some one person—a step parent, a grandparent, an older sibling—with whom he can form a strong, supportive relationship. The fundamental point seems to be that for a child to be able to handle temporary stresses without showing serious behavior problems, he must have *some* close attachment; but it need not be the *first* attachment of infancy.

fancy rather than waiting until the child is of preschool age. The situation is quite different, though, for the profoundly deaf—the child whose hearing loss is so severe that even with assistance his comprehension of sound, especially language, is significantly reduced. I raised some of the issues connected with the early rearing of deaf children in Box 7.3, and you may want to go back and reread that section at this stage. The basic point is that if the emphasis is placed exclusively on *oral* language, the deaf child has very great difficulty developing either

Figure 14.6 These deaf children are being taught sign language. Research on the deaf shows that the children who learn to sign- as well as lip-read when they are very young have the best prognosis.

speech or reading. But if the child is taught sign language *and* lip reading at the same time, the maximum benefit can be derived. *Some* such children can function in a normal school environment, but even with good early training, most deaf children require special schooling.

The Blind Child

If I had asked you, before you read this chapter, to tell me which would be worse, to have been blind or deaf from birth most of you would have said it would be far worse to be blind. Yet from the point of view of the child's ability to function in most normal settings, including school, blindness is a smaller handicap. The blind child can learn to read, can talk with others, can listen to a teacher, and so on. Because of this greater academic potential, there are more options open to the blind adult than to most deaf adults.

Still, there are obviously important limitations for the blind. One of these lies in the earliest relationship with the parent, which I've discussed in Box 14.3. Later relationships may be impaired for the same reasons.

What does seem to be critical, for both the deaf and the blind child, is early intervention with the family as well as with the child. The child can't be "cured," but many of the potential emotional and intellectual problems can be softened if there is early treatment.

Other Physical Problems

Among the most heart-wrenching youngsters are those with multiple handicaps or with physical disabilities so severe that

Box 14.3

Basic Attachments Between Blind Babies and Their Mothers

In Chapter 11, I mentioned Selma Fraiberg's work with blind infants as part of the discussion of the parent's attachment to the child. Because Fraiberg's work is so fascinating, I want to expand on that brief description here.

Fraiberg (1974, 1975) has found that blind babies begin to smile at about the same age as sighted babies (about 4 weeks) but that they smile less often. And at about 2 months, when the sighted baby begins to smile regularly at the sight of the parent's face, the blind baby's smiles become less and less frequent. The blind infant's smile is also less intense, more fleeting.

The other thing blind babies don't do is enter into mutual gaze. They don't look right at their parents, and everything we know about parents' responses to their babies underlines the importance of mutual gaze for the parent's feeling of attachment to the baby. When the blind baby does not look, the parents often report feeling "rejected."

Generally, the facial expressions of the blind infant are muted and sober. Many observers, including parents, conclude that the baby is depressed or indifferent.

Fraiberg found that most of the mothers of the blind babies in her studies gradually withdrew from their infant. They provided the needed physical care, but they stopped playing with the baby, and gave up trying to elicit smiles or other social interactions. They often say they don't "love" this baby.

Fortunately, it's possible to solve this particular problem. Fraiberg found that these mothers could be helped to form a strong bond with their infant if they could be shown how to "read" the baby's other signals. The blind child's face may be sober and relatively expressionless, but her hands and body move a lot and express a great deal. When the child *stops* moving when you come into the room, this means she is listening to your footsteps. Or she may move her hands when she hears your voice rather than smiling as a sighted child would do.

When parents of blind children learn to respond to these alternative "attachment behaviors" in their babies, then the mutuality of the relationships can be reestablished. And when this happens, and the parents are able to provide more varied stimulation, blind children develop more normal behavior in other ways. In particular, they don't show the "blindisms" so often observed in blind youngsters, such as rocking, sucking, head banging, and other repetitive action.

---

they are unable to communicate, move, or play. As an example, some (but by no means all) children with severe forms of cerebral palsy cannot speak, are mentally retarded, and are unable to move without assistance. They require full-time care for their entire lives. Still they *can* learn and love. Among the health care professionals dealing with severely or multiply handicapped children, the move today is toward beginning intervention as early as possible. The family is ordinarily involved from the beginning, not only learning how to care for and stimulate the child but also getting help in developing their own attachment to the child.

Another group of children with significant physical problems is those with chronic diseases, such as muscular dystrophy or cystic fibrosis. The child with muscular dystrophy steadily loses his ability to control his muscles, becoming more and more handicapped over time. The child with cystic fibrosis requires constant medical monitoring and usually becomes progressively worse through the first two decades of life. In every instance, early diagnosis and treatment are critical—not because they can eliminate the disease, but because they may prolong the child's life or the period of comfort and because they can aid the family and the child to come to terms with the conditions and limitations of the disease. (Remember, too, that many of these serious conditions can be identified before birth through amniocentesis, which I discussed in Chapter 2.)

Sex Differences in Atypical Development

The general rule is that boys are substantially more likely to show any form of atypical development. I've put some of the comparisons in Table 14.4.

How are we to explain differences like this? One possibility is that the female, as I mentioned in Box 14.2, is somehow naturally "buffered" against environmental stresses. Girls are less likely to inherit any recessive disease that is carried on the sex chromosomes. Perhaps the double X chromosome provides some general kind of added protection that the boy does not have.

Hormonal differences may also play a role. For example, excess aggression, as in conduct disorders, may have a hormonal basis (see Chapter 11). Sex differences in other areas may result from greater demands being placed on boys, thus creating greater stresses for them to deal with.

Whatever the explanation—and none of the existing explanations is terribly satisfactory to me—it is nonetheless interesting that the girl does seem to be less vulnerable.

Interventions

Treatment of children with atypical development comes in many forms, everything from brief treatment by a school psychologist to lifetime institutionalization. Let me touch on just a few of the options.

Treatment for the Child, Training for the Parents

Probably the most common intervention is some kind of individual therapy or training for the child. In recent years, however, parents have increasingly been involved as well (Tjossem,

Table 14.4 Sex Differences in Incidence of Atypical Development

Type of problem	Approximate ratio of males to females
School problems: children testing below grade level in basic subjects	3 to 2
Physical handicaps	
Visual problems	1 to 1
Hearing problems	5 to 4
Speech defects	3 to 2
Emotional problems	
Conduct disorders (aggressiveness and equivalent)	5 to 1
Anxiety-withdrawal	2 or 3 to 1
Estimated number of children of all diagnoses seen in psychiatric clinics	2 to 1

Sources: Profiles of Children, 1970; Anthony, 1970; Eme, 1979.

1976; Levitt & Cohen, 1977). Parents of children with behavior problems need to examine the pattern of their discipline with their children; parents of physically handicapped children need to learn how to stimulate and play with their children; parents of children with learning problems may be taught specific games or projects to undertake at home that are actually part of the child's treatment.

Programs for retarded children, too, have begun to involve the parents more fully. As one example, a training program for Down's syndrome children at the University of Washington (Hayden & Haring, 1976) includes not only a carefully designed individual training program for each child but instruction for the parent (usually the mother). The mother is given specific tasks to work on with her child in class and at home. Programs like this do not "cure" a Down's syndrome child, but they do help each child develop his maximum potential.

Interventions in the Public Schools: Mainstreaming versus Special Classes

Increasingly, the job of responding to the needs of atypical children is falling on the public school system. The Federal Education for All Handicapped Children Act, passed in 1975, requires that each state have programs for all school-age and preschool handicapped children. Further, it requires that wherever possible, the handicapped child be **mainstreamed**—a word that many of you may have heard bandied about.

What does "mainstreaming" mean? It does *not* mean that every atypical child must be taught full-time in a regular classroom. It does mean that many children who had previously been taught in special, segregated classes will now be spending part or all of their school hours in a regular classroom. Educable mentally retarded children, in most instances, are being assigned full-time to regular classes; children with physical handicaps such as blindness or those with learning problems are spending part of each day in a regular classroom and part with a special education teacher or in a special classroom. The basic rule of thumb is that each child should be assigned to the *least-restrictive environment* he can handle.

The alternative to mainstreaming is some sort of special class (see Figure 14.7)—a system that dominated school treatment of the atypical child until recently. What are the arguments either way? Which works best for the child?

The answer, once again, is that we don't really know, or at least we know a whole lot less than we'd like to. There are a few tentative conclusions. First, the *social* adjustment of mentally retarded or physically handicapped children seems to be better in special classrooms than in regular classrooms (Robinson & Robinson, 1976). Mentally normal and ablebodied children do not ordinarily choose retarded or physically handicapped children as friends or playmates (Karnes & Lee, 1979); so for the child, mainstreaming in a regular classroom may be an isolating rather than a socially integrating experience. That need not be an inevitable result of mainstreaming. It's possible to arrange a classroom and class activities in such a way as to maximize the contact of the special child with other children. But that takes considerable sensitivity and awareness on the part of the teacher.

Second, in support of mainstreaming, there is some indication that the educable mentally retarded child, and probably the physically handicapped child, does a bit better academically in a regular classroom. Since instruction in a special classroom is usually at a slower pace and the teacher may have much lower expectations for her pupils, the child may in fact learn less than he is able to absorb. In a regular classroom, where the expectations are higher and where they are exposed constantly to children who are learning and enjoying it, the same children may develop more rapidly (Goldstein, Moss & Jordan, 1965; Robinson and Robinson, 1976).

Obviously, the information we have at this point doesn't permit an easy choice between these two alternatives. My own feeling about this whole debate is that there is too much discussion of *where* the child will be taught and not enough of *what*

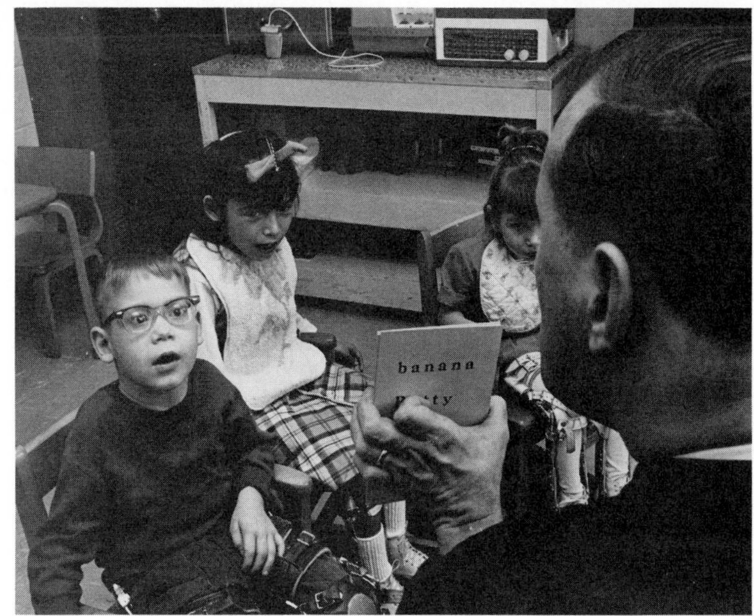

Figure 14.7 **This is a good example of a special class for retarded children carried out within a public school. The class is very small, so there is a great deal of individual instruction. With "mainstreaming" becoming a dominant theme in education for the handicapped, these special classes will become less common but will still exist for children with severe handicaps or significant retardation.**

or *how* he is to be taught. There is also far too little emphasis on the training of the regular classroom teachers who will be asked to instruct physically handicapped or mentally retarded youngsters. It will do little good to place such children in regular classrooms if the teachers are not helped to develop the special skills they will need to teach them and if backup specialists are not available. My assessment of the present situation is that too often these conditions are not being met. In the long run, we cannot know if mainstreaming really "works" unless and until it has been properly tried.

Residential Treatment

A third type of treatment, recommended primarily for those children with such severe handicaps that they cannot readily be cared for at home, is some form of institutional or residential care. With the increasing emphasis on involvement of parents in the treatment of atypical children, the number of children in institutional care has declined. Still, some children can't be handled at home or in schools, so there are still residential treatment facilities in existence. The most common are institutions for profoundly retarded children and adults. Many children in such institutions also have physical handicaps.

Children with severe emotional problems, such as some autistic and schizophrenic children, are also often cared for in institutions. In most cases, the expressed aim of the care is to provide therapy of some kind for the child so that he can be returned to his family. Regrettably, the success of these efforts for the severely disturbed child is not outstanding. Many excellent programs have succeeded in modifying children's behavior sufficiently so that they can live at home, but the beneficial changes often don't last outside the supportive environment of the residential community (Quay, 1979b).

At the present moment, many children who would have been placed in residential care ten years ago are being kept at home, at least for the early years. Supportive training programs for parents and improved programs in the schools aid this move toward home care. But there are still some children for whom residential care is the only reasonable option, and parents should not be made to feel guilty if they make such a choice.

A Final Point

I want to end this chapter, as I began it, by stating strongly that the development of the "atypical" child is really much more like "typical" development than it is unlike it. It is very easy, when dealing with an atypical child, to be overwhelmed by the sense of differentness. But the sameness is there, underneath.

Summary

1. Approximately 15–20 percent of all children will need some form of special assistance because of atypical development.

2. The most common problems are reading difficulties and short-term behavior problems.

3. Children with mental retardation, normally defined as IQ below 70 and significant problems of adaptation, represent approximately $2\frac{1}{2}$ percent of the population.

4. Low IQ should be seen as a symptom rather than a disease. It can change over time or with special intervention.

5. The two basic categories of causes of mental retardation are physical problems, such as genetic anomalies or brain damage, and cultural-familial problems. Children with cultural-familial retardation ordinarily come from families in which the parents have low IQ and provide little stimulation for the child.

6. Interventions with cultural-familial retarded children have been successful in raising the child's IQ to the normal range, but such programs are expensive and still quite scarce.

7. Children with specific learning disabilities make up about 1 percent of the school population. Most display their difficulty in some aspect of reading. The problem *may* arise from some undetected minimal brain damage, but there are other possible explanations.

8. Serious emotional problems, often called psychoses, include autism and childhood schizophrenia. The former develops in the early months of life and includes problems in relating to others and with language. The latter develops later and includes immature behavior, some regression in language skill, and bizarre behaviors.

9. Behavior problems, often of short duration, are commonly divided into several categories, including conduct disorders (ex-

cessive aggressiveness or disruptiveness), anxiety-withdrawal syndrome, and immaturity.
10. Children with conduct disorders frequently come from families in which there is hostility toward the child or rejection accompanied by high levels of physical punishment.
11. Children with anxiety or withdrawal often come from families in which one or the other parent has significantly neurotic behavior patterns and in which there is strict discipline and lack of affection.
12. Whether a child will exhibit a behavior problem or not seems to be heavily influenced by the total level of stress he is asked to cope with at any given moment. When the stress level goes down, the behavior problem may disappear.
13. The best prognosis for the deaf child occurs when identification is made early, hearing aids are used where possible, and the child is taught signing and lip reading from the earliest years of life. Special schooling is usually required.
14. Blind children, in contrast, can often function in regular school classrooms but may have difficulty with personal relationships because of lack of typical attachment behaviors.
15. Boys show almost all forms of atypical development more often than girls do. This may reflect genetic differences, hormone differences, or differences in cultural expectations.
16. Interventions with atypical children increasingly involve the parent as well as the child.
17. "Mainstreaming" of atypical children into regular school classrooms, wherever possible, is now legally mandated. The verdict is still out on the effects of that practice.
18. It is important to remember that the development of atypical children is basically the same as for normal children in most respects.

Key Terms

Adaptive behavior An aspect of a child's functioning often considered in diagnosing mental retardation. Can the child adapt to the tasks of everyday life?

Anxiety – withdrawal syndrome One of several basic patterns of behavior problems in children, including such behaviors as shyness, fearfulness, depression, and withdrawal from relationships with others.

Autism A severe form of emotional/language disorder, appearing in infancy.

Behavior problem The general phrase used to describe mild or moderate forms of emotional difficulty, including aggressiveness, shyness, anxiety, and equivalent.

Brain damage Some insult to the brain, either during prenatal development or later, that results in improper functioning of the brain.

Conduct disorder One of several basic patterns of behavior problems in children, including aggressiveness and disruptive behavior as well as hyperactivity.

Educable mental retardation Label used in school systems for children with IQs in the range of about 50–70.

Genetic anomalies Atypical patterns of genes or chromosomes, resulting in specific physical characteristics such as Down's syndrome. A possible cause of mental retardation.

Giftedness Normally defined as very high IQ, usually above 140 or 150.

Hearing impaired The phrase currently used in place of "hard of hearing" to describe children or adults with significant hearing loss.

Immaturity A pattern of behavior problem including inattentiveness and poor physical coordination, often accompanied by learning problems.

Mainstreaming The word used to describe the placement of atypical children in regular school classrooms wherever possible.

Mental retardation The term used to describe low levels of intellectual functioning and poor adaptation. Normally defined by an IQ of 70 or lower.

Mild mental retardation Equivalent to educable mental retardation (see above).

Moderate mental retardation Equivalent to trainable mental retardation (see below).

Phenylketonuria An inherited metabolic deficiency that can result in mental retardation if not treated from birth.

Profound mental retardation IQ scores below about 20.

Psychoses The collection of severe emotional disturbances, such as schizophrenia and autism in children.

Schizophrenia A severe form of emotional disturbance, seen in both children and adults, characterized by lack of normal relationships with others, bizarre behavior, and often language deficits. Not usually seen in children younger than 4 or 5.

Severe mental retardation IQ scores between 20 and 35.

Specific learning disability (SLD) A disorder in understanding or processing language or symbols. Most often shown in reading problems.

Trainable mental retardation Label used in school systems for children with IQs in the range of 36–50 or so.

Transitory situational disturbances Short-term problem behavior, shown by virtually all children at some times, and *not* an indication of serious emotional difficulties.

Suggested Readings

Edgerton, R. B. Mental retardation. Cambridge, Mass.: Harvard University Press, 1979.
This is an excellent, brief, readable introduction to the whole topic—simpler but less complete than the Robinson and Robinson book listed below.

Farnham-Diggory, S. Learning disabilities. Cambridge, Mass.: Harvard University Press, 1979.
Another excellent, brief introductory discussion from the same series as the Edgerton book.

Gallagher, J. J. Teaching the gifted child. Boston: Allyn & Bacon, 1975.
For those of you who are prospective teachers, this would be an excellent introduction to the topic of giftedness and how to handle gifted children in the school.

Hobbs, N. The futures of children. San Francisco: Jossey-Bass, 1975.
An absolutely first-rate discussion of the whole problem of categorizing and labeling atypical children. Clear and easy to read.

Kaufman, B. N. Son/rise. New York: Harper & Row, 1976.
If you are interested in autism, this book will intrigue you. It was written by the father of an autistic boy and describes the therapy the parents developed. I personally find the style of writing rather flowery, but the message is fascinating.

Robinson, N. M., & Robinson, H. B. The mentally retarded child (2nd ed.). New York: McGraw-Hill, 1976.
The best single text on this subject I know of.

Rutter, M. Helping troubled children. New York: Plenum Press, 1975.
I like Michael Rutter's style very much and think you would find this book an excellent introduction to the full range of emotional problems in children and their treatment.

Preview of Chapter 15

Putting It All Together: The Developing Child

Ann is $2\frac{1}{2}$. She is talking a blue streak now, putting three, four, or even more words together into sentences. Sometimes it seems to her mother that every third sentence has "no" in it, since Ann is definitely asserting her independence. "No milk!" "No more shoes today." "Daddy no coming." But Ann is also beginning to share her toys with the little girl next door when they play together, so it is not all negative. They are also beginning to have some "make believe" play, which is new.

Just recently, Ann started to go to nursery school in the mornings, and her mother noticed that there were a lot of changes. Not only is she talking more and expressing more interest in other children, she also is having trouble eating, which she hasn't done for quite a while. You really have to coax her to get any food into her at all now. And she wakes up more at night. It's a time of great change, fascinating to watch but frustrating at times to live with.

David is 14 and has just started high school. He's taking a science course and a course in algebra, and he complains a little that they are both very hard. He isn't used to having to do experiments. When he's not in school, he and his group of friends play a bit of pick-up basketball in the gym or "hang out" (as they say) at one another's houses. David isn't really dating yet; but there's a group of girls who are friends, and the two groups of kids go to dances together and sometimes sit together at lunch.

David isn't getting along with his parents quite as well these days as he used to. It seems to him that they nag him a lot about getting home on time and that they're too strict about where he goes with his friends. They are also beginning to pressure him about getting good grades, now that he's in high school. "If you want to go to college, you have to think about what classes you're taking and about working hard." David knows he is going to have to face all that, but he doesn't feel ready yet. In fact, he's a little depressed about the whole thing. High school is harder than he thought it would be. And he's really interested in a girl in the crowd he hangs around with, but he's still nervous about asking her out. Sometimes when it all gets to bugging him too much, he yells at his mother and then spends a few hours in his room with the door locked and the music turned up as loud as he dares.

For David's parents, all this is a little bewildering. Two years ago, they all seemed to get along fine. Now they never know what will set him off. He is alternately affectionate and withdrawn. But they're trying to be supportive and realize that "this too shall pass."

Both of these children are imaginary, but I think any parent who has had a child go through one of these periods will recognize the description. (I trust my own children will forgive me for borrowing a bit from them, too!) Each of the two children I've described illustrates two points that I think are vital and that I haven't been able to emphasize as much as I'd like in the rest of the book.

Some Basic Points

The Interlocking Nature of Development

First, all the different threads of development occur together in a complex weave. I've talked about language, perception, thinking, physical changes, social development, and moral development separately in order to give you some sense of the full sweep of changes over time in each "thread" of development. But in the real world, all of these things happen together and interact with each other in complex ways. I need to pull these separate lines together and talk about how they relate to one another.

Transitions and Consolidations

The second point I hope Ann and David illustrate is that I think development proceeds in a series of phases, with alternating periods of rapid growth accompanied by disruption or disequilibrium, followed by times of relative calm or consolidation. Actually, change is going on all the time, from birth through adolescence (and through adulthood and aging, too). But I am persuaded that there are particular times when the changes pile up, when the child develops a whole range of new skills at once, or there are new demands placed on her, such as school

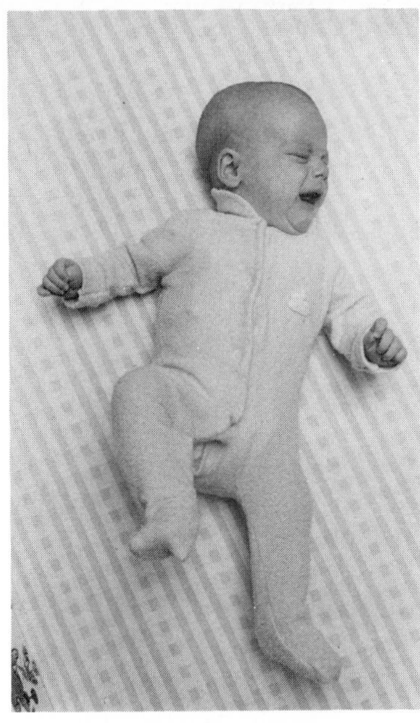

Figure 15.1 The newborn baby can do so many things—see, hear, smell, cuddle, cry. All these abilities help the child elicit caregiving from the adults around her.

or when her body changes rapidly. These "pile ups" of change often seem to result in the child's coming "unglued" for a while. The old patterns of relationship, of thinking, and of talking don't work very well any more; but it takes a while to work out the new patterns. And during the transition, the child may show temporary behavior problems or lose some skills that she had had before.

Generally speaking, these major transitions occur at times when the child changes from one physical state to another (such as prepubescent to pubescent), from one status to another (such as baby to toddler), or from one role to another (such as an at-home child to a going-to-school child). Each of these major changes in role or status creates both a kind of crisis and an opportunity for significant change, for growth.

"Crisis" is really too strong a word for what happens at these transition points. Erikson sometimes uses the word crisis; more often he uses the term **dilemma.** Klaus Riegel (1975) once suggested the phrase **developmental leaps,** which conveys quite nicely the sense of excitement and blooming opportunity that often accompany these pivotal periods. I'm going to use the more pedestrian term **transition** because it sounds less negative than "crisis" and because it is less cumbersome than "developmental leaps."

After each of these transitions has been weathered, the child, and the parent-child relationship, settle into a more stable, steady change period. I have come to use the word **consolidation** for the in-between times. The child is putting together all the new skills, demands, and roles and gradually developing a new equilibrium.

The whole period of childhood—and adulthood as well, in my view—is a series of alternating transitions and consolidations. I'm not altogether happy with the word *stages* as a description of the sort of sequence I'm describing; but for lack of a better term, it will do. So we can think of development as a series of stages, with transitions in between.

Let me apply these concepts to the child's development by looking at all the interlocking threads at each of a series of stages and at the transition periods that lie between each stage.

The Infant from Birth to 2 Months

Louis was active from the first. He cried lustily when he was handled or disturbed, reacting to touch, noises or bright lights with a Moro reflex. . . . Louis was a responsive baby. He quieted to handling, to changes in position, to crooning. He learned quickly to quiet himself by bringing his fist to his mouth and sucking on it. As time went on, he differentiated the two first fingers of his left hand

> and learned to suck on them for comfort, showing how early a lasting pattern like this is established. As he inserted his fingers and began to suck, his arms and legs relaxed. His face became serene and peaceful. . . . He cried every evening. He lay for hours during the day, looking around quietly, but by the end of the day, he semed determined to have his say.
>
> *(Brazelton, 1969, pp. 6, 43)*

In this description, Louis is only a few weeks old. But already you can see some of his important skills and how all those abilities relate to each other. He can quiet himself, and he is responsive to his mother's efforts to soothe him.

To give you some sense of all the different things that happen to a newborn, all the parallel developmental changes going on, I've summarized the skills and changes in Table 15.1. If you read through the information in the table, you'll probably come away with two impressions.

Perhaps most strikingly, there are so many things a newborn baby (like Louis) *cannot* do. He doesn't talk, walk, or think logically. He doesn't smile much yet, and can't tell the difference between mother or father and a total stranger.

But the capacities of the newborn are striking, too. What is even more impressive is the way the child's abilities merge in a way that helps him get taken care of and that help him to focus on the people around him. The baby hears best the sounds that are in the range of the human voice; he focuses his eyes best on things about 8 inches away, so he sees his mother's or father's face clearly when he's being fed or cuddled; he cries when he needs help and then consistently reinforces his parents for picking him up by quieting when they cuddle him, sing to him, or hold him to their shoulder. He can "take turns" during feeding. He pays most attention to things that move and to edges of things.

All of those built-in tendencies help the child focus a lot of his attention on the people around him and help to bring them close to him so they become attached to him. The whole process isn't intentional, of course; but the system is a wonderfully interlocking one, with the baby's physical and perceptual abilities and his sootheability all helping to hook the parents in caregiving and then into full attachment with the baby.

The Transition at 6–8 Weeks

Despite the utility of the newborn's skills, the whole process is very much on "automatic pilot" during the early weeks. Nearly everything the newborn does is based on reflex. He seems to scan edges because his visual system is programmed to do that. In fact, the whole perceptual system during the early weeks appears to be mainly governed by the **reticular formation,** which is a primitive portion of the brain system responsible for such

Table 15.1 The Infant from Birth to 2 Months: A Summary

The physical child	The thinking child	The social child
Many physical and perceptual skills are present at birth. Child can focus both eyes, look systematically at edges and contours, follow a moving object. He can hear well and has good touch and taste sensitivity. Major neurological growth occurs during the early months, including addition of brain cells and myelinization of nerves. Most early activity, though, seems to be controlled by the more "primitive" portions of the brain. Motor control is weak.	This is Piaget's first stage of sensorimotor operations. There is no intentional exploration, only accidental. Actions are governed almost entirely by reflexes. The child has no language and makes only crying and a few pleasure noises.	The baby shows a whole range of very effective attachment behaviors, including crying, cuddling, a little smiling, and occasional eye contact. These are all good "proximity eliciting" behaviors: they lead to the parents' caring for the child. The early parent-child interactions include the first signs of mutuality, as in the "turn taking" during feeding.

basic body rhythms as sleep and breathing. You may remember from Chapter 5 that Gordon Bronson (1974) calls this the **second visual system.** The child is programmed to figure out *where* objects are but not *what* they are.

But somewhere around six to eight weeks after birth, as the cortex develops, the pattern changes rather swiftly as the **primary visual system** enters the picture. The child now begins to look at the objects and people around her in a new way, focusing on eyes, on other facial features, and on specific characteristics of objects, toys, blankets, and cribs.

At the same time, the baby often begins to have a single long sleep period during the night, which is probably related to the changes in the brain as well. He also starts to have eye contact more often with the people holding him, presumably because he's now looking at eyes and not just at the edges of faces. And he begins to smile a lot at about 6–8 weeks, too, which is a terrific turn-on for parents.

Because of all these changes in the baby, and also because it takes the mother six to eight weeks to recover her energy after pregnancy and delivery, there are big changes in the mother–child interaction system during this transition as well. The early weeks involve a great deal of routine caretaking. The baby isn't awake very much, isn't very social, and needs feeding, diapering, and holding. But as the baby changes, and the mother gets more emotionally attached, they begin to spend more time in social interaction, in play, in looking at one another.

The critical aspect of this transition from my perspective is the underlying neurological change in the infant. The baby's cortex develops enough so that he begins to respond to things around him in a less-automatic, less-reflexive way. This, in turn, brings changes in social relationships, in perception, in language, and in the full range of behaviors. I can illustrate the change very clearly by taking a second look at Louis, two months later.

> The third month made the earlier two seem worthwhile. By the end of this period, so much had happened, life was so much easier and more rewarding that [Louis's parents] felt a kind of euphoria. Louis was already an exciting, responsive individual. Indeed, his responses seemed out of proportion to the stimulation he was offered, and he was so delicious that they felt they didn't deserve him. . . . [His father] called him his "dish of ice cream," and constantly played with him, cuddled, and nuzzled him now. Louis gurgled with glee at all of this attention.
>
> *(Brazelton, 1969, p. 98)*

These parents are hooked!

The Baby from 2 to 8 Months

> When Daniel found that he could get himself off the floor, he practiced for hours at pushups. He straightened his legs and arms, his body high like a daddy-long-legs. . . . The game he liked best was the come-and-get-me game. Whenever he saw a parent starting toward him, he squealed happily, scrabbled, and began to push himself away as fast as he could. . . . He had learned to drop his spoon and cup overboard when his mother fed him solids. He dropped them, leaned over to look after them, avoiding the proffered spoon. When [his mother] retrieved them, she found she was soon playing a game with him of picking up his spoon over and over.
>
> *(Brazelton, 1969, pp. 157, 159, 161)*

Daniel is 6 months old and in the middle of the next phase or stage. Obviously, there have been great changes since 2 months. (I've summarized the major things we see in children during this period in Table 15.2.) In the brief description of Daniel I've given, the most striking changes are in his motor skills. Daniel is a particularly active fellow and loves to move, to practice new physical abilities. But the child from 2 to 8 months is a far more social child, too. He smiles a lot and is alert far more of the time, so the parents have more time to play with the child,

Table 15.2 The Child from 2 to 8 Months: A Summary

The physical child	The thinking child	The social child
Huge changes take place in the child's physical skills as the motor and perceptual areas of the brain develop. The baby can sit up and reach for things and has better control of his body. The object concept is also partly developed, and visual acuity improves so that the baby can see the parents more clearly when they are farther away.	This period encompasses Piaget's stages 2 and 3 of the sensorimotor period. The baby explores and examines objects and people more systematically and repeats interesting things. In language, the baby makes cooing sounds, and some infants will begin to babble during this period.	The child now smiles regularly and makes eye contact regularly. He enters into social play with his parents and with others. The first two stages of attachment (initial preattachment and attachment in the making) occur, so most children in this period can still be cared for by several different adults.

to stimulate him, and to take pleasure themselves from these encounters.

The other big change is in the child's cognitive growth. You can see one sign of this in Daniel's looking over the edge of the high chair to search for the spoon or cup he's dropped. For the younger infant, objects are very much "out of sight, out of mind." But the 4–8-month-old begins to develop some concept of the constancy of objects, and this affects his play with both objects and people.

At least two underlying processes seem to be at work during this time. First of all, there are continuing neurological changes. There is no single change in the brain that is quite as marked as what happens at six to eight weeks, but the motor and perceptual areas of the cortex continue to develop. The child is better and better able to control the movements of his body and more and more systematic in his perceptual explorations. The second underlying process is the child's own exploration of everything around him. In Piaget's view (and he certainly seems to be right), these manipulations and explorations of toys, people's hands and faces, spoons, food, blankets, and all the other things within reach are essential for the development of the object concept and for all the other changes in the child's cognitive skills. The child adapts, but he has to have new experiences to encourage those adaptations.

Research on children raised in severely impoverished environments, such as orphanages, during these months of infancy

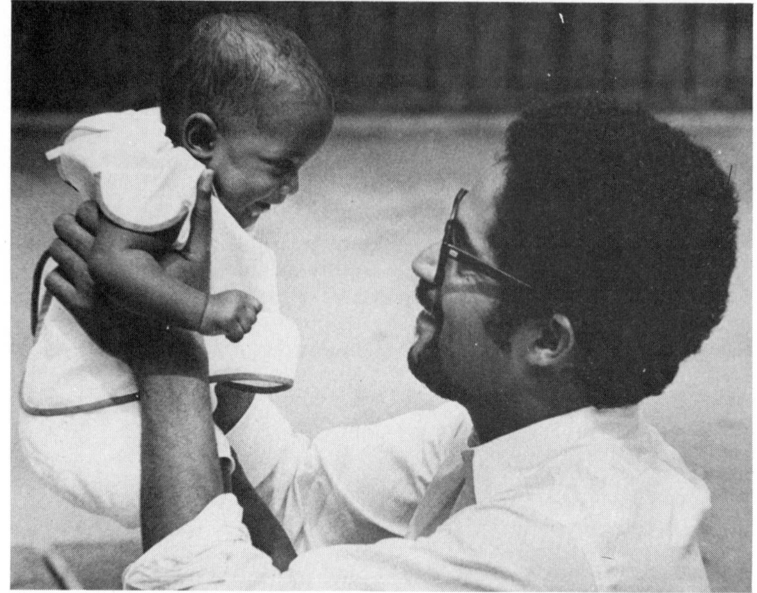

Figure 15.2 During the period from 2 to 8 months, babies become much more social. They smile at the sight of the parent's face, which both fathers and mothers find extremely satisfying.

show us that if the baby doesn't have this kind of opportunity to explore, his cognitive development will be slowed down (Dennis, 1960; White, 1967). In studies of children in family situations, too, opportunities to play with toys or other appropriate objects during these months have been found to be important. Richard Elardo, Robert Bradley, and Bettye Caldwell (1975) found that the availability of "appropriate play materials" at 6 months helped to foster higher IQ scores at age 3. My colleagues and I at the University of Washington, in an ongoing longitudinal study, have found exactly the same thing.

So the child from 2 to 8 months is busy—busy moving, busy exploring, busy developing the early stages of strong attachments to the important people around him.

The Transition at 8 Months

Somewhere in the middle of all this business, I see another transition. The exact timing isn't the same for every child. It depends on when he begins to crawl and when he forms his first really strong individual attachment. But these two events usher in a whole new set of interactions with his parents and with the world around him. And it is the *combination* of these two important changes—one motor, one social—that leads me to see this as an important transition.

One of the characteristics of children who have developed a strong attachment is that they use this most important person as a "safe base" from which to explore the new and exciting—

and somewhat scary—things all around. When the child can crawl and is also attached, the whole process of moving away, coming back to check in, and moving away again begins.

Because of the new ability to crawl, the child of 8 months is also a much more demanding infant to care for than is the less-mobile younger baby. He gets into things and has to be watched almost constantly. And if his strong single attachment is accompanied by fear of strangers, as it usually is at just about this age, then it is harder to leave him with a baby-sitter or even with another family member. The baby is pushing for independence but clings to the familiar at the same time. It is a whole new kind of transaction for the parent and infant—a whole new kind of dance—and requires major adjustments for both.

The cognitive changes that are continuing to take place are not unconnected to this transition. The very existence of a single strong attachment probably depends on the child's development of the object concept in the first place. How can a child become attached to mother, or father, until he not only recognizes the mother or father but understands that the mother or father is a permanent person and continues to exist when not visible? So when the object concept develops, a strong attachment becomes possible. And since the child can now move around more on his own, this has the effect of speeding up his cognitive growth, too, because he can get to so many more places and things and thus must adapt to a wider and wider range of experiences.

The Baby from 8 to 18 Months

> Cautiously, Laura tried to balance with her legs spread wide apart, taking her hands off the couch for short experimental trials. . . . Gradually she gained courage and balance, and by her first birthday, she stood alone. . . . She used her doll in her play—putting her in a rocking chair to be rocked, crooning to her, saying "No" to her. . . . [Her parents] gave Laura a birthday party at the end of her first year. They asked three other babies her age to come. . . . When the others arrived, Laura greeted each one with "Hi Babee." . . . Her mother had never heard her put these sounds together before.
>
> *(Brazelton, 1969, pp. 263, 265, 266)*

This description of Laura at 12 months shows that change continues to be rapid after the transition at 8 months has been mastered. (I've summarized the major changes in Table 15.3.) Obviously, Laura was beginning to talk, which is typical of the child at this age. She was also showing signs of some symbolic play, as when she said "no" to her doll. Psychologists and linguists are still arguing about the relationship between these

Figure 15.3 The child from 8 to 18 months normally has established one strong attachment, as this child shows toward her mother. She also can crawl, which presents new problems for the mother and new vistas for the child.

two lines of development. Does language make new cognitive growth possible or is it the other way around? My own feeling is that language begins when it does partly because the child's brain is now "ready" for it and partly because she has developed her first primitive concepts through explorations and experiments with the objects around her. The early words seem to be labels for categories she has already developed. Whatever the link between the two, it is clear that during this period, the child *does* develop primitive categories or classifications of objects or experiences and that she does use a few words to talk about those groups or classes.

Socially, this period is still dominated by one or several strong attachments to important adults in the baby's life. Typically, an 8–18-month-old child hasn't much contact with other children her own age; but as I pointed out in Chapter 11, children this age will play together a little. Given an option between another child and a toy, though, most infants will still choose the toy (Eckerman & Whatley, 1977).

Increasingly, it appears that the nature of the attachment the child forms to her mother, father, or other significant person during this period plays a critical role in her later success with peers, and possibly in schools as well (Waters, Wippman & Sroufe, 1979; Sroufe, 1978; Lieberman, 1977). Children with secure attachments also seem to be better buffered against later emotional stresses (Rutter, 1979) and are less likely to show behavior problems as school-age children or teenagers (see Box 14.2). These findings certainly fit with Erikson's general pro-

Table 15.3 The Baby from 8 to 18 Months: A Summary

The physical child	The thinking child	The social child
Neurological growth continues rapidly during this period, with the motor and perceptual areas achieving nearly complete development by the end of the period. As a result, the child's motor skills improve very rapidly. She walks during this stretch and gets more and more steady. She also makes progress in using her hands and can hold and pick up smaller objects. Perceptually, she completes the object concept development and her visual and auditory acuity improve, too.	This period includes Piaget's stages 4 and 5 of sensorimotor development. The child experiments and explores intentionally; and because she can now move around on her own, her range of exploration is much wider than it has been. This spurs on even more rapid cognitive development. Primitive concepts seem to be formed during this period. The first words appear now, too, and a few two-word sentences.	Nearly all children have at least one clear-cut, single attachment during this period, which spreads to multiple attachments later. Often fear of strangers appears between 8 and 12 months, too. The child uses her central people as a safe base from which to explore. The security of this first attachment seems to be particularly critical for several aspects of later development.

posal about the centrality of the first dilemma, trust versus mistrust. They also point to the intricate way in which emotional and intellectual growth are intertwined. The insecurely attached child approaches new problems, new objects, and new people in a different way—perhaps more fearfully, perhaps with less vigor, perhaps with less curiosity. Such changes in the child's transactions with the objects and people around her can't help but affect her intellectual growth. The effect is a kind of chain reaction: Lack of security or confidence early results in more restricted experience, which leads to still less confidence.

Despite the importance of the early pattern, however, I think such chains can be broken and the child given greater experience and greater security later on. For example, Lois Murphy and Alice Moriarty (1976) describe a child named Janice, whom they had followed from infancy through adolescence. Janice's mother had been ill a great deal, and the child's initial relationship with her mother had not been at all good. Yet she turned out to cope well with the later tasks of childhood.

> When she was fourteen I discussed with her the fact that her mother had always been unwell and relatively unavailable. I asked her what had helped her to grow up so well. She told me that at about the age of four she had found "another mother" in the mother of her neighbor friend and that this other mother had been very important to her.
>
> *(Murphy & Moriarty, 1976, p. 172)*

In this case, the chain was broken. It illustrates the fact that children *can* recover from early difficulties. But the child with a solid early attachment certainly seems to get off onto the right foot.

The Transition at 18 Months

The transition from "baby" to "child" that occurs at about 18 months seems to be ushered in primarily by the significant cognitive accomplishment of internal representation—substage 6 in Piaget's sensorimotor period. Obviously, the timing of this differs; some children go through this transition at 14–15 months, others not until 2 years or later. But virtually every parent has noticed when his child begins to use words to label things, wants to know the name of everything, and seems to explore in quite a new way. The child's play changes as she becomes able to have objects stand for things; and for a time, her focus seems to be very heavily on her play, on objects, on understanding relationships. From the parents' perspective, an essentially nonverbal baby quite suddenly becomes a talkative, more "intellectual" child. It was this transition that Ann was going through in the description I gave at the beginning of the chapter. It's a tremendously exciting process to watch, though many parents have a feeling of loss, too; their baby is disappearing and a quite different sort of child is taking her place.

The Child from 18 Months to 6 Years

> Mrs. Bond knew the end of a long era was in sight when she heard Joe respond "No! No!—I mean—Yes!" As if on the wind, this sudden change blew in one day in his third year. His automatic "no" was open to discussion or could be considered, and both he and she knew it. Even Mr. Bond noticed a change in Joe which he labeled "growing up." When Mr. Bond suggested that he and Joe pick up the toys in Joe's room, Joe looked at him with the usual "no" but smiled after it, as if he, too, saw the humor in the response. This came as a real change, for just one week before, he would have collapsed screaming on the floor after such a suggestion.
>
> *(Brazelton, 1974, p. 197)*

Joe has passed through the transition I just described and has entered into the long period from 18 months to 6 years—a period I've summarized in Table 15.4. A great deal happens during these four years; enormous changes take place. But I don't see any other major transitions during this period—no other points when a number of changes pile up to produce the need for a whole new reorganization of the child's functioning or of the parent–child system of interacting with one another.

Table 15.4 The Child from 18 Months to 6 Years: A Summary

The physical child	The thinking child	The social child
There are major improvements in the child's motor skills during this period, with much better gross motor skills and fine motor skills. The child walks steadily, runs, climbs stairs, jumps, and so on. He can pick up a pencil, draw, and string beads. His attention becomes more focused and more selective.	The sensorimotor stage ends, and the preoperational stage begins at about 2 and continues through this period. The child's logic is still primitive, but she can have things stand for other things in her play; she uses words with increasing skill and can construct longer and longer sentences. She has *some* ability to take another perspective, but this is still rudimentary. Her classification skills develop, and she develops most of a full gender concept during these years.	Primary attachments to parents are still present and visible when the child is under stress. But the child ranges farther and farther from her "safe base." She develops more and more important relationships with peers, including a few specific friendships toward the end of these years. Her peer interactions become increasingly skillful and more cooperative. Cooperative play largely replaces parallel play. At the same time, physical aggression peaks and then declines during the preschool period. Some same-sex play groups appear now, and there is sex typing of toy choice, too.

One way to think of this period is in terms of consolidation. The major breakthroughs in language and cognition at 18–24 months usher in whole collections of new skills and opportunities. But it takes the child three to four years to master the new skills completely. It's as if the child had discovered a whole new territory which is fascinating and marvelous to explore but which takes years to map thoroughly. It is this "mapping" that takes place during the preschool period.

Another way to look at the preschooler—one which is much more obvious to parents—is in terms of the child's striving for independence. He can get around in his world much better than he could before, and he wants the freedom and opportunity to go his own way. It is this element of the period that Erikson emphasizes in his stages of autonomy versus shame and doubt and initiative versus guilt, both of which he thought occurred during this time.

It's important to realize, though, that the advances in language and cognitive skill, and the push for independence, are by no means separate from one another. Among other things, they combine to influence the form of the child's attachment behavior. When language is rudimentary or nonexistent and the child's locomotion is poor, then clinging, touching, holding, crying, and standing near are just about the only stress-

Figure 15.4 Peers become much more important during the early years of the 2- to 6-year-span. Childrens' groups usually include both boys and girls, but in the later years same-sex play groups become more obvious.

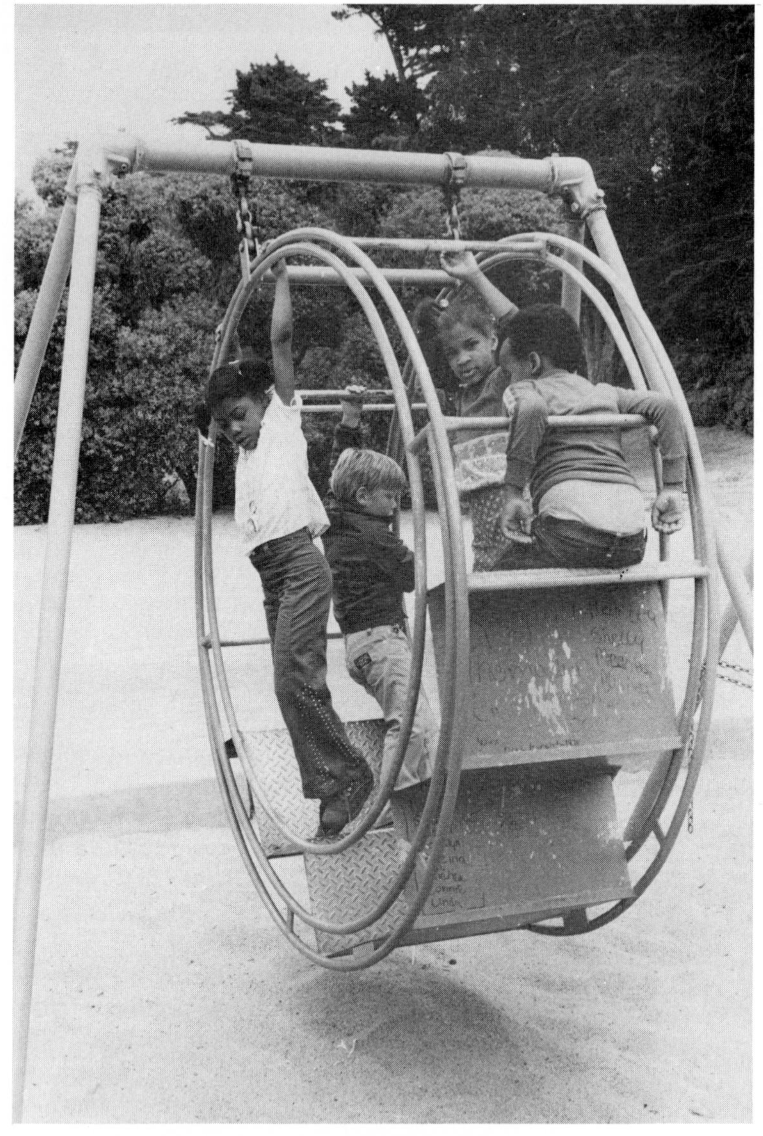

related attachment behaviors available to the child. But as language becomes more skillful, he becomes able to stay in touch with adults and peers around him in new ways. He can call to his mother, "Mommy are you still there?" or ask for attention, "Hey Dad, come and see my pictures." The attachment may be no less strong, but it can be maintained in a greater variety of ways and at greater physical distances. So the child's world broadens both because he can move around so much better and because his language and cognitive skills make it possible for him to move around and still stay in contact.

The new language and cognitive skills and the increased encounters with the world that go with them also clearly have some impact on the child's developing self-concept and sex-role identity. The child now understands that there is a "self," a continuing physical entity. And he can now understand the things that other people say about him, the gender labels that are used, and the comments others make about his skills or difficulties. This information, along with his own explorations and conclusions about himself, all enter into the developing self-concept.

All of these changes make significant new demands on the parents. They must adjust to a child who is demanding far greater independence and who may appear to be far less attached to or interested in being near them. Aggression among peers increases, and the child may begin to express his displeasure toward the parent with aggression, too. This is difficult for many parents to handle, but most parent–child pairs do work out a "modus operandi" by age 4 or 5; so a new level of equilibrium is achieved. The child seems to achieve a cognitive equilibrium as well. She has taken the preoperational skills about as far as she can; she has the new territory mapped well; and she is ready to open the doors to the new territory of concrete operations.

The Transition at Age 5–7

For most children, the next major transition occurs sometime between 5 and 7. Again it seems to be a cognitive shift that is the critical experience, although the fact that most children start school at this time is clearly of vital significance as well. (It's not accidental, in my opinion, that these two occur together. Schooling is begun at about age 5–7 in virtually every culture, presumably because of some recognition that children of that age are now "ready" for the demands of school.) What we know about the effects of schooling suggests that going to school is not necessary for the child to make the transition to concrete operations, but it does seem to speed up the process.

From the child's perspective, new cognitive vistas are opening up as he begins to work out the powerful new cognitive skills Piaget describes as operations, such as addition or multiplication. He learns to use language in a new way as well, such as in helping to remember things, and he can see and deal with new relationships among people and objects. Pretty heady stuff. When he goes off to school, he may be separated from his family for the first time for such a lengthy period and must adjust to a large peer group. Demands are made on him to sit quietly, to concentrate, and to work within a new set of rules.

Figure 15.5 **Children from age 6–12 spend a major portion of their time in school, coping with the developmental task that Erikson calls "industry versus inferiority." There are enormous cognitive gains made during these years, not only in school skills but also in basic logic.**

For children who have been in day care or preschool, some of these challenges are faced at younger ages. But the heavy cognitive demands of elementary school and the increased rules are new for nearly all children.

All of these changes occurring within a relatively short space of time create stress for the child. His ability to adapt is strained; and he may get more colds, show sleep disturbances, lose weight, or have other physical symptoms. But in emphasizing these signs of stress, I don't want to lose sight of the fact that there is real excitement at this time for most children. It is marvelous to be able to do all those things—to discover that you can play tic tac toe with your dad and beat him because you can understand the strategy or to learn how to recognize and draw letters.

I can remember both the joyous and the stressful parts of this period very clearly. When I learned to read enough to make out the signs along the streets, I insisted on reading every one of them out loud. I was terribly proud of my accomplishment; but even more, I was delighted to find out what all the mysterious hieroglyphics meant. (No doubt I drove my parents slightly mad in the process.) But it was during the same period, or a little later (about age 7), that I "ran away from home"—to the local park.

The Child from 6 to 12 Years

Amanda is 6 and has just started first grade. She thinks school is the greatest thing since sliced bread and is completely delighted to

Table 15.5 The Child from 6 to 12: A Summary

The physical child	The thinking child	The social child
Physical growth continues at a steady pace, without big spurts until puberty, which normally begins toward the end of this period (especially for girls). Gross motor skills continue to improve, so that the child in this age group can ride a bike, play ball, and do other tasks that require substantial coordination. Full adult levels of visual and auditory acuity are also reached during these years, and the child becomes better able to focus her attention.	This is the period Piaget calls concrete operations. The child develops skill with all the "operations," which include mathematical operations like addition and subtraction. These things can now be done in the head as well as on paper. The child also grasps conservation and reversibility, becomes able to reason inductively, and generally becomes, over these years, a fairly logical person. The early stages of moral reasoning are apparent during this period, too.	This is the period Freud called "latency" because sexual interests seem to be largely submerged. Peers become very important, but nearly all peer groups are same-sex groups. Children are exploring and learning their sex roles, with boys more narrowly focused on male models than girls are. At this age, there are more girls interested in boys' activities than the reverse. Attachments to parents are less visible but presumably still exist. New attachments to individual friends develop.

be learning to read. She is a child of high intensity, though, and sometimes gets frustrated because things don't go fast enough, or because her friends don't do what she wants. She is fascinated by bugs and other creatures, can play checkers with her Dad now, and is a little bit snooty with her little sister (age 3) who can't do all those things yet. She has also grown an inch and a half in the past six months, and suddenly looks quite differently proportioned.

Amanda and her parents went through some stormy times before she reached this point. She was anxious, angry, excited, and frustrated a lot of the time when she was about 5. But having weathered the transition, she and her parents are now embarked on another long period of "consolidation," of mapping new territory, developing new types of transactions, new rules for the game. As usual, I've summarized the interlocking changes of these years in a table (see Table 15.5).

The cognitive growth during this period is striking. The child moves from primitive concrete operations to full use of inductive logic within this six-year span. She also acquires vital academic tools, such as reading, writing, and basic mathematics.

But these are not the only important changes. Freud talks about this as the "latency" period, as if nothing much was happening; but as you have seen in my earlier discussions of peer relationships and self-concept, this is an important time. Friendships are formed, and ways of playing and working with others are discovered and practiced. Children's leadership status and popularity with peers are also established during this age period (and are hard to change later), and important sex-role learning goes on as well. Again, the word "consolidation" may be appropriate for this period, particularly in the area of social interactions. The patterns are established at 6 and 7, but they are practiced and honed during the remainder of the elementary school years. More important, the child grows steadily in independence during this period, both because he has more abilities—he can get to the library on the bus by himself, for example—and because the parents are more willing to allow him to tackle new tasks on his own.

In many ways, this is a quiet time, as Freud perceived. But it is not at all an empty time. A great deal is happening, but the changes are perhaps more subtle than those we saw in the preschooler or will see in the adolescent.

The 12-Year Transition: Puberty

Some time around age 11 to 13 (earlier for some girls) the pleasant equilibrium of the elementary school child is lost and a new transition begins. The single event which is most critical in ushering in this transition is puberty—that complex collection of physical changes that begins at 9 or 10 for girls and at 12 or 13 for boys. Sharply increased levels of both growth hormones and sex hormones are produced in the body, stimulating rapid physical growth as well as physical sexual maturity.

But the physical changes are not the only ones that are significant at this transition. The final level of cognitive functioning, formal operations, begins to emerge in most children; peer interactions change markedly toward mixed-sex groups and heterosexual pairs; schooling changes, with most children moving from elementary school to junior high school or to some kind of "middle school" in which there are new academic expectations, new responsibilities, and independence; parent–child interactions change, too, both because parents expect more of the now nearly adult in their midst and because the teenager demands greater freedom. This is both a heady and a potentially explosive mixture. At the very least, it disturbs the equilibrium and throws the child into a transition or a "crisis" of some kind.

While it is clear descriptively that all these changes occur at about the same time, the links among them are still largely unknown. In particular, we do not know much about the relationships between hormonal changes and cognitive changes. There are a *few* hints, though, that the physical and cognitive changes could be linked. Deborah Waber, whose 1977 study I men-

Figure 15.6 At adolescence, the search for identity is a dominant theme. The young person must grapple with an occupational identity and a sexual identity. In addition, there are changes in intellectual abilities, in moral judgment, and, of course, in physical maturity that all occur during these years.

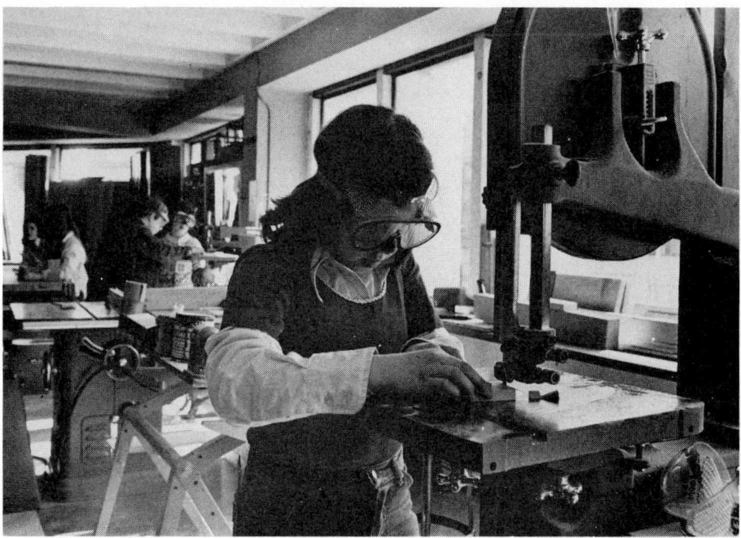

tioned briefly in Chapter 9, has given us some of the most provocative information. She found that teenagers who were early developers were poorer at spatial abilities and better at verbal abilities. In contrast, late-puberty young people were better at spatial tasks and relatively less good at verbal tasks. These findings suggest that the hormones that flood the system during adolescence may affect brain functioning or organization in particular ways. The fact that boys generally go through puberty later than girls do may then help to explain why they are often better at spatial ability tasks than girls are.

Still, the links between the physical changes and the mental changes are pretty fuzzy. We all go through puberty, but many of us do not achieve formal operations. Why is that? Are the two changes unrelated? We don't know, and more research on the connections between physical and cognitive change is clearly needed.

The link between puberty and modification of peer interactions, however, is not speculative. The hormonal changes of puberty awaken (or reawaken, in Freud's view) sexual drives that have been quiescent during elementary school. Freud, Erikson, and other psychoanalytically oriented theorists argue that this new surge of sexual energy reactivates all the old problems—all the unfinished business of the earlier tasks or stages. Whether this is true or not, it is clear that sexual interest at this age period focuses more and more on opposite-sex peers. So the same-sex peer groups that almost totally dominate elementary school interactions are transformed into mixed groups.

Demands for independence, so common among adolescents in our society, are also linked to pubertal changes. The adolescent is, in fact, sexually an adult, or at least capable of conceiving and bearing children. It is quite natural that the teenager would expect other privileges and responsibilities of adult status as well. In many cultures around the world (and in earlier centuries in our own society), that's exactly what happens: The 14- or 15-year-old is an adult in nearly all senses, with adult work responsibilities as well as sexual freedom. But in our society, the several elements of the adult role are not all acquired at the same time. This "discontinuity," as Ruth Benedict called it many years ago (Benedict, 1938), adds to the stress of this transition.

The Young Person from 12 to 20

Henry is a somewhat shy, sensitive, and studious young man. He is taking a college preparatory course, likes physics and math, and is clearly excited about school and what he is learning. He doesn't feel particularly close to any of his teachers, feeling that most of them are strict and sometimes arbitrary and distant. . . . Henry's father is a mechanic—and an alcoholic. Henry feels little relationship with his father and portrays him as a man who, when he is home, "cusses and yells" and makes everyone's life difficult. . . . It is Henry's older brother who has mainly filled the guiding parental role for him. . . . [Henry also has] several close friends with whom he shares his sports activities. He feels that, above all, a friend should be "a helping hand—when someone's in trouble, help them out the best you can."

(Josselson, Greenberger & McConochie, 1977, pp. 38–39)

Table 15.6 The Young Person from 12 to 20: A Summary

The physical person	The thinking person	The social person
Puberty is completed during this period, with *widely* varying rates for both onset and duration of the pubertal changes. Physical growth spurts, and the young person's final height is achieved. Full sexual maturity is reached. There are few other changes in perceptual skills during these years.	Formal operations develop for many young people, but not all, just as principled levels of morality are reached by some, but not all. These two themes are related: Formal operational thinking seems to be necessary but not sufficient for principled levels of morality. The formal operational teenager can reason deductively and generate previously unseen possibilities.	Peer groups become mixed-sex rather than same-sex groups, with individual couples appearing some time during these years for most teenagers. Early maturity contributes to greater popularity among peers during these years. The young person must face Erikson's dilemma of identity versus role confusion, finding both an occupational and a sexual identity. Sex roles are more clearly differentiated during this period, and sex stereotyping is at its strongest, especially among boys.

Henry is an eleventh grader, well into the period I'm talking about here. He is obviously coping pretty well with the problem of defining his occupational identity and has close friends; but he isn't dating yet, and his sexual identity is still fuzzy. He has passed through the transition of puberty but is now struggling with the tasks of adolescence. The summary of changes that take place during this period is in Table 15.6.

Over the past few decades, it has been common to talk about adolescence as a period of "storm and stress," full of upheaval. Many parents dread their children's oncoming adolescence, expecting severe tension. Of course, the transition of puberty does usher in changes; teenagers must work out new rules, new ways of interacting with parents and with one another. But once the transition has been accomplished, this is not a terrifically stormy period for most adolescents. They settle into a fairly stable pattern of family and peer relationships, just as they did between age 6 and 12. Some are popular and some are not; some are studious and some are not; some are involved in athletics, and so on. But for each child, a pattern is developed that continues during the teen years.

What is new at this age is the need to look to the *future* as well as dealing with the present. For the first time, the teenager must consider the ramifications of full independence—getting a job, marrying, raising a family. It is the prospect of these future tasks that may force the adolescent into confronting the problem of **identity,** which Erikson sees as the major dilemma of the period.

The so-called "identity crisis" of youth is not the very beginning of the sense of identity. The 6- or 8-year-old has a concept of self; even younger children see themselves as continuing to exist. But during adolescence, the young person must test the previously developed self-concept against the demands of adolescence and face the future demands of adulthood. Most specifically, the teenager must face the need to find an occupation that will fit with what she knows about herself and what is valued by those around her. To make such a selection involves rethinking old assumptions and questioning parental values. Do I *really* want to be a doctor, or does that only seem logical because my father is a doctor? What do doctors do? Is that what I want to spend my life doing? Do I want to spend the next 20 years as a wife and mother, with no out-of-the-home job? Will that satisfy my needs and use my talents?

Many of the identity issues are not resolved until the late teens or early twenties—a period Kenneth Keniston (1970) calls **youth,** to distinguish it from adolescence and from later adulthood. But the work of James Marcia (1966, 1976) and others, which I mentioned in Chapter 12, does suggest that for most young people, there is a rough progression from a diffuse, nonquestioning period, through a period of questioning and doubt (which Marcia calls **moratorium**), to a final step of identity formation when the issues are at least temporarily resolved and the youth commits himself to an occupational path, to a particular ideology, and to particular sexual and moral values. Some young people sidestep this progression by opting for the values and life-styles of their parents, without questioning—an identity status Marcia calls **foreclosure.** But most adolescents and youth go through at least some period of questioning.

The task of identity formation is not isolated from all the other changes happening from 12 to 20. There are several studies that show that the teenager's success at forming a clear new identity is related both to his cognitive development and to the level of moral reasoning he uses. Specifically, the young person who has moved into formal operations has a somewhat easier time developing a clear identity (Bourne, 1978). Similarly, Marvin Podd (1972) found that those youth who had achieved a principled level of moral reasoning (stages 5 or 6) were most likely to have also achieved a stable identity.

These studies tell us that an individual young person tends to move along three developmental lines at about the same rate —from concrete to formal operations, from conventional to principled moral reasoning, and from diffuse to stable identity. But they don't tell us which tail is wagging the dog. Is some kind of formal operations reasoning *necessary* for the teenager to face the identity crisis successfully? The sort of questioning and doubting, reassessment and reexamination of values that go with the first steps of the identity crisis seem to demand the analytic abilities of formal operational reasoning. But we don't have the longitudinal studies that would tell us which came first. Similarly, we don't know whether identity achievement helps to make more mature kinds of moral reasoning possible or whether it works the other way around. Podd found that there were a few young adults in his study who had diffuse identities but who still used principled moral reasoning, but there were also a few who had achieved an identity and were reasoning at stages 1 or 2 of Kohlberg's moral reasoning stages.

Obviously, the connections among these three lines of development need to be studied further. All I can tell you at this stage is that the young person seems to move at about the same rate on all three. What is striking about all three changes, though, is that they all require the youth to go through a period of disequilibrium—of questioning old values or old strategies—in order to achieve the later, more elaborated forms of thinking, moral reasoning, or individual identity. It may be this pervasive questioning and doubting that gives the period of adolescence and youth the appearance of "storm and stress" so many authors have emphasized.

A Final Point: The Joy of Development

I want to finish this chapter—and the book—by reminding you of something I said at the very beginning. In the midst of all the "crises" and "transitions" and "readjustments," there is a special *joyous* quality to development. When a child masters a new skill, she is not just pleased, she is delighted and will repeat that new skill at length, quite obviously getting vast satisfaction from it. Daniel, at 6 months, showed this sense of joy in his "push ups." A 5-year-old I know learned to draw stars and drew them on everything in sight, including paper, walls, clothes, and napkins. It was so much *fun* to draw stars. A 10-year-old who learns to do cartwheels will delightedly display this new talent to anyone who will watch and will practice endlessly.

I am convinced that this "Oh wow, I can do it!" sense does not desert us when we become adults. I can think of many kinds of joy-in-development times in my own adult years, including the first time I ran 10 miles (at age 39) and the first time I figured out why I got angry whenever someone corrected me. There is joy, too, on the parents's side of the parent–child

Figure 15.8 The joy of discovery!

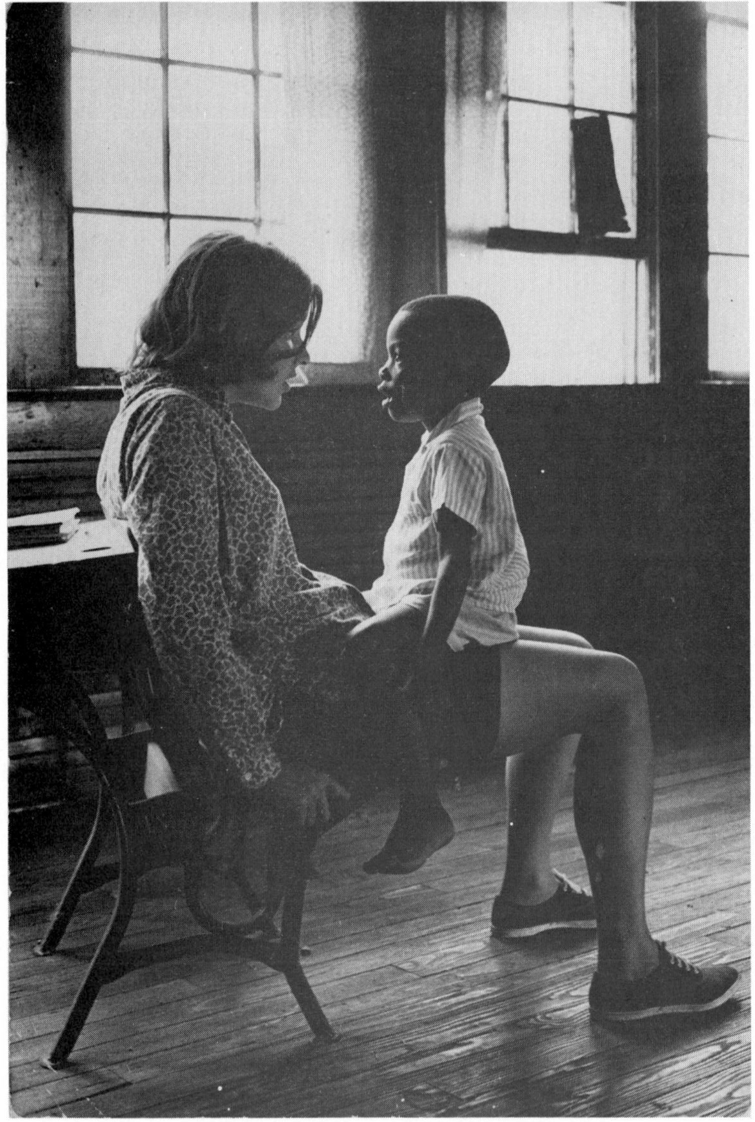

developmental process—joy in seeing your child smile at you for the first time or take his first step, joy when a transition has been successfully weathered and your child once again spontaneously gives you a hug instead of a whine. The whole developmental process is very hard work, but it is also enormously exciting, both for the child and for those who live with and love her.

Summary

1. The years of childhood and youth can be organized into a series of "stages," with "transitions" between each major period. The transitions involve changes in status, role, or physical capacities. The periods of equilibrium between transition points are generally focused around major developmental tasks.
2. People in transition, young children as well as teenagers, often show signs of behavioral disorganization. This is a normal aspect of transition.
3. The infant from birth to 2 months operates mainly on reflex, with "primitive" neurological structures dominating. The transition at two months involves major changes in neurological functioning.
4. From 2 to 8 months, the infant develops more motor skills, becomes much more social, and begins to show some signs of attachment. The transition at about 8 months is marked by the infant's ability to crawl and this single strong attachment.
5. From 8 to 18 months, the infant completes the sensorimotor period, begins to talk, develops attachments to several people, and shows signs of interest in other children. The transition at 18 months is marked by the beginning of the child's ability to manipulate internal representations.
6. From 18 months to 6 years, the preschooler consolidates the earlier gains, with major changes in cognitive skills, language, and social interactions. The child can classify, learns the rudiments of a sex role, and has some ability to take other perspectives. Peers become important. The transition at about age 6 involves a shift from preschool to school child and from preoperational to concrete operational thinking.
7. The "latency" period from 6 to 12 is focused heavily on the tasks of school and on development of friendships and solid peer interactions. Concrete operations are developed; the child becomes able to reason inductively.
8. The transition at age 12 (approximately) is triggered by the physical changes of puberty, along with changes in cognitive functioning and the change in status that goes with leaving elementary school. There are also changes in sex roles that follow from the physical changes of puberty.
9. The period from 12 to 20 is focused not only on the expansion of the formal operations skills and the new social skills, but on the development of a clear identity.
10. Throughout all the transitions and consolidation periods, children and young people experience excitement, joy, and pleasure from successfully mastering developmental tasks.

Suggested Readings

Many of the books I have suggested in earlier chapters are relevant here as well. But let me also suggest several books that give the flavor of particular ages.

Brazelton, T. B. Infants and mothers. Differences in development. New York: Dell, 1969.
This isn't a new book, but it is excellent and still extremely relevant. If you have a newborn child or plan to have a child, I highly recommend this book. Brazelton follows three children through their first year and comments on the changes.

Brazelton, T. B. Toddlers and parents. New York: Dell, 1974.
This is the companion book to the infancy book; it covers children through about age 3 and is just as good. Lots of specific examples and lots of very sensitive advice.

Murphy, L. B., & Moriarty, A. E. Vulnerability, coping and growth. New Haven: Yale University Press, 1976.
This isn't a book about a particular age group, but it deals with a set of issues I have come to see as extremely important. There are many interesting case studies of children followed from infancy through adolescence.

Appendix: Answering Questions

In Chapter 1, I described very briefly the three main strategies for answering questions about development: watching people, asking people, and doing experiments. Let me give you more detail about each of these. In addition, I want to say a bit more about how to interpret the results of research.

Watching People

A great many questions developmental psychologists are interested in can be answered straightforwardly by watching people in natural situations or in specially arranged settings. For example, if you want to know if boys smile more than girls, you could observe the faces of a large number of boys and girls and count their smiles. If you were interested in knowing how teenagers spend their time, you could follow several around for days and keep track of what they did. If you wanted to know about the vocabulary of 2-year-olds, you could listen to and record the language of a number of children. Any of these questions could probably be answered with other techniques, but observation is a good place to start.

Basic Observational Techniques

Generally speaking, observational techniques run from the very general or unfocused type in which you try to observe everything happening to highly focused observations, which may involve looking at, or looking for, only one or two behaviors. Ei-

Figure A.1 Although there are at least four major types of observation, some of them are used infrequently in developmental research. The most common types are the focused observation in natural and in contrived situations.

	Amount of Focus	
Place of Observation	Unfocused: Look at everything	Focused: Watch only certain things
Natural Situation	e.g., "specimen description." Might observe one person over period of time, or groups of children such as day care vs. home-reared.	e.g., observe aggression of nursery school-aged children in nursery school or at home.
Special or "contrived" situation	Not so often done, but could set up special room for mothers with their toddlers and observe all aspects of behavior.	e.g., observe facial expressions of subjects watching selected films or observe attachment behaviors of children in strange situation (or equivalent).

ther type of observation can be done in natural settings—in which you watch people doing their normal things in their normal places—or in more contrived situations, in which you create special circumstances or special environments. If you combine these two aspects of the observation, you get something like Figure A.1.

In the "unfocused-natural" type of observation, one basic technique is called a *specimen description*, advocated particularly by Roger Barker and Herbert Wright (1951). In this strategy, the observer attempts to record as much as possible of what a single subject does over a period of days or weeks. Barker and Wright, for example, wrote an entire book about *One Boy's Day* (1951). In this type of observation, the observer must be deliberately unselective in what he or she watches or writes down; you have to try to set aside your own preconceived notions and write down what *happened*, not what you thought it meant.

As you might guess, this sort of observation is relatively rare. Still, it has its advantages, particularly at the early stages of your thinking about some subject, when you want to get a general "feel" for a given group of people or for a particular kind of situation.

A much more common type of observation is the focused observation in a natural situation. In this technique, we are no

Table A.1 Some Examples of Scoring Categories Used in a Study of Mother–Infant Interaction

Infant behaviors scored	Maternal behaviors scored
Explores toy	Looks at baby
Explores own body	Mutual regard between mother and baby
Explores other person's body	Holds infant
Vocalizes, nondistress (for example, gurglings & cooing sounds)	Touches infant passively
Vocalizes, distress (for example, crying)	Vocalizes to infant
Looks at mother	Vocalizes after infant has made a nondistress sound
Looks at other person	Vocalizes after infant has cried
	Imitates the baby's sound
	Soothes infant
	Smiles at infant
	Provides toy to baby
	Feeds infant

Source: Adapted from Yarrow, Rubenstein & Pederson, 1975, p. 190.

longer trying to write down everything that happens. Instead, we are deliberately selective in what we observe and record, that is, we watch only those things that are relevant for the question we are asking. Usually, researchers who do this kind of observational study develop specific categories of behavior, such as "smiles" or "frowns" or "initiates conversation," and then count how many times each of these behaviors occurs. Table A.1 gives an example of some of the observational categories used by Leon Yarrow and his colleagues (Yarrow, Rubenstein & Pederson, 1975) in a study of mother–infant interaction. They observed each baby and mother in their own home, over a period of about three hours, using a procedure called *time sampling*. The observer would watch the mother and infant for 30 seconds and then would take 60 seconds to write down the types of behavior that had occurred. These 90-second cycles were then repeated for the three-hour observation. This is *very* hard work!

This same type of observation, with predetermined categories of behavior to be counted or described, can be used in an enormous variety of situations. It has the advantage of guaranteeing that you will get the same kind of information about each subject; the disadvantage is that you may miss interesting things about the subject's behavior because it doesn't fit into the categories you are scoring.

Both these same general techniques—the narrative record and the more focused observation—can be used in contrived settings as well. As you have seen throughout the book, this has been done fairly often in studies of children interacting with parents. For example, Mary Ainsworth and her colleagues have observed mothers and infants in the "strange situation" in order to measure attachment (Ainsworth, Blehar, Waters & Wall, 1978). In studies of my own on the origins of cognitive skills in children, I had parents teach their child a specific task and then observed the quality of their teaching (Bee, Van-Egeren, Streissguth, Nyman & Leckie, 1969).

The major advantage of the contrived situation is that every subject is seen in the *same* environment. And by selecting the special environment carefully, the researcher can increase the likelihood that the subject will show the sort of behavior that is being studied. Of course, the disadvantage is that it is not a "natural" situation, and you can't be sure that the same people would behave in the same way in less-contrived situations or in their own homes with no one watching them.

Problems with Observation

As a method of obtaining information, observation quite clearly has many strengths; and for understanding some complex interactions with people, it is probably the best method available. But there are problems with observation, too.

First, there is the problem of objectivity. Particularly in the less-focused observations, there is a great deal of judgment involved. What do you notice? What do you write down? You may try to note everything, but that's clearly impossible. So there is danger that you will unwittingly impose your own biases onto what you see. The more-focused observations, where the observer notes only particular, predetermined behaviors, have been devised to get around this problem.

But even with focused observations, it is not always easy to get two different observers to record the same thing. This is the problem of *objectivity* (often called the *reliability*) of the observation and is usually handled by having two different people score or count the same events. You'd think that if the categories to be observed were carefully defined in advance and if both observers watched the same thing, they would agree on what had happened. When they do, we say that we have high *interobserver agreement*. Unfortunately, what we often get is not agreement but disagreement. If the behavior has occurred very rapidly, the two observers may miss part of the action. Even slow-paced activities may look different from different sides of the room or be interpreted differently by two different people. Researchers using any kind of observational method spend a great deal of effort to make sure their techniques have good interobserver agreement, but it is always a potential source of trouble.

Still a third problem is the influence the observers' presence has on the behavior of the people being observed. If we want to know how Guatemalen children interact with one another and solve problems in their own environment, we are unlikely to find out much by taking middle-class American college student observers into the heart of their villages with clipboards and stopwatches. This is an extreme example, of course, but the problem remains in *any* observation.

A fourth problem, illustrated by the time sampling technique Yarrow used, is that the observer simply can't watch all the time—she has to take some time to record what has happened. Each time she looks down to write, she is missing something that is going on. This becomes especially critical if you are trying to observe long sequences of behavior.

Current Solutions to Observation Problems

Two new techniques—the use of videotape and computer linkups—solve *some* of these problems.

Videotaping of behavior is now becoming quite common, particularly in studies of infants and parent-infant interactions. Barry Brazelton and his associates (Brazelton, Koslowski & Main, 1974), for example, have used videotapes to study "reciprocity" in mothers and infants. Dan Stern (1974) has used the same process to study the development of mutual gaze between baby and adult. In both cases, the videotapes were viewed repeatedly, and subtle kinds of *non*verbal behavior were studied.

Videotaping does solve some problems. It virtually eliminates the problem of interobserver agreement, for instance, since you have a permanent record to go back to and it permits very fine-grained analysis. It is also unbelievably time-consuming and expensive.

Another new strategy is to have observers "type" codes for the behavior they observe directly onto a keyboard that is hooked up with a computer. Each key or combination of keys on the keyboard stands for a particular behavior (for example, "smiles" or "picks up infant"). Once the observer has reached a high level of proficiency at this technique, she can watch continuously while "typing" the scores. This has several advantages. First, since the observer types only when something happens, the computer tape contains information about silences and gaps in the behavior as well as about activity. Second, the sequences in which things happened are recorded and can be analyzed. Finally, having the information go directly onto computer tape saves the time-consuming steps of data coding and keypunching for computer analyses. The problem again is that this is an expensive procedure, and it takes a good deal of training for an observer to become sufficiently skilled to use the system accurately. Despite the difficulties, however, more and more researchers are using this method, since it allows us to look at interactions between people in much more detail than has been possible before.

Asking People

Observation is extremely time-consuming. In part because of this, and because of the difficulty in obtaining good reliability, psychologists have often preferred to ask people instead of watching them. Since babies and young children can't talk very well and can't read the questions on questionnaires, interviews and written instruments have not been widely used in developmental research with children. But both have been used to study parents' attitudes toward and interactions with their children.

Interviews

Twenty years ago, interviewing with parents was a common technique for finding out about "child-rearing techniques." Robert Sears, Eleanor Maccoby, and Harry Levin (1957) used this technique in a major study of the child-rearing antecedents of such behaviors as dependence and aggression. Sears and his colleagues (Sears, Rau & Alpert, 1965) used a similar interview with mothers as part of their study of moral development in children. Interviews with parents to assess their feelings toward and discipline techniques with their children were also part of the methods in most early longitudinal studies (Kagan & Moss, 1962; Bayley & Schaefer, 1964).

Most of these interviews were *structured*, that is, there was a fixed list of questions, and every subject was asked the same questions in the same order. But the subject could—and often did—answer at length. The researchers who used this technique then had to turn those long answers into some sort of score, such as "permissiveness" of child rearing.

Questionnaires

The alternative to the interview is to develop a questionnaire with a more-limited choice of answers for the subject. Or a researcher can use existing questionnaires developed by psychologists interested in specific aspects of personality or behavior. For example, Craig Ramey and his colleagues (Ramey,

Farran & Campbell, 1979), in a recent study of mother–infant interaction, used a questionnaire called the Parental Attitudes Research Inventory (PARI), originally developed by Schaefer and Bell (1958). From this questionnaire, the researchers obtain scores on three broad dimensions: authoritarian control, hostility-rejection, and democratic attitudes. Parents who differ in these dimensions can then be observed directly with their infants and the infants can be tested individually as well.

In studies of child development, both interviews and questionnaires have been most widely used with parents, rather than directly with children. But both are currently being used fairly frequently with teenagers as well. For example, Lawrence Kohlberg's assessment of a young person's stage of moral development (see Chapter 13) is done with a structured interview. James Marcia's measure of identity status among teenagers (see Chapter 12) is also based on a semistructured interview. Forms of interviews are also used with younger children when the experimenter wants to probe the child's understanding of some specific concept, such as perspective taking or sex roles.

In general, whenever we want to know something about an aspect of a person that is not readily visible, such as her attitudes or concepts, an interview or a questionnaire is a reasonable strategy.

Experimental Procedures

When we observe people or ask them questions, ordinarily we are not intervening in any way; we're not trying to change the child's or adult's behavior in some fashion. Rather, we're trying to find out something about how that person behaves or thinks — to answer *what* questions. But experiments are designed to answer both what and why questions.

The Basic Technique

Ideally in an experiment, the experimenter seeks to "hold constant" all factors except the one that he wants information about. Suppose you want to know whether or not reinforcement for aggression will lead to an increase in aggressiveness. One way to go about solving this problem would be to determine how often each of a series of children is reinforced for aggression at home, either by observing directly in a series of homes or by questioning the parents. Then the children would be observed, either at home or in a school setting.

This procedure seems reasonable for many purposes, as it involves natural settings and may tell you something about child-rearing practices and their effects; but there are many uncontrolled variables. For example, you do not control what happens to the child in the school setting. Some children may be permitted to show quite a lot of aggression before the teacher steps in. Others may receive a reprimand from the teacher after only slight aggression. And there is equally little control over the amount of reinforcement or punishment at home, over the type of reinforcement, or over the consistency with which reinforcement or punishment is given for a particular behavior. Surely there is inconsistency in "real life"; and if we want to study what happens in "real life," the less-structured observational procedures will be the method of choice. But observing the full details of the total situation is so enormously complex that it will be difficult, if not impossible, to sort out the real "causes" of aggression. The alternative is to set up an experiment.

Suppose one of your hypotheses about the differences in aggression among children, drawn from learning theory, is that those who are rewarded for aggression will be more aggressive than those who are not rewarded. You want to look at this question under conditions in which you have control over the rewards given to the child. After you recruit a number of children to be in your study, you divide them—at random—into several groups. Children in one group are taken, individually, into a room with some toys that might invite aggression, such as a punching bag, a hammer, or a knife. The child is encouraged to play freely, and each time she shows any aggressive behavior with the toys, you say something like "Good" or "That's the right way to play." With another group of children, the same procedure is followed, except that nothing at all is said to the child about her play. This second group is usually called the *control group*. It is designed to tell something about how children behave if there is no intervention at all, so that the behavior of the *experimental group* can be compared with the behavior of the control group.

The next step is to devise a way to tell whether or not the treatment of the child has had any effect. One way to do so would be to observe children in the nursery school to see whether or not those who had been rewarded for aggression in the experiment showed more aggression in the natural setting than did children in the control group. But there are some problems with this approach. For example, different children will encounter very different experiences in nursery school that might influence how aggressively they play.

A better strategy for a good experiment would be to set up a standard test situation that all the children would undergo. One way would be to have each child, immediately after her original play with the toys, go into a room with another child (usually a child who has not participated at all) and see the two play a game together. If it turns out that during play the experimental group children are more aggressive than the control group, then we can conclude that reward for aggression has at least something to do with the levels of aggression that we see.

Crucial Features of Experiments

If you think about the experiment I have described, you may be able to extract some of the crucial features.

Control of Critical Variables The experimenter must have control over the critical or relevant aspects of the situation. Often this is described as the experimenter having *manipulated* some variable, such as the rewards for aggression.

One Variable at a Time Ordinarily, only one variable is manipulated (varied) at a time, although it is possible to design complex experiments in which several different features are changed.

Independent and Dependent Variables The aspect of the situation that the experimenter alters or controls is called the *independent variable*. The aspect of behavior that is measured—that is thought to change as a result of differences in the independent variable—is called the *dependent variable*. In the experiment on aggression, whether the child was rewarded or not for aggression is the independent variable. The amount of aggression in later play is the dependent variable.

Random Assignment of Subjects Subjects should be assigned randomly to the different treatment groups. In the case of the imaginary experiment on reward for aggression, the experimenter could flip a coin to determine which group each child would be assigned to.

Advantage of the Experimental Procedure

The major advantage of the experimental method is that it allows the researcher to have control over what happens; it permits you to ask quite specific questions about the *relationships* between things and about the effects of *changes* in the environment or in the learning conditions. By devising a series of experiments, we can begin to sort out the various forces at work in any given situation and to look at them one at a time.

Some Problems with the Experimental Method

The major drawback, of course, is that the experiment is always somewhat "artificial." In the "real world," forces don't act on us one at a time. This creates a problem of generalizing from the results of an experiment to the natural environment.

While that's true, it's not as insurmountable a problem as you might think. Most psychologists use experiments as a way of trying to understand the basic *principles* that underlie behavior. Once we think we have a grasp of those principles, we can turn to the problem of applying those principles to the more-complex circumstances of the "real world." A very good example of this is the case of the impact of television aggression on children. Basic research on observational learning has told us a lot about how children and adults learn from watching others perform new tasks. That gave us one of the underlying principles. The next step has been to apply the basic principles to the real-life situation of children watching violent TV. As I've already described in Chapter 11, recent naturalistic studies do show a link between the amount of TV watched and the likelihood of aggressiveness in real-life situations. The important point here is that the later naturalistic research was at least partly guided by the basic experiments on observational learning.

Interpreting Research Results

Once you have performed your experiment, made your observations, or asked your questions, you have some information. Now what do you do with it? What conclusions can you legitimately draw from it?

If all you want to do is to describe what people do in particular situations, you can use information from any of these three methods. That is, all these strategies can help answer the "what" question. If you observed in a natural setting, you may be able to provide basic descriptive information, such as how the interactions of mothers and children change as the child gets older, how mother–infant interaction is different with low-birth-weight infants than with full-term babies, or how 2-year-olds and 4-year-olds differ in their reaction to peer groups.

If you have used a questionnaire or an interview, you will also end up with descriptive data, such as the way children's self-concepts change over time or the attitudes of different groups of parents toward discipline, or equivalent.

Experiments, too, can yield descriptive information, such as the conditions under which a child may or may not be able to perform some task or the effects of increasing stress on a child's reaction to a stranger.

Descriptive information from any of these types of studies is often a vital first step for the understanding of basic developmental processes.

But what about the 'why" question? This moves us into the realm of *causal* relationships. We would like to be able to determine what causes a child's behavior. For answering this question, the various alternative techniques are not equally useful.

From observational and questionnaire studies, the best we can usually do is to discuss relationships among things. We may be able to say, for example, that children who are highly aggressive are more likely to have parents who say they are permissive toward aggression. But that is not the same as saying that permissiveness toward aggression *causes* aggression. All we know is that the two things occur together; we don't know whether one causes the other nor can we *ever* draw a causal statement from such an observation alone.

The statistic you will see in studies and textbooks describing such a relationship is a *correlation*. It is simply a number which can range from −1.00 to +1.00 that describes the strength of a relationship between two variables. A correlation of 0.00 indicates that there is no relationship between the variables. You might expect, for example, to find a 0.00 or nearly 0.00 correlation between the length of big toes and IQ. People with toes of all sizes have high IQs, and those with toes of all sizes have low IQs, too. A correlation of 1.00 or nearly 1.00 means that the two variables are closely related. The length of big toes is probably highly correlated, for instance, with shoe size—the bigger the toe, the bigger the foot. Negative correlations are a little harder to understand because they show that high scores (or big amounts) of something are related to low scores (or small amounts) of something else. There is a negative correlation, for example, between the number of calories you eat when you are on a diet and the number of pounds that you lose. The more you eat, the less you lose.

Perfect correlations (1.00 or −1.00) are not found in the real world, but correlations of 0.80 or 0.90 occur and they suggest very strong relationships between two variables. For example, the correlation between IQ test scores of identical twins is in this range (see Chapter 9). Knowing one twin's IQ, you can predict the other's IQ with considerable accuracy. Overall, the closer the correlation is to 1.00 (or −1.00), the stronger is the relationship between the two variables. Correlations of 0.50 or 0.60, which are fairly common in psychological research, suggest moderate degrees of relationship but with many variations or exceptions.

It is important to remember that correlations as descriptions of relationships, though interesting and suggestive of causes, cannot prove causes in themselves. A fairly silly example may make this clear. It is a fact that there is a correlation between the number of refrigerators sold each year since 1900 and the number of deaths from lung cancer. The more refrigerators sold, the more lung cancer. But neither you nor I would ever draw the conclusion from this correlation that the sale of refrigerators causes lung cancer. Rather, we would suspect that other factors in our environment have changed along with the increase in refrigerators, and that one or more of these factors is probably the cause of increased lung cancer.

The refrigerator example is an easy one because it is so clearly not a causal relationship. But we have to be careful about the way we interpret other findings. For example, it is a fact that the more "difficult" a child's temperament, the more likely he is to be punished by the parents. That is, there is a positive correlation between "difficultness" and punishment. But which causes which? Does the parent punish more because the child is more difficult? Or is the child more difficult because he is punished more? The correlation alone doesn't tell.

An experimental procedure, on the other hand, can often permit us to make causal statements. If we really hold everything constant except the one element that we manipulate, and if we see differences in behavior, we can be quite sure that the cause of the differences in behavior was our manipulation. If children who are rewarded for aggression in an experiment are more aggressive in free play than are children who are not rewarded for aggression, we can conclude that in this setting, previous rewards for aggression were the cause of the increase in aggressive play. Of course, that doesn't mean that *all* aggression is caused by a history of reinforcement. All the experiment tells us is that rewarding aggression may increase it under some conditions. We need to do other experiments to pin down other factors that may also influence aggression.

The point of this discussion is that drawing conclusions from any research is difficult. If you stick with the natural situation, you are unlikely to be able to disentangle cause and effect; if you choose more controlled experimentation, you will have difficulty saying how the behavior you observe in the experiment relates to what may happen in the natural situation. The best strategy is to combine the several techniques. Drawing conclusions from research, in fact, is nearly always a process of adding up findings from several studies done with several methods. If the same conclusion seems to hold up among different reseachers and across research strategies, then our confidence in that conclusion is increased.

How to Evaluate Research

In Chapter 1, I gave you a brief checklist for evaluating the quality of research, but let me now expand on some of the issues.

First, the type of research, whether primarily observational or experimental, does not in itself determine whether the research is good or bad. Which technique is best depends on the questions you are asking and the kind of conclusions you want to draw.

Second, if experimental research is done, it is crucial that the experimenter really does control the situation and has not made some major technical error. To give you an example from another field, I once read an agricultural study in which the experimenter wanted to know whether potatoes would grow better if hay were placed around them while they were growing or whether they'd do better with black plastic around them. Fine so far. But then, instead of using the same variety of potatoes for each treatment, he also varied the type of potato; so one variety was growing under hay and another was growing under black plastic. When he was all done, he couldn't tell whether differences in yield under the two conditions were the result of the variety of potato or the treatment he'd given. This example may sound silly, but it's from a real study. Equally badly designed research is to be found in the human development literature as well, so just because a piece of work is described as an "experiment" does not mean its results are necessarily gospel.

Third, just because a piece of research is new, it is not necessarily better than old research on the same question—there were many marvelous research studies done from the 1920s to the 1960s. It's easy to fall into the habit of putting greater value on the newer work, and that's not always appropriate.

The number of people studied or observed is a fourth important factor. There are some kinds of studies in which it makes sense to include only very small numbers of subjects for observation or clinical investigation. In many intervention studies of the effects of operant conditioning, for example, there is only one subject. A single child is observed before treatment, her reinforcement pattern is changed, and her behavior is observed afterward to see if it has changed. This observation tells us whether or not operant conditioning principles hold for this child and for this particular behavior. In other circumstances, however, you should beware of studies using very small numbers of subjects. We simply cannot generalize as well from a piece of research involving 6 children or adults as from research involving 60 or 600. This is especially true if the 6 are drawn from a select group (like a university nursery school), as they often are.

Finally, I need to say something here about your own personal experience. If you have children of your own or have been around children a good deal, it is terribly tempting to take your own experience as "the truth" and to ignore the findings from carefully controlled research when they don't agree with your own experience. Your experience may be valid, but it is based on a small sample of children under uncontrolled conditions, with your own biases influencing your observations. On the other hand, don't toss out your own observations, hunches, or conclusions. Use them as sources of hypotheses and see how they fit with existing theory and observation. If there is a disagreement between your "intuition" and research results, think about the possible biases in your own observations and about the quality and generalizability of the research, and then see if some kind of synthesis is possible.

Bibliography

Abraham, S.; Collins, G.; & Nordsieck, M. "Relationship of childhood weight status to morbidity in adults." Health Services and Mental Health Administration Health Reports, 1971, *86*, 273–284.

Abramovitch, R., & Grusec, J. E. "Peer imitation in a natural setting." Child Development, 1978, *49*, 60–65.

Achenbach, T. M. Research in developmental psychology: Concepts, strategies, methods. New York: The Free Press, 1978.

Achenbach, T. M. & Weisz, J. R. "A longitudinal study of developmental synchrony between conceptual identity, seriation, and transitivity of color, number, and length." Child Development, 1975, *46*, 840–848.

Adler, G. Studies in analytical psychology. New York: Norton, 1948.

Ahrens, R. "Beitrag zur entwicklun des physionomie und mimikerkennens." Z. F. Exp. U. Angew. Psychol., 1954, *2*, 599–633.

Ainsworth, M. D. S. "Attachment and dependency: A comparison." In J. L. Gewirtz (ed.), Attachment and dependency. Washington, D.C.: Winston, 1972.

Ainsworth, M. D. S.; Bell, S. M.; & Stayton, D. J. "Individual differences in strange situation behavior of one-year-olds." In H. R. Schaffer (ed.), The origins of human social relations. London: Academic Press, 1971.

Ainsworth, M. D. S.; Bell, S. M.; & Stayton, D. J. "Individual differences in the development of some attachment behaviors." Merrill-Palmer Quarterly, 1972, *18*, 123–143.

Ainsworth, M. D. S.; Blehar, M.; Waters, E.; & Wall, S. Patterns of attachment. Hillsdale NJ: Erlbaum, 1978.

Ainsworth, M. D. S., & Wittig, B. A. "Attachment and exploratory behavior of one-year-olds in a strange situation." In B. M. Foss (ed.), Determinants of infant behavior. (Vol. IV). London: Methuen, 1969.

Allport, G. W. Pattern and growth in personality. New York: Holt, 1961.

Almy, M.; Chittenden, E.; & Miller, P. Young children's thinking: Studies of some aspects of Piaget's theory. New York: Teachers College Press, 1966.

Amsterdam, B. "Mirror self-image reactions before age two." Developmental Psychobiology, 1972, *5*, 297–305.

Anastasiow, N. J., & Hanes, M. L. Language patterns of poverty children. Springfield IL: Thomas, 1976.

Angrist, S. S.; Mickelsen, R.; & Penna, A. N. "Sex differences in sex-role conceptions and family orientation of high school students." Journal of Youth and Adolescence, 1977, *6*, 179–186.

Anthony, E. J. "The behavior disorders of childhood." In P. H. Mussen (ed.), Carmichael's manual of child psychology. (Vol. 2, 3d ed.). New York: Wiley, 1970.

Appel, M. H. "The application of Piagetian learning theory to a science curriculum project." In M. H. Appel & L. S. Goldberg (eds.), Topics in cognitive development. (Vol. 1). New York: Plenum, 1977.

Arend, R.; Gove, F. L.; & Sroufe, L. A. "Continuity of individual adaptation from infancy to kindergarten: A predictive study of ego-resiliency and curiosity in preschoolers." Child Development, 1979, *50*, 950–959.

Asher, S. R.; Oden, S. L.; & Gottman, J. M. "Children's friendships in school settings." In L. G. Katz (ed.), Current topics in early childhood education. (Vol. 1). Norwood NJ: Ablex, 1977.

Bandura, A. Social learning theory. Englewood Cliffs NJ: Prentice-Hall, 1977.

Bandura, A., & Walters, R. H. Social learning and personality development. New York: Holt, 1963.

Bane, M. J., & Jencks, C. "Five myths about your IQ." Harper's, 1973, *246*, 28–40.

Barker, R. G., & Wright, J. F. One boy's day: A specimen record of behavior. New York: Harper & Row, 1951.

Barnard, K. B., & Eyres, S. Child health assessment, part 2. Results of the first twelve months of life. Washington, D.C.: U.S. Government Printing Office, 1979.

Barrett, D. E. "A naturalistic study of sex differences in children's aggression." Merrill-Palmer Quarterly, 1979, *25*, 193–203.

Baruch, G. K., & Barnett, R. C. "Implications and applications of recent research on feminine development." Psychiatry, 1975, *38*, 318–327.

Batter, B. S., & Davidson, C. V. "Wariness of strangers: Reality or artifact?" Journal of Child Psychology and Psychiatry, 1979, *20*, 93–109.

Baumrind, D. "Child care practices anteceding three patterns of pre-school behavior." Genetic Psychology Monographs, 1967, *76*, 43–88.

Baumrind, D. "Socialization and instrumental competence in young children." In W. W. Hartup (ed.), The young child: Reviews of research. (Vol. 2). Washington, D.C.: National Association for the Education of Young Children, 1972.

Baumrind, D. "A dialectical materialist's perspective on knowing social reality." In W. Damon (ed.), Moral development. San Francisco: Jossey-Bass, 1978.

Bayley, N. "Comparisons of mental and motor test scores for ages 1–15 months by sex, birth order, race, geographical location, and education of parents." Child Development, 1965, *36*, 379–411.

Bayley, N. Bayley scales of infant development. New York: Psychological Corporation, 1969.

Bayley, N. & Schaefer, E. S. "Correlations of maternal and child behaviors with the development of mental abilities: Data from the Berkeley Growth Study." Monographs of the Society for Research in Child Development, 1964, *29*, (Whole # 97).

Bearison, D., & Isaacs, L. "Production deficiency in children's moral judgments." Developmental Psychology, 1975, *11*, 732–737.

Beckwith, L., & Cohen, S. E. "Preterm birth: Hazardous obstetrical and postnatal events as related to caregiver–infant behavior." Infant Behavior and Development, 1978, *1*, 403–411.

Bee, H. L.; VanEgeren, L. F.; Streissguth, A. P.; Nyman, B. A.; & Leckie, M. S. "Social class differences in maternal teaching strategies and speech patterns." Developmental Psychology, 1969, *1*, 726–734.

Beez, V. "Influence of biased psychological reports on teacher behavior and pupil performance." Paper presented at the annual meeting of the American Psychological Association, San Francisco. 1978.

Bell, S. M. "The development of the concept of object as related to infant-mother attachment." Child Development, 1970, *41*, 291–311.

Belsky, J., & Steinberg, L. D. "The effects of day care: A critical review." Child Development, 1978, *49*, 929–949.

Benedict, R. "Continuities and discontinuities in cultural conditioning." Psychiatry, 1938, *1*, 161–167.

Bereiter, C., & Englemann, S. Teaching disadvantaged children in the preschool. Englewood Cliffs NJ: Prentice-Hall, 1966.

Bereiter, C., Hidi, S.; & Dimitroff, G. "Qualitative changes in verbal reasoning during middle and late childhood." Child Development, 1979, *50*, 142–151.

Berg, J. M. "Aetiological aspects of mental subnormality." In A. M. Clarke & A. D. B. Clarke (eds.), Mental deficiency. The changing outlook. New York: The Free Press, 1974.

Berndt, T. J. "Developmental changes in conformity to peers and parents." Developmental Psychology, 1979, *15*, 608–616.

Best, D. L.; Williams, J. E.; Cloud, J. M.; Davis, S. W.; Robertson, L. S.; Edwards, J. R.; Giles, H.; & Fowles, J. "Development of sex-trait stereotypes among young children in the United States, England, and Ireland." Child Development, 1977, *48*, 1375–1384.

Bianchi, B. D., & Bakeman, R. "Sex-typed affiliation preferences observed in preschoolers: Traditional and open school differences." Child Development, 1978, *49*, 910–912.

Biemiller, A. J. "The development of the use of graphic and contextual information in children learning to read." Reading Research Quarterly, 1970, *6*, 75–96.

Bijou, S. W., & Baer, D. M. Child development I. A systematic and empirical theory. New York: Appleton-Century-Crofts, 1961.

Binet, A., & Simon, T. The development of intelligence in children. Baltimore: Williams & Wilkins, 1916.

Birch, H. G., & Lefford, A. "Intersensory development in children." Monographs of the Society for Research in Child Development, 1963, *28*, (Whole # 89).

Birns, B., & Bridger, W. "Cognitive development and social class." In J. Wortis (ed.), Mental retardation and developmental disabilities. An annual review. (Vol. IX). New York: Brunner/Mazel, 1977.

Bissell, J. S. "Planned variation in Head Start and Follow Through." In J. C. Stanley (ed.), Compensatory education for children, ages 2 to 8. Baltimore: The Johns Hopkins University Press, 1973.

Blanchard, M., & Main, M. "Avoidance of the attachment figure and social-emotional adjustment in day-care infants." Developmental Psychology, 1979, *15*, 445–446.

Blatt, M., & Kohlberg, L. "The effects of classroom moral discussion upon children's level of moral judgment." Journal of Moral Education, 1975, *4*, 169–172.

Blehar, M. C.; Leiberman, A. F.; & Ainsworth, M. D. S. "Early face-to-face interaction and its relation to later infant-mother attachment." Child Development, 1977, *48*, 182–194.

Bloom, L. One word at a time. The Hague: Mouton, 1973.

Bloom, L. "Language development." In F. Horowitz (ed.), Review of child development research. (Vol. 4). Chicago: University of Chicago Press, 1975.

Borke, H. "Piaget's mountains revisited: Changes in the egocentric landscape." Developmental Psychology, 1975, *11*, 240–243.

Bourne, E. "The state of research on ego identity: A review and appraisal. Part I." Journal of Youth and Adolescence, 1978, *7*, 223–251.

Bower, T. G. R. "The visual world of infants." Scientific American, 1966, *215*, 80–92.

Bower, T. G. R. "Infant perception of the third dimension and object concept development." In L. B. Cohen & P. Salapatek (eds.), Infant Perception: From sensation to cognition. (Vol. 2). New York: Academic Press, 1975.

Bower, T. G. R. The perceptual world of the child. Cambridge MA: Harvard University Press, 1977.

Bowlby, J. Maternal care and mental health. Geneva: World Health Organization, 1951.

Bowlby, J. Attachment and loss. (Vol. 1). New York: Basic Books, 1969.

Brackbill, Y. "Obstetrical medication and infant behavior." In J. D. Osofaky (ed.), Handbook of infant development. New York: Wiley, 1979.

Bradley, R. H., & Caldwell, B. M. "Early home environment and changes in mental test performance in children from 6 to 36 months." Developmental Psychology, 1976, *12*, 93–97.

Bradley, R. H., & Caldwell, B. M. "Home Observation for Measurement of the Environment: A validation study of screening efficiency." American Journal of Mental Deficiency, 1977, *81*, 417–420.

Bradley, R. H., & Caldwell, B. M. "Screening the environment." American Journal of Orthopsychiatry, 1978, *48*, 114–129.

Braine, M. D. S. "The ontogeny of English phrase structure: The first phase." Language, 1963, *39*, 1–13.

Braine, M. D. S. "On two types of models of the internalization of grammars." In D. I. Slobin (ed.), The ontogenesis of grammar. New York: Academic Press, 1971.

Brainerd, C. J. "The stage question in cognitive development theory." The Behavioral and Brain Sciences, 1978, *2*, 173–213.

Braun, S. J., & Caldwell, B. M. "Emotional adjustment of children in day care who enrolled prior to or after the age of three." Early Child Development and Care, 1973, *2*, 13–21.

Brazelton, T. B. Infants and mothers. Differences in development. New York: Dell, 1969.

Brazelton, T. B. Toddlers and parents. New York: Dell, 1974.

Brazelton, T. B.; Koslowski, B.; & Main, M. "The origins of reciprocity: The early mother-infant interaction." In M. Lewis & L. A. Rosenblum (eds.), The effect of the infant on its caregiver. New York: Wiley, 1974.

Brenneis, D., & Lein, L. " 'You Fruithead': A socialinguistic approach to children's dispute settlement." In S. Ervin-Tripp and C. Mitchell-Kernan (eds.), Child discourse. New York: Academic Press, 1977.

Brody, E. B., & Brody, N. Intelligence: Nature, determinants and consequences. New York: Academic Press, 1976.

Bromwich, R. M. "Focus on maternal behavior in infant intervention." American Journal of Orthopsychiatry, 1976, *46*, 439–446.

Bronfenbrenner, U. "Developmental research, public policy, and the ecology of childhood." Child Development, 1974, *45*, 1–5.

Bronfenbrenner, U. "Toward an experimental ecology of human development." American Psychologist, 1977, *32*, 513–531.

Bronson, G. W. "The postnatal growth of visual capacity." Child Development, 1974, *45*, 873–890.

Brooks-Gunn, J. & Matthews, W. S. He and she. How children develop their sex role identity. Englewood Cliffs NJ: Prentice-Hall, 1979.

Broverman, I. K.; Broverman, D. M.; Clarkson, F. E.; Rosenkrantz, P. S.; & Vogel, S. R. "Sex-role stereotypes and clinical judgments of mental health." Journal of Consulting and Clinical Psychology, 1970, *34*, 1–7.

Broverman, I. K.; Vogel, S. R.; Broverman, D. M.; Clarkson, F. E.; & Rosenkrantz, P. S. "Sex-role stereotypes: A current appraisal." Journal of Social Issues, 1972, *28*, 59–78.

Brown, R. Social psychology. New York: The Free Press, 1965.

Brown, R. A first language: The early stages. Cambridge MA: Harvard University Press, 1973.

Brown, R. "Introduction." In C. E. Snow & C. A. Ferguson (eds.), Talking to children. Cambridge, England: Cambridge University Press, 1977.

Brown, R.; Cazden, C.; & Bellugi, U. "The child's grammar from I to III." In J. P. Hill (ed.), Minnesota symposium on child psychology. (Vol. 2). Minneapolis: University of Minnesota Press, 1969.

Brown, R., & Hanlon, C. "Derivational complexity and order of acquisition." In J. R. Hayes (ed.), Cognition and the development of language. New York: Wiley, 1970.

Bruner, J. S. "On cognitive growth." In J. S. Bruner, R. R. Olver, & P. M. Greenfield (eds.), Studies in cognitive growth. New York: Wiley, 1966.

Bullock, M., & Gelman, R. "Preschool children's assumptions about cause and effect: Temporal ordering." Child Development, 1979, *50*, 89–96.

Buss, A. H., & Plomin, R. A. Temperament theory of personality development. New York: Wiley, 1975.

Butler, N. R., & Goldstein, H. "Smoking in pregnancy and subsequent child development." British Medical Journal, 1973, *4*, 573–575.

Caldwell, B. M., & Bradley, R. H. Manual for the home observation for measurement of the environment. Little Rock: University of Arkansas, 1978.

Caldwell, B. M.; Wright, C. M.; Honig, A. S.; & Tannenbaum, J. "Infant day care and attachment." American Journal of Orthopsychiatry, 1970, *40*, 397–412.

Campos, J. J.; Langer, A.; & Krowitz, A. "Cardiac responses on the visual cliff in prelocomotor human infants." Science, 1970, *170*, 196–197.

Caron, A. J.; Caron, R. F.; & Carlson, V. R. "Infant perception of the invariant shape of objects varying in slant." Child Development, 1979, *50*, 716–721.

Carr, J. Young children with Down's syndrome: Their development, upbringing and effect on their families. London: Butterworth, 1975.

Cattell, R. The measurement of intelligence in infants and young children. New York: Psychological Corporation, 1940.

Caudill, W., & Frost, N. "A comparison of maternal care and infant behavior in Japanese-American, American, and Japanese families. In U. Bronfenbrenner & M. A. Mahoney (eds.), Influences on human development. Hinsdale IL: Dryden Press, 1972.

Cazden, C. Environmental assistance to the child's acquisition of grammar. Unpublished doctoral dissertation, Graduate School of Education, Harvard University, 1965.

Chall, J. S. Learning to read: The great debate. New York: McGraw-Hill, 1967.

Chase, W. P. "Color vision in infants." Journal of Experimental Psychology, 1937, *20*, 203–222.

Chomsky, N. Aspects of a theory of syntax. Cambridge MA: M.I.T. Press, 1965.

Chukofsky, K. From two to five. Berkeley: University of California Press, 1963.

Clark, E. V. "Knowledge, context, and strategy in the acquisition of meaning." In D. P. Date (ed.), Georgetown University round table on language and linguistics, 1975. Washington, D.C.: Georgetown University Press, 1975.

Clark, E. V. "Strategies and the mapping problem in first language acquisition." In J. Macnamara (ed.), Language learning and thought. New York: Academic Press, 1977.

Clarke-Stewart, K. A. "Interactions between mothers and their young children: Characteristics and consequences." Monographs of the Society of Research in Child Development, 1973, *38*, (Whole # 153).

Clarke-Stewart, K. A. "And daddy makes three: The father's impact on mother and young child." Child Development, 1978, *49*, 466–478.

Clarke-Stewart, K. A.; Vander-Stoep, L. P.; & Killian, G. A. "Analysis and replication of mother-child relations at two years of age." Child Development, 1979, *50*, 777–793.

Clausen, J. A. "The social meaning of differential physical maturation." In D. E. Dragastin & G. H. Elder Jr. (eds), Adolescence in the life cycle. New York: Halsted Press, 1975.

Coates, S. Preschool embedded figures test. Palo Alto CA: Consulting Psychologists Press, 1972.

Connors, C. K. "A teacher rating scale for use in drug studies with children." American Journal of Psychiatry, 1969, *126*, 884–888.

Coopersmith, S. The antecedents of self-esteem. San Francisco: W. H. Freeman, 1967.

Cordua, G. D.; McGraw, K. O.; & Drabman, R. S. "Doctor or nurse: Children's perceptions of sex-typed occupations." Child Development, 1979, *50*, 590–593.

Cornelius, S. W., & Denney, N. W. "Dependency in day-care and home-care children." Developmental Psychology, 1975, *11*, 575–582.

Cowen, E. L.; Pederson, A.; Babijian, H.; Izzo, L. D.; & Trost, M. A. "Long-term follow-up of early detected vulnerable children." Journal of Consulting and Clinical Psychology, 1973, *41*, 438–446.

Crockenberg, S. B., & Nicolayev, J. "Stage transition in moral reasoning as related to conflict experienced in naturalistic settings." Merrill-Palmer Quarterly, 1979, *25*, 185–192.

Crook, C. K. "Taste perception in the newborn infant." Infant Behavior and Development, 1978, *1*, 52–69.

Cummings, E. M. "Caregiver stability and day care." Developmental Psychology, 1980, *16*, 31–37.

Curtiss, S. Genie. A psycholinguistic study of a modern-day "wild child." New York: Academic Press, 1977.

Dale, P. S. Language development: Structure and function. (2d ed.) New York: Holt, 1976.

Davidson, E. S.; Yasuna, A.; & Tower, A. "The effect of television cartoons on sex-role stereotyping in young girls." Child Development, 1979, *50*, 597–600.

Denney, N. W. "Free classification in preschool children." Child Development, 1972, *43*, 1161–1170.

Dennis, W. "Causes of retardation among institutional children: Iran." Journal of Genetic Psychology, 1960, *96*, 47–59.

Derdiarian, J., & Snipper, A. "Effects of maternal employment on sex-role orientation, behavior, and attitudes." Paper presented at the biennial meetings of the Society for Research in Child Development, San Francisco, 1979.

Derwing, B. L. "Is the child really a 'little linguist?' " In J. Macnamara (ed.), Language learning and thought. New York: Academic Press, 1977.

Detterman, D. K. "The effect of heartbeat sound on neonatal crying." Infant Behavior and Development, 1978, *1*, 36–48.

DeVoe, M. W. "Cooperation as a function of self-concept, sex and race." Educational Research Quarterly, 1977, *2*, 3–8.

DeVries, R. "Constancy of generic identity in the years three to six." Monographs of the Society for Research in Child Development, 1969, *34*, (Whole # 127).

The Diagram Group. Child's body. New York: Paddington Press, 1977.

Dickie, J. R., & Strader, W. H. "Development of mirror image responses in infancy." The Journal of Psychology, 1974, *88*, 333–337.

Dicks-Mireaux, M. J. "Mental development of infants with Down's syndrome." American Journal of Mental Deficiency, 1972, *77*, 26–32.

Dickson, W. P.; Hess, R. D.; Miyake, N.; & Azuma, H. "Referential communication accuracy between mother and child as a predictor of cognitive development in the Unites States and Japan." Child Development, 1979, *50*, 53–59.

Dollard, J.; Doob, L. W.; Miller, N. E.; Mowrer, O. H.; & Sears, R. R. Frustration and aggression. New Haven CT: Yale University Press, 1939.

Dominick, J. R., & Greenberg, B. S. "Attitudes toward violence: The interaction of television exposure, family attitudes, and social class." In G. A. Comstock & E. A. Rubenstein (eds.), Television and social behavior. (Vol. III). Washington, D.C.: U. S. Government Printing Office, 1972.

Drillien, C. M. The growth and development of the prematurely born infant. Baltimore: Williams & Wilkins, 1964.

Dunn, H. G.; McBurney, A. K.; Ingram, S.; & Hunter, C. M. "Maternal cigarette smoking during pregnancy and the child's subsequent development: II. Neurological and intellectual maturation to the age of 6½ years." Canadian Journal of Public Health, 1977, *68*, 43–50.

Easterbrooks, M. A., & Lamb, M. E. "The relationship between quality of infant-mother attachment and infant competence in initial encounters with peers." Child Development, 1979, *50*, 380–387.

Eckerman, C. O., & Whatley, J. L. "Toys and social interaction between infant peers." Child Development, 1977, 48, 1645–1656.

Edgerton, R. B. Mental retardation. Cambridge MA: Harvard University Press, 1979.

Edwards, C. P. "Societal complexity and moral development: A Kenyan study." Ethos, 1975, 3, 505–527.

Edwards, C. P., & Lewis, M. "Young children's concepts of social relations: Social functions and social objects." In M. Lewis & L. Rosenblum (eds.), The child and his family. New York: Plenum, 1979.

Ehrhardt, A. A., & Baker, S. W. "Fetal androgens, human central nervous system differentiation, and behavior sex differences." In R. C. Friedman, R. M. Richart, & R. L. Vande Wiele (eds.), Sex differences in behavior. New York: Wiley, 1974.

Eichorn, E. H. "Physical development: Current foci of research." In J. D. Osofsky (ed.), Handbook of infant development. New York: Wiley, 1979.

Eisenberg-Berg, N., & Hand, M. "The relationship of preschoolers' reasoning about prosocial moral conflicts to prosocial behavior." Child Development, 1979, 59, 356–363.

Elardo, R.; Bradley, R.; & Caldwell, B. "The relation of infants' home environments to mental test performance from six to thirty-six months: A longitudinal analysis." Child Development, 1975, 46, 71–76.

Elardo, R.; Bradley, R., & Caldwell, B. "A longitudinal study of the relation of infants' home environments to language development at age three." Child Development, 1977, 48, 595–603.

Eme, R. F. "Sex differences in childhood psychopathology: A review." Psychological Bulletin, 1979, 86, 374–395.

Emmerich, W.; Goldman, K. S.; Kirsh, B.; & Sharabany, R. "Evidence for a transitional phase in the development of gender constancy." Child Development, 1977, 48, 930–936.

Endsley, R. C.; Hutcherson, M. A.; Garner, A. P.; & Martin, M. J. "Interrelationships among selected maternal behaviors, authoritarianism, and preschool children's verbal and non-verbal curiosity." Child Development, 1979, 50, 331–339.

Engel, M.; Nechlin, H.; & Arkin, A. M. "Aspects of mothering: Correlates of the cognitive development of black male infants in the second year of life." In A. Davids (ed.), Child personality and psychopathology: Current topics. (Vol. 2). New York: Wiley, 1975.

Erikson, E. H. Childhood and society. New York: Norton, 1963.

Erikson, E. H. Insight and responsibility. New York: Norton, 1964.

Erikson, E. H. Dimensions of a new identity: The 1973 Jefferson lectures in the humanities. New York: Norton, 1974.

Fagot, B. I. "Sex differences in toddlers' behavior and parental reaction." Developmental Psychology, 1974, 10, 554–558.

Fagot, B. I. "Consequences of moderate cross-gender behavior in preschool children." Child Development, 1977, 48, 902–907.

Fantz, R. L. "A method for studying early visual development." Perceptual and Motor Skills, 1956, 6, 13–15.

Fantz, R. L.; Fagan, J. F. III; & Miranda, S. B. "Early visual selectivity." In L. B. Cohen & P. Salapatek (eds.), Infant perception: From sensation to cognition. (Vol. 1). New York: Academic Press, 1975.

Farnham-Diggory, S. Learning disabilities. Cambridge MA: Harvard University Press, 1978.

Farran, D., & Ramey, C. "Infant day care and attachment behaviors toward mothers and teachers." Child Development, 1977, 48, 1112–1116.

Faust, M. S. "Developmental maturity as a determinant in prestige of adolescent girls." Child Development, 1960, 31, 173–181.

Faust, M. S. "Somatic development of adolescent girls." Monographs of the Society for Research on Child Development, 1977, 42 (Whole # 169).

Feshbach, S. "Aggression." In P. H. Mussen (ed.), Carmichael's manual of child psychology. (Vol. 2, 3d ed.). New York: Wiley, 1970.

Field, T. M. "Effects of early separation, interactive deficits, and experimental manipulations on infant-mother face-to-face interaction." Child Development, 1977, 48, 763–771.(a)

Field, T. M. "Maternal stimulation during infant feeding." Developmental Psychology, 1977, 13, 539–540. (b)

Flavell, J. H. "Developmental studies of mediated memory." In H. W. Reese & L. P. Lipsitt (eds.), Advances in child development and behavior, (Vol. 5). New York: Academic Press, 1970.

Flavell, J. H. Cognitive development. Englewood Cliffs NJ: Prentice-Hall, 1977.

Flavell, J. H., & Wellman, H. M. "Metamemory." In R. V. Kail & J. W. Hagen (eds.), Perspectives on the development of memory and cognition. Hillsdale NJ: Erlbaum, 1977.

Fling, S., & Manosevitz, M. "Sex typing in nursery school children's play interests." Developmental Psychology, 1972. *7*, 146–152.

Fraiberg, S. "Blind infants and their mothers: An examination of the sign system." In M. Lewis & L. A. Rosenblum (eds.), The effect of the infant on its caregiver. New York: Wiley, 1974.

Fraiberg, S. "The development of human attachments in infants blind from birth." Merrill-Palmer Quarterly, 1975, *21*, 315–334.

Fraser, C.; Bellugi, U.; & Brown, R. "Control of grammar in imitation, comprehension, and production." Journal of Verbal Learning and Verbal Behavior, 1963, *2*, 121–135.

Freedman, D. G. "Ethnic differences in babies." Human Nature, 1979, *2*, 36–43.

Freud, S. A general introduction to psychoanalysis. New York: Washington Square Press, 1960.

Friedrich-Cofer, L. K.; Huston-Stein, A.; Kipnis, D. M.; Susman, E. J.; & Cleweet, A. S. "Environmental enhancement of prosocial television content: Effects on interpersonal behavior, imaginative play, and self-regulation in a natural setting." Developmental Psychology, 1979, *15*, 637–646.

Frueh, T., & McGhee, P. E. "Traditional sex role development and amount of time spent watching television." Developmental Psychology, 1975, *11*, 109.

Furth, H. Piaget for teachers. Englewood Cliffs NJ: Prentice-Hall, 1970.

Gallagher, J. J. Teaching the gifted child. (2d ed.). Boston: Allyn & Bacon, 1975.

Gallup, G. G. "Self-recognition in chimpanzees and man: A developmental and comparative perspective." In M. Lewis & L. Rosenblum (eds.), The child and his family. New York: Plenum, 1979.

Garber, H. L. "Preventing mental retardation through family rehabilitation." In B. M. Caldwell & D. J. Stedman (eds.), Infant education: A guide for helping handicapped children in the first three years. New York: Walker, 1977.

Gardner, R. A., & Gardner, B. T. "Teaching sign language to a chimpanzee." Science, 1969, *165*, 664–672.

Gardner, R. A., & Gardner, B. T. "Early signs of language in child and chimpanzee." Science, 1974, *187*.

Garn, S. M.; Clark, D. C.; & Guire, K. E. "Growth, body composition, and development of obese and lean children." In M. Winick (ed.), Childhood obesity. New York: Wiley, 1975.

Gaudia, G. "Race, social class, and age of achievement of conservation on Piaget's tasks." Developmental Psychology, 1972, *6*, 158–167.

Gaulin-Kremer, E.; Shaw, J. L.; & Thoman, E. B. "Mother-infant interaction at first encounter: Effects of variation in delay after delivery." Paper presented at the biennial meetings of the Society for Research in Child Development, New Orleans, 1977.

Gelman, R., & Shatz, M. "Appropriate speech adjustments: The operation of conversational constraints on talk to two-year-olds." In M. Lewis & L. A. Rosenblum (eds.), Interaction, conversation, and the development of language. New York: Wiley, 1977.

Gerbner, G. "Violence in television drama: Trends and symbolic functions." In G. A. Comstock & E. A. Rubenstein (eds.), Television and social behavior. (Vol. 1). Washington, D.C.: U. S. Government Printing Office, 1972.

Gerbner, G., & Gross, L. "Violence profile No. 6. Trends in network television drama and viewer conceptions of social reality 1967–73." Monographs of the Annenberg School of Communications. Philadelphia: University of Pennsylvania, 1974.

Gerson, R. P., & Damon, W. "Moral understanding and children's conduct." In W. Damon (ed.), Moral development. San Francisco: Jossey-Bass, 1978.

Gesell, A. The mental growth of the preschool child. New York: Macmillan, 1925.

Gesell, A., & Thompson, H. "Learning and growth in identical twins: An experimental study by the method of co-twin control." Genetic Psychology Monographs, 1929, *6*, 1–123.

Gewirtz, J. L., & Boyd, E. F. "Does maternal responding imply reduced infant crying? A critique of the 1972 Bell and Ainsworth report." Child Development, 1977, *48*, 1200–1207.

Gibson, E. J. Principles of perceptual learning and development. New York: Appleton-Century-Crofts, 1969.

Gibson, E. J., & Levin, H. The psychology of reading. Cambridge MA: M.I.T. Press, 1975.

Gibson, E. J., & Walk, R. D. "The 'visual cliff.' " Scientific American, 1960, *202*, 80–92.

Ginsburg, H., & Opper, S. Piaget's theory of intellectual development. Englewood Cliffs NJ: Prentice-Hall, 1969.

Gleason, J. B. "Talking to children: Some notes on feedback." In C. E. Snow & C. A. Ferguson (eds.), Talking to children. Cambridge, England: Cambridge University Press, 1977.

Glueck, S., & Glueck, E. Unraveling juvenile delinquency. Cambridge MA: Harvard University Press, 1950.

Golden, M., & Birns, B. "Social class and cognitive development in infancy." Merrill-Palmer Quarterly, 1968, *14*, 139–149.

Golden, M.; Birns, B.; Bridger, W.; & Moss, A. "Social class differentiation in cognitive development among Black preschool children." Child Development, 1971, *42*, 37–46.

Golden, M.; Rosenbluth, L.; Grossi, M.; Policare, H.; Freeman, H.; & Brownlee, E. The New York City infant day care study. New York: Medical and Health Research Association of New York City, 1978.

Goldin-Meadow, S., & Feldman, H. "The development of language-like communication without a language model." Science, 1977, *197*, 401–402.

Goldstein, H.; Moss, J. W.; & Jordan, L. J. "The efficacy of special class training on the development of mentally retarded children." Urbana: University of Illinois, Institute for Research on Exceptional Children, 1965.

Goleman, D. "Special abilities of the sexes: Do they begin in the brain?" Psychology Today, 1978, *12*, 48–59, 120.

Goleman, D. "1,528 little geniuses and how they grew." Psychology Today, 1980, *13*, 28–43.

Goodenough, F. L. Measurement of intelligence by drawings. New York: Harcourt, 1926.

Goodenough, F. L. Anger in young children. Minneapolis: University of Minnesota Press, 1931.

Gordon, T. P.E.T. Parent effectiveness training. New York: Wyden, 1970.

Gottesman, I., & Shields, J. Schizophrenia and genetics: A twin study vantage point. New York: Academic Press, 1972.

Graham, P. "Epidemiological studies." In H. C. Quay & J. S. Werry (eds.), Psychopathological disorders of childhood. (2d ed.). New York: Wiley, 1979.

Gray, S. W., & Klaus, R. A. "An experimental preschool program for culturally deprived children." Child Development, 1965, *36*, 887–898.

Greenberg, M., & Morris, N. "Engrossment: The newborn's impact upon the father." American Journal of Orthopsychiatry, 1974, *44*, 520–531.

Greenfield, P. M., & Smith, J. H. The structure of communication in early language development. New York: Academic Press, 1976.

Grusec, J. E.; Saas-Kortsaak, P.; & Simutis, Z. M. "The role of example and moral exhortation in the training of altruism." Child Development, 1978, *49*, 920–923.

Hagen, J. W.; Jongeward, R. H.; & Kail, R. V. "Cognitive perspectives on the development of memory." In H. W. Reese (ed.), Advances in child development and behavior (Vol. 10). New York: Academic Press, 1975.

Haith, M. M. "Visual cognition in early infancy." In R. B. Kearsley & I. E. Sigel (eds.), Infants at risk: Assessment of cognitive functioning. Hillsdale NJ: Erlbaum, 1979.

Hales, D. J.; Lozoff, B.; Sosa, R.; & Kennell, J. H. "Defining the limits of the maternal sensitive period." Developmental Medicine and Child Neurology, 1977, *19*, 454–461.

Hanson, J. W.; Streissguth, A. P.; & Smith, D. W. "The effects of moderate alcohol consumption during pregnancy on fetal growth and morphogenesis." Journal of Pediatrics, 1978, *92*, 64–67.

Hanson, R. A. "Consistency and stability of home environmental measures related to I.Q." Child Development, 1975, *46*, 470–480.

Hartup, W. W. "Peer interaction and social organization." In P. H. Mussen (ed.), Carmichael's manual of child psychology. (Vol. 2, 3d ed.). New York: Wiley, 1970.

Hartup, W. W. "Aggression in childhood. Developmental perspectives." American Psychologist, 1974, *29*, 336–341.

Hartup, W. W. "The origins of friendships." In M. Lewis & L. A. Rosenblum (eds.), Friendship and peer relations. New York: Wiley, 1975.

Haugen, G. M., & McIntire, R. W. "Comparisons of vocal imitation, tactile stimulation, and food as reinforcers for infant vocalizations." Developmental Psychology, 1972, *6*, 201–209.

Hayden, A. H., & Haring, N. G. "Early intervention for highrisk infants and young children: Programs for Down's syndrome children." In T. D. Tjossem (ed.), Intervention strategies for high risk infants and young children. Baltimore: University Park Press, 1976.

Hayes, C. The ape in our house. New York: Harper & Row, 1951.

Haynes, H.; White, B. L.; & Held, R. "Visual accommodation in human infants." Science, 1965, *148*, 528–530.

Heber, F. R. "Sociocultural mental retardation—A longitudinal study." In D. Forgays (ed.), Primary prevention of psychopathology (Vol. 2). Hanover NH: University Press of New England, 1978.

Heber, R.; Garber, H.; Harrington, S.; & Hoffman, C. "Rehabilitation of families at risk for mental retardation." Unpublished progress report, Research and Training Center, University of Wisconsin, December 1972.

Heinstein, M. I. "Behavioral correlates of breast-bottle regimes under varying parent-infant relationships." Monographs of the Society for Research in Child Development, 1963, *28*, (Whole # 88).

Helfer, R. "Relationship between lack of bonding and child abuse and neglect." In M. H. Klaus, T. Leger, & M. A. Trause (eds.), Maternal attachment and mothering disorders. A round table. Johnson & Johnson Baby Products Col., 1975. (a)

Helfer, R. "Why most physicians don't get involved in child abuse cases and what to do about it." Children Today, 1975, *4*, 29–32. (b)

Henneborn, W. J., & Cogan, R. "The effect of husband participation on reported pain and the probability of medication during labour and birth." Journal of Psychosomatic Research, 1975, *19*, 215–222.

Hennig, M., & Jardim, A. The managerial woman. Garden City NY: Doubleday, 1976.

Hess, E. H. " 'Imprinting' in a natural laboratory." Scientific American, 1972, *227*, 24–31.

Hetherington, E. M. "Effects of father absence on personality development in adolescent daughters." Developmental Psychology, 1972, *7*, 313–326.

Hetherington, E. M.; Cox, M.; & Cox, R. "Beyond father absence: Conceptualization of effects of divorce." Paper presented at the biennial meetings of the Society for Research in Child Development, Denver, 1975.

Hetherington, E. M.; Cox, M.; & Cox, R. "The aftermath of divorce." In J. H. Stevens, Jr., & M. Matthews (eds.), Mother-child, father-child relations. Washington, D.C.: National Association for the Education of Young Children, 1977.

Hetherington, E. M.; Cox, M.; & Cox, R. "Family interaction and the social, emotional, and cognitive development of preschool children following divorce." Paper presented at the biennial meetings of the Society for Research in Child Development, San Francisco, 1979.

Hetherington, E. M., & Deur, J. "The effects of father absence on child development." In W. W. Hartup (ed.), The young child: Review of research. (Vol. 2). Washington, D.C.: National Association for the Education of Young Children, 1972.

Hetherington, E. M., & Martin, B. "Family interaction." In H. C. Quay & J. S. Werry (eds.), Psychopathological disorders of childhood. (2d ed.). New York: Wiley, 1979.

High/Scope Foundation. Research report: Can preschool education make a lasting difference? Results of follow-up through eighth grade for the Ypsilanti Perry Preschool Project. Bulletin of the High/Scope Foundation, Fall, 1977, (4), 1–8.

Hill, R. M.; Craig, J. P.; Chaney, M. D.; Tennyson, L. M.; & McCulley, L. B. "Utilization of over-the-counter drugs during pregnancy." Clinical Obstetrics and Gynecology, 1977, *20*, 381–394.

Hobbs, N. The futures of children. San Francisco: Jossey-Bass, 1975.

Hoffman, L. W. "Maternal employment: 1979." In S. Scarr (ed.), Psychology and children: Current research and practice. American Psychologist, 1979, *34*, 859–865.

Hoffman, M. L. "Moral development." In P. H. Mussen (ed.), Carmichael's manual of child psychology. (Vol. 2, 3d ed.). New York: Wiley, 1970.

Hopkins, J. B., & Vietze, P. M. "Post-partum early and extended contact: Quality, quantity or both?" Paper presented at the biennial meetings of the Society for Research in Child Development, New Orleans, 1977.

Horn, J. L. "Trends in the measurement of intelligence." Intelligence, 1979, *3*, 229–240.

Hubel, D. H., & Weisel, T. N. "Reception fields of cells in striate cortex of very young, visually inexperienced kittens." Journal of Neurophysiology, 1963, *26*, 996–1022.

Hunt, J. McV. "The psychological development of orphanage-reared infants: Interventions with outcomes (Teheran)." Genetic Psychology Monographs, 1976, *94*, 177–226.

Hutt, S. J.; Lenard, H. G.; & Prechtl, H. F. R. Psychophysiological studies in newborn infants." In L. P. Lipsitt & H. W. Reese (eds.), Advance in child development and behavior. New York: Academic Press, 1969.

Ianco-Worrall, A. D. "Bilingualism and cognitive development." Child Development, 1972, *43*, 1390–1400.

Inhelder, B., & Piaget, J. The growth of logical thinking from childhood to adolescence. New York: Basic Books, 1958.

Jacklin, C. N.; Maccoby, E. E.; & Dick, A. E. "Barrier behavior and toy preference: Sex differences (and their absence) in the year-old child." Child Development, 1973, *44*, 196–200.

Jackson, E.; Campos, J. J.; & Fischer, K. W. "The question of decalage between object permanence and person permanence." Developmental Psychology, 1978, *14*, 1–10.

Jencks, C.; Smith, M.; Acland, H.; Bane, M. J.; Cohen, D. K.; Gintis, H.; Heyns, B.; & Michelson, S. Inequality: A reassessment of the effect of family and schooling in America. New York: Basic Books, 1972.

Jensen, A. R. "How much can we boost IQ and scholastic achievement?" Harvard Educational Review, 1969, *39*, 1–123.

Jensen, A. R. Bias in mental testing. New York: The Free Press, 1979.

Jensen, K. "Differential reactions to taste and temperature stimuli in newborn infants." Genetic Psychology Monographs, 1932, *12*, 361–479.

Jones, K. L.; Smith, D. W.; Ulleland, C. N.; & Streissguth, A. P. "Pattern of malformation in offspring of chronic alcoholic mothers." Lancet, 1973, *1*, 1267–1271.

Jones, M. C. "The later careers of boys who were early or late maturing." Child Development, 1957, *28*, 113–128.

Jones, M. D., & Mussen, P. H. "Self-conceptions, motivations and interpersonal attitudes of early and later maturing girls." Child Development, 1958, *29*, 491–501.

Josselson, R.; Greenberger, E.; & McConochie, D. "Phenomenological aspects of psychosocial maturity in adolescence. Part I. Boys." Journal of Youth and Adolescence, 1977, *6*, 25–56. (a)

Josselson, R.; Greenberger, E.; & McConochie, D. "Phenomenological aspects of psychosocial maturity in adolescence. Part II. Girls." Journal of Youth and Adolesence, 1977, *6*, 127–144. (b)

Judd, S. A., & Mervis, C. B. "Learning to solve class-inclusion problems: The roles of quantification and recognition of contradiction." Child Development, 1979, *50*, 163–169.

Juel-Nielsen, N. "Individual and environment: A psychiatric-psychological investigation of monozygotic twins reared apart." Acta Psychiatrica et Neurlogica Scandinavica, Monograph supplement 183, 1965.

Jung, C. G. Analytical psychology. New York: Moffat, Yard, 1916.

Jung, C. G. The integration of personality. New York: Farrar and Rinehart, 1939.

Justice, B., & Justice, R. The abusing family. New York: Human Sciences Press, 1976.

Kagan, J. "Reflection-impulsivity and reading ability in primary grade children." Child Development, 1965, *36*, 609–628.

Kagan, J. Change and continuity in infancy. New York: Wiley, 1971.

Kagan, J.; Kearsley, R. B.; & Zelazo, P. R. Infancy. Its place in human development. Cambridge MA: Harvard University Press, 1978.

Kagan, J.; Lapidus, D. R.; & Moore, N. "Infant antecedents of cognitive functioning: A longitudinal study." Child Development, 1978, *49*, 1005–1023.

Kagan, J., & Moss, H. A. Birth to maturity. New York: Wiley, 1962.

Kagan, J.; Rosman, B. L.; Day, D.; Albert, J.; & Phillips, W. "Information processing in the child: Significance of analytic and reflective attitudes." Psychological Monographs, 1964, 78. (Whole # 578).

Kail, R. V., & Hagen, J. W. (eds.). Perspectives on the development of memory and cognition. Hillsdale NJ: Erlbaum, 1977.

Kamii, C., & DeVries, R. "Piaget for early education." In R. K. Parker (ed.), The preschool in action. (2d ed.). Boston: Allyn & Bacon, 1974.

Kamin, L. J. The science and politics of IQ. Hillsdale NJ: Erlbaum, 1974.

Karmel, B. Z., & Maisel, E. B. "A

neuronal activity model for infant visual attention." In L. B. Cohen & P. Salapatek (eds.), Infant perception: From sensation to cognition. (Vol. 1). New York: Academic Press, 1975.

Karnes, M. B., & Lee, R. C. "Mainstreaming in the preschool." In L. G. Katz (ed.), Current topics in early childhood education. (Vol. II). Norwood NJ: Ablex, 1979.

Kaufman, B. N. Son/rise. New York: Harper & Row, 1976.

Kaye, K. "Toward the origin of dialogue." In H. R. Schaffer (ed.), Studies in mother-infant interaction. New York: Academic Press, 1977.

Keating, D. P., & Clark, L. V. "Development of physical and social reasoning in adolescence." Developmental Psychology, 1980, *16*, 23–30.

Keating, D. P., & Schaefer, R. A. "Ability and sex differences in the acquisition of formal operations." Developmental Psychology, 1975, *11*, 531–532.

Kempe, R. S., & Kempe, C. H. Child abuse. Cambridge MA: Harvard University Press, 1978.

Kendler, H. H., & Kendler, T. S. "Vertical and horizontal processes in problem solving." Psychological Review, 1962, *69*, 1–16.

Kendler, T. S. "Development of mediating responses in children." Monographs of the Society for Research in Child Development, 1963, *28* (Whole # 86), 33–48.

Keniston, K. "Student activism, moral development, and morality." American Journal of Orthopsychiatry, 1970, *40*, 577–592. (a)

Keniston, K. "Youth: A 'new' stage in life." American Scholar, Autumn 1970, 586–595. (b)

Keniston, K. All our children. The American family under pressure. New York: Harcourt, 1977.

Kennedy, W. Z.; Van de Reit, V.; & White, C. C., Jr. "A normative sample of intelligence and achievement of Negro elementary school children in the southeastern United States." Monographs of the Society for Research in Child Development, 1963, *28* (Whole # 90).

Kennell, J. H.; Jerauld, R.; Wolfe, H.; Chesler, D.; Kreger, N. C.; McAlpine, W.; Steffa, M.; & Klaus, M. H. "Maternal behavior one year after early and extended post-partum contact." Developmental Medicine and Child Neurology, 1974, *16*, 172–179.

Kennell, J. H.; Voos, D. K.; & Klaus, M. H. "Parent-infant bonding." In J. D. Osofsky (ed.), Handbook of infant development. New York: Wiley, 1979, 786–798.

Kessner, D. M. Infant death: An analysis by maternal risk and health care. Washington, D.C.: National Academy of Sciences, 1973.

Kilbride, H. W.; Johnson, D. L.; & Streissguth, A. P. "Social class, birth order, and newborn experience." Child Development, 1977, *48*, 1686–1688.

Klaus, H. M., & Kennell, J. H. "Human maternal behavior at first contact with her young." Pediatrics, 1970, *46*, 187–192. (a)

Klaus, H. M., & Kennell, J. H. "Mothers separated from their newborn infants." Pediatric Clinics of North America, 1970, *17*, 1015–1037. (b)

Klaus, H. M., & Kennell, J. H. Maternal-infant bonding. St. Louis MO: Mosby, 1976.

Klaus, R. A., & Gray, S. W. "The early training project for disadvantaged children: A report after five years." Monographs for the Society for Research in Child Development, 1968, *33* (Whole # 120).

Klein, M., & Stern, L. "Low birth weight and the battered child syndrome." American Journal of Diseases of Childhood, 1971, *122*, 15–18.

Kohlberg, L. "Development of moral character and moral ideology." In M. L. Hoffman & L. W. Hoffman (eds.), Review of child development research. (Vol. I.). New York: Russell Sage Foundation, 1964.

Kohlberg, L. "A cognitive-developmental analysis of children's sex-role concepts and attitudes." In E. E. Maccoby (ed.), The development of sex differences. Stanford CA: Stanford University Press, 1966.

Kohlberg, L. "Stage and sequence: The cognitive-developmental approach to socialization." In D. Goslin (ed.), Handbook of socialization theory and research. Chicago: Rand McNally, 1969.

Kohlberg, L. "From is to ought: How to commit the naturalistic fallacy and get away with it in the study of moral development." In T. Mischel (ed.), Cognitive development and epistemology. New York: Academic Press, 1971.

Kohlberg, L. "The cognitive-developmental approach to moral education." Phi Delta Kappan, June 1975, 670–677.

Kohlberg, L. "Moral stages and moralization: The cognitive-developmental approach. In T. Lickona (ed.), Moral development and behavior: Theory, research, and social issues. New York: Holt, 1976.

Kohlberg, L. "Revisions in the theory and practice of moral development." In W. Damon (ed.), Moral development. San Francisco: Jossey-Bass, 1978.

Kohlberg, L., & Elfenbein, D. "The development of moral judgements concerning capital punishment." American Journal of Orthopsychiatry, 1975, *45*, 614–640. (Materials reprinted with permission from the American Journal of Orthopsychiatry: copyright 1979 by the American Orthopsychiatric Assoc. Inc.)

Kohlberg, L., & Ullian, D. Z. "Stages in the development of psychosexual concepts and attitudes." In R. C. Friedman, R. M. Richart, & R. L. Vande Wiele (eds.), Sex differences in behavior. New York: Wiley, 1974.

Kohlberg, L., & Zigler, E. "The impact of cognitive maturity on the devlopment of sex-role attitudes in the years 4 to 8." Genetic Psychology Monographs, 1967, *75*, 84–165.

Kokenes, B. "Grade level differences in factors of self-esteem." Developmental Psychology, 1974, *10*, 954–958.

Kopp, C. B. "Perspectives on infant motor system development." In M. H. Bornstein & W. Kessen (eds.), Psychological development from infancy: Image to intention. Hillsdale NJ: Erlbaum, 1979.

Kremenitzer, J. P.; Vaughan, H. G., Jr.; Kurtzberg, D.; & Dowling, K. "Smooth-pursuit eye movements in the new-born infant." Child Development, 1979, *50*, 442–448.

Kuczaj, S. "The acquisition of regular and irregular past tense forms." Journal of Verbal Learning and Verbal Behavior, 1977, *16*, 589–600.

Kuczaj, S. "Children's judgments of grammatical and ungrammatical irregular past-tense verbs." Child Development, 1978, *49*, 319–326.

Kuczaj, S. "Evidence for a language learning strategy: On the relative ease of acquisition of prefixes and suffixes." Child Development, 1979, *50*, 1–13.

Kuhn, D.; Nash, S. C.; & Brucken, L. "Sex role concepts of two- and three-year-olds." Child Development, 1978, *49*, 445–451.

Labov, W. Language in the inner city: Studies in the Black English vernacular. Philadelphia: University of Pennsylvania Press, 1972.

Lakin, M. "Personality factors in mothers of excessively crying (colicky) infants." Monograph of the Society for Research in Child Development, 1957, *22*, (Whole # 64).

Lamb, M. E. "Effects of stress and cohort on mother- and father-infant interaction." Developmental Psychology, 1976, *12*, 435–443.

Lamb, M. E. The role of the father in child development. New York: Wiley, 1976.

Lamb, M. E. "Father-infant and mother-infant interaction in the first year of life." Child Development, 1977, *48*, 167–181.

Landis, J. T. "A comparison of children from divorced and non-divorced unhappy marriages." Family Life Coordinator, 1962, *21*, 61–65.

Langer, J. Theories of development. New York: Holt, 1969.

Lansky, L. M. "The family structure also affects the model: Sex-role attitudes in parents of preschool children." Merrill-Palmer Quarterly, 1967, *13*, 139–150.

Laosa, L. M., & Brophy, J. E. "Effects of sex and birth order on sex-role development and intelligence among kindergarten children." Developmental Psychology, 1972, *6*, 409–415.

Lavatelli, C. Piaget's theory applied to an early childhood curriculum. Boston: American Science and Engineering, 1970.

LaVoie, J. C. "Ego identity formation in middle adolescence." Journal of Youth and Adolescence, 1976, *5*, 371–385.

Leboyer, F. Birth without violence. New York: Knopf, 1975.

Leifer, A. D.; Leiderman, P. H.; Barnett, C. R.; & Williams, J. A. "Effects of mother-infant separation on maternal attachment behavior." Child Development, 1972, *43*, 1203–1218.

Lenneberg, E. H. Biological foundations of language. New York: Wiley, 1967.

Lesser, G. S.; Fifer, G.; & Clark, D. H. "Mental abilities of children from different social class and cultural groups." Monographs of the Society for Research in Child Development, 1965, *30* (Whole # 102).

Levenstein, P. "Cognitive growth in preschoolers through verbal interaction with mothers." American Journal of Orthopsychiatry, 1970, *40*, 426–432.

Levinger, L. "The intellectually superior child." In J. D. Noshpitz (ed.), Basic handbook of child psychiatry. (Vol. 1). New York: Basic Books, 1979.

Levitt, E., & Cohen, S. "Parents

as teachers: A rationale for involving parents in the education of their young handicapped children." In L. G. Katz (ed.), Current topics in early childhood education. (Vol. I). Norwood NJ: Ablex, 1977.

Lewin, R. "Starved brains." Psychology Today, 1975, *9*, 29–33.

Lewis, M., & Brooks-Gunn, J. "Toward a theory of social cognition: The development of the self." In I. C. Uzgiris (ed.), Social interaction and communication during infancy. San Francisco: Jossey-Bass, 1979.

Liben, L. S. "Long-term memory for pictures related to seriation, horizontality, and verticality concepts." Developmental Psychology, 1975, *11*, 795–806.

Liberman, I. Y., & Shankweiler, D. "Speech, the alphabet and teaching to read." In L. B. Resnick & P. A. Weaver (eds.), Theory and practice of early reading. Hillsdale NJ: Erlbaum, 1977.

Liberman, I. Y.; Shankweiler, D.; Liberman, A. M.; Fowler, C.; & Fischer, F. W. "Phonetic segmentation and recoding in the beginning reader." In A.S. Reber & D. Scarborough (eds.), Reading: Theory and practice. Hillsdale NJ: Erlbaum, 1976.

Lickona, T. "Moral development and moral education." In J. M. Gallagher & J. A. Easley, Jr. (eds.), Knowledge and development. (Vol. 2). New York: Plenum, 1978.

Lieberman, A. F. "Preschoolers' competence with a peer: Relations with attachment and peer experience." Child Development, 1977, *48*, 1277–1287.

Liebert, R. M., & Schwartzberg, N. S. "Effects of mass media." In M. R. Rosenzweig & L. W. Porter (eds.), Annual review of psychology. (Vol. 28). Palo Alto CA: Annual Reviews, 1977.

Light, R. J. "Abused and neglected children in America: A study of alternative policies." Harvard Educational Review, 1973, *43*, 556–598.

Lipsitt, L. P. "The newborn as informant." In R. B. Kearsley & I. E. Sigel (eds.), Infants at risk: Assessment of cognitive functioning. Hillsdale NJ: Erlbaum, 1979.

Lipsitt, L. P., & Kaye, H. "Conditioned sucking in the human newborn." Psychonomic Science, 1964, *1*, 29–30.

Little, A. "A longitudinal study of cognitive development in young children." Child Development, 1972, *43*, 1124–1134.

Locke, J. Some thoughts concerning education. 1690. London: Cambridge University Press, 1913.

Loehlin, J. C.; Lindzey, G.; & Spuhler, J. N. Race differences in intelligence. San Francisco: W. H. Freeman, 1975.

Loehlin, J. C., & Nichols, R. C. Heredity, environment and personality. Austin: University of Texas Press, 1976.

Lorenz, K. On aggression. New York: Harcourt, 1966.

Lovaas, O. I. "A program for the establishment of speech in psychotic children." In J. Wing (ed.), Childhood autism. London: Pergamon Press, 1966.

Lovaas, O. I. Language acquisition programs for nonlinguistic children. New York: Irvington, 1976.

Lytton, H. "Do parents create, or respond to, differences in twins?" Developmental Psychology, 1977, *12*, 456–459.

McCall, R. Infants: The new knowledge. Cambridge MA: Harvard University Press, 1979.

McCall, R. B.; Appelbaum, M. I.; & Hogarty, P. S. "Developmental changes in mental performance." Monographs of the Society for Research in Child Development, 1973, *38* (Whole # 150).

Maccoby, E. E.; Doering, C. H.; Jacklin, C. N.; & Kraemer, H. "Concentrations of sex hormones in umbilical-cord blood: Their relation to sex and birth order of infants." Child Development, 1979, *50*, 632–642.

Maccoby, E. E., & Feldman, S. S. "Mother-attachment and stranger-reactions in the third year of life." Monographs of the Society for Research in Child Development, 1972, *37* (Whole # 146).

Maccoby, E. E., & Jacklin, C. N. The psychology of sex differences. Stanford CA: Stanford University Press, 1974.

Macfarlane, A. The psychology of childbirth. Cambridge MA: Harvard University Press, 1977.

McGraw, M. D. Growth: A study of Johnny and Jimmy. New York: Appleton-Century-Crofts, 1935.

McNeill, C. "The development of language." In P. H. Mussen (ed.), Carmichael's manual of child psychology. (Vol. 1, 3d ed.). New York: Wiley, 1970.

McNeill, D. The acquisition of language. New York: Harper & Row, 1970.

Madden, J.; Levenstein, P.; & Levenstein, S. "Longitudinal IQ outcomes of the mother-child home program." Child Development, 1976, *47*, 1015–1025.

Magenis, R. E. "Parental origin

of the extra chromosome in Down's syndrome." Human Genetics, 1977, *37*, 7–16.

Main, M.; Tomasini, L.; & Tolan, W. "Differences among mothers of infants judged to differ in security." Developmental Psychology, 1979, *15*, 472–473.

Marano, H. "Breast-feeding. New evidence: it's far more than nutrition." Medical World News, 1979, *20*, 62–78.

Marantz, S. A., & Mansfield, A. F. "Maternal employment and the development of sex-role stereotyping in five- to eleven-year-old girls." Child Development, 1977, *48*, 688–673.

Marcia, J. E. "Development and validation of ego identity status." Journal of Personality and Social Psychology, 1966, *3*, 551–558.

Marcia, J. E. "Identity six years after: A follow-up study." Journal of Youth and Adolescence, 1976, *5*, 145–150. (a)

Marcia, J. E. Studies in ego identity. Burnaby, British Columbia: Simon Fraser University. 1976. (b)

Marcus, D. E., & Overton, W. F. "The development of cognitive gender constancy and sex role preferences." Child Development, 1978, *49*, 434–444.

Markman, E. M. "Empirical versus logical solutions to part-whole comparison problems concerning classes and collections." Child Development, 1978, *49*, 168–177.

Martorano, S. C. "A development analysis of performance on Piaget's formal operations tasks." Developmental Psychology, 1977, *13*, 666–672.

Masters, J. C.; Ford, M. E.; Arend, R.; Grotevant, H. D.; & Clark, L. V. "Modeling and labeling as integrated determinants of children's sex-typed imitative behavior." Child Development, 1979, *50*, 364–371.

Mayer, J. "Obesity during childhood." In M. Winick (ed.), Childhood obesity. New York: Wiley, 1975.

Meilman, P. W. "Cross-sectional age changes in ego identity status during adolescence." Developmental Psychology, 1979, *15*, 230–231.

Meredith, H. V. 'Relation between tobacco smoking of pregnant women and body size of their progeny: A compilation and synthesis of published studies." Human Biology, 1975, *47*, 451–472.

Messer, S. B., & Brodzinsky, D. M. "The relation of conceptual tempo to aggression and its control." Child Development, 1979, *50*, 758–766.

Minton, C.; Kagan, J.; & Levine, J. A. "Maternal control and obedience in the two-year-old." Child Development, 1971, *42*, 1873–1874.

Mischel, W. "A social learning view or sex differences in behavior." In E. E. Maccoby (ed.), The development of sex differences. Stanford CA: Stanford University Press, 1966, 56–81.

Mischel, W. "Sex typing and socialization." In P. H. Mussen (ed.), Carmichael's manual of child psychology. (Vol. 2). New York: Wiley, 1970.

Montemayor, R., & Eisen, M. "The development of self-conceptions from childhood to adolescence." Developmental Psychology, 1977, *13*, 314–319.

Mood, D. W. "Sentence comprehension in preschool children: Testing an adaptive egocentrism hypothesis." Child Development, 1979, *50*, 247–250.

Mosher, F. A., & Hornsby, J. R. "On asking questions." In J. S. Bruner, R. R. Olver, & P. M. Greenfield (eds.), Studies in cognitive growth. New York: Wiley, 1966.

Mowrer, O. H. Learning theory and personality dynamics. New York: Ronald Press, 1950.

Mowrer, O. H. Learning theory and the symbolic processes. New York: Wiley, 1960.

Mueller, E., & Brenner, J. "The origins of social skills and interaction among playgroup toddlers." Child Development, 1977, *48*, 854–861.

Muir, D., & Field, J. "Newborn infants orient to sounds." Child Development, 1979, *50*, 431–436.

Mundy-Castle, A. C., & Anglin, J. "The development of looking in infancy." Paper read at the biennial meetings of the Society for Research in Child Development, Santa Monica, 1969.

Murphy, L. B., & Moriarty, A. E. Vulnerability, coping and growth. New Haven CT: Yale University Press, 1976.

Mussen, P. H., & Jones, M. C. "Self-conceptions, motivations, and interpersonal attitudes of late and early maturing boys." Child Development, 1957, *28*, 243–256.

Naeye, R. L. "Relationship of cigarette smoking to congenital anomalies and perinatal death." American Journal of Pathology, 1978, *90*, 289–293.

Nash, S. C. "The relationship among sex-role stereotyping, sex-role preference, and the sex difference in spatial visualization." Sex Roles, 1975, *1*, 15–32.

Neimark, E. D. "Intellectual development during adolescence." In F. D. Horowitz (ed.), Review of child development research. (Vol. 4). Chicago: University of Chicago Press, 1975.

Nelson, K. "Structure and strategy in learning to talk." Monographs of the Society for Research in Child Development, 1973, 38 (Whole # 149).

Nelson, K. "Facilitating children's syntax acquisition." Developmental Psychology, 1977, 13, 101–107. (a)

Nelson, K. "The conceptual basis for naming." In J. Macnamara (ed.), Language learning and thought. New York: Academic Press, 1977. (b)

Newman, H. H.; Freeman, F. N.; & Holzinger, K. J. Twins: A study of heredity and environment. Chicago: University of Chicago Press, 1937.

Nichols, P. L. "Minimal brain dysfunction: Associations with perinatal complications." Paper presented at the biennial meetings of the Society for Research in Child Development, New Orleans, 1977.

Nye, F. I. "Child adjustment in broken and in unhappy unbroken homes." Marriage and Family Living, 1957, 19, 356–361.

O'Donnell, M. Around the corner. New York: Harper & Row, 1966.

Omark, D. R.; Omark, M.; & Edelman, M. "Dominance hierarchies in young children." Paper presented at the International Congress of Anthropological and Ethnological Sciences, Chicago, 1973.

Orlofsky, J. L.; Marcia, J. E.; & Lesser, I. M. "Ego identity status and the intimacy vs. isolation crisis of young adulthood." Journal of Personality and Social Psychology, 1973, 27, 211–219.

Osler, S. F., & Kofsky, E. "Structure and strategy in concept attainment." Journal of Experimental Child Psychology, 1966, 4, 198–209.

Osman, B. B. Learning disabilities: A family affair. New York: Random House, 1979.

Overton, W. F.; Wagner, J.; & Dolinsky, H. "Social-class differences and task variables in the development of multiplicative classification." Child Development, 1971, 42, 1951–1958.

Owen, G. M.; Kram, K. M.; Garry, P. J.; Lower, J. E.; & Lubin, A. H. A study of nutritional status of preschool children in the United States, 1974, 53, Part II, Supplement, 597–646.

Parikh, B. S. "Moral judgment and its relation to family environment factors in Indian and American urban upper middle class families." Unpublished doctoral dissertation, Boston University, 1975.

Parke, R. D. Readings in social development. New York: Holt, 1969.

Parke, R. D. "Some effects of punishment on children's behavior." In W. W. Hartup (ed.), The young child. (Vol. 2). Washington, D.C.: National Association for the Education of Young Children, 1972.

Parke, R. D. "Perspectives on father-infant interaction." In J. D. Osofsky (ed.), Handbook of infant development. New York: Wiley, 1979.

Parke, R. D., & Walters, R. H. "Some factors influencing the efficacy of punishment training for inducing response inhibition." Monographs of the Society for Research in Child Development, 1967, 32 (Whole # 109).

Parmelee, A. H.; Wenner, W. H.; & Schulz, H. R. "Infant sleep patterns from birth to 16 weeks of age." Journal of Pediatrics, 1964, 65, 576–582.

Patterson, G. R. Families. Applications of social learning to family life. Champaign IL: Research Press, 1975.

Patterson, G. R.; Littman, R. A.; & Bricker, W. "Assertive behavior in children: A step toward a theory of aggression." Monographs of the Society for Child Development, 1967, 32 (Whole # 113 & 114).

Peal, E., & Lambert, W. E. "The relation of bilingualism to intelligence." Psychological Monographs, 1962, 76 (Whole # 546).

Pederson, E.; Faucher, T. A.; & Eaton, W. W. "A new perspective on the effects of first-grade teachers on children's subsequent adult status." Harvard Educational Review, 1978, 48, 1–31.

Perfetti, C. A., & Lesgold, A. M. "Coding and comprehension in skilled reading and implications for reading instruction." In L. B. Resnick & P. A. Weaver (eds.), Theory and practice of early reading. Hillsdale NJ: Erlbaum, 1977.

Peskin, H. "Pubertal onset and ego functioning." Journal of abnormal psychology, 1967, 72, 1–15.

Peskin, H. "Influence of the developmental schedule of puberty on learning and ego development." Journal of Youth and Adolescence, 1973, 2, 273–290.

Peterson, G. H.; Mehl, L. E.; & Leiderman, P. H. "The role of some birth-related variables in father attachment." American Journal of Orthopsychiatry, 1979, *49*, 330–338.

Phillips, J. R. "Syntax and vocabulary of mothers' speech to young children: Age and sex comparisons." Child Development, 1973, *44*, 182–185.

Piaget, J. The moral judgment of the child. New York: Macmillan, 1932.

Piaget, J. The origins of intelligence in children. New York: International Universities Press, 1952.

Piaget, J. The construction of reality in the child. New York: Basic Books, 1954.

Piaget, J. "Development and learning." In R. Ripple & V. Rockcastle (eds.), Piaget rediscovered. Ithaca NY: Cornell University Press, 1964.

Piaget, J., & Inhelder, B. The child's conception of space. London: Routledge & Kegan Paul, 1958.

Piaget, J., & Inhelder, B. The psychology of the child. New York: Basic Books, 1969.

Piaget, J., & Inhelder, B. Memory and intelligence. New York: Basic Books, 1973.

Pines, M. "Heredity insurance." The New York Times Magazine, Apr. 30, 1978, 78–92.

Pines, M. "A head start in the nursery." Psychology Today, 1979, *13*, 56–68.

Pitkin, R. M. "Nutrition during pregnancy: The clinical approach." In M. Winick (ed.), Nutritional disorders of American women. New York: Wiley, 1977.

Plomin, R. "Critique of Scarr and Weinberg's IQ adoption study: Putting the problem in perspective." Intelligence, 1978, *2*, 74–79.

Plomin, R., & DeFries, J. C. "Genetics and intelligence: Recent data." Intelligence, 1980, *4*, 15–24.

Podd, M. H. "Ego identity status and morality: The relationship between the two constructs." Developmental Psychology, 1972, *6*, 497–507.

Power, C., & Reimer, J. "Moral atmosphere: An educational bridge between moral judgment and action." In W. Damon (ed.), Moral Development. San Francisco: Jossey-Bass, 1978.

Prader, A.; Tanner, J. M.; & Von Harnack, G. A. "Catch-up growth following illness or starvation." Journal of Pediatrics, 1963, *62*, 646–659.

Prechtl, H. F. R., & Beintema, D. J. The neurological examination of the full-term newborn infant. Clinics in Developmental Medicine, 12. London: Hinemann, 1964.

Premack, A. J., & Premack, D. "Teaching language to an ape." Scientific American, 1972, *227*, 92–99.

Profiles of children. 1970 White House Conference on Children. Washington, D.C.: U.S. Government Printing Office, 1970.

Provence, S. "Development from six to twelve months." In J. D. Noshpitz (ed.), Basic handbook of child psychiatry. (Vol. I). New York: Basic Books, 1979.

Quay, H. C. "Classification." In H. C. Quay & J. S. Werry (eds.), Psychopathological disorders of childhood. (2d ed.). New York: Wiley, 1979. (a)

Quay, H. C. "Residential treatment." In H. C. Quay & J. S. Werry (eds.), Psychopathological disorders of childhood. (2d ed.). New York: Wiley, 1979. (b)

Ramey, C. T.; Farran, D. C.; & Campbell, F. A. "Predicting IQ from mother-infant interactions." Child Development, 1979, *50*, 804–814.

Ramey, C., & Smith, B. "Assessing the intellectual consequences of early intervention with high-risk infants." American Journal of Mental Deficiency, 1976, *81*, 318–324.

Rank, O. The trauma of birth. New York: Harcourt, 1929.

Rapoport, D. "The controversial Leboyer method." The Female Patient, 1978, *3*, 84–86.

Rappoport, L. Personality development: The chronology of experience. Glenview IL: Scott, Foresman, 1972.

Reed, E. W. "Genetic anomalies in development." In F. D. Horowitz (ed.), Review of Child Development Research. (Vol. 4). Chicago: University of Chicago Press, 1975.

Reisman, J. M., & Shorr, S. I. "Friendship claims and expectations among children and adults." Child Development, 1978, *49*, 913–916.

Resnick, L. B. "The future of IQ testing in education." Intelligence, 1979, *3*, 241–254.

Rest, J.; Turiel, E.; & Kohlberg, L. "Level of moral development as a determinant of preference and comprehension of moral judgments made by others." Journal of Personality, 1969, *37*, 225–252.

Rest, J. "The hierarchical nature of moral judgment: A study of patterns of comprehension and preference of moral stages." Journal of Personality, 1973, *41*, 86–109.

Reynolds, N. J., & Risley, T. R. "The role of social and material reinforcers in increasing talking of a disadvantaged preschool child." Journal of

Applied Behavior Analysis, 1968, *1*, 253–262.

Rheingold, H. L., & Cook, K. V. "The contents of boys' and girls' rooms as an index of parents' behavior." Child Development, 1975, *46*, 459–463.

Rice, B. "Brave new world of intelligence testing." Psychology Today, 1979, *13*, 26–41.

Richardson, S. "Ecology of malnutrition: Nonnutritional factors influencing intellectual and behavioral development." In Nutrition, the nervous system, and behavior. Pan American Health Organization Scientific Publication #251, 1972.

Riegel, K. F. "Adult life crises. A dialectic interpretation of development." In N. Datan & L. H. Ginsberg (eds.), Life-span developmental psychology. Normative life crises. New York: Academic Press, 1975.

Ringler, N. M.; Trause, M. A.: & Klaus, M. H. "Mother's speech to her two-year old, its effect on speech and language comprehension at 5 years." Pediatric Research, 1976, *10*, 307.

Ristow, L. W. "Much ado about dropouts." Phi Delta Kappan, 1965, *46*, 461–464.

Rivers, C.; Barnett, R.; & Baruch, G. Beyond sugar & spice. How women grow, learn, and thrive. New York: Putnam, 1979.

Roberge, J. J., & Flexer, B. K. Further examination of formal reasoning abilities. Child Development, 1979, *50*, 478–484.

Robins, L. N. "Follow-up studies." In H. C. Quay & J. S. Werry (eds.), Psychopathological disorders of childhood. (2d ed.). New York: Wiley, 1979.

Robinson, H., & Robinson, N. "Longitudinal development of very young children in a comprehensive day care program: The first two years." Child Development, 1971, *42*, 1673–1683.

Robinson, N., & Robinson, H. B. The mentally retarded child. (2d ed.). New York: McGraw-Hill, 1976.

Roche, A. F. "Secular trends in stature, weight, and maturation." In A. F. Roche (ed.), Secular trends in human growth, maturation, and development. Monographs of the Society for Research in Child Development, 1979, *44* (Whole # 179).

Roe, K. V. "Amount of infant vocalization as a function of age: Some cognitive implications." Child Development, 1975, *46*, 936–941.

Roffwarg, H. P.; Muzio, J. N.; & Dement, W. D. "Ontogenetic development of the human sleep-dream cycle." Science, 1966, *152*, 604–619.

Roper, R., & Hinde, R. A. "Social behavior in a play group: Consistency and complexity." Child Development, 1978, *49*, 570–579.

Rosenkrantz, P.; Vogel, S.; Bee, H.; Broverman, I.; & Broverman, D. M. "Sex-role stereotypes and self-conceptions of college students." Journal of Consulting and Clinical Psychology, 1968, *32*, 287–295.

Rosenthal, R., & Jacobson, L. Pygmalion in the classroom: Teacher expectations and pupils' intellectual development. New York: Holt, 1968.

Rosett, H. L., & Sander, L. W. "Effects of maternal drinking on neonatal morphology and state regulation." In J. D. Osofsky (ed.), Handbook of infant development. New York: Wiley, 1979.

Ross, G.; Kagan, J.; Zelazo, P.; & Kotelchuck, M. "Separation protest in infants in home and laboratory." Developmental Psychology, 1975, *11*, 256–257.

Rosso, R. "Maternal nutrition, nutrient exchange, and fetal growth." In M. Winick (ed.), Nutritional disorders of American women. New York: Wiley, 1977. (a)

Rosso, P. "Maternal-fetal exchange during protein malnutrition in the rat. Placental transfer of a-Amino Isobutyric acid." Journal of Nutrition, 1977, *107*, 2002–2005(b).

Rousseau, J. J. Emile, or concerning education. 1792. Book 2. New York: Dutton, 1938.

Rubin, R., & Balow, B. "Measures of infant development and socioeconomic status as predictors of later intelligence and school achievement." Development Psychology, 1979, *15*, 225–227.

Ruopp, R.; Travers, J.; Glantz, F.; & Coelen, C. Children at the center. Final report of the National Day Care Study. (Vol. 1). Cambridge MA: Abt Associates, 1979.

Rutter, M. "Parent-child separation: Psychological effects on the children." Journal of Child Psychology and Psychiatry, 1971, *12*, 233–260.

Rutter, M. Maternal deprivation reassessed. Harmondsworth, Middlesex: Penguin, 1972.

Rutter, M. "The development of infantile autism." In S. Chess & A. Thomas (eds.), Annual progress in child psychiatry and child development, 1975. New York: Brunner/Mazel, 1975. (a)

Rutter, M. Helping troubled children. New York: Plenum, 1975. (b)

Rutter, M. "Early sources of security and competence." In J. S. Bruner & A. Garton (eds.), Human growth and development. London: Oxford University Press, 1978.

Rutter, M. "Family, area and school influences in the genesis of conduct disorders." In L. Hersov, M. Berber, & D. Shaffer (eds.), Aggression and antisocial behavior in childhood and adolescence. Oxford: Pergamon, 1978.

Rutter, M. "Maternal deprivation, 1972–1978: New findings, new concepts, new approaches," Child Development, 1979, *50*, 283–305.

Rutter, M.; Yule, B.; Quinton, D.; Rowlands, O.; Yule, W.; & Berger, M. "Attainment and adjustment in two geographical areas, III: Some factors accounting for area differences." British Journal of Psychiatry, 1975, *126*, 520–533.

Saario, T. N.; Jacklin, C. N.; & Tittle, C. K. "Sex role stereotyping in the public schools." Harvard Educational Review, 1973, *43*, 386–416.

Sacks, E. "Intelligence scores as a function of experimentally established social relationships between child and examiner." Journal of Abnormal and Social Psychology, 1952, *46*, 354–358.

Salapatek, P. "Pattern perception in early infancy." In L. B. Cohen & P. Salapatek (eds.), Infant perception: From sensation to cognition. (Vol. 1). New York: Academic Press, 1975.

Salatas, H., & Flavell, J. H. "Retrieval of recently learned information: Development of strategies and control skills." Child Development, 1976, *47*, 941–948.

Salk, L. "The effects of the normal heartbeat sound on the behavior of the newborn infant; implications for mental health." World Mental Health, 1960, *12*, 168–175.

Sameroff, A. J., & Cavanaugh, P. J. "Learning in infancy: A developmental perspective." In J. D. Osofsky (ed.), Handbook of infant development. New York: Wiley, 1979.

Sameroff, A. J., & Chandler, J. J. "Reproductive risk and the continuum of caretaking casualty." In F. D. Horowitz (ed.), Review of child development research. (Vol. 4). Chicago. University of Chicago Press, 1975.

Sattler, J. M. Assessment of children's intelligence. Philadelphia: Saunders, 1974.

Scarr, S., & Weinberg, R. A. "Intellectual similarities within families of both adopted and biological children." Intelligence, 1977, *1*, 170–191.

Scarr, S., & Weinberg, R. A. "Nature and nurture strike (out) again." Intelligence, 1979, *3*, 31–39.

Schaefer, E., & Bell, R. "Development of a parental attitude research instrument." Child Development, 1958, *29*, 399–361.

Schaffer, H. R., & Emerson, P. E. "The development of social attachments in infancy." Monographs of the Society for Research in Child Development, 1964, *29* (Whole # 94).

Schaffer, R. Mothering. Cambridge MA: Harvard University Press, 1977.

Schlesinger, H. S., & Meadow, K. P. Sound and sign. Berkeley: University of California Press, 1972.

Scollon, R. Conversations with a one-year-old. Honolulu: University of Hawaii Press, 1976.

Scrimshaw, N. S. "Early malnutrition and central nervous system function." Merrill-Palmer Quarterly, 1969, *15*, 375–388.

Sears, P. S., & Barbee, A. H. "Career and life satisfactions among Terman's gifted women." In J. C. Stanley, W. C. George, & C. H. Solano (eds.), The gifted and the creative. Baltimore: Johns Hopkins University Press, 1977.

Sears, R. R. "Sources of life satisfactions of the Terman gifted men." American Psychologist, 1977, *32*, 119–128.

Sears, R. R.; Maccoby, E. E.; & Levin, H. Patterns of child rearing. Stanford CA: Stanford University Press, 1967, 1977.

Sears, R. R.; Rau, L.; & Alpert, R. Identification and child rearing. New York: Harper & Row, 1965.

Segal, J., & Yahraes, H. "Bringing up mother." Psychology Today, 1978, *12*, 90–96.

Selman, R. L., & Byrne, D. F. "A structural-developmental analysis of levels of role taking in middle childhood." Child Development, 1974, *45*, 803–806.

Shatz, M., & Gelman, R."The development of communication skills: Modifications in the speech of young children as a function of the listener." Monographs of the Society for Research in Child Development, 1973, *38* (Whole # 152).

Sheldon, W. H. The varieties of human physique. New York: Harper & Row, 1940.

Sheridan, M. D. "Final report of a prospective study of children whose mothers had rubella in early pregnancy." British Medical Journal, 1964, *2*, 536–539.

Shields, J. Monozygotic twins brought up apart and brought

up together. London: Oxford University Press, 1962.
Skinner, B. F. Verbal behavior. New York: Appleton-Century-Crofts, 1957.
Skodak, M., & Skeels, H. M. "A follow-up study of children in adoptive homes." Journal of Genetic Psychology, 1945, *66*, 21–58.
Slaby, R. G., & Frey, K. S. "Development of gender constancy and selective attention to same-sex models." Child Development, 1975, *46*, 849–856.
Slaby, R. G.; Quarfoth, G. R.; & McConnachie, G. A. "Television violence and its sponsors." Journal of Communication, 1976, *26*, 88–96.
Slobin, D. I. "Imitation and grammatical development in children." In N. S. Endler, L. R. Boulter, & H. O. Osser (eds.), Contemporary issues in developmental psychology. New York: Holt, 1968.
Slobin, D. I. "Universals of grammatical development in children." In G. B. Flores d'Arcais & W. J. M. Levelt (eds.), Advances in psycholinguistics. New York: Elsevier, 1970.
Slobin, D. I. "On the nature of talk to children." In E. H. Lenneberg & Lenneberg (eds.), Foundations of Language Development. (Vol. 1). New York: Academic Press, 1975.
Slobin, D. I. "A case study of early language awareness." In A. Sinclair, R. J. Jarvella, & W. J. M. Levelt (eds.), The child's conception of language. Berlin: Springer-Verlag, 1978.
Smith, M. E. "An investigation of the development of the sentence and the extent of vocabulary in young children." University of Iowa Studies in Child Welfare, 1926, *3*.
Snow, C. E. "Mothers' speech research: From input to interaction." In C. E. Snow & C. A. Ferguson (eds.), Talking to children. Cambridge, England: Cambridge University Press, 1977.
Snow, C. E., & Ferguson, C. A. (eds.). Talking to children. Cambridge, England: Cambridge University Press, 1977.
Solnit, A. J., & Provence, S. "Vulnerability and risk in early childhood." In J. D. Osofsky (ed.), Handbook of infant development. New York: Wiley, 1979.
Sroufe, L. A. "Wariness of strangers and the study of infant development." Child Development, 1977, *48*, 731–746.
Sroufe, L. A. "Attachment and the roots of competence." Human Nature, 1978, *1*, 50–56.
Staines, J. W. "The self picture as a factor in the classroom." British Journal of Education, 1958, *28*, 97–111.
Stamps, L. E. "Temporal conditioning of heart rate responses in newborn infants." Developmental Psychology, 1977, *13*, 624–629.
Stanley, J. C.; George, W. C.; & Solano, C. H. The gifted and the creative: A fifty-year perspective. Baltimore: Johns Hopkins University Press, 1977.
Staub, E. "A child in distress: The effects of focusing responsibility on children on their attempts to help." Developmental Psychology, 1970, *2*, 152–154.
Staub, E. "To rear a prosocial child: Reasoning, learning by doing, and learning by teaching others." In D. J. DePalma & J. M. Foley (eds.), Moral development. Current theory and research. Hillsdale NJ: Erlbaum, 1975.
Staub, E. Positive social behavior and morality. (Vol. 2). New York: Academic Press, 1979.
Steele, B. F., & Pollock, C. B. "A psychiatric study of parents who abuse infants and small children." In R. E. Helfer & C. H. Kempe (eds.), The battered child. (2d ed.). Chicago: University of Chicago Press, 1974.
Stein, Z.; Susser, M.; Saenger, G.; & Morolla, F. Famine and human development: The Dutch hunger winter of 1944–45. New York: Oxford University Press, 1975.
Stern, D. "Mother and infant at play: The dyadic interaction involving facial, vocal and gaze behaviors." In M. Lewis & L. A. Rosenblum (eds.), The effect of the infant on its caregiver. New York: Wiley, 1974.
Stern, D. The first relationship. Infant and mother. Cambridge MA: Harvard University Press, 1977.
Sternglanz, S. H., & Serbin, L. A. "Sex role stereotyping in children's television programs." Developmental Psychology, 1974, *10*, 710–715.
Steuer, F. B.; Applefield, M. J.; & Smith, R. "Televised aggression and the interpersonal aggression of preschool children." Journal of Experimental Child Psychology, 1971, *11*, 442–447.
Stewart, R. B.; Cluff, L. E.; & Philip, R. Drug monitoring: A requirement for responsible drug use. Baltimore: Williams & Wilkins, 1977.
Streissguth, A. P. "Fetal alcohol

syndrome: An epidemiologic perspective." American Journal of Epidemiology, 1978, *107*, 467–478.

Streissguth, A. P.; Martin, D. D.; & Barr, H. M. "Neonatal Brazelton Assessment and relationship to maternal alcohol use." Paper presented at the annual meeting of the American Psychological Association, San Francisco, 1977.

Subcommittee on Labor and Public Welfare. Education of the gifted and talented. U.S. Senate, March, 1972.

Suls, J.; Gutkin, D.; & Kalle, R. J. "The role of intentions, damage, and social consequences in the moral judgments of children." Child Development, 1979, *50*, 874–877.

Taitz, L. S. "Modification of weight gain by dietary changes in a population of Sheffield neonates." Archives of Disease of Childhood, 1975, *50*, 476–479.

Tanner, J. M. "Physical growth." In P. H. Mussen (ed.), Carmichael's manual of child psychology. (Vol. 1). New York: Wiley, 1970.

Tanner, J. W. "Growth and endocrinology of the adolescent." In L. J. Gardner (ed.), Endocrine and genetic diseases of childhood. (2d ed). Philadelphia: Saunders, 1975.

Terman, L., & Merrill, M. A. Measuring intelligence: A guide to the administration of the new revised Stanford–Binet tests. Boston: Houghton Mifflin, 1937.

Terman, L., & Oden, M. Genetic studies of genius. Vol. 1. Mental and physical traits of a thousand gifted children. Stanford CA: Stanford University Press, 1925.

Terman, L., & Oden, M. Genetic studies of genius. Vol. 4. The gifted child grows up. Stanford CA: Stanford University Press, 1947.

Terman, L., & Oden, M. Genetic studies of genius. Vol. 5. The gifted group at mid-life. Stanford CA: Stanford University Press, 1959.

Terrace, H. S. "How Nim Chimpsky changed my mind." Psychology Today, 1979, *13*, 65–76.

Thomas, A., & Chess, S. Temperament and development. New York: Brunner/Mazel, 1977.

Thompson, S. K. "Gender labels and early sex role development." Child Development, 1975, *46*, 339–347.

Time Magazine. "Outcry over 'Wuf Tickets.' " Aug. 20, 1979, p. 61.

Tjossem, T. D. (ed.). Intervention strategies for high risk infants and young children. Baltimore: University Park Press, 1976.

Tomlinson-Keasey, C.; Eisert, D. C.; Kahle, L. R.; Hardy-Brown, K.; & Keasey, B. "The structure of concrete operational thought." Child Development, 1979, *50*, 1153–1163.

Tomlinson-Keasey, C., & Keasey, C. B. "The mediating role of cognitive development in moral judgment." Child Development, 1974, *45*, 291–298.

Trahey, J. "Down the tube." Working Woman, 1979, *4*, 30.

Trehub, S. E., & Rabinovitch, S. "Auditory-linguistic sensitivity in early infancy." Developmental Psychology, 1972, *6*, 47–77.

Trowbridge, N. "Self-concept and socio-economic status in elementary school children." American Education Research Journal, 1972, *9*, 525–537.

Tuchmann-Duplessis, H. Drug effects on the fetus. New York: Addis Press, 1975.

Tulkin, S. R., & Covitz, F. E. "Mother-infant interaction and intellectual functioning at age six." Paper presented at the biennial meeting of the Society for Research in Child Development, Denver, 1975.

Turiel, E. "An experimental test of the sequentiality of developmental stages in the child's moral judgments." Journal of Personality and Social Psychology, 1966, *3*, 611–618.

Turiel, E. "Conflict and transition in adolescent moral development." Child Development, 1974, *45*, 14–29.

Uzgiris, I. C. "Patterns of cognitive development in infancy." Merrill-Palmer Quarterly, 1973, *19*, 21–40.

Uzgiris, I. C., & Hunt, J. McV. Toward ordinal scales of psychological development in infancy. Champaign IL: University of Illinois Press, 1975.

Vellutino, F. R. "Alternative conceptualizations of dyslexia: Evidence in support of a verbal-deficit hypothesis." Harvard Educational Review, 1977, *47*, 334–354.

von Frisch, K. "Decoding the language of the bee." Science, 1974. *185*, 663–668.

Vygotsky, L. S. Thought and language. New York: Wiley, 1962.

Waber, D. P. "Sex differences in mental abilities, hemispheric lateralization, and rate of physical growth at adolescence." Developmental Psychology, 1977, *13*, 29–38.

Wachs, T. D. "Proximal experience and early cognitive-intellectual development: The physical environment." Merrill-Palmer Quarterly, 1979, *25*, 3–41.

Wachs, T. D.; Uzgiris, I.; & Hunt, J. McV. "Cognitive development in infants of different age levels and from different environmental backgrounds: An explanatory investigation." Merrill-Palmer Quarterly, 1971, *17*, 283–318.

Waldron, S.; Shrier, D. K.; Stone, B.; & Tobin, F. "School phobia and other childhood neuroses: A systematic study of the children and their families." American Journal of Psychiatry, 1975, *132*, 802–808.

Walker, L. J., & Richards, B. S. "Stimulating transitions in moral reasoning as a function of stage of cognitive development." Developmental Psychology, 1979, *15*, 95–103.

Walker, R. N. "Body build and behavior in young children: I. Body and nursery school teachers' ratings." Monographs of the Society for Research in Child Development, 1962, *27* (Whole # 84).

Wallerstein, J. S., & Kelly, J. B. "California's children of divorce." Psychology Today, 1980, *13*, 66–76.

Walters, R. H., & Brown, M. "Studies of reinforcement of aggression. III. Transfer of responses to an interpersonal situation." Child Development, 1963, *34*, 563–571.

Walters, R. H.; Parke, R. D.; & Cane, V. A. "Timing of punishment and the observation of consequences to others as determinants of response inhibition." Journal of Experimental Child Psychology, 1965, *2*, 10–30.

Waterman, A. S.; Geary, P. S.; & Waterman, C. K. "Longitudinal study of changes in ego identity status from the freshman to the senior year at college." Developmental Psychology, 1974, *10*, 387–392.

Waters, E. "The reliability and stability of individual differences in infant-mother attachment." Child Development, 1978, *49*, 483–494.

Waters, E.; Wippman, J.; & Sroufe, L. A. "Attachment, positive effect, and competence in the peer group: Two studies in construct validation." Child Development, 1979, *50*, 821–829.

Watson, J. D., & Crick, F. H. C. "Molecular structure of nucleic acids: A structure for deoxyribose nucleic acid." Nature, 1958, *171*, 737–738.

Wechsler, D. Wechsler Intelligence Scale for Children. New York: Psychology Corporation, 1949.

Weikart, D. P. "Relationship of curriculum, teaching, and learning in preschool education." In J. C. Stanley (ed.), Preschool programs for the disadvantaged. Baltimore: Johns Hopkins University Press, 1972.

Weir, R. Language in the crib. The Hague: Mouton, 1962.

Wellman, H. M.; Somerville, S. C.; & Haake, R. J. "Development of search procedures in real-life spatial environments." Developmental Psychology, 1979, *15*, 530–542.

Werner, E. E.; Simonian, K.; Bierman, J. M.; & French, F. E. "Cumulative effect of perinatal complications and deprived environment on physical, intellectual, and social development of preschool children." Pediatrics, 1967, *39*, 489–505.

Werner, H. Comparative psychology of mental development. New York: Science Editions, 1961.

Werner, J. S., & Wooten, B. R. "Human infant color vision and color perception." Infant Behavior and Development, 1979, *2*, 241–273.

Werry, J. S. "The childhood psychoses." In H. C. Quay & J. S. Werry (eds.), Psychopathological disorders of childhood. (2d ed.). New York: Wiley, 1979.

Weymouth, F. W. "Visual acuity of children." In M. J. Hirsch & R. E. Wick (eds.), Vision of children: An optometric symposium. Philadelphia: Chilton, 1963.

White, B. L. "An experimental approach to the effects of experience on early human behavior." In J. P. Hill (ed.), Minnesota Symposia on Child Psychology. Minneapolis: The University of Minnesota Press, 1967.

White, B. L. The first three years of life. Englewood Cliffs NJ: Prentice-Hall, 1975.

White, C. B. "Moral development in Bahamian school children: Cross-cultural examination of Kohlberg's stages of moral reasoning." Developmental Psychology, 1975, *11*, 535–536.

White, S. H. "Evidence for a hierarchical arrangement of learning processes." In L. P. Lipsitt & C. C. Spiker (eds.), Advances in child development and behavior. (Vol. 2). New York: Academic Press, 1965.

Williams, J. E.; Bennett, S. M.; & Best, D. L. "Awareness and expression of sex stereotypes in young children." Developmental Psychology, 1975, *11*, 635–642.

Wilson, R. S. "Twins and siblings: Concordance for school-age mental development." Child Development, 1977, *48*, 211–216.

Wilson, R. S. "Synchronies in mental development: An epigenetic perspective." Science, 1978, *202*, 939–948.

Winick, M. (ed.). Childhood obesity. New York: Wiley, 1975.

Witkin, H. A.; Dyk, R. B.; Faterson, H. F.; Goodenough, D. R.; & Karp, S. A. Psychological differentiation. New York: Wiley, 1962.

Wolff, P. H. "Observations on the early development of smiling." In B. M. Foss (ed.), Determinants of infant behavior. (Vol. 2). London: Methuen, 1963.

Yarrow, L. J.; Rubenstein, J. L.; & Pederson, F. A. Infant and environment: Early cognitive and motivational development. New York: Halsted Press, 1975.

Yarrow, L. J.; Rubenstein, J. L.; Pederson, F. A.; & Jankowski, J. J. "Dimensions of early stimulation and their differential effects of infant development." Merrill-Palmer Quarterly, 1972, *18*, 205–218.

Yogman, M. "The goals and structure of face-to-face interaction between infants and fathers." Paper presented at the biennial meetings of the Society for Research in Child Development, New Orleans, 1977.

Zack, P. M.; Harlan, W. R.; Leaverton, P. E.; & Cornoni-Huntley, Joan. "A longitudinal study of body fatness in childhood and adolescence." Journal of Pediatrics, 1979, *95*, 126–130.

Zahn-Waxler, C.; Radke-Yarrow, M.; & King, R. A. "Child rearing and children's prosocial initiations toward victims of distress." Child Development, 1979, *50*, 319–330.

Zajonc, R. B. "Birth order and intelligence: Dumber by the dozen." Psychology Today, 1975, *8*, 37–43.

Zajonc, R. B., & Marcus, G. B. "Birth order and intellectual development." Psychological Review, 1975, *82*, 74–88.

Zeskind, P. S., & Lester, B. M. "Acoustic features and auditory perceptions of the cries of newborns with prenatal and perinatal complications." Child Development, 1978, *49*, 580–589.

Zigler, E., & Butterfield, E. C. "Motivational aspects of changes in IQ test performance of culturally deprived nursery school children." Child Development, 1968, *39*, 1–14.

Subject Index

Author Index